Lecture Notes in Computer Science 6016

Commenced Publication in 1973
Founding and Former Series Editors:
Gerhard Goos, Juris Hartmanis, and Jan van Leeuwen

David Taniar   Osvaldo Gervasi
Beniamino Murgante   Eric Pardede
Bernady O. Apduhan (Eds.)

Computational Science and Its Applications – ICCSA 2010

International Conference
Fukuoka, Japan, March 23-26, 2010
Proceedings, Part I

 Springer

Volume Editors

David Taniar
Monash University, Clayton, VIC 3800, Australia
E-mail: david.taniar@infotech.monash.edu.au

Osvaldo Gervasi
University of Perugia, 06123 Perugia, Italy
E-mail: osvaldo@unipg.it

Beniamino Murgante
University of Basilicata, L.I.S.U.T. - D.A.P.I.T., 85100 Potenza, Italy
E-mail: beniamino.murgante@unibas.it

Eric Pardede
La Trobe University, Bundoora, VIC 3083, Australia
E-mail: e.pardede@latrobe.edu.au

Bernady O. Apduhan
Kyushu Sangyo University, Fukuoka 813-8503, Japan
E-mail: bob@is.kyusan-u.ac.jp

Library of Congress Control Number: 2010922807

CR Subject Classification (1998): C.2, H.4, F.2, H.3, C.2.4, F.1

LNCS Sublibrary: SL 1 – Theoretical Computer Science and General Issues

ISSN   0302-9743
ISBN-10   3-642-12155-1 Springer Berlin Heidelberg New York
ISBN-13   978-3-642-12155-5 Springer Berlin Heidelberg New York

springer.com

© Springer-Verlag Berlin Heidelberg 2010
Printed in Germany

Typesetting: Camera-ready by author, data conversion by Scientific Publishing Services, Chennai, India
Printed on acid-free paper   06/3180

Preface

These multiple volumes (LNCS volumes 6016, 6017, 6018 and 6019) consist of the peer-reviewed papers from the 2010 International Conference on Computational Science and Its Applications (ICCSA2010) held in Fukuoka, Japan during March 23–26, 2010. ICCSA 2010 was a successful event in the International Conferences on Computational Science and Its Applications (ICCSA) conference series, previously held in Suwon, South Korea (2009), Perugia, Italy (2008), Kuala Lumpur, Malaysia (2007), Glasgow, UK (2006), Singapore (2005), Assisi, Italy (2004), Montreal, Canada (2003), and (as ICCS) Amsterdam, The Netherlands (2002) and San Francisco, USA (2001).

Computational science is a main pillar of most of the present research, industrial and commercial activities and plays a unique role in exploiting ICT innovative technologies. The ICCSA conference series has been providing a venue to researchers and industry practitioners to discuss new ideas, to share complex problems and their solutions, and to shape new trends in computational science.

ICCSA 2010 was celebrated at the host university, Kyushu Sangyo University, Fukuoka, Japan, as part of the university's 50th anniversary. We would like to thank Kyushu Sangyo University for hosting ICCSA this year, and for including this international event in their celebrations. Also for the first time this year, ICCSA organized poster sessions that present on-going projects on various aspects of computational sciences.

Apart from the general track, ICCSA 2010 also included 30 special sessions and workshops in various areas of computational sciences, ranging from computational science technologies, to specific areas of computational sciences, such as computer graphics and virtual reality. We would like to show our appreciation to the workshops and special sessions Chairs and Co-chairs.

The success of the ICCSA conference series, in general, and ICCSA 2010, in particular, was due to the support of many people: authors, presenters, participants, keynote speakers, session Chairs, Organizing Committee members, student volunteers, Program Committee members, Steering Committee members, and people in other various roles. We would like to thank them all. We would also like to thank Springer for their continuous support in publishing ICCSA conference proceedings.

March 2010

Osvaldo Gervasi
David Taniar

Organization

ICCSA 2010 was organized by the University of Perugia (Italy), Monash University (Australia), La Trobe University (Australia), University of Basilicata (Italy), and Kyushu Sangyo University (Japan)

Honorary General Chairs

Takashi Sago	Kyushu Sangyo University, Japan
Norio Shiratori	Tohoku University, Japan
Kenneth C.J. Tan	Qontix, UK

General Chairs

Bernady O. Apduhan	Kyushu Sangyo University, Japan
Osvaldo Gervasi	University of Perugia, Italy

Advisory Committee

Marina L. Gavrilova	University of Calgary, Canada
Andrès Iglesias	University of Cantabria, Spain
Tai-Hoon Kim	Hannam University, Korea
Antonio Laganà	University of Perugia, Italy
Katsuya Matsunaga	Kyushu Sangyo University, Japan
Beniamino Murgante	University of Basilicata, Italy
Kazuo Ushijima	Kyushu Sangyo University, Japan (ret.)

Program Committee Chairs

Osvaldo Gervasi	University of Perugia, Italy
David Taniar	Monash University, Australia
Eric Pardede (Vice-Chair)	LaTrobe University, Australia

Workshop and Session Organizing Chairs

Beniamino Murgante	University of Basilicata, Italy
Eric Pardede	LaTrobe University, Australia

Publicity Chairs

Jemal Abawajy	Deakin University, Australia
Koji Okamura	Kyushu Sangyo University, Japan
Yao Feng-Hui	Tennessee State University, USA
Andrew Flahive	DSTO, Australia

International Liaison Chairs

Hiroaki Kikuchi   Tokay University, Japan
Agustinus Borgy Waluyo   Institute for InfoComm Research, Singapore
Takashi Naka   Kyushu Sangyo University, Japan

Tutorial Chair

Andrès Iglesias   University of Cantabria, Spain

Awards Chairs

Akiyo Miyazaki   Kyushu Sangyo University, Japan
Wenny Rahayu   LaTrobe University, Australia

Workshop Organizers

Application of ICT in Healthcare (AICTH 2010)

Salim Zabir   France Telecom /Orange Labs Japan
Jemal Abawajy   Deakin University, Australia

Approaches or Methods of Security Engineering (AMSE 2010)

Tai-hoon Kim   Hannam University, Korea

Advances in Web-Based Learning (AWBL 2010)

Mustafa Murat Inceoglu   Ege University (Turkey)

Brain Informatics and Its Applications (BIA 2010)

Heui Seok Lim   Korea University, Korea
Kichun Nam   Korea University, Korea

Computer Algebra Systems and Applications (CASA 2010)

Andrès Iglesias   University of Cantabria, Spain
Akemi Galvez   University of Cantabria, Spain

Computational Geometry and Applications (CGA 2010)

Marina L. Gavrilova   University of Calgary, Canada

Computer Graphics and Virtual Reality (CGVR 2010)

Osvaldo Gervasi   University of Perugia, Italy
Andrès Iglesias   University of Cantabria, Spain

Chemistry and Materials Sciences and Technologies (CMST 2010)

Antonio Laganà   University of Perugia, Italy

Future Information System Technologies and Applications (FISTA 2010)

Bernady O. Apduhan   Kyushu Sangyo University, Japan
Jianhua Ma   Hosei University, Japan
Qun Jin   Waseda University, Japan

Geographical Analysis, Urban Modeling, Spatial Statistics (GEOG-AN-MOD 2010)

Stefania Bertazzon   University of Calgary, Canada
Giuseppe Borruso   University of Trieste, Italy
Beniamino Murgante   University of Basilicata, Italy

Graph Mining and Its Applications (GMIA 2010)

Honghua Dai   Deakin University, Australia
James Liu   Hong Kong Polytechnic University, Hong Kong
Min Yao   Zhejiang University, China
Zhihai Wang   Beijing JiaoTong University, China

High-Performance Computing and Information Visualization (HPCIV 2010)

Frank Dévai   London South Bank University, UK
David Protheroe   London South Bank University, UK

International Workshop on Biomathematics, Bioinformatics and Biostatistics (IBBB 2010)

Unal Ufuktepe   Izmir University of Economics, Turkey
Andres Iglesias   University of Cantabria, Spain

International Workshop on Collective Evolutionary Systems (IWCES 2010)

Alfredo Milani   University of Perugia, Italy
Clement Leung   Hong Kong Baptist University, Hong Kong

International Workshop on Human and Information Space Symbiosis (WHISS 2010)

Takuo Suganuma   Tohoku University, Japan
Gen Kitagata   Tohoku University, Japan

Mobile Communications (MC 2010)

Hyunseung Choo   Sungkyunkwan University, Korea

Mobile Sensor and Its Applications (MSIA 2010)

Moonseong Kim   Michigan State University, USA

Numerical Methods and Modeling/Simulations in Computational Science and Engineering (NMMS 2010)

Elise de Doncker   Western Michigan University, USA
Karlis Kaugars   Western Michigan University, USA

Logical, Scientific and Computational Aspects of Pulse Phenomena in Transitions (PULSES 2010)

Carlo Cattani   University of Salerno, Italy
Cristian Toma   Corner Soft Technologies, Romania
Ming Li   East China Normal University, China

Resource Management and Scheduling for Future-Generation Computing Systems (RMS 2010)

Jemal H. Abawajy   Deakin University, Australia

Information Retrieval, Security and Innovative Applications (RSIA 2010)

Mohammad Mesbah Usddin   Kyushy University, Japan

Rough and Soft Sets Theories and Applications (RSSA 2010)

Mustafa Mat Deris   Universiti Tun Hussein Onn, Malaysia
Jemal H. Abawajy   Deakin University, Australia

Software Engineering Processes and Applications (SEPA 2010)

Sanjay Misra   Atilim University, Turkey

Tools and Techniques in Software Development Processes (TTSDP 2010)

Sanjay Misra   Atilim University, Turkey

Ubiquitous Web Systems and Intelligence (UWSI 2010)

David Taniar   Monash University, Australia
Eric Pardede   La Trobe University, Australia
Wenny Rahayu   La Trobe University, Australia

Wireless and Ad-Hoc Networking (WADNet 2010)

Jongchan Lee   Kunsan National University, Korea
Sangjoon Park   Kunsan National University, Korea

WEB 2.0 and Social Networks (Web2.0 2010)

Vidyasagar Potdar   Curtin University of Technology, Australia

Workshop on Internet Communication Security (WICS 2010)

José Maria Sierra Camara   University of Madrid, Spain

Wireless Multimedia Sensor Networks (WMSN 2010)

Vidyasagar Potdar   Curtin University of Technology, Australia
Yan Yang   Seikei University, Japan

Program Committee

Kenneth Adamson   Ulster University, UK
Margarita Albertí Wirsing   Universitat de Barcelona, Spain
Richard Barrett   Oak Ridge National Laboratory, USA
Stefania Bertazzon   University of Calgary, Canada
Michela Bertolotto   University College Dublin, Ireland
Sandro Bimonte   CEMAGREF, TSCF, France
Rod Blais   University of Calgary, Canada
Ivan Blecic   University of Sassari, Italy
Giuseppe Borruso   Università degli Studi di Trieste, Italy
Martin Buecker   Aachen University, Germany
Alfredo Buttari   CNRS-IRIT, France
Carlo Cattani   University of Salerno, Italy
Alexander Chemeris   National Technical University of Ukraine
                             "KPI", Ukraine
Chen-Mou Cheng   National Taiwan University, Taiwan
Min Young Chung   Sungkyunkwan University, Korea
Rosa Coluzzi   National Research Council, Italy
Stefano Cozzini   National Research Council, Italy
José A. Cardoso e Cunha   Univ. Nova de Lisboa, Portugal
Gianluca Cuomo   University of Basilicata, Italy
Alfredo Cuzzocrea   University of Calabria, Italy
Ovidiu Daescu   University of Texas at Dallas, USA
Maria Danese   University of Basilicata, Italy
Pravesh Debba   CSIR, South Africa
Oscar Delgado-Mohatar   University Carlos III of Madrid, Spain
Roberto De Lotto   University of Pavia, Italy

Jean-Cristophe Desplat	Irish Centre for High-End Computing, Ireland
Frank Dévai	London South Bank University, UK
Rodolphe Devillers	Memorial University of Newfoundland, Canada
Pasquale Di Donato	Sapienza University of Rome, Italy
Carla Dal Sasso Freitas	UFRGS, Brazil
Francesco Gabellone	National Research Council, Italy
Akemi Galvez	University of Cantabria, Spain
Marina Gavrilova	University of Calgary, Canada
Nicoletta Gazzea	ICRAM, Italy
Jerome Gensel	LSR-IMAG, France
Andrzej M. Goscinski	Deakin University, Australia
Alex Hagen-Zanker	Cambridge University, UK
Muki Haklay	University College London, UK
Hisamoto Hiyoshi	Gunma University, Japan
Choong Seon Hong	Kyung Hee University, Korea
Fermin Huarte	University of Barcelona, Spain
Andrès Iglesias	University of Cantabria, Spain
Antonio Laganà	University of Perugia, Italy
Mustafa Murat	Inceoglu Ege University, Turkey
Ken-ichi Ishida	Kyushu Sangyo University, Japan
Antonio Izquierdo	Universidad Carlos III de Madrid, Spain
Daesik Jang	Kunsan University, Korea
Peter Jimack	University of Leeds, UK
Korhan Karabulut	Yasar University, Turkey
Farid Karimipour	Vienna University of Technology, Austria
Baris Kazar	Oracle Corp., USA
Dong Seong Kim	Duke University, USA
Pan Koo Kim	Chosun University, Korea
Ivana Kolingerova	University of West Bohemia, Czech Republic
Dieter Kranzlmueller	Ludwig Maximilians University and Leibniz Supercomputing Centre Munich, Germany
Domenico Labbate	University of Basilicata, Italy
Rosa Lasaponara	National Research Council, Italy
Maurizio Lazzari	National Research Council, Italy
Xuan Hung Le	University of South Florida, USA
Sangyoun Lee	Yonsei University, Korea
Bogdan Lesyng	Warsaw University, Poland
Clement Leung	Hong Kong Baptist University, Hong Kong
Chendong Li	University of Connecticut, USA
Laurence Liew	Platform Computing, Singapore
Xin Liu	University of Calgary, Canada
Cherry Liu Fang	U.S. DOE Ames Laboratory, USA
Savino Longo	University of Bari, Italy
Tinghuai Ma	NanJing University of Information Science and Technology, China
Antonino Marvuglia	University College Cork, Ireland

Pablo Vanegas	Katholieke Universiteit Leuven, Belgium
Piero Giorgio Verdini	INFN Pisa and CERN, Italy
Andrea Vittadini	University of Padova, Italy
Koichi Wada	University of Tsukuba, Japan
Krzysztof Walkowiak	Wroclaw University of Technology, Poland
Jerzy Wasniewski	Technical University of Denmark, Denmark
Robert Weibel	University of Zurich, Switzerland
Roland Wismüller	Universität Siegen, Germany
Markus Wolff	University of Potsdam, Germany
Kwai Wong	University of Tennessee, USA
Mudasser Wyne	National University, USA
Chung-Huang Yang	National Kaohsiung Normal University, Taiwan
Albert Y. Zomaya	University of Sydney, Australia

Sponsoring Organizations

ICCSA 2010 would not have been possible without the tremendous support of many organizations and institutions, for which all organizers and participants of ICCSA 2010 express their sincere gratitude:
  University of Perugia, Italy
  Kyushu Sangyo University, Japan
  Monash University, Australia
  La Trobe University, Australia
  University of Basilicata, Italia
  Information Processing Society of Japan (IPSJ) - Kyushu Chapter
  and with IPSJ SIG-DPS

Table of Contents – Part I

Workshop on Geographical Analysis, Urban Modeling, Spatial Statistics (GEO-AN-MOD 2010)

General Track on Advanced and Emerging Applications

Table of Contents – Part II

Workshop on PULSES V– Logical, Scientific and Computational Aspects of Pulse Phenomena in Transitions (PULSES 2010)

Workshop on Software Engineering Processes and Applications (SEPA 2010)

Workshop on WEB 2.0 and Social Networks (Web2.0 2010)

General Track on Information Systems and Technologies

General Track on Computational Methods, Algorithms and Scientific Application

General Track on Advanced and Emerging Applications

Table of Contents – Part III

Workshop on Mobile Communications (MC 2010)

Workshop on Rough and Soft Sets Theories and Applications (RSSA 2010)

Workshop on Wireless and Ad Hoc Networking (WADNet 2010)

Workshop on Wireless Multimedia Sensor Networks (WMSN 2010)

General Track on Information Systems and Information Technologies

Table of Contents – Part IV

Workshop on Human and Information Space Symbiosis (IWHISS 2010)

Workshop on Information Retrieval, Security and Innovative Applications (RSIA 2010)

Workshop on Collective Evolutionary Systems (IWCES 2010)

General Track on Computational Methods, Algorithms and Applications

Real Estate Values, Urban Centrality, Economic Activities. A GIS Analysis on the City of Swindon (UK)

Francesco Battaglia[1], Giuseppe Borruso[2], and Andrea Porceddu[3]

[1] Savino & Partners, Via San Francesco 9, 34133 Trieste, Italy
battaglia@savinopartners.it
[2] Department of Geographical and Historical Sciences,
University of Trieste, P. le Europa 1, 34127 Trieste, Italy
giuseppe.borruso@econ.units.it
[3] Department of Architectonic and Urban Planning,
University of Trieste, P. le Europa 1, 34127 Trieste
andrea.porceddu@econ.units.it

Abstract[1]. The paper is focused on the analysis of urban shape and structure by means of its constituting physical features, the spatial distribution of population and human activities. In particular we aim at analysing the relations these characteristics have with the house prices distribution in urban areas to examine the spatial form of the city and observe it from different perspectives. GIS and spatial analytical techniques are used to model and visualize the different shapes of a city, helping to understanding the spatial structures related to different urban uses and functions. Recalling the urban geographical theory carried on through the years, we use GIS and point pattern analysis to model such urban features. An ancillary aim of the present research is the exam of urban dynamics and structure relying on freely or publicly available geographical data as valuable elements for providing spatial information.

Keywords: Real Estate Values, Spatial Analysis, GIS, Density Estimation, Swindon (UK).

1 Introduction

Urban space and its shape can derive from human activities relevant for deriving urban hierarchies and density functions of different urban components, as the supply of transport infrastructures (Alonso 1960) and the population distribution (Clarke, as reported in Yeates and Gardner 1976), have long been hypothesized as decreasing

---

[1] The paper derives from joint reflections of the three authors. Paragraph 2 was realized by Francesco Battaglia, paragraphs 1, 4 and 5 ("Results") by Giuseppe Borruso, while paragraphs 3 and 5 ("Limitations") by Andrea Porceddu.

The geographical visualization and analysis, where not otherwise specified, have been realized using Intergraph Geomedia Professional and Geomedia GRID 6.1 under the RRL (Registered Research Laboratory) agreement between Intergraph and the Department of Geographical and Historical Sciences of the University of Trieste (Italy).

D. Taniar et al. (Eds.): ICCSA 2010, Part I, LNCS 6016, pp. 1–16, 2010.
© Springer-Verlag Berlin Heidelberg 2010

from the central areas of the city in terms of urban land use and its value (Knos 1962). Different urban models were considered for describing cities, with the first ones being quite simple considering some circular and concentric structure for urban areas. These were than coupled with sector and radials models organized around a central location in the city. Monocentric models have been recently put in discussion in favor of a polycentric nature of cities (Hoch and Waddel 1993; Waddel, Berry and Hoch 1993), particularly with reference to land values or house prices. In such studies a single central urban nucleus as an organizing element is confronted to the existence of several centers deriving from patterns of development not so homogeneous and uniform, therefore providing images of the city linked to polycentrism(s) related to different characteristics and behavior of living and working population.

In this paper we analyse the city of Swindon (UK) and its urban structure in terms of population distribution, road network structure and the spatial pattern of economic activities. House prices structure is also examined, particularly in terms of new housing in the city deriving from urban redevelopment actions interesting the city in the most recent years. The paper is organized as follows. In paragraph two the Swindon area housing market is described as from UK Land Registry Data available, differentiated according to the different postcode areas and also seen in the wider national UK context of real estate market – this including also considerations on the recent global economic crisis affecting the house markets. In paragraph three the study area is introduced and described. The city of Swindon is described and inserted into the UK context, particularly in terms of urban redevelopment actions and economic framework. Paragraph four is focused on the analysis of data available in terms of urban form and structure, as well as of house prices distribution and characteristics. Here spatial analytical techniques and GIS analysis are used to model urban form and prices. Discussion, concluding remarks and further developments of the research on the spatial characteristics of the city of Swindon follow in paragraph five.

2 The Housing Market in the UK

The housing market is undergoing the effects of the international financial crisis all over the world; the UK market makes no exception to this end: after a decade of substantial growth, started in 1996, the average properties price fell steeply from the peak of the market in autumn 2007 (GBP 184,131.00 - nominal average price) to the minimum of the first quarter of 2009 (GBP 149,709.00) (Fig. 1a). Nowadays, the average price has partially recovered: in October 2009, Nationwide and Halifax, two of the most important English mortgage lenders that regularly issue analytical studies on the UK housing market, estimated the average property price respectively of GBP 162,038 and GBP 165,528[2]. After the brisk downturn of house prices during 2008, last summer a reprise in inflation was noted, however short lasting.

---

[2] Nationwide and Halifax have developed a similar statistical methodology to process their house price index from original lending data for properties at the post survey approval stage; differences reflect the different approach in surveying (http://www.nationwide.co.uk/hpi; http://www.lloydsbankinggroup.com/media1/research/halifax_hpi.asp).

a) b)

Fig. 1. a) Nominal and Real House Price in the UK and b) Real average House Price (value and change rate) compared with GDP growth rate

Source: a) Nationwide Building Society. Nominal House Price is from UK All Properties series - not seasonally adjusted; House Prices adjusted for retail prices uses the Office for National Statistics Retail Price Index (RPI) to convert nominal prices to current prices. b) Office of National Statistics and Nationwide Building Society; GDP growth rate and RHP rate refer to the comparison with the same quarter of the previous year; figures are seasonally corrected.

The analysts are actually very careful about forecasts, since many factors are involved in the crisis outbreak (Nationwide, 2009), in particular: a) the crisis was nested in the real estate market itself, since it was the subprime mortgage crisis that triggered the domino effect in the housing and credit market, finally resulting in a global recession; b) the actual recession that hit the UK real economy from the last quarter of 2008, is not going to recover in short time, while the unsettling effect on the consumer expectations will affect the trend of the market also in the future, although the preliminary estimates show that the Gross Domestic Product will increase from the next year on[3]; c) the UK housing market is not new to "boom and bust cycles" (Fig. 1a), as the last crisis is recorded during the 90's – after the so called "Lawson Boom"[4]; these cycles are caused by structural factors like the limited and therefore inelastic supply of houses and the intrinsic volatility of the mortgage sector, resulting in an highly volatile market, subject to amplified booms and depressions in comparison with the trend of the real economy (Fig. 1b).

With regard to a deeper analysis of the properties price in the United Kingdom, it is noted that the trend path is quite similar in all type of houses, both with reference to their age (Fig. 2a) and their type (Fig. 2b). New houses, quite obviously, are credited slightly more valuable in comparison to the other categories, while in the late years the older, pre WW II built properties have gained a slight increase in their price, surpassing the modern ones.

The type of building, divided in the traditional Anglo-Saxon classes "detached", "semi-detached", "terraced" and "flat", seems to make the real difference in the pricing, depicting a chart in the order mentioned above, with significant gaps between them, and this fact is particularly true with regard to detached houses.

Since the city of Swindon, subject of case study in the present paper, is located in the south-western part of England, we will make some brief consideration on the

---

[3] European Union forecasts for the United Kingdom show an increase in the GDP by 0.9% in 2010 and 1.9% in 2011 (European Commission, 2009).

[4] The "Lawson boom" is named after Nigel Lawson, Chancellor of the Exchequer from June 1983 to October 1989, whose monetary policy and fiscal laxity is considered to be responsible of the heavy inflation of the time (Godley, 2003).

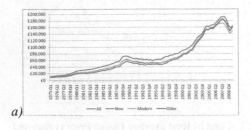 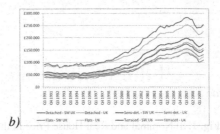

a)

b)

Fig. 2. a) Real House Price in the UK for property ages and b) comparison between UK and South West England, with detail to house type

Source: Nationwide Building Society; older ages refer to pre-WW II properties.

house market of this portion of the United Kingdom. There are in fact some peculiarities compared to the national UK situation (Fig. 2b): particularly, while the correlation between the national and regional datum is very high (>0.99), the average price in this part of England is generally higher, roughly 10% more, with the unique exception of the flats, whose value is almost coincident, lately becoming cheaper than the UK national price.

The house pricing in Swindon is partially consistent with the statistics showing that detached houses are more expensive than in the rest of England, and are highly valued also in comparison with the surrounding region; flats prices diverge for small amounts, but the country values appear to behave similarly. Semi-detached properties' value is more similar to the overall UK value rather than the regional one, and this behaviour is even clearer for the terraced class. Local market factors can provide explanation to these differences: in the sample of 4,749 house sales considered in this work, 1,913 involved terraced houses, 1,119 semi-detached ones, 936 were flats and only 781 detached properties. On this basis, we can hypothesize an excessive supply of semi-detached and terraced houses in the Swindon area, and thus justify the significantly lower local average price, much more in line with the UK standard rather than with the regional value.

With regard to the flow of real estate transactions, the seasonal effect is quite visible (Fig. 3); the decrease of house sales in the winter season is typical, while the sudden summer stop in the sales could reveal two facts: a local condition, linked to the summer holydays that draw the Swindon denizens away from town, and an awareness that the housing market crisis was about to start, resulting in a major change of the customers' expectations.

From the analysis it neatly emerges that, despite the efforts made by the local community to restructure and revitalize the historical centre of the town (corresponding to post zones SN1 and SN2), the most attractive areas of Swindon are still the "green" residential parts (SN25) made of detached houses, aside, separated and kind of "protected" from the city centre car traffic and the surrounding heavy industries. Moreover, the number of sales of the last quarter of 2007 show that the central zones, after an encouraging start at the beginning of the year, seems to suffer a stronger reduction of real estate activities in comparison with other zones of the near suburbs.

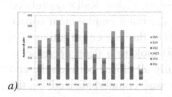 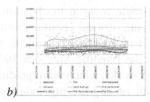 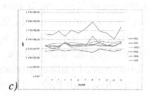

a)   b)   c)

Fig. 3. a) Seasonal effect of the housing market in Swindon – number of transactions per postcode; b) Average daily house prices in Swindon compared to trend polynomial proxy curves referred to house type (6th order polynomial); c) Comparison of average monthly house prices in Swindon, referred to postcode zones, year 2007

Source: Her Majesty's Land Registry 2007 House prices (nominal, non seasoned).

3 The Study Area

3.1 Swindon Urban Area and Evolution

The city of Swindon is located in Wiltshire County (South-Western part of England, inside a rectangle-shaped area whose vertexes are constituted by some important cities such as Bristol, Gloucester, Winchester and Reading) and is accessible by some important transport infrastructure, such as M4 motorway, A420 to Oxford, A419/A417 to Gloucester and the railways line connecting Bristol and London.

The very first urban settlement, corresponding to Old Town area, was located on top of Swindon hill and it was a small market specialised in barter trade; this function characterized Swindon's economy until the first half of 19th Century, when the local economy benefit from the industrial revolution processes.

As in many other towns, Swindon's urban growth is strongly interwoven with the evolution of transport infrastructure: the first urban expansion followed to the realisation of two important infrastructure, Wilts and Berks Canal in 1810 and the North Wilts canal in 1819, which increased accessibility to the local area and gave many more trade opportunities, thus taking to an increase in population and, consequently, to urban structure.

The real boost in urban growth is connected to the evolution of rail transport: in 1840 Swindon was chosen as a site for a new station for the Great Western Railway, with the function of shunting rail flows from London to a potential new rail connection to Gloucester. The station was opened in 1842 and its functioning created a suitable environment for Swindon's urban growth: a new village between the new railway works and Swindon Hill (present Swindon's town centre) was designed by Brunel and built to host workers of the railways company; furthermore, the shunting function of Swindon's station, which required locomotive changes, took to a clustering of rail transport-related activities (in particular rolling stock construction and maintenance) and, consequently, new inhabitants and new services (health and education) which created a skilled and well-educated working class.

During the second half of 19th Century the new city continued to expand along the main rail line connecting Bristol to London until it merged with the original settlement, creating a new single town at the beginning of 1900s. Railways-related activities constituted the engine of local economy and the main employment source (with more than 14,500 workers employed) until the 60s; the last construction of a steam engine locomotive – the Evening Star - in 1960 took to a deep decrease in deliveries of railways-related works, which were gradually all closed between the end of 1970s and 1986. The fall of engineering industry was counterbalanced by the attraction of new economic activities partially related to the previous ones (automotive sector, with multinational companies such as Honda, BMW and Renault), or belonging to the same industrial environment (IT and electronics) or to another one (financing, services, counselling).

This attraction has transformed Swindon economy and urban shape and it has led to an increase in population (in 2007, there are estimates issued by NOMIS of 189,500 inhabitants in the Borough of Swindon, +4.9% compared to 2001 estimates) and to an urban area expansion towards Northern areas like Abbey Meads and Andrew's Ridge (and, more recently, Priory Vale). At the same time, some projects for managing the new expansion of the town and regenerating the original town centre were set up and, in this framework, in 2002 the New Swindon Company was formed with the aim of realizing the tasks of the Regeneration Framework Plan for the town centre, which aimed at creating new office space (969,000 square feet), retail and leisure space (more than 1 million square feet) and 3.000 new homes with investments for over GBP 1 billion across six project areas[5].

According to Knight Frank Research (2009) the future expansion of the town should be realised towards the Southern part of the Borough (so called Southern Development Area, between the town and the M4 motorway): the initial project aimed at creating an additional number of 35,000 homes by 2026, but after the kick-off phase in 2006 it has since been put on hold during the economic recession (Swindon Borough Council, 2009).

Table 1. Swindon development areas

Development areas	Main functional use	Planned works
Union Square	Business oriented	600,000 sq ft offices; retail & leisure, hotel; 450 homes
The Promenade	Cultural centre	New library, museum and art gallery; REGENT CIRCUS: new public square, cinema, hotel, supermarket; 500 homes
The Hub	Retail offer enhancement	300,000 sq ft of new retail space, 250 homes + hotel; new pedestrian facilities
Swindon Central	Gateway to town centre	160,000 sq ft of offices and ancillary retail and leisure facilities; 400 new homes. Enhanced accessibility between the railway station and the town centre
North Star Village and The Campus	Dwellings and education facilities	New University Campus for 4,000 students; linking spaces between the 2 development areas

---

[5] http://www.newswindon.co.uk/regenerationAreas/

3.2 Swindon's Economy

Swindon economy has registered good performances in the period 2002-2007, with an economic growth of +3.1% per year (United Kingdom average level is +2.7% per year) and an employment rate growth of +0.8% per year (compared to United Kingdom values equal to +0.4% per year).

In terms of Gross Value Added per head Swindon economy has the 4th highest value in the Country outside London (Ducalian Property, 2008), with latest figures referring to 2006 equal to GBP 5.2 billion (+4.99% compared to previous year).

In the last four decades Swindon has changed its economic activities structure, switching from an industrial-oriented production to a service and hi-tech based one. The main economic activities both in terms of Gross Value Added and employment are the ones related to banking and financial services, even if it has been deeply hit by the global financial crisis.

Another important economic sector, even if losing its traditional boosting role, is the one of manufacturing activities, which is however re-gaining new development possibilities due to its re-conversion into a knowledge intensive sector. The attraction of automotive and electronic engineering companies, in fact, has already led to the creation of an advanced engineering cluster in the North-Western part of the town, composed by a large number of small suppliers and third-party sub-contractors. This new specialised cluster has boosted new agglomeration economies and the setting of transport and logistics providers which have transformed Swindon in one of the main distribution hub in United Kingdom for retail business. According to Knight Frank Research (2009), the average of take-ups along the M4 has registered an average of 1,2 million of square feet p.a. in the last five years, and there are expansion opportunities in the North-Eastern part of the town, at South Marston area (next to Honda, South Marston Industrial Park and Keypoint area's warehouses).

The presence of Honda, the strategic location along A419 and relative lower costs per acre has created a growing demand for logistics spaces, which however is leading to an oversupply of industrial land, also considering the strong decrease in take-ups registered in 2008 and the consequential rise in availability of floor space (Swindon Borough Council, 2009).

Table 2. Main economic activities in Swindon in terms of GVA and share of total employment

Economic activities	GVA in MGBP			% of Total Employment		
	2004	2005	2006	Jul 05-Jun 06	Jul 06-Jun 07	Jul 07-Jun 08
Manufacturing	1,156	1,154	1,354	18.17%	16.85%	13.30%
Construction	173	182	233	7.31%	7.57%	7.21%
Distribution, Hotels				19.14%	19.58%	19.39%
Transport, Communications	1,223	1,217	1,123	9.68%	10.60%	11.27%
Banking, Finance, etc.	1,571	1,671	1,919	17.85%	17.76%	23.45%
Public Admin etc.	637	709	710	19.87%	19.88%	19.09%

Source: Adapted from Swindon Borough Council (2009).

Logistics-oriented services concentration has allowed a further agglomeration of many retail and leisure activities, which have also been attracted by the new wave of urban regeneration's plans in order to revamp local retail network[6]. Beside the Brunel Centre (with its 100 stores) and many other traditional retail areas like the ones in Old Town, retail supply is completed by two important and peculiar commercial centres (The Parade and Swindon Designer Outlet) and many peripheral retail parks (i.e., Greenbridge, Orbital and West Swindon District Centre). Prime retail rents in central areas show average values of GBP 185 per square feet, but outside the CBD the average value presents high decline levels, with rents level far below GBP 100 per square feet.

Beside retail and leisure sectors, Swindon's development is strongly linked to knowledge-based economy and, since now, it's already showing the attraction of some important activities in this field: one important sector is the one of biotechnology (in particular, the pharmaceutical sub sector) with good possibilities of development depending upon the availability of high quality incubator space and highly skilled job profiles. Another high growing sector is the one of ICT, with the presence of some important companies (Intel, Alcatel Lucent, Motorola) driving increasing trends based on the creation of new markets generated by innovative multimedia technologies and their developments. The presence of some important companies belonging to energy sector (for instance, Johnson Matthey Fuel Cells, RWE nPower) has generated new environmental technologies and related research and consultancy professionals.

Another important sector, whose increasing role is interwoven with building development and urban regeneration programmes issued by local authorities, is the one of construction. Concerning residential areas development, the economic downturn has deeply changed increasing trends in average residential prices (+ 35% over the past five years) which dropped by 15% between January 2008 and February 2009, creating however further investment opportunities. In this framework, Swindon has registered a huge increase in attracting new inhabitants thanks to the relative levels of affordability of house prices (compared to other nearby towns), which is highly valuable for commuters to London's settlement evaluation. Furthermore, the real estate market is enhancing thanks to the presence of many single persons and young cohabiting couples who lust for independence and proper accommodation. Key element to the development of construction sector is constituted by the realisation works of the above mentioned Regeneration Framework Plan, which is attracting new service activities and thus creating inward migration, new offices deliveries and increased demand for residential accommodation.

4   Multilevel Urban Analysis

In order to understand the spatial structures and shapes of the city, the analysis was performed on different datasets, providing different images of the city, in terms of residential occupation, transport network infrastructures, economic activities pattern

---

[6] The New Swindon Company has identified 7 strategic development areas to strengthen retail and leisure services supply: Wharf Green, Canal Walk, The Parade, Regent Street (the main shopping high street), Bridge Street, Havelock Terrace and Wellington Street.

and house market prices. This latter element allowed us to observe the urban dynamics taking place in the area, thus portraying how and if the redevelopment action put in place by the local authorities and regional development agencies of Swindon are shaping the new poles of attractions for people in terms of residentialities. The analyses were performed on different kinds of elements and using different estimators and regarded mainly point pattern analysis to estimate densities of the phenomena observed and local and global estimate measure for examining house prices across the study area.

4.1 The Data

Different datasets for Swindon urban area were used for visualization and analytical purposes. In particular we used census units' polygon data Edline – Enumeration district (303 polygons) – with population figures at census 1991 and 2001 (Study area: 62.5137 km2 Population (2001): 156,016) and OSCAR (© Ordnance Survey Centreline for Roads) as road network data (3,267 points; 6,127 lines. Total length: 529.57 km). As the analysis concerned also some areas external from the Swindon urban area, as the villages and suburbs linked as postcode areas to the urban area, we integrated road network data with OpenStreetMap data for the Borough of Swindon area. These latter data appeared updated and – although quite limited in their attribute's richness – compatible with the official OSCAR data for visualization purposes. From Swindon road network a point dataset for junctions was extracted from the OSCAR data, to be used in a density analysis computation.

Other datasets was also used that needed an extra elaboration. In fact we extracted data on economic activities from UK Yellow Pages for a selected set of categories, and particularly, as macro-categories, banks and insurance companies, retail, real estate and entertainment for a total of 359 records. This set and number of activities was considered sufficient for providing a flavour of the spatial pattern distribution of 'central activities', although many categories were not considered as in other research carried on (Borruso and Porceddu, 2009), where professionals and other sub-categories were counted and mapped. House properties values counted for a 4,744 records dataset on house prices referred to year 2007 derived from Her Majesty's Land Registry[7] at Unit Postcode level. The data contains the house category (Flat, Terraced, Detached and Semidetached houses), price in GBP, date of selling announce and address containing UK Postcode, counting for a total of 1,984 Unit Postcodes. Unfortunately no information on the house dimension was available. Such data, although referred to a period preceding the global economic crisis that affected also the UK real estate market, are however useful in providing a valuable idea on the directions of expansion and development of Swindon and neighbouring areas. Yellow Pages and house prices data needed to pass through different steps, as their collection from websites imposed their organization in different spreadsheets and geocoding[8] in order to be loaded and elaborated in a GIS programme.

---

[7] Data accessed from "This is House Prices" http://www.thisishouseprices.co.uk/ on Dec 2008.

[8] Google Earth Plus was used together with the website http://www.batchgeocode.com. The data precision and correspondence were also tested to avoid errors in representation. Where the position was not available by means of one of the geocoding tools, it was decided to locate the single elements in correspondence to the closest geocoded element.

4.2 The Methods

A Kernel Density Estimation was used to model density and distribution of population, central business district activities and definition of a 'central area', network distribution and, as well, an estimate of a delineation of a central area. The kernel is a 3-D function estimates density of events within its searching radius or bandwidth (τ) weighting them according to their distance from the estimation point (Gatrell et al, 1996).

$$\hat{\lambda}(s) = \sum_{i=1}^{n} \frac{1}{\tau^2} k\left(\frac{s-s_i}{\tau}\right) \qquad (1)$$

where $\hat{\lambda}(s)$ is the intensity at location s, s_i is the observed i^{th} event, and $k(\ )$ is the kernel function, centred in location s, within which events s_i are counted and weighted. Also, KDE as an analytical instrument was calculated over house prices distribution for the year 2007 to highlight areas of major concentration of floor space available. Far from providing an idea of the spatial distribution of the residential built environment, such an index can help in delineating 'hot spots' where city residential improvement projects are developing. House prices' dataset was given a particular attention in order to model spatial distribution of new houses' values over the region. As major urban redevelopment projects are on the ground, the different analyses carried on could reveal patterns and trends in the housing market of the area, although, as stated in the data description, the dataset chosen for the analysis is limited to the year 2007[9].

Spatial trends of prices were measured, with the value in GBP as a function of the distance from the city centre. That was possible using a 2-D scatterplot graph and a 5th order polynomial interpolation curve. To help and integrate this kind of exam, global and local analyses were performed on house prices, both to model a general trend over space and highlighting areas of expansion of the city and to analyse where 'peaks and valleys' in house prices' distribution take place. Global techniques fit a function to the data distribution in order to produce a surface as close as possible to the original point dataset. Local techniques are focused on local variability of the phenomenon under observation, assuming the existence of a local correlation decreasing as distance from the estimated location increases (Kelly and Atkinson 1999). Global estimates were performed using a cubic polynomial regression. That allowed creating 'price surfaces' for the different categories of houses showing a general trend over the study region.

As a local estimate it was decided to interpolate data in terms of their values - price in GBP – and position on a map. The Inverse Distance Weighting (IDW) algorithm was used to create a surface of continuous data from the initial point pattern. As house dimensions were not reported, it was not possible to compute relative prices per house surface. House prices for the Year 2007 were therefore considered as sample values for the study area. The IDW has been used by geographers and spatial analyst to express distance decay factors in spatial behaviors and also to compare other

---

[9] House prices expressed in Postcode areas statistics are referred to a longer timeframe in order to evaluate differences in space and time of prices.

interpolation techniques (Watson 1992). The IDW estimates values at location z' from a set of points z_i according to their distance and can be expressed as:

$$z' = \sum_i^n (1/d_i)^p z_i \Big/ \sum_i^n (1/d_i)^p \qquad (2)$$

where d_i is the distance from z' (estimate) to the locations z_i (set of points) and p the power of distance. The IDW algorithm is based on the assumption that closer values are more similar to each other than farther ones, and therefore it assumes weighting closer values more in interpolating data. In the present research a power function $p = 2$ is used, considering that local interpolation effect is maintained – as it happens when p > 1 - , although the estimator can provide a 'blocky' visualization.

Research is ongoing to limit such effects by using geostatistical approaches (Kelly, Atkinson, 1999) and will be implemented in future works on this topic, where Kriging will be applied on the data available.

4.3 Results and Discussion

Density analysis. The road network junctions were used for a density analysis to highlight areas of transport infrastructure concentration and to analyze urban shapes. A 500 m bandwidth quartic KDE was used coupled with a 20 m cell size (Figure 4 a)[10]. The city centre displays a denser network of streets and roads and represents the core of the city with reference to the network's spatial distribution. Also the residential areas out from the city centre – particularly West Swindon – present high values. It is worth noting also that a 'peak' effect drawn by junctions being close to major access roads is also visible, in areas close to roundabouts in the southeastern and southwestern areas of the Swindon urban area (Borruso, 2003; p. 188).

UK cities generally present a typical pattern of residential areas regularly organized according a hierarchical road network. It is therefore easy to notice a relation between the urban land use and the road network pattern.

With reference to the spatial distribution of population (Figure 4 b) we can notice a general matching of population peaks close to high values of network density. That is particularly true in the same city centre, where the highest network density value is registered, and high population density figures are visible around this area. A stronger matching of density values in the two distributions can be noticed in the residential areas - southwest and southeast of the urban area and study region. This is also visible by comparing the density profiles of the two density surfaces, drawn along different directions, all of them passing through the city centre: North – South; East – West; West-Southwest – Centre – East-Southeast.

A density analysis was performed on some urban activities considered as central, therefore contributing to a formation of the CBD (Figure 4 c).

Here also a density analysis using KDE has been carried on, using a 500 m bandwidth and a 20 m cell resolution. The density surface presents mainly a single peak in what we expect to be "the" city centre of Swindon. A part from the aim of the paper of portraying different functional shapes of the cities according to different perspective, such an analysis

---

[10] Similar bandwidths and cell size were used for the other KDE analysis. That allowed a direct comparison between the different datasets used and suitable for the scale of representation of the area. The choice was done after several tests on different distances.

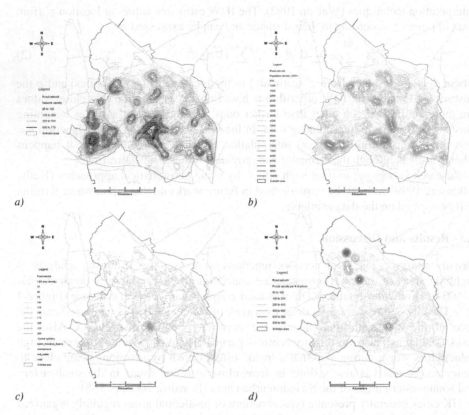

a)   b)   c)   d)

Fig. 4. Kernel density estimation over point datasets. a) junction of road network; b) EDLINE centroids; c) Sample of CBD activities; d) 2007 house prices at UPC level.

was considered important also in order to provide us with a location to be used as the starting point for the distance computation of new houses from the city centre. The centre highlighted by the CBD analysis is also consisted with what seen after the density analysis over the nodes of the urban street network.

The density analysis performed over the spatial distribution of new houses displays a series of peaks in two main areas of Swindon urban area (Figure 4 d). These are the Northwest part of the city, corresponding to postcode SN25, where the highest values as high as 800 events per km^2 are found. The concentration follows a North-Northwest – South-Southeast line. A second area can be found south of the railway line and close to the city centre, corresponding to postcode SN1. Here a smoother peak is visible, although the density estimate here counts for a maximum of 400 events per km^2, with the concentration of new houses following a Northeast – Southwest line.

Global and local analyses. The analysis continued with the exam of the distribution of new houses – and their prices – differentiated by their category and according to the distance from the city centre (Figure 5 a-d). As anticipated in density analysis, an ideal 'centre' of the city was highlighted to serve as a starting point for

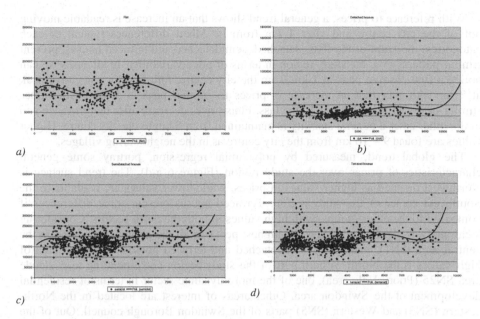

a)

b)

c)

d)

Fig. 5. House prices and distance from city centre. a) flats; b) detached houses; c) semidetached houses; d) terraced houses.

further distance-based analysis. Doing that allowed to compute Euclidean distances for each house price value to the city centre. A first set of analysis allowed representing graphically the spatial distribution of new houses according to distance classes from the city centre.

The results were considered for the different categories of houses available. Although the new houses' location registered span from the city centre to a distance of nearly 11 km from it, as some neighbouring satellite villages around the city of Swindon, the vast majority of events are located within 6 km from the city centre, that is the maximum distance from the border of Swindon urban area, with little figures located over such distance. That is particularly true for terraced houses (95.3% within 6 km), flats (97%), while detached and semidetached houses (87.82% and 91.77% respectively) present a wider distribution over the study region.

Generally new houses are present in the central area of the city within 1 km, with increasing figures at 2 km class. At 3 km there is a reduction in the values and at 4 figures increase again reaching the highest values in the distribution, followed by high but reducing values at 5 and 6 km. These values are differently drawn by the house types considered. Terraced houses, the most represented categories in the distribution (40.32% of all new houses considered), present a similar behaviour as the overall distribution of data. Detached and semidetached houses are nearly absent in the city centre, with the former increasing their values at 4 km, reaching a peak at 5 km and presenting tail values after 6 km, while the latter increases at 2 km, peaks at 4 km and with tail values after 7 km. Flats offer a higher frequency in the city centre and decrease to a minimum at 3 km, steadily increasing again to 6 km where another peak is reached, followed by little figures in the tail values of distance classes.

With reference to prices, a general trend shows that an increase is readable moving out of the city centre and after 4 km from it. Albeit differences typical of each categories, the exam of the flats, detached, semidetached and terraced houses, present similar patterns over the study region in terms of price variability. In all cases we can notice a first positive peak at 1 km from the city centre, followed by a negative peak at 3 km and after that an increase in prices to another peak at 5 km, with values similar or higher than those at 1 km class. Flats prices decrease after that distance and in the other cases a general stability is maintained from 6 km to the city centre. Higher values are found 9 – 10 km from the city centre as in the neighbouring villages.

The global trend, measured by polynomial regression, portray some general characteristics of prices over the study region (Figure 6 a-d). The trend surface is Northwest oriented as higher values in prices, while lower values are readable in the Southwest corner of the study region. Terraced houses present some differences if compared to the other groups, with high values in both the north sectors. Considering local analysis, the IDW displays the highest peaks in all the groups considered in the central area (SN1), mainly for semidetached and terraced houses. A second area of high values is the North-western part of the study region corresponding to postcode area SN25 (Priory Vale area), one of the more dynamic sector in terms of residential development of the Swindon area. Other areas of interest are located in the North-eastern (SN3) and Western (SN5) parts of the Swindon Borough council. Out of the strict study region, some of the surrounding villages appear dynamic as location for new residential development, particularly of higher price houses. Wootton Basset and Wroughton (SN4) present high figures in terms of new realizations and, together with the other villages as Purton, Lydiard Millicent, Chiseldon, they represent the areas of high residential house prices for detached and semidetached houses.

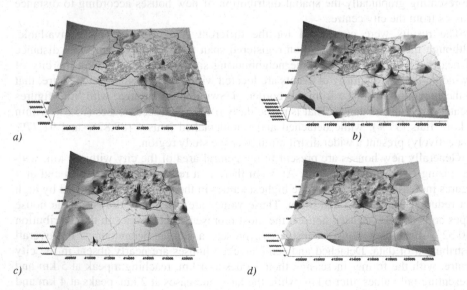

a)

b)

c)

d)

Fig. 6. Global and local analysis for house prices. a) flats; b) detached houses; c) semidetached houses; d) terraced houses. [3D views by elaborations using Golden Software Surfer 8.0].

5 Conclusions

Results. In this paper the analysis of house prices at urban level has been tackled, having in mind different objectives. The paper explored the possibility of examining urban shape and characteristics by means of spatial analytical techniques, and particularly density analysis (KDE) and interpolation techniques (IDW). An ancillary objective was also represented by the possibility of implementing such a research using a limited amount of freely available data, therefore extending the potential of the combination of spatial analytical techniques for modelling urban areas and trends with a limited set of free geographical data. The paper demonstrated also the need to combine qualitative and quantitative analysis to provide elements to understand some of the spatial issues and characteristics of an urban area in terms of house values and development. House prices and their locations were considered as a point pattern and therefore capable of being analysed by means of spatial analytical techniques. The analyses performed allowed to reach a twofold objective. The density analysis on 'pure' locations of new houses allowed mapping the more dynamic areas of the City of Swindon in terms of residential development. On the other side, when considering the house prices distribution, modelling the global trend over the study region and the local effect allowed to highlight also those areas where prices are generally higher and possibly representing the direction of evolution of urban residentialities in the study region. The most dynamic areas of the city of Swindon can be located in the central and centre - south of the city and in the North-western quadrant (SN25) in terms of frequencies of houses available on sale. New houses on sale are located in the area surrounding the city centre at a certain distance from it copying areas already noticed as presenting a high population density, in a process of further housing development.

Limitations. The study concerned house deliveries prices data related to a single year (2007) preceding the economic downturn in real estate market and therefore may have been influenced by a rather "optimistic" view of the short term trend. Crisis period trends usually do not affect consolidated mid-term evolution in real estate market; moreover, year 2007 house prices are quite stable, in comparison with the up-warding trend of the previous years and the following bust of 2008. Another possible limitation is that issues in urban patterns for different house categories prices do not have a clear correlation with the urban re-development policies carried on by local authorities; so, the highlighted concentration of higher price deliveries in North-Western part of the urban area could be explicated by other variables not linked with the benefits of urban re-development policies. From the methodological point of view, there is a need to refine some research methods, as implementing other geographical indicators and tools picking from the most recent ones used in urban land value analysis (GWR and spatial econometrics), as also considering house prices in terms of price per square metre/foot. The use of different data sets, distinguishing the sale offers from the actual transactions concluded, could also help in determining more accurate price projections and finding other variables linked to peculiar locations.

References

Alonso, W.: A Theory of the Urban Land Market. Pap. Proc. Reg. Sci. Assoc. 6, 149–157 (1960)

Bailey, T.C., Gatrell, A.C.: Interactive Spatial Data Analysis. Longman, Harlow (1995)

Borruso, G., Porceddu, A.: A Tale of Two Cities. Density Analysis of CBD on Two Midsize Urban Areas in North-eastern Italy. In: Borruso, G., Lapucci, A., Murgante, B. (eds.) Geocomputational Analysis for Urban Planning. SCI, vol. 176, pp. 37–56. Springer, Heidelberg (2009)

Borruso, G.: Network Density and the Delimitation of Urban Areas. Trans. GIS 7(2), 177–191 (2003)

European Commission: Eurostat database 2009, http://epp.eurostat.ec.europa.eu (acc. December 2009)

Gatrell, A., Bailey, T., Diggle, P., Rowlingson, B.: Spatial Point Pattern Analysis and its Application in Geographical Epidemiology. Trans. Inst. Brit. Geog. 21, 256–274 (1996)

Godley, W.: The awful warning of the Lawson boom 2003, http://www-cfap.jbs.cam.ac.uk/publications/files/Godley%20FT%20060803.pdf (accessed December 2009)

Halifax: Halifax House price index, http://www.lloydsbankinggroup.com/media1/research/halifax_hpi.asp (November 2009, acc. December 2009)

Hoch, I., Waddel, P.: Apartment Rents: Another Challenge to the Monocentric Model. Geog. An. 25(1), 20–34 (1993)

Kelly, R.E.J., Atkinson, P.M.: Modelling and Efficient Mapping of Snow Cover in the UK for Remote Sensing Validation. In: Atkinson, P.M., Tate, N.J. (eds.) Advances in Remote Sensing and GIS Analysis. Wiley, London (1999)

Knos, D.S.: Distribution and Land Values in Topeka, Kansas, Bureau of Business and Economic Research. Lawrence, Mahwah (1962)

Nationwide Building Society: Nationwide Housing Index reviews (2009), http://www.nationwide.co.uk/hpi (acc. December 2009)

Office for National Statistics: Time series data, http://www.statistics.gov.uk/statbase/ (acc. December 2009)

O' Sullivan, D., Unwin, D.J.: Geographic Information Analysis. Wiley, London (2003)

Silverman, B.W.: Density Estimation for Statistics and Data Analysis. Chapman Hall, London (1986)

Swindon Borough Council: Swindon (2010), http://www.swindon.gov.uk (January 2008, acc. November 2009)

Swindon Strategic Economic Partnership: Swindon Economic Profile (2009), http://www.ssep.org.uk (September 2009, acc. November 2009)

The New Swindon Company: Swindon. Challenging your perceptions, http://www.newswindon.co.uk (January 2008, acc. November 2009)

The New Swindon Company: Swindon's Brighter Future, http://www.newswindon.co.uk (June 2009; acc. November 2009)

Waddel, P., Berry, B.J.L., Hoch, I.: Housing Price Gradients: The Intersection of Space and Built Form. Geog. An. 25(1), 5–19 (1993)

Watson, D.F.: Contouring: A Guide to the Analysis and Display of Spatial Data. Pergamon Press, London (1992)

Yeats, M.H., Garner, B.J.: The North American City. New York (1976)

Analysis of Positional Aspects in the Variation of Real Estate Values in an Italian Southern Metropolitan Area[1]

Silvestro Montrone, Paola Perchinunno, and Carmelo Maria Torre

Department of Statistical Science, University of Bari,
Via C. Rosalba 53, 70100 Bari, Italy
s.montrone@dss.uniba.it, p.perchinunno@dss.uniba.it
Department of Architecture and Urban Planning, Polytechnic of Bari,
Via Orabona 4, 70125 Bari, Italy
torre@poliba.it

Abstract. The paper show the use of a fuzzy weighting system to identify the correspondence of real estate value with main socio-physical characters of the urban tissue. The descriptor of the relationship with the real estate value is represented by a set of indicators of the urban decay of housing property and the analysis is tested on a real application of a case study. The study gives support to the development of new approach for localizing cadastral values at a more detailed scale, compared to the current scale used in the Italian Cadastre. The utilized statistical approach has been based on the SaTScan application, as a techniques of fuzzy clustering, and on a test of stability based on the comparison of a "fuzzy semantic distance" among the average real estate values of urban quarters, with the expected crisp distance among the same quarters.

Keywords: Estate value, fuzzy logic, SatScan, semantic distance.

1 Introduction

Property value represents the greatest indicator of quality of market and availability to residential services.

The quality of residential services, and consequently the price, is further associated with physical aspects and external quality, in addition to recognisable aspects of the social context which may be aligned with the significance of intrinsic relative and variable marginal prices which appreciate according to the social and environmental context.

Starting from this assumption, the real estate value is obtained by identifying the belonging to a given market segmentation. If we consider a unique segment of the real estate market, *ceteris paribus*, the only variable affecting the real estate value, is the position. A parameter to define the relationship between value and position can be described modifying by the distance to some reference point (services/amenities).

---

[1] The contribution is the result of joint reflections by the authors, with the following contributions attributed to S. Montrone (chapters 2), to P. Perchinunno (chapters 3 and 5), and to C. M. Torre (chapter 1 and 4).

D. Taniar et al. (Eds.): ICCSA 2010, Part I, LNCS 6016, pp. 17–31, 2010.
© Springer-Verlag Berlin Heidelberg 2010

The classification of the real estates, in the light of their owning to a cluster of the housing market, is managed by Cadastres according to those socioeconomic, architectural, spatial and situational attributes that generate their market value.

But cities are subdivided in homogeneous areas that are not well bounded according to their physical characters.

The way of subdividing the space of the city in the Italian real estate Cadastre (and not only the Italian one) is to sub-divide all urban areas in homogenous sectors that are characterised by rule that "the same type of house has the same price all over the area and varies from an area to another".

This means that the influence of the position on the estate value can not be represented in a continuous function, varying according with the distance, e.g., to some services or to some environmental amenity. This also means that urban fringe should be subdivided in a coherent number of sectors.

The subdivision of cities could be actually more detailed if the information about the real estate value could be spread on the basis of a different and more thick zoning.

For instance, in the city of Bari, South of Italy – one of our case study – the number of cadastral homogeneous areas is nine, while the subdivision in quarters identify more than twenty, physically homogeneous areas.

Table 1. Real Estate Values per Quarter of the City of Bari - 2006

Quarters	New/refurbished($€/m^2$)		Good state ($€/m^2$)		Degraded ($€/m^2$)	
	min estate value	max estate value	min estate value	max estate value	min estate value	max estate value
Carbonara-Ceglie	2.200	2.500	1.900	2.200	1.300	1.700
Carrassi	2.600	3.800	2.200	3.300	1.500	2.600
Japigia	2.400	2.600	2.300	2.500	2.100	2.300
Libertà	2.700	3.500	2.200	2.800	1.800	2.200
Madonnella	2.400	3.500	2.350	3.200	2.300	2.600
S.Girolamo Fesca -Faro	2.200	4.500	2.000	3.000	1.800	2.400
Murat	3.700	5.500	3.200	4.500	3.000	3.500
Palese	2.000	2.600	1.400	1.750	800	1.000
Picone Poggiofr.	2.000	3.500	1.500	2.800	1.100	2.000
S.Nicola	1.500	4.200	1.100	3.000	1.000	2.200
S.Paolo	1.800	2.200	1.400	1.800	1.000	1.400
S.Pasquale	2.600	3.800	2.200	3.300	1.500	2.600
S.Spirito	1.900	2.400	1.300	1.600	800	1.000
Stanic	2.000	2.500	1.500	2.000	1.300	1.800
Torre Mare S.Giorgio	1.400	2.500	1.050	1.500	810	1.250

Source: Our elaboration on the data from the FIAIP Observatory, 2006, II semester.

Furthermore, decennially is possible to analyse the variability of characters of the housing stock and of the social tissue, for more or less the 300 census sections on population and households, that means the possibility of describing the variability inside each quarter on the basis of 60 different sections per quarter.

In our experiment, the attempt is to test the correspondence between a possible ranking of the urban quarters, in the light of their urban attributes with an hypothetic market segmentation implicitly represented by estimated real estate values.

Data referring to the real estate marked derive from the National Italian Confederation of the Real Estates Promoter (FIAIP), drawn from their National Real Estate Observatory. The data are collected from the network of most of the Italian real estate agencies two times per year (each semester). *Table 1* shows the maximum and minimum value for each quarter of the city of Bari, in the South of Italy, reporting the prime prices (that is to say the price of dwellings that are localised in newest and refurbished buildings) and the lowest estate price (that is to say the price of dwellings that are localised in oldest and not well maintained buildings).

2 Measuring Descriptors of the Real Estate Value of Housing Property

2.1 A Multidimensional Approach for the Identification of a Fuzzy Value

At city level, some approach can be addressed by investigating the distribution of housing facilities and of the physical quality of the housing stock, to understand better some peculiar aspects of distribution of real estate values.

The presence of a varied aspects that define the social-physical de-qualification of the urban tissue leads to the necessity of managing a group of indicators. The different scientific research pathways are consequently directed towards the creation of *multidimensional indicators*, sometimes going beyond dichotomized logic in order to move towards a classification which is *"fuzzy"* in nature, in which every unit belongs to the category of distressed areas (*value equal to one*) or high quality areas (*value equal to zero*), and the other values in the interval reflect different levels of decay.

As in previous studies, the approach chosen in order to rich an acceptable synthesis and measure of the relationship urban decay vs real estate value is the *Total Fuzzy and Relative*, based on the use of *Fuzzy Set* in order to obtain a measurement of the level of decay within a urban housing stock, unified with the "social acceptability of social critical aspects, able to de-qualify a given quarter, as anti-amenities, beginning from statistical information gathered from a plurality of indicators" [1].

The development of *fuzzy theory* stems from the initial work of Zadeh [2] and successively of Dubois and Prade [3] who defined its methodological basis. Fuzzy theory assumes that every unit is associated contemporarily to all identified categories and not univocally to only one, on the basis of ties of differing intensity expressed by the concept of degrees of association. The use of fuzzy methodology in the field of "poverty studies" in Italy can be traced back to only a few years ago thanks to the work of Cheli and Lemmi [4] who define their method *"Total Fuzzy and Relative"* (TFR) on the basis of the previous contribution from Cerioli and Zani [5].

This method consists of the construction of a membership function to *the fuzzy totality of the poor* continuous in nature, and able to provide a measurement of the degree of poverty present within each unit [6] [1]. Supposing the observation of k indicators of poverty for every family, the membership function of *i*-th family to the fuzzy subset of the poor may be defined thus [5]:

$$f(x_{i.}) = \frac{\sum_{j=1}^{k} g(x_{i_j}) . w_j}{\sum_{j=1}^{k} w_j} \qquad i = 1,.....,n \qquad (1)$$

For the definition of the function $g(x_{ij})$ please refer to other works [1, 2, 6, 7].

2.2 Defining Indicators of Urban Decay

In order to analyse the phenomena of residential decay on a geographical b asis, this work uses data from the most recent *Population and Housing Census 2001* carried out by ISTAT; this information allows geographical analysis in sections according to the census, albeit hindered by the lack of more recent data. Specifically, the geographical units of the survey are the 1,421 census sections within the City of Bari, of which 109 are uninhabited areas or are designated for other uses (for example parks or universities).

The choice of those indexes to take into consideration has been made according to the analysis of some socio-cultural aspects of the resident population in the City of Bari considered useful in defining urban decay: these are education levels, working conditions and living conditions.

The various indices were classified into *two sets* of *Social degrade*, related to the conditions of the resident population within the various census sections (educational qualifications, working conditions, overcrowding) and *Housing property decay*, related to the housing conditions of dwellings occupied by residents in the various census sections (housing status, lack of functional services such as landline telephone). The indexes have been calculated both at the scale of the census section and at the scale of the neighbourhood.

Table 2 shows average indexes of household decay for each neighbourhood. The analysis of urban decay, referring to the census sections of the City of Bari, shows that the minimum level of school attendance is reached by 55% of citizens aged over 19. This index shows the highest average percentage in a popular neighbourhood (San Paolo) and the old town (San Nicola), and the lowest percentage in the city centre (Murat). The average rate of unemployment is 20%; the worst result is 28% in the San Paolo area, and the best result is 11% in the Murat area. The dwelling space index is 3.42 on average (more or less three inhabitants per 100 square meters). Overcrowding is relevant in the San Nicola area, with five inhabitants per 100 meters (20 square meters per capita) and four inhabitants per 100 meters (25 square meters per capita) in the Stanic and San Paolo areas.

As regards typology of occupation, the index measures the percentage of the total of dwelling occupied by renters. In the City of Bari the average percentage is more or less 29% (while 6% are free used, and 65% are owned by occupants). More specifically, there are 31,558 rented homes, while there are 72,587 owner-occupied homes.

Table 2. Average of indexes [2] per single area of the City of Bari – 2001

Neighborhoods	Index 1	Index 2	Index 3	Index 4	Index 5	Index 6
Carbonara	0.61	0.22	3.55	0.26	0.19	0.07
Carrassi	0.43	0.15	2.92	0.21	0.10	0.07
Ceglie	0.71	0.25	3.61	0.32	0.22	0.08
Japigia	0.50	0.20	3.23	0.29	0.12	0.07
Libertà	0.66	0.22	3.93	0.36	0.18	0.21
Loseto	0.66	0.25	3.49	0.19	0.20	0.03
Madonnella	0.53	0.21	3.30	0.43	0.18	0.20
S.Girolamo F.	0.63	0.21	3.88	0.30	0.21	0.07
Murat	0.28	0.11	2.28	0.24	0.09	0.06
Palese	0.52	0.19	3.25	0.23	0.17	0.04
Picone - Poggiofranco	0.44	0.16	3.13	0.22	0.11	0.06
S.Nicola	0.74	0.25	5.00	0.47	0.33	0.38
S.Paolo	0.84	0.28	4.03	0.46	0.15	0.07
S.Pasquale	0.43	0.16	3.29	0.23	0.13	0.08
S.Spirito	0.58	0.20	3.44	0.30	0.20	0.07
Stanic	0.70	0.27	4.00	0.24	0.27	0.11
Torre a Mare	0.51	0.19	2.85	0.27	0.26	0.08
Bari	**0.55**	**0.20**	**3.42**	**0.29**	**0.17**	**0.10**

Source: Our elaboration of the data from the Population and Housing Census, 2001.

Again, San Nicola (47%), San Paolo (46%) and the Madonnella (43%) show the worst conditions, while the peripheral Loseto area shows the best conditions, even if the property values are not highly rated, and its newest properties are often rented to young couples.

When it comes to facilities, on average 17% of households do not have a contract for a landline telephone and 10% of households do not have heating systems. The critical condition of the San Nicola area is confirmed also by the lack of facilities: 33% of households do not have a contract for a telephone line, 38% of households have no heating systems. The difficulties caused by the lack of facilities are a common problem of the Madonnella and Libertà areas, the most degraded areas in the centre of the city. The Murat area has a

---

[2] Index 1. Lack of education progress: number of ≥ 19 aged without high school diploma on the total.

Index 2. Rate of unemployment: number of ≥15 aged residents searching for job on the whole ≥15 aged workforce.

Index 3. Overcrowding: number of residents per surface unit of their occupied dwellings.

Index 4. Incidence of housing stock for rent. Number of occupied dwellings by rent-payers on the total of residents.

Index 5. Absence of a home-phone landline: number of occupied by residents dwellings without a phone-landline on the total.

Index 6. Absence of home-heating system: number of dwellings occupied by residents without a heating system on the total.

good range of facilities; the property value is quite high, due to the presence of many of historical residential buildings, that have been restored and represent the best quality supply of offices and residence in the city centre area [7].

2.3 The Result of TFR Approach

In Table 3, the TFR measures, estimated for the reality of Bari (the last census data of 2001) are classified into five different level of degradation of the urban property in accordance with the resulting fuzzy value: according to the set of selected indicators, a division of the census sections for conditions of property's decay is produced.

In detail, it rises on the fore that 606 census sections on 1312 (more or less the 46%) do not seem characterized by an evident decay. The lowest level of decay is concentrated in the quarters of Murat and Picone-Poggiofranco (106 census sections). Instead, the 6% of sections shows a condition of high decay. Such sections are localized in the historical quarter of San Nicola (27 sections), in Libertà (16 sections) and Madonnella (11 sections).

Table 3. Composition of absolute fuzzy values of the census sections per single area of the City of Bari - 2001

Neighbourhoods	0,0 - 0,2 property non-decay	0,2 - 0,4 slightly property decay	0,4 - 0,6 almost property decay	0,6 - 0,8 property decay	0,8 - 1,0 Unquestionably property decay
Carbonara	49	40	52	7	4
Carrassi	76	9	6	10	0
Ceglie	13	12	18	2	4
Japigia	51	16	6	3	2
Libertà	23	14	30	25	16
Roseto	5	3	4	1	0
Madonnella	20	6	8	4	11
S.Girolamo F.	21	28	15	6	2
Murat	106	15	5	2	0
Palese	28	16	15	0	1
Picone - Poggiofranco	106	16	13	4	3
S.Nicola	6	8	9	24	27
S.Paolo	12	32	27	11	3
S.Pasquale	40	14	5	7	2
S.Spirito	28	10	16	3	4
Stanic	5	8	6	1	1
Torre a Mare	17	18	14	2	0
Bari	**606**	**265**	**249**	**112**	**80**

Source: Our elaboration on the data from the Population and Housing Census, 2001.

The fuzzy values have been used as weighting set for the real estate appraisal of each sections. More in detail, a function has been structured, giving back the characteristic real estate value of each section, by weighting on the basis of the decay, the minimum and the maximum real estate value of the whole quarter, on each census section.

3 The Geographical Zoning of Real Estate Value

3.1 The Application of Scan Statistics

In order to reason about the possibility of operating by the use of regeneration program, it is necessary to introduce a physical reference to urban spaces. In the field of epidemiological studies many research groups have developed different typologies of software; these are all based on the same approach, but usually differ from each other in the shape of the window.

Among the various methods of zoning, we can remember SaTScan [8] that uses a circular window, FlexScan [9], the Upper Level Scan Statistics [10] and AMOEBA [11]. The research has led to the identification of small areas with high indices of poverty although quite heterogeneous in the observed urban context: know as *hot spots*. Regarding this specific aim, SaTScan seems to be quite efficient [12].

Scan statistics are used to detect and evaluate clusters in a temporal, spatial or space-time setting. This is done by gradually scanning a window across time and/or space, noting the number of observed and expected observations inside the window at each location. In the SaTScan software, the scanning window is either an interval (in time), a circle or an ellipse (in space) or a cylinder with a circular or elliptic base (in space-time). Multiple different window sizes are used. The window with the maximum likelihood is the most likely cluster, that is, the cluster least likely to be due to chance. A p-value is assigned to this cluster [13].

In this case, with the use of the SaTScan model a possible identification of hot spots of discomfort has been obtained from the data generated by a fuzzy analysis starting from two sets of indicators (the first for social difficulty, the second for housing difficulty). SaTScan operates by locating a circular window of arbitrary radius, and calculating the probability of urban difficulty, inside the circle, or the probability of urban difficulty, outside the circle, and consequently by optimizing the dimension of the radius [7].

3.2 The Connection of Hot Spots of Decay with the Real Estate Value

By the use of the above depicted SaTScan Model, it is possible to identify clusters, composed by the number of census sections per level of decay of property.

The internal mean identifies the decay level: the highest value refers to the highest real estate value, that corresponds to the lowest level of decay of the property. It is the same for the opposite: the lowest value refers to the lowest real estate value, that corresponds to the highest level of decay of the property, identified by high degraded areas.

A further aspect to be considered is the p-value that means the highest level of probability of the critical region of the test. The p-value is calculated first of all referring to the cluster that maximizes the likelihood, that is to say the main cluster. After the main cluster other clusters are considered, that do not fit with the main, in decreasing order of overlapping with the statistical test.

There are also a number of measures, based on the geographical location of the point-event, designed to determine whether their spatial distribution and clustering (process aggregate) or dispersed (process repulsive). The *Nearest Neighbor Index* [14] calculates the distance between each crime location and its nearest neighbor's crime location. All the nearest neighbor distances are averaged. If the average distance is less than the average for a hypothetical random distribution, the distribution of the features being analyzed are considered clustered. If the average distance is greater than a hypothetical random distribution, the features are considered dispersed. The index is expressed as the ratio of the observed distance divided by the expected distance. Therefore, the nearest neighbor index (NNI) less than 1 indicates clustering of crime locations whereas the nearest neighbor index greater than 1 indicates a uniform pattern of crime locations. The NNI is given as:

$$NNI = \frac{d(NN)}{d(ran)} . \qquad (2)$$

where numerator is the observed average distance between each crime location and its nearest neighbor and denominator is the expected average distance for the crime location given a random pattern:

$$d(NN) = \frac{\sum_{I=1}^{K} \min(d_{ij})}{N} \quad ; \quad d(ran) = \frac{0.5}{\sqrt{\frac{N}{A}}} \qquad (3)$$

where $\min(d_{ij})$ is the distance between crime location i and its nearest crime location, N corresponds to the total number of crime locations and A is the total study area.

In the case of study four different clusters have been identified: tree of them are characterized by a low estate value (the first, the second and the third cluster); the fourth is the only one characterized by high estate value. The low value characterizing the first tree clusters shows an inside mean of about 2,000 euros per square meter; instead, the high value characterizing the fourth cluster shows an inside mean of about 5,000 euros (Table 4), corresponding to a prestige area, and to a prime estate value.

Table 4. Composition and description of cluster referring to real estate value

Cluster	Number of cases	inside Mean	outside Mean	Standard deviation	p-value	Nearest Neighbour Index
1	59	1,900	2,880	1.04	0.0010	0.41555
2	212	1,970	3,000	0.99	0.0010	0.46437
3	210	2,070	2,980	1.01	0.0010	0.40666
4	114	5,020	2,630	0.82	0.0010	0.15294
Total	**595**					

Putting on the map the cluster, it results that the first cluster identifies the historical area of San Nicola, the second and the third cluster identify some peripherals popular area (Carbonara, Ceglie, San Girolamo Palese and Stanic). The fourth cluster, identifies the downtown quarter of Murat (Fig.1).

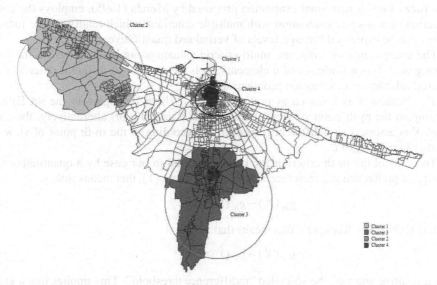

Fig. 1. SaTScan model for the identification of Hot Spots of lowest and highest real estate values in Bari

The easy identification of such areas has been possible due to the low level of variability of real estate values. In the remaining quarters the high level of variability of real estate value forbids a clear identification.

The NNI observed in the present work shows values that are well below one in all clusters (especially for the cluster 4 with high property values), and it consequently shows a good adaptability of data to the identified clusters (Table 4).

4 Interpreting the Positional Parameter in the Real Estate Market by the Use of Semantic Distance

4.1 Housing Market Segmentation and Multidimensional Ranking

The fuzzy analysis carried out on the Census Sections utilizes a wide number of spatial elements in the light of select clusters according to an appropriate statistical identification. At the urban level, at least two further level of spatial classification exist, that can be helpful to describe a relationship between the urban degradation of housing stock and spatial-physical attributes of the urban estates.

The experiment has been carried out by the application of a fuzzy multicriterial ranking, with the consciousness that the spread of values in a quarter, as above reminded, is to be considered imperfectly bounded.

4.2 The Method for a Fuzzy Ranking of the Urban Quarters

The fuzzy multidimensional evaluation proposed by Munda (1995), employs the construction of a discrete evaluation with multiple criteria to which relative value judgements can be expressed through levels of verbal and quantitative grading.

The components of a discrete multi-criteria valuation can be described in the following way: E is a finite set of n elements; m is the number of different criteria considered relevant in a evaluation problem, where:

The element X is assessed as preferable than Y (both belonging to the set E) according to the m-th point of view if $Rank_m(X) > Rank_m(Y)$, or, alternatively, the element X is assessed as indifferent respect to Y according to the m-th point of view if $Rank_m(X) = Rank_m(Y)$.

The rank of the m-th criterion $Rank_m$ is expressed in our case by a quantitative intensity of preference g_m; therefore if $Rank_m(X) > Rank_m(Y)$, this means that:

$$g_m(X) - g_m(Y) > s \qquad (4)$$

and, if $Rank_m(X) = Rank_m(Y)$, this means that:

$$g_m(X) - g_m(Y) \leq s \qquad (5)$$

s is a positive number, the so-called "indifference threshold". This implies that a grey area exists in the interval $(0,s)$, where, in spite of a preference $g_m(X) > g_m(Y)$, we obtain as result of a pairwise comparison, the collocation in the same rank of two generic elements X and Y. This is the representation of non perfect transitivity of such kind of rankings, that was historically evidenced by Luce [15].

Note that it is possible as well to face with a problem of incomparability between X and Y, but we assume that incomparability does not exists in this case of study.

Therefore, the elements composing a multi-criteria evaluation (finalised to have a ranking) are:

- the intensity of preference (when preference is expressed by quantitative criterion scores);
- the number of criteria in favour of a given alternative;
- the eventual weight associated to each single criterion;
- the kind of relationship of each single alternative with all the other alternatives (that is to say preference, indifference or incomparability).

As the regards the last point of above, in order to give a better definition of such area of indifference, some authors introduce the dual concept of "strong preference" and "weak preference" [16].

The "strong preference" and "weak preference", are represented by a couple of thresholds of indifference, instead of one: in this case, if $Rank_m(X) > Rank_m(Y)$, this means that:

$$g_m(X) - g_m(Y) > s_1 + s_2 \tag{6}$$

or this can mean as well that:

$$g_m(X) - g_m(Y) > s_1. \tag{7}$$

In the first case we speak of "strong preference", represented by the overcoming of the sum of two thresholds (s_1 and s_2, representing the weak and strong preference thresholds); in the second, we speak of "weak preference" (s_1, representing only the weak preference threshold).

The final result of the application is that in the two-levels preference the intensity of preference g is associated to a pseudo-ranking of a set of element ordered by pseudo-criteria.

We speak of pseudo-criteria because the ranking is affected by a special kind of uncertainty.

In a second step, other authors [17] identify the possibility that the preference of an alternative with respect to another can be formulated through a fuzzy measure of the difference between the value judgements expressed for the alternative in question; leading to a quantitative transposition for the evaluation of credibility, or rather, the value of the function of the fuzzy membership.

The credibility of the ranking relations between two generic alternatives, X and Y, according to a generic criterion j, can be expressed by judgements (and relationships) as follows:

- $\mu_{>>}(X,Y)_j$ defines the credibility of absolute preference for X with respect to Y (μ $(X,Y)=1$);
- $\mu_{>}(X,Y)_j$ defines the credibility of moderate preference for X with respect to Y (μ $(X,Y)_j$ is between 0,5 and 1);
- $\mu_{\approx}(X,Y)_j$ defines the credibility of moderate indifference for X with respect to Y (μ $(X,Y)_j$ s near by 0,5);
- $\mu_{=}(X,Y)_j$ defines the credibility of absolute indifference for X with respect to Y (μ $(X,Y)_j = 0,5$);
- $\mu_{<}(X,Y)_j$ defines the credibility of moderate preference for Y with respect to X (μ $(X,Y)_j$ is between 0 and 0,5);
- $\mu_{<<}(X,Y)_j$ defines the credibility of absolute preference for Y with respect to X (μ $(X,Y)_j = 0$).

In this way, we set a fuzzy problem, where the different expressions of $\mu(X,Y)_j$ are the elements of the "Universe of Discourse", and we construct a fuzzy function by the use of fuzzy clustering.

In order to provide a further control of the stability of the ranking, it will be possible to assess the "semantic distance". The semantic distance has a general expression of which in our case we use a appropriate reduction.

Let's give a j-th quantitative criterion of a set of m criteria; let's suppose that $f_j(X)$ and g_j (Y) represent the value functions of the criterion to express $Rank_j(X)$ and $Rank_j(Y)$.

In the most general case f_j and g_j can be crisp numbers (this means that the function give a certain result), probabilistic values (this means that f_j and g_j represent expected values), or fuzzy numbers.

In this last case (that is our case) we deal with fuzzy numbers represented by the area bordered by the function f_j and g_j (e.g. a left-right number could be related by a pseudo-Gaussian integral of value equal to 1), as the number "about 1800" and "about 2400", represented in Fig.2, that have a non empty intersection .

The fuzzy number and $g_j(1800)=$"about 1800" has a domain of the ownership function corresponding to the interval (800, 2000), while the fuzzy number $f_j(2400)=$"about 2400" has a domain of the ownership function corresponding to the interval (1000, 2700); the maximum value of "about 1800", that is 2000, is bigger than the minimum value than about 2400, that is 1000.

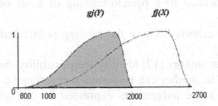

Fig. 2. The fuzzy numbers "about 1800" and "about 2400", has a non empty intersection

Table 5. Expected value of the real estate differential among quarters for prime housing stock

Quarter	Torre a Mare	Stanic	S.Spirito	S.Pasquale	S.Paolo	S.Nicola	Picone	Palese	Murat	S.Girolamo	Madonnella	Loseto	Libertà	Japigia	Ceglie	Carrassi
Carbonara	20	479	-458	-491	154	466	-825	-541	-1554	21	-362	154	-379	-341	179	-512
Carrassi	533	992	54	21	666	979	-312	-29	-1041	533	150	667	133	170	691	
Ceglie	-158	300	-637	-670	-24	287	-1004	-720	-1733	-158	-541	-24	-558	-520		
Japigia	362	820	-116	-150	495	-808	-483	-200	-1212	362	-20	495	-37			
Libertà	400	858	-79	-112	533	845	-445	-162	-1175	400	16	533				
Loseto	-133	324	-612	-645	0	312	-979	-695	-1708	-133	-516					
Madonnella	383	841	-95	-129	516	829	-462	-179	-1191	383						
S.Girolamo	0	458	-479	-512	133	445	-845	-562	-1575							
Murat	1575	2033	1095	1062	1708	2020	729	1012								
Palese	562	1020	83	50	695	1008	-283									
Picone	845	1304	366	333	979	1291										
S.Nicola	-445	12	-924	-958	-312											
S.Paolo	-133	324	-612	-645												
S.Pasquale	512	970	33													
S.Spirito	479	937														
Stanic	-458															

The "Semantic Distance", in this case, is represented by the sum of two double integral:

$$S_d(f_j(x), g_j(y)) = \int_{-\infty}^{+\infty}\int_{X}^{+\infty} |Y - X| g_j(Y), f_j(X) dY dX + \int_{-\infty}^{+\infty}\int_{-\infty}^{X} |X - Y| f_j(X), g_j(Y) dY dX \cdot \qquad (8)$$

In case of empty intersection the hypothesis $f_j(X) < g_j(Y)$ is not proved, and the Semantic Distance is represented by $|\max(f_j(X)) - \max(g_j(Y))|$, that coincides with the expected value of $|X-Y|$ [17].

Our multidimensional ranking is based on the calculation of the values of the fuzzy variable $\mu(X,Y)$ and of the semantic distance Sd for each couple of quarters, referring to each criterion of social/housing difficulty, and to the property value of housing estates.

In the following tables the expected value of $f_j(X) - g_j(Y)$ (in Tab. 5) the semantic distance $Sd(X,Y)$ (in Tab. 6), and the ratio between the absolute value of the expected value of $f_j(X) - g_j(Y)$ and the semantic distance $Sd(X,Y)$ (in Tab. 7) are represented as an example, as regards the criterion "real estate value".

In our assessment the real estate value is a Left-Right fuzzy number, expressing the possible market price per square meter of the housing property.

Data are referring to the year 2006 and measured in monetary unit (thousand of euros per square meter).

Table 6. Semantic distance revealed between quarters for prime housing stock

Quarter	Torre a Mare	Stanic	S.Spirito	S.Pasquale	S.Paolo	S.Nicola	Picone	Palese	Murat	S.Girolamo	Madonnella	Loseto	Libertà	Japigia	Ceglie	Carrassi
Carbonara	328	523	579	540	320	493	809	677	1582	328	464	320	395	429	316	557
Carrassi	655	1050	476	448	694	1004	531	501	1052	655	458	694	383	396	744	
Ceglie	348	326	742	695	270	329	1063	826	1762	348	595	270	558	583		
Japigia	500	860	450	420	543	833	572	489	1237	500	396	543	313			
Libertà	482	848	443	432	524	862	618	472	1224	482	404	524				
Roseto	339	401	722	648	310	383	979	711	1705	339	550					
Madonnella	533	866	534	486	569	871	660	558	1219	533						
S.Girolamo	384	471	644	611	333	488	943	724	1620							
Murat	1620	2080	1105	1132	1706	2035	785	977								
Palese	731	1118	520	500	730	1049	514									
Picone	952	1378	624	611	984	1319										
S.Nicola	478	161	974	989	379											
S.Paolo	339	401	722	648												
S.Pasquale	610	986	529													
S.Spirito	659	1023														
Stanic	478															

Table 7. Ratio between expected value and semantic distance of table 4 and 5

Quarter	Torre a Mare	Stanic	S.Spirito	S.Pasquale	S.Paolo	S.Nicola	Picone	Palese	Murat	S.Girolamo	Madonnella	Loseto	Libertà	Japigia	Ceglie	Carrassi
Carbonara	.06	.92	.79	.91	.48	.95	.02	.80	.98	.06	.78	.48	.96	.79	.57	.92
Carrassi	.81	.94	.11	.05	.96	.98	.59	.06	.99	.81	.33	.96	.35	.43	.93	
Ceglie	.45	.92	.86	.96	.09	.87	.94	.87	.98	.45	.91	.09	.00	.89		
Japigia	.72	.95	.26	.36	.91	.97	.84	.41	.98	.72	.05	.91	.12			
Libertà	.83	.01	.18	.26	.02	.98	.72	.34	.96	.83	.04	.02				
Loseto	.39	.81	.85	.00	.00	.81	.00	.98	.00	.39	.94					
Madonnella	.72	.97	.18	.27	.91	.95	.70	.32	.98	.72						
S.Girolamo	.00	.97	.74	.84	.40	.91	.90	.78	.97							
Murat	.97	.98	.99	.94	.00	.99	.93	.04								
Palese	.77	.91	.16	.10	.95	.96	.55									
Picone	.89	.95	.59	.55	.99	.98										
S.Nicola	.93	.07	.95	.97	.82											
S.Paolo	.39	.81	.85	.00												
S.Pasquale	.84	.98	.06													
S.Spirito	.73	.92														
Stanic	.96															

5   Concluding Remarks

The use of data based on the detail of census section seems to be helpful to give a support for a deeper description of the variability of real estate values. Both the test, based on fuzzy clustering and on the comparison among expected values and semantic distance, show that the geographical identification of highest and lowest values is well supported by the carried out analyses. On the opposite, when values are located at an intermediate level, the quarters are characterized by a high level of variability.

The correct interpretation could be that at the intermediate level we have a more unclear mix among new and degraded housing stocks coexisting in the same place. In fact the highest values and the lowest values are referring to the physically and socially most homogeneous built environments in the urban context of our case study.

References

1. Lemmi, A., Pannuzi, N.: Fattori demografici della povertà, Continuità e discontinuità nei processi demografici. L'Italia nella transizione demografica. 4 Rubettino, Arcavacata di Rende, 211–228 (1995)
2. Zadeh, L.A.: Fuzzy sets. Information and Control 8(3), 338–353 (1965)
3. Dubois, D., Prade, H.: Fuzzy sets and systems. Academic Press, Boston (1980)

4. Cheli, B., Lemmi, A.A.: Totally Fuzzy and Relative Approach to the Multidimensional Analysis of Poverty. Economic Notes 24(1), 115–134 (1995)
5. Cerioli, A., Zani, S.: A Fuzzy Approach to the Measurement of Poverty. In: Dugum, C., Zenga, M. (eds.) Income and Wealth Distribution, inequality and Poverty. Springer, Heidelberg (1990)
6. Perchinunno, P., Rotondo, F., Torre, C.M.: A Multivariate Fuzzy Analysis for the regeneration of urban poverty. In: Gervasi, O., Murgante, B., Laganà, A., Taniar, D., Mun, Y., Gavrilova, M.L. (eds.) ICCSA 2008, Part I. LNCS, vol. 5072, pp. 137–152. Springer, Heidelberg (2008)
7. Montrone, S., Perchinunno, P., Rotondo, F., Torre, C.M., Di Giuro, A.: Identification of Hot Spots of Social and Housing Difficulty in Urban Areas: Scan Statistic for Housing Market and Urban Planning Policies. In: Murgante, B., Borruso, G., Lapucci, A. (eds.) Geocomputation and Urban Planning. SCI, vol. 176, pp. 57–78. Springer, Heidelberg (2009)
8. Kuldorff, M.: A spatial scan statistics. Communication in Statistics: Theory and Methods 26, 1481–1496 (1997)
9. Takahashi, K., Tango, T.: A flexibly shaped spatial scan statistic for detecting clusters. International Journal of Health Geographics 4, 11–13 (2005)
10. Patil, G.P., Taillie, C.: Upper level set scan statistic for detecting arbitrarily shaped hotspots. Environmental and Ecological Statistics 11, 183–197 (2004)
11. Aldstadt, J., Getis, A.: Using AMOEBA to create spatial weights matrix and identify spatial clusters. Geographical Analysis 38, 327–343 (2006)
12. Montrone, S., Bilancia, M., Perchinunno, P., Torre, C.M.: Scan Statistics for the localization of hot spots of urban poverty. In: Conference Proceedings of the Regional Studies Association; Winter Conference; Londra, November 28, pp. 74–77 (2008), ISBN 978-1-1897721-34-6
13. Kulldorff, M.: SaTScanTM User Guide, (August 26, 2006), http://www.satscan.org/
14. Chou, K.C., Cai, Y.D.: Nearest neighbour algorithm for predicting protein subcellular location by combining functional domain composition and pseudo-amino acid composition, Biochem. Biophys. Res. Comm. 305, 407–411 (2003)
15. Luce, R.D.: Semiorders and a theory of utility discrimination. Econometrica 24, 178–191 (1956)
16. Roy, B.: Problem and methods with multiple funtions. Mathemathical programming 1, 239–266 (1971)
17. Munda, G.: Multicriteria evaluation in a Fuzzy Environment. Phisica Verlag, Heidelberg (1995)

A Network Based Kernel Density Estimator Applied to Barcelona Economic Activities

Produit Timothée[1], Lachance-Bernard Nicolas[1], Strano Emanuele[2],
Porta Sergio[2], and Joost Stéphane[1]

[1] Laboratory of Geographic Information Systems, Ecole Polytechnique Fédérale de
Lausanne (EPFL), 1015 Lausanne, Switzerland
[2] Urban Design Studies Unit, Department of Architecture, University of Strathclyde,
131 Rottenrow, Glasgow, G4 ONG, United Kingdom

Abstract. This paper presents a methodology to compute an innovative
density indicator of spatial events. The methodology is based on a modified Kernel Density Estimator (KDE) that operates along road networks,
and named Network based Kernel Density Estimator (NetKDE). In this
research, retail and service economic activities are projected on the road
network whose edges are weighted by a set of centrality values calculated
with a Multiple Centrality Assessment (MCA). First, this paper calculate
a density indicator for the point pattern analysis on human activities in
a network constrained environment. Then, this indicator is modified to
evaluate network performance in term of centrality. The methodology is
applied to the city of Barcelona to explore the potential of the approach
on more than 11,000 network edges and 166,000 economic activities.

1 Introduction

Most of the conventional indicators and spatial interpolation techniques use Euclidean distances for space characterization [21]. In the urban environment, these
approaches do not take into account the road network constraint and its influence
on the location of spatial events.

KDE is widely used as a spatial smoothing technique in many fields such as geography, epidemiology, criminology, demography, hydrology and others (Anselin
[1]; Borruso [4]). In a recent work, Porta *et al.* [18] extended the use of planar
KDE to examine whether the variation of street centralities was reflected in the
intensity of land uses. Recent developments of the same idea have stressed the
network constrained nature of some classes of point events such as crime occurrences or car accidents, therefore exploring the advantages of computing density
on the network (Network based Kernel Density Estimation, or NetKDE) rather
than in the planar space (see Ch. 1.3).

Like these recent works, this paper examines a network oriented approach to
density, but still operated over the 2D space, like the conventional Kernel Density. The research was carried out by computing NetKDE on two kinds of spatial
entities within the city of Barcelona: firstly, retails and services represented as
points; secondly, the road network represented as polylines weighted by a set of

D. Taniar et al. (Eds.): ICCSA 2010, Part I, LNCS 6016, pp. 32–45, 2010.

centrality values resulting from a Multiple Centrality Assessment (MCA) of the same road network (see Ch.1.2).

This paper is divided in three parts. First, the theoretical background of KDE, of network centrality and of the novel NetKDE is presented. Secondly, the methodology to implement NetKDE is explained. And finally, the results of its application to the city of Barcelona case study are presented and discussed.

1.1   Kernel Density Estimation

KDE is a statistical process used for spatial smoothing and/or spatial interpolation [25]. This paper uses KDE to transform the road network MCA measures and the distribution of activities to a common spatial unit (the raster grid). This allows subsequent visual correlation analysis. It is also recognized that the function of density is a means to present analysis and illustrations of complex and technical data in a clear and understandable way to the non-mathematicians [20].

KDE is a well known tool in urban studies. Anselin [1] used the KDE for spatial analysis of crimes to visually simplify their location and to examine the complex characteristics of criminal incidents. Gatrell [13,14] analyzed spatial first-order variation in disease risk with kernel functions. Borruso [4] showed that the KDE applied to an urban system (a density analysis of addresses) allowed a better representation of the phenomenon. He also found out that KDE is less sensitive to size, position and orientation than grid density estimation (GDE). Thurstain-Goodwin and Unwin [22] applied KDE to zip codes data to obtain a continuous surface of density. Associated with indicators of centrality, the kernel density allowed calculation of a composite urban centrality indicator applicable to cities.

KDE is a function balancing events accordingly to their distances and required two parameters. The first is the bandwidth, which is the distance of influence. The choice of the bandwidth has a great impact on the results, some authors used a least-squares cross validation to select the bandwidth [19,24]. Others as Brundson [5] proposed an adaptive KDE with a bandwidth changing accordingly to the cloud of points structure. The second parameter is the weighting function K, which is most often a normal function. Authors agreed that the choice of this function is less critical than the choice of the bandwidth [13].

The technology development of the last decade results in new opportunities in GIS research. Miller [15] pointed out that the hypothesis of a continuous space is too strong for the analysis of events which take place in a one-dimensional sub-space created by a network. Similarly, Batty [2] showed that GIS prevent Euclidean space from being distorted by the constraint of the road network. He also noted that though road network representation is no longer a challenge, further developments on GIS have to take into account this constraint.

1.2   Network Centrality

The urban network has been the object of numerous studies. Its origins can be traced back to Leonhard Euler's solution of the Knigsberg bridges problem, after which the theory of graphs and complex network has been rapidly growing (Euler [11]). Freeman [12] was one of the first researchers to define sets of indices to measure how central is a node with respect to all others. Nowadays, because of this virtually unlimited capacity to represent relationships in most diverse real systems, networks are used in a variety of fields such as ecology, genetics, epidemiology, physics, communications, computing, urban planning and many others (Costa *et al.* [6]).

The specific category of geographical networks is characterized by nodes with well defined coordinates in an embedded space, like street networks. The geography of centrality on such networks has been explored by means of a Multiple Centrality Assessment, as defined by Porta *et al.* [17]. The main characteristics of MCA are: (1) a 'primal' format for the street network; (2) a metric computation of distances along the real street network; (3) an attribution to each street of diverse centrality values (Crucitti *et al.* [7]). This paper presents only one of those computed indices, namely betweenness centrality (BetC). BetC is based on the idea that a node is more central when it is traversed by a larger number of shortest paths connecting all couples of nodes in the network. BetC is defined as:

$$C_i^B = \frac{1}{(N-1)(N-2)} \sum_{j,k \in N; j \neq k; j, k \neq i} \frac{n_{jk}(i)}{n_{jk}} \tag{1}$$

where n_{jk} is the number of shortest paths between nodes j and k, and $n_{jk}(i)$ is the number of these shortest paths that contain node i.

1.3   Network Based Kernel Density Estimation

NetKDE use similar mathematical formula as KDE, but uses distances measured along a network rather than Euclidean distances to compute density values. NetKDE is applicable to polylines and points. Both are balanced by the distance between an event and the point at which the density is estimated.

A study on road accidents demonstrated "*the risks of false positive detection associated with the use of a statistic (K-function) designed for planar space to analyze a network constrained phenomenon*" [27].

Borruso [3] suggested an analysis of density in the space created from the urban network. His network constrained density indicator, named NDE (Network Density Estimation) was applied to the cities of Trieste (IT) and Swindon (UK) for activities related to banks and insurances. He showed up that "*the difference between the KDE and the NDE was not very high, but NDE seems to be more proficient in highlighting linear clusters oriented along a street network*". Borruso also pointed out that the NDE performed better than KDE for the identification of linear patterns along the network. However, the calculated density does not take into account a distance weigthing function such as that of standard KDE.

Xie and Yan [26] came back to an investigation of car accidents as a champion case of network constrained point events: they developed a methodology to reduce the planar 2D KDE to a linear 1D measurement on the basis of a linear unit of conventional length, or "lixel". This reduction however also reduced the real meaning of applying a kernel function, as a simple evaluation of the number of events per linear unit provides far more precise results. Moreover, this study concluded that planar 2D KDE overestimated density as compared with their network KDE. While this conclusion is brought over figures, these are hardly comparable being in different space units (respectively pixel and lixel).

Finally, Okabe [16] developed a KDE to estimate the density of points in a network in order to detect traffic accident hot spots. Three kernel functions were proposed, among which two were unbiased and successfully explained mathematical properties. These functions were implemented in a GIS and are available in the SANET extension. Nevertheless, the calculated density values are attributes of the edges and are not generalized to the entire area of the network.

The methodology of this paper, develop more further the one proposed by Porta [18]. It calculates a NetKDE for both point and linear features. However, the NetKDE operates by extending the bandwidth distance along the street network rather than linearly across the space. This methodology is close to the one used by Downs and Horner [9,10] in traffic accident and animal home range analysis.

2   Methodology

The methodology developed has to deal with very large datasets and has to produce results within reasonable laps of time (around a day for the prototype). Network calculations are time consuming. One simple way to increase the efficiency of scripts is to store data in a specialized relational database management system (RDMS). A RDMS has optimized SQL tools and functions to improve searching and editing of spatial elements and attributes. For the current project, the standard *ESRI* shape files (.shp) were converted to a *PostGIS* format (*PostgreSQL*) using the translating function *shape2pgsql*. The recovery of spatial objects is made within *PostGIS*, external *Python* scripts are used for different calculations, and interactions between data and scripts relied on the *Psycopg API*. (Figure 1).

The implemented algorithm uses three main input files. The first one is the road network with centrality values calculated by a MCA. This network has a clean topology and each node has a unique identifier (ID). The second one is constituted of the activities in the studied area, and the last one is the grid of points used by the KDE and the NetKDE. The KDE of activities and the KDE of edges centrality are calculated with *ArcGIS*. Secondly, on the basis of a *PostGIS* database, different *Python* scripts project activities on network edges, compute shortest path tree (SPT), and compute NetKDE of activities and NetKDE of edge centrality. SPT is a set of connected road network edges that are accessible from a specified location within a maximum trip cost. In our case, this cost is the considered bandwidth. During the development of the methodology several bandwidth have been used (100m, 200m, 400m). These choices were done in respect with city's human scale (walking space), computing resources and the ratio between the raster grid resolution and the bandwidth.

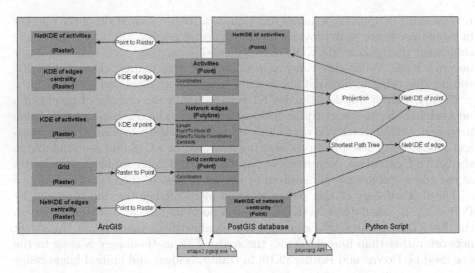

Fig. 1. Algorithm and interaction between the software

2.1   KDE Approach

A sliding window is used over the dataset to estimate the density of events. For the KDE, this sliding window is defined by a 3D function to weight the events according to their distance from the grid point for which the density is evaluated. With x_j being a location vector over the field R and $x_1 \ldots x_n$ the location vectors of the n events, the intensity estimation $f(x_j)$ in x_j is [20,13,14]:

$$\hat{f}_h(x_j) = \sum_{i=1}^{n} \frac{1}{h^2} K(\frac{x_j - x_i}{h}) \qquad (2)$$

$d_{ij} = x_i - x_j$ is the Euclidean distance between the grid point x_j and the event n_i, h being the bandwidth. Actually, several kernel functions are implemented in different GIS. *ESRI ArcGIS Spatial Analyst* module allows only one kernel function for point and line density, known as quadratic or Epanechnikov [21]:

$$K(x_i) = \{ \begin{matrix} \frac{1}{3\pi}(1 - t_i^2)^2 \text{ if } t_i^2 < 1 \\ 0 \text{ otherwise} \end{matrix} \qquad (3)$$

with $t_i = d_{ij}/h$.

The value at each point of the grid j at a distance d_{ij} of the event n_i is obtained from the sum of the individual kernel functions $(K(x_i))$ of the points belonging the bandwidth h. Any activity beyond the bandwidth h from the considered grid point does not contribute to the summation. In case of weighted events, the weight is used as a value of population. Namely, if a point has a value w, the algorithm takes this point into account as if there are w points for this distance d_{ij}. The same approach is applied to edges for which weight is a centrality value as does Porta [18]. Figure 2 shows the Euclidean approach of KDE.

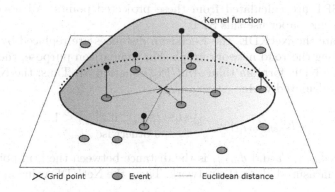

Fig. 2. Kernel function of the Kernel Density estimation

2.2 NetKDE Approach

The NetKDE needs the distance between the grid points and the activities projected onto the road network. The edges of the road network are stored in a database as polyline objects. The attributes of these edges are: From Node ID (FN), To Node ID (TN), FN and TN coordinates, polyline length and centrality values (Figure 1).

The second step of the methodology is to use the Dijkstra's SPT algorithm [8] to create trees of all accessible edges within a specified bandwidth from every grid points (Figure 3). First, the grid points are projected to their nearest edge.

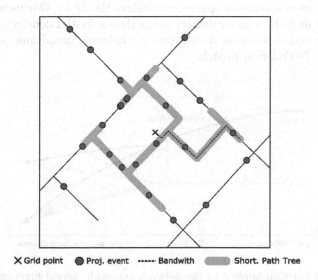

Fig. 3. Shortest Path Tree: The grid point and the activities are projected on the nearest edge

Then, the SPT are calculated from these projected points. All novel indexes presented in this paper use this SPT.

To calculate the NetKDE, the Euclidean distances are replaced by distances measured along the road network graph. For comparison purpose, the NetKDE uses the same KDE formula than *ArcGIS* (Equation 3). Thus, the NetKDE of activities is calculated with:

$$K_{net}(t_{net,i}) = \begin{cases} \frac{1}{3\pi}(1 - t_{net,i}^2)^2 & \text{if } t_{net,i}^2 < 1 \\ 0 & \text{otherwise} \end{cases} \tag{4}$$

with $t_{net,i} = d_{net,ij}/h$ and $d_{net,ij}$ is the distance between the grid point x_j and the event n_i measured along the network. Then, the NetKDE value in grid point x_j is:

$$NetKDE(x_j) = \frac{1}{nh^2} \sum_{i=1}^{n} K_{net}(t_{net,i}) \tag{5}$$

n is the number of events on the SPT for the bandwidth h. NetKDE of edges centrality is calculated in the same way. The edge is reduced to his midpoint and the centrality $BetC_i$ of the edge i is used as a value of population:

$$NetKDE(x_j) = \frac{1}{h^2 \sum_{i=1}^{n} BetC_i} \sum_{i=1}^{n} K_{net}(t_{net,i}) BetC_i \tag{6}$$

This paper makes use of the Epanechnikov kernel function developped for event in an Euclidean space. Nevertheless, for the NetKDE, this function is applied to the events in the non-uniform space created from the SPTs. Our indicator has no unit but refer more to a linear density index than a spatial density index. Okabe [16] proposes kernel function developped for network based analysis. Figure 4 illustrates the NetKDE approach.

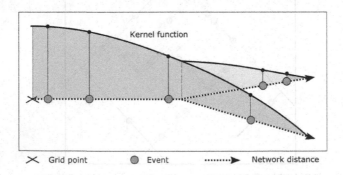

Fig. 4. Kernel function applied to the network approach, kernel function weights the projected events using the distance measured along the network

3 Barcelona Case Study

We applied in two-steps the methodology on the city of Barcelona. Firstly, the methodology algorithms were tested and validated with a sample (500m X 500m) of the Barcelona road network and economic activities and a 10m grid. **For this extract, calculation of the indexes takes less than one hour.** Some of the results from this first exercise are presented in this section. Secondly, once the methodology has been fine tuned and proofed with the data samples, the KDE and NetKDE approaches were applied to the whole city. The complete road network is characterized by 11,222 edges, there are more than 166,311 activities within an area of 92.65km^2, and the 10m resolution raster grid represents 1,890,000 grid points. Activities come from the the the *Agencia de Ecologia Urbana* database describing all the economical, public or associational entities in 2002. For the entire data, the calculation takes approximately 2 days with Intel(R) Core(TM)2 Quad CPU, Q950 @ 3.00GHz, 2.99Ghz, 7.83GB of RAM.

3.1 Results Obtained with Data Samples

This section presents some of the results obtained with the city of Barcelona data samples. Firstly, the KDE of activities and NetKDE of activities are presented.

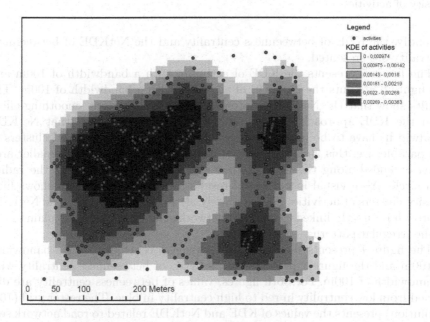

Fig. 5. Kernel Density of activities, bandwidth = 100m, raster cell = 10m, black clusters highlight high density of activities (red dots)

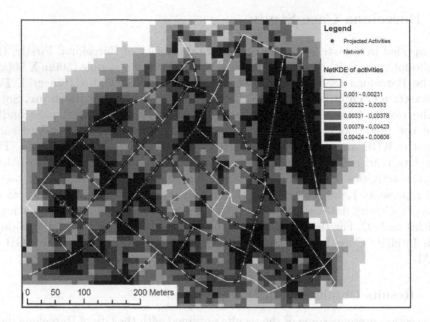

Fig. 6. Network based Kernel Density of activities, bandwidth = 100m, raster cell = 10m, activities are projected on the network, black clusters highlight high NetKDE density of activities

Secondly, the KDE of betweenness centrality and the NetKDE of betweenness centrality are presented.

The figure 5 presents the KDE of activities with a bandwidth of 100m and the figure 6 presents the NetKDE of activities with a bandwidth of 100m. The results show that the NetKDE approach has a less important smoothing effect than the KDE approach for the data samples. We discovered that NetKDE bandwidths have to be larger than those of KDE to produce visual clusters of comparable size; this is no surprise, as the same distance covers a smaller area when extended along the network than when extended linearly as the radius of a circle. Also, visual inspection of results from both approaches shows high density clusters of activities approximately at the same locations. The NetKDE approach is directly linked to the road network geometry and this explains some of the irregular patterns.

The figure 7 presents the KDE of betweenness centrality with a bandwidth of 100m and the figure 8 presents the NetKDE of betweenness centrality with a bandwidth of 100m. For both figures, values of betweeness centrality are displayed from low centrality in red to high centrality in blue. The raster grid (10m resolution) presents the values of KDE and NetKDE related to road network segment centrality. The density clusters is useful to identify clusters characterized by high or low centrality.

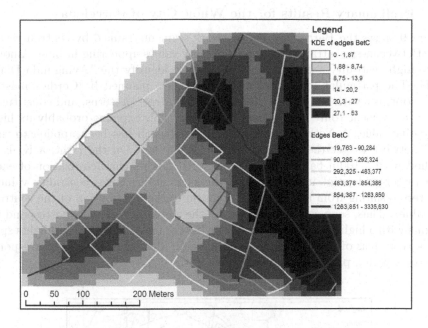

Fig. 7. Kernel Density of Betweenness centrality, bandwidth = 100m. BetC values are calculated from the entire road network.

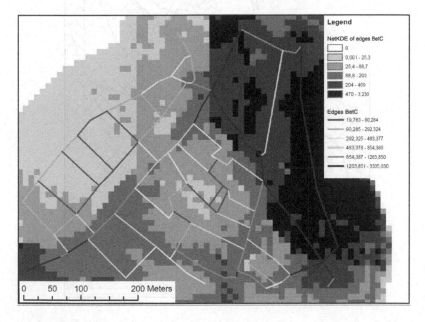

Fig. 8. Network based Density of Betweenness centrality, bandwidth = 100m. BetC values are calculated from the entire road network.

3.2   Preliminary Results for the Whole City of Barcelona

Figure 9 shows the Barcelona road network segments ranked by centrality values (Betweenness centrality), higher centrality values appearing in blue. Among these high centrality segments, it is possible to identify the "Avingunda Diagonal". The particular implantation of this street, planned by Cerda's master plan, contrasts with the rest of the surrounding street patterns, and constitutes a very convenient route in this part of the city. This explains probably its high centrality value. A NetKDE with a 400m bandwidth has been applied to this road network to get the figure 10 shown on the left. On the right, a KDE is applied with a 100m bandwidth. The NetKDE allows characterization of each 10m raster grid point in regard with the surrounding edges centrality values. Clusters resulting from the NetKDE conform to the distribution of the centrality values. Thus, segments highlighted by the global betweenness correspond to regions with a high density indicator. The betweenness centrality highlights specific street areas of the Barcelona road network. Most of these areas correspond to streets with a particular economic role in the city.

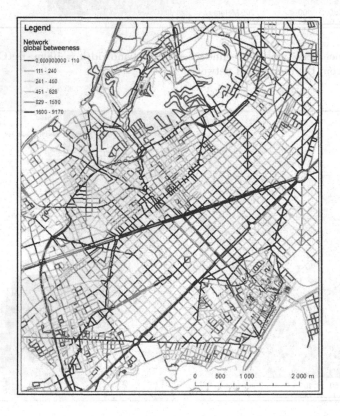

Fig. 9. High value in blue, low value in red: Network of Barcelona ranked by BetC

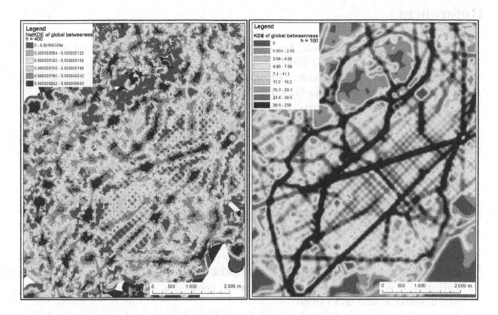

Fig. 10. Density of BetC: High value in blue, low value in red: **Left**: NetKDE of BetC, bandwidth = 400m, raster cell = 10m. **Right**: KDE of BetC, bandwidth = 100m, raster cell = 10m.

4   Discussion

The goal of this research was to improve the analysis of the spatial density of events in urban environment, taking into account network constrains. Firstly, this paper analyzed the distribution of retails and services projected on the road network. Secondly, it analyzed the distribution of edge centralities.

The NetKDE approach works on point events, like economic activities, and linear features, like streets. Instead of calculating linear density of collapsed point events on the network, NetKDE calculates spatial density. The NetKDE approach uses bandwidth constrained by the network rather than Euclidean bandwidth, like previous approaches. This reflects more adequately the reality of urban mobility.

First results clearly highlight the high sensitivity of the methodology to capture high resolution density of retail activities and new possibilities to compare it with the network segment density. Nevertheless, this methodology could already be used in urban analysis for any other type of spatial events. Finally, we could quote Tobler's [23] first law of geography, "everything is related to everything else, but near things are more related than distant things" and add "along the street."

References

1. Anselin, L., Cohen, J., Cook, D., Gorr, W., Tita, G.: Spatial analyses of crime. Criminal Justice 4, 213–262 (2000)
2. Batty, M.: Network Geography: Relations, Interactions, Scaling and Spatial Processes in GIS. Re-presenting GIS, 149–170 (2005)
3. Borruso, G.: Network Density Estimation: A GIS Approach for Analysing Point Patterns in a Network Space. Transactions in GIS 12, 377–402 (2008)
4. Borruso, G.: Network Density and the Delimitation of Urban Areas. Transactions in GIS 7, 177–191 (2003)
5. Brunsdon, C.: Estimating probability surfaces for geographical point data: An adaptive kernel algorithm. Computers & Geosciences 21(7), 877–894 (1995)
6. Costa, L.F., Oliveira Jr, O.N., Travieso, G., Rodrigues, F.A., Boas, P.R.V., Antiqueira, L., Viana, M.P., da Rocha, L.E.C.: Analyzing and Modeling Real-World Phenomena with Complex Networks: A Survey of Applications. arXiv, 0711.3199v3 (2007)
7. Crucitti, P., Latora, V., Porta, S.: Centrality measures in spatial networks of urban streets. Physical Review E 73(3, Part 2) (2006)
8. Dijkstra, E.W.: A note on two problems in connexion with graphs. Numerische Mathematik 1, 269–271 (1959)
9. Downs, J.A., Horner, M.W.: Network-based Kernel Density Estimation for Home Range Analysis. In: Proceedings of the 9th International Conference on GeoComputation, Maynooth, Ireland (2007)
10. Downs, J.A., Horner, M.W.: Characterising Linear Point Patterns. In: Proceedings of the GIS Research UK Annual Conference (GISRUK 2007), Maynooth, Ireland (2007)
11. Euler, L.: Solutio problematis ad geometriam situs pertinentis. Commentarii academiae scientiarum Petropolitanae 8, 128–140 (1741)
12. Freeman, L.C.: Centrality in Social Networks: Conceptual Clarification. Social Networks 1, 215–239 (1979)
13. Gatrell, A., Bailey, T., Diggle, P., Rowlingson, B.: Spatial point pattern analysis and its applications in geographical epidemiology. Transactions of the Institute of British geographers 21, 256–274 (1996)
14. Gatrell, A.: Density estimation and the visualization of Point pattern. In: Hearnshaw, H.M., Unwin, D.J. (eds.) Visualization in Geographical Information Systems, pp. 65–75. John Wiley and Sons, New York (1994)
15. Miller, H.J.: Measuring space-time accessibility benefits within transportation networks: Basic theory and computational procedures. Geographical Analysis 31, 187–212 (1999)
16. Okabe, A., Satoh, T., Sugihara, K.: A kernel density estimation method for networks, its computational method and a GIS-based tool. International Journal of Geographical Information Science 23, 7–32 (2009)
17. Porta, S., Crucitti, P., Latora, V.: The network analysis of urban streets: a primal approach. Environment and Planning B: Planning and Design 33, 705–725 (2006)
18. Porta, S., Latora, V., Wang, F., Strano, E., Cardillo, A., Scellato, S., Iacoviello, V., Messora, R.: Street centrality and densities of retail and services in Bologna, Italy. Environment and Planning B: Planning and Design 36, 450–465 (2009)
19. Row, J.R., Blouin-Derners, G.: Kernels Are Not Accurate Estimators of Home-Range Size for Herpetofauna. Copeia 4, 797–802 (2006)

20. Silverman, B.W.: Density Estimation for Statistics and Data Analysis. Chapman & Hall/CRC (1986)
21. Smith, M.J., Goodchild, M.F., Longley, P.: Geospatial Analysis: a comprehension to principles, techniques and software tools. Troubador Publishing (2006)
22. Thurstain-Goodwin, M., Unwin, D.: Defining and Delineating the Central Areas of Towns for Statistical Monitoring Using Continuous Surface Representations. Transactions in GIS 4, 305–317 (2000)
23. Tobler, W.R.: A computer movie simulating urban growth in the Detroit region. Economic geography 46, 234–240 (1970)
24. Topping, D.T., Lowe, C.G., Caselle, J.E.: Home range and habitat utilization of adult California sheephead, Semicossyphus pulcher (Labriddae), in a temperate no-take marine reserve. Marine Biology 147(2), 301–311
25. Wang, F.: Quantitative methods and applications in GIS. CRC Press, Boca Raton (2006)
26. Xie, Z., Yan, J.: Kernel Density Estimation of traffic accident in network space. Geography, Geology Faculty Publications (2008)
27. Yamada, I., Thill, J.C.: Comparison of planar and network K-functions in traffic accident analysis. Journal of Transport Geography 12, 149–158 (2004)

The Application of Spatial Filtering Technique to the Economic Convergence of the European Regions between 1995 and 2007

Francesco Pecci and Nicola Pontarollo

Department of Economics,
University of Verona, Italy
francesco.pecci@univr.it,
nicola.pontarollo@univr.it
http://dse.univr.it

Abstract. The β-convergence model has been widely used to predict the convergence rates of European regions to their steady states. However, this model has two major limitations. First, it does not take into account the spatial interactions of the economies and, second, it does not include their structural differences. Many authors have overcome the first problem by using spatial econometric techniques such as spatial lag or spatial error, but the latter problem has remained unresolved. In our model we use the spatial filtering technique to manage both spatial dependence and structural differences of the economies. Our results show that European regions have a wide range of convergence rates and in some cases regions with similar structural conditions are clustered. The spatial filtering technique is also able to highlight the scale (local, regional or global) of the phenomena that influence growth. This information is very useful for policy makers.

1 Preface

The β-convergence model developed by Baumol [5], and then revisited by Mankiw, Romer and Weil [29], and Barro and Sala-i-Martin [3]) is a useful tool to evaluate the rate of economic convergence of countries or regions. The economic convergence, together with cohesion and integration, is one of the main purposes of the European policy, and this explains the growing interest in these studies. One of the limits of the β-convergence model is that it considers countries and regions as isolated entities, not taking into account that the economies, mainly in Europe, although structurally different, are mutually interdependent (Mankiw [30], Quah [38]). In addition to this phenomenon, the new economic geography (Krugman [25], Fujita, Krugman and Venabes [19]), predicts that the development perspectives of a region are influenced by the level of development of the surrounding regions: a poor (or rich) region surrounded by other poor (or rich) regions probably will not change their level of development, while a poor region

D. Taniar et al. (Eds.): ICCSA 2010, Part I, LNCS 6016, pp. 46–61, 2010.

surrounded by rich regions is more likely to improve its economic conditions. In order to include the influence of spatial effects on economic growth, many authors (Fischer and Stirböck [17], Arbia and De Amicis [1], Paas and Schlitte [36], Niebuhr [33], among the last) consider convergence models in presence of spatial dependence and spatial heterogeneity. Almost all studies use mainly spatial error and spatial lag methods that lead to a unique convergence rate for all regions; they do not consider the possible existence of heterogeneous steady states and of structural heterogeneity (Durlauf and Temple [11]), that is for Durlauf [10] a realistic hypothesis. To overcome these limitations we propose a different approach that estimates local parameters of regional convergence. This different approach takes into account both the heterogeneities mentioned above. In particular, the model:

a. uses a set of explanatory variables that includes the variables that affect the growth process and their spatial filters, as proposed by Griffith [23];
b. estimates a model of regional convergence to manage structural heterogeneities.

With regard to (a), many studies, among all Fingleton [14] and Le Gallo and Ertur [28], have shown the presence of spatial correlation in the residuals of the traditionally estimated models. The spatial filtering technique allows us to eliminate this phenomenon. In addition, the integration of spatial filters into the model enables us to take into account the effects of spatial interaction taking place among the variables. The integration of spatial filters also allows us to consider the effects of the spatial spillovers (Griffith [22]). As far as (b) is concerned, the spatial regional model is able to split the sample of regions by treating each region together with the surrounding regions as a sub-sample. This avoids the use of arbitrary allocation of the sample and allows us to include the variation of the parameters of all observations.

The proposed model assumes that social, economic and institutional regional similarities may lead to similar convergence rates, that differ territorially. The value of the rate of regional convergence is the algebraic sum of the values of the global and local trends.

Using this model, we can manage both spatial autocorrelation and spatial heterogeneity of the convergence process. On the other hand, unlike the approach proposed in this study, the use of dynamic models based on panel data could cause problems because of distortions related to the range of the analyzed samples and temporal frequency of observations (Islam [24]).

To include spatial effects in the model we use, as mentioned, the technique proposed by Griffith [23] that is based on spatial filters applied to the geographically weighted regression - GWR - (Fotheringham, Brunsdon and Charlton [18]). Unlike the traditional GWR technique, as specified in the following paragraphs, this approach estimates a single OLS equation instead of as many equations as the number of regions.

In the study we analyze the model linked to the concept of social filter proposed by Rodriguez-Pose and Crescenzi [39], which is an extension of the model of Mankiw, Romer and Weil [29].

In the second section we describe the empirical model used in the study of β-convergence, in paragraphs three and four we describe the spatial approach and the spatial model used. Finally in paragraph five we discuss the results.

2   The Empirical Model of β-Convergence

The β-convergence model has been extensively applied in the recent literature on economic convergence to explain differences in country-wide income levels. After some re-parameterization (leading to a linear specification), it can be interpreted as the systematic component of a statistical linear model leading to the estimable equation:

$$\ln y_{i,t} - \ln y_{0,t} = - \left(1 - e^{-\lambda t}\right) \ln y_0 +$$

$$\left(1 - e^{-\lambda t}\right) \left(\frac{\alpha}{1-\alpha} \left(\ln s_k - \ln\left(n + g + \delta\right)\right) + \frac{\beta}{1-\alpha} \ln h\right) + \left(1 - e^{-\lambda t}\right) \ln A_0 + gt$$

$$(1)$$

Where s_k and s_h are time invariant fractions of output invested in physical and human capital, and n, g and δ denote the growth rates of the labour force, technological progress and the depreciation rate of physical and human capital, respectively (Mankiw, Romer and Weil [29]). The parameters α and β ($0 < \alpha < 1, 0 < \beta < 1$) show the production elasticities of physical and human capital, and $1 - \alpha - \beta > 0$ is the elasticity of ordinary labour input. The elasticities also reflect income shares because of the constant returns to scale assumption. Initial values are indicated by 0, and t is time. The parameter $\lambda > 0$ is the speed of convergence. y is the GVA per worker, A_0 the initial index of technology and h the human capital per worker in the steady state. In addition, the constraint that the coefficient $\ln s_k$ and $\ln(n + g + \delta)$ are equal in magnitude but opposite in signe has been set. Since the steady state level of the human capital variable is not observable, it is replaced either by its initial value or an average over the sample period.

Unlike Barro and Sala-i-Martin [3], and considering the critics of Quah [38] and Durlauf and Temple [11], we do not take into account the assumption of uniform structural conditions of regional economies. Our model estimates local parameters and the corresponding regression equation is given by

$$\frac{\left(\ln y_{i,t} - \ln y_{0,t}\right)}{T} = \beta_0 + \beta_1 \ln y_{0,t} + \beta_2 \left(\ln s_{k,t} - \ln\left(n_t + g_t + \delta_t\right)\right) + \beta_3 \ln h + u_t \quad (2)$$

where

$$\beta_0 = \left(1 - e^{-\lambda t}\right) \ln A_0 + gt, \beta_1 = - \left(1 - e^{-\lambda t}\right), \beta_2 = \left(1 - e^{-\lambda t}\right) \alpha/(1 - \alpha),$$

$$\beta_3 = - \left(1 - e^{-\lambda t}\right) \beta/(1 - \alpha)$$

i is the regional index, T the number of time periods in the sample and u the regression error, which follows the white noise properties. The equation (2) for the EU27 in an interval of time between 1995 and 2007, can be rewritten as follows:

$$\frac{(GVAEMP07_i - GVAEMP95_i)}{13} = \alpha + \beta GVAEMP95_i +$$
$$\psi_1 SCEMP03_i + \psi_2 SAVEGVA_i + \psi_3 TECHEMPe_i + \qquad (3)$$
$$\psi_4 LONGUNEMPe_i + \psi_5 EMPAGRI_i + \psi_6 LNLIFLEARe_i + \varepsilon_i$$

where[1]:

- $GVAEMP07_i$ = logarithm of the regional GVA[2] per worker in region i in 2007;
- $GVAEMP95_i$ = logarithm of regional GVA per worker in region i in 1995;
- $SCEMP03_i$ = logarithm of $(\delta + g + n_i)$ where $(\delta + g) = 0.03$, n_i = average growth in employment between 1995 and 2007 in each region;
- $SAVEGVA_i$ = logarithm of the average investment as a per cent of GVA, a proxy for the saving rate in the region i between 1995 and 2007;
- $TECHEMPe_i$ = logarithm of the average workers in high-tech sectors as per cent of total employees in the region i between 1995 and 2007 (Eurostat Regio);
- $LONGUNEMPe_i$ = logarithm of the average of long-term unemployment (more than 12 months) as per cent of the total unemployed in the region i between 1999 and 2007 (Eurostat Regio), an indicator of the rigidity of the labor market (Gordon [21]);
- $EMPAGRI_i$ = logarithm of the average employees in agriculture as per cent of total employees in the region i between 1995 and 2007 (Eurostat Regio);
- $LNLIFLEARe_i$ = logarithm of the participants in programs of long life learning as per cent of total employees in region i between 1999 and 2007 (Eurostat Regio).

The ratio of workers in high-tech sectors compared to the total number of employees helps us to verify the contribution to economic growth of the most innovative and dynamic industries. Furthermore, the variable $TECHEMPe_i$ can be understood as a proxy for the adaptability of a single region to the innovations produced in other regions (Cohen and Levinthal [8], Maurseth and Verspagen [31]). Finally, the percentage of employees participating in the programs of lifelong learning is an indicator of the degree of accumulation of knowledge within the world of regional work. The reference dataset is composed of 259 NUTS2 regions of Europe with 27 members and the data are taken from Cambridge Econometrics' and from the European regional database[3].

---

[1] We verify the presence of multicollinearity among the independent variables through the verification of VIF and the correlation matrix. The responses tend to exclude the presence of multicollinearity among the regressors.

[2] GVA is equal to GDP minus taxes and production subsidies.

[3] The Cambridge Econometrics' database, that comes from Eurostat Regio and national sources, ensures that the data are consistent both across space and over time (Fingleton and McCombie [15]).

3   The Spatial Approach

The externalities related to physical and human capital have an important role in the economic development of surrounding regions. In general, it is conceivable that the influences that a region can exert on their surroundings is inversely proportional to the distance that they have from the i-th region, also in view of the first law of geography by Tobler [44]: *"Everything is related to everything else, but near things are more related than distant things"*. An empirical confirmation of the influence of the spatial spillovers comes from Paci and Pigliaru [35]. The authors note that the propensity to innovate in each region is related to that of the surrounding regions. Furthermore, their results are consistent with the hypothesis of the existence of important spatial spillovers of technological knowledge and they are strong enough to play a role which cannot be ignored in the econometric analysis of the European convergence process. The spatial dependence can be managed through a spatial weights matrix C (globally standardized and symmetrical), which is supposed to be able to capture the spatial structure and intensity of spatial dependence. Since there is no a priori information about the exact nature of spatial dependence, the choice of spatial weights matrix is often arbitrary (Niebuhr [33], Ertur and Le Gallo [13])[4].

The first stage, to test whether the dependent variables are spatially autocorrelated, consists in the application of the Moran's Index that is so specified:

$$I = \frac{n}{\sum_{i=1}^{n} (y_i - \bar{y})^2} \frac{\sum_{i=1}^{n} \sum_{j=1}^{n} C_{ij} (y_i - \bar{y}) (y_j - \bar{y})}{\sum_{i=1}^{n} \sum_{j=1}^{n} (y_i - \bar{y}) C_{ij}} \tag{4}$$

where i and j refer to different spatial units (i.e., cell centroids) of which there are n, and y is the data value in each. The product of differences between two observations (i.e., covariance) determines the extent to which they vary together. The potential interaction between two spatial units varies from -1 (negative spatial autocorrelation) to +1 (positive spatial autocorrelation), and 0 indicating lack of spatial autocorrelation. Positive values closer to +1 indicate high spatial autocorrelation. We use Moran's I because, as written in the following paragraphs, it is strictly linked with the concept of spatial filtering.

In table 1 we can see that all variables are normally distributed and that all Moran's I are statistically significant. Their values are high for almost all variables; only *SCEMP03* has a low value: 0.112. This result implies that the spatial dependence influences the distribution of the variables. The presence of a spatial structure leads to an expulsion of the classical assumption of independence of observations for each variable (Tiefelsdorf and Griffith [43]).

Among the techniques recently introduced to characterize the effects of the spatial interaction and to study the interrelationships between different socioeconomic regions there are the techniques based on spatial filters. The spatial

---

[4] In our case we used a spatial matrix based on a Gabriel graph, which provides that two points P and Q are connected when the circle having as diameter the segment representing the distance between them does not contain any other point.

Table 1. Moran Index of the indipendent variables

Variabile	Moran's I	p-value	P(S-W) of the variable
GVAEMP95	0.8916	< 0.0001	< 0.0001
SCEMP03	0.1115	0.0034	0.0011
SAVEGVA	0.5684	< 0.0001	< 0.0001
TECHEMPe	0.4124	< 0.0001	< 0.0001
LONGUNEMPe	0.6774	< 0.0001	0.0065
EMPAGRI	0.7248	< 0.0001	< 0.0001
LNLIFLEARe	0.7477	< 0.0001	< 0.0001

P(S-W) of the variable: probability of the Shapiro-Wilk test.

phenomena have a great importance especially when we consider both the socioeconomic aspects (Bockstael [6], Weinhold [45]) and the implications for policy making (Lacombe [27]). The presence of spatial patterns that influence (positively or negatively) the economic variables requires a rigorous and systematic assessment of their impact and of their shape. A new interesting research perspective of spatial econometric analysis is that of spatial filters; this analysis tool allows splitting the georeferenced variables into two components, spatial and non-spatial, highlighting the spatial autocorrelation component.

The filtration technique proposed by Griffith [22] exploits, as mentioned, the technique of decomposition of the matrix in its eigenvectors and eigenvalues, allows the extraction from the n x n matrix of uncorrelated numerical orthogonal components (Tiefelsdorf and Boots [42]). This nonparametric approach has the aim of managing the presence of spatial autocorrelation by introducing variables, the eigenvectors, which can be used as predictors instead of not explicitly considered variables (Fischer and Griffith [16]). These variables are derived from the spatial weights matrix C of n x n size:

$$\left(I - 1 I^T \frac{1}{n}\right) C \left(I - 1 I^T \frac{1}{n}\right) \tag{5}$$

where I is the identity matrix of size n x n, and 1 is a vector of one dimension n x 1 and T is the transposed matrix. The particularity of this matrix is that it appears in the numerator of Moran's I (MC). Tiefelsdorf and Boots [42] show that each eigenvalue of the expression (5) is related to different values of MC.

The eigenfunction linked to the geographical contiguity matrix C can be interpreted as the latent spatial association of a georeferenced variable (Getis and Griffith [20]). The first eigenvector, E_1, is the set of numerical values that has the largest value of MC for the given geographic contiguity matrix. The second eigenvector, E_2, is the set of numerical values that has the greatest value of MC for each set of numerical values not correlated with E_1. This sequential construction of eigenvectors continues to E_n, a set of numerical values that has the largest value of MC achievable by any set of numerical values that is uncorrelated with the previous n-1 eigenvectors. These n eigenvectors describe the full range of possible orthogonal, unrelated spatial patterns and can be interpreted as a summary map of variables that describe the nature (positive or negative) and the level (low, moderate, high) of spatial autocorrelation.

4   The Spatial Model

The spatial model used in our work refers to a recent study by Griffith [23] which proposes an approach to GWR model (Fotheringham, Brundson and Charlton [18]), based on the spatial filters through the construction of new variables created by the product between the space filter and the spatial variables.

$$Y = \beta_0(u,v)1 + \sum_{p=1}^{p} X_p\beta_p(u,v) + \varepsilon \tag{6}$$

where Y is an n x 1 vector, and represents the dependent variable, β_j is j_th regression coefficient, X_p is an n x 1 vector of values of the variable p, ε is an n x 1 vector containing the random error terms, and (u, v) indicates that the parameters have to be estimated for each location whose spatial coordinates are given by the pair of vectors (u, v), implicitly assuming that Y, X and ε are georeferenced. A normal linear model with spatial filter incorporates a set P of regressors, $X_p = (k = 1,2,...,P)$, with a k set of selected eigenvectors, $E_k = (k = 1,2,...,K)$, which represent different spatial models, in order to consider the residual spatial autocorrelation in the dependent variable and has the following form:

$$Y = \beta_0 1 + \sum_{p=1}^{p} X_p\beta_p + \sum_{K=1}^{K} E_K\beta_{E_K} + \varepsilon \tag{7}$$

The first two terms in the equation constitute a usual linear regression model (OLS), the third term represents the spatial filter. Griffith [23] proposes to expand the equation (7) with the inclusion of an interaction term between each attribute variable and each candidate eigenvector. The new formulation is:

$$Y = \beta_{0,GWR} + \sum_{p=1}^{p} X_p\beta_{p,GWR} \approx$$

$$\approx \left(\beta_0 1 + \sum_{K_0=1}^{K_0} E_{K_0}\beta_{K_0}\right) + \sum_{p=1}^{p} \left(\beta_p 1 + \sum_{K_p=1}^{K_p} E_{K_p}\beta_{K_p}\right) \bullet X_p \tag{8}$$

where $\bullet$ denotes element-wise matrix multiplication (i.e., Hadamard matrix multiplication), and k_p identifies the eigenvector numbers that describe attribute variable p, with k_p being the total number of these vectors. Equation (8) reveals the presence of the interaction terms in question, namely k_p p $E \bullet X$. The sum of the first and third terms of equation (7) becomes the GWR intercept coefficient expression in equation (8); distributing the $k_p s$ across their premultiplied sums in equation (8), and then rearranging the results yields, when all K candidate eigenvectors are considered, yields:

$$Y = \beta_{0R} + \sum_{p=1}^{p} X_p \bullet I + \sum_{k=1}^{K} E_k \beta_{E_k} + \sum_{p=1}^{P} \sum_{k=1}^{K} E_{K_p} X_p \bullet E_k \beta_{pE_p} + \varepsilon \qquad (9)$$

where the regression coefficients represent global values, and the eigenvectors represent local modifications of these global values; the first two terms (i.e., the global attribute variable coefficients) are multiplied by the vector I, which also is a spatial filter eigenvector. More precisely, the global values are the coefficients needed to construct linear combinations of the eigenvectors, in order to obtain GWR-type coefficients. Estimation of equation (9) needs to be followed by collecting all terms containing a common attribute variable and then factoring it out in order to determine its GWR coefficient, which will be the corresponding sum appearing in equation (7). The GWR coefficients are linear combinations of a subset of the K eigenvectors, with those not in the subset having a regression coefficient value of 0; the GWR coefficients are n-by-1 vectors. Operationally we:

1. computed 71 eigenvectors extracted from the C Gabriel Graph geographic connectivity matrix,
2. computed all of the interactions terms $X_j E_k$ for the P covariates times the K candidate eigenvectors (with $MC \geq 0.25$),
3. selected from the total set, including the individual eigenvectors, with stepwise regression that maximizes value of R^2
4. the geographically varying intercept term is given by:

$$a_i = a + \sum_{k=1}^{K} E_{i,k} b_{E_{i,k}}$$

5. the geographically varying covariate coefficient is given by factoring X_j out of its appropriate selected interaction terms:

$$(b_{i,j} X_j) = \left(b_j + \sum_{k=1}^{K} E_{i,k} b_{E_{i,k}} \right) X_j$$

As mentioned previously, a GWR-type of coefficient can be computed by assembling all selected individual and interaction terms from which the same attribute variable can be factored. For example, *beta* appears in the equation itself and with 7 eigenvector interaction terms. Its GWR-type coefficient can be computed as follows:

$$beta = -0.01469 - 0.06595 E_6 + 0.03642 E_{18} - 0.06540 E_{26}$$
$$+ 0.04771 E_{36} + 0.02629 E_{60} - 0.02146 E_{62} + 0.01071 E_{68}$$

where the regression coefficients were estimated with final variable selections made in the preceding stepwise regression procedure, and the attribute variable *beta* has been factored out of the seven terms.

The result coincides with the sum that appears in equation (7). If two variables have a set of common eigenvectors in whole or in part, it means that they have a component of similarity of their spatial autocorrelation, and conversely, if there are no common eigenvectors, the two variables are not spatially correlated.

5   Estimation Results

In the following table we can observe the results of the classical OLS model and of the GWR-SF model. Since the GWR-SF estimation method is an extension of the GWR, we thought it appropriate to verify the applicability of this technique. The value of the global stationarity test or pseudo F-test (Brunsdon, Fotheringham and Charlton [7]) is not statistically significant and this implies that the GWR method is not suitable. This result gives further support to the application of the spatial filtering technique.

The OLS technique applied to the expanded model (table 2) results in a biased estimation. In particular, we observed the presence of spatial dependence in the error terms, demonstrating the necessity to include the management of spatial effects in the model to obtain more reliable estimations. The β parameter of the model indicates a slow convergence rate: 1% and the R^2 is 0.52. The parameters $GVAEMP95$ and $SAVEGVA$ are statistically significant, proving consistency with the economic theory, while the discount rate is not significant, showing its limited impact on growth. Furthermore $TECHEMPe$ and $LNLIFLEARe$ are significant and positive: they have a positive impact on economic growth; this is also in line with the theory.

In same table 2 we observe the global parameters of the GWR-SF technique and the related diagnostic tests. The number of significant variables increases in comparison to the model estimated with the OLS technique. In this case $LONGUNEMPe$ and $EMPAGRIe$ are significant and negative, meaning that they give a negative contribution to the economic growth. This is easily understandable, since the rigidity of the labor market and a strong employment in agriculture, a sector with low innovation, can be an obstacle to economic development. On the other hand, in this case $LNLIFLEARe$ is not statistically significant.

The above table contains, as mentioned, the global value (the second term of (9)) of the coefficients of the model. These coefficients are useful for making a first comparison with the original OLS estimation but it should be noted that in a second step they are determined at the regional level (the sum of second and fourth term of (9)). This means that we need to study the local values to verify their dynamics and their consistency with the economic theory. The tests on the GWR-SF model show that the null hypothesis of spatial autocorrelation of residuals is rejected. However, it is not possible to reject non-normality of error terms, and heteroschedasticity cannot be excluded since the two tests have different significance. The fit of the GWR-SF model is much higher than the OLS model: the R^2 value exceed 0.96 and also the other tests show better results.

Table 2. Results of the OLS and GWR-SF estimation of the *augmented* model

Variabile	Coefficient OLS	Coefficient GWR-SF
Intercept	0.0998***	0.0767***
(Std. Err)	(0.0099)	(13.466)
GVAEMP95	-0.0107***	-0.0147***
(Std. Err)	(0.0012)	(0.0009)
SCEMP03	-0.0010	-0.0003
(Std. Err)	(0.0007)	(0.0004)
SAVEGVA	0.0181***	0.0069***
(Std. Err)	(0.0024)	(0.0019)
TECHEMPe	0.0064***	0.0019 .
(Std. Err)	(0.0019)	(0.0010)
LONGUNEMPe	-0.0004	-0.0015*
(Std. Err)	(0.0009)	(0.0006)
EMPAGRI	0.0147	-0.0201*
(Std. Err)	(0.0107)	(0.0084)
LNLIFLEARe	0.0304**	0.0089
(Std. Err)	(0.0111)	(0.0091)
Heteroschedasticity test		
Goldfeld-Quandt test	1.6111**	1.5511
Breusch-Pagan test +	35.9154***	139.5108 .
Normality test for the residuals		
Jarque- Brera test	76.4465***	141.7538***
Shapiro-Wilk test	0.9536***	0.9589***
Moran test for spatial autocorrelation		
	0.3619***	-0.2647
Fit of the model		
AIC	-1680.614	-2139.275
R^2(adj.)	0.5194(0.5060)	0.9613(0.9352)
RSS	0.0215	0. 0017

+ studentized Breush-Pagan test (Koenker [26] metodology) robust in presence of
non normal distribution of the residuals
Significance: 0 '***' 0.001 '**' 0.01 '*' 0.05 '.' 0.1 ' ' 1

The table 3 contains the local values of the coefficients of the model; the median of all coefficients coincides with the mean and there is consistency between the signs of global and regional factors. The convergence rate, measured by the coefficients of the variable *GVAEMP95* has a rather wide range, from a minimum of -4.23% to a maximum of 0.08%. The upper range value is represented by one Italian region which tends to diverge, but with very low rates.

These results demonstrate that the 259 European regions have different steady states, converging at different speeds. Finally, the persistence of the positive sign of the variable *SCEMP03* also at regional level, shows that the increase in growth rate of the workforce and / or the discount rate has a positive impact on economic development.

Table 3. Coefficient estimation of GWR-SF *augmented* model

Variabile	Min.	1st Qu.	Median	Mean	3rd Qu.	Max.
Intercept	-0.0651	0.0409	0.0696	0.0767	0.1061	0.3345
GVAEMP95	-0.0423	-0.0192	-0.0142	-0.0147	-0.0092	0.0008
SCEMP03	-0.0118	-0.0029	-0.0004	-0.0003	0.0021	0.0146
SAVEGVA	-0.0226	-0.0009	0.0072	0.0069	0.0147	0.0403
TECHEMPe	-0.0294	-0.0028	0.0013	0.0019	0.0077	0.0247
LONGUNEMPe	-0.0106	-0.0043	-0.0019	-0.0015	0.0011	0.0096
EMPAGRI	-0.2401	-0.0680	-0.0211	-0.0201	0.0227	0.3705
LNLIFLEARe	-0.2153	-0.0392	0.0129	0.0089	0.0598	0.1861

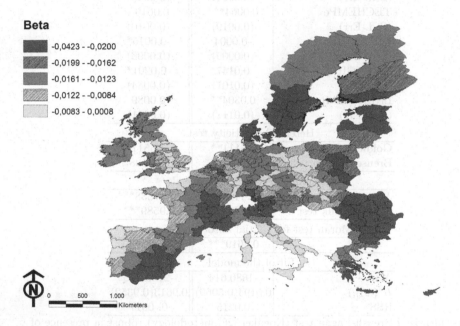

Beta

- -0,0423 - -0,0200
- -0,0199 - -0,0162
- -0,0161 - -0,0123
- -0,0122 - -0,0084
- -0,0083 - 0,0008

0   500   1.000
Kilometers

Fig. 1. Convergence rates

Figure 1, shows the rates of convergence of European regions. As mentioned, only one Italian region diverges by less than a tenth of a percentage point and we can observe many macroregions that exhibit common characteristics. The regions that converge faster, belong mainly to Bulgaria, Romania, Greece, Poland, northern Italy, Austria, northern Germany, Denmark, to southern Sweden and Finland, to southern and central Spain and to the three Baltic republics. Among the regions that converge at a slower rate we can observe some clusters: they are placed especially in central and southern Italy, in Great Britain and in Ireland. We can observe other low convergence areas: one of them goes across Hungary and the Czech Republic up to East Germany, a second one is located in the German regions surrounding Benelux, a third one in western and Atlantic France and the last one in the central and northern regions of Spain and in Portugal.

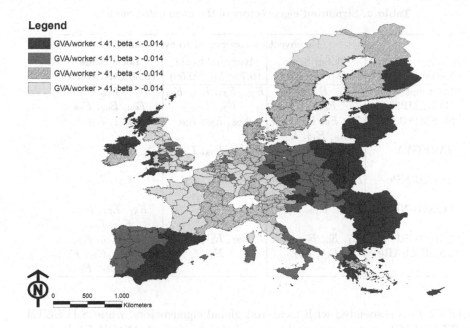

Fig. 2. Correlation between initial GVA per employee and convergence rates

The map represented in figure 2 shows a significant correlation between the initial GVA per employee and the rates of convergence. In the more remote areas, the most economically disadvantaged, the rates of convergence are higher than the median. Conversely, as they approach the most industrialized areas of Europe, the rates of convergence fall. This overview, however, cannot fully explain the phenomenon represented in figure 2 that needs a more detailed analysis. Among the regions with a GVA per worker below the median, only a limited number has a convergence rate higher than the median. Furthermore, only a fraction of the regions with GVA per employee lower than the initial median, have convergence rates that make it possible to foresee, in the long term, an alignment of GVA per employee levels with those of reach regions. Another part, located nearer to richer regions of central Europe has a lower convergence rate.

The spatially filtered model helps understanding the scale of the phenomenon, providing important data for the governance of regional development policy, with particular focus on the growth of regional economies. Furthermore, we are able to recognize the geographic scale of the impact of independent variables by checking the eigenvectors associated to them. The eigenvalue, or MC, connected to every eigenvector enables us to build different sets of eigenvestors. If the values of MC is greater than 0.75 we will discuss global scale, eigenvectors 1 to 24; if the MC value is included between 0.5 and 0.75 we will discuss regional scale, eigenvectors from 24 to 46; and if MC is less than 0.50 we will discuss local scale, eigenvectors from 47 to 71. In the table 4 we can see which are the significant vectors associated with each variable and the intercept. The variable

Table 4. Significant eigenvectors of the *augmented* model

Variabile	Eigenvectors associated to every variable		
	Global Scale (MC>0.75)	Regional Scale (0.75>MC>0.50)	Local Scale (0.50>MC>0.25)
Intercept	E_6, E_{18}, E_{19}	E_{26}, E_{35}, E_{36}, E_{44}	E_{60}
GVAEMP95	E_6, E_{18}	E_{26}, E_{36}	E_{60}, E_{62}, E_{68}
SCEMP03	E_5, E_6, E_9, E_{10}, E_{18}, E_{19}, E_{22}	E_{26}, E_{36}, E_{38}	E_{44}, E_{48}
SAVEGVA	E_6, E_{12}, E_{16}, E_{18}, E_{22}	E_{30}, E_{38}, E_{43}	
TECHEMPe	E_9, E_{10}, E_{16}, E_{19}	E_{26}, E_{30}, E_{36}, E_{38}, E_{43}	E_{51}, E_{69}
LONGUNEMPe	E_5, E_{12}, E_{17}		E_{47}, E_{51}, E_{60}, E_{62}, E_{69}
EMPAGRI	E_1, E_9, E_{11}, E_{24}	E_{27}, E_{31}, E_{38}	E_{46}, E_{50}, E_{70}
LNLIFLEARe	E_{13}, E_{17}	E_{33}	E_{45}, E_{48}, E_{49}, E_{51}, E_{65}, E_{66}, E_{69}

GVAEMP95 is associated with local and global eigenvectors, while *SAVEGVA* and *TECHEMPe* have global and regional eigenvectors, *LONGUNEMPe* local and *EMPAGRIe* local, regional and global eigenvectors.

6 Conclusions

Our work, using a new analysis tool, highlights the existence of different regional convergence parameters Results are different from those of almost all previously conducted analyses, even when models capable of handling spatial dependence were used. The possibility to manage both the spatial effect and the structural differences of the economies is a clear advantage for the economic analysis. This advantage is due to the possibility to verify the hypothesis of the existence of different paths of economic growth among regions, although regions are closely interrelated. This result is also important because it represents an advance into the process of understanding and evaluating the effects of policies at different scales (regional, national, European) inside a reality, the European Union, in which the regional development policies have an important socioeconomic role. Furthermore, this tool could be useful for future research.

While it is possible to compare the global trends identified in the tested model with previous studies, which face the same order of magnitude, it is more difficult to do the same for the regional trends because, with the exclusion of some studies that used the classical GWR approach (Eckey [12], Sassi and Pecci [40]) and a Bayesian model (Ertur, Le Gallo and Le Sage [13]), they lack previous references. The addition of more variables to the model proposed by Mankiw, Romer and Weil [29], brings out, in some cases, a country effect, as noted by Ertur, Le Gallo and Le Sage [13]. The possible interpretation of this country effect is that some variables in regional and global scale, like *TECHEMPe* and *EMPAGRIe*, are sensitive to the national policies and then exert an effect on growth that has common features within each country.

The results of the analysis show a complex reality in which it is necessary to investigate more thoroughly the causes of the different economic behaviors of the European regions. The advantage that the spatial filtering technique can offer to policy makers is that not only the overall contribution of the individual variables can be identified, but also their specific influence. Combining all this information we can draw a picture of all the factors that contribute to the growth of every single region. Finally, the possibility to evaluate the scale of influence of each variable provides policy makers with another powerful tool to handle regional policies.

References

1. Arbia, G., De Dominicis, L., Piras, G.: The relationship between Regional Growth and Regional Inequality in EU and transition countries - a Spatial Econometric Approach. In: ERSA conference papers, ersa05p168 (2005)
2. Barro, R.T., Sala-i-Martin, X.: Convergence Across States and Regions. Brooking Papers on Economic Activity 1, 107–182 (1991)
3. Barro, R.T., Sala-i-Martin, X.: Convergence. Journal of Political Economy 100(2), 223–251 (1992)
4. Barro, R.T., Sala-i-Martin, X.: Economic Growth. McGraw-Hill, New York (1995)
5. Baumol, W.J.: Productivity Growth, Convergence, and Welfare: What the Long-run Data Show. American Economic Review 76(5), 1072–1085 (1986)
6. Bockstael, N.E.: Economics and Ecological Modeling: The Importance of a Spatial Perspective. American Journal of Agricultural Economics 78(5), 1168–1180 (1996)
7. Brunsdon, C., Fotheringham, A.S., Charlton, M.E.: Some notes on parametric significance tests for geographically weighted regression. Journal of Regional Science 39, 497–524 (1999)
8. Cohen, W., Levinthal, D.: Absorptive capacity: A new perspective on learning and innovation. Administration Science Quarterly 35(1), 128–152 (1990)
9. Corrado, L., Martin, R., Weeks, M.: Identify and Interpreting Regional Convergence Clusters Across Europe. The Economic Journal 115, 133–160 (2005)
10. Durlauf, S.: Econometric Analysis and the Study of Economic Growth: A Skeptical Perspective. In: Backhouse, R., Salanti, A. (eds.) Macroeconomics and the Real World. Oxford University Press, Oxford (2000)
11. Durlauf, S., Temple, J.: Growth Econometrics. In: Aghion, P., Durlauf, S.N. (eds.) Handbook of Economic Growth. Elsevier, North-Holland (2005)
12. Eckey, H.F., Dreger, C., Turck, M.: European Regional Convergence in a human Capital Augmented Solow Model. Volkswirtschaftliche Diskussionsbeitr̈age 88/06, Kassel Universitat (2008)
13. Ertur, C., Le Gallo, J., Le Sage, J.: Local versus Global Convergence in Europe: A Bayesian Spatial Econometric Approach. Review of Regional Studies 1, 82–108 (2007)
14. Fingleton, B.: Estimates of time to economic convergence: an analysis of regions of the European Union. International Regional Science Review 22, 5–35 (1999)
15. Fingleton, B., McCombie, J.S.L.: Increasing returns and economic growth: Some evidence for manufacturing from the European Union regions. Oxford Economic Papers 50, 89–105 (1998)

16. Fischer, M., Griffith, D.A.: Modeling Spatial Autocorrelation in Spatial Interaction Data: An Application to PatentCitation Datain the Europeam Union. Journal of Regional Science 48(5), 969–989 (2008)
17. Fischer, M., Stirböck, C.: Regional Income Convergence in the Enlarged Europe, 1995-2000: A Spatial Econometric Perspective. The Annals of Regional Science 37(2), 693–721 (2005)
18. Fotheringham, A.S., Brunsdon, C., Charlton, M.: Geographically Weighted Regression: The Analysis of Spatially Varying Relationships. John Wiley, Sons Ltd., West Sussex (2002)
19. Fujita, M., Krugman, P., Venables, A.J.: The Spatial Economy. MIT Press, Cambridge (1999)
20. Getis, A., Griffith, D.A.: Comparative spatial filtering in regression analysis. Geographical Analysis 34(2), 130–140 (2002)
21. Gordon, I.R.: Unemployment and spatial labour markets: strong adjustment and persistent concentration. In: Martin, R., Morrison, P. (eds.) Geographies of Labour Market Inequality. Routledge, London (2001)
22. Griffith, D.A.: Spatial autocorrelation and spatial filtering: Gaining understanding through theory and scientific visualization. Springer, Berlin (2003)
23. Griffith, D.A.: Spatial Filtering-based contribution to a critique of geographically weighted regression (GWR). Environment and Planning A 40, 2751–2769 (2008)
24. Islam, N.: What have We Learnt from the Convergence Debate? Journal of Economic Surveys 17(3), 309–362 (2003)
25. Krugman, P.: Increasing returns and economic geography. Journal of Political Economy 99, 483–499 (1991)
26. Koenker, R.: A note on studentizing a test for heteroscedasticity. Journal of Econometrics 17, 107–112 (1981)
27. Lacombe, D.J.: Does Econometric Methodology Matter? An Analysis of Public Policy Using Spatial Econometric Techniques. Geographical Analysis 36(2), 105–118 (2004)
28. Le Gallo, J., Ertur, C.: Exploratory spatial data analysis of the distribution of regional per capita GDP in Europe, 1980-1995. Papers in Regional Science 82(2), 175–201 (2003)
29. Mankiw, G.N., Romer, D., Weil, D.N.: A Contribution to the Empirics of Economic Growth. Quarterly Journal of Economics 107(2), 407–437 (1992)
30. Mankiw, N.G.: The Growth of Nations. Brookings Papers on Economic Activity 1, 276–326 (1995)
31. Maurseth, P.B., Verspagen, B.: Europe: One or several systems of innovation? An analysis based on patent citations. In: Fagerberg, J., Guerrieri, P., Verspagnen, B. (eds.) The economic challenge for Europe. Edward Elgar, Cheltenham (1999)
32. Moran, P.A.P.: Notes on continuous stochastic phenomena. Biometrika 37, 13–23 (1950)
33. Niebuhr, A.: Convergence and the Effects of Spatial Interaction, in the EU-25. Jahrbuch für Regionalwissenschaft 21(2), 113–133 (2001)
34. Niebuhr, A., Schlitte, F.: EU Enlargement and Convergence Does Market Access Matter? Eastern European Economics 47(3), 28–56 (2009)
35. Paci, R., Pigliaru, F.: Technological Diffusion, Spatial Spillovers and Regional Convergence in Europe. In: Cuadrado, J.R., Parellada, M. (eds.) The European Monetary Union and Regional Convergence, pp. 273–292. Springer, Heidelberg (2002)
36. Paas, T., Schlitte, F.: Regional Income Inequality and Convergence Process in the EU-25. Italian ournal of Regional Science 2/2008 - Special Issue, 29–49 (2008)

37. Pecci, F.: La crescita dell'agricoltura nelle regioni dell'Europa a 15 negli ultimi due decenni. Rivista di Economia Agraria 1/2008, 151–184 (2009)
38. Quah, D.: Regional convergence clusters in Europe. European Economic Review 40(3-5), 951–958 (1996)
39. Rodriguez-Pose, A., Crescenzi, R.: Research and development, spillovers, innovation systems, and the genesis of regional growth in Europe. Regional studies 42(1), 51–67 (2008)
40. Sassi, M., Pecci, F.: Agricultural and economic convergence in the EU integration process: do geographical relationships matter? In: XIIth EAAE Congress, Ghent, August 26-29 (2008)
41. Solow, R.M.: A Contribution to the Theory of Economic Growth. Quarterly Journal of Economics LXX, 65–94 (1956)
42. Tiefelsdorf, M., Boots, B.: The exact distribution of Moran's I. Environment and Planning A 27, 985–999 (1995)
43. Tiefelsdorf, M., Griffith, D.A.: Semiparametric filtering of spatial autocorrelation: the eigenvector approach. Environment and Planning A 39, 1193–1221 (2007)
44. Tobler, W.R.: A computer movie simulating urban growth in the Detroit region. Economic Geography 46, 234–240 (1970)
45. Weinhold, D.: The Importance of Trade and Geography in the Pattern of Spatial Dependence of Growth Rates. Review of Development Economics 6(3), 369–382 (2002)

Spatial Autocorrelation Analysis for the Evaluation of Migration Flows: The Italian Case

Grazia Scardaccione, Francesco Scorza,
Giuseppe Las Casas, and Beniamino Murgante

Laboratory of Urban and Territorial Systems, University of Basilicata,
Via dell'Ateneo Lucano 10, 85100, Potenza, Italy
firstname.surname@unibas.it

Abstract. During the last decades immigration phenomenon reached a considerable importance, not only in research sector but also at public opinion level. Migration is a complex phenomenon demanding a system analysis which goes beyond demographic and economic considerations. The purpose of this study was to investigate the spatial structure of foreign presence in Italy in order to identify its geographical demarcation line among different interpretations. Traditional statistical analysis suggests different conventional indices allowing to quantify immigration phenomenon. Traditional indices, as Location Quotients and Segregation Index, have been compared to innovative indices including spatial statistics elements, as well as global and local indicators of spatial association. Such indicators have been created on the basis of available data for the case study, but also considering information which can be easily found in great part of national contexts.

Keywords: Foreign Immigration, Location Quotients, Spatial indices of dissimilarity, Spatial Analysis, Spatial Statistics, Global and Local Indicator of Spatial Autocorrelation.

1 Introduction

Migration analysis is an application field involving many disciplines (e.g. geography, economy, social science, etc). Migrations are key factors in population dynamics evolution at different scales, with implications in economy, culture, environment, etc. From an economic point of view: migrations are forms of human capital [1]. In the simplest model of wealth maximization fixed travel costs are balanced by the net present value of earning streams available in the alternative location [2].

Great part of researches on migrations adopt a static framework, basing their assumptions on the link between migration and the "search for better economic conditions" (wealth maximization). This structural concept in the analysis of migrations strongly relies on individual perceptions of Wealth Maximization. Mincer [3] assumes that the location of an individual maximum may not coincide with the location of joint maximum. In this paper, traditional indicators for estimating migrations (location quotient

D. Taniar et al. (Eds.): ICCSA 2010, Part I, LNCS 6016, pp. 62–76, 2010.

and segregation index) have been combined with geostatistical techniques to detect spatial clusters, defining preferential destination areas of migrants.

Such destinations can provide preferential elements for the characterization of migrants joint maximum. Identified clusters become target areas of sectoral policies aimed at overcoming problems of social integration, security, job opportunities (an actual political debate in Europe both at national and community scales).

Modern migrations are mainly characterized by two components, comparable in terms of absolute value: internal migration where part of the population moves within the country; external migration where part of the population reaches the study area (in our case Italy) coming from another country or vice versa.

The present work does not distinguish between these components. The analysis considers both the internal and the external components of migration as a whole, due to problems in data availability. In order to distinguish between these components, it is necessary to manage origin/destination matrix of each migration flow. For internal migration component, such a matrix is not always available and it is very expensive to build-up (in terms of data and processing costs), especially considering detailed scales (our application concerns municipalities). For the external migrations, available data concern sources and destinations per macro geographical regions: continents very far from municipality scale.

This research contributes to the identification of destination areas for migratory flows in Italy, adopting a geostatistical approach using data very easy to find in all countries (resident population, members and deleted, foreigners presence) to propose a fully reproducible methodology. The Italian case is particularly significant in terms of consistency of the phenomenon because of the recent years trends. It is also interesting because, unlike other European countries, Italy has experienced a reversal in migration trends. While in 1960s and '70s Italy was essentially the origin of migration flows mainly oriented to other European countries; in recent decades it has become a destination of migration flows from South Mediterranean countries and, with increasing dimensions, from Eastern EU Countries and Balkans.

2 Materials and Methods

The research has been developed throughout the country, considering municipalities as a independent statistical/geographical minimal unit. This choice reflects the need to represent in detail the phenomenon traditionally described for macro aggregate regions.

Several indicators have been selected in order to measure the impact of foreign population resident in Italy. These indicators have been constructed on the basis of available data for the case study, but also considering that the same information can be easily found in great part of national contexts.

The dataset was provided by the National Institute of Statistics (ISTAT, deputy state body for statistical analysis of territorial dynamics in Italy). Variables are: resident population, present foreign population, members (people who have moved their residence to specific municipalities), erased (people who have removed their residence from specific municipalities). For each variable historical series have been considered. In this paper elaborations concern the period from 1999 to 2007 as epresentative of the latest trends.

2.1 Traditional Approaches for the Analysis of Migration Flows

Techniques adopted in the first phase of analysis provided an evaluation of migrations in global terms. The analysis was based on traditional statistical indicators. More particularly, after referring to the presence of foreigners and the percentage of foreigners in the resident population, we calculated the efficacy index of migration (Ie) in order to obtain information on movement dynamics.

Following traditional approaches, we developed measures of segregation using Location Quotient (LQ) and index of Spatial Segregation. Segregation phenomenon can be analyzed from the socially and spatially point of view. This paper mainly focuses on spatial points of view, assessing two indicators: index of dissimilarity (D), and location quotient (LQ).

These indices allow us to assess levels of territorial differentiation of a group (foreigners) relative to another group (resident population). The measures highlighted heterogeneity of the structure of foreign population in relation to considered study areas. Separating resident population in two groups, Italians and foreigners, the degree of coexistence between them has been measured.

Segregation index focuses on the analysis of phenomena related to residential segregation at urban and regional levels. This kind of approach concerns the evaluation of the risk of social segregation where too high concentration of a single immigrant group is present if compared to local residents (ghetto or 'ethnic islands' effect) [4].

Segregation index generally is the most used indicator in international research concerning geographical mobility. Especially, dissimilarity index (*D*) developed by Duncan and Duncan [5] is widely used.

Its applications generally deal with the comparison of the distribution of national groups in the intra-metropolitan area processing data at a very detailed scale (census blocks). In this work D index had been used to investigate macro regions segregation using municipality data as statistic units for the analysis.

2.1.1 Efficacy Index of Migration

In order to take into account the impact of migration on relative abundance of resident population, we calculated Efficacy Index of migration (Ie). Efficacy Index of migration is defined as:

$$I_e = \left[\frac{(I-D)}{(I+D)} \right] 100 \tag{1}$$

where I = Members (people who have moved their residence to specific municipalities), D = Deleted (people who have cancelled their residence from a specific municipality), (I-D) represents net migration.

Values close to zero indicate that migration exchange in a municipality produces a significant change in population; values close to 100 indicate that the incoming streams are much greater than outgoing ones; and finally, values close to -100 show that emigration flow is prevailing [6].

2.1.2 Location Quotients
"Location Quotient" (LQ) provides an estimation of the degree of specialization of the individual statistical unit (in this case the municipality) to accept foreign population.

LQ provides a measure of relative concentration of a group in a given municipality in connection with average incidence of the same group at National level.
The indicator is defined as:

$$LQ = \frac{(x_i/y_i)}{(X/Y)}$$

(2)

where x_i represents the number of residents of a national group in area unit i (in our case the municipality), X the number of residents in the entire study area (in our case the Country), y_i the foreign population in area unit i and Y the foreign overall population in the study region.

Location quotient is LQ = 1 if the analyzed group holds in the area unit i the same characteristics of the study region; if LQ > 1 than it is overrepresented in area unit i, and if LQ < 1 than it is underrepresented.

Location Quotient (LQ) allows to explore the spatial structure of migrants, as it allows mapping the spatial distribution of the phenomenon according to the most disaggregated zoning system of the study region [7].

2.1.3 Dissimilarity Index
Dissimilarity Index in the formulation of Duncan and Duncan [8] provides an estimation of the segregation degree of two groups of population in the study area. It describes a spatial concentration of population groups.
The index is defined as:

$$D = \frac{1}{2} \sum_{i=1}^{K} | x_i - z_i | \, 100$$

(3)

where:

- x_i is the ratio between the number of residents in the area i and total population in the whole study area;
- Z_i represents a ratio similar to x, for another group;
- k is the number of territorial parts in which we divide the study area.

The index varies between 0 and 100. Values close to 0 indicate a low dissimilarity. High values of this index indicate that the coexistence of the two groups in the same areas is quantitatively limited.

This index allows a direct comparison of different areas, but it is not spatially embedded and it does not explain internal aspects of dissimilarity or segregation.

Although such an index has been used for decades and its family actually dominates the literature [9], it does not provide any indication on the population mix between zones, but just within the whole study area and so it produces results strongly dependent on the zoning system chosen [10].

O' Sullivan and Wong [10] remark that summary indices (such as D) are useful to portray the level of regional segregation and to compare results obtained in different regions. Unfortunately, spatial aspects of phenomena are not accounted, as the possible rise of non-uniformity at local level or the level of segregation across the study area, and do not provide an evaluation of segregation inside a region.

Another critical aspect concerns spatial partitioning system. It strongly affects the evaluation of segregation, generating a 'scale effect' and causing "smaller statistical enumeration units producing higher measured segregation levels" [11].

2.2 Spatial Analysis Techniques Applied to Migratory Phenomena

The identification of representative clusters of the territorial concentration of migration was based on the application of spatial analysis techniques. In particular, measures of spatial autocorrelation have been applied on the dataset.

The concept of spatial autocorrelation is one of the most important issues of spatial statistics and it derives directly from the first law of geography by Tobler [12]: "All Things Are Related, But Nearby Things Are More Related Than Distant Things".

In this study, Moran Index (I), corresponding Moran scatter plots and Local Indicator of Spatial Association (LISA) have been calculated. Moran I provides an overall measure of Spatial Autocorrelation [13], Moran scatter plot [14] allows to achieve a graphic representation of spatial relationships and enables us to investigate possible local agglomerations, LISA allows us to take into account local effects of the phenomenon [15] [16].

2.2.1 Moran's I Statistic
Moran Index [13] can be formalized as follows:

$$I = \frac{n}{S_0} \frac{\sum\limits_{i=1}^{n} \sum\limits_{j=1}^{n} (x_i - \bar{x})(x_j - \bar{x})w_{ij}}{\sum\limits_{i=1}^{n} (x_i - \bar{x})^2} \tag{4}$$

Where:

- X_i is the variable observed in n spatial partitions and $\bar{x}$ is variable average;
- W_{ij} is the generic element of contiguity matrix;
- $S_0 = \sum\limits_{i=1}^{n} w_{ij}$ is the sum of all matrix elements defined as contiguous according to the distance between points-event. In the case of spatial contiguity matrix, the sum is equal to the number of non-null links.

Since the expression of spatial dependence refers to the connection between the nearest unit, prior of autocorrelation concept, there is the problem of expressing the degree of proximity of the areas by defining the concept of spatial contiguity [17].

The concept of contiguity can be defined as a generalized matrix of W weight, usually symmetrical, representing the pattern of connections or ties and their intensity [18], where w_i weights$_j$ denote the effect of the territorial unit on unit i. In our study we used a dichotomic matrix of contiguity where $w_{ij} = 1$ if the i area touches the boundary of j area; and $w_{ij} = 0$ is otherwise.

Index values may fall outside the range (-1, +1). Moreover, in case of no autocorrelation the value is not 0 but is -1/(n-1). So if:

- I < -1/(n-1) = Negative Autocorrelation,
- I = -1/(n-1) = No Autocorrelation,
- I > -1/(n-1) = Positive Autocorrelation.

Moran's index gives an indication of the degree of linear association between the vector of observed values of the variable and the vector of spatially lagged values. A positive and significant value of this statistic indicates that similar values of the variable analyzed tend to characterize contiguous localized areas. In contrast, a significant negative value of Moran-I indicates the presence of dissimilar values of the variable in contiguous areas. The significance of the index does not imply absence of autocorrelation, i.e. the presence of a random distribution of the variable in space. Moran's index, however, does not allow to evaluate if the general positive spatial dependence corresponds to territorial clusters of regions with high or low level of specialization. It is also possible that the degree of spatial dependence between various different groups within the sample is characterized by the existence of a few clusters, located in specific parts of the study region. Considering these limitations, Moran Scatter plot has been adopted.

2.2.2 Moran Scatter Plot
GEODA software [14] allows to build Moran Scatter plot together with the calculation of Moran's I. The graph represents the distribution of the statistical unit of analysis. Moran Scatter plot (Figure 1) shows the horizontal axis in the normalized variable x, and on the normalized ordinate spatial delay of that variable (W_x).

In this representation the first and third quadrants represent areas of values with positive correlations (high-high, low-low) while the second and fourth quadrants represent areas in negative correlation.

If objects are concentrated within the first and fourth quadrants, the correlation is negative. In particular, if statistical units are distributed in the fourth quadrant the relationship is kind of low-elevation and vice versa when they fall in the third

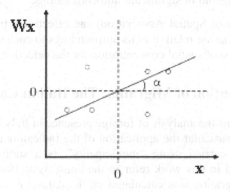

Fig. 1. Moran Scatter plot

quadrant (High-Low). However, Moran Scatter plot gives no information on the significance of spatial clusters. The significance of the spatial correlation measured through Moran's I and Moran Scatter plot is highly dependent on the extent of the study area. In case of a large territory (nation, territorial macro aggregations) the measure does not take into account the presence of heterogeneous patterns of spatial diffusion. Moran's I cannot identify outliers present in the considered statistical distribution. The Local Indicator of Spatial Association (LISA) allows to consider local effects related to the phenomenon.

2.2.3 Local Indicators of Spatial Association (LISA)

The currently most popular index of local autocorrelation is the so called LISA-Local Indicator of Spatial Association [15] [16]. This index can be locally interpreted as an equivalent index of Moran. The sum of all local indices is proportional to the value of Moran one.

The index is calculated as follows:

$$I_j = \frac{\sum_j w_{ij}(y_i - y)(y_j - y)}{\sum_i (y_i - y)^2}$$ (5)

With: $\sum_i Ii = \gamma.I$

It allows, for each location, to assess the similarity of each observation with that of its surroundings. Five scenarios emerge:

- Locations with high values of the phenomenon and high level of similarity with its surroundings (high - high), defined as HOT SPOTS;
- Locations with low values of the phenomenon and high level of similarity with its surroundings (low - low), defined as COLD SPOTS;
- Locations with high values of the phenomenon and low level of similarity with its surroundings (high - low), defined as Potential "Spatial outliers";
- Locations with low values of the phenomenon and low level of similarity with its surroundings (low - high), defined as Potential "Spatial Outliers";
- Location devoid of significant autocorrelations.

LISA (Local Indicator of Spatial Association) can effectively bind a measure of the degree of spatial association relative to its surroundings to each territorial unit, allowing to highlight the type of spatial concentration for the detection of spatial clusters.

3 Spatial Distribution of Migrants: The Italian Case

The case study concerns the analysis of foreign presence in Italy throughout the whole national territory. In particular the application of the indicators described in previous paragraphs has been carried using "municipality" as a statistical minimum unit. Elaborations presented in this work refer to the latest data: 1999, 2002, 2004, 2007. Efficacy Index of Migration was calculated on the dataset covering the years 1999, 2001, 2004 and 2007. Figure 2 shows the results obtained for the most recent dataset.

Fig. 2. Efficacy Index of Migrations calculated for migrants in Italy in 2007 (our elaboration on ISTAT data)

We observed an heterogeneous behaviour of the system that does not allow to identify clustering of origin and destination choices of migration flows. Mountain municipalities have a marked tendency to generate migration confirming depopulation trends.

Regarding the degree of specialization of each municipality to accommodate foreign population it is possible to state, using the Location Quotient, that the greater specialization is localized in central and north-eastern areas of the country (Figure 3).

The index of dissimilarity allowed to measure the heterogeneity of the structure of foreign population (Figure 4).

Segregation indices do not provide guidance on the spatial distribution of the phenomenon, in particular they do not allow to develop assessment of segregation degree within the study area [17].

In order to better identify spatial clusters representative of the concentration of migrants we applied spatial autocorrelation analysis techniques.

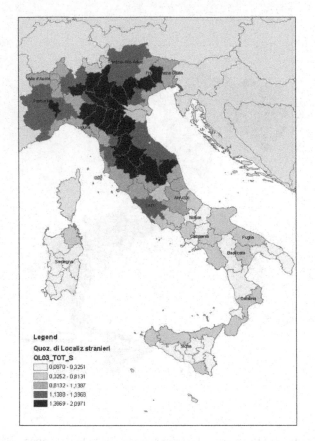

Fig. 3. Location Quotient calculated for resident immigrants in Italy in 2007 (our elaboration on ISTAT data)

In this work, Moran's I coefficient represents the difference between the weighted variance of the ratio of foreign and local resident population and the generalized variance of the same ratio expressed as the weighted variance. It expresses the correlation between the ratio of foreign/population in a given place and the ratio of foreign/population in neighbouring spatial units.

In order to take into account the connections and their intensity we defined a matrix of contiguity W, where $w_{ij} = 1$ if the i area shares boundaries with the j area, i.e. two neighbouring municipalities, and $w_{ij} = 0$ if otherwise. It is possible to consider two main kind of contiguity "Rook contiguity" which accounts only the shared side of the boundaries, and the "Queen contiguity" where the contiguity has been considered also for a shared corner. In this application "Queen contiguity" has been adopted.

Table 1 shows values of Moran (and Z-score) obtained by repeating measures on data for different territorial aggregations using the two basic variables considered in this work: foreign residents and the ratio between foreign residents and total

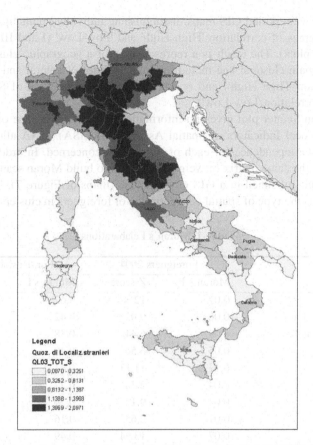

Fig. 4. Dissimilarity Index calculated for resident immigrants in Italy in 2007 (our elaboration on ISTAT data)

population. It has to be noted that spatial correlation is significant for the second variable considered. Therefore it is representative of the considered phenomenon.

To check whether the positive spatial dependence generates territorial clusters with high or low level of specialization we adopted Moran Scatter plot. It allowed us to investigate possible local clusters. The results of Moran Scatter plot were plotted on a map in order to characterize geographic areas with different types of correlation (High-High, Low-Low, High-Low, Low-High). Through this representation we verified the geographical contiguity of regions sharing the same correlation: first identification of homogeneous clusters. Moran scatter plots allowed us to assess type of correlation scaled on the municipality relative to the ratio of foreign residents and total population. In Figure 5 we report the results obtained for 1999, 2002, 2004, 2007.

Moran Scatter plot allowed us to identify extreme cases (outliers). Map representation has the advantage to pinpoint abnormal municipalities and to evaluate if their behaviour depends on geographical location. This is most likely, for example, if outliers are close to each other or are isolated, or if they are border municipalities or islands.

In Figure 6 we reported GIS maps distinguishing individual municipalities in relation to the degrees of correlation 'High High' and 'Low-Low' (I and III quadrants of Moran scatter plots). The result is a representation of a geographic clustering, structured on two main clusters: one including municipalities of central and north-eastern Italy (correlation 'High High') and one comprising municipalities of Southern Italy and islands (correlation 'Low-Low').

Since Moran Scatter plot gives no information on the significance of spatial clusters we used Local Indicators of Spatial Association (LISA). LISA allows measurement of the interdependence for each of the regions concerned. In order to calculate LISA we used the same matrix of weights (W) used to build Moran scatter plot. LISA shows the results obtained in a GIS environment, (maps of Figure 7). "LISA cluster map" highlights the type of spatial concentration of foreigners in clusters.

Table 1. Moran's I elaborations

REGIONS	Foreigners 2004		For./Residents 2004	
	Moran's I	Z-score	Moran's I	Z-score
Italy	0,07	12,3	0,62	94,51
North-Western Italy	0,06	9,02	0,42	39,66
North-Eastern Italy	0,09	6,44	0,48	32,75
Central Italy	0,05	6,56	0,48	25,45
Southern Italy	0,13	11,13	0,41	29,53
Insular Italy	0,04	2,32	0,22	10,54
Piemonte	0,04	9,12	0,24	14,41
Valle d'Aosta	0,07	2,65	0,16	2,48
Lombardia	0,07	13,94	0,49	32,31
Trentino-Alto Adige	0,03	1,45	0,32	10,27
Veneto	0,06	2,08	0,47	19,21
Friuli-Venezia Giulia	0,03	1,13	0,39	9,68
Liguria	-0,04	-2,5	0,42	10,42
Emilia-Romagna	0,03	1,24	0,41	12,46
Toscana	0,1	4,01	0,42	12,02
Umbria	0,07	1,95	0,28	4,56
Marche	0,14	4,14	0,27	7,41
Lazio	0,04	10,7	0,52	16,97
Abruzzo	0,19	5,84	0,33	9,76
Molise	0,05	1,16	0,15	3,13
Campania	0,12	8,68	0,37	14,7
Puglia	0,09	3,09	0,25	6,75
Basilicata	0,17	3,98	0,24	4,89
Calabria	0,02	0,99	0,18	6,2
Sicilia	0,01	0,67	0,24	8,25
Sardegna	0,17	6,9	0,19	6,28

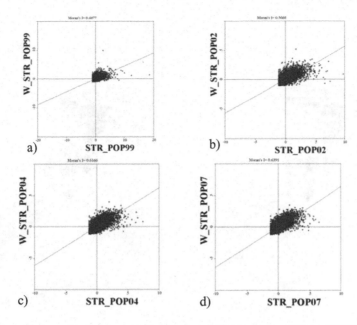

Fig. 5. Moran Scatter plot for the variable Foreigners/Residents in 1999(a), 2002(b), 2004(c), 2007(d) (our elaboration with GeoDa on ISTAT data)

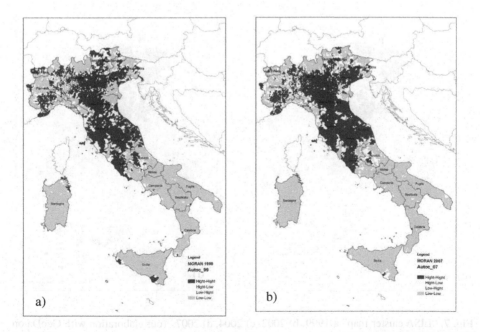

Fig. 6. Moran Scatter plot distribution a) in 1999 and b) in 2007 (our elaboration with GeoDa on ISTAT data)

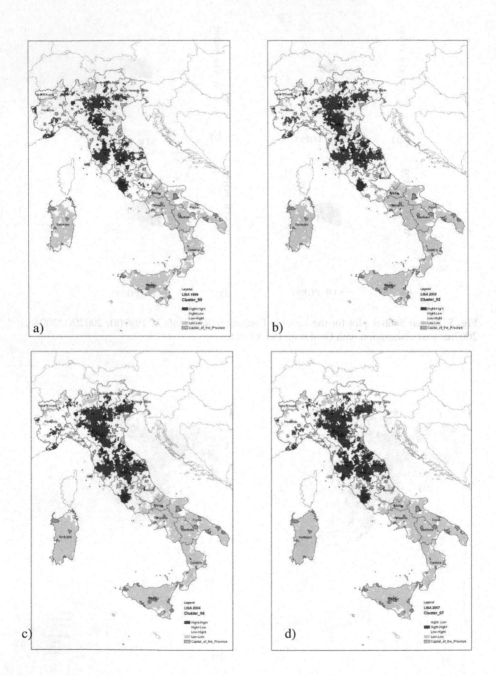

Fig. 7. "LISA cluster map" a)1999, b) 2002, c) 2004, d) 2007. (our elaboration with GeoDa on ISTAT data).

Nevertheless, three agglomerations emerged with different levels of significance:

- The first cluster included values for positive autocorrelation-type high-high increasing over the years, geographically concentrated in north-eastern areas. Such areas are characterized by increasing levels of welfare and therefore they express strong attraction for foreigners linked with employment opportunities.
- The second cluster, always of high-high type affected the central part of the national territory and is explained once again in high levels of income and employment.
- The third cluster, Low-Low type, included the towns of Southern Italy and islands, notoriously characterized by low incomes and few employment opportunities.

The comparison of different LISA areas dates with correlation of High, Low and High-Low type highlighted the trend of the phenomenon. Such clusters are going towards expansion, including other neighbouring municipalities.

4 Conclusions

In recent years the focus on the phenomenon of migration has become more and more important in political and social debates. It coincides with the increase in the size of the phenomenon due to the intensification of migration flows.

The purpose of this study was to investigate the spatial structure of the presence of foreigners in Italy in order to identify, among different interpretations, the geographical demarcation line of foreign presence. In order to define territorial clusters among Italian municipalities, Spatial Autocorrelation Techniques have been adopted.

Clusters have to be intended as target areas for specific policies aimed at overcoming problems of social integration, security and job opportunities.

In the preparation of dataset and indicators, we considered only the component of legal immigrants. Illegal immigrants aliens from the analysis because they are difficult to quantify and every hypothesis brings high uncertainty to the whole study.

Considering the results of the analysis it seems that the interpretations of a state of balance in regional disparities of migration should consider the performance of each area: areas characterized by the same performance (high presence of foreigners or low presence of foreigners) tend to aggregate and to expand including neighbouring municipalities. Therefore an internal movement of foreigners exists but it has not long hauled: this characteristic element fits well with the historical spatial distribution of foreigners in Italy (north-south demarcation line).

References

[1] Sjaastad, L.: The Costs and Returns of Human Migration. Journal of Political Economy 70, 80–89 (1962)
[2] Walker, J.R.: Internal Migration, University of Wisconsin-Madison,
http://www.ssc.wisc.edu/~walker/research/palgrave_6.pdf (Last access 8/11/2009)

[3] Mincer, J.: Family Migration Decisions. Journal of Political Economy 86, 749–773 (1978)

[4] Borruso, G.: Geographical Analysis of Foreign Immigration and Spatial Patterns in Urban Areas: Density Estimation and Spatial Segregation. In: Gervasi, O., Murgante, B., Laganà, A., Taniar, D., Mun, Y., Gavrilova, M.L. (eds.) ICCSA 2008, Part I. LNCS, vol. 5072, pp. 415–427. Springer, Heidelberg (2008)

[5] Duncan, O.D., Duncan, B.: A Methodological Analysis of Segregation Indexes. American Sociological Review 20, 210–217 (1955)

[6] ISTAT, Rapporto Annuale. La Situazione del Paese nel (2007)

[7] Cristaldi, F.: Multiethnic Rome: toward residential segregation? Geojournal (58), 81–90 (2002)

[8] Duncan, O.D., Duncan, B.: Residential Distribution and Occupational Stratification. American Journal of Sociology 60, 493–503 (1955)

[9] Massey, D.S., Denton, N.A.: The dimensions of residential segregation. Social Forces 67, 281–315 (1988)

[10] O' Sullivan, D., Wong, D.W.S.: A Surface-Based Approach to Measuring Spatial Segregation. Geographical Analysis 39, 147–168 (2007)

[11] Wong, D.W.S.: Spatial Dependency of Segregation Indices. The Canadian Geographer 41, 128–136 (1997)

[12] Tobler, W.R.: A computer movie simulating urban growth in the Detroit region. Economic Geography 46(2), 234–240 (1970)

[13] Moran, P.A.P.: The interpretation of statistical map. Journal the Royal Statistical society B, 243–251 (1948)

[14] Anselin, L.: GeoDa 0.9 User's Guide, Spatial Analysis Laboratory, Department of Agricultural and Consumer Economics and CSISS. University of Illinois, p. 125 (2003)

[15] Anselin, L.: Spatial Econometrics: Methods and Models. Kluwer Academic, Boston (1988)

[16] Anselin, L.: Local Indicators of Spatial Association-LISA. Geographical Analysis 27, 93–115 (1995)

[17] O' Sullivan, D., Unwin, D.J.: Geographic Information Analysis. John Wiley & Sons, Chichester (2003)

[18] Badaloni, M., Vinci, E.: Contributi all'Analisi dell'Autocorrelazione Spaziale. Metron 46 (1988)

Using Cellular Automata Model to Simulate the Impact of Urban Growth Policy on Environment in Danshuei Township, Taiwan

Feng-Tyan Lin and Wan-Yu Tseng

National Cheng Kung University, College of Design and Planning,
National Taiwan University, Graduate Institute of Building and Planning
Taipei, 10617 Taiwan (R.O.C)
ftlin@ntu.edu.tw, cindyfish68@gmail.com

Abstract. The impact of urban growth on eco-environment leading to global climate change has attracted great concern. In this research, we use NetLogo, a cellular automation based software, to simulate the development process of Danshuei from an original settlement to a highly developed satellite town of the Taipei Metropolitan area, Taiwan. The study area is a good case showing how to balance between urban development and natural resource protection. The model is validated against the official data extracted from National Land Use Survey of 2008. Four specific scenarios, which have different rules for urban development and strategies for natural resource conservation, are used to simulate the spatial pattern of urban growth. The first scenario simulates the urban growth using slope factor only. The outcome reveals that the areas with lower slope obtain higher potential for urban development. Following the first scenario, the second scenario adds neighbor effect and road gravity as the development rules in the model. The third and fourth scenarios assume a managed growth with moderate and restricted protection of natural resources respectively. The result demonstrates that restricted control could avoid from dramatic loss of forest and agricultural areas.

Keywords: Cellular Automata; urban growth model; policy simulation; environmental impact.

1 Introduction

Urban growth modeling was commenced in the 1960s; however, cities which are open and non-linear systems have not been satisfactorily modeled by the traditional mathematical methods. The complex factors in urban system are difficult to be predicted by traditional mathematical models and therefore the predictions of urban growth were often inaccurate [1]. Consequently, instead of prediction, many researches adopted simulation tools to discuss how the future development will differ and where urban growth is likely to occur by assuming different urban growth scenarios [2]. Advanced technologies in remote sensing and GIS have helped the development of more sophisticated approaches in urban growth models [1] [3-5], such

D. Taniar et al. (Eds.): ICCSA 2010, Part I, LNCS 6016, pp. 77–88, 2010.

as spatial simulation models. Cellular automata (CA) which is a simple but promising approach, has gained great attention from urban researchers in recent years [6] [7]. They have the potential to simulate the complex systems like cities [7] [8].

CA, which is a grid-based model, considers spatial organization in terms of evolution and provides another point of view to spatial evolution [9] [10]. The status of each grid is decided by rule of status of transformation. Its mathematical form is defined in equation 1:

$$S_{ij}^{t+1} = F(S_{ij}^{t}, \Omega_{ij}^{t})$$ (1)

S_{ij}^{t} represents the status of cell at location (i,j) at time t. Ω_{ij}^{t} is a collection of status of neighboring cells at time t. The definition of 'neighbor' is the surrounding cells having k distances to the cell (i,j). F is a transition function. The status of cell (i,j) and its surroundings at time t determine the impact on a particular cell (i,j) at time t+1 [9] [10] . CA model can operate a bottom-up approach of integrating land use factors, which is different from the previous research of top-down process to describe policy governed urbanization [1] [9] [10] . Increasing amount of researches have applied CA model to simulate urban development patterns, the dynamic growth of urban spatial structure, and evaluate environmental impacts. For instance, Hakan [6], Jantz et al.[7], Wu [11] ,Dragicevic et al.[12] and Zhang et al.[13] had used CA model to dynamically simulate the recent hundreds years of development and consequences of land use patterns and changes under different scenarios of land development policies. Syphard [1] forecasted the effects of urban growth on habitat pattern in southern California with three different levels of development prohibited on slope, and evaluated the fragment of landscape. Silva et al. [14], Wu et al. [15] and Hakan et al. [16] had focused on calibration of simulation models using historic images. Amongst, SLEUTH model, formerly the Clarke Cellular Automaton Urban Growth Model, was widely used. SLEUTH is an acronym for the six customized input data of the model: Slope, Land use, Exclusion, Urban extent, Transportation and Hillshade, [6]. These researches revealed that slope, road gravity and land use policy (zoning) are influencing factors to urban growth.

This study uses GIS technique and NetLogo, which is a CA based model (more detail in section 2.1), to simulate the urban growth of Danshuei in Taipei Metropolitan area, Taiwan. The reasons to choose NetLogo as simulation tool includes not only its flexible programming function, but relatively less applied in urban growth model.

Increasing demands of economic growth accelerate the rate of over development of land resources. Inappropriate urban sprawl and unsuitable configuration of land use destructively impact the ecological environment. Urban development with environmental consideration should be considered and this could be achieved by land use planning, policy and government. In view of this, urban growth simulation technique could be an evaluation tool to review the effectiveness of land use policy.

The real estate and transportation development of Danshuei township has been carrying out to reduce the over-dense population pressure of Taipei city, which is the political and financial center of Taiwan. The construction of new infrastructure due to the new development adversely creates significant environmental impact. The study area is a good case showing how to balance between urban development and natural resource protection. Four specific scenarios, which have different rules for urban development and strategies for natural resource conservation, were studied. The impacts on forest and agricultural lands under different level of land use control were also assessed.

2 Materials and Methods

Danshuei township is located at the northwest coast of Taipei County, Taiwan, and north of the estuary of the Danshuei River (Fig. 1). Taipei County governs ten county-controlled cities, four urban townships, and fifteen rural townships, while Danshuei belongs to the urban township. Danshuei encompasses an area of 70.65 Km^2 with a population density of 1968.5 p/km^2, which is the 12th largest among the Taipei metropolitan statistical areas in 2009. Although over 80% of the Taipei county residents live in the 10 county-controlled cities of Taipei County, the recent construction policy on real estate and transportation in Danshuei has attracted developers and urban workers to invest in this place. The population growth of Danshuei township has increased by 87.30% from 1986 to 2009 reaching 139,073. The building coverage has also been significantly increased, from 2.8 km^2 to 7.6 km^2 (Fig. 2).

Danshuei was an important port for the shipping route to the Southeast Asia in the 16th century. Human settlement had been living in this place for more than 7000 years and their living had been relied upon fishery and farming. The aboriginal residents were known as Pepo-frau. Due to its excellent geographical location for business and military purposes, Spanish, Dutch and Japanese developed this place after conquering the north of Taiwan. After the long term colonial development of Danshuei, the place remains with many historical heritages such as forts, schools, transportation stations and traditional streets. The excellent scenery with the historical heritages and golf courses creates huge potential for tourism business.

Fig. 1. Location of Danshuei Township

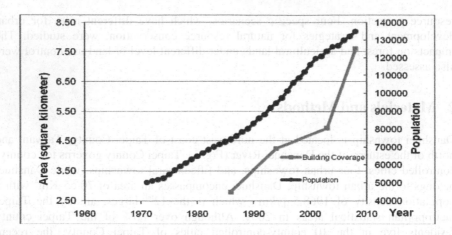

Fig. 2. Population and building coverage growth by year

Apart from the artificial scenery, natural resources like forest and agricultural land are great treasure to the environment and economic income. Danshuei has used to supply a great amount of agricultural products to Taipei County. However, with the agricultural policy being adjusted, the government is now promoting Danshuei and transforming its agricultural industry from production based to recreational and tourism based. Also, since 1980, the Government has been proactively promoting the revitalization of traditional streets, establishment of access roads to Taipei city and neighboring townships and development of new township to promote the tourism industry. However, all of these policies are likely to be risks to the conservation of natural resources, especially when unsuitable configurations of land use are planned. Therefore, this study uses zoning map to adjust coefficients of green resources in the simulation models, and to assess the amount of conserved green resources.

2.1 NetLogo Simulation Tool

NetLogo simulation software was developed by Northwest University, US (http://ccl.northwestern.edu/netlogo/). It can generate complex phenomena through interactions among individuals, and organize macro data and geometric attribute data for spatial analysis. NetLogo has been applied to simulate the complicated mechanism of land use change on urban growth and rural village [17].

NetLogo is adopted in this study because it can simulate and dynamically display the temporal and spatial changes of urban form during the urban growth processes. It has friendly user interfaces and programming functions which are easy to manipulate.

2.2 Input Data, Simulation and Validation

This study uses official topographic maps of 1986, 1994, 2003 and National Land Use Survey data of 2008 as the basic inputs to acquire the land use data and describe the urban growth in Danshuei township. These official topographic maps are firstly digitized, followed by overlaying with 100 by 100 meters square grid in GIS software. Then, 9 categories of terrain features, namely built-up, infrastructure, transportation, agricultural land, forest, grassland, barren land, wetland and water land, are identified according to the maps. These 9 categories are separated into different layers; and the coverage of each category is mapped manually, using a cell-by-cell approach, onto the corresponding layer. The coverage of each category, except the transportation, is graded from 0-4 based on the percentage of the area occupied by that particular category to the total area of the grid The five level corresponds to 0%, 1~20% (10%), 21~50% (35%), 51~80% (65%) and 81~100% (90%) respectively. The transportation layer uses a classification system different from the others. The cell is graded in 4 levels based on the class of road system, such as national high way, provincial highway, prefectural highway and country road. The grading does not consider the area of the road system within the cell but only "existence or non-existence". As for the built-up area category, this study only concerns whether or not the cell is urbanized or non-urbanized but not the grading for built-up area. The cell will be regarded as urbanized once the coverage area is greater than 0.

The model domain in NetLogo simulation software is divided into 18125 (125*145) cells, and Danshuei occupied 7211 cells. Urban growth in the model is determined by growth rules set by users. Starting point (seed) is assigned or randomly placed in a particular cell. The seed begins to grow and occupies one of adjacent cells which are vacant. The newly occupied cell becomes a seed in the next iteration. This process repeats until the maximum number of iterations predefined in the model is reached.

This study considers four scenarios which are interacted by three main parameters that are seeds, growth rules and different restriction levels of policies (Table 1). Each of the four scenarios simulates a particular aspect of the development process. The iterations of the simulation required to reach the ultimate development stage vary with scenarios and cases. In this study 35 Monte Carlo iterations are sufficient.

In this study, the starting points are set according to the six original settlements of Pepo-frau aboriginal residents recorded by historical literatures. The four scenarios of growth models are initialized with these six seeds in time zero. The simulation ceases when settlements grow till stable states are reached. The growth rules are set by three growth coefficients: slope, neighbor effect and road gravity. Slope coefficient considers a seed cell to seek the nearest unoccupied neighbor cell with the lowest

Table 1. Scenarios studied and parameters used in the scenarios

Parameters	Growth Coefficients	Growth Scenarios			
		1	2	3	4
Starting points		six	six	six	six
Growth rules	Slope	▲	▲	▲	▲
	Neighbor effect		▲		
	Road gravity		▲		
Policy Restricted Condition	Non	▲			
	Managed growth with moderate protection			▲	
	Managed growth with restricted protection				▲

slope. Neighbor effect considers the summation of building coverage of nine cells, which are the seed cell and the eight neighboring cells. Road gravity considers the distance from each cell to the nearest cell with road. There are two policies which manage urban growth with moderate or restricted protection.

The process of simulation has two stages: model validation and subsequent prediction. Firstly, the model derives a set of values from physical results, which can effectively describe the urban growth of Danshuei township. The actual growth in 2008 of Danshuei township is used to compare with the ultimate urban development form simulated by the urban growth model. The model accuracy is assessed based on three parameters: predicted accuracy rate, over-predicted rate and less-predicted rate. These parameters describe the amount of land area that accurately, over- and under-predicted the urban growth phenomena. It is to note that over-predicted rate does not mean wrong prediction. They may indicate that the places have a high potential to be urbanized in the future.

Forest and agricultural loss rate are simulated in the four scenarios. As there is no data available before 1986, the loss rate of agricultural and forest areas are calculated based on the data of 1986. The agricultural and forest areas are 27.6 km² and 24.2 km² respectively in 1986.

3   Simulation Results

3.1   Scenario 1

The growth rule of Scenario 1 only considers coefficient of slope. Figure 3 shows the simulation result of building area growth and the comparison to the satellite photo of 2009 acquired from Google Earth map. In the simulation result, red color corresponds to accurate prediction; blue color represents over-prediction; and grey color indicates under-prediction. The gradient of the grey color is indicative of the density of building coverage. Darker grey means higher density of building coverage.

The simulation result shows that comparing with the satellite image of DanShuei as at 2009 the predicted accuracy rate reaches 59.43% and the over-predicted rate reaches 33.59%. Forest and agriculture loss rates reach 27.12% and 38.78% respectively. If the areas, that are rated as over-predicted rate and are feasible to be urbanized, were developed in future, then forest and agriculture loss rates would increase by 13.41 % and 12.47% respectively.

The cause of the over-predicted areas may not be fully explained. However, for example: (1) the white circle in figures 3 indicates the new township planning. Although the site of the new township has few fragmented buildings, the site planning has been done for years. The area circled in white could not be regarded as over-prediction as it will be developed in future. (2) The orange circle shows that the model over-predicts in an area which has a golf course. This again could not be regarded as over-prediction as a golf course could be seen as an occupied/developed land.

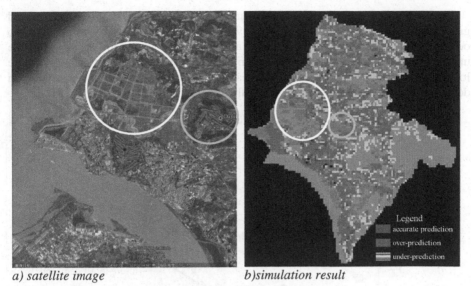

a) satellite image   *b)simulation result*

Fig. 3. The result of scenario 1-1 and comparing to satellite photo

3.2   Scenario 2

This scenario adds road gravity and neighbor effect in the urban growth model. Figure 4 shows the effects of neighbor effect on the predicted accuracy rate and over-predicted rate. When the neighbor effect is ranged from 100 to 900 m^2, the predicted accuracy rate is higher than 50%. However, when the value for neighbor effect is equal or greater than 1,000, the predicted accuracy rate reduces significantly. Based on this observation, it is suggested that the urban development in Danshuei township would spread over an area instead of concentrated at a particular place.

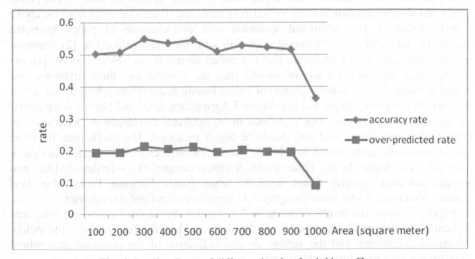

Fig. 4. Predicted rate of different levels of neighbor effect

Figure 5 shows that the predicted accuracy rate increases with the value for road gravity. This suggests that the urban development in Danshuei township tends to occur at a place which is 250m or above away from a road system. However, as the urban development gets further away from a road system, the forest and agriculture loss rate increases. The loss rate is noticeable when the distance between new urban development and a road system is greater than 2000m.

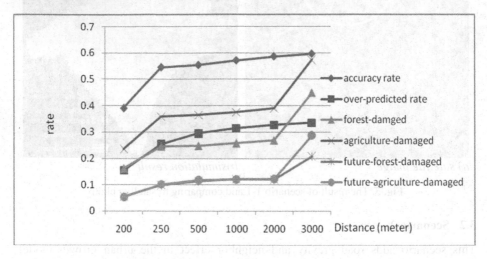

Fig. 5. Predicted rate of different road gravity

4 Environmental Impact Simulations

The first and second scenarios of growth model do not consider policy protection against development. In this situation, natural resources including agriculture land, forest, parks, water and wetland are proven to be exceedingly damaged. Therefore, apart from the above growth scenarios, two additional scenarios with consideration of policy restricted conditions are simulated: (1) managed growth with moderate protection, (2) managed growth with restricted protection. The controlled elements are referenced by present zoning map. Agriculture lands of zoning map are divided into three divisions, one category belongs to Agriculture District of Urban Planning; the others belong to non-urban area which is further categorized into General Agricultural Zone and Special Agricultural Zone. Special Agricultural zone is defined by Agricultural Development Department as high quality agricultural land and should be highly protected. The coefficients for these two scenarios are summarized in Table 2. Other controlled elements include other green resources and water. In the Other green resource category it is further divided into recreational area, general forest districts, urban parks, National Parks, slop land conservation zone. As for water category, it comprises wetland and river district.

Figure 6 shows the results of scenario 3 (a) and 4 (b). In the figures, the pink area indicates the potential area where may be deforested in the future under the policy restricted conditions; and the yellow area is indicative of the potential area where agricultural land may loss in the future.

Table 2. Scenarios studied and parameters used in the scenarios

	Excluded Element From Development		
	Element	Scenario 3	Scenario 4
		Managed growth with moderate protection	Managed growth with restricted protection
Agriculture Land	Agriculture District of Urban Planning		x
	General Agricultural Zone		x
	Special Agricultural Zone	x	x
Other green resources	Recreational area		x
	General forest district		x
	Urban parks		x
	National Parks	x	x
	Slop land conservation zone	x	x
Water	Wetland	x	x
	River District		x

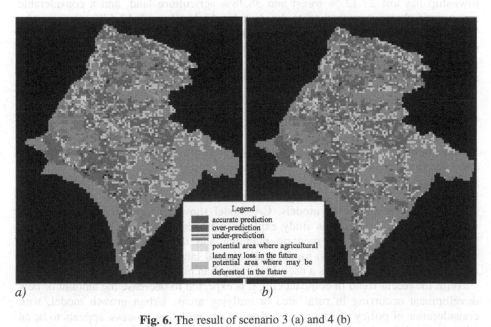

a)   *b)*

Fig. 6. The result of scenario 3 (a) and 4 (b)

Comparing scenario 3 with scenario 1 suggests that the environmental restriction policy can reduce the forest loss rate by 9.2% and the agricultural land loss rate of 8.03%. As in scenario 4, the reduction for forest loss rate and agricultural land loss rate is 11.17% and 9.33% respectively (Table 3). The results show that the environmental restriction policy is an effective method to conserve natural resources.

Table 3. Comparison of scenario results

	S1	S3	S4
Accuracy rate		0.5943	
Over-predicted rate		0.3359	
Forest-damaged rate		0.2712	
Agriculture-damaged rate		0.3878	
Future damaged rate of forest	0.1341	0.0421	0.0224
Future damaged rate of agriculture	0.1247	0.0444	0.0314

5 Results

First scenario assumes that slope is the main factor of affecting urban growth of Danshuei township. It achieves a reasonable accuracy rate comparing to the actual urban growth of 2008. The over-predicted areas are proven to be the high potential development areas. However, it also shows that over-predicted areas occupy some natural resource districts. Results from first scenario indicates that the Danshuei township has lost 27.12 % forest and 38.78% agriculture land, and a considerable amount of them may further to be lost by 13.41 % and 12.47% respectively. Therefore, protection policy strategies are assigned in third and fourth scenarios. The results presents that restricted protection policy will have a distinguished outcome for preservation of natural resource. 11.17% of forest and 9.33% of agricultural land areas can be saved under the most restricted policy in fourth scenario.

6 Conclusion and Discussions

Increasing urban sprawl and its results in degradation of environments has attracted concerns throughout the world. Understanding the driving forces of urban growth and its dynamical evolution is necessary for decision makers and urban planners. Evaluating the impacts of urban growth on the natural resources is also needed to involve into the simulation models. CA model shows an appropriate approach to urban growth modeling. This study explores the adequate achievement of applying NetLogo model for urban scenario planning and decision making process. The visualization of urban growth model and potential land use change areas (forest and agricultural land loss areas) is a useful tool for urban planners and decision makers.

With the recent trend in compact city, it is expected to decrease the amount of new development occurring in rural area or outlying areas. Urban growth model, with consideration of policy restricted conditions in the modeling process, appears to be an effective tool for developing and refining conservation policy strategies. Danshuei township is used as case study. It is a rural area with abundant natural resource and is facing a development pressure on the near future. How to efficiently preserve natural resource avoiding incidentally development from loosen control of zoning alteration has to be addressed in Danshuei. Therefore, this study formulates four scenarios to simulate urban growth and its impacts on forest and agricultural land. The outcomes of these four scenarios show that slope factor is the main driving force of urban growth. Neighbor effect and road gravity applied in the second scenario are lesser influential comparing to slope factor. Scenarios of environmental impact analyses show that restricted zoning control could have considerable preservation of forest and agriculture land in the future.

Three major aspects will be addressed and further investigated in this urban growth modeling study. They are model calibration, investigation of other driving forces/growth rules; and methods for accuracy assessment.

Although the CA model has been successfully used to simulate urban patterns, they have been criticized for not being able to model the urban transformation processes [12]. The reason for this is lacking historical images/data. The same reason defers from a detailed calibration of urban growth model to be performed. As a result, more historical images/data will be collected to undergo a detailed calibration as well as to improve the model capability in modelling urban transformation process.

The driving forces and constraints of urban development adopted in the model play an important role in determining the urban patterns. Yeh [18] mentioned that most of the researches applied CA models under the assumption that urban density in uniform in each cell. Urban density is a critical factor in urban planning and affects urban form substantially. Therefore, to improve the model prediction accuracy, urban density and other social factors will be included in future simulation models; and also combination of the strategies of development constraints will be considered.

The assessment methods for model accuracy applied in this study are predicted accuracy rate, over- and less-predicted rate. Further assessment methods such as Kappa, fuzzy Kappa statistic and other index will be examined in future research.

Acknowledgements. This study has been supported by National Science Council, No. NSC 98-2621-M-002-023.

References

1. Syphard, A.D., Clarke, K.C., Franklin, J.: Using a cellular automaton model to forecast the effects of urban growth on habitat pattern in southern California. Ecological Complexity 2(2), 185–203 (2005)
2. Lin, F.-T.: A review of computational methods on urban and regional studies. Department of Humanities and Social Sciences, National Science Council. In: Conference papers on Research Techniques and database application on Regional, Humanity, and Geographic research, pp. 345–356 (2001)
3. Agarwal, C., Green, G.M., Grove, J.M., Evans, T.P., Schweik, C.M.: A Review and Assessment of Land-Use Change Models: Dynamics of Space, Time, and Human Choice. CIPEC Collaborative Report No.1. USFS Publication NE-GTR-297 Joint publication by the Center for the Study of Institutions. Population and Environmental Change at Indiana University-Bloomington and the USDA Forest Service. Burlington, Vt.: USDA Forest Service Northeastern Forest Research Station (2002)

4. Jones, R.: A Review of land use/land cover and agricultural change models. PIER Energy-Related Environmental Research. CEC-500-2005-056. Stratus Consulting Inc. for the California Energy Commission (2005)
5. Zhao, F., Chung, S.: A Study of Alternative Land Use Forecasting Models. A report to FDOT Systems Planning Office, contract no. BD 015-10 (2006), http://www.dot.state.fl.us/research-center/Completed_Proj/Summary_PL/FDOT_BD015_10_rpt.pdf
6. Hakan, O., Klein, A.G., Srinivasan, R.: Using the Sleuth Urban Growth model to Simulate the Impacts of Future Policy Scenarios on Urban Land Use in the Houston-Galveston-Brazoria CMSA. Journal of Social sciences 2, 72–82 (2007)
7. Jantz, C.A., Goetz, S.J., Shelley, M.K.: Using the SLEUTH Urban Growth Model to Simulate the Impacts of Future Policy Scenarios on Urban Land Use in the Baltimore-Washington Metropolitan Area. Environment and Planning B 31(2), 251–271 (2003)
8. Torrens, P.M., O'Sullivan, D.: Cellular automata and urban simulation: where do we go from here? Environment and Planning B: Planning and Design 28, 163–168 (2001)
9. Clarke, K.C., Gaydos, L.J., Hoppen, S.: A self-modifying cellular automation model of historical urbanization in the San Francisco Bay area. Environment and Planning B 24, 247–261 (1997)
10. White, R., Engelen, G.: Cellular automata as the basis of integrated dynamic regional modeling. Environment and Planning B 24, 235–246 (1997)
11. Wu, F.L., Webster, C.J.: Simulating artificial cities in a GIS environment: urban growth under alternative regulation regimes. Geographical Information Science 14(7), 625–648 (2000)
12. Dragicevic, S., Marceau, D.J., Marois, C.: Space, time and dynamics modeling in historical GIS database: A fuzzy logic approach. Environment and Planning B: Planning and Design 28(4), 545–562 (2001)
13. Zhang, Y., Li, J., Chen, Y.H.: Simulation of Beijing Urbanization Using SLEUTH. Remote Sensing Information 2, 50–54 (2007)
14. Silva, E.A., Clarke, K.C.: Calibration of the SLEUTH urban growth model for Lisbon and Porto, Portugal. Computers, Environment and Urban Systems 26, 525–552 (2002)
15. Wu, X.Q., Hu, Y.M., He, H.S., Bu, R.C.: Accuracy Evaluation and Its Application of SLEUTH Urban Growth Model. Geomatics and Information Science of Wuhan University 33, 293–296 (2008)
16. Hakan, O., Klein, A.G., Srinivasan, R.: Calibration of the Sleuth Model Based on the Historic Growth of Houston. Journal of Applied Sciences 7(14), 1843–1853 (2007)
17. Quang, B.L.: Multi-agent system for simulation of land-use and land cover change: A theoretical framework and its first implementation for an upland watershed in the Central Coast of Vietnam. Ecology and Development Series 29 (2005), http://www.zef.de/fileadmin/webfiles/downloads/zefc_ecology_development/ecol_dev_29_text.pdf
18. Yeh, A.G., Li, X.: A cellular automata model to simulate development density for urban planning. Environment and Planning B: Planning and Design 29, 431–450 (2002)

Improving the Calibration of the MOLAND Urban Growth Model with Land-Use Information Derived from a Time-Series of Medium Resolution Remote Sensing Data

Tim Van de Voorde[1], Johannes van der Kwast[2], Inge Uljee[2],
Guy Engelen[2], and Frank Canters[1]

[1] Vrije Universiteit Brussel, Geography department,
Cartography and GIS research group, Pleinlaan 2, BE-1050 Brussels, Belgium
{Tim.Vandevoorde, fcanters}@vub.ac.be
[2] Flemish Institute for Technological Research (VITO),
Boerentang 200, BE-2400 Mol, Belgium
{Hans.Vanderkwast, Guy.Engelen, Inge.Uljee}@vito.be

Abstract. Calibrating land-use change models requires a time-series of reliable and consistent land-use maps, which are often not available. Medium resolution satellite images have a temporal and spatial resolution that is ideally suited for model calibration, and could therefore be an important information source to improve the performance of land-use change models. In this research, a calibration framework based on remote sensing data is proposed for the MOLAND model. Structural land-use information was first inferred from the available medium resolution satellite images by applying supervised classification at the level of predefined regions using metrics that describe the distribution of sub-pixel estimations of artificial sealed surfaces. The resulting maps were compared to the model output with a selected set of spatial metrics. Based on this comparison, the model was recalibrated according to five scenario's. While the selected metrics generally demonstrated a low sensitivity to changes in model parameters, some improvement was nevertheless noted for one particular scenario.

Keywords: Land-use classification; sub-pixel classification; calibration of land-use change models.

1 Introduction

Urban land-use change processes are affecting the human and natural environment in many ways, and have stressed the need for new, more effective urban management strategies based on the notion of sustainable development. The problem analysis, planning and monitoring phases of a sustainable urban management policy, however, require reliable and sufficiently detailed information on the urban environment and its dynamics, as well as knowledge about the causes, chronology and effects of urban change processes. Land-use change models are useful tools for assisting planners and

D. Taniar et al. (Eds.): ICCSA 2010, Part I, LNCS 6016, pp. 89–104, 2010.
© Springer-Verlag Berlin Heidelberg 2010

policy makers in assessing the impact of their decisions on the spatial system they have to manage. Such models incorporate geospatial data, socio-economic information and knowledge on dynamic urban processes. Their calibration typically requires a time series of land-use maps, which is often lacking. Even if time series are available, inconsistencies in mapping methodologies, legends and scales often induce measured land-use changes that do not represent actual changes in land-use patterns [1]. Manual land-use mapping is, furthermore, time-consuming and expensive.

The extensive archive of medium resolution remote sensing data (e.g. Landsat, SPOT-HRV), with satellite images dating back to the early 1970s, may provide a solution for the lack of reliable land-use information. The likelihood that the required time-series of medium resolution remote sensing images can be successfully obtained is relatively high, and depends on the ground track repeat cycle which is typically between 16 and 26 days. Remote sensing images are also spatially and temporally more consistent than land-use maps, although that depends strongly on atmospheric conditions. Urban land-use change models are typically applied at time intervals of 1 year, with a cell size between 50 and 500 m. This makes the temporal and spatial resolution of medium resolution remote sensing images ideally suited for model calibration. However, although commonly applied image classification algorithms can readily map land cover from the reflective properties of the earth's surface, land-use change modelling requires land-use classes. These are linked to socio-economic activities and, as such, cannot be directly inferred from spectral information [2]. There exists nevertheless a strong relationship between the spatial structure of the built-up environment and its functional characteristics [3]. Visual interpretation of remotely sensed imagery of urban areas, for example, is based on the link between land-use and urban form. This link is the basic concept behind different (semi-)automated approaches for urban mapping that either use the structural and contextual information present in the image, or information derived from ancillary data sources [4]. Spatial metrics have recently been introduced in the field of urban remote sensing as a means to describe various properties of the spatial heterogeneity and configuration of land cover, and to relate these to land-use [5,6]. In this study, spatial metrics are used for two purposes: for inferring urban land-use from medium resolution imagery, and for improving the calibration of a land-use change model.

The calibration framework proposed in this research was developed for the MOLAND (Monitoring Land Use/Cover Dynamics) model [7] that was applied to Dublin (Ireland). The core of this urban and regional growth model is a constraint cellular automata [8] that models the spatial dynamics of the system. The model input consists of five GIS datasets for the geographical area of interest: (1) current land use types; (2) accessibility to the transport network; (3) inherent suitability for different land-uses; (4) zoning status (i.e. legal constraints) for different land-uses and (5) socio-economic characteristics (e.g. population, income, production, employment). The model explores the likely future development of land-use over the next thirty years in time-steps of one year for each grid cell of 4 ha, given alternative planning and policy scenarios and socio-economic trends. The calibration of any model with the level of complexity of MOLAND is not trivial and requires a substantial amount of time and effort. The main reason for this is that in principle every grid cell represents at least one state variable in the model. The goal of calibration is to ensure that the model behaves in a realistic manner, and that it is able to reproduce existing spatial patterns. The calibration of MOLAND is a heuristic procedure based on trial-and-error [7]. It requires a reference (i.e. 'training' or 'historical') land-use map, from which the current or most recently available map is reconstructed. The comparison between the reconstructed and the current land-use maps is performed by means of dedicated goodness-of-fit measures. These consist of a number of statistical indicators such as mean patch area, shape and proximity index, Simpson's diversity index, kappa statistic, kappa histo, kappa location and fuzzy kappa [9]. In addition to the calculation of statistics, comparison is performed by means of GIS procedures. Model calibration entails four steps. First, an initial set of approximate values for the parameters describing the neighbour influence function (push-pull parameters) is determined (1). These parameters are usually taken from previous model applications. Next, a second parameter is fixed: the stochastic parameter α (2), which largely determines the scatteredness of the land-use patterns and patch sizes. Additional information such as suitability maps, accessibility and zoning information are then introduced (3). Finally, the fine tuning of the model starts (4). This involves repeating steps 1 to 3 with a dedicated statistical analysis. All steps are repeated until the reconstructed map satisfactorily matches the current land-use map. For a successful calibration, the calibration period should be sufficiently long in order to give the underlying processes in the system enough time to manifest themselves representatively. The poor availability of high quality and consistent land-use maps often constrains the choice of the calibration period. In the Dublin application of the MOLAND model, used in this study, the required land-use maps are only available for 1990 and 2000, limiting the calibration to this timeframe.

In this paper, we propose a remote sensing based calibration framework that potentially increases the amount data available for the historic calibration of MOLAND, which in turn results in better predictions of the land-use change model. This calibration framework applies newly developed spatial metrics to infer land-use maps from remote sensing images at dates for which no existing land-use maps are available. Spatial metrics are also used for quantitatively comparing the spatial structure and patterns of the model output to the remote sensing derived land-use maps.

2   Study Area, Data and Pre-processing

The study area for this research is Dublin, the political and economical capital of Ireland and home to over 40% of the country's population. Dublin experienced rapid urban expansion in the 1980's and 1990's, fuelled by the building of new roads that drove residential and commercial development rapidly outward into the urban fringe. Three medium resolution satellite images were used to develop the time-series of land-use information: a Landsat 7 ETM+ image acquired on May 24th 2001 and Landsat 5 TM images of September 10th 1997 and June 13th 1988. Because the images were acquired during different illumination and atmospheric conditions, a radiometric rectification was carried out. As a first step, the digital numbers of each image were converted to at-sensor radiances, which were in turn converted to top-of-atmosphere reflectance values [10]. Because this only accounts for predictable changes in solar irradiance and aspect, a relative atmospheric correction based on pseudo-invariant features was also carried out [11]. The Landsat images were geometrically co-registered to a Quickbird image acquired on August 4th 2003 and set in the Irish Grid projection system. A land-cover classification was available for this Quickbird image which provided us with reference sealed surface fractions to build and test sub-pixel classification models. Road network data and land-use maps for 1990 and 2000 were made available by the European MO-LAND project [12].

3 Deriving Land Use from Medium Resolution Images

3.1 Sub-pixel Sealed Surface Mapping

The disadvantage of using medium resolution data for urban analysis is the relatively low spatial resolution, which limits the level of structural detail that can be resolved from the imagery. The sensor's instantaneous field of view (IFOV) is wide in comparison with the IFOV of high resolution images, which makes it very likely that it will cover multiple surface materials with a different spectral response, especially in urban areas. Because image pixels are typically assigned to a single land-cover or land-use class by traditional "hard" classifiers (e.g. maximum likelihood) based on their spectral properties, a mixed spectral response may result in a low mapping accuracy. To overcome this drawback, a sub-pixel or "soft" classification that succeeds in relating a pixel's spectrum to fractions of its surface constituents should be applied.

While many methods are available to approach the mixed pixel problem, the most commonly used is linear spectral mixture analysis (LSMA), whereby a pixel's observed reflectance is modelled as a linear combination of spectrally pure "endmember" reflectances [13,14]. The advantage of LSMA is that it is a physically based model that does not require extensive training data, but only the definition of end-member signatures. Partly for this reason, LSMA has recently received some attention in studies that aim to characterise urban environments. Some of these studies resort to the components of the Vegetation, Impervious surface and Soil (VIS) model proposed by [15] to directly represent the endmembers of the LSMA model (e.g. [16,17]). Although this may seem appealing from a conceptual viewpoint, not all pure vegetation, man-made impervious surface or soil pixels necessarily occupy well-defined, extreme positions in feature space and can, as such, not directly be used as endmembers for linear unmixing. One reason complicating the use of the V-I-S triangle for unmixing urban areas is that pure pixels covering similar land-cover types may be spectrally variable. This is especially the case in urban areas where semantically identical objects such as roofs may demonstrate different reflectance properties depending on the material that is used. According to some authors, most of this spectral variability is related to brightness differences and can be dealt with by applying brightness normalisation prior to the unmixing [18]. Other studies noted that brightness normalisation slightly improved the accuracy of a LSMA model [19], but that it did not completely remove the brightness variation of vegetation [20]. Furthermore, although brightness normalisation accounts for a large part of spectral endmember variability, true spectral confusion between V-I-S components cannot be resolved. For instance, dry bare soils and bright urban surface materials or red-clay roofs and some soil types may take up similar positions in the feature space of multi-resolution imagery. It depends on the spectral characteristics of the study area whether or not this poses a problem.

After examining the mixture space of the Landsat image covering our study area through a visualisation of low order principal components [21], we concluded that no soil endmember could be defined unambiguously. Because exposed soil was nevertheless abundant in the Dublin area at the time of image acquisition (fallow land, construction sites, etc.), we decided to use a multiple regression model in combination with an unsupervised classification. The unsupervised classification was intended to derive a mask that indicates which pixels belong to the urban fabric. These pixels were subsequently unmixed by the regression model, which estimates the fractional cover of vegetation/no vegetation. The urban mask was created through unsupervised classification with a Kohonen self-organising map neural network, and was subsequently enhanced by a knowledge-based post-classification approach [22]. The final classification consisted of 4 classes: urban areas including mixed urban/vegetation pixels, pure vegetation pixels (e.g. crops, pasture), bare soil and water. Pixels belonging to the classes soil, water and pure vegetation were considered to have zero sealed surface cover. Pixels within the bounds of the area belonging to the urban class were considered as mixtures of sealed surfaces and vegetation, and they were therefore subjected to sub-pixel analysis. Because a pixel's sealed surface fraction is the complement of the vegetation fraction within the urban class, a multiple linear regression model that estimates the proportion of vegetation cover for each Landsat pixel could be used. To define the regression model and for validating it, an initial sample of approximately 10 000 pixels was randomly drawn from the part of Landsat image overlapping the high resolution land-cover classification, which was downsampled to calculate reference proportions of sealed surface cover. Pixels in the sample that underwent changes in vegetation cover between the acquisition dates of the Landsat image and the Quickbird image used to derive the land-cover map were filtered out by a temporal filtering technique based on iterative linear regression between NDVI values [19]. From the unchanged sample pixels coinciding with the urban mask, a final sample of 2500 training and 2500 validation pixels was finally selected. The accuracy of sealed surface proportions was assessed for the validation sample with the following error measures. The mean absolute error of the sealed surface fraction (MAE_{Sealed}) was used as a measure of the error magnitude:

$$MAE_{Sealed} = \frac{\sum_{j=1}^{N} |P'_j - P_j|}{N} \tag{1}$$

with

N: the total number of pixels in the validation sample;

P_j: sealed surface fraction inside validation pixel j, derived from the high-resolution classification (ground truth);

P'_j: sealed surface fraction inside validation pixel j, estimated by the sub-pixel classifier.

MAE_{Sealed} quantifies the amount of error and can be interpreted as a mean error percentage. In addition, the mean error (ME_{Sealed}) was used to indicate a possible bias in the proportion estimates (over- or underestimation):

$$ME_{Sealed} = \frac{\sum_{j=1}^{N} (P'_j - P_j)}{N} \tag{2}$$

3.2 Characterising Urban Morphology within Predefined Spatial Regions

Context variables, texture measures and spatial metrics are calculated within a spatial domain, i.e. a relatively homogeneous spatial entity that represents a basic landscape element. Naturally, the definition of the spatial domain directly influences the metrics and will depend on the aims of the study and the characteristics of the landscape [23]. Some authors conduct global comparative analyses of urban form and define an entire city as a single spatial domain [24]. Other studies examine intra-urban growth patterns or land-use changes at a coarse level and divide the urban landscape into relatively large administrative zones [25], concentric buffer zones or large rectangular sample plots [26]. If an analysis of urban morphologies, land-use or change processes is required at a spatially more detailed intra-urban level, the city has to be divided up into smaller and relatively homogeneous units [25]. A commonly used approach in remote sensing data analysis is the use of a moving window or kernel, from which statistical or structural information can be derived. Kernel-based methods, however, have a number of disadvantages compared to region-based approaches, including the difficulty of selecting an optimal kernel size and the fact that the kernel is an artificial construct that does not conform to real urban land-use zones or morphological units [3]. In this study, we defined the spatial domain by intersecting a detailed urban road network with the MOLAND land-use map of 2000. This provided us with a large number of blocks that are relatively homogeneous in terms of land-use for the most recent date of our analysis. Given the resolution of the image data we used, blocks smaller than 1 ha (corresponding to approximately 11 pixels) were topologically removed resulting in a vector layer that consists of 5767 spatial units. The threshold of 1 ha corresponds to the minimum mappable unit employed for urban areas within the MOLAND land-use dataset.

For each spatial entity (block) and for each image in the time-series, the mean of the per-pixel sealed surface fractions was calculated to divide the study area into 4 urban density classes using criteria defined in the MOLAND typology: 0-10% (non-urban land), 10-50% (discontinuous sparse urban fabric), 50-80% (discontinuous urban fabric) and more than 80% (continuous urban fabric). Blocks with less than 10% sealed surfaces were considered as non-urban land (fallow land, large vegetated areas, sea, etc.). Blocks with more than 80% sealed surface cover were labelled as continuous, dense urban fabric. The remaining 3494 blocks with 10%-80% sealed surface cover were further analysed with other approaches because they belonged to different morphological land-use types such as sparse residential areas or industrial zones with empty, vegetated plots, which could not be distinguished based on just the average sealed surface cover.

Spatial variance (SV) is a simple measure for a spatially explicit characterisation of block morphology:

$$SV = \frac{\sum_{i}^{n} \sum_{j}^{k_i} (f_i - f_j)^2}{\sum_{i}^{n} k_i} \tag{3}$$

with n the number of pixels with the block, k_i the number of neighbours of pixel i, and f the sub-pixel sealed surface fraction. To further characterise these blocks, we examined the cumulative frequency distribution (CFD) of the proportion sealed surface cover of the Landsat pixels. Our assumption is that the shape of this distribution function can be related to the morphological characteristics of the block it represents. Low and medium density residential land-use blocks, for instance, contain more mixed sealed surface-vegetation pixels than industrial areas. The abundance of these mixed pixels is reflected by the sigmoid shaped CFD, whereas the predominance of pure sealed surface pixels results in a more exponentially shaped CFD. To express the CFD's shape quantitatively, a function was fitted using a nonlinear least-squares approach. This function's parameters express the shape of the CFD and can be used as variables in a supervised classification to assign the blocks to land-use classes. We transform the logistic function (eq. 4) to fit to the CFD:

$$P_i(f) = \frac{1}{1+e^{-f}} \qquad (4)$$

where $P_i(f)$ is the predicted cumulative frequency within block i of impervious surface fraction f. The point of inflection for this function is 0.5 at a value for f of 0.

The basic form was adapted to allow numerical fitting to a sigmoid shaped CFD, as well as a CFD shape that is typical of non-residential areas by using the convex part of the function, left of the point of inflection. For this purpose, the basic form was scaled and translated along the x and y axes:

$$P_i(f) = \gamma \frac{1}{1+e^{-(\alpha f+\beta)}} + \delta \qquad (5)$$

where α and γ are the scaling parameters of the x and y axis respectively, and β and δ the translation parameters. In our analysis, we were only concerned with the part of the function domain and range that falls within the box defined by the interval $0 \geq f \leq 1$ and $0 \geq P_i(f) \leq 1$.

3.3 MLP-Based Supervised Land-Use Classification

Together with the average amount of sealed surface and spatial variance within the blocks, the 4 parameters of the fitted curve were used as variables in a supervised classification. The primary objective was to assign each block with a sealed surface cover between 10% and 80% (3494 in total) to one of 3 urban classes combined from classes in the MOLAND scheme: other urban (comprised of urban parks, sports and leisure facilities), employment (commercial areas, industrial zones, public or private services) and residential (different types of residential land). The employment and residential classes represent "push" and "pull" land-use functions and are important agents in the MOLAND model. The "other urban" class was included because some urban parks have more than 10% sealed surface cover due to the presence of walkways and small constructions. Blocks with more than 80% sealed surface cover were directly assigned to a sixth class: "continuous urban fabric". These blocks are too densely built to further characterise them with the cumulative frequency distribution of sealed surface pixels. Likewise, pixels with 10% or less sealed surface cover were assigned to the class "non urban land". To obtain reference data for training and validating the classifier, the predominant land-use class of each block was derived from the MOLAND land-use map of 2000 for classifying the 2001 image and from the MOLAND land-use map of 1990 for classifying the 1988 image. The 1997 image, for which no reference data was available, was classified by applying the classification model trained on the 2000 data. We adopted a stratified sampling approach to select training and validation samples. For each class, about 200 blocks were randomly selected. This set was then randomly split in two to obtain independent training and validation samples.

A multi-layer perceptron (MLP) classifier was used to assign the blocks to the land-use classes. MLP is the most commonly used neural network classifier in remote sensing applications [27]. Neural networks have gained popularity in the field because in contrast to statistical classifiers they are non parametric and therefore make no assumptions about the frequency distribution of the data, a property that is particularly interesting when variables from different data sources and distributions are used [28]. Opposed to these potential advantages lies the drawback that the user has to make several design choices, which can have a significant effect on MLP performance: network architecture (number of hidden layers/neurons), parameterisation of the back-propagation algorithm, input/output coding, weight initialisation, etc. [29]. Taking the complex and often ambiguous parameterisation into consideration, we used Neural-Ware's Neuralworks Predict® to develop the MLP. This commercial software package offers the user a set of semantic design choices which optimally set or determine the parameters required to train a neural network.

After a satisfying classification result was obtained, the resulting land-use maps were intersected with urban density maps that were derived by averaging the per-pixel sealed surface fractions within each block and dividing them into the 4 classes discussed earlier (< 10%, 10-50%, 50-80%, > 80%).

4 Calibration Framework

Figure 1 shows the concept of using spatial metrics for the calibration of land-use change models that is proposed in this study. First, morphological land-use classes are derived from a remote sensing image with the approach outlined in the previous section. The remote sensing derived land-use map can then be compared to the output of the land-use change model of the same year with spatial metrics. Depending on the objective of the land-use change model or the stage in its development (calibration or application) the modeller has the choice to optimise: (1) the overall pattern in model predictions, based on landscape-level metrics; (2) patterns within land-use classes, based on class-level metrics and (3) patterns at the moving window-level or pixel level. The spatial metrics used for calibrating land-use change models should be chosen in accordance with the model's objectives. Because this study focused on the evolution of urban sprawl, the metrics should quantify density characteristics, land-use and activity characteristics, fragmentation and scattering, decentralisation characteristics and accessibility characteristics [30]. Four spatial metrics suggested by [30] were used at the landscape level in this research. Shannon's Diversity Index (SHDI) was used to quantify land-use and activity characteristics. The SHDI value reaches zero when there is no diversity at all and increases with increasing

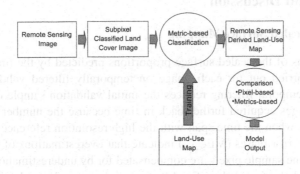

Fig. 1. Concept of using spatial metrics for calibrating land-use change models

diversity. For fragmentation and scattering, the Area Weighted Mean Fractal Dimension (FRAC_AM), Contagion (CONTAG) and the Interspersion and Juxtaposition Index (IJI) were used. The FRAC_AM metric results in a value of 1 when the land-use is unfilled and a value of 2 when the urban landscape is compact. CONTAG was used to calculate the spatial configuration and structure of activities; it is zero for landscapes without fragmentation and 100 for regions that have a maximum fragmentation. IJI is similar, but operates on patches instead of pixels. These four metrics were calculated from model simulations at the landscape level and were compared with metrics derived from existing land-use maps and remote sensing images for optimising the calibration.

The procedure outlined above can be applied each time a remote sensing image is available within the model calibration period (Fig. 2). In this paper, the proposed framework was applied to the Landsat TM5 images of 13 June 1988, 10 September 1997 and the Landsat ETM7 image of 24 May 2001 (Fig. 2). Results were compared with the land-use maps of 1990 and 2000 [7].

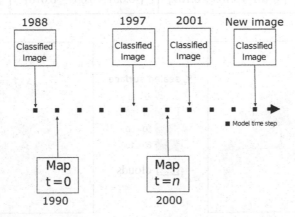

Fig. 2. The proposed remote sensing driven calibration procedure is applied for each image in our time-series and can be repeated when a new image becomes available

5   Results and Discussion

5.1 Sub-pixel Sealed Surface Mapping

Error estimations of the sealed surface proportions predicted by the linear regression models were carried out for each image on temporally filtered validation samples (table 1). The temporal filtering reduces the initial validation sample of 2500 pixels for Landsat images acquired further back in time because the number of unchanged pixels decreases when the time span with the high resolution reference data becomes larger. The low error biases (ME_{Sealed}) indicate that overestimations of sealed surface cover within some sample pixels are compensated for by underestimations within others. This model behaviour is beneficial because our approach involves spatial aggregation of per-pixel proportions to regions. The error magnitudes represented by the mean absolute error (MAE_{Sealed}) are similar for each date, with values around 0.10 (i.e. 10% average error per validation pixel). This is an acceptable result given the constraints put on the sub-pixel proportion estimation in terms of geometrical coregistration, image noise and autocorrelation effects.

The regression models were applied to the entire study area to obtain sealed surface maps for each date (fig. 3). The sealed surface proportions estimated at pixel-level

Table 1. Error assessment of sub-pixel sealed surface fractions estimated by linear regression

	MAE_{Sealed} ($\alpha = 0.05$)	ME_{Sealed} ($\alpha = 0.05$)	# samples
1988	{ $0.101 \leq 0.106 \leq 0.111$ }	{ $-0.005 \leq 0.002 \leq 0.009$ }	1536
1997	{ $0.091 \leq 0.095 \leq 0.099$ }	{ $-0.004 \leq 0.002 \leq 0.008$ }	1961
2001	{ $0.101 \leq 0.105 \leq 0.109$ }	{ $-0.001 \leq 0.005 \leq 0.010$ }	2500

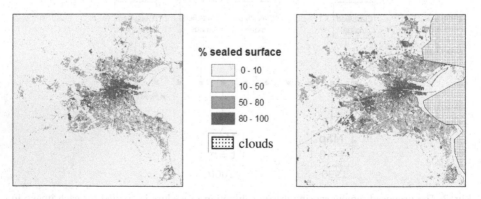

% sealed surface

☐ 0 - 10
10 - 50
50 - 80
80 - 100

▦ clouds

Fig. 3. Sealed surface maps of the Greater Dublin Area for the two most extreme dates in the time-series: June 1988 (left) and May 2001 (right)

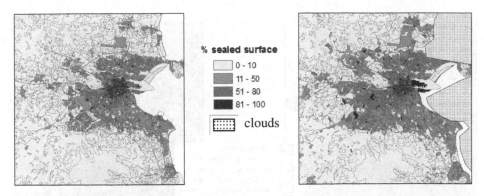

Fig. 4. Urban density maps of the Greater Dublin Area for the two most extreme dates in the time-series: June 1988 (left) and May 2001 (right)

were then spatially averaged to the level of regions to derive built-up density maps (fig. 4). These maps clearly indicate the westward urban expansion of Dublin. The-densification and expansion of industrial estates (Broomhill, Ballymount, Park West) near the M50 motorway in West Dublin and rapid expansion of residential areas in Clonsilla, Hartstown and the new developments in Tyrrelstown are visible.

5.2 MLP-Based Supervised Land-Use Classification

To assign each region to one of the three land-use classes, the 4 function parameters were used together with the average per-block sealed surface cover and spatial variability in a MLP-based supervised classification. Classification accuracies were calculated with an area-based weight, i.e. misclassifying larger regions had a more severe negative impact on overall accuracy than misclassifying smaller regions. For the 2001 image, 86% of the total area covered by the validation samples was correctly classified. This was slightly less for the 1988 image (table 2). This may be caused by the fact that the definition of the regions is partly based on 2000 MOLAND land-use map, which means that some regions may not be homogenous in terms of land-use in 1988. This in turn may influence the signatures (i.e. function parameters) used for training the classifier, but the impact on the output is expected to be limited given the results of the accuracy assessment.

Table 2. Area-weighted producer's accuracy (PA), user's accuracy (UA), and percent correctly classified (PCC) regions for the MLP based land-use classification

Land use	1988 PA|UA		2001 PA|UA	
Residential	70%	80%	71%	79%
Employment	88%	88%	93%	89%
Other urban	58%	51%	77%	83%
PCC (area weighted)	**79%**		**86%**	

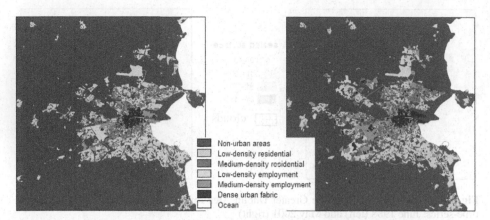

Fig. 5. Land-use maps of the Greater Dublin Area intersected with built-up density maps for the two most extreme dates in the time-series: June 1988 (left) and May 2001 (right)

The output of the region-based land-use classification was intersected with the urban density maps, which results in maps consisting of 6 classes (fig. 5): non-urban land, low density residential, medium density residential, low density employment, medium density employment and dense urban fabric. These classes represent the maximum level of thematic detail that can be derived from medium resolution satellite images with a reasonable accuracy.

5.3 Calibrating the MOLAND Model

Fig. 6 shows the results of the four metrics derived from MOLAND simulations, remote sensing data and land-use maps prior to the calibration. This reference scenario uses neighbour influence parameters and a value for α of 0.4, all copied from a previous application of the MOLAND model [7]. The land-use map of 1990 was used to initialise the model. The simulation results indicate that the diversity of the landscape increases (increasing SHDI) through time, while the landscape gets more filled in (increasing FRAC_AM) and less fragmented in terms of different class pixels (decreasing CONTAG), but with more interspersion of patch types. The land-use maps of 1990 and 2000 point to the same trend. The remote sensing results show the same trend for SHDI, FRAC_AM and CONTAG, but the metric values themselves differ more than those calculated for the land-use maps. For IJI, no trend is visible in the remote sensing results.

The land-use map simulated by the MOLAND model for the year 2000 shows a good resemblance with the actual land-use map of 2000 in terms of metric values for SHDI, IJI and CONTAG. For FRAC_AM the results may be slightly improved by changing the calibration parameters. Since no actual land-use map exists for the period between 1990 and 2000, remote sensing data is the only reference that can be used for calibrating simulation results between these dates. Therefore, the spatial

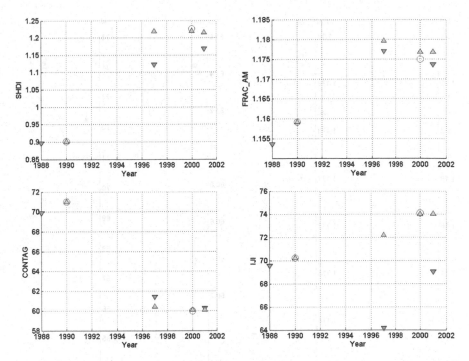

Fig. 6. Spatial metrics derived from MOLAND simulations (▲), remote sensing data (▼) and land-use maps (O), prior to calibration. SHDI = Shannon's Diversity Index, FRAC_AM = Area Weighted Mean Fractal Dimension, CONTAG = Contagion, IJI = Interspersion and Juxtaposition index.

metrics derived from the land-use predicted by the MOLAND simulation of 1997 were compared with the remote sensing derived metrics for that year. This comparison was made for different calibration scenario's (Fig. 7). In scenario 1 to 3, the stochastic parameter α was increased from 0.5 to 0.7, while in scenario 4 and 5 the neighbour influence functions for the residential classes were changed. In general the results indicate that the metrics are not very sensitive to changes in model parameters. On the one hand this may be caused by the thematic generalisation of land-use classes, on the other hand the use of an urban mask restrains the spatial variability of the landscape while most changes take place at the urban fringe and in the suburbs. Nevertheless, some improvements in the calibration scenarios were observed. Which scenario performs best, depends on which metric is used for evaluation. Scenario 4 performs best when the FRAC_AM metric is considered, while for CONTAG the results are worse for scenario's 4 and 5. The other scenarios provide results comparable to the uncalibrated model. No conclusions can be drawn for IJI, because the remote sensing results differ too much from the results obtained from the simulation. For SHDI, all scenarios yield comparable results that are also slightly better compared to the reference scenario.

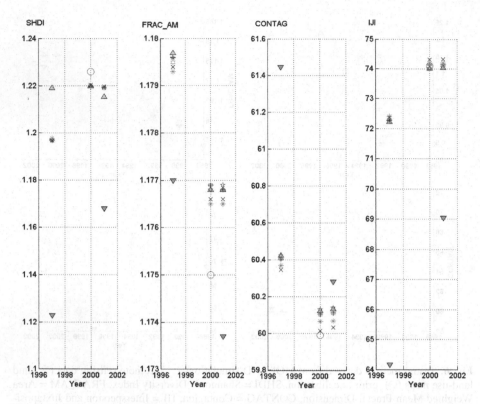

Fig. 7. Spatial metrics derived from remote sensing data (▽) and land-use maps (O), the reference MOLAND (▲) and after calibration according to 5 scenarios: 1(_), 2(E), 3(3), 4(|) and 5(X). SHDI = Shannon's Diversity Index, FRAC_AM = Area Weighted Mean Fractal Dimension, CONTAG = Contagion, IJI = Interspersion and Juxtaposition index.

6 Conclusions

The aim of this study was improving the calibration process of the MOLAND model by comparing spatial metrics derived from satellite images to the same metrics calculated from land-use change simulations. The proposed calibration framework fills up the temporal gaps between available land-use maps by using medium resolution satellite images. The applicability of this method depends on the sensitivity of the chosen metrics to changes in model parameters. The metrics used in this study have a theoretical relation with urban sprawl, but showed low sensitivity to urban land-use changes. This low sensitivity does not only depend on the choice of metrics, but also on the amount of thematic generalisation of classes. The use of more spatially explicit metrics, i.e. at class level or moving window level, could improve the sensitivity to changes in urban morphology. For a particular calibration scenario, the results improved for some metrics, while no improvement was observed for other metrics capturing different aspects of urban morphology. Further research should aim to provide insights on the set of metrics that should be used for evaluating calibration scenario's since this choice will depend on the focus of the model application, i.e. fragmentation, contagion, etc., and the sensitivity of the metric to this phenomenon.

Acknowledgements

The research presented in this paper was supported by the Belgian Science Policy Office in the frame of the STEREO II programme - project SR/00/105. Url: http://www.mamud.be.

References

1. van der Kwast, J., Van de Voorde, T., Uljee, I., Engelen, G., Lavalle, C., Canters, F.: Using Remote Sensing derived Spatial Metrics for the Calibration of Land-use Change Models. In: IEEE 2009 Joint Urban Remote Sensing Event, pp. 1–9. IEEE Press, New York (2009)
2. Gong, P., Marceau, D.J., Howarth, P.J.: A Comparison of Spatial Feature Extraction Algorithms for Land-use Classification with SPOT HRV Data. Remote Sens. Environ. 40, 137–151 (1992)
3. Barnsley, M.J., Barr, S.L.: Distinguishing Urban Land-use Categories in Fine Spatial Resolution Land-cover Data using a Graph-based, Structural Pattern Recognition System. Comput., Environ. and Urban Systems 21, 209–225 (1997)
4. de Jong, S.M., van der Meer, F.: Remote Sensing Image Analysis, Including the Spatial Domain. Kluwer academic publishers, Dordrecht (2004)
5. van der Kwast, J., Engelen, G.: Calibration of Land Use Change Models: the Potential of Spatial Metrics. In: Maktav, D. (ed.) Remote Sensing for a Changing Europe, pp. 402–411. IOS Press, Amsterdam (2009)
6. Herold, M., Scepan, J., Clarke, K.C.: The Use of Remote Sensing and Landscape Metrics to Describe Structures and Changes in Urban Land Uses. Environ. Plan. 34, 1443–1458 (2002)
7. Engelen, G., White, R., Uljee, I.: The MURBANDY and MOLAND models for Dublin - final report. RIKS BV, Maastricht (2002)
8. White, R., Engelen, G., Uljee, I.: The Use of Constrained Cellular Automata for High-Resolution Modelling of Urban Landuse Dynamics. Environ. Plann. B 24, 323–343 (1997)
9. Hagen-Zanker, A., Straatman, B., Uljee, I.: Further Developments of a Fuzzy Set Map Comparison Approach. Int. J. Geogr. Inf. Sci. 19, 769–785 (2005)
10. Irish, R.R.: Landsat 7 Science Data Users Handbook. NASA, Greenbelt MD (2007)
11. Schott, J.R., Salvaggio, C., Volchok, W.J.: Radiometric Scene Normalization using Pseudoinvariant Features. Remote Sens. Environ. 26, 1–16 (1988)
12. MOLAND - Monitoring Land Use/Cover Dynamics, http://www.moland.jrc.it
13. Settle, J.J., Drake, N.A.: Linear Mixing and the Estimation of Ground Cover Proportions. Int. J. Remote Sens. 14, 1159–1177 (1993)
14. van der Meer, F.: Image Classification Through Spectral Unmixing. In: Stein, A., van der Meer, F., Gorte, B. (eds.) pp. 185–193. Kluwer Academic Publishers, Dordrecht (1999)
15. Ridd, M.K.: Exploring a V–I–S (Vegetation–Impervious Surface–Soil) Model for Urban Ecosystem Analysis through Remote Sensing - Comparative Anatomy for Cities. Int. J. Remote Sens. 16, 2165–2185 (1995)

16. Phinn, S., Stanford, M., Scarth, P., Murray, A.T., Shyy, P.T.: Monitoring the Composition of Urban Environments Based on the Vegetation-Impervious-Soil (VIS) Model by Subpixel Analysis Techniques. Int. J. Remote Sens. 23, 4131–4153 (2002)
17. Ward, D., Phinn, S.R., Murray, A.T.: Monitoring Growth in Rapidly Urbanizing Areas Using Remotely Sensed Data. Prof. Geogr. 52, 371–385 (2000)
18. Wu, C.: Normalized Spectral Mixture Analysis for Monitoring Urban Composition using ETM+ Imagery. Remote Sens. Environ. 93, 480–492 (2004)
19. Van de Voorde, T., De Roeck, T., Canters, F.: A Comparison of Two Spectral Mixture Modelling Approaches for Impervious Surface Mapping in Urban Areas. Int. J. Remote Sens. 30, 4785–4806 (2009)
20. Kärdi, T.: Remote Sensing of Urban Areas: Linear Spectral Unmixing of Landsat Thematic Mapper Images Acquired over Tartu (Estonia). Proceedings of the Estonian Academy of Science, Biology and Ecology 56, 19–32 (2007)
21. Small, C.: High Spatial Resolution Spectral Mixture Analysis of Urban Reflectance. Remote Sens. Environ. 88, 170–186 (2003)
22. Van de Voorde, T., De Genst, W., Canters, F.: Improving Pixel-Based VHR Land-Cover Classifications of Urban Areas with Post-Classification Techniques, Photogramm. Eng. Rem. Sens. 73, 1017–1027 (2007)
23. Herold, M., Couclelis, H., Clarke, K.C.: The Role of Spatial Metrics in the Analysis and Modelling of Urban Land Use Change. Comput. Environ. Urban 29, 369–399 (2005)
24. Huang, J., Lu, X.X., Sellers, J.M.: A Global Comparative Analysis of Urban Form: Applying Spatial Metrics and Remote Sensing. Landscape Urban Plan. 82, 184–197 (2007)
25. Ji, W., Ma, J., Twibell, R.W., Underhill, K.: Characterising Urban Sprawl Using Multi-Stage Remote Sensing Images and Landscape Metrics. Comput. Environ. Urban 30, 861–879 (2006)
26. Weng, Y.C.: Spatiotemporal Changes of Landscape Pattern in Response to Urbanization. Landscape Urban Plan. 81, 341–353 (2007)
27. Atkinson, P.M., Tatnall, A.R.L.: Neural Networks in Remote Sensing. Int. J. Remote Sens. 18, 699–709 (1997)
28. Benediktsson, J.A., Swain, P.H., Ersoy, O.K.: Neural Network Approaches Versus Statistical Methods in Classification of Multisource Remote Sensing Data. IEEE T Geosci. Remote 28, 540–551 (1990)
29. Kavzoglu, T., Mather, P.M.: The Use of Backpropagating Artificial Neural Networks in Land Cover Classification. Int. J. Remote Sens. 24, 4907–4938 (2003)
30. Torrens, P.: A Toolkit for Measuring Sprawl. Appl. Spatial Analysis 1, 5–36 (2008)

Design of a Dynamic Land-Use Change Probability Model Using Spatio-Temporal Transition Matrix

Yongjin Joo[1], Chulmin Jun[2], and Soohong Park[3]

[1] Institute of Urban Sciences, University of Seoul, Seoul, Korea
yjjoo75@uos.ac.kr
[2] Dept. of Geoinformatics, University of Seoul, Seoul, Korea
cmjun@uos.ac.kr
[3] Dept. of Geoinformatic Engineering, Inha University, Incheon, Korea
shpark@inha.ac.kr

Abstract. This study aims to analyze land use patterns using time-series satellite images of Seoul Metropolitan Area for the past 30 years, and present a macroscopic model for predicting future land use patterns using Markov Chain based probability model, and finally examine its applicability to Korea. Several Landsat MSS and TM images were used to acquire land-use change patterns and dynamic land-use change patterns were categorized from the classified images. Finally, spatio-temporal transition matrices were constructed from the classified images and applied them into a Markov Chain based model to predict land-use changes for the study area.

Keywords: land-use change prediction, spatio-temporal transition matrix, Markov Chain, urban growth model.

1 Introduction

Urban economist and planners have consistently studied how urban areas have developed and what primary factors have affected. However, those research efforts have not sufficiently presented theoretical models. That's because the aspect of urbanization is different between countries and varies with time. In addition, the process of urbanization is so complicated that proposing theoretical validity is difficult through feasible verification [10].

Detecting an urban spatial structure and predicting changing trend is very important information in establishing the efficient urban policies. In Korea, however, there have been minimal research efforts regarding analysis and prediction of the characteristics of dynamic changes of land use. In order to predict land use change, models represented in terms of space-time is needed and a variety of variables and data supporting the model are also required [11]. The models in the previous studies, with insufficient time-series data, show limitations in incorporating the past tendencies of urbanization and explaining the past land use changes. Investigating the current state of land use and comparing with the past ones requires significant time and efforts. In

D. Taniar et al. (Eds.): ICCSA 2010, Part I, LNCS 6016, pp. 105–115, 2010.
© Springer-Verlag Berlin Heidelberg 2010

the areas as Seoul Metropolitan Area (SMA), which shows fast population growth and development, detecting the land-use variations happened in the past is very difficult. In this situation, utilizing remote sensing data is a practical alternative for monitoring visible change of urban spaces.

First of all, in this study, we examine the characteristics of land use transitions through the time-series images of Landsat in SMA. Then, we develop a prediction model for land-use change based on Markov chain methods and apply it to the simulation of the land-use transition processes. Finally, we examine the validity of prediction result using the actual data of1984, 1992. Before the implementation of the model, we set up the prototype of the model through the consideration of the spatial characteristics of the study area, the definition of model components, establishing input variable data, and designing basic algorithm for the model. Satellite images (MSS, TM), digital maps and data of the limited development district were used to establish the prediction model. In other words, input data which are relevant to land-use changes (topography and social phenomenon) and land cover data are developed. Then, by calculating the land use conversion rate, a transition matrix was composed on two periods-- 1972~1984, 1984~1992. The suitability of the model was evaluated by using a validation method comparing the derived results with the actual data (1984, 1992).

2 Markov Transition Model

2.1 Model Framework

Analysis of Markov Chain, a statistical method was used for predicting how topographical and social variations affect on the land use changes in the future through examining dynamic characteristics of the past. It is based on the process of probability called Markov Chain, which assumes that present state is determined only by the immediate previous state. It is composed of the system state and transition probability. The changes of states are called transitions, and the probabilities associated with various state-changes are called transition probabilities.

When a probability analysis can be performed on matrix of random events accompanied by time, $\{X_t\}$, the row of random variables of each event is referred to as stochastic process. If random variables $X_t(t=1,2,...)$ change into one of state sets(S_1, S_2, ... S_k) at a certain moment, transforming from state S_i to S_j is called a step. And when the transition probability from S_i to S_j (P_{ij}) is only related to the immediate previous state S_i, such probability process is Markov Process. The following formula (1) indicates the transition probability.

$$P_{ij} = P\{X_n = S_j \mid X_{n-1} = S_i \wedge P\} = P\{X_n = S_j \mid X_{n-1} = S_i\} \tag{1}$$

The transition matrix of P_{ij} defined as follows;

$$p = \begin{bmatrix} P_{11} & P_{12} & ... & P_{1k} \\ P_{21} & P_{21} & ... & P_{2k} \\ P_{k1} & P_{k1} & ... & P_{kk} \end{bmatrix} \text{ for } 0 <= P_{ij} <= 1 \sum P_{ij} = 1 \tag{2}$$

In its simplest form, the state vector X(t) can be described if types of land use are categorized into urban, water, forest, and agriculture. The formula is defined as follows;

$$X(t) = \begin{bmatrix} X1(t) \\ X2(t) \\ X3(t) \\ X4(t) \end{bmatrix} \quad (3)$$

In the above formula, vector x(t) is land use/cover, transition probability P is land use and land-use change from time t to $t+1$ is defined as. $X(t+1) = P * x(t)$. Each element of transition matrix P_{ij} is the probability to move from i type of land use in time t to j type of land use in time $t+1$. For example, let's suppose there are 100 pixels of forests in t time. If, after 20 years, there still remain 78 pixels of forests, 12 pixels change into agricultural area and 10 pixels to urban area, then P_{ij} is described as;

- $P_{31} = 10 / 100 = 0.10$
- $P_{32} = 0 / 100 = 0.00$
- $P_{33} = 78 / 100 = 0.78$
- $P_{34} = 12 / 100 = 0.12$

With the transition matrix being described as;

$$p = \begin{bmatrix} P_{11} & P_{12} & P_{13} & P_{14} \\ P_{21} & P_{22} & P_{23} & P_{24} \\ P_{31} & P_{32} & P_{33} & P_{34} \\ P_{41} & P_{42} & P_{43} & P_{44} \end{bmatrix} = \begin{bmatrix} \cdots & \cdots & \cdots & \cdots \\ \cdots & \cdots & \cdots & \cdots \\ 0.10 & 0.00 & 0.78 & 0.12 \\ \cdots & \cdots & \cdots & \cdots \end{bmatrix} \quad (4)$$

2.2 Problems of Spatial Influence Algorithm

Markov model has been used to predict aspects of land-use changes by human activities and understand the changing processes of natural forms [8]. The probability of a land cover change in this model is based on spatial influence algorithm with neighborhood effects having influence on adjacent land cover [12]. On the whole, this algorithm supposes that change of a cell is carried out by transition probabilities. The range of influence that adjacent cells reach can be set up with 4 or 8 neighbor cells. The values are set in two-dimensional square cells and transition state of land use class from previous time (t1) to next time (t2) is calculated. After that, change of cell in the space can be simulated by the time according to calculated transition probability.

Markov model is easily computed by using digital image or raster-based GIS data and has an advantage to reflect transition tendency of current land use effectively. Even though time passes along, transition matrix is always constant and applied equally to all locations [7]. However, actual land use doesn't change exactly according to the assumption of Markov and obtaining the transition probability through independent measurement is difficult. Also, the factors for land-use transition are more affected by political and economic factors rather than biophysical ones [1]. Therefore, in case we apply previous algorithm to our study area, the Seoul metropolitan area where urbanization has been on the rise at an extremely rapid rate for a short period in Korea, some anticipated problems are as follows;

First of all, limited development districts (also called green-belt areas) have been set in South Korea since 1972. It has been playing an important role in controlling spread of urbanization and preserving green spaces. Because the change of center pixel is affected only by the land uses of adjacent cells, it leads to a spread of habitation inside the limited development areas. Secondly, one of the most important factors relevant to land-use change is the slope. The high slope prevents the regions from being developed and populated by the development permit system in Korea. Unless the physical properties of the land are considered, habitation cells located in hill sides and low mountains will spread into neighboring cells.

In this paper, we thus improved previous model into a more practical land-use model engrossed in urban structural change, which can incorporate the concept of multi-dimensional spatial filter. In other words, political factor of land use regulation (green-belt policy) is considered to prevent urbanized cells in green area and green-belts from spreading. More importantly, we developed the methodology for dynamic probabilities of transition matrix with the help of practical multi-temporal satellite images accumulated for long periods.

3   Design of Land-Use Change Model

Land-use change model that we suggest is based on Cellular automata (CA), which are both a body of knowledge and set of techniques for solving complex dynamic-systems problems [9]. The model includes four components: a grid space, local states, neighborhoods and a transition rule. Though these components, the model evolves in discrete time steps by updating their local state according to a universal rule that is applied to each cell synchronously at each time step. The value of each cell is determined by a geometrical configuration of neighbor cells, and is specified in the transition rule. Updated values of individual cells then become the inputs for the next iteration. In this chapter, we specify each element for design of land-use change model in detail.

Grid space: The first element of this model is grid spaces, which mean regular grid of cells where interactions for urban sprawl are carried out. Theoretically, there is no restriction to the tessellation of a grid space and it could be various forms of shape. In general, however, square cells are the most common form in CA applications due to their inherent convenience of implementation in computation. Therefore, grid space in this study consists of regular square cells of 2 dimensions. Besides, because grid spaces are determined by the spatial resolution of satellite images, input data (land cover, green-belt, and slop) are determined as 60m grids according to Landsat MSS, the lowest size of the sensor resolution.

Local states: The second element of the model is the local state. The local states mean the status of each cell encoded by numerical values at a given time step. The range of its values is defined in the transition rules and depends on the actual implementation of model. In raster GISs, these local states are directly analogous to the values of each grid cell in a layer. The local states in our study represent the land-use characteristics of cells, that is, values assigned in all cells. Table 1 shows the cell state of input data that we used in our experiment.

Table 1. The cell states of input data

Thematic Data		State	Grid Space(m)	Data type
Land cover	Urban	1	60 × 60	Integer
	Water	2	60 × 60	
	Forest	3	60 × 60	
	Agriculture	4	60 × 60	
Green-belt	Exclusive region	1	60 × 60	Byte
	Non-Exclusive region	0	60 × 60	
Gradient map	Slope	0 × 90	60 × 60	Integer

Neighborhood cell: Neighborhood is a set of cells located adjacent to focus cell. Such a neighborhood concept is very similar to the mask or moving window of spatial filters in digital image processing and GIS. In theory, there is no limitation to the size of a neighborhood and usually the configuration of a neighborhood can be extended to the temporal dimension as well as the spatial dimensions. In this study, the Neighborhood of Moor was used as the neighborhood definition. In fig 1, the cell in the 3 x 3 window (i.e, the neighborhood) is changed in a discrete time step according to the transition rule.

Transition rule: GIS data such as land cover data of time series built from satellite images, digital elevation models (DEM), and green-belt data are considered as input variables. The local transition rule and constraints are applied to grid spaces repeatedly resulting in state transitions from time t to time $t +1$. This transition rule defines how each cell changes every time step, and models the process that a state of a cell changes constantly in accordance with the effects of neighboring cells. As the process of this algorithm, transition matrix is calculated by using time-periodic transition probability in the study area. Transition index is calculated through examining the state of the focus cell and the adjacent state of 8 cells representing land use followed by the computation of the transition index. The transition index is the maximum value j of $N_j \times P_{ij}$ (where N_j is the number of land use elements in the current window size and P_{ij} is the element in the transition matrix from i to j). If the returned value of transition index is urban, then model checks for such constraints as green-belt and slope. In case agricultural cell in green-belt is changed into urban, then its state is maintained. Lastly, transition index is assigned to the cell and move on to next cell. Process and algorithm for model execution are as shown in figure 1.

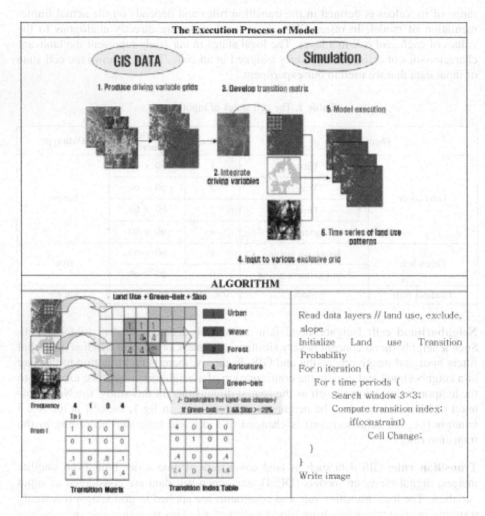

Fig. 1. Process and algorithm for model execution

4   Construction of Land-Use Change Model

4.1   Data Set

In order to apply the proposed land-use change model, we built input data on factors for the past 30 years related with land-use change (topography and social phenomenon) by utilizing the satellite images (MSS, TM), digital maps, and green-belt data. Transition of land use in the study area was analyzed using the land cover maps. We utilized MSS(1972) images, TM(1984, 1992,2000) images for land cover maps. Finally, the water bodies, greenbelt and DEM were used to limit the land-use change.

In Korea, the green-belt system has been established since 1971, and we collected green-belt data from that time to the present. Gradient maps were used by extracting contours and layers only from digital topographic maps, interpolating them in TIN (Triangulated Irregular Network), and then transforming into DEM (Digital Elevation Model) or a percent form. After creating the DEM by using a contoured digital topographical map, we used it as slope for the study. Because the elevation value was less changeable over time, we used the DEM values in the 1990s as substitutes for the 1970s, 1980s and 1990s data. The major characteristics of images and the input data are shown in figure 2.

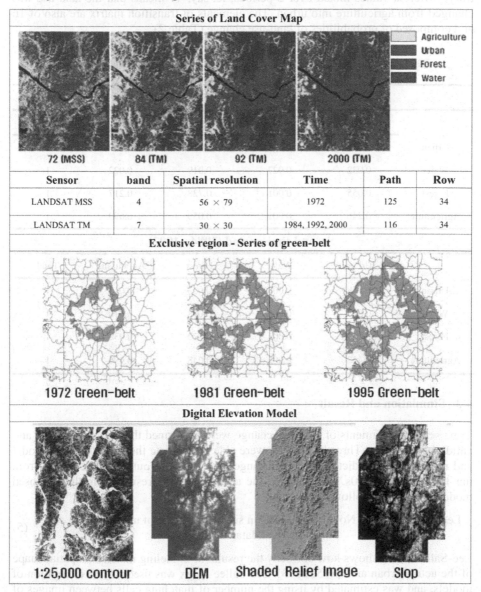

Series of Land Cover Map

72 (MSS)   84 (TM)   92 (TM)   2000 (TM)

Agriculture
Urban
Forest
Water

Sensor	band	Spatial resolution	Time	Path	Row
LANDSAT MSS	4	56 × 79	1972	125	34
LANDSAT TM	7	30 × 30	1984, 1992, 2000	116	34

Exclusive region - Series of green-belt

1972 Green-belt   1981 Green-belt   1995 Green-belt

Digital Elevation Model

1:25,000 contour   DEM   Shaded Relief Image   Slop

Fig. 2. GIS databases for the study

4.2 Transition Matrix Configuration

In order to configure transition matrix with change type by time, we combined each result of classification into 1972~1984, 1984~1992 respectively. So each mixing type becomes $4^2(16)$ different types for each has 4 categories of 2 periods. In other words, change type has values between 11 and 44. For example, same values mixed over 2 periods such as 11, 22, 33, and 44 means that land use doesn't change. On the contrary, different values mixed over 2 periods, let say, 41 means that the land use was changed from agriculture into urban. The elements of transition matrix are also of 16 and composed of probabilities of land-use change (Table 2).

Table 2. Configuration of transition matrix using time-series land-cover map

First time period (1972 - 1984)					
	Urban	Water	Forest	Agriculture	Total
Urban	0.939	0.011	0.014	0.037	1
Water	0.032	0.927	0.019	0.022	1
Forest	0.055	0.001	0.728	0.217	1
Agriculture	0.240	0.001	0.059	0.699	1
Second time period (1984 - 1992)					
	Urban	Water	Forest	Agriculture	Total
Urban	0.958	0.008	0.023	0.011	1
Water	0.027	0.956	0.008	0.010	1
Forest	0.090	0.001	0.870	0.038	1
Agriculture	0.452	0.003	0.048	0.496	1

4.3 Simulation and Result

Time series experiments of land-use change were performed through simulations and validation methods. Through this, we were able to evaluate the validity of the model and reliability of predicted land-use change. The range of our experiment was from the 1970s to the 1990s. We analyzed the accuracy of the results from the proposed model by using the following formula;

$$\text{Lee-Sallee Index} = \text{No. of urban cells in simulation} / \text{No. of urban cells in actual data} \quad (5)$$

Lee-Sallee Index shows how correctly the results of modeling match the spatial shape of the actual urban area [4, 5, 6, 13]. Lee-Sallee index was used for the calibration of models, and was estimated by using the number of matching cells between images of

Table 3. The validation result using the Lee-Salle index

Test	1984	1992
Cells of predicted urban areas	116,799	128,611
Cells of actual urban areas	102,657	115,173
No. of iteration	32	82
Lee-Sallee Index (×)	0.68647	0.61972

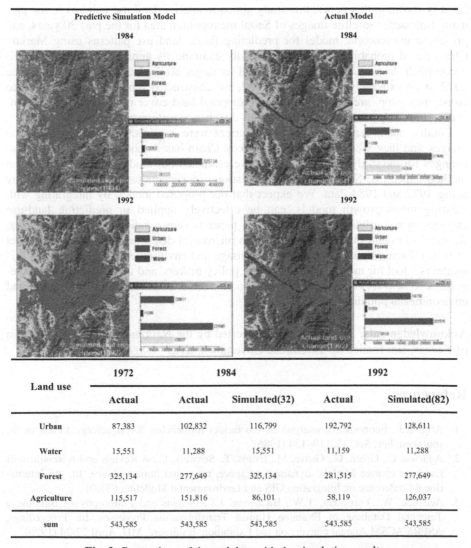

Land use	1972	1984		1992	
	Actual	Actual	Simulated(32)	Actual	Simulated(82)
Urban	87,383	102,832	116,799	192,792	128,611
Water	15,551	11,288	15,551	11,159	11,288
Forest	325,134	277,649	325,134	281,515	277,649
Agriculture	115,517	151,816	86,101	58,119	126,037
sum	543,585	543,585	543,585	543,585	543,585

Fig. 3. Comparison of the real data with the simulation results

urbanized areas and those of from the simulation at a standard point of time. Table 3 shows the results of Lee-Sallee indexes which have the highest spatial similarity.

As a result, following figure 3 represents the results of the simulation through the predictive images calibrated by Lee-Sally index. They were compared against the actual land cover map to verify our proposed model.

(Simulated (n) indicates the simulation images obtained from n times of model processes.)

5 Conclusions

As it is shown in this paper, this study aimed to analyze land use patterns in the past using time-series satellite images of Seoul metropolitan area for the past 30 years, and present a macroscopic model for predicting future land use patterns using Markov Chain-based probability model, and finally examine its applicability to Korea. To accomplish this, we, first, selected Seoul as target area which has urbanized since 1972 at an extremely rapid rate. Second, we constructed input data with regard to constraints (slop, green-belt) and spatio-temporal land cover maps from satellite images, which help categorize dynamic land-use change patterns.

Finally, spatio-temporal transition matrices were constructed from the classified images and they were applied to a Markov Chain-based model to predict land-use changes for the study area. In addition, we evaluated our model through a validation method called Lee-Sally index and simulation experiments to predict 1984, 1992 by using 1972 and 1984 data. We expect that our proposed model, by integrating with existing urban growth models, can be effectively applied in predicting land-use changes in non-urban areas. Though this paper is shown satisfactory consequences, we need to extend our proposed model to microlevel deterministic simulation model in urban domain by using transportation usage and environmental impact so that this model is a tool for use by urban planners, policy makers, and other community stakeholders to help formulate and evaluate combinations of land use, transportation and environmental policies.

Acknowledgments. This work was supported by the National Research Foundation of Korea Grant funded by the Korean Government (NRF- 2009-413-D00001).

References

1. Alig, R.J.: Econometric analysis of the factors influencing forest acreage trends in the southeast. For. Sci. 32, 119–134 (1986)
2. Agarwal, C., Green, G., Grove, M., Evans, T., Schweik, C.: A Review and Assessment of Land-use change Models: dynamics of space, time, and human choice. In: 4th International Conference on Integrating GIS and Environmental Modeling (2000)
3. Acevedo, W., Foresman, T.W., Buchanan, J.T.: Origins and Philosophy of Building a Temporal Database to Examine Human Transformation Processes. In: Proceedings, ASPRS/ACSM Annual conversion and Exhibition, Baltimore, MD, April 22-24 (1996)

4. Clark, S., Starr, J., Foresman, T.W., Prince, W., Acevedo, W.: Development of the Temporal Transportation Database for the Analysis of Urban Development in the Balimore-Washington Region. In: Proceeding, ASPRS/ACSM Annual Convention and Exhibition, Balimore, MD, April 22-24, vol. III, pp. 101–110 (1996)
5. Clarke, K.C., Hoppen, S., Gaydos, L.: Methods and techniques for rigorous calibration of a cellular automaton model of urban growth. In: Third International Conference/Workshop on Integrating GIS and Environmental Modeling, Santa Fe, New Mexico, January 21-25, Santa Barbara: National Center for Geographic Information and Analysis (1996)
6. Clarke, K.C., Hoppen, S., Gaydos, L.: A Self-modifying Cellular Automata Model of Historical Urbanization in the San Francisco Bay Area. EPB 24, 247–261 (1997)
7. Huang, O., Cai, Y.: Simulation of land use change using GIS- based stochastic model: the case study of Shiqian County. Stoch. Env. Res. Risk Assess. 21, 419–426 (2007)
8. Jenerette, G.D., Wu, J.: Analysis and simulation of land-use change in the central Arizona - Phoenix region. Landscape Ecology 16, 611–626 (2001)
9. Jung, J.J.: Development of Cellular Automata Model for the Urban Growth. Seoul University (2001)
10. Park, S.: Design and Implementation of an Integrated CA-GIS System. Geographic Information System Association of Korea 5(1), 99–113 (1997)
11. Park, S., Joo, Y.-G., Shin, Y.-H.: Design and Development of a Spatio-Temporal GIS Database for Urban Growth Modeling and Prediction. The Geographical Journal of Korea 36(4), 313–326 (2002)
12. Turner, M.G.: Spatial simulation of landscape changes in Georgia: a comparison of three transition models. Landscape Ecology 1, 29–36 (1987)
13. Kang, Y., Park, S.: A Study on the Urban Growth Forecasting for the Seoul Metropolitan Area. Journal of the Korean Geographical Society, 621–639 (2000)

Forecasting Space-Time Land Use Change in the Paochiao Watershed of Taiwan Using Demand Estimation and Empirical Simulation Approaches

Hone-Jay Chu, Yu-Pin Lin, and Chen-Fa Wu

Department of Bioenvironmental Systems Engineering,
National Taiwan University, 1, Sec. 4, Roosevelt Rd.,
Da-an District, Taipei City 106, Taiwan, R.O.C
honejaychu@gmail.com, yplin@ntu.edu.tw
Department of Horticulture, National Chun Hsing University,
250, Kuo Kuang Rd., Taichung 402, Taiwan, R.O.C
cfwu@dragon.nchu.edu.tw

Abstract. This study applies two empirical approaches such as logistic regression, and artificial network (ANN) to combine Conversion of Land Use and its Effects (CLUE-s) model to predict urban sprawl in the Paochiao watershed in Taipei County, Taiwan. The current investigation projected land-use dynamics for the next twenty years using demand prediction models such as the Markov chain and cellular automata model. Accordingly, the empirical models integrating with CLUE-s then simulated land-use patterns for future periods based on the predicted demands.

Results show that land-use patterns predicted by the model tended to fragment and intersperse future patterns. The predicted land-use patterns have significant impact on urban sprawl in the Paochiao watershed. The study is an effective means of enhancing land-use monitoring and managing urbanized watersheds.

Keywords: Markov chain; land use change; landscape metrics; ANN; CLUE-s.

1 Introduction

The impact of land use changes has received considerable attention from ecologists, particularly with respect to the effects on aquatic ecosystems and biodiversity [1, 2]. Land use change can be characterized by the complex interaction of behavioral and structural factors associated with demand, technological capacity, and social relations, which affect both demand and environmental capacity, as well as the natural environment in question [3]. Landscape patterns can be quantified using spatial landscape indices to characterize and quantify landscape composition and configuration. The composition of a landscape denotes the features associated with the variety and abundance of patch types within a landscape. The spatial configuration of a landscape denotes the spatial character and arrangement, position, or orientation of patches within a class or landscape [4]. These

D. Taniar et al. (Eds.): ICCSA 2010, Part I, LNCS 6016, pp. 116–130, 2010.

metrics may include the number of patches, area, patch shape, total edge of patches, nearest neighbor distance, landscape diversity, interspersion and contagion metrics to represent landscape patterns, including compositions and configurations. Recent studies have applied landscape metrics to quantify landscape patterns [5, 6]. Moreover, landscape metrics may also be useful as a first approximation of broad-level landscape patterns and processes, and for characterizing differences among planned and design alternatives, and have been suggested as an appropriate tool for land use planning and design [7, 8].

Numerous studies have developed modeling approaches to simulate the pattern and consequences of land use changes. Stochastic models, optimization models, dynamic process-based simulation models, cellular automata, and empirical-statistical models are examples of approaches that have been used to explore land-use changes [9]. Each type of model has its own potential and constraints with respect to the requirements and expectations of land use planners. One such land use model is the conversion of land use and its effects model (CLUE-s), developed to simulate land use change using empirical quantified relationships between land use and its driving factors. The CLUE-s is a spatial simulation model which explores changes in land-use patterns within user-specified rules of permissible change and rates of change. Driving factors that influence changes from one land-use type to another are defined by combining spatially explicit data on land use and supposed driving factors in a logistical regression analysis (named Logistic-CLUE-s in the following) [10, 11]. Based on the competitive advantage of each land use at a location, the model simulates the competition among land uses for a particular location [10]. In recent years, a number of researchers have successfully applied ANN models in land-use change modeling (e.g., Pijanowski et al. (2002), Dai et al. (2005), Pijanowski et al. (2005)). This study combines ANN and CLUE-s, or the ANN-CLUE-s model to simulate land use change. The ANN directly accounts for the nonlinear complex relationship between driving variables and changes in land-use [12, 13, 14]. The ANN generates probabilities for each land-use category. Finally, using land-use patterns simulated by the ANN-CLUE-s model, this research identifies the differences in land-use patterns compared to the Logistic-CLUE-s.

Researchers have widely used the Markov chain to model land use changes including both urban and nonurban areas for large spatial scales [15, 16, 17, 18, 19]. A Markov process is a random process in which the future is independent of the past, given the present. Most of these studies use first-order Markov chain models. Stationary and first-order are usually assumed except in a few studies testing the stationary or the order of the Markov chain [16]. As land use and cover change reflects the dynamics and interplay of economic, social, and biophysical factors over time, expecting stationarity in land use/ cover data is implausible. However, regarding land use/cover change to be reasonably stationary during a short time span might be practical. Recent studies have applied the Markov chain to quantify landscape demand [20, 21, 22]. These methods should apply to regions with rapid land-use change. The current study combines the Markov chain process and the empirical land use model to simulate land use change in the Paochiao watershed of Taiwan. This study first validates the ANN-CLUE-s compared to the Logistic-CLUE-s. Then the study analyzes CLUE-s simulation results based on Markov model demands, compared with the demands from SLEUTH, a cellular automaton model calibrated using historical urban development patterns [23]. This investigation uses landscape metrics to analyze spatial patterns of land use change between the two demand models.

2 Methods and Materials

This study uses the Markov model analyzing the stochastic nature of the land use data and cellular automata model [6] to find the demand of each land use category for the next twenty years. After annual land-use demand is performed, land use change models (i.e. Logistic-CLUE-s and ANN-CLUE-s) implements a land-use allocation procedure. Both models are used to simulate various land use scenarios based on driving factors for the Paochiao watershed in northern Taiwan. Then, landscape metrics at the class level are calculated using the landscape pattern analysis package Patch Analyst.

2.1 Markov Chain

A Markov process is a system that can be in one of several states, and can pass from one state to another each time step according to fixed probabilities. Markov chain models have several assumptions. One basic assumption regards land use and land cover change as a stochastic process, and different categories are the states of a chain [21].This paper assumes land use change as a finite first-order Markov chain with stationary transition probabilities, and different categories are the states of a chain. A Markov chain is defined as a stochastic process having the property that the value of the process at time t, X_t, depends only on its value at time $t-1$, X_{t-1}, and not on the sequence of values X_{t-2}, X_{t-3}, ... X_0 that the process passed through in arriving at X_{t-1}. The chain can be expressed as:

$$\Pr\{X_t = j \mid X_0 = i_0, X_1 = i_1, ... X_{t-1} = i \}$$
$$= \Pr\{X_t = j \mid X_{t-1} = i\} \tag{1}$$

The $\Pr\{X_t = j \mid X_{t-1} = i\}$, known as the one-step transitional probability, gives the probability that the process makes the transition from state i to state j in one time period [21]. Treatment of the Markov chain in this study will be limited to a first order homogeneous Markov chain. In this event:

$$\Pr\{X_t = a_j \mid X_{t-1} = a_i\} = P_{ij} \tag{2}$$

where P_{ij} can be estimated from observed data by tabulating the number of times the observed data transitions from state i to j. As the time-stationary Markov chain advances in time, the land-use distribution $s(t+1)$ after t th transition period is

$s(t+1) = s(t)P$, where P is the Markov transition matrix in the land-use categories [22]. When a sufficiently large time steps occurs, the chain reaches a steady state. The limiting distribution $s^* = \lim_{t \to \infty} s(0)P^t$, is independent of the initial distribution. The estimation is obtained by maximizing the maximum likelihood function subject to the constraint that $\sum_j P_{ij} = 1$, and this yields

$$P_{ij} = n_{ij} / n_i \tag{3}$$

where n_{ij} is the total number of observed cells from state i to j; n_i is the total number of cells transiting from state i. Moreover, the Chi-square (χ^2-test) is used to test whether the change matrix meets the Markov chain [24].The study passes the test and then assumes a stationary and first order Markov process.

2.2 Logistic -CLUE-s & ANN-CLUE-s

The CLUE-s model allocates land use changes based on regional land requirements, zoning restrictions and preference maps. The non-spatial module calculates the area of change for all land-use types at an aggregate level, and the spatial module in CLUE-s translates demands into land-use changes at various locations within the study region [10]. In the CLUE-s model, the probability maps for all land-use types were compiled with the logistic regression models described in previous studies [10, 11]; (We called it Logistic-CLUE-s later). The relationships between land uses and their drivers were evaluated by the following logistic regression [10]:

$$p'_i = \frac{\exp\left(\beta_0 + \sum_{j=1}^{k} \beta_j y_{ji}\right)}{1 + \exp\left(\beta_0 + \sum_{j=1}^{k} \beta_j y_{ji}\right)}, \tag{4}$$

where p'_i is the probability of a land-use type occurring in a grid cell i; k is the number of driving factors; y_{ji} is the driving factor of each cell i in the driving factor j ; β_0 is the estimated coefficient; and β_j is the coefficient of each driving factor in the logistic model.

This paper uses the ANN to replace the logistic regression [25]. The functions for a two-layer neural network can be written as in the following.

$$O_j = f(net_j), net_j = \sum_i w_{i,j} O_i - b_j \tag{5}$$

where O_j d.enotes the output for node j in the output layer; O_i denotes the input for node i in the input layer; f is the transfer function; $O_{i,j}$ denotes a connected weight between jth node in the output layer with ith node in the input layer; b_j represents bias value in the output layer. After fitting the ANN model to all land uses, the current study specifies restricted area and land-use transition rules for the study watershed. Finally, land-use change is allocated in the following iterative procedure based on probability maps, while decision rules are combined with actual land use maps and demand for different land uses.

The model allocates land-use changes by an iterative procedure that utilizes probability maps, decision rules specifying which transitions are possible and allowed, and a series of conversion elasticities accounting for the current land-use maps [10].

2.3 Landscape Metrics

Landscape ecology studies provide many useful conceptual and analytical tools to bridge the gap between planning and ecology [26]. Of these, landscape metrics are particularly promising because they are readily applicable. To assess simulated land-use patterns, this work calculated landscape metrics using the Patch Analyst [27] in ArcView 3.2. This study used seven landscape indices, namely Number of Patches (NP), Mean Patch Size (MPS), Mean Shape Index (MSI), Total Edge (TE), and Mean Nearest Neighbor (MNN) to present the land-use composition and configuration in the Paochiao watershed. Detailed descriptions of the above metrics can be found in McGarigal and Marks (1994) [4, 27].

2.4 Study Watershed and Data

The Paochiao watershed is an urbanized watershed in the Tamsui River Basin. The watershed borders the Taipei metropolitan area (Figure 1) to the south. The Paochiao watershed is approximately 98.61 km^2 with a mean elevation of 214.8 m. Due to expansion of the Taipei metropolitan area, land use and its patterns in the Paochiao watershed have changed over the last decade. Total population in 2000 was 237,861. The watershed area is large, but numerous population results in crowded and thriving land usage. Under increasing population, the watershed has become a high-density urbanized watershed, especially in the downstream watershed area.

Four SPOT images were purchased from the space and remote-sensing research center in Taiwan, and selected for watershed land-use classification on March 27, 1990, December 25, 1993, July 16, 1998, and January 2, 2000. Supervised classification and fuzzy convolution were performed using the software ERDAS IMAGINE with 1/5000 black and white aerial photographs [6]. Land uses were classified into the following six categories: forest; built-up land; cultivated land; grassland; water; and, bare land. Land-use classes of forest, built-up land, cultivated land and grassland had high classification accuracies (92%~96%, 85%~96%, 73%~90% and 63%~90%), while bare land classes had low classification accuracies (42%~60%). Land uses in 2000 were 74.78%, 15.26%, 8.24%, 0.83%, 0.65%, and 0.24% for forest, built-up land, cultivated (agricultural) land, grassland, water, and bare land, respectively (Figure 1).

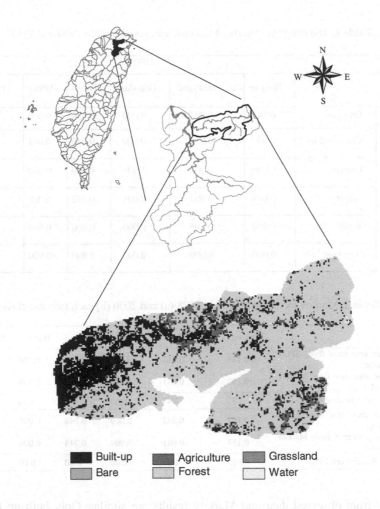

Built-up   **Agriculture**   **Grassland**
Bare   **Forest**   **Water**

Fig. 1. The location of the Paochiao watershed and land use patterns in 2000

3   Results and Discussion

3.1   Demand from Markov Model

This research obtains the transition matrix associated with the system based on land-use classification images in 1990 and 1993 (Table 1). The area percentage of land use for each category in 1990~2050 is simulated by the Markov model. The major land use types in the area are forest, built-up, and cultivated land. To validate the Markov model, this work validates the Markov results compared to reference maps in 1998 and 2000 in Table 2. Results show that the total land area ratio in each land use

Table 1. The transition matrix of land use category between 1990 and 1993

		1993					
		Built-up	Cultivated land	Grassland	Forest	Water	Bare land
1990	Built-up	0.844	0.002	0.000	0.154	0.000	0.000
	Cultivated land	0.006	0.950	0.000	0.043	0.001	0.000
	Grassland	0.000	0.000	1.000	0.000	0.000	0.000
	Forest	0.045	0.002	0.001	0.952	0.000	0.000
	Water	0.000	0.005	0.000	0.000	0.995	0.000
	Bare land	0.000	0.000	0.000	0.000	0.000	1.000

Table 2. Markov model validation in 1998 (a) and 2000 (b) each land use class

	Built-up	Cultivated land	Grassland	Forest	Water	Bare land
(a) The area ratio from SPOT 1998 image	0.138	0.083	0.009	0.762	0.006	0.002
The area ratio from Markov model	0.142	0.081	0.009	0.759	0.006	0.002
Relative error (%)	2.82	2.47	0.00	0.40	0.00	0.00
(b) The area ratio from SPOT 2000 image	0.153	0.082	0.009	0.748	0.006	0.002
The area ratio from Markov model	0.154	0.081	0.009	0.748	0.006	0.002
Relative error (%)	0.65	1.23	0.00	0.00	0.00	0.00

category from observed data and Markov results are similar. Only built-up land in 1998 overestimates by 2.28 % but improves in 2000. This implies that the Markov model performs more effectively. The Markov probabilities estimated from the full period predict the distribution of land use change. However, the CLUSE-s simulates land use patterns each year while the time step in the Markov process is three years. For downscaling, yearly demand relationships are necessary to interpolate by the linear regression model. All results of linear regression models were significant at the $p \leq 0.01$ level. Figure 2 (a) shows the yearly Markov demand based on interpretation results in 2001~2020. The figure clearly shows a considerable change. The built-up land area in the study area increased 22.92% from 240.8 ha in 2000 to 296.0 ha in 2020, and cultivated land in the study area vanished to 22.0 from 130.0 ha in 2000 to 108.0 ha in 2020, with a loss rate reaching 16.95%. Forest land over the next twenty years decreased 36.2 ha from 1179.9 ha in 2000 to 1143.7 ha, and the loss rate reached 6.27%.

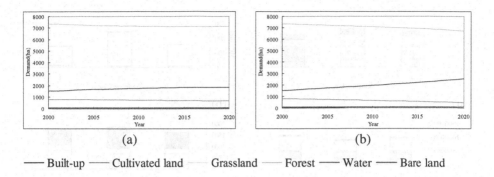

(a)   (b)

—— Built-up —— Cultivated land —— Grassland —— Forest —— Water —— Bare land

Fig. 2. The demand each land use category in 2000~2020 (a) using the Markov model (b) using SLEUTH model

3.2 ANN-CLUE-s and Logistic-CLUE-s Comparison

The current work uses ANN and logistic regression in the CLUE-s to predict probabilities for all land-use classes and measure the relationships between probabilities and driving factors [25]. This section sets the demands in the Logistic-CLUE-s and ANN-CLUE-s according to simulation results obtained by the Markov model for 2001–2020. However, most land-use types are impacted by socio-economic factors, suggesting that urbanization impacts land use in the watershed study. For example, studies included a distance to built-up land depends on the exception of the built-up land in the Paochiao watershed. The population density increases urbanization and generates land-use changes in the watershed. The models defined an area with a slope > 21% as a restricted area. In the models, land-use transition rules indicate that forested, cultivated land, grassland, and bare land can be converted between any of these land-use classes and built-up land, while the water body remains unchanged. The simulated results of Logistic-CLUE-s and ANN-CLUE-s in 1993 and 1998 are validated and summarized using the Kappa, and landscape metrics in the following.

The simulation results of ANN-CLUE-s and Logistic-CLUE-s can be quantified using the Kappa statistic.The results show that the overall accuracy of land-use simulation in 1993 using ANN-CLUE-s and Logistic-CLUE-s in this study reaches 92% and 86%, and the Kappa values are 0.8 and 0.64 respectively. In 1998, the overall accuracy of land-use simulation in ANN-CLUE-s and Logistic-CLUE-s reaches 91% and 85%, and the Kappa values are 0.75 and 0.6 respectively. According to Kappa values, the map agreement is good based on the criteria [14] and simulation accuracy satisfies the requirements of further analysis. The ANN-CLUE-s reveals a high predictive power compared to the Logistic-CLUE-s.

This work uses landscape metrics to assess the abilities of the two techniques such as ANN-CLUE-s and Logistic-CLUE-s models to predict the probabilities of land-use changes, and to demonstrate landscape metrics each land-use class among the simulated maps and the referenced maps in 1993 and 1998 (Figures 3 and 4). Landscape metric values such as the NP, MPS, PSSD, TE, ED, MSI and MNN of the ANN-CLUE-s simulated land-use patterns are more similar in the referenced land use

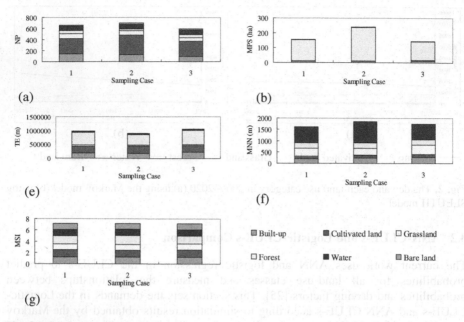

Fig. 3. Model validation in 1993 using landscape metrics (a) NP, (b) MPS, (c) TE (d) MNN (e) MSI in ANN-CLUE-s (Case 1) and Logistic-CLUE-s (Case 2) when compared to the referenced map (Case 3)

classes compared to those of the Logistic-CLUE-s, especially the MPS and MNN. According to the validation statistics, ANN-CLUE-s is superior compared to Logistic-CLUE-s during the validation period. In addition, index analysis shows that forest is the major patch in the studied area but bare land area is minimal. A large number of patches and edge density exist in the built-up area. These indices show the fragmented land-use patterns due to urban sprawl in the Paochiao watershed.

3.3   Future Land Use Change Analyzed Using Landscapes Matrices

The current study analyzes ANN-CLUE-s simulation results based on the two demands from the Markov model and the SLEUTH model for 2001–2020. The SLEUTH model is a cellular automaton pattern-extrapolation model that combines urban growth and the land-cover change model for Monte Carlo growth simulations [6, 28], and calibrates using urban development patterns in the past, forecasting these patterns into the future [6, 25]. Details in SLEUTH modeling could refer to Lin et al., 2008 [6]. Figures 5 and 6 present land-use maps for 2005, 2010, 2015 and 2020, using ANN-CLUE-s with Markov and SLEUTH demands. The ANN-CLUE-s results show that urbanization expansion is more serious from the SLEUTH demand (Figure 2 (b)) than from the Markov demand (Figure 2 (a)). The most developed and frequently changed areas are located in the eastern part of the downstream area and along the major stream of the Paochiao watershed, especially in areas with low elevations. The most cultivated land change occurs in the downstream built-up land. A remarkable

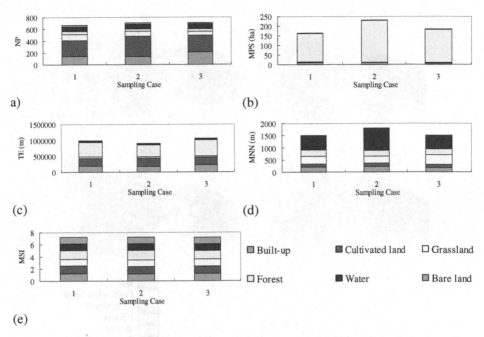

a)   (b)

(c)   (d)

(e)

Fig. 4. Model validation in 1998 using landscape metrics (a) NP, (b) MPS, (c) TE (d) MNN (e) MSI in ANN-CLUE-s (Case 1) and Logistic-CLUE-s (Case 2) when compared to the referenced map (Case 3)

urbanization phenomenon shows that urbanized cell distribution scatters, due to urban sprawl. The urbanized grid cells induce a high probability of urbanization in nearby grid cells. Simulation results indicate that present urbanization priorities include forest, cultivated land, grassland, and bare land in that order.

Landscape metrics are a good judge of changing land use patterns. Comparing landscape metrics of the study can help to understand changes in landscape patterns as well as land-use and detect the differences from two types of predicted demand. The major land use types that depend on areas and change sharply are the forest, cultivated and built-up land. Figures 7 and 8 show the values of landscape metrics for the built-up, and agricultural land patches during the next twenty years in ANN-CLUE-s. The Number of Patch (NP) values of predicted trend decreased in cultivated land and increased in build-up land from 2001 to 2020 significantly (Figures 7 (a) and 8 (a)). Findings clearly show that built-up patches increased sharply with increased urbanization in this region. For built-up areas, the NP calculation using SLEUTH demand increases sharply compared to that using the Markov chain ten years later (Figure 7 (a)). For agricultural land, the NP calculation using SLEUTH demand decreases sharply compared to that using the Markov demand ten years later (Figure 8 (a)).

The values of Mean Patch Size (MPS) of predicted land-uses simulated decreased from 2001 to 2020 in the built-up, agricultural land patches (Figures 7~8 (b)). In Figure 7 (b), the MPS decreased in the built-up class from both demands the first ten years. However, The MPS slightly decreased from Markov demand while MPS

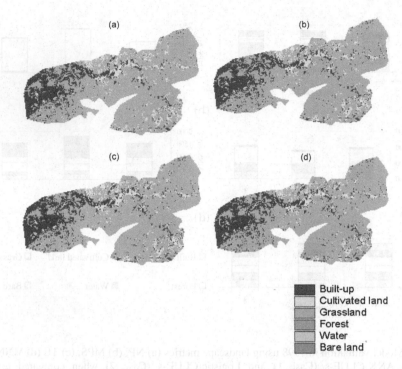

Fig. 5. Spatial land-use distribution in the Paochiao watershed simulated using the Markov model demand: (a) 2005 (b) 2010 (c) 2015 and (d) 2020

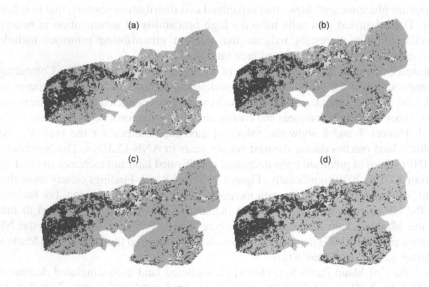

Fig. 6. Spatial land-use distribution in the Paochiao watershed simulated using the SLEUTH model demand: (a) 2005 (b) 2010 (c) 2015 and (d) 2020

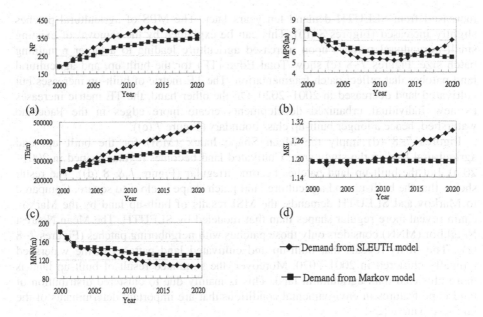

Fig. 7. The dynamic simulated landscape matrices in built-up land (a) NP (b) MPS(c) TE (d) MSI (e) MNN in ANN-CLUE-s

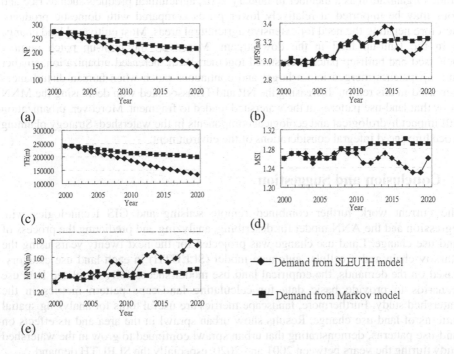

Fig. 8. The dynamic simulated landscape matrices in cultivated land (a) NP (b) MPS(c) TE (d) MSI (e) MNN in ANN-CLUE-s

increased from SLEUTH demand ten years later. The MPS of agricultural patches slightly increased (Figures 8 (b)). This can be explained by the removal of existing small agricultural patches upon increased agriculture leading to a larger remaining patch size. Figures 7~8 (c) show Total Edge (TE) for the built-up, and agricultural land patches that reflect patch fragmentation. The TE metric of built-up increases but cultivated land decreased in 2001~2020. On the other hand, the TE metric increases as new individual urbanized developments create more edges in the Paochiao watershed, hence a longer built-up class boundary (Figure 7 (c)).

Figures 7~8 (d) imply the Mean Shape Index (MSI) for the built up, and agricultural land in the study area. Cultivated land becomes regular shaped in 2001–2020, but the built-up land patches become irregular (Figure 7 & 8 (d)). The result shows that the built-up and agriculture land patch shape is close to square. Compared to Markov and SLEUTH demands, the MSI results of built-up land by the Markov chain reveal more regular shapes than that modeled by SLEUTH. The Mean Nearest Neighbor (MNN) considers only those patches with neighboring patches (Figures 7~8 (e)). The MNN reveals that built-up and cultivated land patterns in the watershed typically clustered in 2001–2020. Moreover, the simulated result of built-up land is more clustered than agricultural land. This is mainly due to clustered distribution of landscape features in environmental conditions that are important determinants of the land-use pattern [29].

From landscape metrics analysis, the patch number and edge in cultivated land decreased but patch sizes increased slightly. Since Taiwan was accepted by the World Trade Organization as a member in January 2002, agricultural products such as rice and flour may be imported at relatively lower prices compared with domestic products, therefore negating the need for extensive agricultural areas. Most cultivated land change is in the built-up land in the downstream. Moreover, the built-up patch number increased and built-up patches clustered together. With increased urbanization, smaller built-up patches merged into a larger and continuous patch when human disturbances increased in this region. Increasing the NP and TE associated with decreasing the MNN show that land-use patterns in the watershed tended to fragment. Moreover, urbanization will impact hydrological and ecological components in the watershed. Strategy planning procedures need integral considerations of the environment.

4   Conclusion and Suggestion

The current work further combined remote sensing and GIS technologies with regression and the ANN model for describing, analyzing and predicting the process of land use change. Land use change was projected for the next twenty years using the Markov chain and a cellular automata model (SLEUTH) in each land use category. Based on the demands, the empirical land use model successfully simulated land use scenarios to provide basic data for calculating landscape pattern metrics in the watershed study. Furthermore, landscape metrics are useful tools for analyzing spatial patterns of land use change. Results show urban sprawl in the area and its effects on land-use patterns, demonstrating that urban sprawl continued to grow in the watershed study during the years between 2001 and 2020, especially the SLEUTH demand.

Future studies could apply this method to other case studies. This study will further research the integration of Markov chain and cellular Automata for land-use modeling and hydrological processes associated with land use change.

Acknowledgements. This study has been supported by National Science Council of Taiwan (No.NSC98-2621-M-002-023). Authors are grateful to the anonymous helpers for their contributions to this study.

References

1. Turner, M.G., Gardner, R.H., O'Neill, R.V.: Landscape Ecology in Theory and Practice: Pattern and Process, pp. 108–109. Springer, New York (2001)
2. Kumar, S., Stohlgren, T.J., Chong, G.W.: Spatial heterogeneity influences native and nonnative plant species richness. Ecol. 87(12), 3186–3199 (2006)
3. Verburg, P.H., van Eck, J.R.R., de Nijs, T.C.M.: Determinants of land-use change patterns in the Netherlands. Environ. Plan. B – Plan. Design 31(1), 125–150 (2004)
4. Mcgarigal, K., Marks, B.J.: FRAGSTATS: Spatial Pattern Analysis Program for Quantifying Landscape Structure. Reference Manual, Forest Science Department, Orgon State University, Corvallis, Oregon, 38–53 (1994)
5. Herold, M., Goldstein, N.C., Clarke, K.C.: The spatiotemporal form of urban growth: measurement, analysis and modeling. Remote Sens. Environ. 86(3), 286–302 (2003)
6. Lin, Y.P., Lin, Y.B., Wang, Y.T., Hong, N.M.: Monitoring and predicting land-use changes and the hydrology of the urbanized Paochiao watershed in Taiwan using remote sensing data, urban growth models and a hydrological model. Sensors 8(1), 658–680 (2008)
7. Jongman, R.H.G.: Landscape ecology in land use planning. In: Wiens, J.A., Moss, M.R. (eds.) Issue in Landscape Ecology. International Association for Landscape Ecology, Guelph, Ontario, pp. 112–118 (1999)
8. Corry, R.C., Nassauer, J.I.: Limitations of using landscape pattern indices to evaluate the ecological consequences of alternative plans and designs. Landscape Urban Plan. 72, 265–280 (2005)
9. Agarwal, C., Green, G.M., Grove, J.M., Evans, T.P., Schweik, C.M.: A Review and Assessment of Land-use Change Models: Dynamics of Space, Time, and Human Choice. US Department of Agriculture, Forest Service, Northeastern Research Station, 12–27 (2002)
10. Verburg, P.H., Soepboer, W., Veldkamp, A., Limpiada, R., Espaldon, V., Sharifah Mastura, S.A.: Modeling the spatial dynamics of regional land-use: the CLUES model. Environ. Manage. 30(3), 391–405 (2002)
11. Castella, J.C., Verburg, P.H.: Combination of process-oriented and pattern-oriented models of land-use change in a mountain area of Vietnam. Ecol. Modl. 202(3-4), 410–420 (2007)
12. Pijanowski, B.C., Brown, D.G., Shellito, B.A., Manik, G.A.: Using neural networks and GIS to forecast land-use changes: a Land Transformation Model. Computers, Environment and Urban Systems 26, 553–575 (2002)
13. Dai, E., Wu, S.H., Shi, W.Z.: Modeling change-pattern-value dynamics on land-use: an integrated GIS and Artificial Neural Networks approach. Environmental Assessment 36(4), 576–591 (2005)

14. Pijanowski, B.C., Pithadia, S., Shellito, B.A.: Calibrating a neural network-based urban change model for two metropolitan areas of the Upper Midwest of the United States. International Journal of Geographical Information Science 19(2), 197–215 (2005)
15. Bourne, L.S.: Physical adjustment processes and land use succession: a review and central city example. Econ. Geogr. 47, 1–15 (1971)
16. Bell, E.J.: Markov analysis of land use change: an application of stochastic processes to remotely sensed data. Soc. Econ. Plan. Sci. 8, 311–316 (1974)
17. Robinson, V.B.: Information theory and sequences of land use: an application. The Prof. Geogr. 30, 174–179 (1978)
18. Jahan, S.: The determination of stability and similarity of Markovian land use change processes: a theoretical and empirical analysis. Soc. Econ. Plan. Sci. 20, 243–251 (1986)
19. Muller, R.M., Middleton, J.: A Markov model of land-use change dynamics in the Niagara region, Ontario, Canada. Landscape Ecol. 9, 151–157 (1994)
20. Brown, D.G., Pijanowski, B.C., Duh, J.D.: Modeling the relationships between land use and land cover on private lands in the Upper Midwest. J. Environ. Manage. 59(4), 247–263 (2000)
21. Weng, Q.: Land use change analysis in the Zhujiang Delta of China using satellite remote sensing, GIS and stochastic modeling. Journal of Environmental Management 64, 273–284 (2002)
22. Wu, Q., Li, H.Q., Wang, R.S.: Monitoring and predicting land use change in Beijing using remote sensing and GIS. Landscape Urban Plan. 78(4), 322–333 (2006)
23. Clarke, K.C., Gaydos, L.J.: Loose-coupling a cellular automaton model and GIS: long-term urban growth prediction for San Fransisco and Washington/Baltimore. Int. J. Geogr. Inf. Sci. 12(7), 699–714 (1998)
24. Billingsley, P.: Statistical methods in Markov chains. Ann. Math. Stat. 32(1), 12–40 (1961)
25. Lin, Y.P., Chu, H.J., Wu, C.F., Verburg, P.H.: Predictive ability of logistic regression, auto-logistic regression and neural network models in empirical land-use change modeling - a case study. Int. J. Geogr. Inf. Sci. (revised)
26. Leitão, A.B., Miller, J., Ahern, J., McGarigal, K.: Measuring Landscapes: A Planner's Handbook. Island Press, Washington D.C (2006)
27. Elkie, P.C., Rempel, R.S., Carr, A.P.: Patch Analyst User Manual: A Tool for Quantifying Landscape Structure. NWST Technical Manual TM- 002. Ontario (1999)
28. Clarke, K.C.: Land Transition Modeling With Deltatrons. In: Proceedings of the Land Use Modeling Conference (1997)
29. Verburg, P.H., Kok, K., Pontius Jr., R.G., Veldkamp, A.: Modeling Land-Use and Land-Cover Change. In: Lambin, E.F., Geist, H.J. (eds.) Land-Use and Land-Cover Change: Local Processes and Global Impacts. The IGBP Series, Springer, Heidelberg (2006)

Should Neighborhood Effect Be Stable in Urban Geosimulation Model? A Case Study of Tokyo

Yaolong Zhao[1], Fei Dong[1,*], and Hong Zhang[2]

[1] South China Normal University, Guangzhou, Guangdong 510631, P.R. China
yaolong@scnu.edu.cn, kmdongfei@gmail.com
[2] Yunan University of Finance and Economics, Kunming, Yunan 650221, P.R. China

Abstract. Neighborhood effect is one of the most important components in the construction of cellular automata (CA) – based urban geosimulation models. Although some literatures have focused on the neighborhood effect in the study of land-use changes, mechanism of the effect still keeps unknown. Purpose of this paper is to explore the dynamics of neighborhood effect in the case study of the Tokyo metropolitan area of Japan. Neighborhood effect in urban dynamics is evaluated for the four time intervals of 1974-1979, 1979-1984, 1984-1989, and 1989-1994 of the Tokyo metropolitan area using a neighborhood interaction model. The results show that neighborhood effect is quite different for the transition of different land-use types. But for one certain land-use type, although the regressed coefficient, which can represent the neighborhood effect, has a slight difference in different time interval, the general trends of coefficient show similar. This finding indicates that neighborhood effect essentially keeps stable during certain long time period.

Keywords: Urban geosimulation model, neighborhood effect, GIS, cellular automata, Tokyo (Japan).

1 Introduction

Urban geosimulation is an effective approach to discern, interpret, and especially forecast the changes of urban land-use pattern and urban form in the process of urban dynamics [1-3]. This approach, generally which is based on Geographic Information Systems (GIS) and Cellular Automata (CA), also becomes a hot issue in the field of GIS [4-6], urban study, complexity science, and even computational science [7]. Especially, urban geosimulation systems have shown powerful function in the field of urban planning [8, 9]. Using such system, the predicted result of urban form and structure in the future, which can be controlled in the system by inputting alternative policy factors, provides intuitional and visual likely subsequences of planning or not planning the future of the cities to urban planners for their spatial decision-making. For achieving such purpose, urban geosimulation system always is calibrated using urban land-use maps, which are the snapshots of urban dynamics, or remote sensing

---

* Corresponding author.

D. Taniar et al. (Eds.): ICCSA 2010, Part I, LNCS 6016, pp. 131–139, 2010.

images at one or more time intervals, generally more than 5 years. The chief purpose of calibration is to estimate the values of parameters in the system which controls the location simulation and the repercussions of activity through time [10]. Generally, the calibration is determined through precision evaluation. Then the system performs the prediction of urban form and structure in the calibrated parameter environment, which commonly is deemed to keeps stable in the process of simulation [11]. Therefore, users' confidence in the predicted results depends on their cognition on urban theory used in the model and the characteristics of assumed stability of parameters. Nevertheless, are the parameters stable in the process of urban dynamics? This question should be answered unambiguously before urban planners can accept the predicted urban form and structure. This paper tries to focus on this issue.

There is an important component in urban geosimulation systems: the local spatial interaction between neighborhood land-use types (i.e. neighborhood interaction) [12, 13]. It affects the transformation of land-use types in the process of urban simulation. Neighborhood effect plus exogenous (like spatial interactions between cities) and endogenous factors (like transportation network in urban area) determine the spatial process of urban land-use changes [14]. In fact, neighborhood interaction between the location of facilities, residential areas and industries has been given more attention in some literatures [12, 15, 16], and it is often addressed as the main factors which decide urban dynamics as other factors like natural constraints and institutional controls (land-use policies) are comparatively stable in spatial process of urban dynamics for a certain period. Neighborhood also has been considered as an important research scale in urban study, such as domestic architecture [17], community culture [18], crime [19], disease and ethnicity [20], poverty and employment [21], and so forth. These literatures emphasized the significance of neighborhood scale in urban dynamics.

In the same way, as one important factor, neighborhood effect in CA-based urban geosimulation models also is always assumed as a constant, which keeps stable in past and future process of urban dynamics, in the process of urban geosimulation implementation [11, 22]. However, question of whether neighborhood interaction should keep stable or not in the process has not been fully examined at both aspects of theoretical and empirical. This status undoubtedly affects user's confidence in simulated results for predicting future urban development using such models. This research aims at providing an empirical analysis of the dynamics of neighborhood effect in the process of urban dynamics to support urban geosimulation models using the Tokyo metropolitan area as a case study.

2 Methodology

2.1 CA-Based Urban Geosimulation

CA has led urban modeling to a new era of geosimulation [1]. It is a rule-based algorithm that has been long employed in computer science to explore social and physical phenomena [23]. CA has shown many advantages for modeling urban phenomena, including their decentralized approach, the link they provide to complexity theory, the connection of form with function and pattern with process, the relative ease with which model results can be visualized, their flexibility, their dynamic approach, and also their affinities with GIS and remotely sensed data [24]. For some time now, CA has been in popular use for urban geosimulation [4, 5, 13, 14, 22, 25-31].

2.2 Study Area and Data

The Tokyo metropolitan area comprises most areas of 5 prefectures of Tokyo, Saitama, Ibaraki, Chiba and Kanagawa, with 143 towns and cities (Fig 1). Total area is 6383 km^2.

In Japan, the period of High Economic Growth which began in the latter half of the 1950s and ended in 1974 led to a massive migration of population from rural to urban areas as well [32, 33]. The concentration of population on Tokyo metropolitan area is particularly noteworthy. Accompanying the increase of population, urbanized area expanded rapidly at an unthinkable speed into the surrounding region. From 1974, the speed of economic growth declined because of the petroleum shock and the period with low-speed growth started. However, urban growth did not stop either in two or three dimensions and turned into a period with correspondingly stable growth. The trend would continue until 2014 according to the result of population projection by National Institute of Population and Social Security Research of Japan. Therefore, Tokyo metropolitan area is a typical study area in understanding urban dynamics.

The data set of "Detailed Digital Information (10m Grid Land Use) Metropolitan Area" of Tokyo is used, which was produced by the Geographical Survey Institute of Japan, and surveyed in 1974, 1979, 1984, 1989, and 1994. The data set was released in 1998 (Geographical Survey Institute 1998). Herein, original 10m grid was grouped into

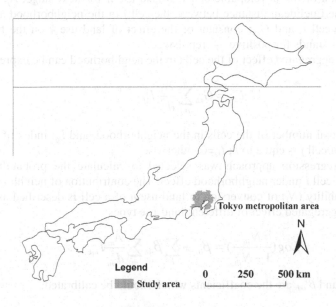

Fig. 1. Study area

100m in a majority rule, and land-use classification with 15 land-use types was set up into 10 categories: vacant, industrial, residential, commercial, road, public, and special, Forest & wasteland, cropland, water. Vacant, industrial, residential, commercial, road, public, and special land are located in the urbanized area, and Forest & wasteland, cropland are in non-urbanized area. Where, vacant, industrial, residential, and commercial land are active features; road, public, and special are active passively; Forest & wasteland and cropland are passive; and water is fixed.

2.3 Neighborhood Interaction Model

Zhao-Murayama neighborhood interaction model is used for analyzing the dynamics of neighborhood effect. This model has been well verified in simulating urban growth of the Tokyo metropolitan area [12]. The integrated model is based on the theory of Tobler's first law of geography, Reilly's law of retail gravitation as well as logistic regression approach. The extended neighborhood area in the urban geosimulation model consists of total 196 cells within the radius of 8 cells from the central cell. It is assumed that in cellular environment all the cells in the neighborhood contribute to the conversion of developable cell i (central cell). The contribution of one cell is associated with the state of itself and the distance to the developable cell i. It can be expressed as follows:

$$f_{kh} = G_{kh} \frac{A_j}{d_{ji}^2}. \tag{1}$$

Where, f_{kh}: constribution of one cell j with land-use k in the neighborhood to the transformation of the developable cell i to land-use h for next stage; A_j: area of the cell j; d_{ji}: the Euclidean distance between the cell j in the neighborhood area and the developable cell i, and G_{kh}: constant of the effect of land-use k on the transition to land-use h. + stands for positive, − repulsive.

Then the aggregated effect of the cells in the neighborhood can be expressed as:

$$F_{kh} = G_{kh} \sum_{j=1}^{m} \frac{A_j}{d_{ji}^2} I_{kj}. \tag{2}$$

Where, m: total number of the cells in the neighborhood, and I_{kj}: index of cells. $I_{kj}=1$, if the state of cell j is equal to k; $I_{kj}=0$, otherwise.

Logical regression approach was selected to calculate the probabilities of the transition of cell i under neighborhood effect. The contribution of neighborhood effect to the probability (N_i) of conversion to land-use h of a cell is described as a function of a set of aggregated effect of different land-use types:

$$Log(\frac{N_{ih}}{1 - N_{ih}}) = \beta'_{0i} + \sum_{k} \beta'_{ikh} \sum_{m} \frac{A_m}{d_{mi}^2} I_{mk}. \tag{3}$$

Where, β'_{oi} and β'_{ikh} are the coefficients which should be calibrated.

2.4 Significance of Regression Coefficients

Regression coefficients β'_{ikh} in formula 3 stand for the effect of different land-use types in the neighborhood on the change of transformation odds $(N_{ik}/(1-N_{ik}))$ of central cell i to land-use type k. If β'_{ikh} is positive, the odds will add with the increase of aggregated effect of land-use type k; and vice versa. If one of the coefficients does not pass hypothesis test at 0.05 level, $\beta'_{ikh} = 0$. This indicates that corresponding land-use type does not affect the transformation of central cell i. In addition, value of the coefficients represents the intensity of effect on the odds. The bigger the value is, the more intensity of the effect. It is obvious that the coefficients are such indices to analyze the effect of land-use types in neighborhood on the transformation of cells. Herein, the coefficients were adopted to analyze the dynamics of neighborhood effect in the process of urban dynamics.

3 Results and Discussions

Urban dynamics of the Tokyo metropolitan area was divided into four stages: 1974-1979, 1979-1984, 1984-1989, and 1989-1994. Obviously, changes of urbanized area and pattern in one stage are different from that in other stages. Neighborhood effect model was used to regress the coefficient β'_{ikh} of different land-use types in the neighborhood for every stage. The coefficients were compared among four stages (Fig 2). Where, horizontal-axis stands for the land-use types which affect the transformation of four active land-use types: vacant, industrial, residential, and commercial land in the neighborhood. Vertical-axis is the value of regression coefficients β'_{ikh}.

3.1 Characteristics of Neighborhood Effect

Fig 2 indicates that neighborhood effect is different for the transformation probability to every active land-use type at each stage. For the transformation to vacant land, values of the coefficient of land-use types are correspondingly small except that of vacant (Fig 2a). This phenomenon comes from the complexity of definition of vacant land, location of which would be determined mostly by other factors rather than neighborhood effect. Fig 2b illustrates that at local interactions, the transformation to industrial land is mostly from the effect of vacant, commercial and itself. Although effect of residential is low, residential land shows a little repulsive to the transformation. In Fig 2c, all the land-use types do not show strong effect on the transformation to residential land. For the transformation to commercial land (Fig 2d), commercial land shows stronger effect than other types. Effect of vacant, residential and public land shows slight compared with others.

In addition, no matter in which stage, the effect value of regression coefficient of each active land-use type on its own transformation is always more than that of other land-use types, especially industrial and commercial land. This phenomenon represents the effect of spatial autocorrelation in the spatial process of urban dynamics in the Tokyo metropolitan area.

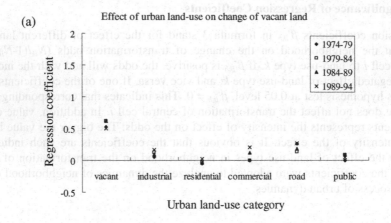

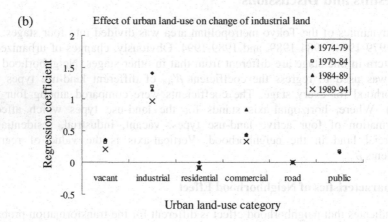

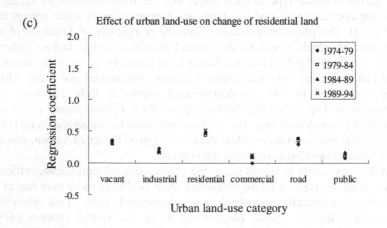

Fig. 2. Comparison of regression coefficient in neighborhood interaction model between the stages of urban dynamics

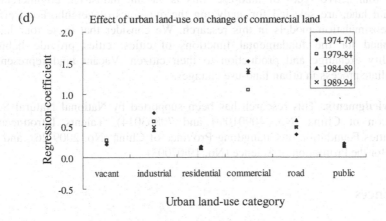

Fig. 2. Continued

3.2 Dynamics of Neighborhood Effect

Comparison of the values of coefficient among four stages indicates the dynamics of neighborhood effect. Although changes of urbanized area and pattern in one stage are different from that in other stages, values of regression coefficient of one land-use type do not shows very obvious variety among stages for every active land-use type generally. This phenomenon shows that neighborhood effect during certain long time period keeps stable in the process of urban dynamics of the Tokyo metropolitan area. The finding empirically supports the conceptual framework of urban geosimulation models for predicting future urban forms. It indicates that such urban geosimulation models based on this neighborhood effect model have ability and confidence to predict future urban form and structure.

Nevertheless, for industrial and commercial land, the differences of effect value of regression coefficient of some land-use types among stages are a little bigger. This maybe represents the change of neighborhood effect of some land-use types on the transformation to one land-use type along with time going. In addition, the slight difference also would be derived from measure or computation errors. This needs further investigation at next step.

4 Concluding Remarks

Neighborhood effect is an important component in CA-based urban geosimulation models. This research empirically indicates that although neighborhood effect is different for the transformation probability of every active land-use type, during certain relatively long time period it keeps stable in the process of urban dynamics. The results empirically support the conceptual framework of urban geosimulation models, and confirm the ability and confidence of urban geosimulation models based on the calibration using past dataset for predicting future urban form and structure.

Only four active types of land-use, this is vacant, industrial, commercial, and residential land, are selected for analyzing the dynamics of neighborhood effect in urban geosimulation models in this research. We consider that these four land-use types stand for the fundamental functions of cities: cities provide habitation, commodity exchange and production to their citizen. Vacant land represents the intermediate process in urban land-use changes.

Acknowledgments. This research has been supported by National Natural Science Foundation of China (No. 40901090 and 70863014), Talents Introduced into Universities Foundation of Guangdong Province of China (No. 2009-26), and Japan Society for the Promotion of Science (No. 19·07003).

References

1. Benenson, I., Torrens, P.M.: Geosimulation: Automata-based Modeling of Urban Phenomena. John Wiley & Sons, Chichester (2004)
2. Torrens, P.M., David, O.S.: Cellular automata and urban simulation: where do we go from here? Environment and Planning B 28, 163–168 (2001)
3. Batty, M.: New ways of looking at cities. Nature 377, 574–574 (1995)
4. Batty, M., Xie, Y., Sun, Z.: Modeling urban dynamics through GIS-based cellular automata. Computers, Environment and Urban Systems 23, 205–233 (1999)
5. Clarke, K.C., Gaydos, L.J.: Loose-coupling a cellular automaton model and GIS: long-term urban growth prediction for San Francisco and Washington/Baltimore. International Journal of Geographical Information Science 12, 699–714 (1998)
6. Goodchild, M.F.: Geographical information science. International Journal of Geographical Information Systems 6, 31–46 (1992)
7. Dragicevic, S.: GeoComputation: Modeling with spatial agents. Computers, Environment and Urban Systems 32, 415–416 (2008)
8. Stevens, D., Dragicevic, S., Rothley, K.: iCity: A GIS-CA modelling tool for urban planning and decision making. Environmental Modelling & Software 22, 761–773 (2007)
9. Yeh, A.G.O., Li, X.: A constrained CA model for the simulation and planning of sustainable urban forms by using GIS. Environment and Planning B 28, 733–753 (2001)
10. Batty, M.: Modeling cities as dynamics systems. Nature 231, 426–428 (1971)
11. White, R., Engelen, G.: Cellular automata and fractal urban form: a cellular modelling approach to the evolution of urban land-use patters. Environment and Planning A 25, 1175–1199 (1993)
12. Zhao, Y., Murayama, Y.: A new method to model neighborhood interaction in Cellular Automata-based urban geosimulation. In: Shi, Y., van Albada, G.D., Dongarra, J., Sloot, P.M.A. (eds.) ICCS 2007. LNCS, vol. 4488, pp. 550–557. Springer, Heidelberg (2007)
13. White, R., Engelen, G., Uljee, I.: The use of constrained cellular automata for high-resolution modeling of urban land-use dynamics. Environment and Planning B 24, 323–343 (1997)
14. White, R., Engelen, G.: High-resolution integrated modelling of the spatial dynamics of urban and regional systems. Computers, Environment and Urban Systems 24, 383–400 (2000)
15. Phipps, M.: Dynamic behavior of cellular automata under the constraint of neighborhood coherence. Geographical Analysis 21, 197–215 (1989)

16. Yang, Y., Billings, S.A.: Neighborhood detection and rule selection from cellular automata pattern. IEEE Transactions on Systems, Man, and Cybernetics - Part A: Systems and Humans 30, 840–847 (2000)
17. Mock, J.: Social impact of changing domestic architecture in a neighborhood in Sapporo, Japan. City & Society 2, 41–49 (1988)
18. Halperin, R.H.: Practicing Community: Class, Culture and Power in an Urban Neighborhood. University of Taxas Press, Austin (1998)
19. Zhang, L., Messner, S.F., Liu, J.: An exploration of the determinants of reporting crime to the police in the city of Tianjin, China. Criminology 45, 959–984 (2007)
20. Cotter, J.V., Patrick, L.L.: Disease and ethnicity in an urban environment. Annals of the Association of American Geographers 71, 40–49 (1981)
21. Holloway, S.R., Mulherin, S.: The effect of adolescent neighborhood poverty on adult employment. Journal of Urban Affairs 26, 427–454 (2004)
22. Wu, F.: Calibration of stochastic cellular automata: the application to rural-urban land conversions. International Journal of Geographical Information Science 16, 795–818 (2002)
23. Wolfram, S.: A New Kind of Science. Wolfram Media, Champaign (2002)
24. Torrens, P.M.: How cellular models of urban systems work. Centre for Advanced Spatial Analysis (CASA), University of College London (2000)
25. Yeh, A.G.O., Li, X.: A cellular automata model to simulate development density for urban planning. Environment and Planning B 29, 431–450 (2002)
26. Yeh, A.G.O., Li, X.: Sustainable land development model for rapid growth areas using GIS. International Journal of Geographical Information Science 12, 169–189 (1998)
27. Li, X., Yeh, A.G.O.: Modeling sustainable urban development by the integration of constrained cellular automata and GIS. International Journal of Geographical Information Science 14, 131–152 (2000)
28. Wu, F.: SimLand: a prototype to simulate land conversion through the integrated GIS and CA with AHP-derived transition rules. International Journal of Geographical Information Science 12, 63–82 (1998)
29. Batty, M.: Urban evolution on the desktop: simulation with the use of extended cellular automata. Environment and Planning A 30, 1943–1967 (1998)
30. Barredo, J.I., Kasanko, M., McCormick, N., Lavalle, C.: Modelling dynamic spatial processes: simulation of urban future scenarios through cellular automata. Landscape and Urban Planning 64, 145–160 (2003)
31. Clarke, K.C., Hoppen, S., Gaydos, L.: A self-modifying cellular automaton model of historical urbanization in the San Francisco Bay area. Environment and Planning B 24, 247–261 (1997)
32. Murayama, Y.: Japanese Urban System. Kluwer Academic Publishers, Dordrecht (2000)
33. Okawa, I.: Regional transformation of the Tokyo metropolitan area. Taimeido, Tokyo (1989) (in Japanese)

A Fuzzy Cellular Automata Modeling Approach – Accessing Urban Growth Dynamics in Linguistic Terms

Lefteris A. Mantelas[1], Thomas Hatzichristos[2], and Poulicos Prastacos[1]

[1] Regional Analysis Division, Institute of Applied and Computational
Mathematics, Foundation for Research and Technology-Hellas,
GR 71110, Heraclion Crete, Greece
mantelas@iacm.forth.gr,
poulicos@iacm.forth.gr
[2] Department of Geography and Regional Planning, National
Technical University of Athens, I.Politechniou 9,
GR 15786, Zografou, Greece
thomasx@survey.ntua.gr

Abstract. This paper presents a methodological framework for urban modeling which accesses the multi-level urban growth dynamics and expresses them in linguistic terms. In this approach a set of parallel fuzzy systems is used, each one of which focuses on different aspects of the urban growth dynamics, different drivers or restriction of development and concludes over the suitability for urbanization for each area. As a result the systems' structure and connection merge the input variables into a single variable providing an information flow familiar to the human conceptualization of the phenomenon. At the same time, the structure does not pose severe data requirements while the utilization of parallel connection between fuzzy systems allows the user to add or remove variables without altering the ways in which other variables affect the knowledge base. Following, a fuzzy system that incorporates cellular automata techniques simulates the horizontal and vertical urban growth. The proposed model is applied and tested in the Mesogeia area in the Attica basin (Athens) and fits reality in average by 76% (LeeShalle index) while the average cell error is 19%. Nevertheless, the benefits obtained in the herein presented approach lie in the information management and representation.

Keywords: Urban Growth, Rule-based Modeling, Cellular Automata, Fuzzy Logic, Mesogia Athens.

1 Introduction

Urban growth is a global phenomenon and one of the most important reforming processes effecting both natural and human environment through many ecological and socioeconomic aspects. It is a phenomenon inherent to human civilization and present in various forms in different stages of human history; from a social point of view, it could be described as a spontaneous spatially referenced tradeoff between different types of human needs and expectations. Given the recent urban population growth

D. Taniar et al. (Eds.): ICCSA 2010, Part I, LNCS 6016, pp. 140–151, 2010.
© Springer-Verlag Berlin Heidelberg 2010

rates and the fact that urban society's needs in space, services, facilities and energy, increase faster than its population does, it is of major importance that urban growth occurs in an planned way, maximizing the benefits for urban population while minimizing both economical and environmental cost. What is equally important is that growth should occur in a sustainable way providing the future societies with the opportunity to deal with their needs.

The term 'modeling' refers to creating a strictly defined analog of real world by subtraction [1]. Yet there is no rigorous framework for modeling such a spatiotemporal phenomenon as urban growth since there lies great inherent spatial, temporal and decision-making heterogeneity [2], which results from socio-economic and ecological heterogeneity itself. Moreover there is something special regarding the spatiotemporal nature of the urban growth. Urban growth does not simply evolve in time; it also spreads in space and not always continuously. That means that apart from the difficulties of studying a spatial phenomenon, when studying urban growth we may (actually it's rather impossible not to) come across first-seen qualitative phenomena and interactions, that cannot be modeled mathematically in an easy way. The problem seems to be that our knowledge, both theory-driven and data-driven, is not really describing urban growth dynamics in general, but instead the part of the urban growth dynamics that have already occurred and have been observed and experienced. What is more, knowledge about the operational scale(s) of urban form and process, and the interaction and parallelism among different scales, is poor [3].

We deal with a phenomenon which exists but it is also recreated in space, extending itself both continuously and discontinuously in space while evolving in time. Moreover, its dynamics evolve in time as well and all there is for modeling urban growth is our experience of the phenomenon itself, which might be inaccurate for describing its future evolution. Considering further that an urban growth model is a spatial planning tool, it's clear that the usability of the estimations and the knowledge provided by the model are as much important as the model's consistency to the real world.

While most contemporary urban models go through an in depth analysis of selected parameters, we propose a modeling structure that allows the parallel "in-width" analysis of any given spatial or spatially referenced variable. Our approach uses spatial – and potentially temporal – rules that may be either data-driven or theory-driven; hence they may fit better to reality allowing the user to overcome the limitations of the available data by using exogenous knowledge adapted to the model by empirical similarity patterns. Empirical rules are enabled by the fact that the knowledge base is expressed in common language, which makes this model friendly and usable, especially to the non-expert users. We propose a structure of fuzzy systems that are serial, parallel or encapsulated to each other. Apparently the model's structure and the systems' connection are tightly related to the model's efficiency, the information's flow and the interpretability of the extracted knowledge. Each system receives different input and concludes over certain aspects of the overall dynamics while the system that estimates the evolution of the urban growth further incorporates cellular automata (CA) techniques. Both CA and fuzzy logic are briefly introduced in the next session.

2   Cellular Automata and Fuzzy Logic

Cellular Automata (CA) is a computational methodology that has been applied to various science fields, such as numerical analysis, computational fluid dynamics, simulation of biological and ecological systems, traffic analysis, growth phenomena modeling, etc. In CA the system under study is divided into a set of cells with each cell interacting with all other cells belonging to predefined neighborhoods through a set of simple rules [4]. The interactions take place in discrete time steps with each cell's state at any time period estimated by considering the state of the neighboring cells. This approach is repeated continuously in a self-reproductive mechanism with no external interference. Growth is thus simulated through a bottom up approach and this makes CA an appropriate technique for simulating complex phenomena that is difficult to model with other approaches. There is a great variety of highly sophisticated crisp approaches concerning CA based urban growth modeling. Among them, the stochastic approach of Mulianat et al [5], the object-oriented approaches of Cage [6] and Obeus [7], the approach proposed by Morshed [8], the environment Laude that combine CA and Genetic Algorithms and other widely applied models, such as Sleuth [3]. These models are either quantitative or qualitative. Quantitative numerical models focus on the efficiency of the estimations and may provide accurate results. What such models are not capable of is to map and express the qualitative characteristics of urban growth phenomenon, which are a result of the socio-economic decision making of the urban population. Qualitative rule-based models on the other hand are capable of such mapping and expression since they focus on the quality of causes and effects. Nevertheless, in the binary world of classical rule-based systems, qualities, objects and relations are strictly defined and they either exist or not. There is no such thing as partial, uncertain or imprecise fact, membership or relation and this is not the way it works in real world.

Fuzzy logic allows the continuous analysis between "false" and "true" and bridges the gap between qualitative and quantitative modeling. Fuzzy logic was originally proposed by Zadeh [9] as a generalization of binary logic and is used to model imprecision, vagueness and uncertainty in real world. Fuzzy logic does not comply with the binary property of dichotomy; hence fuzzy variables may consist of partially overlapping fuzzy sets. When a fuzzy set is meant to manage quantitative (numerical) information, it is fully described by a membership function which returns a membership value (μ) within [0,1] for a given object in the fuzzy set. Otherwise we refer to them as fuzzy symbols. For each fuzzy set, a linguistic variable familiar to its quality is used. Linguistic variables, apart from describing primitive fuzzy sets, are also used to define new sets, based on the primitive ones. This is accomplished by applying fuzzy hedges which are verbal definitions, such as 'more or less', 'not', 'very' etc. Each hedge is joined to a numerical expression which is applied to the membership function of the primitive set. Linguistics in fuzzy logic, allow the management of information in a way closer to this of human conceptualization.

The knowledge base is represented as "IF…THEN" rules, connecting hypotheses to conclusions through a certainty factor. The most frequently used inference engines are the Mamdani and the Sugeno approach. In the Mamdani approach, the inference engine is divided into the stages of aggregation, implication and accumulation [10][11]. Aggregation returns the fulfillment of hypothesis for every rule individually, implication combines aggregation's result to the rule's certainty factor (CF) resulting to the degree of fulfillment for each rule's conclusion, while accumulation corresponds to compromising different individual conclusions into a final result. The Sugeno approach is very similar, the main difference being that the rule's conclusion may either be a constant or a function of the rule's hypothesis [11][12]. In our case, fuzzy logic provides a proper framework for managing both qualitative and quantitative information and describing facts and relations using linguistic terms.

Recently a few fuzzy approaches have been proposed; Dragicevic [13] and Liu et al [14] introduce single fuzzy systems in CA based urban modeling. They both propose the use of transition functions that are influenced by the various input variables. Dragicevic uses a single variable function for each type of transition (from a certain land use to another) while Liu uses a set of predefined functions, only one of which is applied in each cell for a single step. These approaches resemble to the Sugeno approach. The key concept in those approaches is familiar to the model we herein propose but there are many differences and technical advantages. First of all we propose a structured set of fuzzy systems instead of a single system; this way we may analyze separately the effect of various parameters to the urbanization process. What is more, we emphasize on the specialized use of fuzzy algebra and suggest a new operator so that we can deal with the urbanization process in both a qualitative and a quantitative way. Spatial expansion is simulated by a Mamdani inference engine while intensification is simulated by a Sugeno inference engine. What is more, we incorporate simple rules to improve the knowledge interpretability and introduce fuzzy hedges and spatial variability for more efficient simulation and more accurate description of the urban growth patterns. Finally, instead of predefined (Liu) or undefined (Dragicevic) rules we developed a transferable generic rule-extraction module that is used to produce an initial knowledge base. More technical information is given in the next session.

3 Modeling Shell Structure

We have developed a modeling structure (figure 1) based on our previous work [15][16] that attempts to describe a work flow familiar to the human perception of the urban growth process. A structure based upon the relations between facts and procedures so that even partial results may be helpful to the better understanding of the process. Moreover, a generic form of the model is sustained to avoid data limitation (more data provide better results, less data still provide results though); hence the model is fully transferable to both data-rich and data-poor applications. Initially a group of qualitative fuzzy systems is used to process the input data and estimate the suitability for urbanization for separate sets of variables. The themes that can be used depend on data availability with physical (slope, soil), natural (land use), accessibility (road networks) being the obvious ones. Rules in these systems have a plain hypothesis premise and depict the average distribution of urban status appearance for each value of each variable within the set and conclude over thematic suitability indexes that consist of three ordered fuzzy symbols (low, average, high).

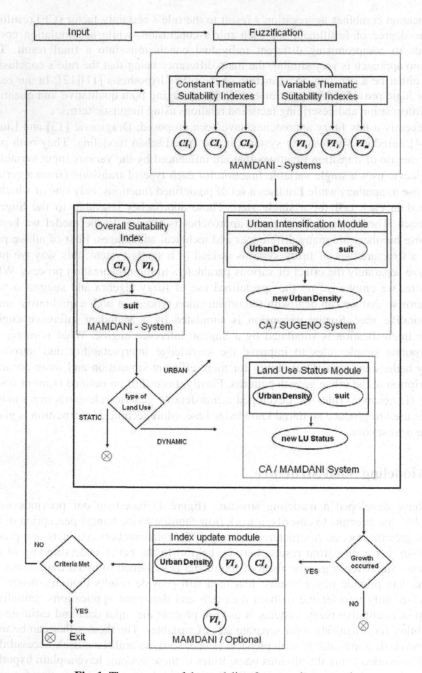

Fig. 1. The structure of the modeling framework proposed

These thematic indexes are either static (i.e. physical) or variable in time (i.e. accessibility) and may alter in subsequent stages if knowledge about their evolution is acquired or in order to simulate alternative scenarios. Following, thematic suitability indexes are merged into a single overall suitability index which depicts the propensity of each cell to support urbanization process - overall suitability consists of two fuzzy symbols (low-high). This is accomplished by a separate fuzzy system that uses exclusively the Algebraic Sum as an accumulation operator in the paradigm of the Dempster-Shafer theory of evidence [17]. The basic notion of this operator is that the more rules that lead to the same conclusion, the less likely it is for this conclusion to be false. Its advantage is that it takes into account not only the strength of each result but also the number of rules that conclude to this specific result; it's disadvantage on the other hand is that since it tends to return higher values as the number of rules increase it takes a finer tuning to work efficiently. Moreover this operator should apply to rules whose hypotheses are relatively independent from each other.

The suitability systems, apart from providing useful intermediate results, are used for three purposes. To start with, they result into decreasing the number of variables used in the following systems, making thus easier the further analysis and allowing the user to use more simple and hence more comprehensible rules; for modeling, simplification is both necessary and useful [18]. What is next, each thematic system focuses on both the relations and the diversifications of the input variables (i.e. if density of road network is positive, then obviously the distance from road network is zero and vice versa) and as a result the outputs – the thematic indexes – tend to be less correlated to each other than the input variables. Finally, it is much easier and less risky to update the (variable) thematic indexes rather than the initial variables.

Thematic fuzzy systems run only once and afterwards, the area of study is divided into three groups – static non urban, dynamic non urban and urban. The static and dynamic non-urban groups are described by a crisp set (membership is 0/1) while urban is a fuzzy set. Static areas remain untouched by the model and no growth takes place in these cells – these cells might be covered by forests, have very high slopes or similar criteria that may originate by statistical analysis, empirical knowledge or combination.

Dynamic non urban areas are then processed by a hybrid Mamdani fuzzy system that incorporates CA techniques in order to simulate the transition from non urban to urban while (dynamic) urban areas are managed by a hybrid Sugeno fuzzy system. In the Sugeno system a new exponential operator has been introduced to simulate the vertical growth of partially urbanized cells. While the linguistic syntax of the rule is the same, the computational difference is that the new operator raises the membership value of the conclusion premise in the power of the hypothesis complement. Given the fact that membership values, certainty factors and aggregation results are bounded in [0,1], if the hypothesis of the rule is not met at all, such a rule results to no change in the fuzzy set of the conclusion; it returns the initial membership value. On the other hand if the hypothesis is fully met and the rule is deterministic, it results to a certain conclusion – a membership value 1. In any other case it returns a membership value within (m,1) where m is the initial membership value. Both urban systems use Moore neighborhood of various radius.

Once the whole area has been processed, a last qualitative system may be applied in the areas that any type of growth (expansion or intensification) has occurred, updating the variable thematic suitability indexes. This takes place if knowledge about the evolution of dynamic variables is acquired (i.e. road network development) or if alternative scenarios are to be populated. The whole process runs iteratively until exit criteria are met; that is to allocate the projected urban cover which is an exogenous parameter to the model.

Though the main idea of combining CA and fuzzy logic exists in previous approaches, the herein presented approach presents some advantages, namely:

- it does not require specific data to calibrate and apply,
- a reducible/extensible form of knowledge base is used,
- fuzzy hedges are enabled both in rule's hypothesis and conclusion,
- spatio-temporal parameters may be taken into consideration within each rule's certainty,
- both qualitative and quantitative management of information is enabled.

In order to extract the rules for the qualitative non-CA fuzzy systems we calculate the fitting between each fuzzy set of each input variable and each fuzzy set of the urban cover variable (the output). This takes place upon data that refer to the starting time point excluding the areas that are considered static. This way, each fuzzy set of each input variable forms the rule's hypothesis while as the correspondent certainty factor is taken the value of the fitting without any further calibration being required at this stage; i.e. the sets "low distance from secondary road network" and "high urban cover" fit each other by 56%, hence the rule becomes:

IF *"distance from secondary road network"* is LOW, THEN *"urban cover"* is HIGH
| CF=0.56

A more sophisticated approach would be to consider not only single attributes – simple rules, but combinations of attributes – complex rules with fuzzy sets intersections as well [19]. In that case the accuracy of the model could be improved, but it would affect the simplicity and hence the interpretability and the generality of the knowledge base. What we gain by keeping the rules simple, is that if another variable is to be added, then all we need to do is add the rules that describe its own effect to the phenomenon, without altering any of the initial rules.

In the hybrid fuzzy systems we use simple empirical or common sense rules that are subjected to a calibration process to determine the certainty factors. Due to the (in general) irreversible nature of CA, data for two time-points may depict the result of the CA process but not the dynamic or the specific form of its transition engine; in such a system, simulation is the only way to predict outcomes [20]. At this stage, having already reduced the number of variables that are used, it is relatively easy - and even kind of fun in a more literal sense of Urban Gaming Simulations [21] to experiment with each rule's syntax and its parameters fine tuning.

Rules (in all systems) may be spatial, which means that the same rule performs differently in different locations. Spatial variability is gained by expressing rules' certainty factors in terms of a spatial 2-D fuzzy variable with 9 fuzzy sets which expresses the relative location of a cell within the study area (figure 2). Temporality (the same rule changing behavior as time – steps – passes) can be introduced likewise if a sufficient time-series of data is available.

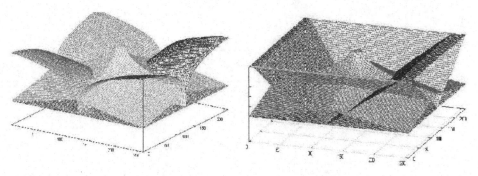

Fig. 2. graphs of the fuzzy sets of the 2-D spatial variable, the horizontal level is a square re-parameterization of the area under study while the vertical axis is the membership values for each spatial fuzzy set (center, N, S, E, W on the right and NE, NW, SE, SW on the left) that are represented with different colors

4 Case Study

The model was applied in the Mesogia area (figure 3) at the eastern part of the Attica basin (Athens), an area of 632 square km that is located within 25km from the historical center of Athens, yet it used to be agricultural until 15-20 years ago when it started to develop rapidly; more specifically, from 1988 till today urban cover in Mesogia has been doubled. Recently the new international airport, the extension of the subway and train lines and the construction of a new highway in Mesogia have influenced urban growth not only in terms of the growth rate but also in terms of the location of the growth. What is more, Mesogia can be considered relatively autonomous when studying urban growth since it is physically separated by the mount of Hemmetus in the West and Aegean Sea in the East, while neither Northern, nor Southern areas are significantly urbanized.

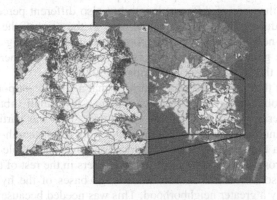

Fig. 3. Mesogia - the wider and specific area under study

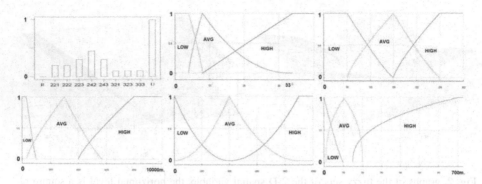

Fig. 4. membership functions of the fuzzy sets(low, average and high) for each input variable (clockwise) corine (singleton), slope, density and distance from primary and secondary road network

In our study the available data for Mesogia include the Corine Land Cover database (100X100m for 1990 and 2000 available from European Environmental Agency and a Corine based classification for 2004 produced by GeoInformation SA). Most of the area is classified as Agricultural or Forest/Semi-natural while the vast majority of Artificial Surface is mainly Urban Fabric with the exception of the airport. The road network for years 2000 and 2004 was provided by Infocharta Ltd while an estimation of the road network for 1990 was produced based on a satellite image of the area for 1990. Road network data were classified in primary and secondary and layers of distance and density were derived. What is more, a 90m resolution DEM of the area was acquired from the SRTM webpage. Land Use data were represented as singletons (one for each corine class) while for each quantitative variable three fuzzy sets (low, average and high) were empirically defined (figure 4).

The period 1990-2000 was used in order to extract knowledge base and calibrate the model while the period 2000-2004 was used to check the fitting of the model to the real world. Initially, these two periods appear not to be directly comparable to each other, since they are of different length but also different percentages of urban growth occurred during them. Nevertheless, due to the airport, the metro/train line extension and the new highway that were completed in 2001 among other reasons for the 2004 Olympic games, the growth observed – in absolute numbers - during 2000-2004 is similar to the growth observed during 1990-2000.

First results for the 1990-2000 period showed that a significant portion of the error occurred in the south-east part of the area where a few small urban clusters grow faster than the average growth rate of the whole area. This was partially dealt by increasing the certainty factor of the suitability rules only for the south-east area and not for the whole area under study. If the CFs increases over the whole area, significant overestimation error occurs around large urban clusters in the rest of the areas. Spatial variability was also introduced in both knowledge bases of the hybrid systems, in order to use locally a greater neighborhood. This was needed because in CA, information may propagate at most at a distance equal to the neighborhood radius used per iterative step. An alternative approach would be to search for qualitative measures that distinguish those specific areas from the others, but this was not possible at this

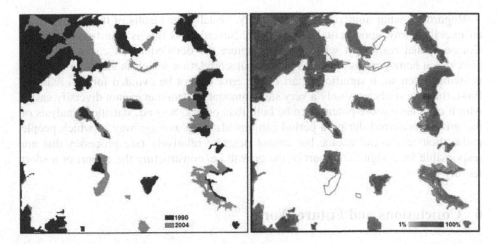

Fig. 5. Actual urban cover for 1990 (blue) and 2004 (green) – left – and estimation of the 2004 urban cover based on 1990 – right

level of analysis with such few available data. Visual comparison between results and reality introduced fuzzy hedges in the final knowledge base which produced estimation for urban cover in 2000 based on 1990 with an average error of 20% or 0.75 LeeShalle index.

Following, these rules were applied on the 2000 data to provide estimations for 2004. The results fit the actual 2004 urban cover by 82% (or 18% average error per cell) while the LeeShalle index reaches 0.77. As a final test, the same knowledge base was used to simulate urban growth for the period 1990-2004 during which urban cover in the area grew from 90 square km to 142 or by 55%. The model's estimations for 2004 based on 1990 (figure 5) fit real data by 0.74% (LeeShalle) while the average cell error is and 25%.

While the error indexes (table 1) suggest that the model can provide useful estimations of future urban growth, a more thorough view of the error indexes and specifically their evolution over the iterations of the algorithm suggests that the optimum – in terms of error indexes – is reached a few steps before the algorithm exits and hence error is slightly increased during the last few steps. This is partially due to the exit criterion which introduces dependencies between the two types of possible error - either a rural cell is considered urban or vice versa. That means that, more or less, for each mistakenly considered urban cell there is another cell, mistakenly considered rural and after some steps more cells are allocated inaccurately rather than accurately.

Table 1. Error indexes for cases studied

Period	Average Cell Error	LeeShalle
2000 I 1990	20%	0.75
2004 I 2000	18%	0.77
2004 I 1990	25%	0.74

Regardless what numerical indexes imply, visually the results of the models fit in an excellent way upon actual urban cover. Nevertheless this is also because of the Corine spatial resolution which cannot capture the detailed urban cover but rather provides a homogenous shape with high autocorrelation which is easier to simulate growing. Even so, a significant part of the error cannot be avoided for two reasons. First, the case study uses only a very small amount of data that cannot diversify easily which cells have more potential to be built than others. Second, statistical analysis of the growth occurred during a period can elucidate the average way in which people make their residential choice but cannot describe relatively rare processes that are responsible for a significant part of the growth i.e. constructing the airport or a sport facility etc.

6   Conclusions and Future Work

We developed and presented an urban model that provides a parallel connection be-tween input variables and can easily be transferred to both data rich and data poor cases. The model was calibrated and applied in Mesogia area in east Attica (Athens) and is capable of providing satisfactory estimations of the future urban growth pat-terns at least in the short-term. The fitting indicators suggest that the model simulates efficiently the qualitative patterns of the urban expansion in the study area which is further certified by visual comparison. This is partially due to the CA techniques incorporated, that are proved very efficient in simulating the spread of existing urban cover. What they lack, and this is because of the CA nature, is the ability to capture the urbanization of detached areas. For that reason we intend to introduce agent-like rules in the next version of the model.

Fuzzy logic is an advisable way to deal with vague data and stochastic relations since it enhances the potential qualitative resolution of the model and provides the proper tools for uncertainty management. It allows the process of information in both a qualitative and a quantitative way and expresses the dynamic of the phenomenon in common linguistic terms. The rules syntax is kept simple and hence comprehensible; as a result the user can easily calibrate the model empirically and introduce changes such as spatial variability or fuzzy hedges to improve the performance of the model. Both the parallel accumulation operator and the polynomial implication operator improve the model's behavior despite their need for fine tuning. Finally, temporal rules are in general supported by this model but the available data set is not rich enough to allow the extraction of a temporal knowledge base. Acquiring rich data to experiment on temporal rules is one possible direction towards which future work could be directed. More challenging though is to test this model in data of higher spatial resolution that are less auto-correlated and present more complex patterns of growth.

Acknowledgements. The research leading to these results has received funding from the European Community's Seventh Framework Programme FP7/2007-2013 under grant agreement n° 212034.

References

1. Κουτσόπουλος, Κ.: Γεωγραφικά συστήματα πληροφοριών και ανάλυση χώρου, Εκδόσεις Παπασωτηρίου, Αθήνα (2002)
2. Cheng, J., Masser, I.: Understanding Urban Growth System: Theories and Methods. In: 8th International Conference on Computers in Urban Planning and Urban Management, Sendai City, Japan (2003)
3. Dietzel, C., Clarke, K.C.: Replication of Spatio-Temporal Land Use Patterns at three Levels of Aggregation by an Urban Cellular Automata. In: Sloot, P.M.A., Chopard, B., Hoekstra, A.G. (eds.) ACRI 2004. LNCS, vol. 3305, pp. 523–532. Springer, Heidelberg (2004)
4. Krawczyk, R.J.: Architectural Interpretation of Cellular Automata. Presented at NKS 2003, Boston (2003)
5. Mulianat, I., Hariadi, Y.: Urban Area Development in Stochastic Cellular Automata. In: Urban/Regional, EconWPA (2004)
6. Blecic, I., Cecchini, A., Prastacos, P., Trunfio, G.A., Verigos, E.: Modelling Urban Dynamics with Cellular Automata: A Model of the City of Heraclion. In: 7th AGILE Conference on Geographic Information Science. University of Crete Press, Heraklion (2004)
7. Benenson, I., Kharbash, V.: Geographic Automata Systems and the OBEUS Software for their Implementation. In: Complex Artificial Environments, pp. 137–153. Springer, Heidelberg (2006)
8. Morshed, A.: Land Use Change Dynamics: a Dynamic Spatial Simulation. PhD Thesis (2002)
9. Zadeh, L.A.: Fuzzy Sets. Information and Control (8), 338–353 (1965)
10. Kirschfink, H., Lieven, K.: Basic Tools for Fuzzy Modeling. Tutorial on Intelligent Traffic Management Models in Helsinki (1999)
11. Hatzichristos, T.: GIS and Fuzzy Logic in Spatial Analysis. Educational notes, NTUA (2001)
12. http://www.mathworks.com/access/helpdesk/help/toolbox/fuzzy/fp49243.html
13. Dragicevic, S.: Coupling Fuzzy Sets Theory and GIS-based Cellular Automata for Land-Use Change Modeling. In: Fuzzy Information, IEEE Annual Meeting of the Processing NAFIPS 2004, Banff, Canada, vol. 1, pp. 203–207 (2004)
14. Liu, Y., Phinn, S.R.: Developing a Cellular Automaton Model of Urban Growth Incorporating Fuzzy Set Approaches. Proceedings of the 6th International Conference on Geo-Computation, University of Queensland, Brisbane, Australia (2001)
15. Mantelas, L., Hatzichristos, T., Prastacos, P.: A Fuzzy Cellular Automata Based Shell for Modeling Urban Growth – A Pilot Application in Mesogia Area. In: 10th AGILE International Conference on Geographic Information Science, Aalborg University, Denmark (2007)
16. Mantelas, L., Hatzichristos, T., Prastacos, P.: Modeling Urban Growth using Fuzzy Cellular Automata. In: 11th AGILE International Conference on Geographic Information Science, Girona, Spain (2008)
17. Ahmadzadeh, M., Petrou, M.: An Expert System With Uncertain Rules Based on Dempster-Shafer Theory. In: IEEE International Geoscience and Remote Sensing Symposium, IGARSS, Sydney, Australia (2001)
18. Ness, G.D., Low, M.M.: Five Cities: Modelling Asian Urban Population-Environment Dynamics, pp. 43–67. Oxford University Press, Oxford (2000)
19. Cuesta, R.C., Diaz, I., Cuadrado, A.A., Diez, A.B.: A Visual Approach for Fuzzy Rule Induction. In: Proceeding Emerging Technologies and Factory Automation conference, Lisbon, Portugal (2003)
20. Clarke, K.C., Hoppen, S., Gaydos, L.: A Self-Modifying Cellular Automaton Model of Historical Urbanization in the San Francisco Bay Area. Environment and Planning B, Planning and Design 24, 247–261 (1997)
21. Cecchini, A., Rizzi, P.: Is Urban Gaming Simulation Useful? Simulation Gaming 32(4), 507 (2001)

Computer-Based Methods for a Socially Sustainable Urban and Regional Planning - CoMStaR

Jens Steinhöfel, Frauke Anders, Hermann Köhler, Dominik Kalisch,
and Reinhard König

Bauhaus-University Weimar, Faculty of Architecture,
Chair Computer Science in Architecture,
Belvederer Allee 1, 99421 Weimar, Germany
{Jens.Steinhoefel,Dominik.Kalisch,Frauke.Anders,
Hermann.Koehler,Reinhard.Koenig}@uni-weimar.de

Abstract. Global restructuring and urbanisation presents a great challenge for urban and regional planning and highlights a pressing need for sustainable planning strategies. The research project CoMStaR aims to provide a methodical instrument that takes into account the social dimension of sustainability by making it possible to assess current models of urban planning from the viewpoint of social sustainability.

Simulation techniques such as agent-based models and graph-based analytical procedures help to reveal new ways of approaching relevant planning issues. By combining these with large-scale empirical data it is possible to investigate the effects of built structure on the spatial organisation of inhabitants and vice versa. Through a comparison of simulation models and empirical data, one should be able to derive theoretical concepts which can in turn be used to evaluate specific built structures. Such concepts can be used to provide recommendations for sustainable approaches to urban planning.

Keywords: Urban planning theory and methodology, computer-based planning systems, spatial and agent-based simulation models, graph-based analysis methods, quantitative urban research.

1 Introduction

In urban planning concepts of sustainability, the social dimension has until now been neglected to a great extent. Thus, the consequences that generally recognized urban planning sustainability strategies like densification, mixed use, and polycentrality [1] have for the social structure of cities are unknown. The unintentional intensification of conflicts that arise from the spatial separation of different population groups should be avoided. There is difficulty in estimating what effects spatial restructuring measures have on the social structure of cities. In addition, suitable methods that enable the qualified evaluation of the influences of spatial structures on the social-spatial organization of the population must urgently be developed. The central question consists of examining how concepts of sustainable city and regional planning can be developed and verified, taking into account the interrelationship between spatial and social

D. Taniar et al. (Eds.): ICCSA 2010, Part I, LNCS 6016, pp. 152–165, 2010.

structures. On the one hand, the unintended social effects of planning conceived in terms of ecological or economic sustainability should be prevented or estimated in advance, and on the other hand, unintentional social developments should be recognized very early.

1.1 Sustainability

The general principle of sustainable development that maintains its effect in the long term promises to address the needs of the current world population without interfering in the possibilities of future generations [2]. Sustainability is generally discussed on the ecological, economic and social level, which is why there are often references to the "three E's" - environment, economy and equity [3]. Occasionally, these three levels are supplemented by other ones - for example in [4], by the level of values and that of culture.

In the international professional discourse on sustainable urban planning, the social dimension of sustainability is treated peripherally at best, in that reference is made to the general influence of built space on human coexistence [5][6]. "In contrast to the ecological dimension for a socially sustainable development up to now no action principles or aims about which to a great extent agreement exist" [7]. That the problems of disadvantaged residential areas are meanwhile also perceived from the governmental side is shown by the German project "Social City" ("Soziale Stadt") (cf. the reports of the Bundestransferstelle Soziale Stadt[1]) which tests, in different cities, concrete measures for civil cooperation, the improvement of job market conditions, infrastructure, residences, and the living environment, as well as the design of district centers (Guidelines for the organization of the communal initiative "Social City", 2005). The CoMStaR plan approaches the question of socially sustainable urban planning strategies from another vantage point: For us, it is a matter of investigating the interaction between the built urban structure and the social organization of the inhabitants.

1.2 Hypotheses and Aims of the Project

The following hypotheses should serve as aims of the project:

1. Generative methods permit the automatic creation of a broad spectrum of spatial structures. In connection with graph-based analysis procedures and valid simulations of residential segregation, these offer useful support in the development of urban planning concepts. It is sensible to design a generative system in such a way that it generates the topological relations in the form of a graph in the first step, and in a second, to offer geometrical solutions therefrom.

2. Graph-based analysis procedures allow meaningful measurements of different qualities of the built structures of a city. Based on a topological-functional representation of a city, residential segregation processes can be simulated by means of an agent-based model.

3. If one looks at the built structure of a city at different levels of scale, influences on the social-spatial organization of the population can be demonstrated on every

---

[1] See: http://www.sozialestadt.de/veroeffentlichungen/ (last viewed on 14.10.2009).

level. We assume that residential areas with comparable spatial structures exhibit similarities in social organization and vice versa. Moreover, we expect that in residential areas with homogeneous population, the use habits of the residents can be explained as a function of the spatial structure.

The project is split into three parts:
Module 1: Generation of spatial structures
Module 2: Graph analysis & simulation
Module 3: Empirical social space analysis

2   Generation of Spatial Structures

For the creation of very detailed spatial-geometric structures that are independent of a grid, we generally rely on the shape grammar procedure [8]. Using a set of rules that is to be precisely defined, variations of geometric structures are created with this method. Parish and Müller have shown in the area of computer graphics that with this technology, very realistic urban structures can be generated [9]. Duarte et. al. have extended the shape grammar technology to an urban grammar and have demonstrated the generation of a town structure using the example of an urban quarter in Marrakesh [10]. However, the very realistic results require the implementation of a multitude of micro-rules (controlling parameters) for all the combinations of streets and properties that occur.

In order to be able to manage the complicated interaction of micro-rules, for further development of their approach, Duarte and colleagues suggest using a genetic algorithm in the search for optimally sustainable structures. The disadvantages of the shape grammar procedure come from the fact that the rules pertain to purely geometrical circumstances and must be fixed at the beginning in great detail. Furthermore, the generative functionality of shape grammar systems is limited to certain typologies. With [10], this was the dense, historical built structure of an old city quarter in Marrakesh; with [9] these are modern, single buildings in "Manhattan style".

In module 1 of the CoMStaR project, we will deal with generating typologically extensive settlement patterns, which firstly get by with few controlling parameters and secondly, can be optimized with regard to general criteria of sustainability (energy consumption, daylight exposure, ventilation). In addition, the shape grammar procedure will be combined with an evolutionary strategy, as was used, for example, by [11] for plan generation.

3   Graph Analysis and Simulation

A special form of network analysis in the realm of urban research is represented by the space syntax method [12][13][14], which has become established for the analysis of urban road networks or residential plans. With this investigation method, the intensity of the use of different streets is primarily calculated. After the streets are transferred into a view axis network, various centrality measures can be determined [15]. The investigation of [16] is especially relevant for the present project, because it associates the calculated values of integration with the distribution of the population according to income, and shows how small-scale population data from geographic information systems (GIS) can be correlated to values of space syntax methods. A restriction of the space syntax method exists in the fact that, until now, the analyses can be applied either to the road system of a city or the internal building circulation. There is no connection between both subsystems. To create this connection, and to illustrate and analyze the circulation structure from the apartment to the main street in a continuous graph will be an important component of module 2 of the CoMStaR project.

At the interface between urban geography and urban sociology, agent-based systems are used for the simulation of segregation processes [17] [18]. In the process, the organization of the population at a macro-level is explained by the behavior of individual households at the micro-level. At the same time, the individual decisions about place of residence are dependent on the overall urban population structure, which itself results from the individual decisions. For our interests, the agent-based system for residential segregation from [19] seems especially important, because other investigations on the dynamic behavior of the model were carried out based on it [20] and qualified proofs of the validity of the simulations could be produced [21] [22]. Another important component of module 2 of the CoMStaR project will consist in transferring the simulation model of residential segregation onto a graph as a representation of the spatial structure of a city. In this way, using unchanged control parameters for the inhabitant's behavior, the effects of different spatial configurations can be investigated in the model. Further, module 2 will be concerned with deriving heuristics for the perception of the townspeople amongst each other as a function of the built structure. Pointers can be found, e.g. in the study by [23], in which it was shown that the sum of the residents of a street who know their neighbors is inversely proportionally to the traffic volume of the street; as well as in an investigation by [24], in which the communal sense and communication of the residents were clearly dependent on the spatial factors of individual settlement patterns.

3.1 Graph Analysis

A first step to investigate the structure of urban development is to establish the connection between roads and buildings. The physical affiliation of buildings with a certain road is usually not given in a data set but may be coded in indices relating to a street number and a house number. However often the data does not cover such information or the code is not a familiar one. In this case the connection between the houses and the roads is not a simple task. A first approach can be seen in the calculation of the minimum distance between a point and a line, whereas the point is representing the centroid of the house and the line is representing a road. The shortest distance regarding the whole road network can be taken as the access path to the house. This approach gives good results however many special arrangements have to be considered to avoid mismatches and to preserve the typical structure of building alignments. [25] shows an algorithm to detect building alignments for generalisation purposes which can be adapted for this module. Figure 1 shows first results of the connection between buildings and roads.

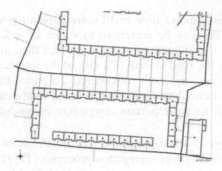

Fig. 1. Connection of the road graph with the buildings – calculation of the access paths

These access paths are inserted in the existing graph structure resulting in a combined network. The graph structure of the road network is already described in earlier publications [26] which dealt with the automatic detection of patterns in road networks.

The complete graph can now be investigated in terms of the space syntax method. Characteristics like "Integration" (an indicator for centrality) and "Choice" (an indicator for the frequency of transport use) give first information about the structure of the network and some outstanding roads with global sphere of influence.

However to examine the local structures of an urban development – and to take into account the milieus described in chapter 4 – we separate the network and build smaller spatial units according to the milieu data. This milieu information is given as points representing usually 5 households. A characteristic milieu class is attributed to the point. Figure 2 shows such a distribution of milieu points on the example of the city of Dresden.

Fig. 2. Microm data points representing the dominant milieu. The colour corresponds to the colour of the Sinus-milieus described in chapter 4.

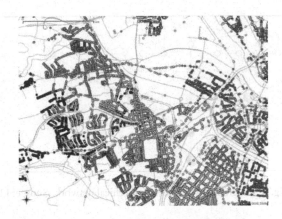

Fig. 3. Cluster of the Microm data points. A single colour represents a single cluster.

To separate the network we cluster the points representing the milieu data with the help of WEKA [27]. The boundary box of the points belonging to a single cluster will be calculated and intersected with the network graph, which contains the roads and access ways to buildings. Thus we achieve partitions of the network graph, which correspond to the present milieu situation. At this moment it is not of interest whether these partitions are consistent with existing administrative urban districts, because we just would like to investigate milieu segregation.

According to the space syntax theory and the research of [28] and [29] we calculate typical characteristics for every single graph partition like "continuity", "connectivity", "depth", "density", "integrity" etc. Furthermore we investigate the partitions regarding typical patterns like a grid structure or access ways formed like a comb. On the basis of this data a verification is done whether there are significant differences or not. With these analyses we would like to infer the relationship between a dominant milieu and the choice of location of people belonging to this milieu. The issue is to answer the question whether there are individuals/social groups with special preferences for a special site affected by particular spatial conditions. For example the well-to-do group inhabits the periphery with low road density and low centrality – in contrast the non-established and poorer classes of population live in high density residential areas with a high density of road network and a high connectivity.

That data gives a first indication for the socio-spatial distribution of a town and its correlation with structures of urban development. It should be possible to draw conclusions from that case study so that clues for further quantitative research can be given. With the help of gained knowledge and indicators described we also can attribute the agents in our simulation model to manipulate a realistic behaviour.

3.2 Simulation

Regarding J.M. Epsteins "If you didn't grow it, you didn't explain it." [30] the agent-based simulation (also referred as agent based model –ABM) has been choosen in this project as the method to explain correlation patterns between infrastructure and social structure. The ABM consists of three major parts:

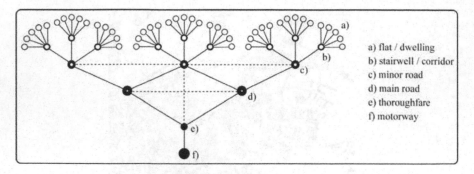

Fig. 4. Diagrammatic urban hierarchical network. Source: [31].

- the infrastructure submodel,
- the social submodel and
- the status transition rules.

One important reason for choosing an ABM is that the infrastructure explicitly is to be modeled in a very detailed degree from the motorway down to the single flat as shown in figure 4 to make sure that high resolution influences of infrastructure on social structure and vice versa are not lost. High degrees of heterogeneous topological and spatial detail cannot be represented in a classical equation-based model in a reasonable manner. While still widely used and clearly an excellent choice in many situations cellular automata models are obviously not an option in this case for the same reason. Furthermore the value of GIS-based infrastructure modeling in agent-based simulation has been pointed out quite early, e.g. in [19].

Beside the infrastructure submodel described above a social submodel is needed to take the social side of the project into account. As the natural way to model human societies and human behavior [19][30] and because there is the detailed infrastructure model the social submodel is done in a detailed way as well having households populated with humans as its major objects as shown in figure 5.

Looking at the residential behavior the model approach abstracts from having the households and humans move around in the city infrastructure, e.g. commute to work etc. Therefore the only static or "status" connection between the two submodels is the residential location of a household. All other connections are expressed by the rules which determine the status transitions of both submodels.

All the parts of the model must be complex enough to address the research topic of social sustainability in relation to the built infrastructure, but simple enough to stay manageable and to be of explanation value [32][30].

There are many important properties of agents in the social submodel as size of household, age, income, education level, phase of life etc. To reduce the complexity we use the classical approach of combined status variables, especially the milieu approach which is described in chapter 4.

In the infrastructure model a similar technique is applied to build combined status variables for different real world properties. An example is shown in figure 6. Centrality measures provided by Space Syntax methods as described in chapter 3 are taken into account.

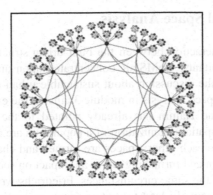

Fig. 5. Households of different milieu occupying dwellings in an abstract infrastructure network graph. Source: [31].

The rules which connect the two submodels and care for the transition of one model state to another are developed by a minimum approach, starting with a minimum set of rules. Special attention is payed to calibrate the model to match the development of socially stable and socially unstable regions in the example city of Dresden during the simulation period. The base data to calibrate the model available to the project at the moment covers 6 respectively 10 years of city development. After being well calibrated to the city of Dresden we aim to use the model to perform predictions of large-scale social reactions to changes in the infrastructure.

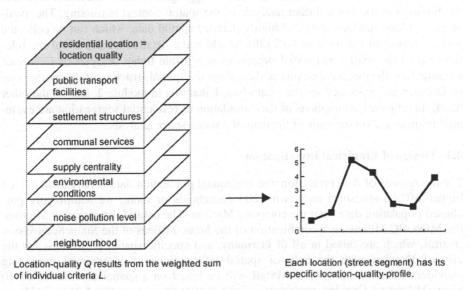

Location-quality Q results from the weighted sum   Each location (street segment) has its
of individual criteria L.   specific location-quality-profile.

Fig. 6. Combining different housing quality criteria into a joint quality profile variable

4 Empirical Social Space Analysis

By investigating the interaction between the built urban structure and the social organization of the inhabitants, CoMStaR concentrates upon an aspect that has been neglected until now in the discussion about sustainable urban and regional planning. In so doing, the social space analysis in module 3 aims at the empiric investigation of these connections. Bernd Hamm has already pointed to the social importance of space: "The social and spatial organization of a population are mutually dependent on each other and related to each other: spaces are formed and changed by social activities (…), and their design and furnishings have an impact on social relations and problems" [33]. Concerning the same circumstances, Friedrichs writes: "Definable forms of social organization regularly lead to certain forms of spatial organization. Moreover, it remains to be investigated, what repercussions the respective spatial organization has on the social" [34].

The empirical studies carried out during the last 20 years in the field of settlement sociology generally equate space with social space that distinguishes itself by the composition of the population in a certain area. How the population composition of a residential quarter affects the individuals living in it was investigated by considering, for example, the duration of poverty situations [35]. Thus, although a precise description of the investigation areas is found in the study by [36], built structure no longer plays a role in the actual investigation. Only the furnishings of the apartments are given attention.

Similar results are ascertained in the test of Schelling's tipping point theory by [37]. Here, a distinction was made between the aggregate levels of the house rows and the building block, but a further analysis of the spatial context is missing. The availability, at least fundamentally, of highly detailed spatial data, which can be collected and evaluated on the basis of GIS [38], would make detailed studies about the relationship of the spatial and social organization possible today. As part of CoMStaR module 3, on the one hand empirical data about the spatial structure of the partner city of Dresden are processed for the graph-based analyses in module 2, and on the other hand, thereby the (assumptions of the) simulation of residential segregation are evaluated in module 2 on the basis of the data of a social space analysis.

4.1 Design of Empirical Investigation

For the reasons of data protection, the communal population data is only available on bigger official statistical areas with 200 households or more, we additionally purchased population data from the company Microm. The data of the company Microm, the MOSAIC Milieus, is a combination of the Sinus-Milieus of the Sinus Sociovision Institut, which are raised in all of Germany, and specific spatial projections for the city of Dresden with the help of spatial informations of commercial marketing providers[2]. Thus the project CoMStaR will be based on a spatial distribution of 10 Sinus-Milieus of Dresden, each point of the distribution aggregates 5 households on

---

[2] http://www.microm-online.de/Deutsch/Microm/Sekundaernavigation/Glossar/M/index.jsp, last viewed on 01.11.09

average. In this way we are able to make statements on a small-scale level such as houses or street-segments for the years 2002, 2004, and 2008.

In order to make sure the spatial projection of the Sinus-Milieus is approximate to reality, we match this data with the official communal data of the statistical areas of Dresden. Additionally, a survey is planned in different spatial areas, which is not only for matching empirical knowledge with the spatial projection of the Sinus-Milieus, but to provide a better understanding of the interrelationship between spatial and social structure, too.

4.2 Milieu Approach

The milieu approach consists of not only socio-demographic variables, such as age, gender, income and education, but also of the aspects of modern, individual lifestyle such as cultural activities and preferences of residential location [39]. These two directions, vertical (social structure) and horizontal (degree of modern lifestyle), are shown in this milieu-diagram (Fig. 7). For instance, the milieu of the conservatives on the upper left hand side, the milieu of the classical middleclass in the middle and the milieu of the hedonists on the lower right hand side.

Each of these various milieus has special preferences of residential location according to statistical analysis of the German Socio-Economic-Panel. These preferences are important indicators of how each household of the corresponding milieu would behave in terms of effort made for the relocation.

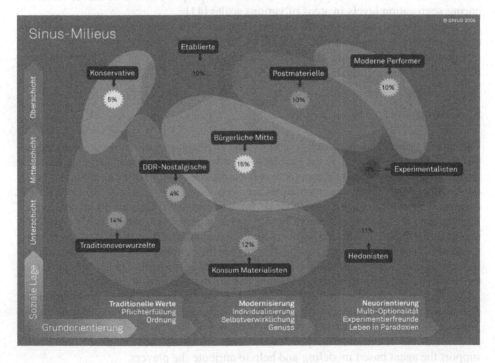

Fig. 7. Sinus-Milieus of Dresden

4.3 Spatial Indices of Segregation

With the help of the detailed MOSAIC Milieu data we are able to identify socio-spatial areas approximating the reality - without depending on communal statistical units. This is carried out with the aid of statistical methods such as cluster and factorial analysis.

The central question here is which level of socio-spatial areas - from building block to city level – is the decisive factor in order to claim statements of segregation and gentrification.

Therefore the proceeding of the project is first to measure segregation indices of different spatial levels and second to evaluate the results by theoretical approaches of segregation and gentrification.

Segregation is commonly measured by means of an index of dissimilarity. A "boundary modified" version of the index was formulated by [40]. It was based upon the concept that segregation is a separation created by spatial structure imposed upon the social space and thus interaction between racial or social groups is limited. The index takes into account one of the spatial elements – contiguity – but ignores the others [41].

The approach of David Wong argues that the length of the common boundary between two areal units and the shape of the areal units are important spatial components in determining segregation. Thus a family of segregation indices is derived by incorporating these spatial components and can be applied to various spatial configurations. One of the indices possesses a distinctive property which is useful for comparing segregation levels in areas of various scales [41].

Particularly the last-mentioned index represents a suitable tool to measure residential segregation for the project CoMStaR.

For the evaluation of the results by theoretical approaches of segregation authors like [42] and [43] will be discussed.

5 Conclusion

The article presents an approach to address the challenges of urbanisation and restructuring of our cities as well as the problems of segregation. The basic elements for such an investigation are infrastructural analyses on the one hand and socio-cultural studies on the other hand. Simulation techniques are needed to design scenarios of urban development with respect to the behaviour of humans and modifications in infrastructure. The purpose of simulation in agent based models is to provide a new way of bringing together the socio-cultural and infrastructural opportunities in a city and to learn more about the "natural" processes accompanying urban development. We would like to support decisions regarding the future design of a city by providing better knowledge of the influence and the interaction of humans and urban environment.

The research described in the paper is still in the beginning. There are many open questions to be solved in the near future. Concerning graph analysis as well as the generation of spatial structures, algorithms identified in Section 2 and 3 will be implemented and tested with respect to different scenarios. Sociological studies will support the agent based modeling and help to attribute the players.

The methods rely on geometric operations in vector data, network analysis and statistical investigations of the social components. While the first step is to extract elementary information chunks with the help of graph analysis and sociological studies, the next challenge is the combination of these pieces of information in the simulation model to achieve a higher level interpretation. The simulation model will be of use for urban planners as well as politicians, who can use the results to impact future developments and to avoid such undesirable phenomena like segregation.

Acknowledgements

This work is supported by the DFG (German Research Foundation). We thank the city of Dresden, especially the town planning office for providing several spatial and social data sets.

References

1. Gaebe, W.: Urbane Räume. Verlag Eugen Ulmer, Stuttgart (2004)
2. Hauff, V.: Unsere gemeinsame Zukunft: Der Drundtland-Bericht der Weltkommission für Umwelt und Entwicklung. Greven (1987)
3. Bullard, R.: People-of Color Evironmentalism. In: Wheeler, S.H., Beatley, T. (eds.) The Sustainable Urban Development Reader, 2nd edn., pp. 143–149. Routledge, New York (2006)
4. Spitzer, H.: Fünf Ebenen der Nachhaltigkeit. In: Birzer, M., Feindt, P.H., Spindler, E.A. (eds.) Nachhaltige Stadtentwicklung: Konzepte und Projekte, pp. 60–70. Economica Verlag, Bonn (1997)
5. Wheeler, S.M.: Planning for Sustainability: Creating Livable, Equitable, and Ecological Communities. Routledge, London (2004)
6. Williams, K., Burton, E., Jenks, M.: Achieving Sustainable Urban Form. E & FN, New York (2000)
7. Werheit, M.: Monitoring einer nachhaltigen Stadtentwicklung. In: Dortmunder Beiträge zur Raumplanung ed., vol. 113, Institut für Raumplanung (IRPUD), Fakultät Raumplanung, Universität Dortmund (2002)
8. Stiny, G., Gips, J.: Shape Grammars and the Generative Specification of Painting and Sculpture. IFIP Congress (1971)
9. Parish, Y.I.H., Müller, P.: Procedural Modeling of Cities. In: SIGGRAPH, Los Angeles, CA (2001)
10. Duarte, J.P., Rocha, J. D. M., Soares, G.D.: Unveiling the structure of the Marrakech Medina: A shape grammar and an interpreter for generating urban form. Artificial Intelligence for Engineering Design, Analysis and Manufacturing 21 (2007)
11. Elezkurtaj, T., Franck, G.: Algorithmic Support of Creative Architectural Design. Umbau 19, 129–137 (2002)
12. Hillier, B.: Space is the machine: a configurational theory of architecture (2007), http://www.spacesyntax.com/tool-links/downloads/space-is-the-machine.aspx
13. Hillier, B., Hanson, J.: The social logic of space. Cambridge University Press, Cambridge (1984) (reprinted paperback edition 2003 ed.)

14. Hillier, B., Leaman, A., Stansall, P., Bedford, M.: Space syntax. Environment and Planning B: Planning and Design 3(2), 147–185 (1976)
15. Jansen, D.: Einführung in die Netzwerkanalyse: Grundlagen, Methoden, Forschungsbeispiele, 3rd edn. VS Verlag, Wiesbaden (2006)
16. Omer, I., Gabay, R.: Social Homogeneity and Space Syntax of Towns in Israel. In: 6th International Space Syntax Symposium (2007),
    http://www.spacesyntaxistanbul.itu.edu.tr/papers/shortpapers/
    108%20-%20Omer%20Gabay.pdf
17. Schelling, T.: Dynamic models of segregation. Journal of Mathematical Sociology 1, 143–186 (1971)
18. Schelling, T.: Micromotives and Macrobehavior (Rev. ed.). W. W. Norton, New York (1978)
19. Benenson, I.: Multi-Agent Simulations of Residential Dynamics in the City. Computers, Environment and Urban Systems 22(1), 25–42 (1998)
20. Portugali, J.: Self-Organization and the City. Springer Series in Synergetics. Springer, Heidelberg (2000)
21. Benenson, I.: Agent-Based Modelling: From Individual Residential Choice to Urban Residential Dynamics. In: Goodchild, M.F., Janelle, D.G. (eds.) Spatially Integrated Social Science: Examples in Best Practice, pp. 67–95. Oxford University Press, Oxford (2004)
22. Benenson, I., Omer, I., Hatna, E.: Entity-based modelling of urban residential dynamics: the case of Yaffo, Tel Aviv. Environment and Planning B: Planning and Design 29, 491–512 (2002)
23. Appleyard, D.: Livable Streets. University of California Press, Berkeley (1981)
24. Hinding, B.: Zur Bedeutung der Nachbarschaft für die Förderung nachhaltiger Konsummuster. In: Maier, K., Michelsen, G. (eds.) Nachhaltige Stadtentwicklung: Eine Herausforderung für Umweltkommunikation und Soziale Arbeit, pp. 254–265. Verlag für Akademische Schriften, Frankfurt am Main (2003)
25. Christophe, S., Ruas, A.: Detecting Building Alignments for Generalisation Purposes. In: Symposium on Geospatial Theory, Processing and Applications, Ottawa, Canada (2002)
26. Heinzle, F., Anders, K.-H., Sester, M.: Automatic Detection of Pattern in Road Networks - Methods and Evaluation. In: Proc. of Joint Workshop Visualization and Exploration of Geospatial Data, Stuttgart, vol. XXXVI - 4/W45 (2007)
27. Hall, M., Frank, E., Holmes, G., Pfahringer, B., Reutemann, P., Witten, I.H.: The WEKA Data Mining Software: An Update. SIGKDD Explorations 11(1) (2009)
28. Marshall, S.: Streets and Patterns. Spon Press, Taylor and Francis Group, London (2005)
29. Jiang, B., Claramunt, C.: A Structural Approach to the Model Generalisation of an Urban Street Network. GeoInformatica 8(2), 157–171 (2004)
30. Epstein, J.M.: Generative Social Science. Princeton University Press, Princeton and Oxford (2006)
31. Koenig, R.: Simulation und Visualisierung der Dynamik räumlicher Prozesse: Eine computergestützte Untersuchung zu den Wechselwirkungen sozialräumlicher Organisation und den baulichen Strukturen städtischer Gesellschaften (VS Research ed.). VS Verlag, Wiesbaden (in press)
32. Grimm, V., Railsback, S.F.: Individual based modeling and Ecology. Princeton University press, Princeton (2005)
33. Hamm, B.: Einführung in die Siedlungssoziologie. Beck, München (1982)
34. Friedrichs, J.: Stadtanalyse: Soziale und räumliche Organisation der Gesellschaft, 3rd edn. Westdeutscher Verlag, Opladen (1983)

35. Farwick, A.: Segregierte Armut in der Stadt: Ursachen und soziale Folgen der räumlichen Konzentration von Sozialhilfeempfängern, vol. 14. Leske + Budrich, Opladen (2001)
36. Friedrichs, J., Blasius, J.: Leben in benachteiligten Wohngebieten. Leske + Budrich, Opladen (2000)
37. Kecskes, R., Knäble, S.: Der Bevölkerungsaustausch in ethnisch gemischten Wohngebieten: Ein Test der Tipping-Theorie von Schelling. In: Friedrichs, J. (ed.) Soziologische Stadtforschung, vol. 29, pp. 293–309. Westdeutscher Verlag, Opladen (1988)
38. Benenson, I., Omer, I.: High-resolution census data: a simple way to make them useful. Data Science Journal 2, 117–127 (2003)
39. Bourdieu, P.: Die feinen Unterschiede. Suhrkamp, Frankfurt/Main (1987)
40. Morrill, R.L.: On the measure of geographic segregation. Geography Research Forum 11, 25–36 (1991)
41. Wong, D.W.S.: Spatial Indices of Segregation. Urban studies 30(3), 559–572 (1993)
42. Häußermann, H., Kapphan, A.: Berlin: von der geteilten zur gespaltenen Stadt? Sozialräumlicher Wandel seit 1990. Leske + Budrich, Opladen (2002)
43. Dangschat, J.S.: Soziale Ungleichheit, gesellschaftlicher Raum und Segregation. In: Dangschat, J.S., Hamedinger, A. (eds.) Lebensstile, soziale Lagen und Siedlungsstrukturen. Akademie für Raumforschung und Landesplanung, Forschungs- und Sitzungsberichte der ARL, Band 230, Selbstverlag, Hannover (2007)

A Comparison of Evolutionary Algorithms for Automatic Calibration of Constrained Cellular Automata

Ivan Blecic, Arnaldo Cecchini, and Giuseppe A. Trunfio

Laboratory of Analysis and Models for Planning (LAMP)
Department of Architecture and Planning - University of Sassari,
Palazzo Pou Salit, Piazza Duomo 6, 07041 Alghero, Italy
{ivan,cecchini,trunfio}@uniss.it

Abstract. We present a comparative study of seven evolutionary algorithms (Generational Genetic, Elitist Genetic, Steady State Genetic, $(\mu/\rho, \lambda)$ Evolution Strategy, $(\mu/\rho + \lambda)$ Evolution Strategy, generational and elitist Covariance Matrix Adaptation) for automatic calibration of a constrained cellular automaton (CCA), whose performance are assessed in terms of two fitness metrics (based on Kappa statistics and Lee-Salee Index). Two variations of the CCA (one with 14 and one 27 parameters) were tested jointly with different number of time steps targeted by the calibration procedures. Besides offering some methodological suggestions for this kind of comparative analysis, the findings provide useful hints on the calibration algorithms to be expected to perform better in the application of cellular automata of sort for the simulation of land-use dynamics.

Keywords: cellular automata, urban modelling, land-use model, evolutionary algorithms, automatic calibration.

1 Introduction

Cellular automata (CAs) models of land use are increasingly used as a tool for assessing spatial and urban planning policies. A recurring issue with the operational use of CA models is their calibration. This consists of adapting their parameter-dependent transition rules to have the modelled urban phenomena best matching the observed reality. Clearly, the estimation of model parameters to improve such agreement must be considered an essential phase of the model design. However, CA calibration is often a challenging task, as it involves large search spaces whose dimension grows remarkably with the number of parameters to be calibrated. It is known that the calibration of typical CAs used for land-use simulations through trial and error processes based only on expert knowledge is time consuming and usually leads to unreliable results. Instead, the current research trend in the field suggests the employment of formal, well-structured and automated optimisation procedures.

At present, many optimisation algorithms have been used for the automatic calibration of CAs, including techniques based on exhaustive search [1,2], the *ad hoc* designed search procedures [3,4] as well as Evolutionary Algorithms (EAs) [5-9].

D. Taniar et al. (Eds.): ICCSA 2010, Part I, LNCS 6016, pp. 166–181, 2010.

A class of well known and widely applied CAs for land use simulation is represented by the so called Constrained Cellular Automata (CCAs) [10,11] in which the land-use demand is modelled as exogenous to the cellular model.

For the automatic calibration of CCAs, some effort has been dedicated by researchers in employing *ad hoc* heuristics. In particular, in [3] the authors have developed an automatic calibration procedure specifically designed for CCAs. Their method involves an empirical search technique in which the 'erroneous' neighbourhoods are first indentified and then the parameters are adjusted to reduce the error. However, the method assumes that there exists a set of maps available on a year-by-year basis, which is rarely the case in practice. In [4] a further development of that method has been discussed, where it is suggested an empirical technique to correct the calibration procedure in order to cope with the unavailability of maps covering each step of the calibration interval. Nevertheless, it is not clear to what extent such empirical adjustments affect the quality of the final solution.

On the other hand, although many studies reported the results of automatic calibrations of various CAs using general-purpose heuristics [5-9], to our knowledge none has been devoted to the comparison of the performances achieved by standard, but yet advanced, search methods for the calibration of a CCA, notwithstanding the fact that in the recent years an ongoing research in the field of search heuristics provided some potentially well-suited techniques for the optimisation of black-box multimodal functions. For these reasons, we have undertaken a comparative study of several evolutionary-algorithm strategies (from fairly standard to few state-of-the-art such as Covariance Matrix Adaptation ES) in different CCA experimental settings, the results of which are hereby presented and discussed.

The paper is organised as follows. In section 2 the CCA used for the numerical experiments is presented together with the formalisation of the calibration problem. In section 3 the algorithms object of comparison are outlined and the studied experimental space is described. Section 4 illustrates the results of the numerical experiments and section 5 concludes the paper.

2 A Constrained CA Model

The CCA used in the present work is composed of square cells which form a raster representation of a geographical area. The relevant component of the state of every cell represents its land-use class (such as residential, industrial, commercial, agriculture). Starting from a known configuration, the automaton evolves in discrete steps, typically equivalent to one year, simulating the land-use dynamics of the area.

A CCA model is "constrained" in the sense that at each time step the aggregate level of demand for every land use is fixed by an exogenous constraint. This constraint is defined on a macro level by external a-spatial demographic, economic and environmental models. In this sense, the CCA can be viewed as a way to determine the spatial distribution of a given aggregate land-use demand, taking into account for the local interaction between different land uses.

With respect to the CCA discussed in [25,26,27], the model used in our calibration experiments is of a simplified kind, as it has been devised for studying the performance of the calibration methods rather than for simulating the land-use dynamics of a specific area. In this CCA model, besides the land use, other cell's properties represent its relevant static characteristics. These are: *(i)* the cell *accessibility* $A \in [0,1]$, reflecting to what extent the cell is serviced by the transportation network infrastructure; *(ii)* the cell *suitability* $S_j \in [0,1]$ taking into account, for each land use j, features like slope or other terrain aspect; *(iii)* a Boolean value Z_j defining the exclusion of the j-th land use (for example due to zoning regulations or physical constraints). The state of the cell also includes its current *transition potentials* $P_j \in [0,1]$ expressing the propensity to acquire the j-th use type. The cell neighbourhoods are circular regions of a given radius around the cell.

In the CCA, the first phase of the transition function consists of computation of the transition potentials for every cell, according to the equation:

$$P_j = \nu A S_j Z_j N_j \qquad (1)$$

where ν is a random perturbation factor and $N_j \in [0,1]$ is the so called *neighbourhood effect*. The latter represents the sum of all the attractive and repulsive effects of land uses and land covers within cell's neighbourhood, on the j-th land use which the current cell may assume. Since, in general, more distant cells in the neighbourhood have smaller influence, in our calibration study the factor N_j is computed, as suggested in [12], on the basis of an exponential decay function:

$$N_j = \frac{1}{2} + \frac{1}{n_c} \left[\frac{I_k}{2} + \sum_{c \in V} \frac{a_{ij}}{1 + e^{\frac{\gamma\,(d-s)}{d_{ij}}}} \right] \qquad (2)$$

where:

- the summation is extended to all cells of the neighbourhood V (which does not include the owner cell itself);
- the current land use of the cell $c \in V$ is denoted by i;
- $n_c = \sharp V + 1$ where $\sharp V$ is the number of cells in the neighbourhood;
- s is the cell size;
- d is the distance between the cell c of the neighbourhood and the current cell;
- $a_{ij} \in [-1,1]$ represents the maximum influence (positive or negative) of the land use i on the use j;
- $d_{ij} \in [0, d_{\max}]$ is the distance in correspondence of which the contribution to the neighbouring effect is a fraction α of the maximum value (currently $\alpha = 0.05$) and $\gamma = \ln((1-\alpha)/\alpha)$;
- the term $I_k \in [0,1]$, where k denotes the current land use of the cell for which the transition potential is under evaluation, accounts for the effect of the cell on itself (zero-distance effect) and represents an inertia due to the costs of transformation from one land use to another.

In the second phase of the transition function, which takes place on a non-local basis, *(i)* the yet untransformed cell c_k with the highest potential towards the yet unsatisfied land use k is found; *(ii)* cell c_k is assigned to the land use k; *(iii)* if there are still unsatisfied land uses and untransformed cells the procedure is iterated.

More details about the model implementation used in this work, which is based on the MAGI C++ class library, can be found in [13].

In general, the CCA above described includes both static land uses (i.e. not changing during the simulation) and dynamic land uses. Thus, using expression (7), a CCA with n_T land uses, n_s of which static and n_d dynamic, depends on $n_p = n_d + 2\,n_T\,n_d$ scalar parameters, namely on n_d parameters $I_k \in [0,1]$ and on $n_T\,n_d$ couples (a_{ij}, d_{ij}) which define the exponential decay functions.

2.1 The Calibration Problem

In the CCA outlined above, the transition function depends on a vector of scalar parameters $\mathbf{p} = [I_1, \ldots, I_{n_d}, a_{11}, \ldots, a_{n_T n_d}, d_{11}, \ldots, d_{n_T n_d}]^T$ which belongs to the space Λ of all possible parameters. In the model under consideration, all of the local transition functions, acting simultaneously on each cell, can be thought of as an overall parameter-dependent function Φ which acts on the entire automaton and gives the global configuration $\omega^{(t+1)}$ at the step $t + 1$ (i.e. the set of all cells' states):

$$\omega^{(t+1)} = \Phi(\omega^{(t)}, \mathbf{p}, \mathbf{f}(t)) \tag{3}$$

where $\mathbf{f(t)}$ is a vector collecting the demand for each land use at the step t.

Thus, the iterative application of the function Φ to the successive configurations, starting from an initial one $\omega^{(0)}$, leads to the dynamic process:

$$\omega^{(0)} \xrightarrow{\Phi} \omega^{(1)} \xrightarrow{\Phi} \cdots \xrightarrow{\Phi} \omega^{(t)} \tag{4}$$

where the automaton configuration at the time step t depends: *(i)* on the initial configuration; *(ii)* on the parameters; *(iii)* on the history of the given external constraints on the land uses for each time step; *(iv)* on the structure of the CA model.

With respect to the parameters vector $\mathbf{p}$, the model can be optimised to minimise the misfit between the simulated patterns and the observed ones. Formally, let us suppose the existence of a spatio-temporal dataset $\bar{V}_T$ (which we call "training set") collecting some automaton configurations corresponding to the historical data in the form of a sequence of thematic maps of the geographical area under study. In particular, let $\bar{V}_T$ be composed of a series of q automaton configurations:

$$\bar{V}_T = \left\{ \bar{\omega}^{(k)} : k \in \{0, \tau_1, \ldots, \tau_q\} \right\} \tag{5}$$

where the attribute τ_i indicates the time step in which the configuration $\bar{\omega}^{(k)}$ is known. Therefore, starting from the configuration $\bar{\omega}^{(0)}$, and given a vector $\mathbf{p}$ of parameters, the process (4) can be executed for the computation of the $q - 1$ automaton configurations:

$$V = \left\{ \omega^{(k)} : k \in \{\tau_1, \ldots, \tau_q\} \right\} \tag{6}$$

where $\omega^{(k)}$ is given by the process (4).

In general, it is desirable that the model be able to reproduce different aspects of the evolution of the real system, both in space and time. Thus, in order to measure the agreement between the real spatio-temporal sequence and the simulated one, in general, g measures $\Theta_i\left(\bar{\mathcal{V}}_T, \mathcal{V}\right)$ of fitness can be defined where each metric Θ_i accounts for a specific aspect of the agreement between the simulated and the observed spatial pattern. Therefore, the calibration process consists of the following multi-objective maximisation problem:

$$\max_{\mathbf{p}\in\Lambda}\Theta_i\left(\bar{\mathcal{V}}_T, \mathcal{V}\right) \qquad i = 1,\ldots,g \qquad (7)$$

In other words, we need to determine the value of the parameter vector which leads to the optimal agreement between the observed data and the corresponding simulated data.

Often the problem (7) is defined as a single objective optimisation, either considering only one measure of agreement or by combining the multiple objectives into a single one. However, as shown in [7,8], the latter approach has some drawbacks, and a suitable alternative consists in conducting a full multi-objective optimisation that identifies a set of non-dominated or Pareto solutions [14].

As to the solution of the optimisation problem (7), it is worth to point out that in general, as already shown in [3], even in the case of a single objective optimisation, calibration procedures do not, in the line of principle, yield a unique solution. In other words, depending upon the structure of both the CA and the fitness function, the same configuration of the CA could be obtained using different parameter vectors $\mathbf{p}$.

Ideally, besides the training set $\bar{\mathcal{V}}_T$, a validation set $\bar{\mathcal{V}}_V$ is available containing further known CA configurations with $\bar{\mathcal{V}}_V \cap \bar{\mathcal{V}}_T = \emptyset$. This allows for the validation, in correspondence to the elements of $\bar{\mathcal{V}}_V$ and with suitable measure of agreements, of the CA parameters obtained with the optimisation procedure according to (7).

2.2 Automatic Calibration

Automatic calibration consists of solving the problem (7) through the use of a suitable search algorithm. In the present study we use different evolutionary algorithms (EAs) to tackle the automatic calibration of the CCA illustrated in section 2.

EAs are population-based probabilistic optimisation algorithms grounded on the principles of evolution through mutation and selection of the fittest. Starting with an initial population of μ individuals called "parents" (i.e. candidate solutions) and given the corresponding objective function value, called fitness (i.e. the measure of agreement obtained through a CCA simulation in our case), an offspring population of λ candidate solutions is created from the parents using specific variation operators. The latter can be directed to the production of diversity into the population or to foster the convergence towards the optimum. Variation operators of the first type typically change each single parent $\mathbf{p}$ randomly according to a specific probability distribution (i.e. the mutation operator) or involve more than one parent in the variation (i.e. the recombination operator). Operators of the second type are the so-called selection operators, which are designed to choose those offspring individuals as parents for the next generation which exhibit a higher fitness.

Depending on how the variation and selection operators are designed and on how the individuals are represented (e.g. string of bits or real-valued vectors), different classes of EAs have been proposed. Among these are Evolution Strategies (ES) [15] and Genetic Algorithms (GA) [16]. For a comprehensive overview, the reader is referred to [17].

3 Experimental Setup

For the convenience of easing the reader's understanding, it is of purpose to schematically present the space of experimental settings hereby considered. This space is defined by four "dimensions": (1) the evolutionary algorithm (EA) used for the calibration, (2) the fitness function employed for measuring the performance of the EA, (3) the CCA model to be calibrated, and finally (4) the CA-simulation time steps targeted by the calibration algorithm.

Subsequently, we present a more detailed characterisation of each of the four dimensions of the experimental space.

3.1 Evolutionary Algorithms

The calibration procedures in this study were based on an implementation of the following EAs:

1. **Generational Genetic Algorithm** (GGA). In this fairly standard Genetic Algorithm [16], a population of bitstrings, each encoding a candidate solution (i.e. the set of parameters) is evolved through the iterative application of the operators of selection, recombination and mutations. In the present work, each parameter of the CCA was encoded on a string composed of 10 bits. The algorithm uses standard 1-point crossover applied with probability $p_c = 0.6$, while the mutation operator is the standard bit flipping with a fixed probability per bit defined as $p_m = 1/n_b$, being n_b the number of bits composing the individual. The standard Roulette Wheel Selection [16] was applied in the context of a generational replacement scheme (i.e. the entire population is replaced at once).
2. **Elitist Genetic Algorithm** (EGA). This algorithm is identical to GCA except for the replacement scheme, always preserving the best individual in the population from generation to generation.
3. **Steady State Genetic Algorithm** (SSGA). This is a variant of the GGA in which at each generation only n_{rep} offsprings are generated for replacing the worst individuals of the parent population (we use $n_{rep} = 5$ in this work).
4. **$(\mu/\rho, \lambda)$ Evolution Strategy** ($(\mu/\rho, \lambda)$-ES). This is a rather standard evolution strategy [15] usually applied to continuous optimisation, in which a population of individuals is evolved through the iterative application of the recombination, mutation and selection operators. Each individual is composed of two real-valued vectors representing a set of CCA parameters and the corresponding mutation step sizes (i.e. the standard deviations of the normal distribution used for the mutation operator), respectively. The algorithm uses a population of μ parents, ρ of which are randomly selected to produce λ offsprings each through recombination

(in this work we assumed $\rho = 2$). In particular, discrete recombination is used for the CCA parameters, while intermediate recombination is applied for step sizes [15]. Mutation is performed by adding a zero-mean normally distributed random value $N(0, \sigma_i^2)$ to each CCA parameter p_i, while the step sizes σ_i are subjected to a log-normal distributed standard adaptation. The selection operator is deterministic and is based on the fitness ranking. In particular, the μ parents are only selected among the λ offsprings (the previous parent generation is completely discarded).

5. $(\mu/\rho + \lambda)$ **Evolution Strategy** $((\mu/\rho + \lambda)$-ES). The only difference with respect to the $(\mu/\rho, \lambda)$-ES, reflects the fact that the selection operator selects the μ best individuals out of the union of parents and offsprings to form the next parent generation.

6. **Covariance Matrix Adaptation evolution strategy** (CMA). CMA [18] is similar to the above described $(\mu/\rho, \lambda)$-ES but, as the main difference, exploits a multivariate normal distribution as the mutation operator instead of the $N(0, \sigma_i^2)$ based on the step sizes σ_i. In particular, candidate solutions are mutated according to a covariance matrix which describes the pairwise dependencies between the variables in a multivariate normal distribution. The covariance matrix of the mutation distribution is updated during the evolution through an adaptive process which tries to learn a second-order model of the underlying objective function.

7. **Elitist Covariance Matrix Adaptation evolution strategy** (ECMA). This algorithm is identical to CMA except for the fact that the best individual in the population is always preserved by the selection operator.

Usually, in the automatic calibration of the CAs, the computationally most expensive operation is by far the CA evaluation. For this reason it appeared meaningful to make comparisons among search algorithms assigning a limited budget of evaluations of the CCA to each. In addition, it is well known that in optimisations based on EAs the result might depend on the particular initialisation of the population. Therefore, for each of the heuristics, the search strategy was structured as follows: *(i)* a number of n_{run} automatic optimisations, each initialising the random number generator with a different seed, were executed with a limited budget of n_{sim} CCA evaluations; *(ii)* the most promising optimisation run was then restarted with an additional number of n_{ref} CCA evaluations available.

Moreover, in order to assess the characteristics of the heuristic search procedures, avoiding the unessential complications related with the presence of a noisy objective function, a deterministic version of the CCA model described above was used (in other words, it was assumed that $\nu = 1$ in eq. (1)).

In our experiments we have applied the calibration heuristics to the data obtained with the CCA itself, using a set of parameters generated within meaningful intervals. This guarantees the existence of a zero-error solution of the calibration problem, thus allowing for an unbiased evaluation of the calibration procedures.

The numerical experiments were executed using the SHARK Machine Learning Library [19] on a standard PC based on a Intel Core 2 Quad (Q9400) CPU.

3.2 Fitness Functions

In order to evaluate candidate solutions in the context of the evolutionary search (i.e. to measure the agreement between the simulation outcomes and the training set), we are employing fitness functions based on two metrics: the Kappa statistics (K) and an adaptation of the Lee-Salee Index (LS).

1. The Kappa statistic [20] is a well known approach for the measurement of the level of cell-by-cell agreement between two maps. It performs a correction in order to account for the statistically expected agreement related to the actual number of cells of each land use class that are contained in the two maps object of comparison. A Kappa value greater than 0 indicates that there is more similarity than random and the value 1 means there is perfect agreement of the two maps. Thanks to its suitable properties, the standard Kappa statistic, together with its improved variants proposed in the literature (e.g. [21,22]) in the latest years, is one of the most used measures for model validation.

2. The second statistics used, an adapted Lee-Salee Index [23], gives rise to a different fitness function defined as:

$$\Theta_{LS}^{(j)} = \left(\prod_{k=1}^{n_d} \frac{\left\| \bar{A}_k \cap A_k^{(j)} \right\|}{\left\| \bar{A}_k \cup A_k^{(j)} \right\|} \right)^{\frac{1}{n_d}} \tag{8}$$

where n_d is the number of land uses actively modelled, $\bar{A}_k$ is the region in the training map covered by the k-th land use, $A_k^{(j)}$ is the region of the simulated map at j-th step covered by the k-th land use, while $\|A\|$ indicates the area of the region A. The shape index given by Eq. (8) is adapted from the Lee-Salee index used for the calibration of the urban growth model included in SLEUTH [1,2].

3.3 CCA Model Variations

For the purpose of this study, we have taken under consideration two variations of the CCA model. In regard of the calibration problem addressed in this paper, the most relevant distinction between the two is the number of parameters to calibrate: 14 in the first case, 27 in the second. In both cases, the model was applied on a map representing a region in the western part of Sicily (Italy) using a grid of 135×135 square cells of size 400×400 meters.

1. In the first variation of the CCA model, the cell land uses were limited to the set {residential, industrial, others}. Here, the first two land uses were actively modelled (i.e. their dynamics was simulated) while the third was a static class collecting all the remaining land uses contained in the map. According to the model presented above, such assumption leads to a CCA depending on 14 scalar parameters. Starting from the initial configuration $\bar{\omega}^{(0)}$ corresponding to the real situation in 1970, 30 steps of simulation were carried out using the parameters' values shown in Table 1 and the trend lines describing a linear increase of the aggregate land use demand for the dynamic land uses. Afterwards, for each calibration problem, the simulated maps were used for constructing different training sets $\bar{V}_T$ and validation sets $\bar{V}_V$.

Table 1. the set of parameters used for the generation of the training set for the 14-parameter CCA calibration exercises (for a_{ij} and d_{ij} the first column corresponds to the index i)

I_k		a_{ij}		d_{ij}	
		Residential	Industrial	Residential	Industrial
Residential	0.8	1.0	-0.2	1000.0	1000.0
Industrial	0.4	-0.6	1.0	1000.0	1000.0
Others	/	0.3	0.5	1000.0	1000.0

Table 2. the set of parameters used for the generation of the training set for the 27-parameter calibration exercise (for a_{ij} and d_{ij} the first column corresponds to the index i)

I_k		a_{ij}			d_{ij}		
		Residential	Industrial	Commercial	Residential	Industrial	Commercial
Residential	0.8	1.0	-0.2	0.8	1000.0	1000.0	1800.0
Industrial	0.4	-0.65	1.0	0.2	1000.0	1000.0	800.0
Commercial	0.6	0.5	0.2	0.3	1000.0	1500.0	1500.0
Other	/	0.2	0.75	-0.2	1000.0	1000.0	500.0

The calibration exercises discussed in the present section were executed assuming $n_{run} = 10$ and $n_{sim} = n_{ref} = 500$. Moreover, the GGA, EGA, SSGA algorithms operated on a population of 25 individuals, for the ESs the parents where $\mu = 10$ and the offsprings $\lambda = 30$ and for the CMAs $\mu = 6$ and $\lambda = 24$ was assumed.

2. The second variation of the CCA model used by us increases the dimension of the search space, for another, fourth, land use class was introduced in the model. Here the set of land uses was defined as {*residential, industrial, commercial, others*}, with the first three classes dynamically updated during the simulation. According to the model presented in section 2, such assumption leads to a CCA depending on 27 scalar parameters. The corresponding calibration problems are considerably harder than before because of the exponentially increased cardinality of the search space.

In this case also, the initial configuration $\bar{\omega}^{(0)}$ corresponded to the real situation in 1970 of the mentioned geographical area and 30 steps of simulation were carried out using the parameters' values shown in Table 2, together with the demand for the three dynamic land linearly increasing. Differently from the previous case, the EGA operated on a population of 30 individuals while for the ECMA it was assumed that $\mu = 6$ and $\lambda = 24$. Moreover, the calibration exercises were executed assuming $n_{run} = 20$ and $n_{sim} = 2000$ and $n_{ref} = 0$.

3.4 The CA-Simulation Time Steps Targeted by the Calibration Algorithms

For calibration, target CA configurations for specific time steps should be provided as training sets to the EAs. Here, we have used three such time-steps targeting. The first two are single-time-step training sets, corresponding to the CA configurations after respectively 5 and 15 steps. The third tested case is composite, for both configurations after 5 and after 15 steps were simultaneously provided as the training set to the EAs.

For the purpose of labelling of experiments, the three mentioned time step targets will be named respectively "S5", "S15" and "S5.15".

4 Calibration Exercises and Discussion

Given the hitherto described characterisations of the experimental space, each single computational experiment can be singled out in terms of the said dimensions. To reflect this, in the presentation and discussion of results of EAs' performances, we will henceforth label the experiments according to their CCA model (CA14 or CA27), the fitness function used (K or LS) and the time steps targeted by the EA (S5, S15 or S5.15).

The following discussion is divided into two subsections, first presenting the results for the simpler model (CA14), then for the more parameter-rich one (CA27).

4.1 Three Land Uses (14 parameters) Calibration Examples

In the first experimental setting, labelled CA14-K-S5, the training set included only the configuration corresponding to the step 5, that is: $\bar{V}_T = \{\bar{\omega}^{(5)}\}$.

Table 3 shows a summary of the results obtained for the calibration problem CA14-K-S5 using the experimental setup described above. In particular, the first four rows of statistics were obtained over 10 independent runs of the algorithms, each on a fixed budget of 500 CCA evaluations, while the last data row refers to the optimisation obtained by the best run of the 10, on a budget of 1000 CCA evaluations. According to the obtained results, the $(\mu/\rho + \lambda)$-ES leaded to the best Kappa value of 0.96. The best average value on 500 evaluations was instead obtained by the ECMA method that also presented the lowest value of the standard deviation. The latter statistic is important because it indicates a lower sensitivity of the solution provided by the algorithm to the initialisation of the population.

In the second experimental setting, labelled CA14-LS-S5, the previous CCA model (CA14) and target time step (S5) was studied using the LS-based fitness function.

In Fig. 1 the convergence paths of the best run for each of the experimented search heuristics are shown for CA14-LS-S5.

The optimisation results obtained for the same problem, both in terms of Kappa index and LS metric, are reported in Table 4. Interestingly, the use of the LS index as fitness happens to lead to an improved optimisation result for all heuristics except for the $(\mu/\rho + \lambda)$-ES. In particular, the elitist CMA method gave the best Kappa value of 0.988 after 1000 CCA evaluations.

Table 3. Summary of the results obtained for CA14-K-S5 in terms of Kappa statistic

		GGA	EGA	SSGA	$(\mu/\rho, \lambda)$-ES	$(\mu/\rho + \lambda)$-ES	CMA	ECMA
	Min	0.836	0.868	0.863	0.710	0.889	0.868	0.911
	Max	0.911	0.939	0.912	0.788	0.926	0.974	0.933
K	Avg.	0.874	0.893	0.872	0.811	0.895	0.918	0.925
	Std.dev.	0.034	0.027	0.025	0.062	0.071	0.046	0.010
	Max$_{1000}$	0.871	0.956	0.940	0.821	**0.960**	0.963	0.945

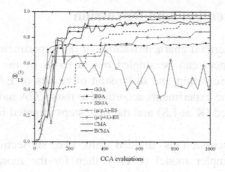

CCA evaluations

Fig. 1. Convergence behaviour of the best run of each heuristic for the CA14-LS-S5 calibration exercise. At the end of the 1000 CCA evaluations, the elitist CMA method achieved a fitness value of 0.972 whichcorresponded to a Kappa value of 0.988.

Table 4. Summary of the results obtained for CA14-LS-S5 in terms of both Kappa statistic and LS index (the latter was used as driving fitness for the evolutionary algorithms)

		GGA	EGA	SSGA	$(\mu/\rho, \lambda)$-ES	$(\mu/\rho + \lambda)$-ES	CMA	ECMA
	Min	0.867	0.892	0.763	0.520	0.861	0.870	0.911
	Max	0.902	0.955	0.901	0.863	0.902	0.958	0.982
K	Avg.	0.884	0.908	0.880	0.601	0.884	0.934	0.941
	Std.dev.	0.022	0.027	0.041	0.066	0.051	0.036	0.028
	Max_{1000}	0.915	0.982	0.955	0.863	0.935	0.978	**0.988**
	Min	0.408	0.668	0.431	0.335	0.653	0.426	0.481
	Max	0.752	0.894	0.824	0.692	0.742	0.887	0.964
LS	Avg.	0.684	0.763	0.626	0.576	0.689	0.605	0.730
	Std.dev.	0.164	0.092	0.134	0.269	0.042	0.209	0.226
	Max_{1000}	0.759	0.950	0.902	0.692	0.845	0.923	0.972

Table 5 shows the set of parameters corresponding to the best found Kappa value obtained for the CA14-LS-S5. In spite of the relatively low calibration error, indicating that configurations $\bar{\omega}^{(5)}$ and $\omega^{(5)}$ are almost identical, a comparison between Table 1 and Table 5 shows that the values of the corresponding parameters are significantly different (although of the same sign). This may indicate either the convergence of the evolutionary algorithm towards a different (possibly sub-optimal) maximum or just a slow convergence, with respect to the allocated budget of CCA evaluations, towards the exact solution in Table 1.

Table 5. the set of parameters corresponding to the best found Kappa statistic obtained for CA14-LS-S5 (for a_{ij} and d_{ij} the first column corresponds to the index i)

	I_k	a_{ij}		d_{ij}	
		Residential	Industrial	Residential	Industrial
Residential	0.425	0.2384	-0.4902	899.2	892.6
Industrial	0.253	-0.1611	0.7600	331.2	736.9
Others	/	0.2322	0.5777	455.9	754.3

Table 6. Summary of the results in terms of Kappa statistic obtained for CA14-LS-S15 (the LS index was used as driving fitness for the evolutionary algorithms)

	GGA	EGA	SSGA	$(\mu/\rho, \lambda)$-ES	$(\mu/\rho + \lambda)$-ES	CMA	ECMA
Min	0.824	0.858	0.815	0.653	0.683	0.892	0.801
Max	0.895	0.916	0.900	0.859	0.923	0.921	0.954
Avg.	0.871	0.887	0.850	0.749	0.814	0.906	0.916
Std.dev.	0.029	0.021	0.031	0.073	0.101	0.013	0.065
Max_{1000}	0.854	0.951	0.919	0.884	0.921	0.900	**0.959**

A third calibration exercise, labelled CA14-LS-S15, was experimented with only difference with respect to CA14-LS-S5 being that the training set $\bar{V}_T$ included the configuration corresponding to the step 15 of the simulation, instead of the step 5 (in other words $\bar{V}_T = \{\bar{\omega}^{(15)}\}$). In Table 6 the corresponding results obtained through the used optimisation heuristics are shown, while the convergence paths of the best run for each of the experimented search heuristics are depicted in Fig. 2. On the assigned budget of CCA evaluations, the best found result of 0.959 for Kappa was obtained trough the elitist CMA method. As supposable, the optimum obtained for CA14-LS-S5 was slightly better with respect to the one obtained for CA14-LS-S15. In fact, the latter calibration problem is harder because of the superior nonlinearity of the fitness function to optimise. Table 7 shows the set of parameters corresponding to the optimum obtained for the CA14-LS-S15.

Table 7. the set of parameters corresponding to the best found Kappa statistic obtained for CA14-LS-S15 (for a_{ij} and d_{ij} the first column corresponds to the index i)

	I_k	a_{ij}		d_{ij}	
		Residential	Industrial	Residential	Industrial
Residential	0.340	1.000	-0.229	888.9	648.2
Industrial	0.596	0.183	0.455	667.2	1018.9
Others	/	0.212	0.545	258.7	860.7

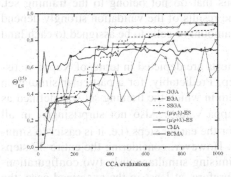

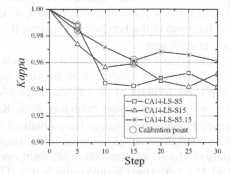

Fig. 2. Convergence behaviour of the best run of each heuristic for the CA14-LS-S15 calibration exercise. The elitist CMA method achieved a fitness value of 0.912 which corresponded to a Kappa value of 0.959.

Fig. 3. Validation in terms of Kappa statistic of the solution obtained for CA14-LS-S5, CA14-LS-S15 and CA14-LS-S5.15 over a 30-steps simulation period

Table 8. the set of parameters corresponding to the best found Kappa statistic obtained for CA14-LS-S5.15 (for a_{ij} and d_{ij} the first column corresponds to the index i)

I_k		a_{ij}		d_{ij}	
		Residential	Industrial	Residential	Industrial
Residential	0.564	0.721	-0.781	864.0	505.7
Industrial	0.745	-0.433	0.410	522.4	958.5
Others	/	0.243	0.390	69.51	888.4

A further experiment based on the same CCA was carried out, labelled CA14-LS-S5.15, in which the target fitness to optimise was defined considering simultaneously both the configurations at steps 5 and 15.

Here, it was necessary to measure the fitness of not only one, but two configurations in the training sets (S5 and S15) in comparison to the respective configurations obtained with the parameters tested by the EAs. For that purpose, we need to define a LS-based fitness function aggregating the two LS measures for S5 and S15. We thus used the geometric mean of the two as the fitness function, *viz.*:

$$\Theta_{LS}^{(5,15)} = \sqrt{\Theta_{LS}^{(5)} \Theta_{LS}^{(15)}} \tag{9}$$

Also in the case of CA14-LS-S5.15, given the assigned budget of CCA evaluations, the best found set of model parameters was obtained with the elitist CMA method. The solution is shown in Table 8 while the corresponding best found Kappa values were 0.984 for the step 5 and 0.962 for the step 15.

With respect to the calibrations based on a single configuration, addressing simultaneously the measures of agreement at different time steps leaded to comparable Kappa values in terms of the optimisation targets.

A further investigation was then carried out, comparing the validation results of the best found solutions obtained for the test problems CA14-LS-S5, CA14-LS-S15 and CA14-LS-S5.15. As mentioned above, in the validation phase the obtained set of parameters are tested against configurations that do not belong to the training set. Clearly, in the particular case of a CCA, the results of the validation strongly depend on the form of the function $\mathbf{f(t)}$ giving the amount of cells to be assigned to each land use at each step.

In Figure 3 the results of the validation tests are depicted in terms of Kappa statistic expressed as a function of the time step. Predictably, for a particular simulation step i, the solution of the calibration problem in which the training set was defined as $\bar{\mathcal{V}}_T = \{\bar{\omega}^{(i)}\}$ presented relatively high Kappa values. Also not surprisingly, in all cases higher Kappa values were obtained for the earlier steps (i.e. it is easier to simulate configurations close to the initial one). However, considering the entire 30-steps period, the set of parameters obtained optimising simultaneously two configurations (S5.15), performed significantly better. Therefore, at least in the examined case, the simultaneous use of more target configurations could improve the overall quality of the calibration without affecting the required effort in terms of CCA evaluations. Considering the increased availability of remotely sensed spatial data today, the latter outcome confirms that the quality of the calibration result can take significant advantages from richer training sets.

4.2 Four Land Uses (27 Parameters) Calibration Examples

For the harder CCA variation, namely CA27 (see above 3.3.-2. for details), we explored the EAs' performance for the experimental setting CA27-LS-S5.15.

As shown in Figure 4 and in Table 9, after 2000 CCA evaluations both EGA and ECMA heuristics provided solutions with an acceptable agreement between the simulation and the target maps. However, the ECMA algorithm performed better in terms of the fitness function and Kappa statistic at the calibration steps 5 and 15.

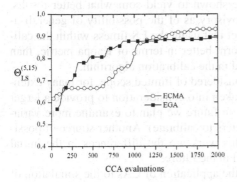
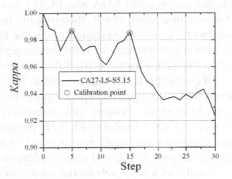

Fig. 4. Convergence behaviour of the best run of each heuristic for theCA27-LS-S5.15 calibration exercise

Fig. 5. Validation in terms of Kappa statistic of the solution obtained through the ECMA for CA27-LS-S5.15 over a 30-steps simulation period

Table 9. Summary of the results in terms of Kappa statistic obtained for CA27-LS-S5.15

	Step 5		Step 15	
	EGA	ECMA	EGA	ECMA
Min	0.903	0.909	0.887	0.930
Max	0.947	**0.988**	0.974	**0.986**
Avg.	0.931	0.940	0.938	0.961
Std.dev.	0.021	0.033	0.041	0.026

Table 10. The set of parameters of the best found solution obtained for the CA27-LS-S5.15 calibration exercise (for a_{ij} and d_{ij} the first column corresponds to the index i)

I_k	a_{ij}			d_{ij}		
	Residential	Industrial	Commercial	Residential	Industrial	Commercial
Residential	1.000	-0.553	0.652	1003.0	146.5	1843.1
Industrial	-0.394	-0.588	-0.626	874.4	345.8	231.2
Commercial	0.401	0.216	0.431	778.6	232.3	251.1
Other	-0.0534	0.495	0.566	495.5	695.2	288.9

The best solution provided by the ECMA algorithm, which is shown in Table 10, was validated against all the steps comprises in the interval 0-30 of the simulation.

The validation results are depicted in Figure 5, where the typical behaviour of a two-point calibration can be recognised: the Kappa statistic gets relatively high values at the calibration points, assumes lower values between the calibration points, and drops rapidly outside the calibration interval.

5 Conclusions and Future Work

The results presented in this paper offer some evidence on the performances of different EAs for calibrating CCAs. In particular, within the space of the studied experimental settings, the EGA and ECMA have shown to yield somewhat better results. Another interesting result, though quite provisory as of the possibility of generalisation worth of further investigation, is the fact that using the LS fitness within the calibration algorithm may to some extent perform better in terms of Kappa metric, than when the Kappa metric is itself directly used in the calibration algorithm.

Of course these findings are still to be considered of limited scope, for many extensions to the experimental space should be taken into consideration to provide a larger body of evidence. Among such extensions, in future we plan to examine more variations of the CCA model (with more parameters to calibrate). Another source of possible variability not taken into account in this work are the differences in the initial configurations, which will also be addressed in the future.

Finally, of a more substantial nature for the application of CAs to the simulation of the real-world spatial dynamics, would be to consider not only zero-error training sets (i.e. configurations which can be obtained exactly with the given CCA model), but also the cases where, besides that of the calibration error, there exists the possibility of what we might call "model error" (no set of parameters can yield the desired target configuration) and that of the "information noise" (where there are uncertainties or fuzziness in the target configuration land uses). These, clearly essential for the operational application of CAs on real territorial cases where both such situations are common, will be studied in the research to come.

References

1. Clarke, K., Hoppen, S., Gaydos, L.: A self-modifying cellular automaton model of historical urbanization in the San Francisco Bay Area. Env. Plan. B 24, 247–261 (1997)
2. Project Gigalopolis, NCGIA (2003),
   http://www.ncgia.ucsb.edu/projects/gig/
3. Straatman, B., White, R., Engelen, G.: Towards an automatic calibration procedure for constrained cellular automata. Computers, Environment and Urban Systems 28, 149–170 (2004)
4. Engelen, G., White, R.: Validating and Calibrating Integrated Cellular Automata Based Models of Land Use Change. In: The Dynamics of Complex Urban Systems: an Interdisciplinary Approach, pp. 185–211. Springer, Heidelberg (2007)
5. Spataro, W., D'Ambrosio, D., Rongo, R., Trunfio, G.A.: An evolutionary approach for modelling lava flows through cellular automata. In: Sloot, P.M.A., Chopard, B., Hoekstra, A.G. (eds.) ACRI 2004. LNCS, vol. 3305, pp. 725–734. Springer, Heidelberg (2004)

6. Goldstein, N.C.: Brains vs. brawn comparative strategies for the calibration of a cellular automata based urban growth model. In: Proceedings of the 7th International Conference on GeoComputation (2003)

7. Trunfio, G.A.: Exploiting Spatio-temporal Data for the Multiobjective Optimization of Cellular Automata Models. In: Corchado, E., Yin, H., Botti, V., Fyfe, C. (eds.) IDEAL 2006. LNCS, vol. 4224, pp. 81–89. Springer, Heidelberg (2006)

8. Avolio, M.V., D'Ambrosio, D., Di Gregorio, S., Lupiano, V., Rongo, R., Spataro, W., Trunfio, G.A.: Evaluating Cellular Automata Models by Evolutionary Multiobjective Calibration. In: Umeo, H., Morishita, S., Nishinari, K., Komatsuzaki, T., Bandini, S. (eds.) ACRI 2008. LNCS, vol. 5191, pp. 114–119. Springer, Heidelberg (2008)

9. Shan, J., Alkheder, S., Wang, J.: Genetic Algorithms for the Calibration of Cellular Automata Urban Growth Modeling. Photogram. Eng. Rem. Sens. 74(10), 1267–1277 (2008)

10. White, R., Engelen, G., Uljee, I.: The use of constrained cellular automata for high-resolution modelling of urban land use dynamics. Env. Plan. B 24, 323–343 (1997)

11. White, R., Engelen, G.: High-resolution integrated modelling of the spatial dynamics of urban and regional systems. Comp., Env. and Urb. Sys. 24, 383–400 (2000)

12. Hagen-Zanker, A., Martens, P.: Map Comparison Methods for Comprehensive Assessment of Geosimulation Models. In: Gervasi, O., Murgante, B., Laganà, A., Taniar, D., Mun, Y., Gavrilova, M.L. (eds.) ICCSA 2008, Part I. LNCS, vol. 5072, pp. 194–209. Springer, Heidelberg (2008)

13. Blecic, I., Cecchini, A., Trunfio, G.A.: A General-Purpose Geosimulation Infrastructure for Spatial Decision Support. Trans. on Comput. Sci. VI, LNCS 5730, 200–218 (2009)

14. Pareto, V.: Cours d'Economie Politique, vol. I, II. F. Rouge, Lausanne (1896)

15. Beyer, H.-G., Schwefel, H.-P.: Evolution strategies: a comprehensive introduction. Natural Comput. 1(1), 3–52 (2002)

16. Goldberg, D.: Genetic Algorithms in Search, Optimization, and Machine Learning. Addison Wesley, Reading (1989)

17. Bäck, T., Hammel, U., Schwefel, H.-P.: Evolutionary computation: comments on the history and current state. IEEE Trans. Evol. Comp. 1(1), 3–17 (1997)

18. Hansen, N., Ostermeier, A.: Completely derandomized self-adaptation in evolution strategies. Evol. Comp. 9(2), 159–195 (2001)

19. Igel, C., Heidrich-Meisner, V., Glasmachers, T., Shark: J. Mach. Learn. Res. 9, 993–996 (2008)

20. Cohen, J.: A coefficient of agreement for nominal scales. Educat. Psychol. Meas. 20(1), 37–46 (1960)

21. Hagen, A.: Fuzzy set approach to assessing similarity of categorical maps. Int. J. Geogr. Inf. Sci. 17(3), 235–249 (2003)

22. Hagen-Zanker, A.: An improved Fuzzy Kappa statistic that accounts for spatial autocorrelation. Int. J. Geogr. Inf. Sci. 23(1), 61–73 (2009)

23. Lee, D., Sallee, G.: A method of measuring shape. Geographical Review 60, 555–563 (1970)

The Calculation Method of Heating and Cooling Energy Saving Potential in Urban District

Shin Do Kim, Im Hack Lee*, and Sung Moon Cheon

#312, 2nd engineering building,
Department of Environmental Engineering, University of Seoul,
13 Siripdaegil, Dongdaemun-Gu, Seoul 130-743, Korea
imhack@empal.com

Abstract. We used to be focus in concerns by taking particulate matters, NOx, VOCs and CO_2 emission by combustion of fossil fuels, i.e. coal, crude oil and natural gas. The combustion of these fuels has been a major source of environmental pollution posing health hazards. The goal of this study was to examine the relationship between the monthly fuel energy demand and the weather variable, such as the temperature, and in this paper, a few energy usage patterns were introduced by using the energy saving potential calculation method. These can result for forecasting the analysis of the heating and cooling energy demand of urban city, and we can produce the reliable emission data for various environmental modeling tools.

Keywords: heating, cooling, energy, electricity, gas, saving, potential.

1 Introduction

Energy consumption of the residential sector accounts for 16–50% of that consumed by all sectors, and averages approximately 30% worldwide [1]. This significant consumption level warrants a detailed understanding of the residential and commercial sector's consumption characteristics to prepare for and help guide the sector's energy consumption in an increasingly energy conscience world; conscience from standpoints of supply, efficient use, and effects of consumption. In response to climate change, high energy prices, and energy supply/demand, there is interest in understanding the detailed consumption characteristics of the residential and commercial sectors in an effort to promote conservation, efficiency, technology implementation and energy source switching, such as to on-site renewable energy. The commercial service sector is estimated to exhibit the highest relative potential for energy savings. The measures proposed to realize these potentials include implementing energy management systems, promoting public–private energy efficiency funds or financing packages and energy audits in small and medium-sized companies and in the public sector [2]. Seasonal energy consumption calculations play an important role in calculating heating and cooling loads of any household and commercial building [3].

---

* Corresponding author.

D. Taniar et al. (Eds.): ICCSA 2010, Part I, LNCS 6016, pp. 182–192, 2010.

Precipitation and temperature records provide important information about a region's weather conditions. In addition to the effects of changes in temperature on agriculture, architecture, energy production and consumption, and melting of snow, icing and freezing affect transportation systems, flowering and harvest days, heating-cooling electric power and gas energy at buildings, and air conditioning systems. All of these are dependent on daily and hourly outside temperatures and system design values [4]. Although there are other complex methods for energy analysis in buildings, the degree-day method is one of the simplest and reliable energy estimation techniques [5]. Air conditioning engineers working in domestic and foreign firms use design data in the energy analysis of buildings, and thus heating and cooling conditions should be analyzed with regard to the design of internal thermal comfort in buildings.

Heating degree-days (HDD) and cooling degree-days (CDD) provide considerable ease in estimating heating and cooling loads of buildings, energy planning, and determining the dimensions of HVAC systems [6]. The use of degree-day methods in the energy analysis of buildings is presented in several studies [7–12]. The goal of this study was to examine the relationship between the Korean monthly energy demand and the weather variable, such as the temperature. In this paper different energy using patterns are introduced in the estimations. We concentrate on the analysis of the monthly effects of possible dynamic patterns on the energy demand-temperature relationship. In particular, we focus on the consequences of correlations. These can result for forecasting the heating and cooling energy demand of urban city in Korea.

2 Data and Method

Urbanization was one of the key issues in Korean economic development. Rapid urbanization was often the cause of enormous pressure on rural and natural environments. Urbanizing population growth, industrialization particularly contributed to the oil industry, vehicles utilization and other anthropogenic activities have increased the amount of energy consumption such as coal, natural gas, crude oil, petroleum oil and electricity. Along with rapid industrialization, the industrial sector had a greater share of energy consumption. The Republic of Korea is a non-negligible player in the world energy market because of its export driven economy, relatively large domestic energy market and heavy dependence on imported energy. In the world, Korea ranks 25th in population, 11th in total production (GDP), 12th in export amount, and 12th in import amount. In comparison, Korea is the 10th in primary energy consumption, the sixth in oil consumption, the fifth in energy import and the third in oil import. Korean dependency on imported energy amounts to a dazzling 97% (83% when excluding nuclear energy) [13].

The heat loss is divided into two groups: (i) the heat transmission losses through the confining walls, floor, ceiling, glass, or other surfaces, and (ii) the infiltration losses through cracks and openings, or heat required to warm outdoor air used for ventilation. Heat loss by conduction and convection heat transfer through any surface is given by:

$$Q = k * A * (T_i - T_0) \tag{1}$$

Where,

> Q = heat transfer through walls, roof, glass, etc. (heat load)
> k = air-to-air heat transfer coefficient
> A = surface areas
> T_i = indoor air temperature
> T_0 = outdoor air temperature

A significant scientific interest in the relationship between energy consumption and weather has led to an important number of papers exploring the role of weather variability and change on energy consumption. Most of these papers model electricity demand as a function of seasonal climate factors. Different electricity statistical models can be developed using two sets of independent variables (Sailor and Munoz, 1997) such as temperature, precipitation, relative humidity and derived variables including heating degree-days, cooling degree. Most models show that the key weather variable is the outdoor air temperature both in its primitive and derived HDD, CDD forms.

$$(HDD)_{T_i} = \int \|T_i - T_0\| dT = (1 day) \sum_{days} \|T_i - T_0\| \qquad (2)$$

$$(CDD)_{T_i} = \int \|T_0 - T_i\| dT = (1 day) \sum_{days} \|T_0 - T_i\| \qquad (3)$$

Where, HDD is Heating Degree Days, CDD is Cooling Degree Days.

2.1 Electricity and Gas Consumption Data

The electricity and gas consumption data used in this study comprised of the monthly electricity demand given in kilowatts hour(kWh) and monthly gas demand given in cubic meters(m^3) by dong (Korean local district unit ; Seoul has 522 dongs) base in Seoul from January 2005 through December 2005, and these energy data were transformed to the data of giga-calory unit base.

In the capital city of Seoul, which accounts for 23.3% of the residential consumption of energy in Korea, a significant number of households have switched from oil and coal to gas and electricity. Especially in urban areas, where, in 1987, natural gas began to be supplied and the rate of consumption increased dramatically thereafter, the rate of consumption has increased at an average rate of 6.9% per year. As of 2001, natural gas was the main source of energy for households in Seoul, accounting for 55.4% of the residential consumption of energy [14]. The supply chain for gas in urban areas in Seoul is structured as follows. Natural gas is imported in liquid form (LNG) from foreign countries and is then supplied to domestic gas companies (wholesale companies and a monopolized public utilities company that is owned by the Korean government). It is also supplied to regular, urban, gas companies (for-profit retail companies and private firms) that supply to households, businesses, and industries. The electricity supply system in the Republic of Korea consists of a single tightly interconnected grid that serves the entire country. Power is not generally used in areas adjacent to the power plants where it is generated. This so-called 'circle-network system' connects the whole country in an electric ring structure [16].

2.2 Weather Data

Previous studies have shown that temperature is usually the most significant weather variable influencing electricity consumption. For this reason we have used this variable for the present study, and the possible influence of other weather variables is left for future work. In particular, we have used the mean monthly outdoor temperature.

The mean monthly temperatures were assessed at 25 weather stations distributed across Seoul, representing 25 different climatic sub regions. Each weather station produces the temperature data by per one hour, and we calculate the monthly average data with these hourly data. Actually each weather station logged relative humidity, precipitation, wind speed, wind direction, so we can analyze the relationships between energy consumption and other weather properties.

2.3 Methodology

Generally, electricity and gas energy consumptions can be divided three areas of energy usages called heating, cooling, lighting and machine operation (TV, refrigerator, computer etc.) for electricity consumption and called heating, cooling, cooking and hot water for gas consumption. In this study, energy conservation potential was taken into account in heating and cooling area. To divide total energy consumption by each area, we used the following method.

First, the energy consumption of each month was calculated and the month was collected that had the minimum energy using consumption by comparison the monthly data of 2005 year.

Second, the differences between the each monthly energy using datum and minimum monthly datum that calculated in the first step were produced. When this difference value is zero, the monthly average temperature was assumed base level temperature, and we assumed that the energy consumptions that were equal with minimum monthly energy using data were lighting and machine operation for electricity consumption part and were cooking and hot water for gas consumption part. When the monthly averaging temperature is lower than the base level temperature, the differences between the each monthly energy using datum and minimum monthly datum was called heating energy, and When the monthly averaging temperature is higher than the base level temperature, the differences between the each monthly energy using datum and minimum monthly datum was called cooling energy.

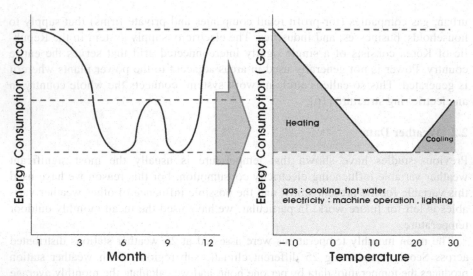

Fig. 1. This shows the energy dividing method. When the energy consumption differences between the each monthly energy using datum and minimum monthly datum is zero, the monthly average temperature at that time was assumed base level temperature.

3 Result

Monthly gas consumptions of eunpyeong-gu from January 2005 to December 2006 are shown in Fig. 2. a.. Seoul has 25 gus that have about 20 dongs for each gu, where eunpyeong-gu shows 19 dongs' data, and the area of each dong can be calculated as mean value 1.3 km². As the real gas consumption difference values among dongs in each gu are various, we can not show the energy consumption pattern curve in the same graph with real energy using values. So we divided monthly gas usage consumption values by annual average values, and we could get normalized monthly gas usage data of each dong of which patterns can be described in serial graph diagram for each gu unit at the same time. The monthly gas consumption patterns in eunpyeong-gu are very simple and typical because of that Korean has 4 seasons.

The outdoor temperatures of Dcc. or Jan. are so low that decrease to -15℃, and people have to use the gas energy to heat indoor spaces, by contrast, Korean people have to use the cooling energy when the ambient temperature increase to 35℃ in Jul. or Aug., so we can obtained the typical energy usage concept of Korea. The city character or concept of eunpyeong-gu is bed town image with many old residential buildings, so we can assume that energy using patterns of dongs in eunpyeong-gu have typical concept that show high heating energy usage in winter and show low energy usage in summer. Monthly electricity consumptions of eunpyeong-gu from January 2005 to December 2006 are shown in Fig. 2. b. We could see that electric energy using patterns of dongs in eunpyeong-gu have a concept that show high heating energy usage in winter and show high cooling energy usage in summer because of using electricity energy for indoor space heating and cooling activities.

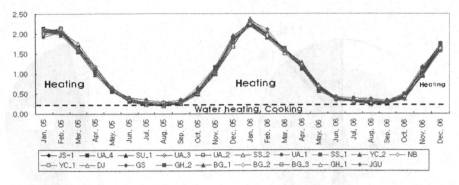

(a) Gas consumption

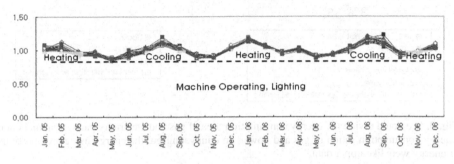

(b) Electricity consumption

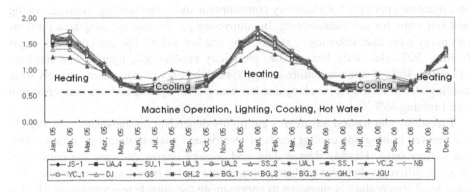

(c) Gas and Electricity consumption

Fig. 2. These data shows energy consumption of eunpyeong-gu. (a) is Monthly gas consumptions, (b) is electricity consumptions, and (c) is the sum data of (a) + (b) for two years.

By analyzing the normalized electricity and gas time serial energy consumption patterns among dongs, we could divide the energy consumption area of gas and electricity parts of annual data in Fig. 3. In this paper, we divided electricity and gas energy consumptions by three areas of energy usages called heating, cooling, lighting

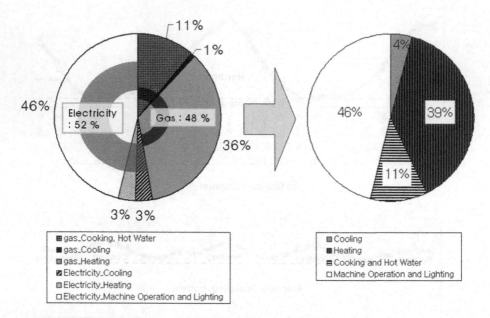

Fig. 3. We could divide the energy consumption area of gas and electricity parts of annual data. Energy consumption ration of gas and power. In eunpyeong-gu, the energy using area portions of energy were like upper data.

and machine operation for electricity consumption and called heating, cooling, ooking and hot water for gas consumption. In eunpyeong-gu, the energy using area portions of energy were like followings ; gas cooking and hot water 11%, gas cooling 1%, gas heating 36%, electricity heating 3%, electricity cooling 3%, lighting and machine operation 46%. If not concerning energy types, the energy using area portions were cooling 4%, heating 39%, cooking and hot water 11%, lighting and machine operation and Lighting 46%.

Electricity and natural gas usages are highly dependent on the weather. In Fig. 4., we showed heating and cooling loads of electric and gas consumptions versus ambient temperatures. Heating degree days and cooling degree days are the number of degrees difference between ambient temperature and a base level temperature. The base level temperature is supposed to approximate the outside temperature at which a person inside a house or office would need to turn on the heat or turn on a cooling system in order to remain comfortable.

Historically, 18℃ has often been selected as that base level temperature. Heating degree day base 18℃ is the number of degrees where the ambient temperature is colder than 18℃. The method of using HDDs and CDDs based at 18℃ in the regression assumes that the load response is essentially V, U and similar line shaped. But in this paper, we analyzed other shapes that showed area patterns at various base level temperatures.

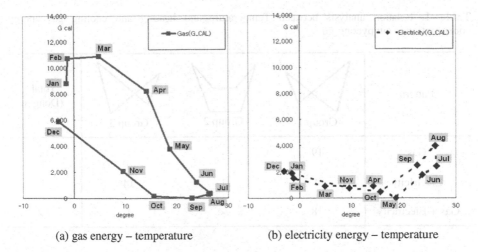

     (a) gas energy – temperature   (b) electricity energy – temperature

Fig. 4. We showed heating and cooling loads of electric and gas consumptions versus ambient temperatures. These figures are the circulation pattern examples between temperature and heating, cooling energy.

Table. 1. showed pattern counting results which show the inter-relationship between the monthly average electricity, gas consumption for heating, cooling and the monthly mean temperature. The cooling energy consumption increases when the temperature rises that is higher than the base level temperature and the heating energy consumption increases when the temperature rises that is lower than the base level temperature.

The reason why these area shape patterns occur was not analyzed until now, but by calculating the inner areas of the energy-temperature relation shapes, we may define energy saving potentials, namely, in same temperature condition we can use lower monthly energy consumption. For example, in Fig. 5. a., we can use the gas heating energy amount of December in -2 ~3℃ condition rather than the amount of January or February, and we can use the gas heating energy amount of October or September in 13~23℃ condition rather than the amount of April or May or June. In Table 1., If the area of shape patterns in the other gu was more than that of area of shape patterns in eunpyeong-gu, it means that the energy saving potential of the other gu is larger than that of eunpyeong-gu, and with this calculating method we can produce the energy using data and energy saving potentials in local government, regional government, and national government, and we can produce environmental emission data for air dispersion models If we convert these dong base data format to 1 km x 1 km grid base format.

By calculating method of the energy potential in eunpyeong-gu, we got the heating and cooling energy potential results like followings; When the total energy consumption in eunpyeong-gu, Seoul, Korea was 4,479,255 G-cal, the gas heating and cooling energy potential was 7.67 %, and the electricity heating and cooling energy potential was 3.48 %, so we could get the total electricity heating and cooling energy potential in eunpyeong-gu, Seoul was 11.15 % (499,437 G-cal).

Table 1. Relation analysis between Temperature and heating and cooling gas energy consumption in eunpyeong-gu

Pattern	Group 1	Group 2	Group 3	Total (Dongs)
Gas	19	-	-	19
Electricity	4	1	14	19
Gas + Electricity	18	-	1	19

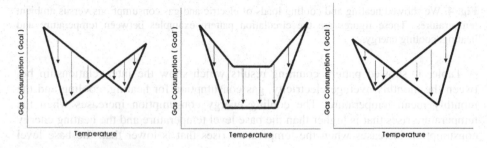

Fig. 5. We could obtain the different heating and cooling energy consumption data in the same ambient temperature condition. So we thought the energy difference between months in the same ambient temperature condition could be the target of saving Energy saving potential examples of energy-temperature patterns.

4 Conclusion

The visibility, ambient ozone concentration, and the global climate change are the internationally known most vital problems of current environmental issues. In conjunction with this, we used to be focus in concerns by taking particulate matters, NOx, VOCs and CO_2 emission by combustion of fossil fuels, i.e. coal, crude oil and natural gas. The combustion of these fuels has been a major source of environmental pollution posing health hazards. Although there are other complex methods for fossil fuel energy consumption analysis in buildings, the degree-day method is one of the simplest and reliable energy estimation techniques. Air conditioning engineers working in domestic and foreign firms use design data in the energy analysis of buildings, and thus heating and cooling conditions should be analyzed with regard to the design of internal thermal comfort in buildings. Heating degree-days (HDD) and cooling degree-days (CDD) provide considerable ease in estimating heating and cooling loads of buildings, energy planning, and determining the dimensions of HVAC systems. The goal of this study was to examine the relationship between the Korean monthly fuel energy demand and the weather variable, such as the temperature, and in this paper, several energy using patterns were introduced in the estimations.

Generally, the correlation curve is V, U and similar line shaped but in this paper, the area shape patterns could be seen such as butterfly shapes with the big right wing (group 1), butterfly shapes with the big left wing (group 2), smile shapes (group 3). Group 1 was analyzed that we have to focus on reducing heating energy consumption, and group 2 was analyzed that we have to focus on reducing cooling energy consumption and group 3 was analyzed that we have to focus on reducing mid-term heating and cooling energy consumption.

After dividing electricity and gas energy consumptions by three areas of energy usages called heating, cooling and others, we could calculate the inner areas of the heating/cooling energy-temperature relation shapes, and we may produce energy saving potentials. With this calculating method we can produce the spatial energy using data and energy saving potentials in spatially various governments, and we can produce environmental emission data for air dispersion models using for making environmental policies

With the result of this paper, we may produce dynamic environmental emission source data that can be used to analyze and assess the environmental impacts by air dispersion models. So, we have the plan to develop the energy using database of urban city that can produce data of B.A.U. (Business As Usual) and data of the case after energy decreasing scenarios in the near future.

Acknowledgments. This work was supported by the National Research Foundation of Korea(NRF) grant funded by the Korea government(MEST) (No. 2009-413-D00001).

References

1. Swan, L.G.: Modeling of end-use energy consumption in the residential sector: A review of modeling techniques. Renewable and Sustainable Energy Reviews 13, 1819–1835 (2009)
2. Schleich, J.: Barriers to energy efficiency: A comparison across the German commercial and services sector. Ecological Economics 68, 2150–2159 (2009)
3. Duryamaz, A., Kadıoglu, M., S¸en, Z.: An application of the degree-hours method to estimate the residential heating energy requirement and fuel consumption in Istanbul. Energy 25, 1245–1256 (2000)
4. Seṇ, Z., Kadıoglu, M.: Heating degree-days for arid regions. Energy 23, 1089–1094 (1997)
5. Bu yu kalaca, O., Bulut, H., Yılmaz, T.: Analysis of variable-base heating and cooling degree-days for Turkey. Applied Energy 69, 269–283 (2001)
6. Satman, A., Yalçınkaya, N.: Heating and cooling degree-hours for Turkey. Energy 24, 833–840 (1999)
7. Matzarakis, A., Balafoutis, C.: Heating degree-days over Greece as an index of energy consumption. International Journal of Climatology 24, 1817–1828 (2004)
8. Bodescu, V., Zamfir, E.: Degree-days, degree-hours and ambient temperature bin data from monthly-average temperatures (Romania). Energy Conversion & Management 40, 885–900 (1999)

9. Sarak, H., Satman, A.: The degree-days method to estimate the residential heating natural gas consumption in Turkey: a case study. Energy 28, 929–939 (2003)
10. Lorusso, A., Maraziti, F.: Heating system projects using the degree-days method in livestock building. Journal of Agricultural Engineering Research 71, 285–290 (1998)
11. Bellia, L., Mazzei, P., Polombo, A.: Weather data for building energy cost-benefit analysis. International Journal of Energy Research 22, 1205–1215 (1998)
12. Christenson, M., Manz, H., Gyalistras, D.: Climate warming impact on degree-days and building energy demand in Switzerland. Energy Conversion & Management 47, 671–686 (2006)
13. Kim, S.H., et al.: Korean energy demand in the new millennium: outlook and policy implications, 2000-2005. Energy Policy 29, 899–910 (2001)
14. Seoul Metropolitan Government. Regional energy plan of Seoul city, Seoul (2003)
15. Yoo, S.-H., et al.: Estimating the residential demand function for natural gas in Seoul with correction for sample selection bias. Applied Energy 86, 460–465 (2009)
16. Lee, K.-M.: Life cycle inventory analysis for electricity in Korea. Energy 29, 87–101 (2004)

GIS-Based Estimation of Wetland Conservation Potentials in Europe

Christine Schleupner

Research Unit Sustainability and Global Change, ZMAW & Hamburg University,
Bundesstr. 55,
20146 Hamburg, Germany
christine.schleupner@zmaw.de

Abstract. In the EU socio-economic considerations and economic activities play an important part in land use management and conservation planning. However, conservation studies that offer high-accuracy landscape information at the European level are often recommended by policy makers, but rarely realized. This study contributes to this problem by optimal combination of existing spatial datasets to obtain the spatial distribution of wetlands by definition of flexible knowledge rules. The resulting distribution model distinguishes between existing wetlands and sites suitable for wetland restoration at 1 km resolution. It differentiates several wetland types and covers 37 European countries. The results of the model may help to locate sites suitable for restoration programs, or for the introduction of faunistic corridors.

Keywords: Land use planning, restoration ecology, spatial analysis.

1 Introduction

Land utilization in Europe is diverse and complex because of its settlement history. As a consequence, many natural ecosystems such as wetlands are altered and experience degradation, fragmentation and biotope loss. It is estimated that more than two thirds of all wetlands in Europe have been lost since beginning of the 20th century [1] because economically profitable land utilization requires drainage of wetlands leaving them to be among the world's most threatened ecosystems. Wetland loss has most recently also been made responsible for unprecedented flooding events and species declines [2]. Often wetland terms and definitions are not standardized. In this study we concentrate on the natural freshwater or inland wetlands whose types are based on definitions by [3], [4], and [5]. The definition of inland wetlands also includes marshes and wet meadows dominated by herbaceous plants that are most often human made as well as shrub- or tree-dominated swamps. In Europe, inland wetlands are most common on floodplains along rivers and streams, along the margins of lakes and ponds, and in other low-lying areas where the groundwater intercepts the soil surface or where precipitation sufficiently saturates the soil (vernal pools and bogs). Many of these wetlands are seasonal and may be wet only periodically. Open waters are considered separately.

D. Taniar et al. (Eds.): ICCSA 2010, Part I, LNCS 6016, pp. 193–209, 2010.

Due to growing shortage of natural habitat latest conservation efforts include the option of restoration and creation of wetlands to meet the targets set out by the European Commission to halt biodiversity decline. But changing land use for food and, increasingly, biofuel production constitutes a great challenge to nature conservation. In the past the integration of conservation concerns in agricultural as well as forestry production land use models has often been neglected [6]. One reason is lack of accurate and consistent basis data. Usually, economic land use models refer to country statistics as base data. These data differ in spatial accuracy, reliability, acquisition data and class definition. Aggregating statistical and spatial data from many sources into one database often causes low spatial accuracy and complicates comparability, as is often the case between data of eastern and western European countries, for example. Thus, the spatial distribution of wetlands in Europe is not well known except for large wetland areas or for wetlands of special ecological interest [7]. Even those wetland areas, which have been identified on the behalf of European Environment Agency (EEA), correspond to wetland areas of ecological interest and represent only a rather small part of all wetland areas. The use of existing global wetland data, e.g. [8] for conservation studies in European scale is inappropriate because the spatial resolution is coarse and wetlands are seldom differentiated in detail. The most detailed consistent information about wetland habitats in Europe offers the EUNIS Database [9]. However, the corresponding EUNIS habitat type map [10] has been created using mainly aggregated CORINE data. Also CORINE biotopes data [11] [12] are based on reported NATURA2000 sites and neither represent the existing wetlands completely, nor illustrate its area extension spatially. At present, CORINE [13] is the most detailed land cover database covering the European Union. One disadvantage is the heterogeneity of the classes determined by functional land use and not by land cover itself. The digital map of the potential natural vegetation of Europe [14] shows a detailed classification and potential distribution of wetland vegetation types across Europe. However, this distribution is irrespective of human influences and therefore only conditionally suitable because river regulation, peat extraction or urbanization on former wetland areas often lead to changed wetland restoration potentials. In all it becomes clear that there are no digital land cover or vegetation maps of the EU that show detailed wetland distribution.

This study contributes to the problem by compiling spatially consistent information on wetlands differentiated by wetland types and characteristics using GIS-based techniques. GIS has been used before for wetland studies by many authors (e.g. [15], [16], [17], [18], [19], [20]). However, the analyses refer to catchment areas at the largest extent and no application to larger areas is discussed. The study presented here is an attempt to extend the distribution modeling process to a broad continental scale by keeping the spatial accuracy as high as possible. This is important because European wetlands are often fragmented ecosystems of small extent. Many wetlands are smaller than one 1km². But improvements in data quality and availability as well as simplifications in earth observation techniques make the more detailed studies feasible. As a result the narrow stripes of alluvial forests or small isolated bogs may be better represented in broad-scale analyses of wetlands. Through the model not only existing wetland habitats are documented but also potential wetland restoration sites by considering actual land use options. Decision makers of European land use policies demand spatial ecosystem information at holistic scales. The resulting wetland distribution model is integrated into the mathematical bottom-up land use assessment model EUFASOM (European Forest and Agricultural Sector Optimization Model), which is used to study synergies and trade-offs between wetland conservation efforts, greenhouse gas mitigation options including carbon sinks and bioenergy, and agriculture and forestry of Europe [21].

2 Locating Wetland Potentials

The spatial wetland distribution model "Swedi" is developed as extraction tool to denote wetland allocations in Europe. In this respect GIS and spatial modeling are used as instrument to locate existing wetland areas as well as to identify the most suitable areas for wetland regeneration measures. This GIS model aims to depict the distribution of wetland areas at regional level and also at coarse geographic scale. This involves the integration of a variety of GIS datasets and multiple iterations of expert review and interpretation to delineate the potential wetland areas of Europe. We used the GIS tool ArcGIS9 for analysis. Figure 1 gives an overview of the Swedi model structure and its core input data. It is described in more detail in the following methodological section that is subdivided into two parts. The first deals with the evaluation of existing wetlands in Europe, and the second with the modeling of potential convertible sites for wetland restoration management.

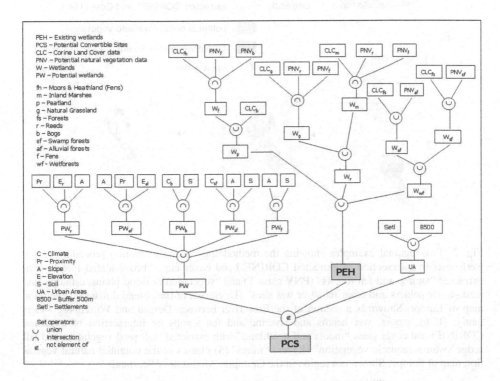

Fig. 1. The spatial wetland distribution model "Swedi"

2.1 Existing Wetland Habitats (PEH)

Existing wetland biotopes are defined as areas where wetlands with state close to nature actually appear within Europe. The analysis is executed with Model Builder and the Spatial Analyst Extension of ArcGIS9.

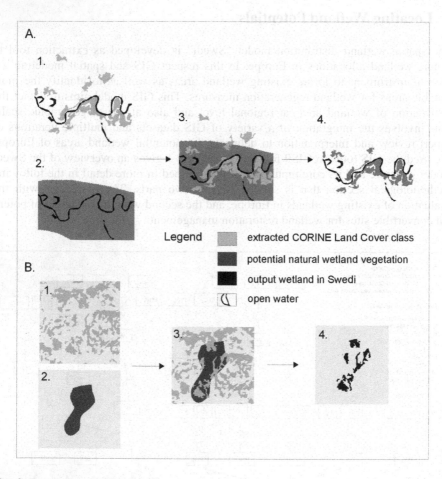

Fig. 2. Two regional examples showing the methodology of the extraction procedure A. for wetforests by intersection of extracted CORINE Land cover class "broad-leafed forest" with extracted "swamp and fen forests" (PNV class T) and "vegetation of flood plains, estuaries and fresh-water polders and other moist or wet sites" (U) classes of the potential natural vegetation map of Europe. Shown is a section of the Elbe river between Dessau and Wittenberg / Germany. B. for moors, wet heaths and riverine and fen scrubs by intersection of extracted CORINE Land cover class "moors and heathland" with extracted "tall reed vegetation and tall sedge swamps, aquatic vegetation" (R) and "mires" (S) classes of the potential natural vegetation map of Europe. Shown is a region in the Grampian Mountains / Scotland.

The Corine land cover map 2000 with spatial resolution of 100 m serves as core base map [13]. From the CORINE data, the following land cover classes have been extracted: moors & heathland (3.2.2.), inland marshes (4.1.1.), peat bogs (4.1.2.), inland waters and estuaries (5.1. and 5.2.2.), natural grassland (3.2.1.) and forests (3.1.). The EEA [22] gives detailed definitions of each class. Within the spatial model the land cover class "peat bogs" serves as the only one that does not need to be altered to show existing "bog" wetlands, whereas all other selected land cover classes have to be split up separately: out of the generalized forest classes, only the wet forests, namely alluvial forests next to river courses and fen or swamp forests, are extracted through rule based statements using set operators. The CORINE classes "natural grassland" as well as "inland marshes" serve as base data for the model parameter "natural wet grasslands". In addition, moors, wet heaths, riverine and fen scrubs are extracted from the general class "moors and heathland". The map of the potential natural vegetation (PNV) of Europe [14] has been selected as source to locate the wetland sites within these CORINE land cover classes. The PNV map in general distinguishes following wetland types: a. tall reed vegetation and tall sedge swamps, aquatic vegetation (PNV class R), b. mires (S), c. swamp and fen forests (T), d. vegetation of flood plains, estuaries and fresh-water polders and other moist or wet sites (U). These types can then be further subdivided. We extracted the wetland types and intersected them with the corresponding CORINE data. Only those sites matching both attributes were considered as present existing wetland site. The remaining sites were assumed to be non-wetland. However, this does not exclude the probability of the non-wetland areas to be potential wetland restoration sites as is explained in more detail below. Figure 2 gives examples of the intersection and extraction procedure.

In order to verify the accuracy of the distribution of existing wetlands in Swedi, resulting outputs must be compared with an independent data set [23] [24]. A description of general CORINE Land Cover data accuracy is found in [25]. In this study we use the CORINE biotopes database and parts of the RAMSAR list of wetlands of international importance [26] for comparative analyses. The Corine biotopes (Version 2000) database is an inventory of major nature sites. The aim of the database was to enhance reliable and accessible information about vulnerable ecosystems, habitats and species of importance as background information for community environmental assessment. The wetland sites of the database are - among others - attributed with the size of the wetland. Site coordinates are included for easy localization of the biotopes within a GIS. We selected 50 freshwater wetlands from the database and compared their occurrence in the Swedi model considering spatial accuracy and wetland size. The same procedure has been applied to 50 selected RAMSAR sites. Additionally, the spatial extends of denoted NATURA2000 wetland sites as well as available biotope maps of individual sites are compared to the existing wetlands of Swedi.

2.2 Potential Convertible Sites (PCS)

The second part of the GIS assessment evaluates potential convertible wetland sites. These areas may be used for location of restoration programs or habitat creational measures. The distribution of wetlands is explained by many dependent and explanatory variables. Important factors are the climatic, hydrological, geological, ecological and socio-economic conditions of the area. The classification of wetland distribution is therefore preferably based on analysis of these independent variables [27]. The connection between the respective information of the database and the probable appearance of the wetlands is determined by assuming that there is a relationship between environmental gradients such as soil, climate, or slope and wetland distribution [28]. We use traditional statistical methods based on observed correlation as well as geographically weighted regression analysis to analyze environment-wetland relationships. This proved to be useful concerning European scale analyses, because it allows for regional differences in relationships by estimating regression parameters that vary across space [29]. Characteristic soil parameters, climate conditions, slope angles, and elevations are worked out for every wetland type on the basis of several literature resources ([30], [31], [32]). Through this, rule-based statements are derived about the potential appearance of the target wetland types. In combination with geographical data these statements allow the identification and localization of potential wetland sites within a GIS. Table 1 illustrates the resulting factors that characterize each wetland type.

Former wetland areas are considered as most suitable for wetland recreation ([33], [34]). These might be arable fields, pasture lands, fallow or forested areas on sites of former wetlands that have been intensely changed. Actual soil conditions might give hints for potential wetland biotopes. We use the European soil database [35] of 1 km grid resolution and extract following potential wet- and peatsoil-classes: gleysols, fluvisols, gleyic luvisols, histosols, gleyic podzol. The wetland types bogs, swamp forests and fens are considered to be soil dependent. The climate parameter is only applied for the parameters bogs and swamp forests; all other wetland types are rated as azonal and therefore relatively climate independent [36]. The climate variables of the wetland types shown in table 2 are extracted from the explanatory text of the map of the Natural Vegetation of Europe [32]. We use the attributes temperature (max temp of warmest month, min temp of coldest month, average annual) and precipitation (average annual) of the Bioclim and Worldclim data at spatial grid resolution of 30 arc-seconds (~ 1 km²).

Table 1. Rating factors that characterize each wetland type ([24], [25], [26])

	Soil	Slope Angle	Climate	Proximity to open waters	Elevation
Fen	X	X			
Bog	X		X		
Swamp Forest	X	X	X		
Alluvial Forest		X		X	X
Reeds		X		X	X

Table 2. Wetland type characteristics concerning their climate ranges of occurrence

Wetland type	Average annual temperature (in °C)	Average precipitation (mm/year)	Max temp av. warmest month (°C)	Min temp av. coldest month (°C)
Bogs	3 - 6	300 – 1 000	12 - 17	-15 – (-2)
	9 - 11	1 200 – 2 000	13 - 15	5 – 7
	3 - 8	1 400 – 2 400	10 - 12	-2 - 0
	5 – 9,5	550 – 1 500	14 - 19	-3 - 5
	4 – 5,5	900 – 1 400	11 - 12	-3 – 0
	3.5 – 7.8	530 - 630	17.5 - 19	-10 – (-2)
	- 10 - 1	200 - 500	8 - 13	-25 – (-10)
Aapa mires (fens)	- 3 - 5	250 - 700	8 - 15	-17 – (-5)
transitional mires (fens)	0 - 5	500 - 870	8 - 14	-12 – (-3)
degraded bogs, now wet forests	8 - 9	600 – 1 200	15 - 16	0 – 4
wet forests	6 - 11	450 – 1 000	16 - 21	-5 – 0
	14 - 15	> 1 000	20 - 22	6 – 8
	9 - 10	550 – 1 000	15 - 16	4 - 5

The analyses of elevation dependent wetland types might also refer to climate or relief conditions [7]. However, we are confined to the statements of highest occurrences of respective wetland types by the explanatory text of the PNV map of Europe [32]. The base elevation data for Europe are taken from GTOPO30 data a global digital elevation model at spatial resolution of 30 arc-seconds (sheets: W020N90, E020N90, W020N40, E020N40) [31]. In addition to that the bio-geographical regions map of Europe [38] contribute to the elevation parameter by dividing the height variables into several bioclimatic regions that better reflect the height-limits than country based distinctions of regions. Table 3 shows the wetland type characteristics concerning their maximum elevation occurrence range.

Table 3. Wetland type characteristics concerning their maximum elevation occurrence range

Wetland type	Biogeographical Region	Elevation (m)
Reeds	Boreal, alpine (scand.)	<= 500
Reeds	Alpine (other), all others	<= 800
Alluvial forests	Boreal, alpine (scand.)	<= 500
Alluvial forests	Alpine (other), all others	<= 1 200

The map of bio-geographical regions is based on [14]. It distinguishes between six bio-geographical regions in the EU-25, namely Alpine, Boreal, Continental, Atlantic, Mediterranean, and Pannonian. Alluvial forests and reeds are considered elevation dependent, less because of climatic conditions, but more due to loss of suitable ground conditions ([32], [39]). The climate dependent wetlands are assumed to limit their height occurrence by this parameter itself. An elevation constraint is therefore not necessary. Only the fens are assumed neither climate nor elevation dependent. They solely refer to soil conditions and the slope parameter.

The slope parameter is evaluated based on the elevation data using the Spatial Analyst extension of ArcGIS9. Only those areas with a slope angle below 1° are assumed suitable for the wetland types reeds, alluvial forests, swamp forests and fens [39]. Due to scale reasons the slope angle is set to this maximum extension and does not distinguish slope angles below that point as has been done in case studies of larger scale [40]. The delineation of floodplains that may be obtained directly from DEMs using a topographic index [41] is scale dependent as well and thus not applicable on the scale of this study.

The proximity to inland waters or to existing inland peatland is an important criterion for localization of target areas if other parameters are fulfilled. The proximity criterion has been initially set to 500 meters. But this border may be handled flexible. For implementation in the GIS-based model we establish multiple ring buffers around inland waters and other bog areas with radius of the defined proximity. The extension of potential water surrounding wetland sites like alluvial forests can be detected by a combination of the proximity with other parameters. Highly populated areas as are towns and cities provide very limited space for wetland restoration or construction. For this reason, potential convertible sites are only modeled for agriculturally used areas, grasslands and forests by using pseudo-absences for urban areas (cf. [42]). Urban areas including a buffer zone of 800 meters are omitted by the model. We use the Corine Land Cover 2000 data for determination of these sites.

For accuracy assessment the potential wetland sites are correlated with the spatial distribution of the existing wetlands. And in a last step, the existing wetland sites are subtracted from the preliminary results to obtain only data on potential convertible areas. All data encompass the whole EU-25 states boundaries with exception of Malta and Cyprus that are not included in the analysis.

3   Results

The outcomes of Swedi are spatially explicit data on wetland distribution in Europe. The results may be illustrated through wetland distribution maps. Figure 3 shows the spatial distribution of existing habitats (dark grey) and potential convertible sites (light grey) exemplarily for selected areas. The comparison of existing wetlands with samples of independent data sets (RAMSAR wetlands and CORINE biotopes) shows that all selected wetlands of the databases are also represented in Swedi. The differences lie in the area extent of the respective wetlands: In over 70% of the cases the model overestimates the size of an existing wetland. One reason is the fact that the existing wetlands module of the Swedi model accepts uncertainties about the state of the wetland ecosystem also due to scale reasons. We are not able to distinguish

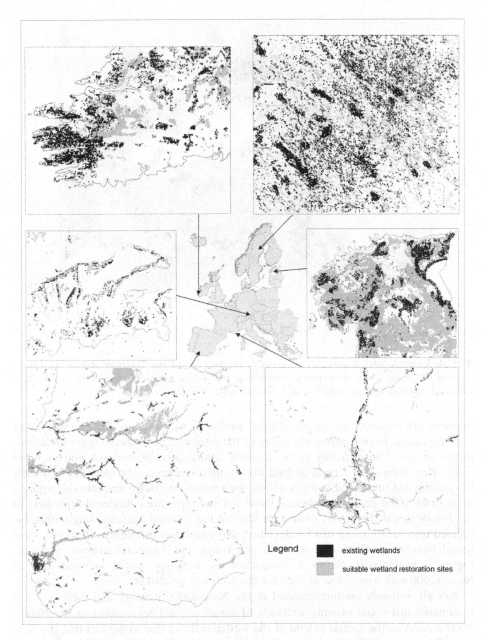

Fig. 3. Detailed examples of the spatial distribution of potential existing habitats (dark grey) and potential convertible sites (light grey) of Swedi. The whole illustrated data set is available for download at http://www.fnu.zmaw.de/Dipl-Geogr-Christine-Schleupner.5728.0.html.

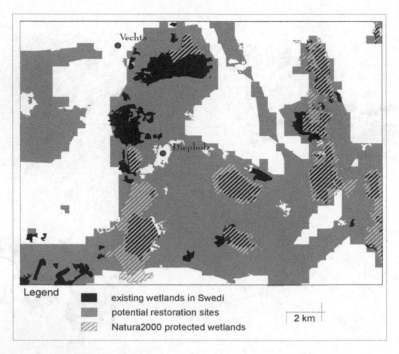

Fig. 4. Example of the accuracy assessment in the case of the Dümmer Region in Lower Saxony / Germany. We used spatial information of wetlands implemented in the Natura2000 sites and correlated them to the wetland distribution of Swedi.

between afforestations or natural alluvial forests in a floodplain, for example, what also might lead to overestimation errors of the results. 26% of the sites are underestimated in size. The difficulty is the accurate demarcation of wetlands and its types from open waters and terrestrial land due to their dynamic characteristics and their fluctuating and undefined borders. Often open waters are integrated into the wetland definitions of the databases whereas these wetland types are considered separately in the Swedi model. However, more than 85% of the selected wetlands stay within the defined uncertainty range of 15% deviation. No significant differences in accuracy are found between northern and southern or eastern and western European wetlands. Figure 4 exemplarily shows a comparison of available spatial wetland data of Natura2000 with Swedi data as used for the accuracy assessment.

Not all wetlands are implemented in the Natura2000 network and therefore it is reasonable that some existing wetlands of Swedi are not represented in the Natura 2000 data. Also the spatial extend of the wetlands differ due to the fact that the wetland dimensions are difficult to define and that often the Natura2000 data include other biotopes combined in biotope complexes or buffer zones as well. Despite its inconsistencies in extent, more than 91 % of the Natura 2000 wetlands data are also represented in Swedi. A weakness of Swedi is that wetlands below a certain extent are not well represented and therefore some present wetlands may be underestimated or indicated as restoration site. At the same time the restoration sites overestimate the extent of potential wetland sites because of coarse base data in elevation or soil that do not respect geographic diversity at landscape scale. Problems in comparability arose by drawing comparisons with a simple per-country aggregation of Swedi- derived wetland areas to results of the Pan European Wetland Inventory (PEWI) [43]. This may simply be due to the fact that both datasets apply to different wetland type determinations and basis data. Whereas the Swedi data are spatially explicit and rely on other spatial and geophysical data, the PEWI data are on country scale and rely on different kinds of national wetland inventories or statistics.

An analysis of the Swedi map reveals that about 4% of the EU-25 land area consists of potentially existing wetlands and an additional 21% of the land areas are potential convertible to wetland sites. This constitutes a maximum share of wetlands of one fourth of the total land area of the EU-25. Figure 5 gives a general overview of the total area of existing and the potential convertible wetland sites per country derived from Swedi.

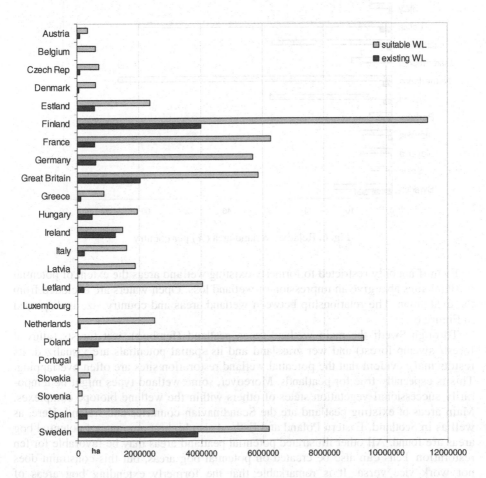

Fig. 5. Total wetland area (in 1000 ha) per country distinguished after existing wetlands and suitable restoration sites

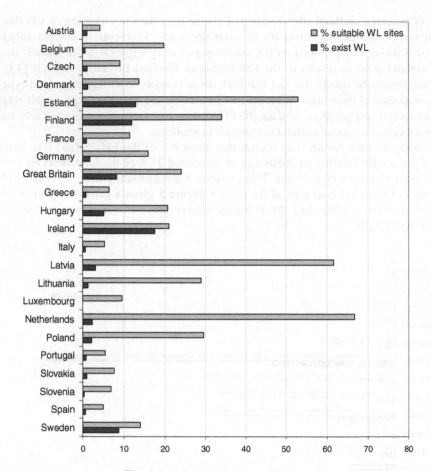

Fig. 6. Relative wetland area (%) per country

Even if not only restricted to formerly existing wetland areas the extent of potential wetland sites also give an impression of wetland loss. Open waters are excluded from the evaluation. The relationship between wetland areas and country size is displayed in Figure 6.

Through Swedi the main wetland types peatland (fen/bog), wet forests (alluvial forest/ swamp forest) and wet grassland and its spatial potentials are visualized. Its results make evident that the potential wetland restoration sites are often overlapping. This is especially true for peatlands. Moreover, some wetland types might be temporarily successional vegetation states of others within the wetland biotope complexes. Main areas of existing peatland are the Scandinavian countries and Ireland. Here, as well as in Scotland, Eastern Poland and Estland also highest amounts of potential bog areas are found. All other illustrated potential peatland areas may be favorable for fen restoration. Fens can also be created on potential bog areas, but this constraint does not work vice versa. It is remarkable that the formerly extending bog areas of North-Western Germany, that have been mainly drained and exploited during the last centuries, show fen instead of expected bog potentials in Swedi. This might be due to model uncertainties or errors, but can as well be a hint that the bogs have developed under different climatic conditions from the end of the last ice age and are relicts only. The destruction of these bog areas possibly means an unrecoverable demise of the ecosystem. Like wet grasslands also wet forests are found along water courses and in the proximity of other open waters. Especially the swamp forests are constricted to wet soils and to specific climate conditions. Main areas of potential swamp forest sites are therefore found in Central and Eastern Europe but also in the UK. In northern and western European countries the wet forested area does not exceed the peatland areas whereas in Germany and Poland and further south wet forests are the most extending wetland types. Extending areas of potential wet grassland sites are shown in Scandinavia, Estland, and Ireland, but also in Hungary. Wetland areas need to have at least a size of one hectare to be included into the spatial model. Therefore, often reeds along lakeshores are not shown in the results and Finland even counts no wet grasslands even though there are reeds growing along many waters.

Summarizing the total PCS areas distinguished after the main wetland types for the European countries one gets following results: a maximum area of respectively 1 329 200 km², 643 300 km² and 305 700 km² could be potentially used for additional bog, additional fen as well as additional wet forest creation. It must be noted that these data are no absolute numbers, but moreover provide an informative basis of potential wetland restoration area.

3 Discussion

There is a growing demand of policy makers and researchers for high-accuracy landscape information at the European level. Despite numerous data on land use in Europe, a detailed analysis of the distribution of wetlands and potential restoration sites has been lacking so far. We developed a detailed wetland distribution map in European scale with high spatial resolution. Not only does it distinguish between different wetland types but also between existing and potential convertible wetland restoration sites; information that has not been available before. Whereas the evaluation of existing wetlands relies on a cross-compilation of existing spatial datasets, the potential wetland restoration sites are determined by definition of flexible knowledge rules in combination with geographical data. The orientation towards physical parameters and the allowance of overlapping wetland types characterizes the Swedi model. The detailed spatially explicit wetland classification of Swedi allows connections to other habitat databases, for example EUNIS, as well.

The accuracy of Swedi is strongly restricted by the availability and quality of geographical data. For example, the soil information is generally poor and often misleading from the standpoint of wetland functionality. The same holds for the elevation and slope data. Also the water factor is only indirectly integrated into the model through climate and soil data. As long as these detailed Pan-European data are unavailable provides Swedi a static estimation of wetland potentials suitable for broad scale studies that may be analyzed at landscape scale in more detail. The utilization of GIS makes the methodology highly applicable and easily to improve concerning data sources. The accuracy assessment showed uncertainties in the wetland size and extent that can be explained through base data uncertainties but also through differences in wetland definition and its assignment. Varying analogies in accuracy of different wetland types is more a reason of scarce and inhomogeneous reference data and less of dissimilar modeling precision. Due to the fact that with Swedi only those wetlands with an area extent of more than 1 ha are displayed, the total wetland distribution may be underestimated. Many wetlands, especially those in central and southern Europe, are very small-sized and its implementation in broad scale maps is still not realized. However, we found no differences in accuracy between northern and southern wetlands. Another uncertainty is the state of the ecosystem of the existing wetlands. In Swedi we are not able to make statements about the naturalness of the site. Nevertheless, the comparison of Swedi with independent datasets of wetland biotopes proved high accuracy of the existing wetland sites in the Swedi model and the area extent is mainly reproduced within the uncertainty range. The direct use of country aggregated Swedi data by simple polygon measurement as shown in the results section should be regarded with caution. The data give useful results but the European scale should be used with care for area estimation because it can give strongly biased results. In principle, the direct use of such data for estimation is only acceptable when no other data are available [44]. And for the spatially explicit estimation of wetland distribution no other homogeneous data exist in Europe.

The knowledge of the extent and distribution of wetlands is important for a variety of applications. The data on wetland ecosystems in European scale presented here can be used as ground information for further studies, for example helping to locate sites suitable for renaturation programs, or for the introduction of faunistic corridors respecting the Natura 2000 network of sites. The application of the model in nature conservation issues may favor the success in regional conservation planning. By integrating the spatially explicit biotope information of Swedi into the economic land use model EUFASOM [21], the costs and potentials of different land utilizations as well as optimal conservation opportunities are evaluated. Furthermore, Swedi builds the base within systematic biodiversity conservation studies of endangered European wetland species. It is of utmost importance to provide accurate base data for the management and planning of conservation areas. This study offers some first guidelines but is also intended for an impulse of discussion on improvements of such data. The next enhancing step of Swedi, besides basc data refinements, is to make this static extraction tool dynamic through the integration of hydrologic parameters for questions concerning climate change, conservation and land use planning options.

Acknowledgments. This study has received financial support from the Michael Otto Foundation for Environmental Protection, the cluster of excellence "Integrated Climate System Analysis and Prediction" (CliSAP), and from the European Commission under the FP6 projects European Non-Food Agriculture (ENFA) and Global Earth Observation - Benefit Estimation: Now, Next, and Emerging (GEOBENE). It has been improved by constructive comments of anonymous referees.

References

1. LIFE (ed.): Europe's wetlands – status and trends. LIFE Focus, pp. 3–11 (2007)
2. Dahl, T.E.: Status and trends of wetlands in the conterminous United States 1998 to 2004. US Department of the Interior, Fish and Wildlife Service, Washington DC (2006)
3. Cowardin, L.M., Carter, V., Golet, F.C., LaRoe, E.T.: Classification of wetlands and deepwater habitats of the United States. US Fish & Wildlife Service, Washington DC (1979)
4. Mitsch, W.J. (ed.): Global Wetlands: Old World and New. Elsevier, Amsterdam (1994)
5. Sanderson, M.G.: Global Distribution of Freshwater Wetlands for use in STOCHEM. Hadley Centre Technical Note 32 (2001)
6. Franklin, J.F., Swanson, M.E.: Forest Landscape Structure, Degradation and Condition: Some Commentary and Fundamental Principles. In: Lindenmayer, D.B., Hobbs, R.J. (eds.) Managing and Designing Landscapes for Conservation: Moving from Perspectives to Principles. Conservation Science and Practice Series 1, pp. 131–145. Blackwell Publishing, Oxford (2007)
7. Merot, P., Squividant, H., Aurousseau, P., Hefting, M., Burt, T., Maitr, V., Kruk, M., Butturini, A., Thenail, C., Viaud, V.: Testing a climato-topographic index for predicting wetlands distribution along an European climate gradient. Ecological Modelling 163(1-2), 51–71 (2003)
8. Lehner, B., Döll, P.: Development and validation of a global database of lakes, reservoirs and wetlands. Journal of Hydrology 296(1-4), 1–22 (2004)
9. Moss, D., Davies, C.: Cross-references between the EUNIS habitat classification and the nomenclature of the CORINE land cover. CEH project No. CC00389 (2002)
10. European Topic Centre on Biological Diversity (ed.): Introduction to EUNIS database (1993–2006), http://eunis.eea.europa.eu/
11. European Commission: CORINE biotopes. The design, compilation and use of inventory of sites of major importance for nature conservation in the European Community. EUR 13231 EN. Brussels (1991)
12. EEA (ed.): CORINE Biotopes Database (2010), http://dataservice.eea.eu.int/dataservice
13. EEA (ed.): CORINE Land Cover 2000 Database, 100 m (2000), http://dataservice.eea.eu.int/dataservice
14. Bohn, U., Neuhäusel, R., with contributions by Gollub, G., Hettwer, C., Neuhäuslová, Z., Raus, T., Schlüter, H., Weber, H.: Karte der natürlichen Vegetation Europas / Map of the Natural Vegetation of Europe. Scale 1: 2 500 000. Landwirtschaftsverlag, Münster (2003)
15. Palmeri, L., Trepel, M.: A GIS-Based Score System for Siting and Sizing of Created or Restored Wetlands: Two Case Studies. Water Resources Management 16, 307–328 (2002)
16. Malczewski, J.: GIS-based land-use suitability analysis: a critical overview. Progress in Planning 62, 3–65 (2004)
17. Roise, J.P., Gainey, K.W., Shear, T.H.: An approach to optimal wetland mitigation using mathematical programming and geographic information system based wetland function estimation. Wetlands Ecology and Management 12, 321–331 (2004)
18. Zacharias, I., Dimitriou, E., Koussouris, T.: Integrated water management scenarios for wetland protection: application in Trichonis Lake. Environmental Modelling & Software 20, 177–185 (2005)
19. Alexandridis, T.K., Lazaridou, E., Tsirika, A., Zalidis, G.C.: Using Earth Observation to update a Natura 2000 habitat map for a wetland in Greece. Journal of Environmental Management 90, 2243–2251 (2009)

20. Rebelo, L.-M., Finlayson, C.M., Nagabhatla, N.: Remote sensing and GIS for wetland inventory, mapping and change analysis. Journal of Environmental Management 90, 2144–2153 (2009)

21. Schneider, U.A., Balkovic, J., De Cara, S., Franklin, O., Fritz, S., Havlik, P., Huck, I., Jantke, K., Kallio, A.M.I., Kraxner, F., Moiseyev, A., Obersteiner, M., Ramos, C.I., Schleupner, C., Schmid, E., Schwab, D., Skalsky, R.: The European Forest and Agricultural Sector Optimization Model – EUFASOM. FNU-156, Hamburg University and Centre for Marine and Atmospheric Science, Hamburg (2008)

22. EEA (ed.): CORINE Land Cover. Part 2: Nomenclature (1995), http://reports.eea.europa.eu/CORO_landcover/en

23. Verbyla, D.L., Litaitis, J.A.: Resampling methods for evaluating classification accuracy of wildlife habitat models. Environmental Management 13, 783–787 (1989)

24. Araújo, M.B., Pearson, R.G., Thuiller, W., Erhard, M.: Validation of species-climate impact models under climate change. Global Change Biology 11, 1504–1513 (2005)

25. EEA (ed.): The thematic accuracy of Corine Land Cover 2000. Assessment using LUCAS (land use/cover area frame statistical survey). European Environment Agency, Copenhagen (2006)

26. RAMSAR Bureau: The list of Wetlands of International Importance, Gland, Switzerland (2008), http://www.ramsar.org

27. Guisan, A., Zimmermann, N.E.: Predictive habitat distribution models in ecology. Ecological Modelling 135, 147–186 (2000)

28. Franklin, J.: Predictive vegetation mapping: geographic modelling of biospatial patterns in relation to environmental gradients. Prog. Phys. Geogr. 19, 474–499 (1995)

29. Miller, J., Franklin, J., Aspinall, R.: Incorporating spatial dependence in predictive vegetation models. Ecological Modelling 202, 225–242 (2007)

30. Brinson, M.M.: Hydrogeomorphic Classification for Wetlands. US Army Corps of Engieneers, Wetland Research Program. TR: WRP-DE-4, Washington DC (1993)

31. Succow, M., Joosten, H. (eds.): Landschaftsökologische Moorkunde. E. Schweizerbert'sche Verlagsbuchhandlung, Stuttgart (2001)

32. BfN (ed.): Explanatory Text to the Map of the Natural Vegetation of Europe. Landwirtschaftsverlag, Münster (2004)

33. Wheeler, B.D., Shaw, S.C., Fojt, J., Robertson, R.A. (eds.): Restoration of temperate wetlands. John Wiley & Sons, New York (1995)

34. Schultink, G., Van Vliet, R.: Wetland identification and protection: North American and European policy Perspectives. Departement of Resource Development. Michigan State University (1997), http://rdserv1.rd.msu.edu/wetlands/wims/wims_nort.doc

35. Joint Research Centre: European Soil Database (v 2.0), European Soil Bureau Network and the European Commission, EUR 19945 EN (2004)

36. Walter, H., Breckle, S.W.: Vegetation und Klimazonen, 7th edn. Ulmer, Stuttgart (1999)

37. USGS (ed.): GTOPO30 (1996), http://www.edcdaac.usgs.gov/gtopo30/gtopo30.html

38. EEA (ed.): The Biogeographical Regions Map of Europe. – European Environment Agency, Copenhagen (2002), http://dataservice.eea.eu.int/dataservice

39. Mulamoottil, G., Warner, B.G., McBean, E.A.: Wetlands: Environmental Gradients, Boundaries and Buffers. Lewis Publishers, New York (1996)

40. Tsihrintzis, V.A., John, D.L., Tremblay, P.J.: Hydrodynamic Modeling of Wetlands for Flood Detention. Water Resources Management Journal 12(4), 251–269 (1998)

41. Manfreda, S., Sole, A., Fiorentino, M.: Can the basin morphology alone provide an insight on floodplain delineation? In: Flood Recovery Innovation and Response I, pp. 47–56. WIT-press, Southampton (2008)
42. Chefaoui, R.M., Lobo, J.M.: Assessing the effects of pseudo-absences on predictive distribution model performance. Ecological Modelling 210, 478–486 (2008)
43. Nivet, C., Frazier, S.: A review of European wetland inventory information. Report prepared in the framework of "A pilot study towards a Pan-European wetland inventory". In: Taylor, A.R.D., van Eerden, M. (eds.) Wetlands International, RAMSAR (2004)
44. Gallego, J., Bamps, C.: Using CORINE land cover and the point survey LUCAS for area estimation. International Journal of Applied Earth Observation and Geoinformation 10(4), 467–475 (2008)

G.I.S. to Support Environmental Sustainability in Manufacturing Areas. Case Study of the Apulian Region in Southern Italy

Francesco Selicato, Grazia Maggio, and Francesco Mancini

Dept. of Architecture and Urban Planning, Bari Polytechnic,
Via Orabona n.4, 70125 Bari, Italy
selicato@poliba.it

Abstract. This work addresses the potential of using Geographic Information Systems (G.I.S.) to support urban planning. In the case in point, the tool has been adopted to carry out a census of all the manufacturing plants in the Apulian Region, in the context of a working agreement between the Apulian Regional Board and the Department of Architecture and Urban Planning of Bari Polytechnic. After analysing the need to identify territorial governance systems that can support sustainable management of industrial areas, the work illustrates the data collection methods, how the dedicated Geodatabase structure was set up, what data were collected and some analyses that could then be made. In conclusion, the potential of using G.I.S for urban planning in manufacturing areas is discussed, as well as some critical elements. Among these, the need for continual data updating to fully exploit this potential is underlined.

Keywords: Geographic Information Systems, urban planning, sustainable management of industrial areas.

1 Sustainability in Manufacturing Areas

The first and foremost economic development strategy adopted by the European Union is based upon an ideal balance among the economic, social and environmental sectors. It underlines the need for an economy to guarantee high living standards and employment rates, based on sustainable grounds. The development of local manufacturing systems cannot be divorced from the wider view of development of the whole territory, not only from a purely geographic-physical viewpoint but also and above all from the social, economic and institutional standpoints, taking into account all those factors that contribute to determine the competitiveness of an area.

In accordance with this view, development does not only respond to a quantitative economic logic and does not stem from top-down actions; on the contrary, specific local conditions must be seen as extraordinary, non reproducible resources: these elements are determinant of endogenous development practices [13]. In this sense, "surveys of local resources" are the core on which actions must be based [5] and the approach to development must be bottom-up. This approach has led to the identification of overall strategic goals that should be achieved in local development policies:

D. Taniar et al. (Eds.): ICCSA 2010, Part I, LNCS 6016, pp. 210–223, 2010.
© Springer-Verlag Berlin Heidelberg 2010

- promoting the action of local subjects to produce innovation;
- reinforcing the quality of local contexts to improve competitiveness;
- setting up institutional mechanisms to help combine different resources and actors, both public and private;
- promoting cooperative behaviors among the different subjects, thus "forging local society" [1].

In particular, manufacturing activities have an impact on the local ecosystem, characterized by specific, well-defined environmental aspects. Indeed, we have only to think of the environmental impact on companies localized in an industrial district of their proximity to a zone of naturalistic interest. These companies will have to take account of the same critical aspects of the local ecosystem that are potentially exacerbated by the territorial concentration of industrial activities.

The "industrial zones" originated not only for reasons of logistic efficiency but also as a solution to an excessive effect of man-made and industrial activities on the area. They were emarginated from areas where a better quality environment was required to ensure the health of the citizens, and became – during the intense growth of industrial activities in the 1970s and '80s – a sort of "zona franca" where the limits and effects of environmental regulations tended to be waived in favour of the importance of the economic gains.

Nowadays, these industrial areas can be seen as areas where the balance between development and the environment needs to be restored. In fact, a correct approach to the creation of new developments and verification of the environmental sustainability of existing plants can contribute to minimize the risks of impact of these areas on the surrounding environment. These tasks can be facilitated by the adoption of suitable territorial planning and monitoring tools like the Geographic Information Systems [14] [4] [3].

It is no longer possible nowadays to dismiss manufacturing areas as reject functional areas with a unique purpose, relegated to less sensitive zones from the landscape standpoint. On the contrary, reconsidering the forms and types of industrial landscapes means taking into account the problems of environmental compatibility, plurifunctional spaces and the need to offer quality, liveable areas. Industrial areas (to be reclaimed or built from scratch) can thus become a central element around which the manufacturing system can be recreated in an environmentally sustainable key. To do this, the structural (identifying) elements of a territory need to be assigned their rightful role, as well as the relations among the subjects, both institutional and private citizens, that live and operate in that territory.

Up to now, the environmental aspects of manufacturing activities have been dealt with, also by national and EU norms only at the level of the single manufacturing site. Only recently was it realized that a wider territorial scale, like that of the entire industrial area or district, would be a more efficacious way of ensuring a correct, environmentally sustainable management of the whole area. Shifting the focus from the individual company or site to the whole industrial area means, in terms of promoting sustainability, not only widening the territorial scale but also the issues under discussion. To assess the environmental sustainability of manufacturing areas it is also important to understand:

a) the planning quality of the intended work, paying particular attention to how it harmonizes with the landscape, the connections with geomorphological aspects, the external appearance and the homogeneity of the proposed building;

b) how the environmental aspects were identified and assessed when selecting the area for a particular manufacturing activity;

c) the assignment of priority, on receipt of applications to build new areas in which to set up industrial and craftsmanship activities, to ecologically sustainable plans, in order to foster and promote their development, while also promoting adequate processes of re-localization, reclaiming and re-qualification of the existing manufacturing systems.

In sustainable planning and management of industrial areas it is also important to encourage discussion among experts in the different fields (territorial planning, economics, ecology) and the Public Authorities. In fact, cooperation among local bodies is the institutional equivalent of the concept of sustainable development. Inter-institutional coordination aims to reinforce the local economic-productive potential and to ensure that the work is compatible with the need to improve the quality of life and, in general, the well-being and social integration of the citizens. The institutional actors need to operate outside the industrial system, coordinating and supporting those companies involved in the shift toward a sustainable model of development.

The companies may find themselves in the position of interacting with the local authorities and controlling bodies in a dialogic atmosphere offering space for negotiation, or else with institutional subjects that apply the letter of the law and insist on strict conformity with all the limits and constraints. The different attitude of the institutions towards the companies operating in a given manufacturing area can attenuate or exacerbate the environmental pressure. Moreover, some local authorities may be particularly active in promoting conjoint solutions (consociations or consortiums) to the most urgent and severe environmental problems in the local context, acting as catalysers of collaboration among different enterprises and a synergic use of resources.

Thus, sustainable development of productive areas needs to be carried out through a succession of phases, including planning of a vast area, urban planning and subsequent routine management, employing various tools each of which has its own peculiarities.

It is in this context of planning and control that G.I.S become powerful methods supporting governance of a territory by the local bodies. The requirement to integrate many heterogeneous types of data and sources, whose overall quality and reliability may vary greatly, stems directly from the needs discussed above. As pointed out by several authors who have addressed similar topics [2] [7] [6] [8] [10] [11] [12] [15], Geographic Information Systems (G.I.S.) may offer a solution to the needs to process spatial-related information in order to support decision making procedures. This is true of urban planning activities and, more generally speaking, of the governance of cities, suburban zones and industrial districts. This last category, industrial settlements, is the focus of the present paper.

2 Monitoring Industrial Areas in Apulia

In Apulia, in the last few years the regional government has assigned strong priority to the generation of industrial policies founded on sustainable governance of the territory, individuating not only single companies or sectors as possible fields of application of such policies but also entire territories and industrial areas. To combat assessment of transformations and construction work only on the basis of economic criteria (e.g. the number of jobs created by the company) as it was made in the last decades of the regional policies, the Apulian Region is nowadays facing the challenge of safeguarding local systems of resources. It is attempting to foster networks of local actors, in order to encourage the development of innovative capacities. In fact, the new regional policies are oriented to reinforce public intervention, paying a greater attention to quality not just quantity, and promoting cooperation among the different institutional boards. However, some local contexts are still very "immature", showing poor concentration powers and tending to privilege consolidated routines that are difficult to interrupt in order to introduce innovations.

Another important reference framework of regional programming in recent years is the policy of "Promoting the Information Society", with particular regard to the Public Administration, Public Education and Manufacturing sectors, with the aim of fostering internationalization of Apulian companies and transfrontier and transnational economic integration.

In such processes, the G.I.S., and information technology in general play leading role. They provide a better knowledge of the reference territory, contribute to identify goals to be gradually achieved and the appropriate measures to be adopted to attain and monitor achievement and maintenance of such goals. These tools can foster cooperation among local bodies and between institutions and companies, simplify bureaucratic procedures and, finally, territorial marketing operations, thus contributing to trigger sustainable processes and actions.

In the management renewal currently ongoing in the Apulian Region, the creation of a Territorial Information System covering the entire region is the main platform intended to support the creation of an updated, reliable overall knowledge picture of the various levels, tools and subjects involved in regional territorial planning.

The management, maintenance and implementation activities of the regional portal "SistemaPuglia" for the development and promotion of the territory and enterprises come under the framework of Measure 6.2 Action b) "Marketing Territoriale e Attrazione degli Investimenti" POR (Programma Operativo Regionale) Puglia 2000/2006. In particular, to implement the contents of the Section "Monitoring Industrial Zones" of this portal the Polytechnic of Bari, on request by the regional government, has undertaken the survey, analysis and monitoring activities of the Manufacturing Zone Plans (PIP[1] areas). An overall strategic approach has been adopted, oriented to

---

[1] The "Piani di Insediamento Produttivi" (PIP) (Manufacturing Zone Plans) were introduced by Law n. 865/1971 and had the aim of reorganizing the territorial set-up of manufacturing activities within the Municipality and boosting local production. In fact, these areas were set aside exclusively for manufacturing activities and especially for small enterprises of local concern and craftsmanship workshops. These Plans are very detailed and regard areas expropriated by the Municipality and ceded (at cost price, plus the cost of the relative urbanization work) to those companies and enterprises presenting an application. The areas are assigned as rights of property (for quotas not exceeding 50% of the overall volume of the entire Plan) and rights of surface use (for the remaining quota), to set up manufacturing plants of an industrial, craftsmanship, commercial or tourist nature. No time limit is set for the concession of rights of surface use to public bodies to create public services and plants; in all the other cases the concession is granted for a minimum of 60 and a maximum of 99 years.

promote the attraction of new investments in the manufacturing sector, also thanks to offering a clear picture of the degree of current occupation of these areas.

The local administrative context in which this work fits is quite different from the intentionality of renewal promoted in recent years by the regional government. In most local municipality in southern Italy an emergency culture (in which the art of "getting by" is still predominant) is commonly present. Some local administrations have shown themselves quite incapable of seeing the GIS as an opportunity to insert innovative elements in the territorial management process. Among local actors there is still too local an idea of territorial governance. There is often a lack of interaction among the different levels of authorities, that in some cases creates a truly conflicting situation among institutional representative bodies.

In these organizational spheres, the skills are not always up to the tasks required of a local technical-administrative facility. Among other things, they deal with single sectors and are therefore totally inadequate to contend with the interdisciplinary nature of the modern approach to territorial management. In this context, the territorial management activities are largely limited to carrying out checking and control operations of the ongoing territorial transformation processes and, moreover, these checking activities are confined to a simple review that the operations conform to the current laws, taking practically no account of any proper analysis of their real impact on the territory. In this context there is no need to use information technologies and methodologies in the management of public goods.

Thus in manufacturing areas G.I.S. respond to the need to facilitate collection, implementation and updating of the volume of information regarding the productive area. It is clear that the first census will have to be followed by periodic surveys and so by continual updating. The tool can thus support decision making about planning, investments and territorial management by the public administrations[2]. The present product therefore addresses:

1) monitoring of changes being wrought in manufacturing areas and assessment of their relative environmental compatibility;

2) experimentation of new forms of cooperation among local authorities at all levels;

3) the creation of a state-of-the-art territorial marketing system.

3   The Geographical Information System Approach

In this section the G.I.S. design and implementation will be addressed, and discussion will be made of problems related to the centralized collection of the huge volumes of data available at the archives of the local Apulian administrations, and their preliminary screening.

---

[2] In fact, the PIP is a tool that allows local authorities to draw up an ordered planning and management diagram of the industrial areas, preventing fragmented development. This planning tool satisfies the needs of public administrations to express their strong intentions to exert a guiding action on urban transformations, coordinating the planned settlements and manufacturing activities.

3.1 Data Collection

During the first step, all the information and documentation related to each of the industrial settlements established within the Municipalities of the Apulian Regional territories were required to be presented to the 258 local Offices dedicated to this purpose, or were searched for in the main archives of the Apulian Region. This census activity also involved the collection of deliberations, tables, maps and existing plans, as well as further information contributing to describe the PIP areas. In addition, questionnaires were administered to the technical municipal staff appointed to control each aspect. Table 1 resumes the amount of data collected and products generated by their processing.

Existing plans are outdated and many times incomplete. The executives working in this kind of environment limit their actions to routine tasks and believe that the information they possess – for the tasks they normally carry out – is complete and fits their job description. Moreover, within the administrative machine there is often a lack of ability (for cultural reasons) and in some cases also the will, to recognize the existence of new skills outside the public administration and involve them actively in the decision making processes. The involvement of local authorities can be difficult, not quickly and above all the collection of local government information and data (especially about environmental, economic and social aspects) requires the need to involve other territorial management bodies scattered throughout the region with a great waste of energy and resources.

Because the industrial settlements were built at the end of the 1970s without the aid of digital media, all the planning documentation was available only as traditional hard maps. It must also be pointed out that in some cases these maps detailing the planned industrial settlements were based (overlaid) upon topographical, cadastral or photogrammetric maps using non-uniform cartographical reference frames (national geodetic, cadastral, arbitrary or none) and map scales. Moreover, many different styles of map

Table 1. Resume of data related to PIP areas that were processed in the preliminary collection phase. Data are related to each of the administrative districts of the Apulia Region (BA: Bari, BR: Brindisi, FG: Foggia, LE: Lecce, TA: Taranto).

	Documents collected from regional archives					Documents other than regional archives					Total					Overall
	BA	BR	FG	LE	TA	BA	BR	FG	LE	TA	BA	BR	FG	LE	TA	
Digitized maps	229	156			154	106	54	53	199	160	335	210	53	199	314	1111
Processed raster maps	221	126			140	83	27	21	178	45	304	153	21	178	185	841
Georeferenced raster maps	211	126			128	64	29	14	128	41	275	155	14	128	169	741
Maps available in vector format						371	52	25	62	111	371	52	25	62	111	621
Reports, acts, deliberations etc						79	25	22	30	37	79	25	22	30	37	193
Orthophoto used in georeferencing						37	16		63	27	37	16	24	63	27	167
Used Ground Control Points files	211	126			128		30	26	86	42	211	156	26	86	170	649
Stored file	872	534	0	0	550	740	233	161	746	463	1612	767	185	746	1013	4323
Intermediate products	1540	984	0	0	813	854	257	188	496	366	2310	1016	282	987	1358	5953
Total products (archived + intermediate)	2412	1518			1363	1594	490	349	1242	829	4249	1980	539	1912	2605	11285

drawing were encountered, featuring a different graphic accuracy and overall reliability of the maps representing the industrial area. The requirement for homogeneous data was therefore the first problem that had to be faced. In order to create a digital raster and georeferenced dataset all over the five Apulian Provinces, about 1100 hard documents were scanned with a large format scanner at an average resolution of 400 dpi (dot per inch), and georeferenced. This raster dataset was subsequently adopted as the basemap for the creation of the geometrical database after vectorialization in the GIS environment. More than 10,000 documents were handled during this phase.

In the vectorialization procedure standards and format listed by commissions involved in the Global Spatial Data Infrastructure (http://www.gsdi.org/gsdicookbookindex) and international membership organization engaged in a co-operative effort to create open computing specifications in the area of geoprocessing (OGC, Open GIS Consortium, http://www.opengis.org). Format and data structure used meet the requirements of interoperability which where defined at the time of the products design and data implementation. The GIS created within this work is therefore able to perform on several software platform and GIS environment.

When geometrical properties, such as areas and perimeters, have to be estimated or spatial analysis carried out by GIS analysis tools, all the potential positional errors affecting the dataset have to be carefully evaluated. With particular regard to the procedures listed and discussed in this section, the possible source of errors related to the scanning and georeferencing phases will be briefly summarized below.

The scanned raw digital data were then radiometrically enhanced to better define the contrast and hence the readability of old and sometimes deteriorated maps. The scanning procedures constitute the first source of errors and distortions in the derived raster dataset. It must be borne in mind that the scanning of a 1:5000 scale map at a resolution of 400 dpi produces a pixel size of 0.3 meters at the ground. The pixel size represents the smallest possible graphic uncertainty of the raster map generated, which has to be added to the scanner inner deformation.

The next step, georeferencing, affects the planimetric accuracy of maps in two different ways. Firstly, the georeferencing procedure is itself a source of error, but, depending on the selected algorithm, it could also reduce the deformation errors stemming from the scanning procedure thanks to the use of an adjustment procedure based on the minimum squared criteria. Basically, the positional uncertainty of a geocoded map depends on the algorithm adopted and on the accuracy of the Ground Control Points (GCPs) used, that have to be easily recognized and non ambiguous in the digital images to be processed. The GCPs (natural or man-made) used for georeferencing were obtained from a series of ortophotos recently released by the local Authorities with a planimetric accuracy of 2 m and a pixel size of 0.5 m. Each raster dataset required a different number of GCPs (corners of buildings, road intersections and regular geometric features) and the overall planimetric accuracy of the georeferencing phase was quantified on the basis of the algorithmic residuals around the GCPs (pixels or distance) and comparison of the positions with respect to an external dataset.

Georeferencing of the whole raster dataset, by polynomial procedures, produced mean planimetric errors of 5-6 m in the worst cases (low map scale and coarse geometric definition). Instead, the internal map inconsistencies related to paper deformations or native geometric inaccuracies, was usually lower than 0.5 m. A rigorous control of positional errors is fundamental when different settlements have common boundaries or in cases of later modifications of earlier settlements.

3.2 The G.I.S. and DataBase Creation

The implemented G.I.S deals mainly with geometric features and alphanumerical parameters collected in an object-based Geodatabase that relies on the definition of hierarchic and geometrical dependencies among the data. The geometric features are derived from the vectorialization of all the entities included in the raster georeferenced map. For all the geometric features entered in the G.I.S. environment, users are required to specify a series of alphanumerical properties in order to complete the data entry phase related to that entity. The procedure ends with the validation of the geometric entities, according to a few predefined rules. In Figure 1 an overview of the data collected and missing is shown, in addition to a typical geometric detail representing an industrial area.

Subsequently, to enable the database to be planned and structured in such a way as to uniform the differences among the various PIP (in terms of nomenclature and classifications), the documentation (reports, technical norms, etc.) of many plans had to be preliminarily analyzed and compared. This analysis made it possible to identify the main urban planning and typology parameters to be inserted in the analysis and so in the G.I.S. Representation of these items by means of defining appropriate indicators resulted in a first homogenization of the data contained in the different plans and then a contextual analysis of all the information collected during execution of the project.

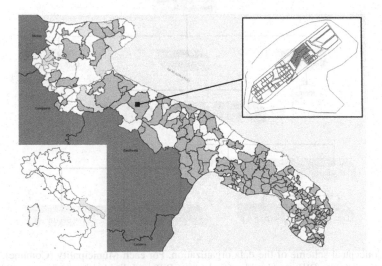

Fig. 1. Overview of the available data. Dark grey area: local administrations with a complete set of data (137); light grey area: local administrations with missing or incomplete documentation (40); white area: local administrations with no established industrial area.

The data collected per area selected as manufacturing zones are listed below, subdivided by heading. These data were then organized in the dedicated database created to serve this project.

General Information: includes the following indications referred to the Municipality the PIP area belongs to: Name of Municipality; Mean height above sea level; Seismic class (defined in accordance with the national norms). All this in view of the fact that several PIP areas may belong to the same Municipality and so it is not necessary to repeat the same information for all the PIP areas in that jurisdiction. However, since some indexes may change even in the same PIP area, depending on the plot group, a subordinate PIP level has been created denominated "Sub-area".

Surfaces and other urban planning aspects: includes indications referring to the single PIP areas: Maximum height of buildings; Mean price of land (mean price of land surfaces selected as manufacturing zones); Building Index; Built-up surface/total surface ratio; Surface available for new building; Maximum buying plot surface available; Minimum buying plot surface available; Mean/maximum time for obtaining building concessions.

Services and infrastructures: includes indications referring to the single PIP areas: Availability and mean costs of water (aqueduct, sewage, water purifying systems); Purifying and relative costs; Airports (minimum distance); Ports (minimum distance); Viability (minimum distance from main roads); Railways (minimum distance from main railway stations).

The conceptual scheme of the data organization can be represented as shown in the following figure 2.

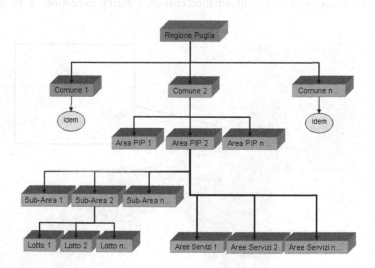

Fig. 2. Conceptual scheme of the data organization. For each Municipality (Comune), various areas destined to the PIP may be identified (Area PIP), subdivided into sub-areas (Sub-Area) detailing the minimum unit represented (Lotto). Each of the "PIP Area" include one or several areas devoted to services (Area Servizi). A hierarchy between geometric features as well as between variables and attributes is therefore established, allowing all the subsequent inquiry selected by the users.

4 Results

Some of the results obtained are illustrated in this section, pointing out both the critical elements and the opportunities for the future that emerged.

4.1 Some Analyses of the Entered Data

The inserted data can be analyzed and successively displayed in the GIS environment to gain both a first reading at regional level and a detailed description of the single areas selected as PIP. Some of the aspects of particular interest include:

- number of PIP per Municipality;
- ratio of surfaces selected as PIP to built-up areas;
- distance of PIP areas from the main infrastructures (ports, airports, railways, main roads);
- areas with a residual building capacity (freehold surface areas and permitted volumes);
- mean cost of surfaces selected for building;
- state of progress of primary and secondary urbanization work;

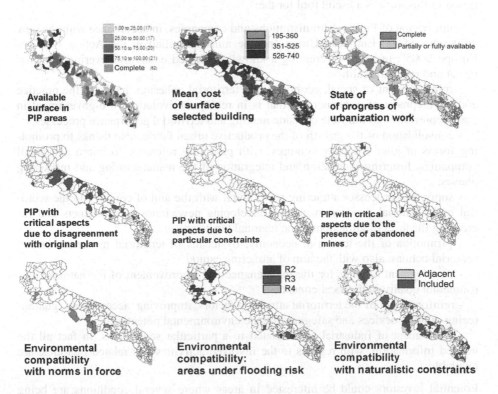

Fig. 3. Some strengthens and weaknesses of the regional industrial districts processed in the GIS

- critical aspects of the whole manufacturing area, such as: (i) the presence of plots not built in accordance with the plans, (ii) green spaces, parking areas or areas under particular constraints occupied by industrial plants;
- state of environmental compatibility of the localities selected as manufacturing zones according to the urban planning norms in force (Municipal and above) and, in general, to the main characteristics of the territorial area structure;
- critical environmental aspects in the manufacturing area: relations with superficial groundwater, with nature, the coast, and areas at hydro geological risk;
- characteristics of the existing manufacturing zones inside the PIP areas (defining the manufacturing sectors);
- analysis and assessment of the building opportunities.

Figure 3 shows some examples related to possible analysis able to highlight strengthens and weakness of the regional industrial districts.

4.2 Opportunities and Critical Elements: Future Prospects

The present case study unveils some opportunities and critical elements associated with the use of G.I.S. The benefits have to do with both the territory and the institutional and socio-economic contexts. In fact, a G.I.S. with a structure like the one proposed in this work is a useful tool for the:

- innovation of Public Administrations and companies, in accordance with the new guidelines of the European Union and the aims identified in the Action Plan "e-Europe 2005", in terms of creating a knowledge-based economy covering both national and regional realities;
- reinforcement of social, economic and territorial cohesion thanks to the practice and development of e-democracy, that is in reality an evolution of e-government in that it contributes to innovate decision making and territorial governance processes;
- consolidation of the growth of the productive urban fabric, also thanks to promoting forms of joint company ventures, with particular reference to micro and small companies, fostering innovation and integration of the manufacturing and marketing phases;
- support of processes attracting new capital with the aim of completing the sectorial and territorial production chains, developing new, innovative products and increasing the level of attraction of the regional territory;
- promotion of the territorial economy, by means of territorial marketing and/or sectorial actions, also with the aim of attracting capital;
- development of tools for the maintenance and improvement of the natural environmental quality in the local context;
- reinforcement of the territorial attraction factors, improving accessibility, guaranteeing quality services and safeguarding the environmental potential;
- assessment of industrial risks related to a particular settlements. In fact all the needed information, with regards to the involved activities and related facilities, are available.

Potential investors could be interested in areas where several conditions are being accounted for. A simulation of such research might be carried out by searching in the GIS under certain requirements like the following: distance from main infrastructures, progress in the urbanization work and hypothesis on warehouse dimension, minimum and maximum free-space within the plot and available parking area. Lets suppose to be interested in a warehouse not far than 1km from main roads, with 4m of minimum elevation, a free surface between 1000 and 1600mq and a parking area not lower than 4000mq. A requests such the these will produce the output of figure 4.

Analyses supported by the GIS addressing the main environmental features of the territory can support the various policies promoting environmental sustainability and quality landscape in productive areas, such as ecological reclaiming, delocalization of industrial plants posing risks, reinforcing productive districts and the connections between them and the local agricultural system. All this can be achieved by means of various actions such as: adopting a gully, reclaiming buildings facing the road, reforesting at the edge of manufacturing plants, disimpermeabilising the area, identifying good building practices.

At the same time, this case reveals some critical elements largely linked to the local context. There were difficulties in collecting and homogenizing the data, defining the processes involved in planning (design, implementation) that cannot always be deduced from the technical documentation or represented using information technologies. Reliability, comprehensibility, completeness and adequacy are, in general, the essential requisites for setting up any knowledge base. They lay the necessary conditions to prevent the data from being distorted, circumvented or manipulated (Forester, 1989).

In this context, the Municipal administration boards and technical-administrative offices of the local bodies, and especially the Municipal technical offices, are encouraged to make a fundamental, and often exclusive, contribution to creating G.I.S for PIP zones.

In situations like the one analyzed herein, however, that reflects conditions that are fairly widespread over southern Italy, a true involvement of the local bodies is difficult to obtain and very time-consuming. This is largely due to the immense delay that has accumulated in the South as regards setting up a new approach to planning, more-oriented toward dialogue and collaboration. Great endogenous resistance of various types is observed, determined by the generalized poor propensity to accept changes in consolidated organizational behaviors and systems, that are still bound to a historically self-referencing urban planning culture.

The utility of tools like the one we propose is seen only in economic terms as the chance to acquire funding, without taking advantage of the possibility to trigger

Fig. 4. Simulation of data retrieval by a generic user under 3 different requirements. Map on the right highlight PIP areas that meet all the requirements the user is searching for.

changes in practices and above all the cultural approach. In any case, our experience has shown that in contexts like ours in the south of Italy, the presence of strong supra-local institutional actors, regional in this case, played an important role in pushing through some mechanisms of change, even if not truly innovative.

The tool we describe can encourage the various institutional subjects to cooperate, and interface with the same platform, and the same rules. This can constitute an example of institutional integration built ex post (during and after the creation of the tool) not ex ante (i.e. while building the tool).

In this light, the G.I.S. is important not only at the time of implementation, but also and above all during management. It must again be emphasized that the usefulness of a dynamic database like the one we describe depends on how updated it is, and continues to be over time. Updating can be done by activating specific procedures, mainly of a electronic nature, that enable the insertion of all new data on PIP zones and continual maintenance of the entire system. Firstly, it is important to identify all those elements in the database likely to vary over time and those that, on the contrary, may be regarded as invariant. Then, for the former, the best updating interval must be established, bearing in mind that these data may be alphanumerical or geometric (vectorial) and that in both cases data entry must follow the same procedures used in this work in order to guarantee data homogeneity and quality.

A second problem to be faced is the architecture of the G.I.S. management system, that requires a central reference and coordination structure to execute data management. This role can be carried out directly by the technical offices, as in our case by the Apulian Region, or by third parties. Some possible organizational scenarios are listed below:

- Local Bodies that autonomously operate their updating (respecting precise operative standards) of the information to be sent to the "control centre" where it is verified, validated and finally memorized in the main Geodatabase;

- Local Bodies (Technical Offices) that operate on the data within their jurisdiction by on-line editing using procedures implemented thanks to Web-GIS interfaces;

- "control centres" that operate using the same methodology as has been employed to create the G.I.S, i.e. by continuing to monitor the data on the individual Municipalities, that in turn periodically communicate data variations on the PIP zones in their area.

5 Conclusions

Our experience demonstrates that the issue of sustainable management of manufacturing areas must necessarily take into account the need to program suitable opportunities for communication and dialogue among the various subjects that operate and live in a given territory. A more open, dialogic communication is more efficacious, as it allows the needs of the actors to be listened to and understood, guaranteeing the construction of more efficient, productive relations.

In these processes, tools like the G.I.S can be very important because they allow the creation of reliable, objective information that the various institutional actors can assess, and on which their decision making can be based. They also satisfy the citizens' demand for clear, exhaustive and objective information. Information systems and their associated advantages contribute to motivate the different subjects, institutional and private, operating on a territory to take an active part in creating a shared knowledge base and to realize the resulting added value conferred by the integration of different knowledge and skills in the long term.

Acknowledgements. Authors are grateful to all have partecipated at the Project. The working group employed during the data collection, GIS creation and data entry was composed of the following: prof. Carmelo Torre (Eng.), Pasquale Balena (BSc) and the group of engineers involved: Francesco Aportone, Michele Cera, Carla Chiarantoni, Davide Del Re, Antonella Di Giuro, Francesco Fiorito, Milena Miglionico, Giuseppe Orlando, Giuliano Ritrovato and Vittoria Greco. The personnel of Regione Puglia kindly provided all the PIP data and FINPUGLIA co-operated during the whole project.

References

1. Bonomi, A.: Il capitalismo molecolare, Einaudi, Torino (1998)
2. Brazier, A.M., Greenwood, R.L.: Geographic Information Systems: a consistent approach to land use planning decisions around hazardous installations. Journal of Hazardous Materials 61, 355–361 (1998)
3. Campagna, M.: GIS for Sustainable Development. Taylor & Francis Group - CRC (2005)
4. Craglia, M., et al.: SDI Developments in Western Europe. In: Craglia, M., et al. (eds.) Geographic Information in the Wider Europe, European Commission, p. 17 (2003)
5. Cremaschi, M.: I programmi integrati – Opportunità e Vincoli, Donzelli Editore, Roma (2001)
6. Du, G.: Using GIS for analysis of urban systems. GeoJournal 52, 213–221 (2001)
7. Dai, F.C., Lee, C.F., Zang, X.H.: GIS-based geo-environmental evaluation for urban land use planning: a case study. Engineering geology 61, 257–271 (2001)
8. Fang, Y.P., Raymond, P.C., Rong, Q.: Industrial sustainability in China: Practice and prospects for eco-industrial development. J. Environ. Manage 83, 315–328 (2007)
9. Forester, J.: Planning in the face of Power, Berkeley CA, University of California (1998)
10. Gaicomelli, A., Lodo, S.: Il Sistema Informativo Territoriale per le Aree Industriali della Sardegna. MondoGIS, 45–48 (2001)
11. Kohsaka, H.: Applications of GIS to urban planning and management: Problems facing Japanese local governments. GeoJournal 52, 271–280 (2001)
12. Meng, Y., Zhang, F.R., An, P.L., Dong, M.L., Wang, Z.Y., Zaho, T.: Industrial land-use efficiency and planning in Shunyi, Beijing. Landscape and Urban Planning 85(1), 40–48 (2008)
13. Magnaghi, A.: Il territorio dell'abitare. Lo sviluppo locale come alternativa strategica, Franco Angeli, Milano (1990)
14. Mothi Kumar, K.E., Kundu, B.S., Rao, T.B.V.M., Nigam, R.K., Manchanda, M.L.: Integrated Management of Natural Resources for Sustainable Development Through Remote Sensing and GIS. In: Muralikrishana I V (JNTU) Int. Con. on Remote Sensing & GIS, - ICORG 1997. Edited by Hyderabad, pp. 546–554 (1997)
15. Okunuki, K.: Urban analysis with GIS. GeoJournal 52, 181–188 (2001)

Estimating and Classifying Spatial and Temporal Distributions of Flow Conditions for Fish Habitats by Using Geostatistical Approaches with Measured Flow and Fish Data

Yu-Pin Lin, Cheng-Long Wang, Hsiao-Hsuan Yu, and Yung-Chieh Wang

Department of Bioenvironmental Systems Engineering,
National Taiwan University, 1, Sec. 4, Roosevelt Rd.,
Da-an District, Taipei City 106, Taiwan, R.O.C.
yplin@ntu.edu.tw
Department of Civil and Environmental Engineering,
Georgia Institute of Technology, 790
Atlantic Dr. Atlanta, GA 30332-0355, USA

Abstract. This study investigated the relationship between the distribution of Sicyopterus *japonicus*, current velocity and water depth in four reaches along Datuan Stream in northern Taiwan during winter of 2007 and spring of 2008. The spatial distributions of current velocity and water depth were estimated by kriging from the stream mouth to the upstream section. The empirical rule method and the Froude number method with kriging estimated distributions of the current velocity and water depth were incorporated into a geographical information system (GIS) and used to classify flow conditions at the investigated reaches. Indicator kriging was used to estimate the probability of the presence of *S. japonicus* and superimposed on the estimated flow conditions at each reach. The field results showed that, in each investigated season, the average current velocity was low in the downstream and upstream reaches, but high in the middle stream reach. The flow conditions based on kriging estimated distribution of water velocity and water depth at the investigated reaches accurately reflect flow conditions at each reach along the stream. Geostatistical approaches, such as kriging and indicator kriging, can be used to estimate the flows and the appearance probability of fish accurately. Moreover, the overlapping maps of the flow conditions and the probabilities indicate that the preferences of *S. japonicus* vary in different reaches and seasons. Based on the migration behavior of *S. japonicus*, the classification of the empirical rule flow classification method with geostatistical approaches in GIS can be used to estimate the preferences of *S. japonicus* in Datuan stream effectively.

Keywords: Geostatistical approach, Kriging, Indicator kriging, GIS, Fish habitat, Flow condition, Freshwater.

D. Taniar et al. (Eds.): ICCSA 2010, Part I, LNCS 6016, pp. 224–237, 2010.
© Springer-Verlag Berlin Heidelberg 2010

1 Introduction

Streams are notoriously heterogeneous environments where organisms exhibit patchy distributions on a spatially and temporally variable physical arena. In stream systems, complex physical variables have to be demarcated by velocity and depth, and joining river cross-sections, slope, substrate are capable of explaining a greater proportion of the variation than a single variable alone [1] [2], to improve the accuracy of flow conditions judgment. In streams, the flow conditions may be understood as a mosaic of mesohabitat patches which are clearly illustrated by different combinations of current velocity, depth and others [3]. Habitat models used for predicting the amount of stream habitat suitable for fish are commonly based on four key variables: water depth, water velocity, substrate composition and in-stream cover. Basing on velocity and water depth, empirical model [2] and Froude number method [1] [4] [5] [6] have been widely used in classification of flow conditions in the studies of associations of fishes and flow conditions.

To increase accuracy of flow condition and fish probability with sampling data, geostatistical models are now being used in environmental sampled data in spatial or temporal scales [7] [8] [9]. Geostatistics uses spatial autocorrelation techniques to estimate or simulate variables of interest [9] [10]. In geostatistics, variograms provide a means of quantifying commonly observed relationships between the values of samples and the samples' proximity to one another [9] [10] [11]. Using sample data and geostatistical methods, biologists can make optimal predictions about spatially dependent biological variables (e.g., species richness) at potential sites where data has not been collected previously [12]. Kriging, a geostatistical technique, is a linear interpolation procedure that provides a best linear unbiased estimator (BLUE) for quantities that vary in space. At an unsampled location and for a given variogram, a kriging estimate can be thought simply as an optimally weighted average of the surrounding sampled data. Kriging has been applied to map fish distributions, flow conditions, and further to various estuaries and stream system studies. As for indicator kriging, assumptions are not made about the underlying invariant distribution, and 0–1 indicator transformations of data render the predictor robust to outliers [13]. Therefore, indicator kriging can be used to estimate and map the probabilities of estimates that appearance of fishes.

The major species, S. japonicus, stay at the pool/riffle sequence more often in various seasons in the Datuan stream. In this study, we applied kriging to estimate velocity and water depth distributions and flow conditions classification [2] [6] with our investigated data to estimate the flow condition requirement of S. japonicus, in order to find the preference of S. japonicus in reach scale (from downstream to upstream) and discover the relation between the classifications of flow conditions and S. japonicus in the seasonal variations. Then, comparing the differences between the two flow condition classification methods, we discussed the suitability of both classification methods applying to the study area. Indicator kriging with fish investigated data was applied to estimate the probability of appearance of S. japonicus in each reach. Finally, the probability maps are superimposed with estimated flow conditions to estimate associations between S. japonicus and flow conditions in each reach in four seasons in ArcGIS [14].

2 Methods and Materials

2.1 The Study Area

Located in northern Taiwan, Datuan stream (Fig. 1) has a total length of 14.5 km and ranges in altitude from approximately 1066.0 m to 0.0 m. Upstream, the Datuan stream flows through Yangming-Shan National Park, a heavily forested area; the midstream section flows through a designated agricultural area; and the downstream portion flows through a mixed developed and agricultural area. The major species, *S. japonicus,* has been found in the Datuan stream. As a species of sympatric amphidromous grazing Gobiidae fish, *S. Japonicus* reproduces during the summer in the mid and upstream sections of rivers. The fish spawn in fresh water. After hatching, the young fish are passively transported to a more saline environment downstream [15]. They return to the fresh water upstream approximately 6 months after hatching [15].

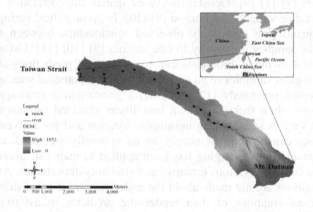

Fig. 1. Study area (Datuan stream)

2.2 Field Surveys of Fishes and Flow

The sample reach were 50 m in length and were selected based on their accessibility of fish assemblages and habitats. Because of the short nature of the stream (14.5 km) and the absence of fishes in the lowermost 5 km, this sampling scheme resulted in 4 reaches covering 8000 m of stream (Fig. 1). The sampling equipment was a battery operated backpack electroshocker. Each sampling crew comprised three individuals, with one operating the equipment while the other two collected the fish samples. The fish were stored in aerated buckets for identification, enumeration, and measurement. The survey methods were based on the freshwater bio-monitoring methods [16].

2.3 Kriging and Indicator Kriging

Kriging, a geostatistical method, is a linear interpolation procedure that provides the best linear unbiased estimator (BLUE) for quantities varying in space [10]. In this study, the current velocity and water depth in each $0.5m \times 0.5m$ grid is estimated using kriging at each reach (reaches 1 to 4). An initial step of kriging estimating water velocity and water depth is to calculate experimental variograms, which graphically show semivariance calculated directly from the data for each lag distance [9] [10] [11]. Experimental variogram is denoted by equation 1,

$$\gamma_{uu}(h) = \frac{1}{2n(h)} \sum_{i=1}^{n(h)} [u(x_i + h) - u(x_i)]^2 \cdot \tag{1}$$

Where h denotes the lag distance that separates pairs of sampling sites; $u(x)$ is the fish count and assemblage value at location x; $u(x + h)$ denotes the number of fish at location $x+h$; and $n(h)$ represents the number of pairs separated by the lag distance h.

At an unsampled location and for a given variogram, a kriging estimate can be viewed simply as an optimally weighted average of the surrounding sampled data [10]. Additionally, the weights, which depend on the correlation structure exhibited, are determined by minimizing the estimation variance. In this context, kriging estimates (Best Linear Unbiased Estimator) are considered the most accurate of all linear estimators. Therefore, using kriging, this study estimates the value of the investigated variable at an unsampled location x_0 based on the measured values in the following linear form [10]:

$$u^*(x_0) = \sum_{i=1}^{N} \lambda_{i0} u(x_i) \cdot \tag{2}$$

where $u^*(x_0)$ is the estimated value at location x_0, λ_{i0} is the kriging estimate of the weight of $u(x_i)$; x_i is the location of the sampling site for the variable u; and N is the number of the variable u involved in the estimates. The kriging estimation variance can be calculated by adopting the Lagrange method to minimize the estimation variance based on non-biased constraints, i.e.

$$\sigma^2_{kriging} = \sum_{i=1}^{N} \lambda_{i0} \gamma_{uu}(x_i - x_0) + \mu \cdot \tag{3}$$

where μ is a Lagrange Multiplier. The Lagrange multiplier in kriging estimation is multiplied by a factor for ease of subsequent computation of minimizing the estimation variance [17].

To provide adequate signs of fishery status, the probability of fish appearance in each reach was determined by indicator kriging [18], by which we estimated the probability that define 1 as the maximum value given when S. japonicus is captured and 0 as the minimum value where no one is captured over the study area in each season. For this purpose, the fish data were transformed from a continuous to a binary scale to apply ordinary indicator kriging. The probabilities in a square $(0.5m \times 0.5m)$ grid comprised of 1309 cells transferred to the GIS system for display are estimated using Indicator kriging. Indicator kriging estimates the probability of exceeding specific threshold values, z_k, at a given location [11]. In indicator kriging, the data, z(x), is transformed into an indicator as follows:

$$i(x, z_k) = \begin{cases} 1, & if \quad z(x) \le z_k \\ 0, & otherwise \end{cases} \quad (4)$$

At an unsampled location, x_0, the probability $z(x) \le z_k$ can be estimated using a linear combination of neighbouring indicator variables. This ordinary indicator kriging estimator is

$$\Pr ob[z(x_0) \le z_k /(n)]^* = \sum_{\alpha=1}^{n} \lambda_\alpha i(x_\alpha; z_k). \quad (5)$$

where $i(x_\alpha; z_k)$ denotes the indicator values at x_α ; $\alpha = 1, \cdots, n$; and λ_α represents the kriging weight of $i(x_\alpha; z_k)$ determined by solving the following kriging system when estimating $\Pr ob[z(x_0) \le z_k /(n)]$. The resulting maps displayed continuous data in the range 0–1, showing a contour of fish probability in each reach.

The experimental variograms, indicator variograms, kriging and indicator kriging for flow and fish data were performed by using GS+ [19]. For fitting variogram models, a relatively consistent set of best-fit models with minimum Model Reduced Sum of Squares (RSS), maximum r^2 values were generated using the least squares model fitting [19].

2.4 Flow Classification in Geographical Information System

In this study, flow conditions of estimated velocity and water depth values are classified by Froude number and Wong's empirical classification. The index requires the velocity and depth in each unit for open surface flow in channels. The Froude number (Fr) relates inertial and gravity forces in flows and is a measure of flow criticality. It is given as:

$$Fr = \frac{V}{\sqrt{gd}}. \quad (6)$$

where V is mean velocity (ms^{-1}), d is water depth (m) and g is acceleration of gravity (ms^{-2}). Jowett [6] explored the utility of the Froude number (among other variables) as a means of discriminating pools (Fr < 0.18), runs (Fr = 0.18 ~ 0.41) and riffles (Fr > 0.41) using analysis of variance statistics.

3 Results

3.1 Investigated Velocity and Water Depth

Fig. 2 shows investigated average velocity and water depth values at each reach and season. Fig. 2a shows that the average current velocity was mostly located from 0.2m/s to 0.4m/s in winter and spring, but it reached up to 0.6m/s (maximum value) in reach 2 of winter then decreased from 0.6m/s to nearly 0.4m/s. Meanwhile, the trend of reach 4 in spring was similar to that in winter. Generally, the average velocity in upstream was greater than that in downstream. During the spring, the water depth in reach 1 and 4 was greater than which in reach 2 and 3, but the average depth in winter decreased from downstream to upstream.

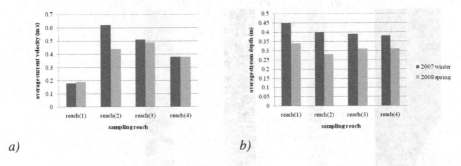

a)   *b)*

Fig. 2. (a) The average current velocity in each reach from winter to spring. (b) The average stream width in each reach from winter to spring.

3.2 Estimated and Classified Flow Conditions

In Fig. 3e and f, the result was close to Fig. 3a and b, but part of run occurred at the estuary. Pool and riffle occupied the stream area in reach 3. The case considerably differed from the result in the empirical method (Fig. 3c and g). Run appeared at the most area of reach 4, but some pools were distributed in the upper section. The range of pool distribution is more widely spread in the Froude number method than that in the empirical rule (Fig. 3d and h).

In the case of downstream in spring, the major flow conditions were pool in reach 1 and riffle in reach 2. However, reach 2 had high heterogeneity of the flow condition which also includes the other types of flow (pool, run and slack). Slack always appeared along the river bank. This phenomenon confirmed with the description of slack from the empirical rule method. In the midstream and upstream, run and riffle had the most two great area in the reach 3 and 4 (Fig. 4c and d). In addition, the flow condition in reach 4 had high heterogeneity the same as which in reach 2. However, the singular phenomenon occurs only in spring but the other seasons. In comparison with the empirical rule, the downstream (reach 1 and 2) was mainly categorized as pool and run (Fig. 4e and f). Comparing to the empirical rule method, riffle (Fig. 4b) was easy to be identified with run (Fig. 4f) in reach 2. Run covered the most part of

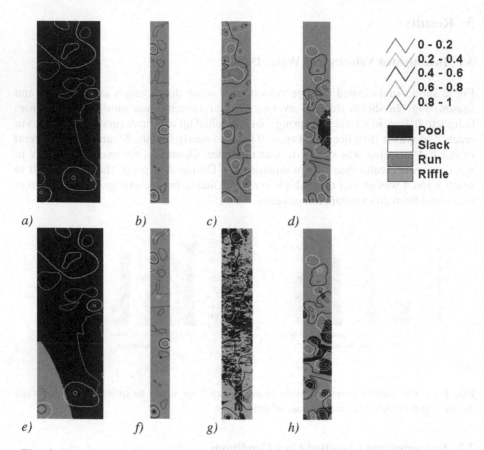

Fig. 3. The flow conditions and fish probability overlapped mapping in winter (a)~(d) reaches 1, 2, 3 and 4 by empirical method; (e)~(h) reaches 1, 2, 3 and 4 by Froude number method

reach 3 (Fig. 4g). There was a quite disparity between the two flow condition classifications. In reach 4, the result in the Froude number method was the same as the empirical rule method; besides, part of pool and riffle were inlayed in reach 4 (Fig. 4h).

3.3 Appearance Probability of Fish

In our study, we used the indicator kriging to estimate the appearance probability of *S. japonicus*, and the result was mapped and superimposed by GIS. According to the method in the result of winter, the contours in reach 1 were not smooth, and the area of the highest probability interval (0.8~1) was reduced at the estuary (Fig. 3a and e). The condition represented that the density of *S. japonicus* in winter was low. In reach 2, most sections in the reach have the appearance probability of *S. japonicus* from 0.8 to 1, which showed that the density of *S. japonicus* was high besides three places near

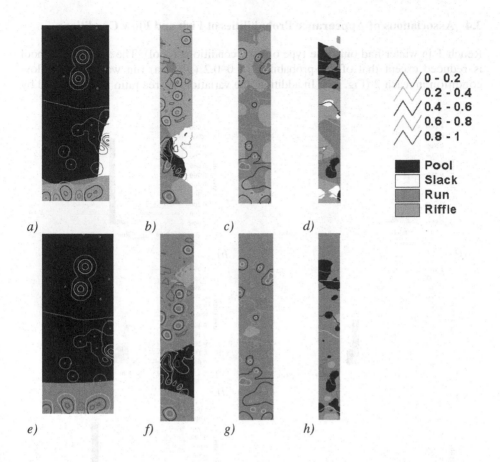

Fig. 4. The flow conditions and fish probability overlapped mapping in spring (a)~(d) reaches 1, 2, 3 and 4 by empirical method; (e)~(h) reaches 1, 2, 3 and 4 by Froude number method

the river bank (Fig. 3b and f). The result of reach 3 was similar to reach 4, and it was different with the situation in the other reach (Fig. 3c, d, g and h). Meanwhile, the appearance probability of fish in reach 3 and 4 in winter were high, which exhibited the migrant of *S. japonicus*. The probability maps also showed that the high density areas of fish were discovered at the estuary in the spring (Fig. 4a and e). The contours which represented low probability were assembled in the lower reach 2, but the area of high probability was widespread with the upper reach (Fig. 4b and f). The mapping of contours could not be identified clearly. In terms of the contour in reach 3 (Fig. 4c and g), the probability of fish in the center was higher than other areas. Overall, the probability in reach 3 in spring was greater than the other seasons, which showed that *S. japonicus* could migrate to the upper stream. After all, the area of probability was cut into several regions.

3.4   Associations of Appearance Probabilities of Fish and Flow Conditions

Reach 1 in winter had only one type of flow conditions (pool). The area ratio of pool is reduced except that of the probability of 0~0.2 (Fig. 5a) run was the only flow condition in reach 2 (Fig. 5b). In addition, the variation of area ratio was increased by

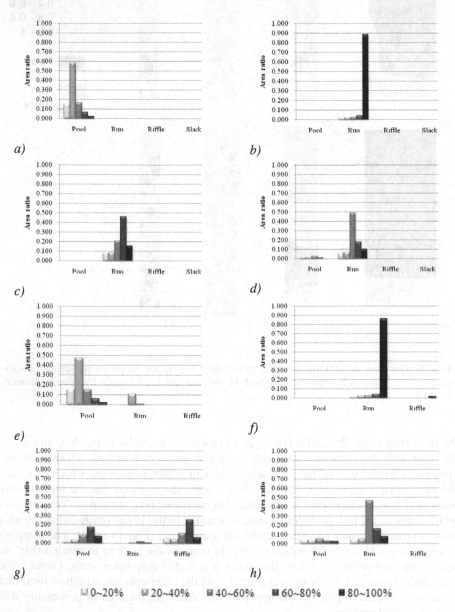

Fig. 5. The histograms of the classifications of flow conditions in winter. (a)~(d) from reach(1)~(4) by empirical method ; (e)~(f) from reach(1)~(4) by Froude number method.

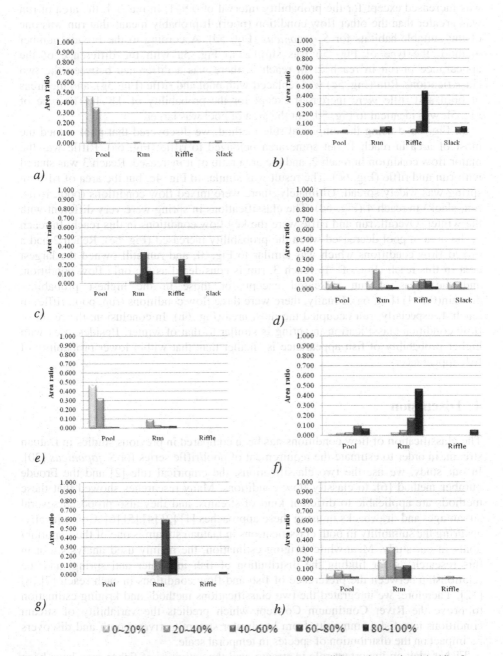

Fig. 6. he histograms of the classifications of flow conditions in spring.(a)~(d) from reach(1)~(4) by emperical ; (e)~(f) from reach(1)~(4) by Froude number method.

the raising of probability. Run occupied the area of reach 3 (Fig. 5c), the area of run was increased except for the probability interval of 0.8~1. In reach 4, the area of run was greater than the other flow condition (pool). It probably means that run was one of the suitable habitats for *S. japonicus* (Fig. 5d). According to the Froude number method, the type of Fig. 5e was similar to Fig. 5a with the difference of the appearance of run in reach 2. In reach 3, there was a difference between the two classifications. Run (Fig. 5c) was replaced with pool and riffle (Fig. 5g), and the areas of pool and riffle were increased except for the probability of 0.8~1. The type of Fig. 5h was identical to Fig. 5d, but the area of pool was larger.

In Fig. 6a~d using the empirical rule method, we discovered that pool owned the most of area in reach 1, but some area belonged to riffle (Fig. 6a). Riffle was the major flow condition in reach 2, and the area ratio of it increased. Reach 3 was shared with run and riffle (Fig. 6c). The result was similar to Fig. 4c, but the area of riffle in spring was widely spread. Ultimately, there were mixed flow conditions (pool, riffle, run, slack) in reach 4 (Fig. 6d). The classifications in spring were very different with the winter. Overall, run and riffle were the key flow conditions in this reach. In reach 1, the area of pool decreased when the probability increased (Fig. 6e). Reach 2 had a mixed flow conditions which was similar to Fig. 3f, and run still owned the largest area in this reach (Fig. 6f). In reach 3, run is considered as the only flow condition, and the areas of run increased except for those in the highest probability domain(0.8~1) (Fig. 6g). Finally, there were three flow conditions (run, pool, riffle) in reach 4, especially, run occupied the most area (Fig. 6h). In conclusion, the result of flow condition classification in spring is similar to that of winter. Besides, area with higher probability of fish appearance is smaller than that within lower probability of fish appearance.

4 Discussion

The classification of flow conditions has been compared in previous studies in Datuan stream, in order to estimate the requirement of pool/riffle series for *S. japonicus* [20]. In our study, we use the two classifications, the empirical rule [2] and the Froude number method [6], to classify flow conditions. Many researches showed that these methods are applicable to different kind of streams, and they also proposed several advantages and drawbacks in using these approaches [1] [2] [4] [5] [6]. Consequently, ensuring the suitability in both classifications in Datuan stream is one of the important goals in our study. Meanwhile, kriging estimation, the mainly used analysis tool in this research, is for finding the distribution of fish in winter and spring, and the relationship between the preference of fish and flow conditions in each reach [7] [8] [12]. Therefore, we integrated the two classifications methods and kriging estimation to prove the River Continuum Concept which predicts the variability of stream conditions in a fish community from headwater stream to river mouth and discovers its impact on the distribution of species in temporal scale.

Fishes play an important role in stream, and the activities of fishes may have been great influenced by freshwater system, particularly flow conditions [20] [21]. In this study, the two key factors, current velocity and stream depth, were considered as the most important factor by determining the habitat preference of fish. The pool/riffle series are usually related with rank erosion and the type of substrate, such as boulders and cobbles in the reach [21]. For instance, the crevices between boulders could produce high velocity, and attract fishesby sufficient dissolved oxygen which promotes the growth rate of algae [22]. The result of the two classifacations were not identical, especially in areas from downstream to middle stream under construction, and the classifications may also lose their accuracy due to the artificial ditubances.

The empirical rule was first built up by Wong [2], and the approach has been applied in many rivers of Taiwan to provide the estimation of pool/riffle series [2]. Nevertheless, in the empirical rule, the limits of water depth and current velocity are 0.3m and 0.3m/s. In some specific sections of reaches, the data of the two hydrological factors are close to 0.3m and 0.3m/s, which indicate that some sections could not be precisely categorized as pool, riffle, run, or slack. Despite of the defect in the empirical rule, a number of ecologists still utilize this method because of its convenience and immediateness [1].

The *S. japonicus* passed for migration and reproduction in winter and spring at the mouth of the stream. Thus deeper pools can provide excellent refugia for them to rest and to save their energy [21]. The migration of fish becomes more frequent when spring comes, for the reason that higher current velocity in riffle facilitates fish moving in water and stimulates the photosynthetic rate thus affords more dissolve oxygen attracting the algae growth. Pool and riffle in the first reach would be regarded as resting habitat and food source [15]. The other result of habitat preference classification is from pool/run in winter to pool/run in spring. The outcome of classification of pool agrees with that of Wong [2]. The difficulty of personal identification through stream conditions results in difference of the level classified at the estuary area. For example, pools are usually erroneously regarded as runs (in winter), and riffles are easily mixed up with runs (in spring). These disparities generally come from the terms considered when computing the Froude number. If the term of current velocity and water depth is too close to 0.3m, the result of classification could be totally different by person. Azzellino and Vismara [4] applied the Froude number method in 370 hydraulic sections to aid identifying four main morphological units (pools, deep pools, and slow and fast riffles). According to these researches, the classification of stream conditions by Jowett [6] requires few modifications when applying at the mouth of river.

5 Conclusion

To be effective in confirming the preference of *S. japonicus*, the researchers, biologists, and river managers have tried to establish the classification of stream conditions (i.e. pool, riffle, run, slack) in order to find those stream areas with higher fish abundance and heterogeneity. Almost all the strategies are based on the predicted distribution of *S. japonicus* with spatial and temporal variation. To the best of our knowledge, this study is the first one which combines the kriging method with two flow conditions classifications [2] [6] to study the fish distribution and its habitat preference throughout the stream catchment in Taiwan. The flow conditions classifications are applied to assign all the hydrological data (current velocity and depth), which were interpolated by ordinary kriging, and then overlapped the probability of *S. japonicus* by indicator kriging. These mappings not only describe the abundance and heterogeneity of *S. japonicus* throughout the stream with seasonal changes, but also quantify the area ratio of the combination of fish probability and flow conditions in each reach. The result shows that the measurement to classify the flow conditions [2] is more appropriate than the others for Datuan stream [6]. Flow condition classification measurement could efficiently reduce the financial cost and provide information for engineers when designing and constructing ecological engineering, which could supply the suitable habitats for the life-history (i.e. shelter, reproduction, food source) of *S. japonicus*. Moreover, according to the migration behavior of *S. japonicus*, the classification of the empirical rule method with geostatistical approaches in GIS can be used effectively to estimate the habitat preference of *S. japonicus* in Datuan stream. For future work, the investigation of *S. japonicus'* distribution and the basic information in these reach will be included to extend, improve, and validate our further results.

Acknowledgements. The authors would like to thank National Science Council of Taiwan for partial financial support of this research under contract no. NSC-97-2628-H-002-026-MY3. In addition, we appreciate the support given by the Fisheries Agency of the Council of Agriculture at the Executive Yuan. Finally, we would also like to thank Min-Hua Chen, Po-Hui Yang, Yien-Tan Wang, Yien-Hauo Hwang, and Mr. Tung for helping with the field investigations.

References

1. Joanna, L.K., David, M.H., Giuseppe, A.C.: The habitat-scale ecohydraulics of rivers. Ecological Engineering 16, 17–29 (2000)
2. Wong, C.M.: Water resources education at Da-Chia stream. Water Resources Agency, Ministry of Economic Affairs, 30–45 (2000)
3. Francisco, L., Lilian, C., Helena, S.G., Andre, B.D.C., Denise, D.C.R.F.: Riffle and pool fish communities in a large stream of southeastern Brazil. Neotropical Ichthyology 3(2), 305–311 (2005)
4. Azzellin, A., Vismara, R.: Pool Quality Index: New Method to Define Minimum Flow Requirements of High-Gradient, Low-Order Streams. Journal of Environmental Engineering 127(11) (2001)
5. Deborah, S., Dan, R.: Hyfraulic habitat composition and diversity in rural and urban stream reaches of the north Carolina Piedmont(USA). River. Res. Applic. 24, 1082–1103 (2008)
6. Jowett, I.G.: A method for identifying pool, run, and riffle habitats from physical measurements. J. Mar. Freshwater Res. 27, 241–248 (1993)
7. Durance, I., Lepichon, C., Ormerod, S.J.: Recognizing the importance of scale in the ecology and management of riverine fish. River Research and Application 22, 1143–1152 (2006)
8. Torgersen, C.E., Gresswell, R.E., Bateman, D.S.: Pattern detection in stream networks: quantifying spatial variability in fish distribution. In: Nishida, T., Kailola, P.J., Hollingworth, C.E. (eds.) Proceedings of the Second Annual International Symposium on GIS/Spatial Analyses in Fishery and Aquatic Sciences, Japan, Fishery GIS Research Group, Saitama, pp. 405–420 (2004)

9. Wang, Y.C., Lin, Y.P., Cho, T.H., Wang, C.L.: Estimating scale-dependent hierarchical variations and longitudinal distribution of stream fish abundance–Datun stream, Taiwan. In: International Statistical Ecology Conference (2008)

10. Lin, Y.P., Yeh, M.H., Deng, D.P., Wang, Y.C.: Geostatistical Approaches and Optimal Additional Sampling Schemes for Spatial Patterns and Future Samplings of Bird Diversity. Global Ecology and Biogeography 17, 175–188 (2008)

11. Lin, Y.P., Chen, B.Y., Shyu, G.S., Chang, T.K.: Combing a Finite Mixture Distribution Model with Indicator Kriging to Delineate and Map the Spatial Patterns of Heavy Metal Pollution in Soil. Environmental Pollution 158, 235–244 (2010)

12. Carroll, S.S., Pearson, D.L.: Detecting and modeling spatial and temporal dependence in conservation biology. Conservation Biology 14, 1893–1897 (2000)

13. Cressie, N.A.C.: Statistics for spatial data, revised edn. Wiley 506 Interscience, New York (1993)

14. ESRI (2009), http://www.esri.com

15. Shen, K.N., Tzeng, W.N.: Formation of a metamorphosis check in otoliths of the amphidromous goby Sicyopterus japonicus. Marine Ecological Progress Series 228, 205–211 (2002)

16. Liang, S.H.: Developing models for freshwater bio-monitoring. In: National Park Workshop, Taipei (2005)

17. Wackernagel, H.: Multivariate geostatistics: An introduction with applications, vol. 607. Springer, Heidelberg (2003)

18. Seijo, J.C., Caddy, J.F.: Uncertainty in bio-economic reference points and indicators of marine fisheries. Marine and Freshwater Research 51, 477–483 (2000)

19. Gamma Design Software, GS+: Geostatistics for the environmental sciences. Version 5.0. Gamma Design Software, Plainwell, MI (2004)

20. Inoue, M., Miyayoshi, M.: Fish foraging effects on benthic assemblages along a warm-temperate stream: differences among drift feeders, benthic predators and grazers. Oikos 114, 95–107 (2006)

21. Abe, S., Iguchi, K., Ito, S., Uchida, Y., Ohnishi, H., Ohmori, K.: Habitat use of the grazing goby (Sicyopterus japonicus) in response to spatial heterogeneity in riparian shade. Journal of Freshwater Ecology 18, 161–167 (2003)

22. Dettlaff, T.A., Ginsburg, A.S., Schmalhausen, O.I.: Sturgeon fishes: developmental biology and aquaculture. Springer, Berlin (1993)

Service Path Attribution Networks (SPANs): Spatially Quantifying the Flow of Ecosystem Services from Landscapes to People

Gary W. Johnson[1,2], Kenneth J. Bagstad[2], Robert R. Snapp[1],
and Ferdinando Villa[2]

[1] Department of Computer Science
[2] Ecoinformatics Collaboratory, Gund Institute for Ecological Economics
University of Vermont, Burlington, VT 05405, USA
{gwjohnso,kbagstad,rsnapp,fvilla}@uvm.edu
http://ecoinformatics.uvm.edu

Abstract. Ecosystem services are the effects on human well-being of the flow of benefits from ecosystems to people over given extents of space and time. The Service Path Attribution Network (SPAN) model provides a spatial framework for quantifying these flows, providing a new means of estimating these economic benefits. This approach discovers dependencies between provision and usage endpoints, spatial competition among users for scarce resources, and landscape effects on ecosystem service flows. Particularly novel is the model's ability to identify the relative density of these flows throughout landscapes and to determine which areas are affected by upstream flow depletion. SPAN descriptions have been developed for a number of services(aesthetic viewsheds, proximity to open space, carbon sequestration, flood mitigation, nutrient cycling, and avoided sedimentation/deposition), which vary in scale of effect, mechanism of provision and use, and type of flow. Results using real world data are shown for the US Puget Sound region.

Keywords: ecosystem services, ecosystem service assessment, SPAN model, service path attribution network, environmental planning, service flows, flow modeling, flow density, flow criticality.

1 Introduction

The concept of Ecosystem Services (ES) provides a cohesive scientific view of the many mechanisms through which nature contributes to human well-being[5]. Focusing on both the biophysical mechanisms of ES provision and the economic implications of ES use can allow our societies to balance the sides of the "nature vs. economy" equation, leading to better management and governance[10]. Natural systems provide valuable physical resources to support daily life, regulation of local through global processes within ranges appropriate for human survival, and cultural benefits that satisfy psychological, emotional, and cultural needs. These values, which can be determined by the careful application of ecological

D. Taniar et al. (Eds.): ICCSA 2010, Part I, LNCS 6016, pp. 238–253, 2010.

and economic principles, should be factored into decisions that influence the state of natural systems and the services they provide[5,11,10].

Understanding and modeling the complexities of coupled human-natural systems requires researchers to combine techniques from both socio-economics and the physical sciences. A major hurdle to this union is in overcoming the very different underlying assumptions, scales, and applications of the main modeling techniques used in these fields. Additionally, even with the best of intentions, many of the interactions between humans and their environments remain as of yet unknown[9].

For these reasons, concrete techniques for supporting quantification, spatial mapping and economic valuation of ES have lagged behind the popularity of the concept, making it difficult to productively use ES as a basis for scientific investigation and accurate decision-making [3,17]. Virtually all methodologies employed or proposed [4,6,12,15] to quantify ES and their values convert proxy categorical information, chiefly land cover type, into coarse assessments of value or potential provision through the use of aggregated coefficients. Such approaches ignore the complex, multi-scale dynamics of ES provision, use, and flow and are insufficiently precise to enable detailed scenario analyses or inform spatial planning decisions. Current approaches tend to address the following three points unsatisfactorily:

1. **Scalability:** Ecosystem services are provided and used at a wide variety of spatial and temporal scales[8,7]. However, most current spatial ES models are calibrated to operate on one fixed scale. A robust model would be able to adapt its scale and associated complexity to match each problem.

2. **Generalizability:** The algorithms used in the model analysis should be transparent enough for decision-makers in the field of ecosystem services to understand (and modify as necessary), while being robust enough to handle a variety of different services and applications.

3. **Benefit-Centrism:** Although earth system simulation modeling is a well established field, especially with respect to climate and hydrologic modeling, these models focus largely or exclusively on describing and predicting how physical environmental systems behave under varying conditions. The effects of the environmental system on the human economic system (and vice versa) must be central to the model, as assessing these is the heart of ecosystem service assessment and valuation[3,17,1].

This contribution addresses these issues through a combination of network analysis, dynamic programming, parallelism, and agent-based techniques. The end result is a model which emphasizes service *flows* rather than their in situ production, reflecting the definition of ecosystem services given in [16]: the effects on human well-being of the flow of benefits from an ecosystem endpoint to a human endpoint at given extents of space and time. This algorithm, called the Service Path Attribution Network (SPAN), discovers dependencies between provision and usage endpoints, spatial competition among users for scarce resources, and landscape effects on ecosystem service flows. Particularly novel is the model's ability to identify the relative density of these flows throughout landscapes and to determine which areas are affected by upstream flow depletion. SPAN descriptions have been developed for a number of services(aesthetic viewsheds, proximity to open space, carbon sequestration, flood mitigation, nutrient cycling, and avoided sedimentation/deposition), which vary in scale of effect, mechanism of provision and use, and type of flow. Due to page limitations, we concentrate on results obtained using real world data for the aesthetic viewshed service in the US Puget Sound region. Results for other services will be available online and in forthcoming publications[1].

2   Structure of the Model

In the SPAN model, both potential producers and beneficiaries of ecosystem services are spatially identified on the landscape, and the service flow from these ecosystems to their economic endpoints becomes the focus of the analysis. In this way, we can reach a more thorough understanding of which benefits are received by which people. We can also determine the degree to which landscape features and other human activities affect service flows and can use this information to suggest land management scenarios to decision makers that will increase or decrease these flows to meet their needs.

2.1   Mapping from Geospace to Vertices

A SPAN is implemented over a directed acyclic graph that represents the spatial relationships between those geographic areas that participate in the production, use, transport, or absorption of a given ecosystem service. Each spatial region is represented by a vertex in the graph, along with its underlying feature measurements. Each boundary element between adjacent regions is represented by a directed edge indicating the direction of service flow (see Figure 1).

Because the number of vertices in our network must be finite to perform this analysis, an initial step in building a SPAN is selecting the study scale and discretizing the overall region of interest into a set of spatially disjoint locations according to the particular service's production, use, and flow characteristics. Given the underlying georeferenced data set, this spatial segmentation process may be automated via techniques from image analysis, computer vision, or spatial data mining or may even be manually supplied using a predetermined partitioning, such as a map of geopolitical or bioregional boundaries.

Although many natural processes are often approximated by continuous models (e.g. hydrologic or atmospheric dynamics), we believe a discrete paradigm offers several advantages. First, environmental datasets are almost always comprised of discretely-sampled measurements. These usually come in the form of either polygon maps or regular grids with associated feature values at each measured location. Using discrete regions in the SPAN model allows us to match our algorithms to the same scale and representation as that of the underlying data. The second advantage is that agent-based algorithms can be readily applied to the data to identify

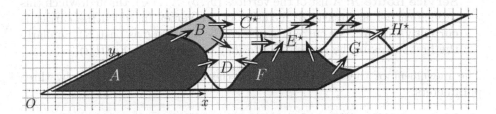

Fig. 1. Pixelated landscape segmented into regions by underlying feature measurements. Each region corresponds to a vertex in the SPAN, and the arrows depict the direction of service flow between regions. *A* and *F* are *source* regions, *B* is a service *sink*, and regions *C*, *E*, and *H* contain potential service *users*, denoted by an asterisk on the region's label.

flow pathways between service providers and beneficiaries. A third and final advantage is that the computational complexity of some models can be reduced by aggregating high resolution data within each region into simpler representations, such as probability distributions or functional approximations, which the agent system may then use as input. A caveat to this is that acceptable scales for downsampling must be fine enough to accurately represent the movement of the given service and are thus constrained by its flow properties.

2.2   Service Medium and Service Carriers

In order to simulate the flows of ecosystem services through the model, the analysis of a SPAN requires an additional component, called the *service medium*. This is the particular form of matter, energy, or information that transmits the chosen service between geospatial locations and therefore also through the SPAN to which they are mapped. Depending on the service, the medium's propagation may represent the movement of a benefit (like food, clean water, or scenic views) or a detriment (like the movement of excessive sediment, nutrients, or floodwater). We term the former services *provisioning services*, as the provision of the service medium by an ecosystem to a human beneficiary group represents a benefit.[1] We term the latter services *preventative services*, since the benefit is provided by an ecosystem's prevention of the service medium reaching a beneficiary. Thus for some ecosystem services, accumulation of the medium by beneficiaries provides economic value, while for other services, the value is accrued by preventing this accumulation.

In the network, the service medium is reified as a collection of service carrier agents, represented as pairs (W, R) with the following meaning:

– **Service Weight** W: A numeric (or otherwise quantifiable) representation of the quantity or quality of the service medium that a service carrier is transporting through the network.

---

[1] This definition of the term *provisioning services* differs from that given in the Millenium Assessment, in which it is used to mean physical goods obtained from ecosystems.[10].

– **Service Route R:** A list of the vertices $(v_1, v_2, \ldots, v_N)$, through which this service carrier has traveled, inclusive of the vertex in which the carrier is currently located. The current vertex can be addressed as Last(R). Similarly the first vertex in the carrier's route may be accessed as First(R).

The movement of these carriers through the SPAN is then specified by three parameters:

1. **Movement Function,** Move : $(W, R) \rightarrow ((W, R)*)$: This function maps a carrier (W_0, R_0) to a list of new carriers $((W_1, R_1), (W_2, R_2), \ldots, (W_N, R_N))$, where N is the number of outgoing edges from Last(R_0). These represent the next steps of the service carrier through the SPAN. Each new carrier route is formed by appending one of the vertices reachable by an outgoing edge from Last(R_0) onto R_0. All vertices directly reachable by an outgoing edge are represented without repetition. The weights associated with these routes describe the amount of service medium which follows each particular route away from Last(R_0). If a carrier moves into a vertex with no outgoing edges, then Move((W, R)) evaluates to an empty list.

2. **Decay Function,** Decay : $(W, R) \rightarrow W'$: Some service media may decay in quality or importance as a function of the distance they travel or by some limiting effect of the route they follow. For example, the view of a mountain becomes less impressive the further away it is. We represent this in the SPAN by a function that maps a service carrier to a new weight $W' \leq W$ which is the remaining weight after applying the decay effects along the route R. In order to reverse this calculation (as required by Section 3.3), a corresponding function Undecay : $(W', R) \rightarrow W$ must also be supplied.

3. **Transition Threshold,** θ_{trans}: This is the minimum weight that any carrier in the network must have in order to be a candidate for the Movement function. Should a service carrier's weight W ever become less than θ_{trans}, then the carrier expires and the medium it bears ceases to propagate any further. Increasing this value will decrease the maximum route length for carriers.

2.3   Location Properties

With the study area partitioned and the service medium identified, each vertex v in the SPAN is assigned eight properties (see Table 1), which describe its region's effects on the service medium. Those properties labeled *Concrete* are expressed in physical units. Those labeled *Abstract* are represented with a unitless value from $[0, 1]$. The properties that saturate represent limited absorption or usage capacities. Regions with these values will not absorb or use quantities of the service medium greater than these limits during the flow analysis. Conversely, the non-saturating properties represent amounts of absorption or usage that are entirely dependent on the amount of the service medium encountered.

For many but not all ecosystem services, either the absolute or the relative forms of the source, sink, and use functions are defined. In general, cultural and aesthetic services (e.g. scenic viewsheds, proximity to open space, or preservation of a cultural icon) are most easily modeled using relative source, sink,

Table 1. Location properties assigned to each vertex in the SPAN

Location Property	Function	Unit Type	Saturating	Relationship to Medium
Absolute Source	$\text{Source}_{abs}(v)$	Concrete	N/A	Amount produced
Absolute Sink	$\text{Sink}_{abs}(v)$	Concrete	Yes	Amount potentially absorbed
Minimum Absolute Use	$\text{Use}_{abs}^{min}(v)$	Concrete	Yes	Amount potentially unusable
Maximum Absolute Use	$\text{Use}_{abs}^{max}(v)$	Concrete	Yes	Amount potentially usable
Relative Source	$\text{Source}_{rel}(v)$	Abstract	N/A	Amount produced
Relative Sink	$\text{Sink}_{rel}(v)$	Abstract	No	Percent potentially absorbed
Minimum Relative Use	$\text{Use}_{rel}^{min}(v)$	Abstract	No	Percent potentially unusable
Maximum Relative Use	$\text{Use}_{rel}^{max}(v)$	Abstract	No	Percent potentially usable

and use values. Concrete values are better suited to represent services based on the movement of matter or energy across landscapes (e.g. water provision, flood mitigation, or carbon sequestration). In this case, the absolute source value of a region represents the amount of the medium (i.e. runoff or carbon sequestration – including avoided release of stored carbon) that it produces during the simulation. Since the SPAN model currently operates statically in time, this source value is based on a predefined time window or a particular event, such as a 100-year storm.

Of particular interest are the minimum and maximum use values. For a provisioning service, a region's minimum use value denotes the amount of the service medium which cannot be used by the beneficiaries within its bounds, stated in either physical units or as a percentage of the total quantity encountered. Maximum use indicates the total that can be captured by beneficiaries. These may be used to represent both institutional constraints as well as physical or technological limitations on the extraction process. For a preventative service, the minimum use value should be interpreted as a limit on the amount of the service medium encountered which will not cause any measurable damage to the beneficiaries in a region. Maximum use then represents the amount beyond which no further damage is caused (because all assets of note have already been ruined).

A final property of service usage is that it may be either destructive or nondestructive on the service medium. This is correlated with the rivalness[2] of the resource being analyzed. For example, with water provision, the extraction and use of water is clearly rival and destructive of the resource since collecting it in one region prevents its use by all downstream regions. The same applies to carbon sequestration, as a finite quantity of carbon sequestration capacity must be shared among all users in order to maintain the atmospheric carbon

---

[2] A rival good is one whose use or consumption by one party leaves less available for use or consumption by others[13]. Most physical goods and commodities bought and sold in the market are rival goods. A non-rival good is one that can be used by multiple parties without leaving less available for others. Examples include public safety, information in the public domain, and most regulating and cultural values provided by ecosystems.

balance at a safe level. However, in the case of flood mitigation, the same water that causes flood damage in one region may cause further damage in others. Thus, by providing the service of flood mitigation to one area, many areas may simultaneously receive the same benefit depending on their spatial configuration. The same non-rivalness may often hold for the informational or accessibility-based services. As an example, the availability of scenic viewsheds may benefit many users in different regions without competition for this resource.

2.4   Property Thresholds

As a means of restricting service flow calculations to parts of the system deemed more important than others, a positive, real-valued threshold may be associated with each of the above location properties. These shall be labeled as follows:

$$\theta_t^m, \quad \text{where, } m \in \{\text{abs}, \text{rel}\}, t \in \{\text{source}, \text{sink}, \text{use}\}.$$

These thresholds will be used to determine the vertex sets S, K, and U in the following section.

2.5   The Graph Specification

Now that the mapping from geospace to vertices has been detailed and all the necessary terminology introduced, we can present the graph specification of our SPAN model in detail. A SPAN is built on a directed graph $G = (V, E)$, possessing the following six properties:

1. Every vertex $v \in V$ represents a single geospatial area, whose polygon-bounded region is distinct and does not overlap topologically with that of any other vertex $v' \in V$.
2. Every directed edge $(u, v) \in E$ represents a path along which a service carrier may travel from location u to location v. This path may represent an adjacency relationship (shared boundary) between u and v in the georeferenced space, but it may also connect two spatially separated locations in the event that the service medium's flow may be better modeled in such a manner. For example, two cities which are accessible along the same train line may be connected by an edge in the SPAN for services which may travel along human transportation networks.
3. A subset $S \subseteq V$ contains those vertices which we shall call *service sources*. For each $s \in S$, either $\text{Source}_{\text{abs}}(s) \geq \theta_{\text{source}}^{\text{abs}}$ or $\text{Source}_{\text{rel}}(s) \geq \theta_{\text{source}}^{\text{rel}}$, depending on whether the source is absolute or relative.
4. A subset $K \subseteq V$ contains those vertices which we shall call *service sinks*. For each $k \in K$, $\text{Sink}_{\text{abs}}(k) \geq \theta_{\text{sink}}^{\text{abs}}$ or $\text{Sink}_{\text{rel}}(k) \geq \theta_{\text{sink}}^{\text{rel}}$, depending on whether the sink is absolute or relative.
5. A subset $U \subseteq V$ contains those vertices which we shall call *service users*. For each $u \in U$, $\text{Use}_{\text{abs}}^{\max}(u) \geq \theta_{\text{use}}^{\text{abs}}$ or $\text{Use}_{\text{rel}}^{\max}(u) \geq \theta_{\text{use}}^{\text{rel}}$, depending on whether the use is absolute or relative.
6. S, K, and U need not be disjoint.

This completes the description of the SPAN model's structure, parametrization, and correspondence to the underlying spatial data. Next, we must connect the regions providing services with their beneficiaries.

3 Flow Analysis

Thus far, the ecosystem service properties of our study area have been determined within each region without regard to the relationships between regions. We call these values the *theoretical* source, sink, and use estimates of our service assessment because without determining where the service medium generated at the sources will flow, we cannot determine who, if anyone, will receive its benefits or which sinks will actually impede its movement. This highlights an important aspect of the SPAN model's definition of service provision: unless the generated benefit is actually made accessible to human beneficiaries, no service is attributed to the ecosystem. Furthermore, since services can flow to beneficiaries from different sources, it is important to correctly assign value to sources that are actually used.

The algorithm that determines these spatial relationships consists of four phases: Discovering the Flow Topology, Sorting Routes by Dependence, Applying Sink and Rival Use Effects, and Analyzing the Carrier Paths.

3.1 Discovering the Flow Topology

First, each vertex v in the graph is assigned two empty sets, which we shall call its *carrier caches*, $\mathrm{Cache}_{\mathrm{possible}}(v)$ and $\mathrm{Cache}_{\mathrm{actual}}(v)$. A service carrier is initialized in each source vertex $s \in S$ with its weight and route (W, R) set as either $(\mathrm{Source}_{\mathrm{abs}}(s), (s))$ or $(\mathrm{Source}_{\mathrm{rel}}(s), (s))$, depending on the service medium. Each carrier is then used as the root node of a depth-first tree traversal in which $\mathrm{Move}((W, R))$ is used as the successor function at each step. During this phase of the traversal, the weight values of the carriers are only reduced by path branching (i.e. when a parent's weight is divided among multiple children) or distance decay as computed by the $\mathrm{Decay}((W, R))$ function. The leaf nodes on this carrier graph are both those for which $\mathrm{Move}((W, R))$ returns no children as well as those for which $\mathrm{Decay}((W, R)) < \theta_{\mathrm{trans}}$. Whenever a carrier (W, R) is created for which $\mathrm{Last}(R) \in K \cup U$, a new carrier $(\mathrm{Decay}((W, R)), R)$ is appended to $\mathrm{Cache}_{\mathrm{possible}}(\mathrm{Last}(R))$.

3.2 Sorting Routes by Dependence

Let $\mathrm{Carriers}_{\mathrm{unsorted}} = \bigcup_{v \in V} \mathrm{Cache}_{\mathrm{possible}}(v)$. Let $\mathrm{Carriers}_{\mathrm{sorted}}$ be a list containing all the members of $\mathrm{Carriers}_{\mathrm{unsorted}}$ ordered according to the following constraint: Given a carrier (W, R) in $\mathrm{Carriers}_{\mathrm{unsorted}}$, select the last vertex r in R that belongs to K, or that belongs to $K \cup U$ if the service is rival, excluding $\mathrm{Last}(R)$. All carriers in $\mathrm{Cache}_{\mathrm{possible}}(r)$ must appear before (W, R) in $\mathrm{Carriers}_{\mathrm{sorted}}$.

3.3   Applying Sink and Rival Use Effects

Next, we want to determine the degree to which landscape sinks and human users along the flow paths deplete the service carrier weights which they encounter. We first establish the following definitions:

$$\text{Input}_{\text{actual}}(v) = \begin{cases} \displaystyle\sum_{(W,R)\in\text{Cache}_{\text{actual}}(v)} W, & \text{if } |\text{Cache}_{\text{actual}}(v)| > 0 \\ 1, & \text{otherwise} \end{cases}$$

$$W_{\text{contrib}}(w,v) = \frac{w}{\text{Input}_{\text{actual}}(v)}$$

$$W_{\text{sink}}(w,v) = \begin{cases} w \times \text{Sink}_{\text{rel}}(v), & \text{if } \text{Sink}_{\text{rel}}(v) > 0 \\ W_{\text{contrib}}(w,v) \times \\ \quad \min\left(\text{Input}_{\text{actual}}(v), \text{Sink}_{\text{abs}}(v)\right), & \text{otherwise} \end{cases}$$

$$W_{\text{unusable}}(w,v) = \begin{cases} w \times \text{Use}_{\text{rel}}^{\min}(v), & \text{if } \text{Use}_{\text{rel}}^{\min}(v) > 0 \\ \min\left(w, W_{\text{contrib}}(w,v) \times \text{Use}_{\text{abs}}^{\min}(v)\right), & \text{otherwise} \end{cases}$$

$$W_{\text{used}}(w,v) = \begin{cases} (w - W_{\text{unusable}}(w,v)) \times \text{Use}_{\text{rel}}^{\max}(v), & \text{if } \text{Use}_{\text{rel}}^{\max}(v) > 0 \\ \min\left(w - W_{\text{unusable}}(w,v), \right. \\ \quad \left. W_{\text{contrib}}(w,v) \times \text{Use}_{\text{abs}}^{\max}(v)\right) & \text{otherwise} \end{cases}$$

Select the first carrier (W, R) in Carriers$_{\text{sorted}}$ and retrace its route, allowing the sink and use regions along it, if any, to reduce its service weight as follows:

Compute the route's undecayed weight value Undecay$((W, R))$. Initialize w to this value, and let it represent the remaining weight after each successive reduction. Let v assume the values sequentially between First(R) and Last(R). Whenever $v \in K$, subtract $W_{\text{sink}}(w, v)$ from the weight remaining and call this w. If the service is rival and $v \in U$, subtract $W_{\text{used}}(w, v)$ from the post-sunk weight. Finally, apply Decay to w at this step, and if it is greater than θ_{trans}, continue to the next value of v.

After all sink and use effects along route R have been applied, append a new carrier (w, R) to Cache$_{\text{actual}}$(Last(R)). Repeat this algorithm for each successive carrier in Carriers$_{\text{sorted}}$. By generating these carriers in the order determined by the path sorting phase, each Cache$_{\text{actual}}(v)$ will be fully populated before any $W_{\text{sink}}(w, v)$ or $W_{\text{used}}(w, v)$ calculations that depend on it will be performed.

At this point, for all $v \in V$, Cache$_{\text{possible}}(v)$ has been populated with service carriers (W, R) which indicate the amount of benefit W that could be transmitted along route R if the effects of sinks and rival uses were nullified. For each such carrier (W, R) in Cache$_{\text{possible}}(v)$, Cache$_{\text{actual}}(v)$ contains a corresponding carrier

(w, R), which denotes the amount of benefit w expected to travel along R when the effects of sinks and rival uses are factored in.

3.4 Analyzing the Carrier Paths

Once the flow model has completed execution, the two carrier caches are analyzed to determine the total amount of service each location receives from each producer, which sinks and rival use effects block downstream access to the service medium, and what parts of the landscape exhibit the greatest flow density. All of these calculations are possible because the weighted routes stored during the simulation record spatial information about each of these effects on the flow.

The results of this path analysis are several:

1. **Theoretical Source, Sink, Use:** The names given to the in situ location properties of each site determined prior to flow analysis as described in Section 2.3. These are included for completeness and comparison.
2. **Possible Source, Sink, Use, Flow:** Source amounts reachable by users along flow paths determined by landscape topology and topography and the medium's flow characteristics, estimates of sink absorption and usage capacity actualized along these flow paths as functions of the quantity of the medium encountered, and flow density through each region in the study area. All values are calculated by disregarding the effects of sink and rival use locations upstream of each region. This provides an upper bound for the landscape's service flow potential if development scenarios are implemented which minimize these effects.
3. **Actual Source, Sink, Use, Flow:** Same as the Possible values, except that sink and rival use effects are included in their calculation. This provides a snapshot of the actual state of ecosystem service flows in the region.
4. **Inaccessible Source, Sink, Use:** The difference between Theoretical and Possible values. Unreachable source production, unutilized sinks, and unsaturated use capacity due to flow topology.
5. **Blocked Source, Sink, Use, Flow:** The difference between Possible and Actual values. Unreachable source production, unutilized sinks, and unsaturated user capacity due to sink and rival use effects.

For provisioning services, the use values calculated in this stage represent met (or unmet) user demand, sinks are considered detrimental, and source regions are valued according to the amount of service they produce which is received by human beneficiaries. Because receipt of the service medium is desirable, the landscape features which facilitate its transport through intermediate regions are also of value.

For preventative services, greater use indicates greater damage incurred due to encounters with the service medium. Regions with high source estimates or flow densities are undesirable, and sinks along flow paths become the providers of value to human beneficiaries. This approach can be used to quantify the effectiveness of landscape features in mitigating or blocking flow propagated threats, such as flood waters, wildfires, or mudslides.

This information, in combination with maps of the flow topology and density, can be used to target spatial planning decisions that intend to change or preserve service flows as well as to identify the comparative effects on ecosystem services of different development actions before they are enacted.

4   Results

The SPAN model described above has been implemented as a core component of the NSF-funded "ARtificial Intelligence for Ecosystem Services"(ARIES) project's software infrastructure. In this context, spatial environmental and economic datasets for model calibration and testing have been made available by case study partners in the Puget Sound[3] and Madagascar[4]. Discretization of the landscape was performed by converting all geographic data to a common resolution pixel-grid (raster) format. The location properties (see Table 2.3) were described using Bayesian networks, which were initially designed based on literature reviews and were later vetted and extended by local experts in each case study area (see Acknowledgements). Move and Decay functions, θ_{trans}, and the property thresholds were also provided by experts associated with each project for each service under study.

4.1   Aesthetic Viewsheds

As a first example, we examine benefits provided by unimpeded views of natural landscapes (e.g. the economic value of views of mountains and water bodies as measured using hedonic analysis[2]). In this case, the service medium is a measure of "scenic beauty" that is propagated by a movement function which follows lines of sight to potential beneficiaries. $\text{Source}_{\text{rel}}(v)$ assigns each grid cell v a qualitative beauty measure with respect to all other cells in the study area. $\text{Use}_{\text{rel}}^{\text{max}}(v)$ highlights potential users of this service (for example, property owners in a given development district). Finally, $\text{Sink}_{\text{rel}}(v)$ depicts the presence of landscape features whose presence along a line of sight may detract from the view quality (i.e. billboards, clearcuts, industrial development). $\text{Decay}(W, R) = W/4\pi|R|^2$ so that the impact of a view drops off quadratically with distance, and θ_{trans} is set arbitrarily small enough to allow carrier propagation across the entire study area. Optionally, increasing θ_{trans} restricts smaller carriers from transmitting service and can be used as a filter for discovering which areas receive the most service from each provision region.

In the following diagrams, the pre- and post-flow estimates of the source, sink, use and flow density values are shown for the landscape surrounding the city of Kent, WA in the US Puget Sound region. Note, in particular, that the possible source which is available to beneficiaries in Kent is much less (denoted by its lighter shading) than the theoretical source due to the visually detracting effects of commercial and industrial development around the city.

---

[3] Earth Economics: http://eartheconomics.org
[4] Conservation International: http://www.conservation.org

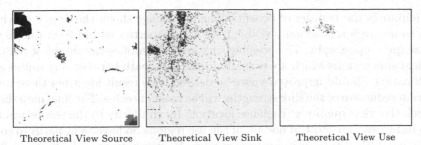

Theoretical View Source   Theoretical View Sink   Theoretical View Use

The dark area in the upper left of the first image is part of the Puget Sound and that in the lower right is the portion of Mount Rainier within the study area. These and the smaller water bodies and hills scattered across the map are detected as sources of scenic beauty by the $Source_{rel}$ function. The second image shows potential sink zones (here denoted by commercial, industrial, and transportation-related development). The final image depicts the potential beneficiaries of the aesthetic view service: residential properties within the city of Kent.

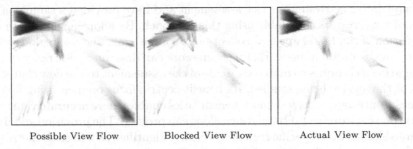

Possible View Flow   Blocked View Flow   Actual View Flow

These three maps indicate the flow densities between provision and use regions. The darkness of each path indicates the usable quality of the scenic beauty as it radiates from its point of origin toward the properties in Kent. The first shows all possible lines of sight along which the service medium may travel. The second depicts those flows which are blocked due to landscape sinks (i.e. obstructions and visual blight). The last shows the actual view quality when sink effects are taken into account.

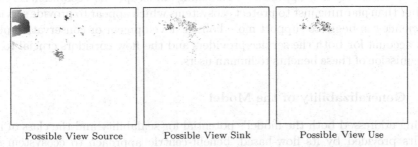

Possible View Source   Possible View Sink   Possible View Use

In contrast with the theoretical (pre-flow) projections, the possible (post-flow) source and sink values are significantly lower across the study area, demonstrating the utility of flow information in filtering out those regions which do, in fact, participate in the transfer of benefits. The first image shows the degree to which each source region is actually visible from the properties within Kent due to the landscape's topography. The possible sink image identifies the subset of the theoretical sink regions which are actually in the view path between any source and use location. Should improved views be desired, this result identifies those areas wherein reduction of the sink strengths will be most effective. The final map shows the relative view quality at each use location. Its similarity to the theoretical use map indicates that most, if not all, of the use regions do have sight paths to some of the aesthetically beautiful source regions. However, since sink effects on flow quality are not taken into account in these maps, the reader should be aware that the substantial amount of visual blight will have a significant impact on reducing these values in the actual source, sink, and use maps.

5 Discussion

We have described in this paper the structure and operation of the SPAN model for quantitative ecosystem service assessment and have provided a sample of the kinds of novel results calculable using this approach. By adopting a discrete representation of the landscape as a collection of source, sink, and use regions which map to an abstract flow network, this framework can draw on a wide range of data aggregation techniques to match the scale of the assessment to the flow characteristics of the service being studied. Its benefit-centric focus on measuring flows of services from ecosystems to human beneficiaries enables more accurate value estimates than environmental simulations alone can provide. The provision and usage relationships between specific regions are clearly identified as well as the detrimental effects on service flows of both landscape features and human consumption. In instances in which different beneficiary groups compete for a finite resource, the flow paths clarify which groups have the earliest and/or easiest access. In cases of preventative services, the SPAN's multi-stage flow calculations make it possible to identify exactly how much flow (which represents potential threats) each sink region blocks from reaching each use region. Finally and perhaps most interestingly, discovering and mapping the flow densities for particular services opens the door to an entirely new approach to managing landscapes for ecosystem services. Rather than planning just to protect ecosystems which appear to provide services, ES science can begin to support more holistic development or conservation plans that account for both the service providers and the flow corridors crucial to the transmission of these benefits to human users.

5.1 Generalizability of the Model

Having addressed both the model's potential for scalability and the class of new results provided by its flow-based, benefit-centric approach to ecosystem services, the last element to discuss is its generalizability across services. Due to page limitations, only one service was described in detail in Section 4. To provide a wider range of examples, the following table maps a number of ecosystem services into the SPAN formalism. Although only a subset of the commonly described services[10], we believe these are sufficiently representative of the larger list as to enable the creation of mappings for other services. The examples shown vary in the type of benefit provided (provisioning or preventative), rivalness of the resource, units of representation (concrete or abstract), scale of effect, and movement function.

Service	Aesthetic Viewsheds	Proximity to Open Space
Benefit Type	Provisioning	Provisioning
Medium	Scenic Beauty	Open Space
Units	Abstract	Abstract
Scale	Viewshed	Walking Distance
Movement	Line of Sight (Ray Casting)	Walking Simulation
Decay	Inverse Square	Gaussian
Rival?	No	No
Source	Mountains & Water Bodies	Open Spaces in Urban Areas
Sink	Visual Blight	Walking Obstructions (Highways & Fences)
Min Use	0	0
Max Use	Property Value	Property Value
Service	Carbon Sequestration	Flood Mitigation
Benefit Type	Provisioning	Preventative
Medium	CO_2 Absorption	Water (Runoff)
Units	Concrete	Concrete
Scale	Global	Watershed
Movement	Atmospheric Mixing	Hydrologic Flow
Decay	None	None
Rival?	Yes	No
Source	Sequestration & Storage Capacity	Rainfall & Snowmelt
Sink	0	Water Absorption by Soil and Vegetation
Min Use	0	Minimum Water for Flood Damage
Max Use	Carbon Emissions	Minimum Water for Total Damage
Service	Nutrient Cycling	Avoided Sedimentation/Deposition
Benefit Type	Provisioning	Preventative
Medium	Nutrients in Water	Sediment
Units	Concrete	Concrete
Scale	Watershed	Watershed
Movement	Hydrologic Flow	Hydrologic Flow
Decay	None	None
Rival?	Yes	No
Source	Landscapes along Waterways	Landscapes along Waterways
Sink	Filters in Waterways	Riparian Zones
Min Use	Determined by Nutrient	Determined by Beneficiary
Max Use	Determined by Nutrient	Determined by Beneficiary

5.2 Open Problems and Next Steps

To conclude, we provide a short list of problems still to be addressed in order to improve the SPAN model's scalability, generalizability, and applicability to decision processes as well as to continue extending the frontiers in quantitative ecosystem service assessment.

First, upper limits on downsampling spatial datasets must be determined for each service flow type, below which total reconstruction of the flow path can be accurately determined. This problem is related to the Nyquist-Shannon sampling theorem and the aliasing problem[14]. Second, extending the SPAN formalism to operate over graphs with cycles will enable the assessment of new services such as those related with tidal or marine systems. Third, making movement functions and location property calculations non-deterministic will allow the modeling of unpredictable service media such as storms or wildfires. Fourth, investigating flow path substitutability will add further detail to maps of critical flow regions by making irreplaceable flow corridors more valuable than others.

Finally, the SPAN model can be used as a basis for spatial optimization techniques concerned with finding landscape configurations which maximize ES flow given cost (or other) constraints on spatial development activities.

Acknowledgments. Funding for this work was provided by the National Science Foundation, grant 9982938. We thank the ARIES partner organizations of Conservation International (CI) and Earth Economics (EE) for providing spatial data and an improved understanding of regional ecosystem service dynamics: in particular, Rosimeiry Portela, Miroslav Honzak and Nalini Rao of CI and Dave Batker of EE. Marta Ceroni (UVM) aided in setting up the case studies, Sergey Krivov (UVM) investigated probabilistic modeling and decision support frameworks, and Joshua Farley (UVM) led work on economic valuation of ecosystem services in ARIES.

References

1. Bagstad, K.J., Johnson, G.W., Villa, F., Krivov, S., Ceroni, M.: From ecosystems to people: Characterizing and mapping the beneficiaries of ecosystem services. Ecological Economics (in review)
2. Bourassa, S.C., Hoesli, M., Sun, J.: What's in a view? Environment and Planning A(36), 1427–1450 (2004)
3. Boyd, J., Banzhaf, S.: What are ecosystem services? the need for standardized environmental accounting units. Ecological Economics 63, 616–626 (2007)
4. Costanza, R., d'Arge, R., de Groot, R., Farber, S., Grasso, M., Hannon, B., Limburg, K., Naeem, S., O'Neill, R.V., Paruelo, J., Raskin, R.G., Sutton, P., van den Belt, M.: The value of the world's ecosystem services and natural capital. Nature 387, 253–260 (1997a)
5. Daily, G.C.: Nature's services: Societal dependence on natural ecosystems. Island Press, Washington (1997)

6. Farber, S., Costanza, R., Childers, D.L., Erickson, J., Gross, K., Grove, M., Hopkinson, C.S., Kahn, J., Pincetl, S., Troy, A., Warren, P., Wilson, M.: Linking ecology and economics for ecosystem management. Bioscience 56, 121–133 (2006)
7. Fisher, B., Turner, R.K.: Ecosystem services: Classification for valuation. Biological Conservation 141, 1167–1169 (2008)
8. Hein, L., van Koppen, K., de Groot, R.S., van Ierland, E.C.: Spatial scales, stakeholders, and the valuation of ecosystem services. Ecological Economics 57(2), 209–228 (2006)
9. Limburg, K.E., O'Neill, R.V., Costanza, R., Farber, S.: Complex systems and valuation. Ecological Economics 41, 409–420 (2002)
10. Millennium Ecosystem Assessment (MA). Millennium Ecosystem Assessment: Living beyond our means - Natural assets and human well-being. Washington, D.C., World Resources Institute (2005)
11. National Research Council (NRC). Valuing ecosystem services: toward better environmental decision-making. National Academies Press: Washington, DC (2005)
12. Nelson, E., Mendoza, G., Regetz, J., Polasky, S., Tallis, H., Cameron, D.R., Chan, K.M.A., Daily, G.C., Goldstein, J., Kareiva, P.M., Lonsdorf, E., Naidoo, R., Ricketts, T.H., Shaw, M.R.: Modeling multiple ecosystem services, biodiversity conservation, commodity production, and tradeoffs at landscape scales. Frontiers in Ecology and the Environment 7(1), 4–11 (2009)
13. Samuelson, P.A.: The pure theory of public expenditure. The review of Economics and Statistics 36(4), 387–389 (1954)
14. Shannon, C.E.: Communication in the presence of noise. Proc. Institute of Radio Engineers 37(1), 10–21 (1949)
15. Tallis, H., Polasky, S.: Mapping and valuing ecosystem services as an approach for conservation and natural-resource management. Annals of the New York Academy of Sciences 1162, 265–283 (2009)
16. Villa, F., Ceroni, M., Bagstad, K., Johnson, G., Krivov, S.: ARIES (artificial intelligence for ecosystem services): A new tool for ecosystem services assessment, planning, and valuation. In: Proceedings of the 11th Annual BIOECON Conference on Economic Instruments to Enhance the Conservation and Sustainable Use of Biodiversity (2009)
17. Wallace, K.J.: Classification of ecosystem services: Problems and solutions. Biological Conservation 139, 235–246 (2007)

Facing the Archaeological Looting in Peru by Using Very High Resolution Satellite Imagery and Local Spatial Autocorrelation Statistics

Rosa Lasaponara[1] and Nicola Masini[2]

[1] CNR-IMAA (Istituto di Metodologie di Analisi Ambientale),
C.da S. Loja 85050 Tito Scalo (PZ), Italy
[2] Archaeological and Monumental heritage institute, National Research Council,
C/da S. Loia Zona industriale, 85050, Tito Scalo (PZ), Italy

Abstract. In many countries of Southern America, Asia and Middle East clandestine excavations affect more than other man-made and natural risks archaeological heritage. Direct and aerial surveillance are not always suitable for protection and monitoring sites of cultural interest. This favoured the use of Very high resolution satellite data for the detection of looting pits.

This paper is focused on results we obtained from ongoing research focused on the use of VHR satellite images and spatial autocorrelation statistics, such as Moran's I, Geary's C, and Getis-Ord Local Gi index, for the identification and monitoring of looting.

A time series of satellite images (QuickBird-2 and World-View-1) has been exploited to analyze and monitor archaeological looting in Cahuachi, a large Ceremonial Centre built by the Nasca Civilization in Southern Peru. The spatial autocorrelation statistics enabled us to extract spatial anomalies linked to illegal excavations and to recognize and quantitatively characterize looting patterns over the years.

The results obtained encourage the application of satellite by means of cluster analysis techniques for the monitoring of archaeological sites.

Keywords: looting, NASCA, satellite, Spatial autocorrelation statistics.

1 Introduction

In the last decade, the increasing development of Earth Observation (EO) techniques (ground, aerial and space) and the tremendous advancement of computer science has determined an increasingly importance of remote sensing tools in archaeological research (see for example, [1]). EO techniques can uncover unique and invaluable data, from the detection, to the management and preservation of cultural resources and landscape. Space and airborne remote sensing based on active and passive sensors can be fruitfully used for archaeological research to search larger areas, to obtain accurate quantitative information on ancient landscape and to detect archaeological features in a more rapid manner compared to traditional survey techniques [2,3].

In particular EO data can be fruitfully exploited for the quantification of damage from looting. The protection of archaeological heritage from looting is generally

D. Taniar et al. (Eds.): ICCSA 2010, Part I, LNCS 6016, pp. 254–261, 2010.

based on a direct surveillance, but it is time consuming, expensive and not suitable for remote archaeological sites, characterized by difficult accessibility. In the 20th century, aerial surveillance has been the most common manner to prevent looting and locate clandestine excavations; but it is not suitable for extensive areas and non practicable in several countries due to military or political restrictions.

In such conditions, Very high resolution (VHR) satellites (GeoEye, WolrdView1-2, QuickBird2, Ikonos) offer a suitable chance thanks to their global coverage and frequent revisitation times.

Recently, satellite VHR images helped to quantify looting and damage affecting the archaeological heritage of Iraq [4], and other countries of Middle East involved in war [5].

Since 2007, two institutes of the Italian CNR are experiencing VHR satellite data to support archaeological investigations as well as to analyze and monitor archaeological looting in Cahuachi [6,7].

It is the largest adobe Ceremonial Centre in the World, built in the southern desert of Peru by the Nasca Civilizations.

The archaeological evidences are characterized by around forty semi-artificial mounds, spread out on the south bank of the Nasca river (figure 1) and facing the Pampa de San Jose, where the majority of the famous geoglyphs (listed in the World Heritage) were etched. The archaeological investigations in the last 25 years [8,9, 10] allowed the understanding of the functional and cultural evolution of the site between 400 B.C. – 400 A.D.. It was at the beginning a shrine (Huaca), then a ceremonial centre and later the Theocratic Capital of the Nasca State.

The difficult environmental setting of the Nasca territory favoured an intense ceremonial activity with rituals, precious offerings and sacrifices to propitiate the gods, to have rich harvests and prevent natural disasters (earthquakes and flash floods).

Today, the enormous quantity of precious offerings and rich tombs is a very tempting target for looters.

A time series of panchromatic and multispectral satellite images allowed the mapping of looting over the years. The reliability of the detection was evaluated by field surveys carried out on some test sites. The evaluation has shown a rate of success was very high in some areas and unsatisfactory for other areas. This suggested to experience different data processing methods. The paper shows the results obtained by means of an approach based on local spatial autocorrelation statistics.

2 Satellite Data

VHR satellite images from QuickBird (QB) and WorldView-1 (WW1) have been used for this study. QB has panchromatic and multispectral sensors with resolutions of 61-72cm and 2.44-2.88m, respectively, depending upon the off-nadir viewing angle (0-25 degrees). The panchromatic sensor collects information at the visible and near infrared wavelengths and has a bandwidth of 450 – 900 nm. The multispectral sensor acquires data in four spectral bands from blue to near infrared (NIR).

WW1 has panchromatic sensor with a resolution varying from 50 cm to 59 cm, depending on the off-nadir viewing angle (0-25 degrees).

The QB data used for this study were acquired: i) on the 16th September 2002 at 15:17 with an off-nadir of 7°.90 and Ground sample distance (GSD) of 61,90 cm; ii) on the 25th March 2005 at around 15:29 with an off nadir view angle of 11°.90 and GSD=63,40.

WW1 data were acquired on the 31st July 2008 at 15:26 with an off-nadir of 23°.90 and Ground sample distance (GSD) of 58,10 cm.

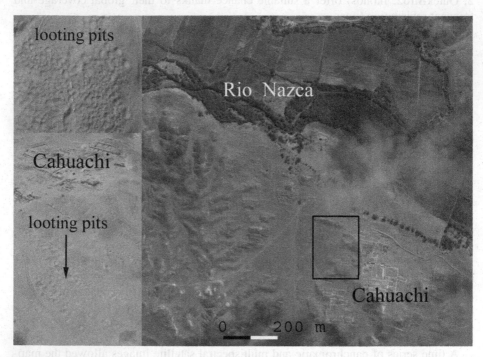

Fig. 1. Location of Cahuachi. Black rectangular box indicate the investigated test site characterized by looting pits. On the left details of looting pits.

3 Method

Spatial autocorrelation statistics measure the degree of spatial dependency among observations, the similarity of objects within an area, the level of interdependence between the variables, the nature and strength of the interdependence. In the context of image processing, spatial autocorrelation statistics can be used to measure and analyze the degree of dependency among spectral features.

Spatial autocorrelation is generally described thought some indices of covariance for a series of lag distances (or distance classes) from each point. The plot of the given indices against the distance classes d is called correlogram, that illustrates autocorrelation at each lag distance. The distance at which the value of spatial autocorrelation crosses the expected value, indicates the range of the patch size or simply the spatial range of the pattern.

In the context of image processing, for each index and each lag distance, the output is a new image which contains a measure of autocorrelation.

Classic spatial autocorrelation statistics include a spatial weights matrix that reflects the intensity of the geographic relationship between observations in a neighborhood. Such spatial weights matrix indicate elements of computations that are to be included or excluded. In this way it is possible to define ad hoc weights to extract and emphasize specific pattern. As an example, if the source dataset was polygonal, as in the case of agricultural tracts, adjacency weights might be chosen to reflect the relative lengths of shared boundaries.

In this study we used the statistics from Local Moran's I, Geary's C, and Getis-Ord Local Gi index [11,17].

The Moran's I index is defined according to formula 1.

$$I = \frac{1}{p} \frac{\sum_i \sum_j w_{ij}(z_i - \bar{z})(z_j - \bar{z})}{\sum_i (z_i - \bar{z})^2} , \text{ where}$$

$$p = \sum_i \sum_j w_{ij} / n$$

(1)

Moran's I computes the degree of correlation between the values of a variable as a function of spatial lags. This coefficient is structurally comparable to a Pearson's product–moment correlation coefficient and computes the deviation between the values of the variable and its mean.

Moran's I varies from -1 (negative autocorrelation) to 1 (positive autocorrelation).

The Geary's C Index is defined according to formula 2.

$$C = \frac{1}{p} \frac{\sum_i \sum_j w_{ij}(z_i - z_j)^2}{\sum_i (z_i - \bar{z})^2}$$

(2)

$$p = 2 \frac{\sum_i \sum_j w_{ij}}{n-1}$$

Geary's c, measures the difference among values of a variable at nearby locations. It behaves somewhat like a distance measure and varies from 0 for perfect positive autocorrelation, to about 2 for a strong negative autocorrelation. In the absence of significant spatial autocorrelation, the expected value is 1.

Spatial autocorrelation statistics such as Moran's I and Geary's C are global in the sense that they estimate the overall degree of spatial autocorrelation for a dataset. The possibility of spatial heterogeneity suggests that the estimated degree of autocorrelation may vary significantly across geographic space.

Local Moran's I and Geary's C statistics provide estimates disaggregated to the level of the spatial analysis units, allowing assessment of the dependency relationships across space.

One of the most widely used local spatial autocorrelation statistics is Getis & Ord (1992). G statistics compare neighbourhoods to a global average and identify local regions of strong autocorrelation. As mentioned before, local versions of the I and C statistics are also available.

The Getis and Ord global spatial association measure is defined as follows:

$$G_i^* = \frac{\sum\limits_{j=1}^{n} w_{i,j} x_j - \bar{X} \sum\limits_{j=1}^{n} w_{i,j}}{S \sqrt{\dfrac{\left[n \sum\limits_{j=1}^{n} w_{i,j}^2 - \left(\sum\limits_{j=1}^{n} w_{i,j} \right)^2 \right]}{n-1}}} . \tag{3}$$

where x_j is the attribute value for feature j, $w_{i,j}$ is the spatial weight , n the number of features, X is the average of x_j and S is given in formula 4.

$$S = \sqrt{\frac{\sum\limits_{j=1}^{n} x_j^2}{n} - \left(\bar{X} \right)^2} \tag{4}$$

The Getis-Ord Gi index permits the identification of areas characterized by very high or very low values (hot spots) compared to those of neighboring pixels.

It should be noted that the interpretation of G is different from that of Moran's I. In detail the Getis-Ord Gi enables us to distinguish the clustering of high and low values, but does not capture the presence of negative spatial correlation.

The Moran's I is able to detect both positive and negative spatial correlations, but clustering of high or low values are not distinguished.

Of course the interpretation of results from these statistics is depended on some critical issues, among them it is important to define the similarity and homogeneity.

(i) Local Moran's I index identifies pixel clustering. It has values that typically range from approximately +1, representing complete positive spatial autocorrelation, to approximately -1, representing complete negative spatial autocorrelation:

(ii) the Local Geary's C index allows us to identify edges and areas characterized by a high variability between a pixel value and its neighboring pixels,

(iii) the Getis-Ord Gi index permits the identification of areas characterized by very high or very low values (hot spots) compared to those of neighboring pixels.

Geostatistical analysis tools are available in several commercial software, such as GIS and image processing. We used ENVI packages for the current study.

4 Data Processing and Results

The time series of panchromatic and multispectral satellite images described in section 2 has been used to map looting in Cahuachi from 2002 to 2008.

Looters' holes are usually recognizable by their small and circular pits (0.7-3 m diameter), somewhat filled with sand, and by scattered remains (human and animal bone, pottery fragments) (see figure 1, upper left).

The comparative visual inspection of the available satellite dataset put in evidence that the panchromatic images are more suitable than pansharpened spectral bands to emphasize both the pitting holes and archaeological features (shallow to outcropping walls). This is due to the fact that for the study area there are no significant spectral variations in the four bands of QB imagery.

On the basis of these results, we focused only on satellite panchromatic scenes.

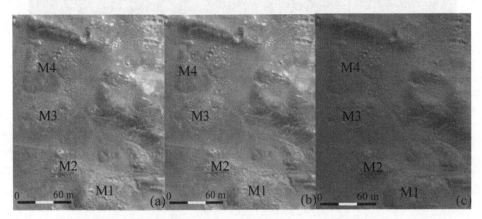

Fig. 2. (a) 2002 QB panchromatic image; (b) 2005 QB panchromatic image; (c) 2008 WW1. M1-M4 indicate mounds characterized by the typical circular pits dug by grave looters. The spatial resolution of satellite images is not enough to appreciate significant variation between 2002 and 2008.

The reliability of the detection was evaluated by field survey carried out (November 2008) on some test sites selected on mounds and flat areas. The evaluation has shown that the rate of success was very high for flat areas (higher than 90%) but unsatisfactory for mounds (30-80%), due to the effect of wind erosion and geomorphological features.

To overcome this drawback, an approach, based on local spatial autocorrelation statistics applied to panchromatic imagery, such as Moran's I, Geary's C, and Getis-Ord Local Gi index, has been employed.

They enable to recognize and quantitatively characterize patterns of spatial dependence at multiple scales, thus making them useful in detecting archaeological features. Such approach has been already experienced by the same authors of this paper, providing satisfactory results, for some Neolithic settlements in Southern Italy [18].

In Cahuachi, the detection of looting pits on mounds has been significantly improved (75-90%) by applying local spatial autocorrelation statistics. Such improvement is still more evident if we compare the panchromatic satellite time series with the correspondent time series processed by local spatial autocorrelation statistics.

Figures 2a-c show the panchromatic scenes (2002, 2005 and 2008) related to four mounds characterized by the typical circular pits dug by grave looters. Such traces of looting are visible thanks to the micro-relief, but the spatial resolution is not enough to appreciate significant variation between 2002 and 2008.

Figures 3a-c show the RGB composition of Moran; Getis; and Geary indices which does emphasize these pits enhancing their edges (yellow coloured).

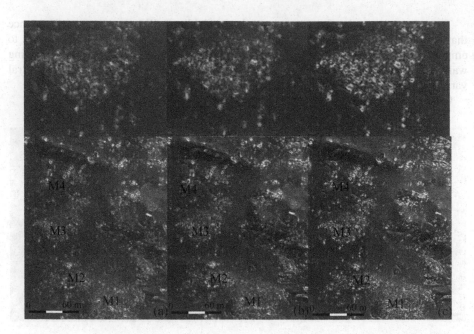

Fig. 3. RGB composition of Moran, Getis and Geary indices (R:Moran; G: Getis; B: Geary) applied to panchromatic images of 2002 QB (a), 2005 QB (b) and 2008 WW1 (c). As in the previous figure 2 M1-M4 indicate mounds characterized by pits dug by grave looters; up of each figure a zoom of Mound M3 can be observed. RGB composition of Moran; Getis; and Geary indices emphasize pits enhancing their edges (yellow coloured). The multitemporal comparison of the three RGB images clearly show an increasing number of pits from 2002 to 2008 and, therefore, the intensification of the looting phenomenon over the years.

The multitemporal comparison of the three RGB images clearly show an increasing number of pits from 2002 to 2008 and, therefore, the intensification of the looting phenomenon over the years.

5   Conclusion

Clandestine excavations is one of the biggest man-made risks which affect the archaeological heritage, especiali in some countries of Southern America, Asia and Middle East.

To contrast and limit this phenomenon a systematic monitoring is required. In this context, VHR satellite imagery can play a fundamental role to identify and map looted areas.

The Cahuachi study case herein presented put in evidence the limits of VHR satellite imagery in detecting features linked to looting activity. This suggested to experience local spatial autocorrelation statistics which allowed us to improve the reliability of satellite in mapping looted area.

References

1. Lasaponara, R., Masini, N. (eds.): Advances in Remote Sensing for Archaeology and Cultural Heritage Management. In: Proc. of I International EARSeL Workshop "Advances in Remote Sensing for Archaeology and Culturale Heritage Management", Rome, Aracne Roma, September 30 -October 4 (2008)
2. Lasaponara, R., Masini, N.: Detection of archaeological crop marks by using satellite QuickBird multispectral imagery. Journal of Archaeological Science 34, 214–221 (2007)
3. Lasaponara, R., Masini, N.: Full-waveform Airborne Laser Scanning for the detection of medieval archaeological microtopographic relief. Journal of Cultural Heritage 10S, e78–e82 (2009)
4. Stone, E.C.: Patterns of looting in southern Iraq. Antiquity 82, 125–138 (2008)
5. Parcak, S.: Satellite remote sensing methods for monitoring archaeological tells in the Middle East. Journal of field archaeology 32(1), 65–81 (2007)
6. Masini, N., Rizzo, E., Lasaponara, R.: Teledeteccion y Investigaciones geofísicas en Cahuachi: primeros resultados. Nasca. El Desierto de los Dioses de Cahuachi, Graph Ediciones Lima (2009)
7. Masini, N., Lasaponara, R., Orefici, G.: Addressing the challenge of detecting archaeological adobe structures in Southern Peru using QuickBird imagery. Journal of Cultural Heritage 10S, e3–e9 (2009)
8. Orefici, G.: Nasca. Archeologia per una ricostruzione storica. Jaca Book (1992)
9. Silverman, H.: Cahuachi in the Ancient Nasca World. University Of Iowa Press (1993)
10. Orefici, G., Drusini, A.: Nasca: Hipótesis y Evidencias de su Desarrollo Cultural, Centro Italiano Studi e Ricerche Archeologiche Precolombiane, Brescia (2003)
11. Getis, A., Ord, J.K.: The analysis of spatial association by use of distance statistics. Geographical Analysis 24, 189–206 (1992)
12. Anselin, L.: Local Indicators of Spatial Association LISA. Geographical Analysis 27, 93–115 (1995)
13. Moran, P.: The interpretation of statistical maps. Journal of the Royal Statistical Society 10 (1948)
14. Geary, R.: The contiguity ratio and statistical mappingâ. The Incorporated Statistician 5 (1954)
15. Ripley, B.D.: Spatial Statistics. Wiley & Sons, New York (1981)
16. Shabenberger, O., Gotway, C.A.: Statistical methods for spatial data analysis. Chapman & Hall, Sydney (2005)
17. Illian, J., Penttinen, A., Stoyan, H., Stoyan, D.: Statistical analysis and modelling of spatial point patterns. Wiley, Chichester (2008)
18. Ciminale, M., Gallo, D., Lasaponara, R., Masini, N.: A Multiscale Approach for Reconstructing Archaeological Landscapes: Applications in Northern Apulia (Italy). Archaeological Prospection 16, 143–153 (2009)

U-City: New Trends of Urban Planning in Korea Based on Pervasive and Ubiquitous Geotechnology and Geoinformation

Myungjun Jang[1] and Soon-Tak Suh[2]

[1] Institute of Urban Sciences
and
[2] Department of Urban Administration,
University of Seoul
Siripdae-gil 131 Jeonnong-dong 90
Dongdaemun-gu, Seoul, S. Korea, 130-743
getz74@hanmail.net, stsuh@uos.ac.kr

Abstract. The concept of Ubiquitous Computing Environment leads new paradigm change in urban space creation. In Korea, new concept of Ubiquitous-City (U-City) draws a lot of attentions now. It is trying to fuse high-tech infrastructure and ubiquitous information service into the urban area. It is also thought to bring innovations of urban functions. At last, it is advancing to the ubiquitous society, intelligence-based society where humans, things, and computers are combined. This paper introduces U-City's definition, characteristics, trend, status, and future research work.

Keywords: U-City, Ubiquitous computing environment, Context Based Systems, Location Based Service (LBS).

1 Introduction

A user called Ubiquitous computing is not aware of network or computer, and be independent of location, and mean the information communication environment which can connect to network [19] [20]. Speaking further in detail, ubiquitous means 'exists everywhere at anytime' was derived from Latin language. And, it indicates the environment where user can connect to computer or network without being aware of them. While Mark Weiser of Xerox used term called 'Ubiquitous computing' in 1988, it appeared for the first time. Ubiquitous computing joined to main frame and personal computers (PC), and it would lead the third information revolution. By the way, this is normally written with a form like Ubiquitous communications, Ubiquitous network etc. This is not to add to any additional function to computer. This will put computer to any appliances or things like car, refrigerator, glasses, clock, stereo equipment etc. And then, this new information technology (IT) environment or the information technology paradigm makes them communicate between each other [17].

Recently, new concept of ubiquitous city (U-city) is noted in the Korea [2] [5]. The concept has received most attention in South Korea, which is planning to build new 15 ubiquitous cities .The first U-City, Hwaseong-Dong tan U-Citys, has been partially

D. Taniar et al. (Eds.): ICCSA 2010, Part I, LNCS 6016, pp. 262–270, 2010.
© Springer-Verlag Berlin Heidelberg 2010

completed and operated. It characterizes diverse U-Services that include U-Traffic, U-Parking, and U-Crime Prevention service, one stop administrative service [10]. It also enables automating communication because 'U-city' amalgamates advanced IT infra and Ubiquitous information service to urban space. U-city can show future shape of city where it is possible to develop self controlling urban space. In this article, we would like to introduce U-city's concept and characteristic, trend, current situation and future research work.

2 Definition and Characteristics of U-City

2.1 Definition of U-City

'U-City' is a 21st century futurist city which enables the service such as one-stop administration service, automatic traffic, crime prevention, fire prevention system and home-networking of residential places which fused high-tech infrastructure and ubiquitous information service into the urban area. Meanwhile, ubiquitous means 'existing anywhere' in Latin, and means that the environment user can access to the network regardless of the place and not being aware of the computer/network. It is the futurist high-tech city that maximizes the quality of life and value of a region by innovating every function of the city by fusing high-tech infrastructure and ubiquitous service into the urban area. U-City is the next-generation informatization city that can innovate every function of the city such as increase in convenience of urban life, improvement of quality of life, security guaranteeing by systematic city management, improvement of citizen welfare and new industry creation [3] [13]. That is, U-City means the 21st Korean neo-city that speeches convergence with construction, home-appliance, contents and converges the capacity of IT totally which is developed in the country as a representative business model of ubiquitous IT [11].

2.2 Characteristics of U-City

We can analyze U-City in terms of intelligence, network, platform and service [4]. U-City features intelligence of urban function that manages and optimizes various situations intelligently which are related to urban function, wired and wireless communication network connection, which is the basis of electronic spatial embodiment, common platform and integrative management that pursue universal service anywhere and anytime, variation and application of the applied service that pursues practical service by which ubiquitous technology is grafted. The following figure 1 illustrates the conceptual format of U-City.

2.3 Types of U-City Service

The service type of U-City is divided into u-Home, u-Work, u-Traffic, u-Health, u-Environment, u-Public service and u-Education largely according to the application range of service, and this u-City service is realized by contents combination such as ①communication infrastructure wired and wireless service(ex: xDSL, FTTH, RFID, Wi-bro, mobile communication), ②construction infrastructure such as high-tech

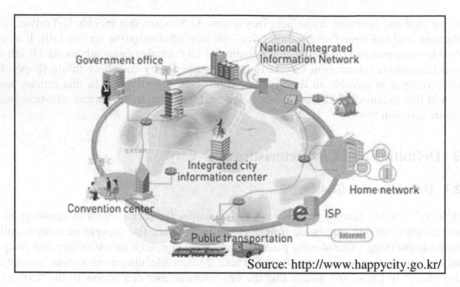

Source: http://www.happycity.go.kr/

Fig. 1. Conceptual format of Ubiquitous City

intelligent building and intelligent road, ③solutions such as home networking, building management system, ④e-Learning, IP-media, etc [10] [14].

3   Trend and Status of U-City

3.1   Market Opportunity of U-City

U-City, 21C Korean neo-city of which searching convenience of urban life combining ubiquitous IT and IT infrastructure to the urban area and is thought to bring innovation of urban function is embossed as a place where domestic IT industry's total ability is converged, and convergence with construction, home-appliance and culture are unfold developmentally [8]. We grasped the market opportunity and potentiality of u-City based on the investigation results about the common people and suggested policies and strategic assignments for activation. Analysis has shown positive overall evaluation of common people towards u-City and a lot of households wanted to move into u-City and u-Health, and u-home-networking are embossed as killer service. They were favored more by communication service provider's u-City business model [9] [10]. Figure 2 shows examples of ubiquitous services in progress currently.

3.2   Current Research about U-City

3.2.1   Previous Work
Hong Kong's cyber port, Dubai's entrepreneur city, Malaysia's MSC project, Finland's Aribianranta project and Germany Cologne's media part are the outstanding promotion cases of overseas u-City [5]. Integrating these overseas cases, they are being promoted in the direction that can raise urban competitiveness emphasizing the

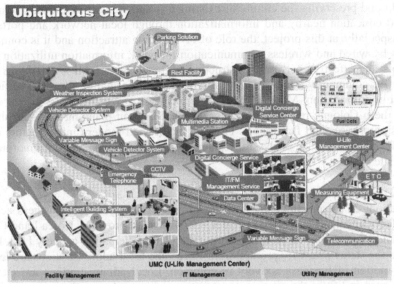

Fig. 2. Examples of Ubiquitous Services

features and advantages of each city in maximum, and they all display increasing effect through connection with peripheral industries and realize self-sufficient city that provides pleasant service of life above the simple urban dimension. We can describe each case of overseas u-City as follows. Hong Kong is making an effort to realize cyber port targeting strategic cluster that can support service such as finance, communication, trade, advertisement, and amusement to realize ideal environment where multinational companies can work at as the cross-section of local economy activity. For this, they are promoting intelligent building management, super-high networking connection between offices, informatization of the whole region and connection of optic communication between the campuses of the schools to realize intelligence office actively [16].

Dubai has oriented global hub of information industry since the late 1990s, and has pursued internet city, media city, knowledge village first time in the world, and is forming 'Technology and Media Free Zone'. Especially, internet city is promoting ICT hub with e-business through entering of famous international enterprises such as MS, Oracle, HP and IBM after 1999, and is alluring global broadcasting media enterprises such as CNN, CNBC under the motto of creative freedom for them. Also, it is pursuing knowledge village such as alluring famous universities, and is providing optimal living environment to promote foreign investment environment through healthcare city by 2010 [4]. Malaysia's MSC(Multimedia Super Corridor) is the smart town project started from 1996 and is aiming at constructing multimedia complex. For this, it constructed Kuala Lumpur international airport, Technology Parks, info-industry complex and new cyber information city and is maximizing the synergy effect. The Arbianranta project of Finland features redeveloping small cities within

Helsinki and preserving the culture of existing city and connecting industry related to arts and education nearby and informatization through local network and portal service. Especially, at this project, the role of IT is getting attraction and it is connecting regions by wired and wireless communication for quick information utilization to the residents and effective network construction to the enterprises. It is providing portal service for community information for the residents, information for the specific user and public information. Media Park of Cologne, Germany changes the freight site of the northern Cologne region into a new city under urban planning and it is alluring famous enterprises and facilities as IT basic facility and modern infrastructure of the city and the convenience of the traffics and creating employment and promoting it as tourist sites [1].

3.2.2 Development in Korea

Now, about 20 local administrations are promoting and planning business actively and KT(communication service provider), SI/NI service provider, Korea Land Corporation and Korea National Housing Corporation are participating actively [12]. Looking into the status of u-City promotion in Korea, the local administrations are leading the promotion of business actively in common. Local administrations are pursuing convenience in life of the citizens constructing various urban activities as intelligent service through IT and ubiquitous IT. They are groping local city economic activation actively by selecting specialized industries that fit to the features of the regions. That is, each local administration constructs safe and convenient living environment through u-City and promote specialized business having been connected to the social and cultural features and industrial development strategies of each region in common. U-City in Korea has the world best level wired and wireless infrastructure, and is retaining related industry that is competitive such as construction and is assessed to be highly successful as there are broad and high level user basis. And ubiquitous IT technology is developing rapidly and there are many demands by the common people, and this is the engine of u-City.

3.2.3 Comparison of the Cases between Korea and Overseas

In Korea, Republic of Korea has come to raise maturity in many technological factors for IT developing country in the future through promotion strategy called u-Korea. This is not just a concept in Korea but also used in Japan. In Japan, they want to realize virtual interface and equipments that can interact and realize ubiquitous society anytime, anywhere without personal terminal, which is the expanded network concept of present Japanese environmental factors(limits by local features, communicative limits and physical limits) through the IT strategies of the government, ubiquitous-Japan [6] [7].

After all, what is completed by this strategy is ubiquitous society. Looking deeply into it, it is the service-targeting region in the village, city and earth based on ubiquitous computing/network. Social ubiquitous computing service can be interpreted by the examples as follow. It provides opportunity factors that people might come to that park again after visiting once to the amusement park, or making people feel dynamically, not making them watch undermined pictures at the museum to improve their understandings. In that meaning, the strategy of Japan is realizing ubiquitous system after creating profits through mobile communication, informatized residence, and game. While Japan presents their strategy like the above, Korea illustrates "IT839" as its uKorea strategy from the Ministry of Information and Communication [12]. It is predicted that it will lead the social structure change throughout the whole national society such as public administration, living service and economic industry. Easily explaining IT839, it is the abbreviation to realize future ubiquitous environment. That is, it will construct 3 large infrastructures at early times for 9 large neo-growth engines and 8 large service core infrastructure provisions, and is also constructing information protection infrastructure for reliability and safety of u-Korea. Recently, the direction of strategy was established. What the Ministry has added in IT service as one of the 8 large services of new u-IT839 strategy is that it will develop software industry which is expanding in its weight day after day as a core business of the nation [11].

4 Future of U-City

To secure future leading technology, it is important to learn advanced technology and develop it in advance, but the more important thing is the answer for whether it can give useful added value to humans combining these technologies in some way. Rather than the concept of ubiquitous, it is the computing based on the life style of the humans. Computing must learn about people now, and after all, it is the future of ubiquitous that computing can see it as one personal object. Through internet expansion and service integration, it is advancing to the ubiquitous society, intelligence-based society where humans, things and computers are combined. At this period of change, each nation in the world is making lots of effort in studying ubiquitous computing to secure national competitiveness and market preoccupation in the future. USA(computing), Japan(network and mobile) and EU (apply IT to the general materials, computing within people's lives) [2]. Each country is investing much to the fields that fit to its reality.

5 Core Success Factors and Activation Direction of U-City

To activate u-City, we need to access in a new form where IT and construction technology are fused in a different way from the neo-city development or informatization business in the past.

First, the most basic factor for u-City success is the construction of ubiquitous IT infrastructure. With the urban construction which has urban basic facilities and high-tech intelligent buildings, providing infrastructure where communication technology and IT solution are combined are the necessity of u-City. Especially, not only the communication infrastructure but also the strategic development that forms good circulation with the domestic IT industry development connecting the IT 839 strategy of u-City and government must be the foundation.

Second, furthering investment environment and expanding the self-sufficient function of the city is the way that leads u-City into success. It is needed to further business conditions by which many enterprises in and out of the country can realize strategic cluster and install education institute for employee suppliance and connect the grouping regions for consumption and expanding self-satisfactory function that expands traffic network and convenient facilities. U-City must prevent to fall into a bed-town and consumptive city as a satellite city which is the new city format of the past and must be the self-sufficient space that enjoys society based infrastructure, leisure of life and convenience.

Third, the development of successful business model and distribution of u-City raises the possibility of u-City to succeed early through benchmarking. Especially, it is needed to develop specialized application service through various urban industry developments that has reflected regions in each new city and industrial features.

Fourth, it must reinforce differentiated urban industry strategy and reinforce specialization of the city which promotes u-City strategy. It must develop differentiated industry through u-City promotion that is combined with the features of the region and it is demanded to promote portfolio among the industries through harmony with the traditional industry or cultural industry of the region as well as high-tech industry.

At last, participation and cooperation of various interested parties with government departments, local administrations, communication service providers, SI/NI service provider, construction enterprises and CP (Contents Provider) are needed, and it is demanded to create synergy through connected development and competitiveness reinforcement of the whole value chains of u-City. Also, laws and policy support to eliminate obstacles and support u-City by policies must be backed up.

6 Conclusions

U-City that can respond to the demands which cities may need, not the u-City of policy! It is the informatization city and intelligent city, which is the congregation of concentrated technological growth engine. We said it is u-City; nominated as a futuristic next generation technology and the market applying this urban concept and ubiquitous. In that meaning, Ministry of Land, Transport and Marine Affairs and Korea Institute of Construction Technology are deciding many policies with the theory as a happy, fresh and intelligent city and now, u-City legislative bills are drawn up. In many other countries, they do not turn their cities into ubiquitous cities, but they want to provide environmental factors that their residents needs. The most representative examples are Helsinki's Arabianranta city's network community [15]. Here, it is a planning virtual village. Helsinki is No.1 in national competitiveness for this filed. As it is an economic cluster where industries and academics cooperate well, they realize a demo project by villages that are more efficient in Arabianranta and realize information network that the residents of the village can automatically solve the problem of job position creation.

The successful informatization city is as the example above, and our country might as well construct a city that is realizable by realistic technology, not u-City of policies. Basically, the strategy to realize ubiquitous city and society are finding out the technological and service factors that can be cash cow and can be performed next on. Also, only if the technology can accept the parts local features demand well, it can be a happier and more effectively operating city. Generally, it perceives ubiquitous as intelligent space, we misapprehend it is realized only by new technology, but ubiquitous is the innovative way of thought we can give new added value. Now, looking at the status of members of u-City forum, there are many countries which are participating to the u-City project with interest, but there are numerous cases where it doesn't suggest concrete service, and by the technological and limited factors, it is suggested that it is hard to be realized. So, for u-City to be realized, cooperative project with the enterprises and schools must be performed by the governmental support, and the standard must be built on. Also, from the period where the laws related to u-City are drawn upon, I think people can keep optimistic point of view about u-City only if the policies that are free, eco-friendly and everybody dreams of can be established, not the city where it is controlled.

Acknowledgements. This work was supported by the National Research Foundation of Korea Grant funded by the Korean Government (NRF-2009-413-D00001).

References

1. Choi, N.: Plan and Requirement for Ubiquitous City. Ubiquitous IT Korea Forum (2005)
2. ETRI, U-City Infrastructure Activation Plan: Electronics and Telecommunications Research Institute (2007)
3. Jagoe, A.: Mobile location services: the definitive guide. Pearson Education, London (2002)
4. Jeong, K.: Implementation Strategies for Future Ubiquitous Cities Based on u-City Service Model. Entrue Journal of Information Technology 6(1), 81–100 (2007)
5. Jung, B., Lee, S., Lee, K., Park, Y., Kim, J., Park, J., et al.: Korean U-City Model Proposal: National Information Society Agency (2005)
6. Kang, H.: U-city Tutorial: Ubiquitous IFEZ: Department of the Incheon Free Economic Zone (2005)
7. Kang, H.: U-City Development Status: Korea U-City Association (2007)
8. Kim, J.: Enabling Technologies and Organizational Infrastructure: New Songdo City Development, LLC (2005)
9. Kim, J., Jo, C., Han, S.: The National Strategies for the Realization of U-City: Korea Research Institute for Human Settlements (2008)
10. KNHC, U-City Business Plan: Korea National Housing Cooperation (2007)
11. Lett, D.: In pursuit of status: the making of South Korea's 'new' urban middle class. Harvard University Press, Cambridge (1998)
12. MIC. IT 839 Strategy: the Road to $20,000 GDP/capita: Ministry of Information and Communication, Republic of Korea (2004)
13. MIC. U-City Policy Development Plan: Ministry of Information and Communication, Republic of Korea (2007)
14. Mountain, D., Raper, J.: Modelling human spatio-temporal behaviour: A challenge for location-based services. In: Proc. of the 6th Internat. Conference on GeoComputation. University of Queensland, Brisbane, Australia, pp. 24–26 (2001)
15. Sagong, H.: National GIS Policy Plan in Ubiquitous Generation: Korea Research Institute for Human Settlements (2007)

16. Schiller, J., Voisard, A.: Location-Based Services. Morgan Kaufmann, San Francisco (2004)
17. Schmidt, A.: Ubiquitous Computing - Computing in Context. PhD Thesis, Computing Department, Lancaster University, U.K (2002)
18. Tolmie, P., Pycock, J., Diggins, T., MacLean, A., Karsenty, A.: Unremarkable Computing. Paper presented at the ACM conference on human factors in computing systems CHI 2001 Minneapolis, MN (2001)
19. Weiser, M.: The computer for the 21st Century. Sci. Am. 265(3), 94–104 (1991)
20. Weiser, M., Gold, R., Brown, J.: The origins of ubiquitous computing research at PARC in the Late 1980s. IBM Syst. J. 38(4), 693–696 (1999)

Settlement-Preference Patterns and Characteristics of Households in Urban Renewal Area

Jin-Kyung Lee, Seungil Lee, and Kyu-Il Kim

University of Seoul, Institute of Urban Sciences
13 Siripdae-gil, Dongdaemun-gu, Seoul, 130-743, Korea
jinklee@uos.ac.kr, silee@uos.ac.kr, amigokki@hanmail.net

Abstract. To solve Seoul's a localized imbalance between demand and supply of housing by redevelopment, this research was to analyze relationship between the settlement-preference pattern and characteristics of householders such as average monthly income, household head's job location. For this task, The polytomous logistic regression model (PLRM) was then chosen to test the attitude-need recognition relationship. There are three findings, 1) when household head's job location is nearby of original site, respondents are more likely to prefer nearby. For settlement-preference in same district, household head's job flocation is impact factor. 2) Low income households and high income households intend to prefer settlement within the Seoul. 3) For settlement-preference within the Seoul, householder's characteristic is not impact factors, but householder's asset or investment preference would be impact factors. The results would contribute to making the urban renewal policies to establish effective settlers' strategies.

Keywords: Settlement-Preference; Urban Renewal; Polytomous Logistic Regression Model.

1 Introduction

In common with other OECD countries, the housing stability is a key to government's green growth and social sustainability of our cities and communities. Because unstable housing threatens labor stability, unstable labor, in turn, impacts into industry added value, decreasing added value hurts sustainable urban development [18]. Seoul is also joining the mainstream in its lack of affordable housing.

Research released recently by the Seoul Government Residential Improvement Committee (SGRIC) shows that the most salient issue Seoul faces is the prevalence of unstable dwellings, caused by the decreasing housing stocks available for low income groups, high rent, a gap of housing affordability between income groups, a localized imbalance between demand and supply of housing by redevelopment, and the increased cost for single and aged households. SGRIC proposed that Seoul set out housing policy's strategies for expanding the affordable housing supply and helping the affordability of households.

D. Taniar et al. (Eds.): ICCSA 2010, Part I, LNCS 6016, pp. 271–282, 2010.
© Springer-Verlag Berlin Heidelberg 2010

Especially, in Seoul, 50% of all new house supply stocks are reconstruction and redevelopment projects. These projects usually involve demolishing small, various, and low price homes, and only one type of apartment is being developed (project's 98%). As the promotion of these projects increases, the number of old houses decreases in which low-income households have previously lived. Because these householders all generally want to move to a nearby village, the sudden increase in demand leads to an increase in the price for rental and buying. It should threaten housing stability of households [17]. However, the substantial advances of the subject have not witnessed both conceptually and empirically. Significant amount of empirical work has not also appeared in settlement-preference literature. In Korea, previous researches of the subject have focused on housing types and ownership types of household, and they have used data sets of general households [8] [9] [19] [20].

Here, to support particular evidence in concerning settlement-preference of households living in Urban Renewal Area (URA), the paper is designed to contribute to the field by applying a conceptual model based on expectancy-value theory to the study of settlement-preference of households in URA with two specific objectives: 1) identifying a preference pattern of URA, and 2) examining the relationship between the elements of the settlement pattern and the characteristics of households in URA.

2 Conceptual Foundations

2.1 Expectancy-Value Theory

Various Attitude or Preference studies in general marketing literature are guided by two types of conceptual foundations, normative and expectancy-value models [22]. Normative approaches have relationships that physical stimuli (e.g. product attributes) first influence customers' perceptions and then influence their affects or preferences (e.g. attitude), which in turn cause their final choices [6]. Criticism of normative approaches focuses on their failure to incorporate motivational elements with cognitive elements [22]. Lancaster (1966) suggested that consumers chose the attributes possessed by goods rather than goods themselves, and the perceptions of these attributes were used as the input to assess the utility of goods [16]. The attributes involved in decision making must be self-important to the consumers. The Lancaster's proposition became the theoretical foundation of expectancy-value models, which are also known as multi-attributes attitude models or linear compensatory models. Among them, the Fishbein model is the most widely applied in attitude research. The expectancy-value models suggest that an individual's attitude towards an object is a function of their beliefs about the attributes of the object and their evaluations towards these attributes [6] [12] [13]. The expectancy-value models accommodate both cognitive and motivational elements of consumer behavior. They can be defined as:

$$A_{object} = \sum_{i=1}^{n} F_i I_i \qquad (1)$$

Where,

A_{object} = attitude toward an object
I_i = intensity of favorability
F_i = favorability to attribute I
n = the number of salient attributes towards an object

According to Engel, Blackwell, and Miniard (1995), favorability is one of the core properties of attitude. Researchers have traditionally focused on the cognitive elements in explaining the favorability. Ajzen (1975) suggested that the attitude measurement should also be based on attitude towards action. More recently, researchers proposed that attitude consist of three components: cognition, affect, and conation [4] [11] [21]. Cognition refers to awareness, beliefs, and knowledge of an attitude object. Affect, also termed evaluative aspect, involves emotion and feelings of like or dislike to the object. Conation refers to behavioral intention with regard to the object.

Baloglu (1998) suggested that cognition influences affect, which in turn influences conation in destination choice [7]. However, Zinkhan & Fornell (1989) found that the hierarchical orders of the three components were different due to different levels of involvement. For low-involved customers, conation is an antecedent of affect, because their attitudes are based on behavioral learning. For high-involved customers, affect is prior to conation, since their attitudes are based on cognitive information or knowledge. Furthermore, even though two individuals consider some attribute as favorable in a similar manner, they may have different evaluations of the strength or intensity of the favorability. An evaluation of an attribute can be located in a continuum ranging from positive extremity to negative extremity [11]. The work by Haugtvedt, Schumann, Schneier, and Warren (1994) emphasized the strength or intensity of favorability in consumer attitude research [14].

In numerous households and their choice for settlement, need recognition can be the first stage of multi-stage household's decision of settlement process, followed by information search, evaluation of alternatives, choice of settlement such as multi-stage consumer's buying process. The paper is to adopt Expectancy-Value Model to examine the relationship between the attitudes of settlement and characteristics of households.

2.2   The Situation of Urban Renewal Area and Housing in Seoul

In Seoul, 50% of all new house supply stocks are reconstruction and redevelopment projects. About 336 projects have been promoted for improving their dwelling environment. However, they involve demolishing small, various, and low price homes, and only one type of apartment is being developed (project's 98%). As the promotion of these projects increases, the number of old houses decreases. Especially, figure a) and b) showed because NE1 has houses need to improve their quality, NE1 faces strongly to above problem. Also, Settlers of NE1 impact into rising sharply a housing price. Householder's approval percent to Urban renewal and dwelling satisfaction percent show that Seoul couldn't avoid developing renewal projects. To achieve effective urban plan including land use, above all, decision-makers understand spatial characteristics and householder's preference in urban renewal area.

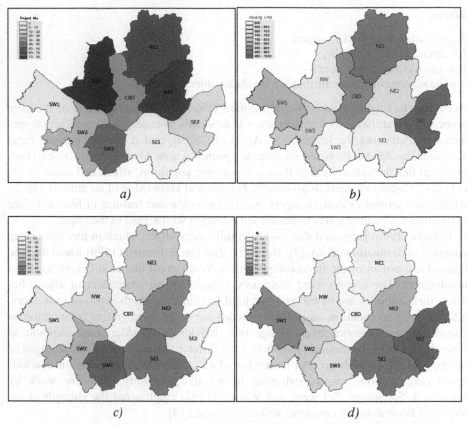

Fig. 1. The situation of urban renewal area and housing in Seoul. Urban Renewal Projects of 9 Life Zones (a), House Units per 1000 Households of 9 Life Zones (b), Householder's Approval to Urban Renewal Projects of 9 Life Zones (c), Dwelling Satisfaction of 9 Life Zones (d).

3   Methods and Analysis

3.1   Data

This study used data from 28 URA's Households Survey in Seoul. The data was collected by the Seoul Government Residential Improvement Committee (SGRIC) in 2008 to investigate dwelling situations in URA and to develop policies improving their problems. The households data of this survey was selected by systematic sampling among households living in 28 URA or owners of houses in there. A systematic sampling method was used to select the representative samples. The respondents were eligible respondents who were willing to participate in face-to-face, in-home interviews. A total of 1,014 in-home personal interviews were conducted.

There are two business types, redevelopment projects and reconstruction projects, for urban renewal in Korea. Redevelopment projects and reconstruction projects were proximately half and half. The respondents were classified into five segments according to their need recognition about their settlement. They were 1) *nearby of original site* (where is a radius of pedestrian including original project's site), 2) *same district* (Seoul has 25 districts), 3) *within the Seoul*, 4) *without the Seoul (where is Seoul Metropolitan Area) 5) others.*

Table 1 summarized the sample profile. Male and female were 37.4% and 62.6%. More than 80 percent of respondents fell into the age range of over 40 and their distribution in this age range was quite even. Approximately, 52.1 percent of respondents

Table 1. Sample profile

Contents		Sample No.	%
Total		1,014	100.0
Project type	Redevelopment	550	54.2
	Reconstruction	464	45.8
9 Zones of life	North-East 1	177	17.5
	North-East 2	190	18.7
	North-West	250	24.7
	South-West 1	84	8.3
	South-West 2	147	14.5
	South-West 3	48	4.7
	South-East 1	93	9.2
	South-East 2	25	2.5
	CBD	0	0
Occupancy type	Owners	499	49.2
	Tenants	515	50.8
Respondents status	Household head	528	52.1
	Household mate	443	43.7
	Others	43	4.2
Gender	Male	379	37.4
	Female	635	62.6
Age	20-29	41	4.0
	30-39	158	15.6
	40-49	248	24.5
	50-59	216	21.3
	60 or older	351	34.6
Income (U.S. $)	1000 & under	285	31.0
	1001-2000	247	24.4
	2001-3000	192	18.9
	3001-4000	144	14.2
	4001 & over	117	11.5
Dwelling Period	2years & under	84	8.3
	2~4years	181	17.9
	5~9years	223	22.0
	10~19years	206	20.3
	20years &over	320	31.6

were household head, followed by household mate at 43.7%. Owner and tenant were proximately half and half. About 33 percent of respondents had monthly household income at U.S. $ 2,001-4,000, and 24.4 percent of respondents earned $ 1,001-2,000 per month. Three quarters of respondents lived in their URA during 5 years and over, while less than 10 percent of respondents lived about 2 years.

3.2   Model

The polytomous logistic regression model (PLRM) was then chosen to test the attitude-need recognition relationship. PLRM may be extended beyond the analysis of dichotomous variables to the analysis of categorical (nominal or ordinal) dependent variables with more than two categories. In the literature on logistic regression the resulting models have been called polytomous, polychotomous, or multinomial logistic regression models. Here the terms dichotomous and polytomous will be used to refer to logistic regression models, and the terms binomial and multinomial will be used to refer to logit models form which polytomous logistic regression models may be derived. For polytomous dependent variables, the logistic regression model may be calculated as a special case of the multinomial logit model [1] [2] [10] [15].

Mathematically, the extension of the dichotomous logistic regression model to polytomous dependent variables is straightforward. One value (typically the first or last) of the dependent variable is designated as the reference category, $Y=h_0$, and the probability of membership in other categories is compared to the probability of membership in other categories is compared to the probability of membership in the reference category. For nominal variables, this may be a direct comparison, like the indicator contrasts for independent variables in the logistic regression model for dichotomous variables. For an ordinal variable, contrasts may be made with successive categories, in a manner similar to repeated or Helmert contrasts for independent variables in dichotomous logistic regression models.

For dependent variables with some number of categories M, this requires the calculation of M-1 equations, one for each category relative to the reference category, to describe the relationship between the dependent variable and the independent variables. For each category of the dependent variable except the reference category we may write the equation.

$$g_h(X_1, X_2,...,X_k) = e^{(a_h + b_{h1}X_1 + b_{h2}X_2 + ... + b_{hk}X_k)}$$
$$h = 1, 2, ..., M-1 \tag{2}$$

Where the subscript k refers, as usual, to specific independent variables X and the subscript h refers to specific values of the dependent variable Y. For the reference category, $g_0(X_1, X_2, ..., X_k) = 1$. The probability that Y is equal to any value h other than the excluded value h_0 is

$$P(Y = h | X_1, X_2,...,X_k)$$

$$= \frac{e^{(a_h + b_{h1}X_1 + b_{h2}X_2 + ... + b_{hk}X_k)}}{1 + \sum_{h=1}^{M-1} e^{(a_h + b_{h1}X_1 + b_{h2}X_2 + ... + b_{hk}X_k)}} \tag{3}$$

$$h = 1, 2, ..., M-1,$$

and for the excluded category $h_0 = M$ or 0,

$$P(Y = h_0 | X_1, X_2, \ldots, X_k)$$

$$= \frac{e^{(a_h + b_{h1}X_1 + b_{h2}X_2 + \ldots + b_{hk}X_k)}}{1 + \sum_{h=1}^{M-1} e^{(a_h + b_{h1}X_1 + b_{h2}X_2 + \ldots + b_{hk}X_k)}} \tag{4}$$

$$h = 1, 2, \ldots, M - 1,$$

For the five-category dependent variable, the PLRM in this study was expressed with four log-linear functions as follows:

$$\log(p_1 / p_5) = \beta_{10} + \beta_{11}X_1 + \beta_{12}X_2 + \ldots + \beta_{1j}X_k \tag{5}$$

$$\log(p_2 / p_5) = \beta_{20} + \beta_{21}X_1 + \beta_{22}X_2 + \ldots + \beta_{2i}X_k \tag{6}$$

$$\log(p_3 / p_5) = \beta_{30} + \beta_{31}X_1 + \beta_{32}X_2 + \ldots + \beta_{3i}X_k \tag{7}$$

$$\log(p_4 / p_5) = \beta_{40} + \beta_{41}X_1 + \beta_{42}X_2 + \ldots + \beta_{4i}X_k \tag{8}$$

where,

$p_i = $ *probability of event i* for $i = 1, 2, 3, 4, 5$
β_{1j}s, β_{2j}s, β_{3j}s, and β_{4j}s are parameters with $0 \leq j \leq m$
X_ks are independent variables with $1 \leq k \leq m$

Similar to binary logistic regression, parameters can be interpreted as the effect of variable Xs on the log odds of any outcome M versus reference outcome. Maximum likelihood estimation was employed in this method, where a smaller likelihood ratio Chi-square with higher less-than-one p-value indicates a better goodness-of-fit.

4   Results and Discussion

Table 3 presents the output from SPSS PLRM with settlement as a dependent variable on types of urban renewal project, average monthly household income, and job location. The sample includes 536 respondents with valid data on settlement and the three independent variables (See Table 2).

PLRM relied on maximum likelihood procedures to estimate the model coefficient. The model worked fairly well, as indicated by the statistically significant model Chi-square and the McFadden R^2 of 0.060. PLRM had -2LL(0) of 419.570 and -2LL(k) of 357.809. The Chi-square was 61.760 with p-value of 0.005 in 36 *df*, which indicated a very good overall model fit. To evaluate goodness of fit of the model, SPSS computed two measures of the pseudo-variance explained, Cox and Snell R^2 of 0.109 and Negelkerke R^2 of 0.121.

Table 2. Variables of PLRM

Variables		Categories
Dependent	Settlement	Settlement 1: nearby of original site(S1, reference category) Settlement 2: same district (S2) Settlement 3: within the Seoul (S3) Settlement 4: without the Seoul (S4) Settlement 5: others (S5)
Independent	Type of Urban Renewal Project	Redevelopment(RD) Reconstruction(RC=1)
	Average Monthly Household Income	1000 & under (I1) 1001-2000 (I2) 2001-3000 (I3) 3001-4000 (I4) 4001 & over (I5=1)
	Job Location	Job Location 1: nearby of original site (J1=1) Job Location 2: same district (J2) Job Location 3: within the Seoul (J3) Job Location 4: without the Seoul (J4) Job Location 5: others (J5)

In Wald significant, nearby of original site compared with same district was impacted from job location, but average income and types of urban renewal project was not statistically significant. Especially, when household head's job location is nearby of original site, respondents are more likely to prefer nearby. Also, estimated B supported that low income households and high income households intend to prefer settlement within the Seoul.

Types of urban renewal project affected Preference of within the Seoul. When households decide their settlement, their average monthly income and types of urban renewal project were statistically significant factors.

Finally, for settlement-preference in same district, household head's job location is impact factor. For settlement-preference within the Seoul, householder's characteristic is not impact factors, but householder's asset or investment preference would be impact factors.

Dividing the coefficients in the column labeled B by the standard errors in the column labeled S.E. gives the z ratio, which can be interpreted with the usual z table and selected levels of significance. Squaring the ratio of the coefficient to the standard error gives Chi-square values-presented as the Wald statistic. Based on the chi-square distribution, the probability associated with each Wald statistic follows in column headed Sig.

Table 3. Parameter Estimates of PLRM

Settlement [a]		B	S.E.	Wald	df	Sig	Exp(B)
S2 (vs.S1)	Intercept	-2.403	0.573	17.570	1	0.000	
	RD	0.405	0.301	1.808	1	0.179	1.499
	RC	0 [b]	.	.	0	.	
	I1	0.167	0.514	0.106	1	0.745	1.182
	I2	-0.537	0.447	1.442	1	0.230	0.525
	I3	-0.122	0.440	0.077	1	0.781	0.885
	I4	0.330	0.439	0.566	1	0.452	1.391
	I5	0 [b]	.	.	0	.	.
	J1	0.830	0.478	3.011	1	0.083	2.293
	J2	0.024	1.152	0.000	1	0.984	1.024
	J3	0.807	0.497	2.637	1	0.104	2.242
	J4	0.957	0.523	3.348	1	0.067	2.604
	J5	0 [b]	.	.	0	.	.
S3 (vs.S1)	Intercept	-1.709	0.710	5.794	1	0.016	
	RD	-0.977	0.431	5.131	1	0.023	0.376
	RC	0 [b]	.	.	0	.	
	I1	0.355	0.714	0.247	1	0.619	1.426
	I2	-0.175	0.662	0.070	1	0.791	0.839
	I3	-1.105	0.897	1.517	1	0.218	0.331
	I4	0.217	0.754	0.083	1	0.773	1.243
	I5	0 [b]	.	.	0	.	.
	J1	0.046	0.580	0.006	1	0.936	1.047
	J2	-18.626	0.000	.	1	.	8.147E-09
	J3	-0.461	0.679	0.462	1	0.497	0.630
	J4	-0.873	0.893	0.957	1	0.328	0.418
	J5	0 [b]	.	.	0	.	.
S4 (vs.S1)	Intercept	-3.125	0.936	11.149	1	0.001	
	RD	0.102	0.522	0.038	1	0.846	1.107
	RC	0 [b]	.	.	0	.	
	I1	-0.616	1.000	0.379	1	0.538	0.540
	I2	0.281	0.703	0.160	1	0.690	1.324
	I3	-0.520	0.851	0.373	1	0.541	0.595
	I4	-1.131	1.182	0.916	1	0.339	0.323
	I5	0 [b]	.	.	0	.	.
	J1	0.358	0.787	0.207	1	0.649	1.431
	J2	-18.264	0.000	.	1	.	1.170E-08
	J3	0.985	0.768	1.644	1	0.200	2.678
	J4	0.017	1.002	0.000	1	0.986	1.018
	J5	0 [b]	.	.	0	.	.

Table 3. (*continued*)

	Intercept	-1.071	0.446	5.781	1	0.016	
	RD	-0.729	0.233	9.760	1	0.002	0.482
	RC	0[b]	.	.	0	.	.
	I1	1.059	0.433	5.968	1	0.015	15984047
	I2	0.223	0.408	0.298	1	0.585	8297216
S5	I3	0.056	0.432	0.017	1	0.897	8642131
(vs.S1)	I4	0.319	0.463	0.473	1	0.492	10458066
	I5	0[b]	.	.	0	.	.
	J1	0.057	0.341	0.028	1	0.868	1.058
	J2	-19.347	0.000	.	1	.	3.959E-09
	J3	0.127	0.351	0.131	1	0.717	1.135
	J4	0.088	0.410	0.046	1	0.831	1.092
	J5	0[b]	.	.	0	.	.

Note.   a : S's reference category is S1 of 1,
         b : this parameter is set zero because it is redundant.

5   Concluding Remarks

Recently, the most salient issue Seoul faces is the prevalence of unstable dwellings, caused by the decreasing housing stocks available for low income groups, high rent, a gap of housing affordability between income groups, a localized imbalance between demand and supply of housing by redevelopment, and the increased cost for single and aged households.

To improve Seoul's renewal area problems, this research was firstly to analyze relationship between the settlement-preference pattern and characteristics of householders such as average monthly income, household head's job location. In numerous households and their choice for settlement, need recognition can be the first stage of multi-stage household's decision of settlement process, followed by information search, evaluation of alternatives, choice of settlement such as multi-stage consumer's buying process. The paper adopted Expectancy-Value Model to examine the relationship between the attitudes of settlement and characteristics of households, using the polytomous logistic regression model.

According to the results, when household head's job location is nearby of original site, respondents are more likely to prefer nearby. Also, estimated B supported that low income households and high income households intend to prefer settlement within the Seoul. For settlement-preference in same district, household head's job location is impact factor. For settlement-preference within the Seoul, householder's characteristic is not impact factors, but householder's asset or investment preference would be impact factors.

The results would contribute to making the urban renewal policies to establish effective settlers' strategies. In Seoul, 50% of all new house supply stocks are reconstruction and redevelopment projects. These projects usually involve demolishing small, various, and low price homes, and only one type of apartment is being developed (project's 98%). As the promotion of these projects increases, the number of old houses decreases, such as the Dagagu, Dasedai, and detached houses, in which low-income households have previously lived. Because these householders all generally want to move to a nearby village, the sudden increase in demand leads to an increase in the price for rental and buying. Renewal development projects transfer private initiatives to public initiatives, which mean that public sectors intervene directly and/or indirectly in the projects to secure confidence and drive out absurdities. Furthermore, public sectors can expect a filtering effect as the supply of diverse types of houses for low-income households move from the projects. Before applying the results for the URA, the model should be tested in consideration of the other factors for fitting the model. This requires more empirical researches in the future.

Acknowledgements. This work was supported by the National Research Foundation of Korea Grant funded by the Korea government (NRF- 2009-413-D00001).

References

1. Agresti, A.: Categorical data analysis. Wiley, New York (1990)
2. Aldrich, J.H., Nelson, F.D.: Linear probability, logit and probit models. Sage University Paper Series on Quantitative Applications in the Social Sciences CA (1984)
3. Allen, C.T., Machleit, K.A., Kleine, S.S.: A comparison of attitudes and emotions as predictors of behavior at diverse levels of behavioral experience. Journal of Consumer Behavior 18(4), 493–504 (1992)
4. Arnould, E.J., Price, L.L., Zinkhan, G.M.: Consumers. McGraw-Hill, Boston (2002)
5. Bagozzi, R.P.: Expectancy-value attitude models: an analysis of critical measurement issues. International Journal of Research in Marketing 2, 43–60 (1985)
6. Bagozzi, R.P.: The rebirth of attitude research in marketing. Journal of the Market Research Society 30(2), 163–195 (1988)
7. Baloglu, S.: An empirical investigation of attitude theory for tourist destinations: A comparison of visitors and nonvisitors. Journal of Hospitality and Tourism Research 22(3), 211–224 (1998)
8. Choi, M.J., Lim, Y.J.: Empirical Analyses of the Relationships between Household Characteristics and Preference of Residential Location and Housing Types. Journal of the Korea Planners Association 36(6), 69–81 (2001) (in Korean)
9. Choi, S.A., Kim, T.H., Ko, D.K., Kim, H.K.: Analysis of Relocation Behavior of Tenants in Redevelopment Area. Journal of the Architectural Institute of Korea 21(11), 235–242 (2005) (in Korean)
10. DeMaris, A.: Logit modeling. Sage University Paper Series on Quantitative Applications in the Social Sciences CA (1992)
11. Engel, J.F., Blackwell, R.D., Miniard, P.W.: Consumer behavior, 8th edn. The Dryden Press, Chicago (1995)
12. Fishbein, M.: An investigation of relationships between beliefs about an object and the attitude toward that object. Human Relations 16, 233–240 (1963)
13. Fishbein, M., Ajzen, I.: Belief, attitude, intention, and behavior: An introduction to theory and research. Addison-Wesley, Reading (1975)
14. Haugtvedt, C.P., Schumann, D.W., Schneier, W.L., Warren, W.L.: Advertising repetition and variation strategies: Implications for understanding attitude strength. Journal of Consumer Research 21(1), 176–189 (1994)
15. Knoke, D., Burke, P.J.: Log-Linear models. Sage University Paper Series on Quantitative Applications in the Social Sciences CA (1980)
16. Lancaster, K.J.: A new approach to consumer theory. Journal of Political Economy 74, 132–157 (1966)

17. Lee, J.-K., Ha, S.-K.: Measuring inequality of housing allocation and housing affordability in Seoul. In: 2009 AsRES-AREUEA Joint International Conference LA (2009)
18. Evans, L.: Moving Towards Sustainability: City-Regions and Their Infrastructure. Canadian Policy Research Networks Canada (2007)
19. Mun, T.H., Jeong, Y.Y., Jeong, K.S.: Determinant Factors and Probabilities of House Type Choice-Case Study in Jinju City. Journal of the Korea Planners Association 43(2), 87–98 (2008) (in Korean)
20. Nam, J., Hwang, I.J.: A Study on the Determinant Factors of the Rental Housing Choice of Tenants in the Housing Redevelopment Area. Journal of the Korea Planners Association 41(3), 69–82 (2006) (in Korean)
21. Onkvisit, S., Shaw, J.J.: Consumer behavior: Strategy and analysis. Macmillan College Publishing Company, New York (1994)
22. Feng, R., Cai, L.A., Zhu, Y.: Logn-Haul Travel Attitude Construct and Relationship to Behavior: the case of French travelers. Purdue Tourism & Hospitality Research Center (2005), http://www.stat.purdue.edu/~yuzhu/Papers/AttitudeNeed.doc
23. Soon-Kwi, K., Dong-Bin, J., Yong-Sool, P.: Understanding Logistic Regression and its Applications using SPSS. Hannarae Seoul (2008) (in Korean)
24. Menard, S.: Applied Logistic Regression Analysis, pp. 91–102. Sage Publications, London (2002)

Ontologies for Urban Regeneration Could Be Useful for Managing Cohesion Policies?

Francesco Rotondo

University of Polytechnic of Bari, Department of Architecture and Town Planning
Via Orabona 4, 70125 Bari, Italy
f.rotondo@poliba.it

Abstract. This paper describes the building of an urban regeneration ontology for managing cohesion policies focused on revitalizing cities. After a discussion of the background of the ontology subject, and about the experience in which the prototype of an ontology for urban regeneration has been developed, first user needs and requirements for ontology specification are described starting from this prototype. The prototype has been developed in the "Towntology software", by the LIRIS Laboratory at the University of Lyon (France). It has been tested in the Italian Apulia Region offices for Spatial planning and Environmental Management; as described in the paragraph "OUR first training". The test has shown interesting address and suggestions for user needs and requirements that are discussed in the paragraph "OUR suggestions". The reported experience is not over, hence not all what can be said has been written or observed, but these first results are useful to trace possible future perspectives for research.

Keywords: Urban Regeneration; Ontology; User needs.

1 Preface

The European Union (EU) Community Strategic Guidelines 2007-2013 place particular emphasis on the specific needs of certain zones, such as urban and rural areas. The guidelines encourage an "integrated approach" towards cohesion policy, not only stimulating growth and creating jobs, but also pursuing certain social and environmental objectives.

The success of the URBAN Community Initiative is in no small measure due to the integrated approach. URBAN has targeted social and economic cohesion in parallel, removing barriers to employability and investment at the same time as promoting social and environmental goals. The mobilisation of a broad range of partners with different skills has underpinned this approach.

The next EU urban regeneration policies try to confirm these successes with new policies oriented to regeneration of deprived urban areas, such for example the JES-SICA[1] policy. In this context ontologies could play a significant role in developing and managing these new policies strengthening integration, shared vision and

---

[1] Joint European Support for Sustainable Investment in City Areas (JESSICA).

D. Taniar et al. (Eds.): ICCSA 2010, Part I, LNCS 6016, pp. 283–292, 2010.

knowledge of the urban regeneration problems offering an instrument capable to show concepts, their shared definitions and relations between them, in a multilingual tool, in this European Union matter.

Nowadays, in the institutional offices dedicated to the management of these regeneration policies at all level, EU, regions, municipalities, the understanding of different interpretation of the same words made by an architect, a planner, an ecologist, an economist, is really difficult because the discipline approaches are quite different.

For example a cycle path is a simple line in a network of nodes for a transport engineer, a space for urban project for an architect, a way to improve urban sustainability for a planner, a way delimited by a vegetal hedge, a biological corridor for an ecologist, and so on.

Urban regeneration could means different things in different disciplines. Ontologies could be a useful tool for ordering, integrate and making transparent all these meanings of the policy.

It appears particularly useful in such European context, where the coherence of different actions in the same field is often difficult to find from the European level to the municipal one.

2 The Multiple Components of Urban Regeneration and Its Basic Elements

Urban regeneration is an integrated urban policy approach mixing multiple dimensions: economic, social, cultural, spatial and environmental.

New urban planning [4] and design methods replaced rationalist architectural codes and conventions by locating some key points which echo the aspirations of urban regeneration policies and strategies. In response to the Leipzig Charter[2], the same questions where developed during the Slovenian Presidency of the Council of the European Union in 2008, as demonstrated by the Ljubljana Declaration on Urban Regeneration & Climate Change (Ljubljana, 17 June 2008).

This, may be expressed, for example, in the upgrading of the physical environment and encouraging sustainable urban transport, the strengthening of the local economy and labour markets, or in the promotion of proactive education and training policies for children and young people in deprived urban areas.

All these elements are of a crucial importance for deprived urban neighbourhoods reducing inequalities, preventing social exclusion, improving their physical environment. That's why EU new initiatives, JASPERS[3] and JESSICA, and some measures of the European Regional Development Funds (ERDF) will support from 2007 to 2013, these policies of urban regeneration.

After these brief introduction on the urban regeneration goals and about some European policies which are promoting these goals, it appears evident the multiple dimension of an urban regeneration process, encouraged by the European Union.

---

[2] The *Leipzig Charter on sustainable European cities* is available on line at: http://europa.eu.int/comm/regional_policy/index_en.htm
[3] Joint European Resources for Micro to Medium Enterprises (JASPERS).

So, for a region implied in these European policies it's fundamental to manage this multiple dimension of the same problem, using different competencies, sharing the same physical, economical and social words and objects [5].

Ontologies could be a way to organize this complex and multifaceted work.

3   A Possible Ontology for Urban Regeneration (OUR)

Guarino [7] defines an Ontology as a set of logical axioms designed to account for the intended meaning of a vocabulary. Ontologies are usually enshrined in computer programs. They determine what can be represented and what can be said about a given domain through the use of information techniques.

Accordingly "ontology designers have to make conscious and explicit choices of what they admit as referents in a particular system or language" [8].

The way to make these choices is an important subject of research given their practical implications over the long-term.

According to Gruber [6], an ontology is an explicit, formal and shared conceptualization of a particular domain. The conceptualization process represents the attribution of unambiguous meanings to terms defining knowledge in that precise domain (domain ontology).

So, a domain ontology for urban regeneration is expected to express the viewpoints and satisfy the information needs of multiple stakeholders and interest groups, including but not limited to town planners, environmental agencies, municipalities, police departments, owners and sellers of real estate, third sector associations.

These actors use different jargons and pursue different, occasionally conflicting tasks, also if they manage similar and related domains.

Reports from ontology development experiences in many fields of applications, underline that different jargons and information needs are hard to accommodate in a consensual ontology[10][4].

In the case of OUR, it's not strictly necessary to have a unique definition of a term, if it results impossible to have, but it is sufficient that all the agents involved in the same or in similar activities at least are informed and have the possibility to know the others definitions.

For example in an objective 1 region[5] as Apulia in Italy, it is necessary that the environmental management office, the regional planning office, the transport bureau, the economic planning bureau, are, at least, aware of the others definitions to avoid that each of theme promote different incoherent funding policies on the same urban regeneration objects, based on the same EU definition, as already happened.

This is what we have founded in different funds on the cycle paths in the precedent phase of cohesion policies (2000-2006), that is one of the objects of urban regeneration, promoted by the transport bureau, more related to a vision of this object as a functional one, useful to enlarge the possibilities of movement in the urban context, not related to a definition of cycle paths as an element related to leisure and nature which could be build with natural materials such as compact sand and green hedges,

---

[4] Examples of ontologies are available at http://protege.stanford.edu/download/ontologies.html
[5] An objective 1 region is a region where the gross development product is below the 75% of the European Union average.

useful in the tourist routes in the countryside. This last vision of these elements has been funded by the environmental management office.

In the same period the regional planning office has promoted urban regeneration process in which it funded also the same objects to encourage an alternative way to reach the working place, schools etc.

An ontology for urban regeneration related to the regional geographical information systems, that starts to be a common platform for spatial policies, could perhaps avoid these bad communications and lack of knowledge specially in the biggest organizations as a regional one (Apulia region has actually more than 3000 employees). The ontologies vary according to the size of the community they address.

It is conceivable that the type of ontology might differ depending on the purpose and breadth of the community it seeks to support.

According to Barone and Di Pietro [1], ontologies could introduce an administrative simplification, a better control of the public expenditure and a simplification of policies management.

Indeed, a domain ontology could show all the different definitions of the policies and the object related, in a semantic integration of n... databases, and in the software Towntology, produced by the LIRIS, Institut National des Sciences Appliquées de Lyon, offers also the possibility to use images to represents concepts, so that for example is possible visualising different way to build the same object (this is not possible with others ontology software as, for example, Protégé[6]).

It is really important in the urban regeneration domain the possibility of seeing objects described, because the same thing could be build in many different ways. So it is relevant for a user visualizing images to find a shared definition of objects.

4   OUR First Training

The scope of the case studies depended heavily on the availability of and access to information and actors within studied organisations. Thinking to the case of the Apulia region, well representing a large number of situations specially in the "objective one" regions of EU, in the case of OUR, we have started to build the ontology from a town planner point of view and then we have submitted to others agents the 110 terms identified to describe the domain, identifying different definitions of concepts and objects related, illustrating them with images and their relations in a dynamic chart changing its representation with the interests of the agent who manage the ontology.

The chosen agents are all interested to develop policies at the regional level about urban regeneration and they are implied in the elaboration of the specific regional measures to apply the European programmes such as the next JESSICA, or what is called Operative Program in the ERDF.

They have been involved five persons, a civil engineer working in the field of the nets of public systems, a biologist, specialised in ecology, an architect urban planner, an agronomist, an economist working on the management of the structural funds.

They have been guided in the survey by the author and one of his student.

---

[6] http://protege.stanford.edu/

Fig. 1. The meeting between the professionals involved in the Apulia Region

The survey has been conducted using the well known SWOT (Strengths, Weaknesses, Opportunities, Threats) analysis method, trying to enlightening if the ontology could be a useful tools for their public administration offices, if the prototype has used the basic words and definitions and if there was some conflicts or disagreement about definitions and relations.

After an illustration of the subject of the meeting they have been put on the ontology to analyse it.

The Editor page of the software is the door to entry definitions and relations between terms, as shown in the figure 2.

In the OUR we have introduced, until now, 110 definitions in the urban regeneration domain, starting from very general and complex terms such as urban decline or social and economic cohesion to arrive at the object definitions such as cycle path or chicane or green corridor.

For each definition there's the possibility to indicate the reference and an url with a link to a representative image (as shown in the figure 3), trying to clarify the disciplinary knowledge at the base of the term, so that also from different backgrounds it is possible to enlarge the knowledge base.

After editing the ontology, the Townto-Browser offer the possibility to surf the ontology showing relations, the level of integration of terms, their general value.

After the building of OUR it has been tested with the groups of agents described above working in different departments of Apulia Region.

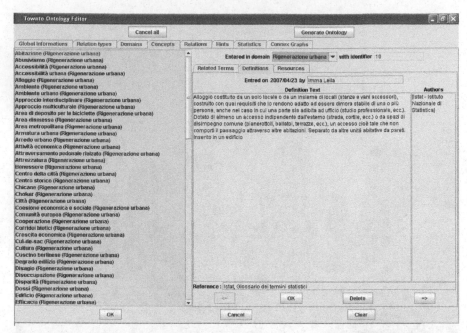

Fig. 2. The Towntology editor offer the possibility to add how many definitions it's necessary just using the arrows. Here the definitions of the term "abitazione" (house), in the Italian language.

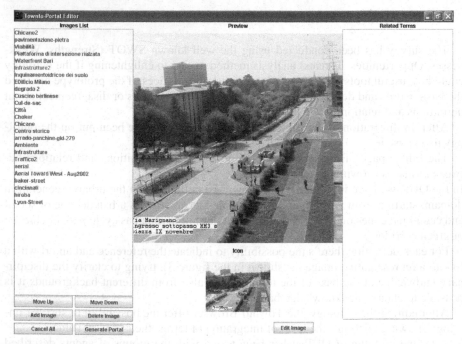

Fig. 3. A typical scene of the Portal Editor showing the image of a complex space with a pedestrian precinct, a pedestrian platform to cross the road, a bus stop and a green hedge

The "testing phase" has been conducted firstly with a meeting between all the agents involved (see figure 1), then discussing on line with "skype" trying to find an agreement on terms and definitions.

They have modified 25 definitions of the original 110 and they have add others 9 definitions of existing terms, showing no possibilities of agreement about those.

The largest difference has been notice between the definitions made by the transport department and those made by the environment management department.

The next step could be the integration of the ontology into GIS of the Apulia Region (that now is under construction) linking terms to real examples in the region focusing on each city where regional departments are planning an urban regeneration policy.

Having a unique domain ontology could reduce the overlapping of similar decision integrating them each time it could be possible, sharing the same knowledge base. In fact thinking to the ontology running on a GIS, it could be possible to represent places where urban regeneration policies have been applied or are in course of action, with all its related terms and relations.

5 OUR Suggestions

The main goal of selecting and developing this case study was to examine the impact of ontologies (implied or otherwise) on an big size organization working in the broad area of environment and urban development.

The rationale was that a better understanding of the impact of ontologies in practice will inform the development of future ontologies. The case study is intended to provide the 'raw material' for analysis and discussion of issues surrounding the use of ontologies in practice.

Reflecting on the case study above it has been noted that people are often not aware of using ontologies. Ontologies are implicit but not revealed during many everyday activities connected to urban planning and design. But without knowing it, people are using ontologies that are embedded in the systems (software and otherwise). It is often only when the software comes to the fore that its ontological underpinnings are exposed.

In a second type of usage, an ontology can be developed specifically to reveal characteristics of a problem in the urban modelling domain. By focusing on an ontological description, it forces its developers to clarify the entities and relations inherent in the problem and from which a possible solution may emerge.

The results of this first OUR case study depended heavily on the availability of and access to information and actors within studied organizations. Since this type of work tends to be labour - intensive, it is difficult to conduct detailed studies without significant funding or other resources.

The general aim of this task is to investigate the use of ontologies in real organizations. The specific objectives were:

- to identify methods of studying ontologies in action;
- to identify and describe specific problems resulting from the use (or absence) of ontologies in this field;

- to develop a deeper understanding of how ontologies impact on the practices of organizations working in the urban environment;

The case study used methodologies depending on the application and the domain under investigation. The methods used included literature reviews and interviews with key stakeholders in the organization involved, and participant observation during use of ontologies.

After these first, yet significant, experiences [9] [2] in collecting impressions from participants it is possible to outline some user requirements:

- OUR could perhaps be of most use if used as an integrated tool within usual policies and policy making, rather than as an exceptional instrument;
- In order for OUR to be effective it has to be available on the web or at least on the intranet of the public office or institution involved;
- A unique multitask interface could be developed within the "Towntology" software with which the user would simultaneously be able to locate the list of terms (possibly with a multilingual description), their definitions, their relationships and any associated imagery where applicable.

As it seems it has been done in the release n°2 of the software Towntology represented in the following image.

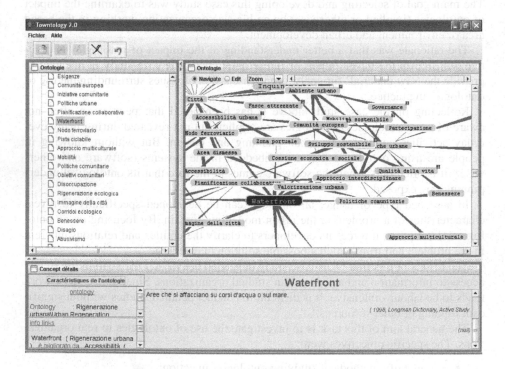

Fig. 4. The new interface of Towntology software

The availability of multiple on-line ontologies takes on a particular importance, especially when considering EU policies given that:

- Public organizations are predominantly divided into a range of departments with a high level of specialization yet a low level of integration. If ontologies were to become an integrated tool which could be applied to even standard policy, or better still if applied on a GIS, public organizations could potentially arrive at a greater integration of policy content.
- Ideally, OUR would be available on-line or at least on the intranet of the organization in question, as its value is determined by the possibility of being utilized by anyone involved in urban regeneration regardless of their physical working location. In this way the glossary will grow and every definition could be discussed and eventually shared in a unified way.
- EU cohesion policies are frequently multifaceted and complex, often with various possible implementation choices, deriving in part from the particular characteristics of the nation in which it is applied.

In the case therefore of single large-scale organizations, ontologies could lead towards a better cohesion in the way that different member states may apply the same EU policy.

Although yet to be sufficiently experimented and diffused, considering the initial results of first experiences, it may be possible to assume that OUR is potentially a tool which could foster improved communication between stakeholders.

Possible future directions for research in the field of ontologies for urban regeneration with reference to EU policies could be a compared evaluation between ontologies as seen within different languages and cultures as, for example, with a French urban renewal ontology, as has been developed by the EDU Laboratory in Lyon [2], alongside another in English thereby making an ontology available in the official language of EU.

A step beyond this would perhaps be the conception of a more extensive experiment involving EU offices, in which regeneration policies are developed and managed.

The possibility of using OUR in practice is strictly related to the wider diffusion of ontologies within public administration routine. From the first definition by Gruber [6] of an ontology in the sphere of Artificial Intelligence, only within the last few years have we seen some experiences.

The greater the increase in the availability of data sets, the more an ontology lends itself to being a useful instrument in providing clear definitions and corresponding relationships within a specific domain.

Acknowledgements. This study has been supported by the European Science Foundation funded COST Action C21, "Urban Ontologies for an improved communication in urban civil engineering projects".

It should be added that the views expressed in this paper do not necessarily reflect those of the scientific group working with the EU COST Action C21 which sustained the project. The Author is grateful to the LIRIS Laboratory at the University of Lyon (France), which has developed the prototype of the "Towntology software" used in this experience.

References

1. Barone, A., Di Pietro, P.: Ontologia. Elemento Chiave per la Costruzione della Società della Conoscenza. IterLegis 5-6, 9–15 (2005)
2. Berdier, C., Roussey, C.: Urban Ontologies: the Towntology Prototype towards Case Studies. In: Teller, J., Lee, J., Roussey, C. (eds.) Ontologies for Urban Development, pp. 143–155. Springer, Berlin (2007)
3. European Council of Town Planners: The New Charter of Athens 2003. Alinea Firenze (2003)
4. Dutton, J. A.: New American Urbanism: Re-forming the Suburban Metropolis. Skira Milano (2000)
5. European Commision, Commission Staff Working Document. State Aid Control and Regeneration of Deprived Urban Areas. Vademecum (2006),
   http://europa.eu.int/comm/regional_policy/index_en.htm
6. Gruber, T.R.: A Translation Approach to Portable Ontologies. Knowledge Acquisition 5(2), 199–220 (1993)
7. Guarino, N.: Formal Ontology in Information Systems. In: Guarino, N. (ed.) Proceedings of FOIS 1998, Trento, Italy, June 6-8, pp. 3–15. IOS Press, Amsterdam (1998)
8. Kuhn, W.: Ontologies in Support of Activities in Geographic Space. International Journal of Geographical Information Science 15(7), 613–631 (2001)
9. Rotondo, F.: Future perspectives in Ontologies for urban regeneration. In: Teller, J., Cutting-Decelle, A.F., Billen, R. (eds.) Urban ontologies for an improved communication in urban development projects. Les Editions de l'Université de Liège, Liège, pp. 51–59 (2009)
10. Rotondo, F.: Ontologies for urban regeneration: opportunities and weakness for their development in cohesion policies for cities. In: Teller, J., Tweed, C., Rabino, G. (eds.) Conceptual Models for Urban Practitioners, Società Editrice Esculapio, Bologna, pp. 149–158 (2008)

The Effect of School Facility Allocation to City Center Development Base on Dynamic Spatial Structure Model

Shyh-Haw Chyan[1], Hsiao-Lan Liu[2], and Feng-Tyan Lin[3]

[1] Lan-Yan Technological Institute, Department of Architecture
261 Yiland County, Taiwan
Ph. D, National Taipei University, Graduate Institute of Urban Planning
c_moneydc@yahoo.com.tw
[2] Professor, National Chengchi University, Department of Land Economic
Taipei City, Taiwan
slliou@nccu.edu.tw
[3] Dean, National Cheng Kung University, College of Planning and Design
Tainan City, Taiwan
slliou@nccu.edu.tw

Abstract. The Dynamic Spatial Structure Model of multi-centric City, which integrated the rent function of Alonso and the neighborhood model of Cellular Automata (CA), is a useful model to study the development of urban spatial structure [11]. In this study aims to (1) understand the rent distribution of dynamic multi-centric city with school, and (2) discover the effect of school allocation to a city's core. The facility, school and road, occupied quite area and quantity on urban space, and affect the transportation cost of family. The location of facilities directly affects the urban structure, especially on developing city. This study simulated the city development with primary school and two-tier road by DSSM to understand the effect of urban spatial structure. It uses the spatial structure, the hierarchy of cores, the Turbo-cornutus (Tanabe, 1970)[1] and location sensitivity to analysis the effect of multi-centric city.

Keywords: Spatial Structure, Urban Dynamics, School Facility, Commuting Cost, Artery Road.

1 Introduction

The city public facility supplies the convenience of family living to reduce the transportation cost and increase the housing rent. The studies of Urban Rent focus on the investigation of land rent, and the calculation of mathematical rent function. The former is as the study of Topeka, Kansas (Knos1962)[2]; the land price has opposite change with the distance of city centre. Hartshorn (1992)[3] studied the

---

[1] Scargill, David Ian, (1979), *The Form of Cities*, p.251[1].
[2] Chien, Hsueh-Tao, (2001), Principle and Practice of Urban Planning, p,159[1].
[3] Hsueh, Yi-chung, (2006), *Urban Geography*, p.178[3].

D. Taniar et al. (Eds.): ICCSA 2010, Part I, LNCS 6016, pp. 293–308, 2010.
© Springer-Verlag Berlin Heidelberg 2010

distribution of American city's land price; the price in the city center had a highest price dropping fast outwards. The land prices in commercial node of periphery went up slightly and in the suburban center were higher. Scott (1970)[4] compared the relation of commercial store category with land rents, the department store and women's dress store were in the city center. Besides, the scholars used the mathematical calculation to analysis the bid rent function. Alonso [4] represented the urban spatial structure with bid rent function. He added the transportation cost to production function and utility function of variety land user to transform bid rent function determined the user's distribution. It proved the Concentric Zone Model of Burgess (1923)[5]. Fujita [6] used comparative statics to analysis equilibrium and optimal land use of multiple types' user in single center. Liu [7] did bid rent functions analysis for two sectors of firm and householder to study the ring structure. In multiple nuclei model, White [8] used the differential equation of the householder's utility function of linear city, and it get the sub-centers of loop road will improve the welfare of all family. Wieand [9] added the cash flow and development agency to utility function that used planar polygon to analyzed two centers city. Sasaki [10] simulated the growth of the three-centers-two-levels linear city with utility function and production function on time series to analyze the breaking point of two land users. The DSSM (Dynamic Spatial Structure Modeling, Chyan and Liu [11]) was a bid rent simulating model of interactive multi-users. It discussed the development of multiple nuclei city and studied the spatial structure and developing series of the core-periphery. Chyan [12] uses the DSSM modeling to simulate the growth of the Cultural Center area of Yilan County. It compared with the aerial photography and discussed the issues of realistic planning.

The allocation of public facilities influences land user's life convenience. The general family will choose to be close to the places of some facilities in the house, as primary school, market or public garden, in order to reduce to the traffic cost of going to these facilities, and raise the price of land. The tradition market in city is a commercial center of community, and its market range demonstrates the level in the scale and urban spatial structure of the community. The primary school has its scale, service population and radius. A lot of families will influence the local price and development of the community while closing to the school.

The dynamic model of the city expand investing multiplier model in to the cores change model. In the urban economic model (Forrester [13], p.148), the school was a grand public investment of a city, which is a variable of dynamic model on public expenditure multiplier. The market area of commercial cores was distributed with hierarchy system (Christaller [3], p.142), the distribution of commercial cores was effected by market scale coefficient k on the equal agricultural area, and the core markets with different levels had different service level. The DSSM set up the travel cost of working and consuming to figure out the rent of cells on the GIS package, it created a simulation method of multi-level cores city development, which find the variation style and reason of highest-level cores.

---

[4] Hsueh, Yi-chung, (2006), *Urban Geography*, p.197[3].
[5] Chen, Kun-Hong ,(1994), Theories, Methodology and Planning on Study of Spatial Structure, p.91[5].

This study integrates the position factor of the primary school and traffic cost of student in DSSM model. It analyzes the multi-level cores distribution for facility construction, and also analyzes the effect of primary school for community development. First, it added the school and road factors on DSSM model. Second, it did the simulation of multi-core city with travel costs of employment, consume, and go to school. Final, it studies the effect of facility for city spatial development with spatial structure, Turbo- cornutus[1], and location sensitivity.

2 The Model Construction

Before to simulate a dynamic city, it is needed to suppose the city system, the economic model of land user, the neighborhood model of city development, road constructed model, the scale and location selection model of school, and integrated the above five parts.

2.1 The City System

There are four basic sectors, residents, retails & services, land and road, to supply goods and service, labor, land, and traffic, in city system of DSSM, as Figure 1. They need to pay cost of goods and service, salary, rent, and traffic coast (Chyan, Liu and Chan [14]). Besides, in this study, the primary school provides the compulsory education, and the students of family need to pay the traffic coast of going to school.

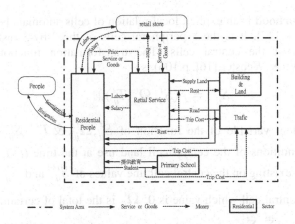

Fig. 1. The city system of DSSM with the primary school, retail, and transportation system

2.2 The Economic Model of Land User

Every land user in city has his economic model. The utility function of residential (Fujita, 1989) is

$$\max_{r,z,s} U(z,s), \quad \text{subject to} \quad z + R(r)s = Y - T(r), \tag{1}$$

the z is the total amount of consumer goods for a resident, s is the land area of resident occupied, $R(r)$ is the rent the per unit land at r, y is the income of unit time, and $T(r)$ is the traffic cost at r.

This study supposes every household unit has same house land area, same income and utility level, and hence has the same quantity of consumer goods. The budget of household unit is

$$B_C \cdot P_C + R \cdot T_h = W \cdot B_w - (t_w \cdot B_w \cdot u_w + t_c \cdot B_C \cdot u_c) \tag{2}$$

t_{wa} is the commuting trip distance of artery, t_{ws} is the commuting trip distance of alley, u_{wa} is the unit trip cost of commuting in the artery, u_{ws} is the unit trip cost of commuting in the alley, t_{ca} is the consuming trip distance of artery, t_{cs} is the consuming trip distance of alley, u_{ca} is the unit trip cost of consuming in the artery, u_{cs} is the unit trip cost of consuming in the alley, B_l is the student number of family, t_{la} is the going to school trip distance of artery, t_{ls} is the going to school trip distance of alley, u_{la} is the unit trip cost of going to school in the artery, and u_{ls} is the unit trip cost of going to school in the alley.

2.3 Neighborhood Model of City Development

The bid rent function of economic model is a relation of the location of land users and city's cores and it doesn't involve the environment of neighborhood and the demand threshold of market area. This study adopts the General Neighborhood and Threshold Neighborhood.

General Neighborhood is an explicit local relation of cells automata behavior model (Leao etc., [15], p.147). It is the 8 peripheral cells of the 3-by-3 raster decide the empty condition of the central cells. The transformation function of General Neighborhood (Wu & Webster,[16], p.106) is

$$S_{ij}^{t+1} = f(S_{ij}^t, \Omega_{ij}^t, T_{ij}^t), \tag{3}$$

S_{ij}^{t+1} is a dependent variable of the function of $S_{ij}^t, \Omega_{ij}^t, \& T_{ij}^t$. S_{ij}^{t+1}, and S_{ij}^t are respective the conditions of the central cell land use at the time $(t+1)$ and time (t). When one user is existing on the central cell, the values of S_{ij}^{t+1} and S_{ij}^t are 1, and the user no-use the central cell which value is 0. Ω_{ij}^t is the total of certain use of central cell's neighbor, $\Omega_{ij}^t = \sum_{i=i-x}^{i+x} \sum_{j=j-y}^{j+y} n_{ij}$, x, y are the vertical and horizontal displacement of cell on i, j location for summing. n_{ij} is the value of the cell at i,j, 1 and 0 represent use and no-use for certain use. T_{ij}^t is the condition of Ω_{ij}^t value for transformation rule, when it is greater than and equal to a criterion to transform. The resident and firm have the general Neighborhood, their $t+1$ conditions are S_{ij}^{t+1} & S_{ij}^t and the transformation rules are T_{hij}^t & T_{gij}^t, as the Function (4) and (5).

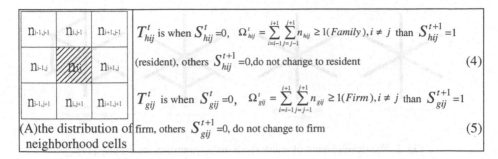

T_{hij}^{t} is when $S_{hij}^{t}=0$, $\Omega_{hij}^{t}=\sum_{i=i-1}^{i+1}\sum_{j=j-1}^{j+1}n_{hij}\geq 1(Family), i\neq j$ than $S_{hij}^{t+1}=1$

(resident), others $S_{hij}^{t+1}=0$, do not change to resident   (4)

T_{gij}^{t} is when $S_{gij}^{t}=0$, $\Omega_{gij}^{t}=\sum_{i=i-1}^{i+1}\sum_{j=j-1}^{j+1}n_{gij}\geq 1(Firm), i\neq j$ than $S_{gij}^{t+1}=1$

firm, others $S_{gij}^{t+1}=0$, do not change to firm   (5)

(A) the distribution of neighborhood cells

Threshold Neighborhood model is the threshold of a firm emerging in neighborhood. If a firm does not have enough amount of threshold consumer for managing a firm, the firm does not emerge in a neighborhood. The translation condition of new retail firm emerging in a neighborhood is

$$T_{Ngij}^{t} \quad when \quad \Omega_{gij}^{t}=\sum_{i=i-x}^{i+x}\sum_{j=j-y}^{j+y}n_{hij}\geq the\ amount\ of\ threshold\ consumer= turnover\div(family\ size\times consumption), i\neq j$$

$$than \quad S_{gij}^{t+1}=1, change\ as\ firm,$$

$$others \quad S_{gij}^{t+1}=0, does\ not\ change\ as\ firm \quad (6)$$

The threshold neighborhood condition T_{Ngij}^{t} of a retail store is $\Omega_{gij}^{t}=\sum_{i=i-x}^{i+x}\sum_{j=j-y}^{j+y}n_{hij}$ of around housing cells large than the threshold of retail managing at i, j position, than cell at i, j emerge the retail, $S_{rij}^{t+1}=1$, others the retail dose not exist, $S_{gij}^{t+1}=0$. The x, y is according to the threshold's demanded quantity to decide the displacement distance, the number of external loop for center cell 6. When a new center-periphery emerging, for keeping manage, the total consuming volume large than the turnover of all retails on the center, $Bc \times Nh \times Pc \square G \times Pg$ (Bc is the family size, Nh is the amount of family on periphery, Pc is everyone's amount of money of consumption, G is the amount of retailer at center, Pg is the turnover of a retailer).

2.4 The Road Development Model

The road development model is trying to explore of the impact of road systems on urban development in a simplified manner. This paper supposes two kinds of road: artery and alley. The time cost of alley is the twice of artery road. In simulation, we create the artery road developing modeling of the raster system in GIS to reflect the developing of core-periphery: On the plain of equal, the city center has three artery roads to the intersection, un-right angle intersection, as

Figure 2(a). The artery roads pass through the plain to connect other cities. On the growing population and expanding city's area, the city government constructs the new arteries to contact the growing area and other artery roads, as Figure 2(c) and 2(d).

---

[6] If the turnover of retail is NT 400000, consume money of per person is NT10000, the volume of family is 4, the retail threshold on the neighborhood is 10 family, about $x=y \fallingdotseq 3$.

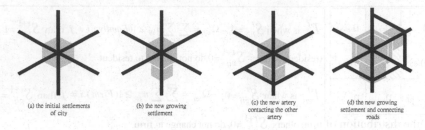

(a) the initial settlements of city   (b) the new growing settlement   (c) the new artery contacting the other artery   (d) the new growing settlement and connecting roads

Fig. 2. The development of artery roads and settlements for the city [17]

2.5   The Assumption of School Size and Location Selecting

The school size is according to the criterion of Taiwanese regulation; the area of a primary school is 2 hectare[7], about a circular with 80m radius, 143 cells of 12m*12m. The school district of primary school supposes a 56 hectare with 15000 people, every 3 family has a student, and the radius of school district is about 420m[8]. Capacity of Every school is 1250 student, and every grad has 200 students for very class has 30~40 students. The school has a gate on the artery road. The principle of the school location is supposed as Figure 3, the new school is located in the middle of two school districts, and there most residents in the school district.

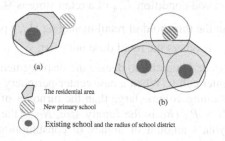

(a)

    The residential area
    New primary school   (b)
    Existing school and the radius of school district

Fig. 3. The principle of the school location

2.6   The Expenditure Cost and Trial Balance of a Family

The employee number of a family is 1.5 people. Wages is 40,000 NT dollars for each employee. Each person of family consumes 10,000 NT dollars for goods of every month. The cost of 10,000 NT dollars goods is 3000 NT dollars. The transport cost of going to work and school on artery road is 800 NT dollars per kilometer in each person's each month, and cost of alley road is 1200 NT dollars. Every family has one children studying in primary school. The transport cost of consuming on artery road is

---

[7] The criticism standard of Public Facility Land.

[8] There are 1250 students of a school. There is a primary student in every three families. There are 1250 students in the school, and there are 3750 families and 15000 people in the school district. 3750 families need 54 hectares and school of 2 hectares, it is 54 hectares altogether. Its radius of 54 hectares in area and round is about 420m.

Table 1. The test sheet of rent in different position

Item	Case 1 at center	Case 2 50m artery 50m alley	Case 3 500m artery 500m alley
Employee number, B_w	1.5	1.5	1.5
Wage, W	40,000	40,000	40,000
The family income, $B_w \times W =$	60,000	60,000	60,000
Employee number, B_w	1.5	1.5	1.5
Trip cost of artery road in commuting, u_{wa}	800	800	800
Commute distance of artery road, t_{wa}	0	0.05	0.5
Trip cost of alley road in commuting, u_{ws}	1,200	1,200	1,200
Commute distance of alley road, t_{ws}	0	0.05	0.5
$B_w \times (u_{wa} \times t_{wa} + u_{ws} \times t_{ws}) =$	0	150	1500
Number of consumer in family, B_c	4	4	4
Trip cost of artery road in consuming, u_{ca}	240	240	240
Consuming distance of artery road, t_{ca}	0	0.05	0.5
Trip cost of alley road in consuming, u_{cs}	360	360	360
Consuming distance of alley road, t_{cs}	0	0.05	0.5
$B_c \times (u_{ca} \times t_{ca} + u_{cs} \times t_{cs}) =$	0	120	1200
Number of going to school in family, B_l	1	1	1
Trip cost of artery road in schooling, u_{la}	800	800	800
School distance of artery road, t_{la}	0	0.05	0.5
Trip cost of alley road in schooling, u_{ls}	1,200	1,200	1,200
School distance of alley road t_{ls}	0	0.05	0.5
$B_l \times (u_{la} \times t_{la} + u_{ls} \times t_{ls}) =$	0	100	1000
Consumption of every one, P_c	10,000	10,000	10,000
Number of consumer in family, B_c	4	4	4
$P_c \times B_c =$	40,000	40,000	40,000
Total Rent, $R \times T_h =$	20,000	19,630	16,300

240 NT dollars per kilometer in each person's each month, and cost of alley road is 360 NT dollars. The turnover of every retail firm, the retail and service shop, is 400000 NT dollars.[11].

The municipal government constructs the school on the peripheral expansion of the city for the need of growing people. The student of family goes to school a week for five days. As Table 3, the family has a student to go school with the 500m artery and 500m alley distance, the cost of going to school accounts for the total cost is 27.03%, and the trip cost of consumption accounts for 32.43%. Under reducing the cost on the road, so many families choose the housing near shopping and going to school. If the housing located at artery road, it will save 60% cost for commuting. So the house will not be too far from the arterial road, in other words, the households all hope to have convenient transportation.

The condition of the new core to emerge on periphery is that the new house rent at new core-periphery boundary is equal to the rent at old core-periphery boundary,

$$Y_j - [(d_{ij} + t_j) \times u_w \times B_w + t_j \times u_c \times B_c] = Y_i - (t_i \times u_w \times B_w + t_i \times u_c \times B_c) \quad (7)$$

Table 2. The trip cost of working, shopping, and going to school

(a) The compare of 1km Artery and 1km Alley

Item	Trip cost of commute	Trip cost of shopping	Trip cost of going to school	Sum
Arterial Road				
People	1.5	4	1	
Kilometer	1	1	1	
Trips per Time	2	2	2	
Times per month	20	6	20	
NT dollars per Kilometer	20	20	20	
Total	1200	960	800	2960
Alley				
People	1.5	4	1	
Kilometer	1	1	1	
Trips per Time	2	2	2	
Times per month	20	6	20	
NT dollars per Kilometer	30	30	30	
Total	1800	1440	1200	4440
%	40.54%	32.43%	27.03%	100.0%

(b)The compare of 1km Artery, and 1km Alley, 500m artery & 500m alley

Item	Artery	Alley	Total	Save the proportion
Artery 1000m	2960		2960	33.3%
Alley 1000m		4440	4440	
Artery1000m	2960		2960	20.0%
Artery 500m+ Alley 500m	1480	2220	3700	

Yj is the income of new family income at new core-periphery (C_j). dij is the distance between C_i and C_j, as Figure 4 The Parameters of Function 10. Bw is the worker number of family. ti and tj are the distances of periphery boundary to core. uw and uc is the unit distance cost of commute and shopping. Bc is the consumer number of family.

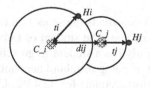

Fig. 4. The Parameters of Function 10

2.7 The Modeling Integration

This section integrates fore interactive modeling, the rent modeling, the neighborhood modeling, the road development modeling, and the school location selection modeling. As Figure 5, the new core emerges at the boundary of old core-periphery which has an iso-rent line of new core-periphery with rent modeling (Figure 5 (I)). In the iso-rent line, the number of different user is threshold neighborhood modeling (Figure 5 (II)). If the new core-periphery is larger than original, city constructs the new artery road to connect the radiation artery (Figure 5 (A)). If the newly increased population is larger than the schooling district population of exist schools, city set up new school at the middle of the area of newly increased population or the service radius having population most (Figure 5 (B)). The new residents aggregate with general neighborhood modeling on the suburb out (Figure 5 (III)). If the number of new residents is larger than the threshold of retail store, the new retails emerge on the out of periphery (Figure 5 (IV)). The population grows continually on the iso-rent lines. Select the location of the new retails at the supreme rent of boundary (Figure 5 (V)).

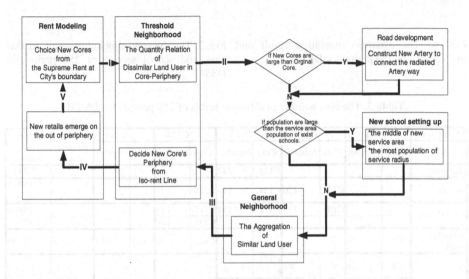

Fig. 5. The DSSM integration model of road development and primary school

3   The Simulation Result and Discuss

After 250 developing simulation, as Figure 6, there are 23 core-peripheries, 122916 people, 30729 house units, and 1647 retail units. The locations and schooling districts of seven schools are as Figure 7. There are 14 cores at artery, 9 cores are at alley, the cores of artery accounts 61% for all. They are divided into five levels, as 錯誤! 找不到參照來源。, C1, C121, C123, C124, and C133[9] are the main cores of different levels. The quantity rate of core levels is 1:3:7:12 (the biggest: bigger: middle (slightly big + slightly small): small (smaller+ smallest)). The k factor of urban hierarchy $\fallingdotseq$ 2 is small than the k=3 of Central Place Theory. The core-periphery structure of every period has the phenomenon of cell quantity increasing.

---

[9] After C10, C111, C112 are C11 _ 1 and C11 _ 2 simplification, representative the same period in C11, _ 1 and _ 2 is different cores of the same period.

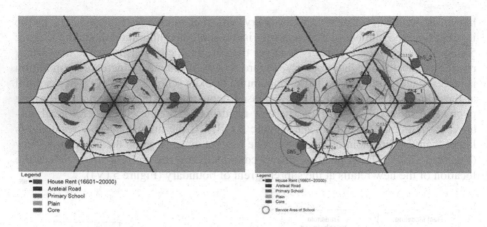

Fig. 6. The dynamic simulation result and market area of 250 period for DSSM

Fig. 7. The dynamic simulation result, market area, and school service of 250 period for DSSM

Table 3. The core number of different levels of 250 periods for DSSM

Main Core / Level	C1 Core	C1 Number	C121 Core	C121 Number	C123 Core	C123 Number	C124 Core	C124 Number	C133 Core	C133 Number	The number of core	The range of cell number
Biggest					C123	242					1	242
Bigger			C121	150	C134	147	C124	145			3	150~145
Slightly big			C101	138	C111	112	C112	133			4	138~112
							C132	120				
Slightly small	C1	50					C122	50	C133	77	3	77~50
Smaller	C6	29	C9	41	C131b	32					7	41~28
	C8	34	C131a	35								
	C5	36										
	C7	28										
Smallest	C2	9							C102b	11	5	14~7
	C3	7										
	C4	14										
	C102b	7										
The number of cores	9		4		4		4		2		Total	
The core at artery	14		The core at alley		9		The number of arterial core/ Total		61%		23	242~7

The development situation of 250 periods is the illustration of Figure 8. It is started from C1 core-periphery, the 502 housing units and the 50 retail units. The development of the 43rd period has had the C2 core and the three circles expansion, the 91st period develops C3 core-periphery, and the 125th period emerges the C5 core-periphery. The cores of C111 and C112 appear at the 163rd period, the four cores of

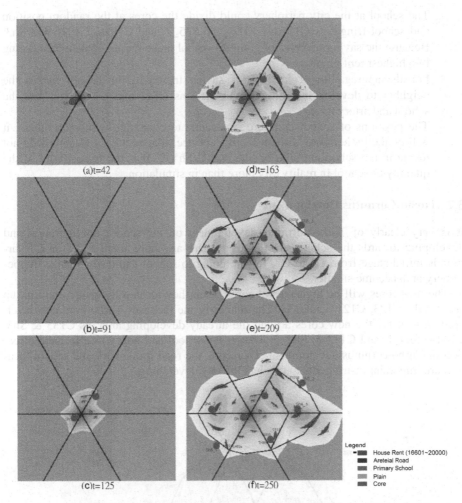

Fig. 8. Six development stage of 250 periods for DSSM simulation

C13s come on at the 209th period, and at the 250th period the periphery of C13s has developed.

The simulation discovers the core-periphery shape affected by Concentric Zone Model. The fringe of core-periphery is consisted some arcs and the new core at the fringe is a crescent. The emergence of high level core is until C10 large than C1, that is later than the study of Chyan and Liu (2006). It is may affected by the traffic cost of going to school. The increase of the traffic cost lets greater core-periphery not be easy to present.

3.1 The Result of Simulation

1. Observing the C1 and Sh1, the core is developed to the direction of the school. It is saving trip-cost for living near the school. The C112 core and Sh4_2, C5 and Sh2 have same phoneme.

2. The school at the city periphery could divide the cores at the random position and school fringe, as C131a, C131b, and Sh5_2, and C102a, C102b and Sh3. Because the saving trip cost of going to school make the iso-rent-line emerging two highest rent points.

3. For the aggregation of facility for saving trip cost, the school makes the neighbor to develop more high level core, as C111 and C112, they has the school and artery road.

4. The positions of school and core are unable to cooperate with each others; it will be the higher core without facility service, like as the C134 core does not locate in the schooling area of Sh5_1 and Sh5_2. It is the reason why of the quantity of school in reality city more than in simulation.

3.2 Turbo-Cornutus Development

It is very clearly of Turbo-cornutus development on the school configuration and developing towards the school. As Figure 9, there are more small cores on C1 surrounds initial stage from C2 to C8, for the going to school trip-cost to make the periphery area become smaller.

The new cores will be higher level cores when they locate on outside and link up artery, like C123, C121, andC132. The school is one factor of Turbo-cornutus development to make the new cores around the already developing area, as C133 & Sh3, C111& Sh4_1, and C112 & Sh4_2. That is the school and artery to affect the direction of Turbo-cornutus development. Therefore, the road framework and school location are important instruments to conduct the city developing.

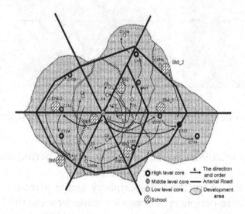

Fig. 9. Turbo-cornutus development of DSSM with primary school

3.3 The Sensitive Analysis of Facility and City Core Position

This sensitive analysis is study the effect of the facility at different distance and axis. There are two part of analysis: one part is the new core and school at same road axis, as Figure 10 a, other part is the school and new core at different axis, as Figure 10 b.

At same axis, where the school is the next-door neighbor of new core, as Figure 11 a, the size of core-periphery is 40-405 cells. The length of core to edge of periphery (depth) is 225m. Where the school is at the edge of core (130m), as Figure 11 b, the size of core- periphery is 46/464 cells and the depth is 281m. If the school position is at out, 520m, as Figure 11 b', the size of core-periphery is 20/209 cells and the depth is 246m. If the school position is at out, 770m, as Figure 11 b'', the size of core-periphery is 3/26 cells and the depth is 105m. There is the school at 920m, as Figure 11 b''', people don't immigrate to the periphery for school.

School and core at different axis, there are same condition happened. As Figure 11 c, the between of school and new core has a 30 degree angle, the size of core-periphery is 46/459 cells and the depth is 172m. The between of school and new core has a 60 degree angle, as Figure 11 c', the size of core-periphery is 17/167 cells. The two positions has a 120 degree angle, the school do not attract the people to live on the new core's periphery. When the new core's periphery is the schooling area of original school, as Figure 11 c''', the size of core-periphery is stilly 8/81 cell units.

According the study data, the position of school affects the core-periphery's size directly, as Table 4 and Figure 12. The school at the core edge, the size of core-periphery is largest. Keeping away from or close to the cores will reduce the size of core-periphery.

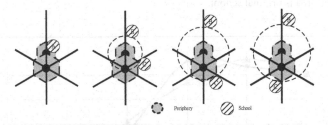

Fig. 10. The diagram of the sensitiveness of the core scale in the school position

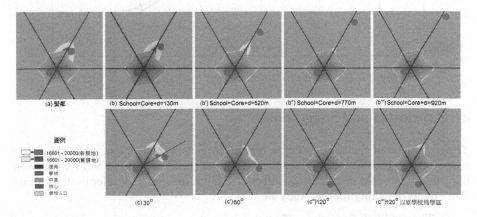

Fig. 11. The Sensitive Condition of distance for Axis and Angle Type

Table 4. The Quantity Table of Sensitive Condition Of Distance for Axis and Angle Type

Axis type					
Item	(a)	(b)	(b')	(b")	(b''')
The distance of school and new core (m)	0	130	520	770	920
Depth(m)	255	281	246	105	0
The number of core's cells	40	46	20	3	0
The number of periphery's cells	405	464	209	26	0
The increase number of per 100 meter		45.4	-49.0	-23.8	-2.8
Angle type					
Item	(a)	(c)	(c')	(c")	(c''')*
The distance of school and new core (m)	0	270	520	760	760
Depth(m)	0	30	60	120	120
The number of core's cells	255	172	65	0	90
The number of periphery's cells	40	46	17	0	8
The increase number of per 100 meter	405	459	167	0	81
Item		18.0	-97.3	-27.8	

*The schooling area is original school.

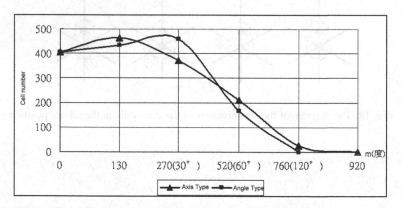

Fig. 12. The Sensitive Trend of distance for Axis and Angle Type

4 Conclusion and Suggestion

The simulation of facilities based on rent function surmounts the tradition discussion scope of Bid Rent Theory. Except the analysis of the core position and rent distribution, this paper also discusses the effect of facility on spatial development of a city. The effects of facility for this study are,

1. The facility's figuration affects to delay the emergence time of higher level cores, until C101. Chyan and Lui [11] studied the emergence of higher level core is C5.

2. The facility with high trip costs could be separating the core developed at that time into two places, as C102 and C131. Some retails aggregate on the out of school, the others aggregate at high rent point.
3. It is unsuitable that giant facility and core are very near, as school. They will limit the development of core area.

On the spatial policy, the government can utilize the facilities to strengthen or weaken central development. Like as we know, a new university will create a business center at the out of its gate. If they want a CBD improving the level, it has to consider moving the giant and low service efficiency facility. Taipei City government moved the factory at East Area to create the Hsin-Yi Planning District improving the level of east, the Taipei New CBD.

This simulation with rent function has only three item of trip cost, the most part of trivial cost for a family. But different live style of citizen has different trip cost item. How to consider different style people's transportation cost in models, it will be a great challenge of studying in the future.

Acknowledgements. This study has been supported by National Science Council for the project of 97WFA0102340, Authors are grateful to Dr. Chan, Shih-Liang for the technology of spatial analysis of GIS.

References

1. Scargill, D.I.: The Form of Cities. St. Martin's Press, New York (1979)
2. Chien, H.-T.: Principle and Practice of Urban Planning. Mao Rong Books Inc., Taipei (2001)
3. Hsueh, Y.-c.: Urban Geography. Sanmin Bookstore, Taipei (2006)
4. Alonso, W.: Location and Land Use. Harvard University Press, Cambridge (1964)
5. Chen, K.-H.: Theories, Methodology and Planning on Study of Spatial Structure. Ming Wen Book Store, Taipei (1994)
6. Fujita, M.: Urban Economic Theory- Land Use and City Size. Cambridge University press, New York (1989)
7. Liu, H.-L.: Two-sector nonmonocentric urban land-use model with variable density. Environment and Planning A 20, 477–488 (1988)
8. White, M.J.: Firm suburbanization and urban subcenters. Journal of Urban Economic 3, 323–343 (1976)
9. Wieand, K.F.: An extension of monocentric urban spatial equilibrium model to a multicenter setting: the case of the two-center city. Journal of Urban Economic 21, 259–271 (1987)
10. Sasaki, K., Mun, S.-I.: A Dynamic Analysis of Multiple- Center Formation. Journal of Urban Economic 40, 257–278 (1996)
11. Chyan, S.-H., Liu, H.-L.: The Initial Frame and Simulation of Dynamic Spatial Structure Modeling for Multi-centric City. Journal of Planning 33, 1–20 (2006)
12. Chyan, S.-H.: The Development of Ring Urban and the Simulation of Initial Stage Development for Yiland New County Center Area. In: The 2009 Academic Conference of Taiwan Institute of urban planning association of 2009/12/5, Taipei, Taiwan (2009)
13. Forrester, J.W.: Urban Dynamics. Pegasus Communications Inc., Waltham (1999)
14. Chyan, S.-H., Liu, H.-L., Chan, S.-L.: The Preliminary Framework and Simulations of Dynamic Spatial Structure Modeling (DSSM) on Right and Un-right Angular Artery Framework. Journal of Architecture and Planning 8(3), 205–221 (2007)

15. Liu, H.-L.: Two-sector nonmonocentric urban land-use model with variable density. Environment and Planning A 20, 477–488 (1988)
16. Wu, F., Webster, C.J.: Simulation of land development through the integration of cellular automata and multi-criteria evaluation. Environment and Planning B: Planning and Design 25, 103–126 (1998)
17. Chyan, S.-H., Liu, H.-L., Chan, S.-L.: The Preliminary Framework and Simulations of Urban Spatial Structure Dynamic Model (USSD Model) on Two-Tier right and un-right Angular Roadway. In: 2007 PRSCO, 20th Conference for the Pacific Regional Science, Vancouver, May 6-9 (2007)

A Fuzzy Reasoning Based Approach for Determining Suitable Paths between Two Locations on a Transport Network

Indira Mukherjee and S.K. Ghosh

School of Information Technology
Indian Institute of Technology, Kharagpur 721302, India
indira.mukherjee.23@gmail.com, skg@iitkgp.ac.in

Abstract. One of the major applications of geospatial information is to find the path or route between two locations. Though, several works have been carried out in finding the shortest or optimal path(s) between two locations; but not much efforts have been given in evaluating the *suitability* of a path with respect to various path attributes. In this paper, a fuzzy reasoning based approach has been proposed to find the *suitability* of a path/route based on its dimension, quality (i.e., texture and width) and the type of vehicle. The set of paths between two geographic locations are first determined using spatial topological reasoning. Then, the *suitability* of a path for a particular vehicle type is determined based on its *length* and *quality*, using fuzzy logic. The applicability of the proposed method has also been demonstrated.

Keywords: Geospatial Information, Transport Network, Fuzzy Logic.

1   Introduction

Geospatial information is becoming an integral part of many decisions making and query resolution processes. One of the major applications of such data is to find the route(s) or path(s) between two geographic locations. Many web based commercial geoinformatic systems, like, Google Earth[1], MapQuest[2], Yahoo Maps[3] have successfully addressed the problem of finding shortest path between a given pair of source and destination in a transportation network. However, the vehicle navigation literatures present that in addition to the length of the path, various other impedance factors plays a significant role in deciding the suitable route(s) or path(s) between two locations [1] [2] [3]. Further, the route having less congestion [1], simplest path [3] are some of the works related to route determination process. An approach based on genetic algorithm has been proposed in [1] to solve the problem of finding least congested path between a source

---

[1] http://earth.google.com
[2] http://www.mapquest.com
[3] http://www.maps.yahoo.com

D. Taniar et al. (Eds.): ICCSA 2010, Part I, LNCS 6016, pp. 309–319, 2010.

and destination in a set of location points. Algorithms for finding shortest path in a dynamic road network have been proposed in [4] [5]. The traffic in a path varies with respect to time and the algorithm calculates shortest path in a dynamic fashion. Ronga et al. [6] proposed a method by combining knowledge and algorithm for way finding. Duckham et al. [3] examined numerous cognitive studies and conveys that along with length of the route, route instruction complexity is important factors to human navigators. The research proposes an algorithm for finding simplest paths (easy to describe) in a network. The aim of simplest path algorithm is to minimize the route description complexity. Although the route navigators provide a general idea about what constitutes optimal route but it is difficult to express in search interfaces [7]. Again, the relative importance of route selection criteria often depends upon route alternatives, type of vehicle, smoothness of the route etc.

In this paper, an approach has been proposed to determine the suitable *paths* between a source and destination in a given transport network using fuzzy logic [8]. The *suitability* of a *path* is calculated based on *vehicle type* used for transportation, *road texture, road type* [9] and *route length*. In this work, the following aspects have been considered to determine the *path suitability - length, quality (roughness, width)* of the paths and the *vehicle type*.

The organization of the rest of the paper is as follows. Section 2 describes the overall methodology for finding suitable paths between two points in a given network. Section 3 presents a case study where roads between two geographic locations has been determined based on proposed framework.

2   Suitability of a Path

In a given transport network, several paths may connect two geographical locations. Geo-spatial portal, liek, Google Earth, can determine the shortest path between two geographical locations. However, for traveling from one location to another, shortest path may not be the only criteria. Some other properties have to be taken into consideration, viz. traffic condition of the path, quality of the path and so on. In this work, the *suitability* of the routes/paths are determined based on *route texture,route length* and *vehicle type*. For example, a given route is suitable, if *length* of the route is short and quality of the path is *good*. Again the *quality* of a path is *good* if the route is wide and texture of the route is smooth. Therefore, it can be shown as follows

$path$ suitability $\longleftarrow$ (path length($\mathcal{P}_L$), $path\ quality(\mathcal{P}_Q)$)
$path\ quality$ $\longleftarrow$ (path width($\mathcal{P}_L$), average roughness($\mathcal{R}_a$))

The *suitability* evaluation method has following steps:

1. Locations (source, destination) and type of vehicle
2. Determination of the routes that connect the given source and destination, for a given transport network, using spatial reasoning [10] [11]

3. Determination of fuzzy membership functions [8] based on route properties (*length, width, texture*)
4. Determination of the *suitability* of the route based on attributes/properties of the route, their fuzzy membership functions and the vehicle type.

For a given source and destination on a transport network, all the routes are determined using graph analysis and spatial reasoning. For example, in section 2.2, three paths have been considered for navigation between a source and destination pair.

In the next section, the fuzzy membership functions of the attributes have been determined. These membership functions have been subsequently used for determination of the *suitability* of a path or route.

2.1   Fuzzy Membership Functions for Suitability Analysis

In this section the fuzzy membership functions for *path suitability* based on *path length* and *path quality* have been determined (refer Fig. 1).

The *suitability* of a route with respect to *path length* and *path quality* is determined by membership value. The fuzzy membership functions for *path suitability*

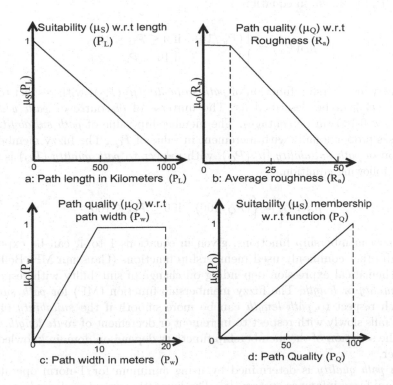

Fig. 1. Membership functions for determining route *suitability*

$[\mu_S(\mathcal{P}_L)]$ with respect to *path length* $(\mathcal{P}_L)$can be described as: Universe of discourse of *path length* in $\mu_S(\mathcal{P}_L)$ is 0-1000 in kilometers. For larger route network the universe of discourse *path length* $(\mathcal{P}_L)$ can range from 0 to ∞. The *suitability* of a route decreases with increase in *path length* $(\mathcal{P}_L)$. Therefore, the *suitability* membership value (μ_S) falls with increase in *path length*. The *path suitability* membership function $[\mu_S(\mathcal{P}_L)]$ w.r.t *path length* $(\mathcal{P}_L)$ is given in equation 1.

$$\mu_S(\mathcal{P}_L) = \begin{cases} 1\text{-}(\mathcal{P}_L/1000) & \text{if } 0 \le \mathcal{P}_L \le 1000, \\ 0 & \text{if } \mathcal{P}_L \ge 1000 \end{cases} \tag{1}$$

Similarly, the fuzzy membership function of *path quality* $[\mu_Q(\mathcal{R}_a)]$ with respect to average roughness $(\mathcal{R}_a)$ is given by equation 2.

$$\mu_Q(\mathcal{R}_a) = \begin{cases} 1 & \text{if } 0 \le \mathcal{R}_a \le 10, \\ (50 \text{-} \mathcal{R}_a)/40 & \text{if } 10 \le \mathcal{R}_a \le 50, \\ 0 & \text{if } \mathcal{R}_a \ge 50 \end{cases} \tag{2}$$

The fuzzy membership function of *path quality* $[\mu_Q(P_w)]$ with respect to *path width* (P_w) is shown in equation 3.

$$\mu_Q(\mathcal{P}_w) = \begin{cases} (\mathcal{P}_w/10) & \text{if } 0 \le \mathcal{P}_w \le 10, \\ 1 & \text{if } 10 \le \mathcal{P}_w \le 20 \end{cases} \tag{3}$$

The fuzzy membership function of *path suitability* $(\mu_S(P_Q))$ with respect to *path quality* (P_Q)can be described as: The universe of discourse of *path width* in $\mu_S(P_Q)$ is 0-100 (in percentage). The membership value of *path suitability* (μ_S) increases proportionally with increment in value of P_Q. The fuzzy membership function of *path suitability* $[\mu_S(\mathcal{P}_Q)]$ with respect to *path quality* $(\mathcal{P}_Q)$ is given by the following equation.

$$\mu_S(\mathcal{P}_Q) = \left\{ (\mathcal{P}_Q/100) \quad \text{if } 0 \le \mathcal{P}_Q \le 100, \right. \tag{4}$$

The fuzzy membership functions, given in equations 1 to 4, can be expressed through other commonly used membership functions (Gaussian MF, Bell MF) or mathematical expression depending on change of suitability with respect to path *quality* or *length*. The fuzzy membership function (MF) for *path suitability* with respect to *path length* can be more smooth if the *suitability* of *path* rise or falls slowly with respect to increment or decrement of *route length*. However, the selection of the membership functions depend on domain knowledge of the user.

The *path quality* is determined by using minimum for T-norm operator in Mamdani fuzzy inference system [8]. The linguistic terms (*good, medium, poor*)

Table 1. Linguistic terms of *path quality*

Path Quality	α-cut
poor	$0 \leq \min(\mu_Q(R_a), \mu_Q(P_w)) \leq 0.3$
medium	$0.3 \leq \min(\mu_Q(R_a), \mu_Q(P_w)) \leq 0.6$
good	$0.6 \leq \min(\mu_Q(R_a), \mu_Q(P_w)) \leq 1.0$

are used to define the quality of a path. Further, each linguistic term is defined by α-*cut* set (refer Table 1). The α- *cuts* offer a way to limit attention to a subset of a fuzzy set and also offer a complete characterization of a fuzzy set that can be easily compared to other fuzzy sets [12].

2.2   Determining Path Suitability

In a given transport network, routes connecting two geographical locations are determined (refer Fig. 2) using spatial reasoning based query. Once the routes between the location are known the attributes (*length, width ,average roughness*) of the route is determined through spatial query. For example (refer Fig. 2), given two locations X and Y, there are three paths, namely *path a, path b, path c*.

- Path a: (a1, a2, a3, a4, a5, a6)
- Path b: (b1, b2, b3)
- Path c: (c1, c2, c3, c4, c5, c6)

For *path a*, $a1, a2, a3, a4, a5, a6$ are the nodes and $e_{X,a1}$, $e_{a1,a2}$, $e_{a2,a3}$, $e_{a3,a4}$, $e_{a4,a5}$, $e_{a5,a6}$, $e_{a6,Y}$ are the edges. Similarly, the nodes and the edges of *path b*

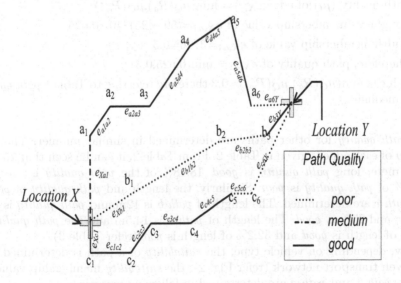

Fig. 2. Route network between two locations

and *path c* are determined. The attributes of the individual edges of each path is determined through spatial query (refer Table 2). Now, depending on type of vehicle, the *suitability* of a path is calculated. In this work, three types of vehicles are considered, namely, *heavy weight*, *light weight* and *two-wheeler*.

Table 2. Path length, path texture and path width of each edge of path a

Length	Roughness	Width	Path Quality
$e_{X,a1}$=4km	25 R_a	3m	medium
$e_{a1,a2}$=2km	18 R_a	6m	good
$e_{a2,a3}$=2.5km	19 R_a	6m	good
$e_{a3,a4}$=4km	20 R_a	6m	good
$e_{a4,a5}$=2.5km	18 R_a	6m	good
$e_{a5,a6}$=4.5km	18 R_a	6m	good
$e_{a1,Y}$=2.5km	35 R_a	1.5m	poor

From table 2,
Length of *path a* = sum of edges ($e_{X,a1}$, $e_{a1,a2}$, $e_{a2,a3}$, $e_{a3,a4}$, $e_{a4,a5}$, $e_{a5,a6}$, $e_{a6,Y}$) = $4 + 2 + 2.5 + 4 + 2.5 + 4.5 + 2.5 = 22$ meters
The *path quality* of all the edges of the *path a* are determined and shown in Table 2. The *path quality* of edge $e_{X,a1}$ is shown as follows.

- Path quality (μ_Q)of edge $e_{X,a1}$= $\min(\mu_Q(R_a), \mu_Q(P_w))$
- Roughness membership value of $e_{X,a1}$=$(50 - 25)/40$=0.625
- Width membership value of $e_{X,a1}$=3/10=0.3
- Therefore, path quality of $e_{X,a1}$= $\min(0.625, 0.3)$
- Value of $\min(\mu_Q(R_a), \mu_Q(P_w))$=0.3 therefore referring to Table 1 *path quality* is medium.

The *path quality* for other paths are determined in similar manner. The *path quality* of each edge is given in Table 2. From Table 2, it can be seen that 75.45% of 22 meter long *path quality* is *good*, 18.18% of the *path quality* is *medium*, 11.36% of *path quality* is *poor*. Similarly, the length and *path quality* of *path b* and *path c* are determined. The length of *path b* is 12m and *path quality* is 75% is *poor* and 25% is *good*. The length of *path c* is 14.5m and the *path quality* of 67.8% of length is *good* and 32.2% of length is *poor*(refer Table 3).

Now, depending on vehicle type, the *suitability* of a path is determined. For the given transport network (refer Fig. 2), the *suitability* membership values of *path a*, *path b* and *path c* are determined in following manner.

Table 3. Path length, path quality of the connecting paths between Location X and Location Y

path	Length	path quality
path a	22m	good=75.45%, medium=18.18%, poor=11.36%
path b	12m	good=25%, poor=75%
path c	14.5m	good=67.8%, poor=32.2%

$$\text{Suitability membership value of } path \ a = \min(1\text{-}(P_L/1000), P_Q/100)$$
$$= \min(1\text{-}(22/1000), 75.45/100)$$
$$= \min(0.978, 0.75)$$
$$= 0.75$$

Similarly, the *suitability* membership values of *path b* and *path c* can been derived.

$$\text{Suitability of } path \ b = \min(0.988, 0.25)$$
$$= 0.25$$
$$\text{Suitability of } path \ c = \min(0.985, 0.67)$$
$$= 0.67$$

Table 4. Suitability of *path a*, *path b* and *path c*

path Name	$\mu_{suitability}(path)$
path a	0.75
path b	0.25
path c	0.67

The α-*cut* set for *suitability* set of a path is defined in equation 5. The value of α changes with respect to vehicle type.

$$suitability_\alpha = \text{path}|\mu_{suitability}(path) \geq \alpha \tag{5}$$

From equation 5, it can be seen that all paths in the *suitability* set of a path have a membership value($\mu_{suitability}$(path))$\geq \alpha$. For example, if α is set to 0.40 (for *light* vehicle) then *path a* and *path c* are included in *suitability* set since these paths have membership values ($\mu_{suitability}(path)$)≥ 0.4 (refer Table 4). In Fig. 3, only two paths *path a* and *path c* for *light* vehicle are determined based on the α-*cut* suitability set. The linguistic terms (refer Table 5) are used to define the *suitability* of the routes.

In the next section, a suitability analysis has been carried out using the road network of a geographical region.

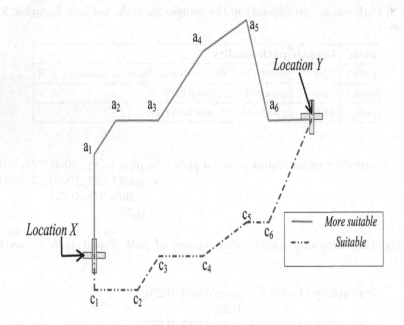

Fig. 3. Path suitability for light weight vehicle traversal

Table 5. Suitability Terms for light weight vehicle

Suitability membership value	Linguistic Term
0.96-1.0	Highly suitable
0.86-0.95	Most suitable
0.76-0.85	More suitable
0.66-0.75	Suitable
0.60-0.65	Somewhat suitable
0.40-0.59	Almost suitable

Table 6. Suitability Terms for heavy weight vehicle

Suitability membership value	Linguistic Term
0.96-1.0	Highly suitable
0.86-0.95	Most suitable
0.76-0.85	Suitable
0.6-0.75	Almost suitable

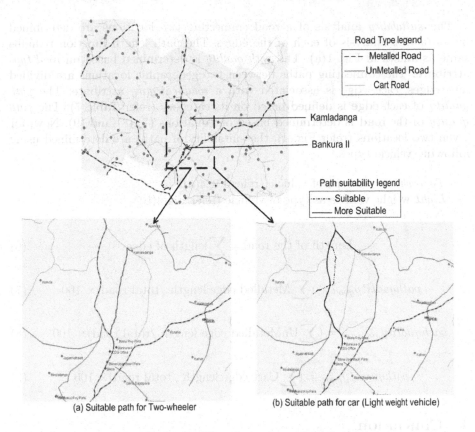

Fig. 4. Path suitability for various type of vehicle

3   Suitability Analysis of Roads between Two Geographic Locations

In this section the *suitability* of roads connecting two locations of a geographic region have been determined. There are three categories of roads namely, *Cart* road, *UnMetalled* road and *Metalled* road. The *path quality* of the road are defined based on their categories (refer Table 7).

Table 7. Path quality for each category of road

Road Category	Path Quality
Metalled Road	Good
UnMetalled Road	Medium
Cart Road	Suitable

The *suitability* analysis of a road connecting two locations are determined by *suitability* analysis of each of the edges. The path length function remains same as ahown in Fig. 1(a). The *path quality* is determined based on *road type* attribute. The connecting paths between two geographic locations are divided into edges, each edge is associated with a *road category* attribute. The *path quality* of each edge is defined based on its category (refer Table 7). The *path quality* of the road is determined based on equations (7),(8) and (9). Now, for given two locations (refer Fig. 4), the suitability of paths are determined using following vehicle types.

- *Two-wheeler* as type of vehicle (refer Fig.4(a))
- *Light* weight vehicle as type of vehicle (refer Fig.4(b))

$$\text{Length of the road} = \sum \text{length of edge} \tag{6}$$

$$pathquality_{good} = \left(\sum \text{Metalled edge length } / \text{total road}\right) \times 100 \tag{7}$$

$$pathquality_{medium} = \left(\sum \text{UnMetalled edge length } / \text{total road}\right) \times 100 \tag{8}$$

$$pathquality_{poor} = \left(\sum \text{Cart edge length } / \text{total road}\right) \times 100 \tag{9}$$

4   Conclusion

In a real transport network, the shortest or optimal route(s) between two locations may not be suitable for all types of vehicles. Further, the route or path may have several characteristics, namely, *path length, path width, path roughness/texture* etc. This paper proposes a methodology for determination of *suitable* route(s)/path(s) between two geographic locations, using fuzzy logic. The *suitability* of the path is calculated taking into consideration the *path length, path quality* (texture, width etc) and the *vehicle type*. The fuzzy reasoning is used to calculate the *suitability* of each path in the path set. The efficacy of the proposed approach has also been demonstrated with help of a case study. Other dynamic factors like, *traffic congestion, road on repair* factors are not considered in this work. The proposed methodology illustrates a technique to determine suitable paths which are more realistic than other shortest or simplest path determination methods where the crisp result is returned. The proposed approach can be employed to classify the *suitability* of a path in a realistic manner, like, *more* or *less* suitable etc. In future, the dymanic factors, like, *traffic congesion* etc, will be considered.

References

1. Haque, M., Raunak, M.S., Rahim, M., Delwar, T., Haque, A.: Artificial intelligence approach of optimal route selection in telematics. In: Proceedings of the 3rd International Conference on Electrical and Computer Engineering, pp. 210–214 (2004)
2. Thirumalaivasan, D., Guruswamy, V.: Optimal route analysis using gis. In: 5th annual international conference and exhibition in the field of Geographic Information Sciences, pp. 312–315 (2002)
3. Duckham, M., Kulik, L.: Simplest paths: automated route selection for navigation. In: Kuhn, W., Worboys, M.F., Timpf, S. (eds.) COSIT 2003. LNCS, vol. 2825, pp. 169–185. Springer, Heidelberg (2003)
4. Zhimin, A.W., Xianfeng, B.L.: The model and algorithm for finding the optimal route in a dynamic road network. In: Proceedings of Intelligent Transportation Systems, vol. 2, pp. 1495–1498 (2003)
5. Alivand, M., Alesheikh, A., Malek, M.: New method for finding optimal path in dynamic networks. World Applied Sciences Journal 3, 25–33 (2008)
6. Ronga, Q., Min, W., QingYun, C.Z.: Combining algorithm with knowledge for way-finding 37, 937–940 (2008)
7. Hochmair, H.H.: Optimal route selection with route planners: Results of a desktop usability study. In: North American Fuzzy Information Processing Society, pp. 312–315 (2007)
8. Jang, J., Sun, C., Mizutani, E.: Neuro-fuzzy and Soft Computing. Pretice Hall, Upper Saddle River (1997)
9. Min, W., Hehai, W., Qingyun, D.: A heuristic and hierarchical wayfinding algorithm based on the knowledge of road network 31, 360–363 (2006)
10. Sharma, J.: Heterogeneous Spatial Reasoning in Geographic Information Systems. PhD thesis, Department of Spatial Information Science and Engineering, University of Maine (1996)
11. Yang, H., Cobb, M., Ali, D., Rahimi, S., Petry, F., Shaw, K.: Fuzzy spatial querying with inexact inference. In: Proceedings of the 15th ACM International Symposium on Geographic Information Systems, pp. 377–382. IEEE Press, Los Alamitos (2002)
12. Clark, T., Larson, J.M., Mordeson, J.N., Potter, J.D., Wierman, M.J.: Fuzzy Set Theory. In: Shapiro, E. (ed.) ICLP 1986. LNCS, vol. 225, pp. 29–63. Springer, Heidelberg (1986)

Assessing Macroseismic Data Reliability through Rough Set Theory: The Case of Rapolla (Basilicata, Southern Italy)

Fabrizio Gizzi[1], Nicola Masini[1], Maria Rosaria Potenza[1], Cinzia Zotta[1], Lucia Tilio[2], Maria Danese[2], and Beniamino Murgante[2]

[1] Archaeological and monumental heritage institute, National Research Council, C/da S. Loia Zona industriale, 85050, Tito Scalo (PZ), Italy
{f.gizzi,n.masini,m.potenza,c.zotta}@ibam.cnr.it
[2] Laboratory of Urban and Territorial Systems, University of Basilicata, Via dell'Ateneo Lucano 10, 85100, Potenza, Italy
firstname.surname@unibas.it

Abstract. This paper deals with the analysis of the reliability of information concerning damages caused to buildings by earthquakes.

This research was started after analyzing a huge amount of written sources drawn up after 1930 Irpinia (southern Italy) earthquake. The analysis led to delineate damage 'scenarios', useful in trying to mitigate seismic risk for most affected towns.

Once analyzed the effects induced by the quake, it was suitable to assess the reliability of the retrieved information. To face up this subject the town of Rapolla (PZ, Basilicata, southern Italy) was chosen as test bed. The whole data set, concerning administrative-technical aspects of 1930 earthquake, was analyzed through Rough Set Approach, a non-parametric statistic methodology.

Considering that the town of Rapolla represents a piece of the entire *corpus* of information available for 1930 earthquake, this paper shows preliminary insights about the subject.

Keywords: Rough Set Theory, earthquake, damage pattern, macroseismic data.

1 Introduction

Natural events such as earthquakes, floods, and landslides occur all over the world, and have the potential to become deadly disasters, or economically destructive events.

Strategies aimed to reduce the impact of natural events require a better knowledge of vulnerable areas to allow prevention development and prediction actions to reduce financial, structural and human losses in future events. By using historical data (manuscripts, iconographic sources, newspapers, and scientific records), we can increase our knowledge about specific aspects of natural phenomena.

For example, analysing the effects of past earthquakes on towns, using high spatial resolution, helps to better identify most seismically 'vulnerable' urban areas [1]. The damage caused by past earthquakes is the result of a natural test to which the building-soil system (especially in the historical centre) was subjected.

D. Taniar et al. (Eds.): ICCSA 2010, Part I, LNCS 6016, pp. 320–330, 2010.
© Springer-Verlag Berlin Heidelberg 2010

In this way, it is possible to gather geological and anthropological features of the site (seismic amplification, landslides, geo-technical failure of soils, and/or building vulnerability) influencing the severity of damage in some areas. This will help to setup proper strategies aimed to assess and to reduce seismic risk (e.g. areas with higher historical damage will be considered as a priority to perform surveys and investigations).

However, a proper analysis of past natural events requires reliable historical records.

Starting from these preliminary remarks, a research on damage caused by 23 July 1930 earthquake in towns of Basilicata, a southern Italian region in a seismic-prone area, began. For this event a rich primary documentation (thousands of dossiers)is available, useful to delineate building-by-building damage pattern in each town [2], [3]. The analysis and the GIS implementation of the whole corpus of information is still ongoing.

Data contain information about damage, post-seismic repairing procedures with building techniques description of the housing units and technical-economic-administrative data. The availability of different kinds of data allows to perform cross-correlated analysis to evaluate information reliability.

This aspect was tackled by Rough Set Theory, a non-parametric statistic methodology. A preliminary case study, concerning macroseismic data analysed for the town of Rapolla, is proposed here. Further investigation, based on the database of all Basilicata towns damaged by 1930 earthquake, will allow to refine the consideration about information reliability.

2 Methodology

Rough set theory allows to tackle imprecise, vague and uncertain knowledge [4], classifying elements in indiscernible way, using the available information. The central concept in rough set theory is the indiscernibility relation. As an example, the most famous one, if we consider two persons showing the same symptoms, we will associate them to the same diagnosis, and they will be considered as a cluster of indiscernible elements, concerning the only available information (that is information about symptoms) [5].

Formally, these two persons are elements of a set U, that we call Universe, and that is finite and not empty, $U = \{x_1, ..., x_m\}$, and symptoms are elements of a set A, that is finite and not empty; for each symptom (temperature, or cough, etc.), that is $\forall a \in A$, there is a set of values V_a, called domain of A, $\exists f_a : U \to V_a$. U and A are an Informative System: $IS = \{U, A\}$. When a decision attribute d influences classification, then it can be defined a Decision System $DS = \{U, A \cup d\}$.

If we consider a subset of A, $B \subset A$, and two elements of U, x_i ed x_j, $x_i, x_j \in U$, we can define an indiscernibility relation, Ind(B) on U, and we can say that x_i and x_j are indiscernible if $b(x_i) = b(x_j), \forall b \subset B$. Then, Ind(B) is an equivalence relation and each element of U belonging to Ind(B) can be denoted as $[x_i]_{Ind(B)}$. Any set of all indiscernible elements is called elementary set, and it represents the littlest block of knowledge about data.

A problem that typically has to be faced is the need to define membership of equivalence classes to a defined set $X \subset U$: considering available information, it can result that some equivalence classes surely belong to X, some others do not surely belong, but some others potentially belong to X. Figure 1 shows this situation:

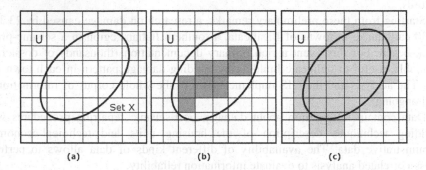

Fig. 1. Lower and Upper approximation

In (b) the simplest situation is represented: equivalence classes are included into X, so that they surely belong to X; the union of all equivalence classes for which this condition is verified is called lower approximation, and indicated as $\underline{BX}$. Formally, lower approximation is defined as follows: $\underline{BX} = \{x_i \in U: [x_i]_{Ind(B)} \subset X\}$. In (c) the other situation is represented: equivalence classes are not completely included into X, nor they are completely outside. The intersection of these equivalence classes with X is not empty; the union of all equivalence classes for which this condition is verified is called upper approximation, and indicated as BX. Formally, lower approximation is defined as follows: $BX = \{x_i \in U: [x_i]_{Ind(B)} \cap X \neq 0\}$.

The difference between upper and lower approximation is the Boundary Region of X. When a boundary region exists – i.e. when $BX - \underline{BX} \neq 0$ – then X is a Rough Set.

In particular, X can be further classified depending on lower and upper approximation characteristics [6], as summarized in table 1.

Table 1. Classification of Set X depending on Lower and Upper Approximation

Classification		Conditions		
X "*roughly definable*"	on U when	$\underline{BX} \neq 0$	and	$BX \neq U$
X "*externally undefinable*"	on U when	$\underline{BX} \neq 0$	and	$BX = U$
X "*internally undefinable*"	on U when	$\underline{BX} = 0$	and	$BX \neq U$
X "*totally undefinable*"	on U when	$\underline{BX} = 0$	and	$BX = U$

Approximation accuracy depends on the ratio between cardinality of lower and upper approximation:

$$\mu_B(X) = \frac{card(\underline{B}X)}{card(\overline{B}X)} \tag{1}$$

Accuracy is defined so that $0 \leq \mu_B(X) \leq 1$. It is evident that if $\mu_B(X) < 1$, then X is undefinable.

Indiscernibility relation can be useful in identifying dependence between attributes: in fact, if $Ind(A) = Ind(A - a_i)$, then a_i is superfluous, depends on other attributes and his contribute is not relevant for knowledge on IS; then, it can be eliminated without information loss. If $Ind(A) \neq Ind(A - a_i)$, then a_i is necessary and it cannot be eliminated or omitted. The minimal subset of condition attributes discerning all objects discernible by the original information table is called reduct [7]. The Common part of all reducts, i.e. intersection, is the core.

Rough Set Analysis allows to identify patterns and to extract relations, identifying cause-effect relations. Identified patterns are represented through a decisional rule set, where rules are expressed in the "if...then" form. Objects are assigned to a decision class if it satisfies the conditions of an identified rule; rule strength is determined by number of objects satisfying that condition; at the same time, this number of points also gives a measure of uncertainty into decision class assignment.

3 Study Case

Rough set theory was tested on a macroseismic data set concerning the effects of 1930 Irpinia earthquake (Me=6.7) on the historical centre of Rapolla (PZ, Basilicata, southern Italy), which was heavily shaken by this natural event (VIII in Mercalli-Cancani-Sieberg macroseismic scale).

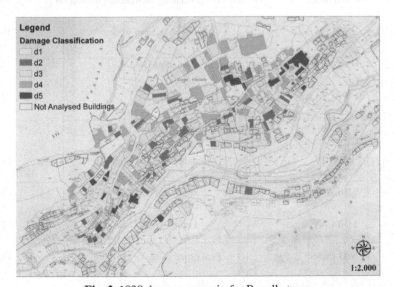

Fig. 2. 1930 damage scenario for Rapolla town

Table 2. Description of database

FIELD CODE	NAME	DESCRIPTION	TYPE
a	DITTA	Name of company that contracted works for reconstruction/renovation	String
b	I_D	Building ID	Double
c	MAPPALE	Information concerning dossier cataloguing	String
d	BUSTA	Information concerning dossier cataloguing	String
e	FASCICOLO	Information concerning dossier cataloguing	String
f	VIA	Information concerning dossier cataloguing	String
g	DISTRUTTA	Destruction condition after earthquake	String
h	CONFINI	Information concerning neighbouring	String
i	EDPUB	Information concerning public property	String
j	EDREL	Information concerning religious usage	String
k	ELABORATI	Information concerning availability of other documents	String
l	SUSSIDIORE	Information concerning subventions revocation	String
m	IMPPER	Estimated cost of works	Double
n	DATAPER	Survey Date	Date
o	DATACOLL	Test Date	Date
p	IMPCONT	Recorded cost of works	Double
q	IMPREV	Financed cost of works	Double
r	INLAV	Starting Work Date	Date
s	FINELAV	Ending Work Date	Date
t	VALIMM	Real estate values of Building	Double

Table 2. (*continued*)

u	REDANNUO	Owner Annual Income	Double
v	TIRANTI	Adoption of tie-beam	String
w	INTCOPERTU	Roof rebuilding	String
x	RISLESIONI	Cracks rebuilding	String
y	SCUCICUCI	Scuci-Cuci (technical procedure for walls rebuilding)	String
z	DEMMUR	Walls demolition	String
aa	DEMVOLTE	Vaults demolition	String
ab	DEMSOLAI	Floors demolition	String
ac	NUOVAMUR	New walls	String
ad	NUOVISOLAI	New floors	String
ae	AMMORSATUR	Toothing interventions	String
af	TFM	Shearing stress of masonry (technical procedure for walls rebuilding)	String
ag	DANNO	Damage description	String
ah	DD	Declared Destroyed (if the building was declared not reconstructable)	String
ai	DANNO_EMS	Damage Level according EMS	String
aj	PROBABILE	Other information	String
ak	GROTTOES	Presence of caves under the building	String

A detailed analysis of technical-administrative dossiers compiled by engineers of Civil Defence allowed to build a rich database, where about 730 buildings of Rapolla are described by several kinds of information, summarized in Table 1.

These data were analyzed through a Rough Set Approach, with the aim to verify the dependence of damage level attribution to each building from some socio-economical local dynamics, and to identify patterns, able to create a cross-data control.

Analysis was carried through ROSE (Rough Set Data Explorer)[1] software, and results, in terms of rules, were mapped on GIS. Before data analysis, some considerations have been made concerning data preparation: observing the data table, it has been highlighted that a non-negligible part of buildings shows missing values, and, at the same time, several attributes seem not completely compiled; it has been considered necessary to test analysis on different datasets. Totally, six analyses have been run, and finally the last one has been taken into account for data interpretation.

The zero analysis considered the original data set, without any change. As synthesized in table 2, quality of classification was really small as well as number of elementary sets, and there was only a reduct; this bad result is due to the manipulation that ROSE executes during pre-processing, in order to manage missing values, and carried out using the most frequent value for each attribute. Even if in some cases this kind of approximation produces good results, in this one it was not correct. In fact, it has to be considered that data concern historical information about reconstruction, with economic values, dates of works, etc., and such values normally are different for each building, with no statistical relation.

This observation led to modify the original dataset, and to run the analysis number 1, where missing values have been replaced by 0. As expected, quality of classification, number of atoms, number of reducts increased.

In order to obtain a better result, other intermediate analyses have been run, considering other changes in dataset, in number of attributes included into the analysis, in number of buildings, in decisional variables and so on. Attempts stopped at the sixth data configuration, which at present can be considered satisfying.

Table 3. Synthetic results of analysis

	Quality of classification	# of Atoms	# of Reducts	# of attributes in Core
Analysis 0	0,2665	189	1	17
Analysis 1	0,3887	287	8	9
Analysis 2	0,3874	281	12	4
Analysis 3	0,7084	264	12	8
Analysis 4	0,7411	276	1	9
Analysis 5	0,7057	265	2	8

Induced rules (produced by ROSE software) have been mapped on GIS and grouped according to damage classification. ROSE identified 97 rules, 88 of which were considered exact and 8 approximate.

---

[1] ROSE [8] is a modular software system implementing basic elements of rough set theory and rule discovery techniques, developed at the Laboratory of Intelligent Decision Support Systems of the Institute of Computing Science in Poznan.

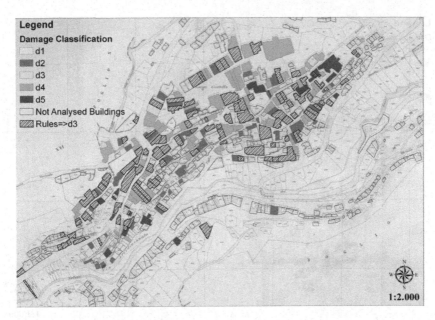

Fig. 3. Mapped rules grouped according to damage classification. Here, rules inducing damage level d3.

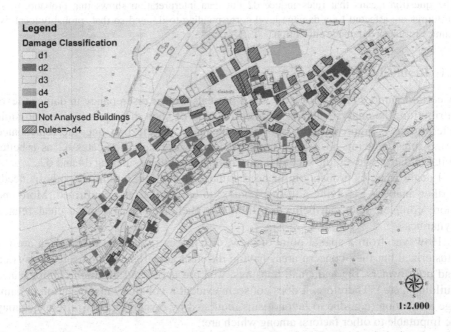

Fig. 4. Mapped rules grouped according to damage classification. Here, rules inducing damage level d4.

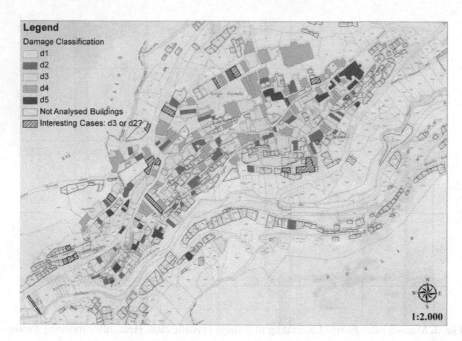

Fig. 5. Some of the rules with clear discrepancy in damage level attribution. Here, d2 or d3? The question means that rules induce d2 but data interpretation shows that probably those buildings are affected by a damage level corresponding to d3, and so that probably local dynamics influenced damage attribution.

3.1 Results Interpretation

A certain number (25/88) of exact rules presents a clear discrepancy in damage level attribution: the analysis allows the identification of such discrepancy and a possible interpretation. Figure 5 and 6 show two examples: in the first one, are represented some rules inducing d3, whose interpretation, nevertheless, indicates d2 as a better suitable damage level; the second one is analogous, but considering d4 and d2.

Local dynamics probably influenced damage attribution, but this hypothesis needs further analyses involving a larger context to be verified and confirmed. More and more complete data can better highlight this phenomenon, and make clear related dynamics.

However, from a spatial point of view, differences in damage distribution are not clusterized but they concern areas having different social and building features (rich and poor owners, big and small housings, well preserved and lacking in maintenance buildings, etc.). Therefore, it does not seem evident a voluntary manipulation in damage attribution (e.g. due to favouritisms requested by owners), rather differences may be imputable to other factors, among which are:

1. Rough surveys of damage conditions (so that damage attribution was limited only to a survey on the outside or to some rooms);

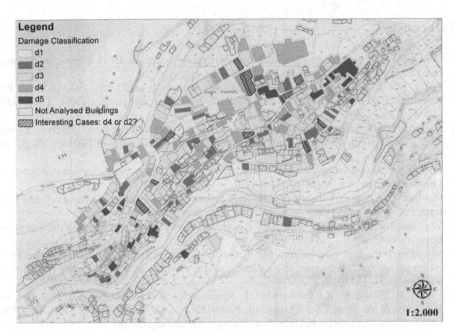

Fig. 6. Some of the rules with clear discrepancy in damage level attribution. Here, d4 or d2? The question means that rules induce d4 but data interpretation shows that probably those buildings are affected by a damage level corresponding to d2, and so that probably local dynamics influenced damage attribution.

2. Different vocational training of engineers entrusted to survey affected housings;
3. Improvements and/or works extensions not connected to seismic event included in damage description in first phases of post-seismic event;
4. Insufficient descriptive data.

4 Discussion and Future Development

The paper discusses about the use of Rough Set Approach to evaluate information reliability concerning damages caused by earthquakes.

Preliminary results have allowed to show some insights about the assessment of the information. However, for a more robust interpretation it is compulsory to have as large as possible data sets.

Therefore, the next step will be to address all the efforts to complete the implementation of a GIS of the retrieved information for the eight towns of Basilicata more damaged by 1930 earthquake.

Analyses will be run also using other intelligent methods, such as Visual Analytics, multiform Bivariate Matrix, Self-Organising Map (SOM) and Parallel Coordinates Plot (PCP), in order to compare RSA results.

References

1. Gizzi, F.T.: To what degree can historical seismicity records assist in seismic microzonation? Engineering Geology 87, 1–12 (2006)
2. Gizzi, F.T., Masini, N.: Damage scenario of the earthquake on 23 July 1930 in Melfi: the contribution of the technical documentation. Annals of Geophysics 47(5), 1641–1665 (2004)
3. Gizzi, F.T., Masini, N.: Historical damage pattern and differential seismic effects in a town with ground cavities: A case study from Southern Italy. Engineering Geology 88, 41–58 (2006)
4. Pawlak, Z.: Rough set approach to knowledge-based decision support. European Journal of Operational Research 99, 48–57 (1997)
5. Pawlak, Z.: Rough set theory and its applications to data analysis. Cybernetics and systems 29(7), 661–688 (1998)
6. Walczak, B., Massart, D.L.: Tutorial - Rough sets theory. Chemometrics and intelligent laboratory systems 47, 1–16 (1999)
7. Soetanto, D.P., Van Geenhuizen, M.: Technology incubators and knowledge networks: a rough set approach in comparative project analysis. Environment and Planning B: Planning and Design 34, 1011–1029 (2007)
8. Predki, B., Slowinski, R., Stefanowski, J., Susmaga, R., Wilk, S.: ROSE – Software Implementation of the Rough Set Theory. In: Polkowski, L., Skowron, A. (eds.) RSCTC 1998. LNCS (LNAI), vol. 1424, pp. 605–608. Springer, Heidelberg (1998)

Utilization of LiDAR and IKONOS Satellite Data for Security Hotspot Analysis Based on Realism of 3D City Model

Mazlan Hashim, Maged Marghany,
Mohd Rizaludin Mahmud, and Mohd Hafiz Anuar

Institute of Geospatial Science & Technology (INSTEG)
Universiti Teknologi Malaysia, 81310 UTM Skudai, Malaysia
mazlanhashim@utm.my

Abstract. This paper highlights the study on realism of 3D city urban model for security hotspot analysis using remote sensing data and spatial analysis approach. New advanced remote sensing data, namely LiDAR (Light Detection and Ranging) and IKONOS satellite data were used to obtain the spatial information of the urban features which used to simulate the 3D urban city model. This study examines the threats from the snipers using multi-criteria algorithm, emphasizing on viewshed and distance analysis on 3D urban city model of Dataran Merdeka, Kuala Lumpur, Malaysia, one of the most frequently selected venue for many public events. The main output of the study is the identification of potential spots, best to enclave prospective snipers given the effective shooting ranges and clear viewshed to the target of interest. Rainfall effects, a common environmental factor that hinders clarity of snipers viewshed in tropical cities has also been considered in the identification of these potential risky spots. The identified risk spots were later confirmed fully with in-situ verifications, hence demonstrated the utility of such technique for applications in the security hotspot analysis.

Keywords: Security Hotspot, Remote Sensing, 3D City Model, LiDAR, IKONOS.

1 Introduction

Monitoring public security has been a serious and continuous issues debated worldwide. A great challenge has been faced by scientists to introduce an efficient, simple and yet robust technique from existing technology to the related authorities in assessing security in one area [7], [2], and [8]. In this context, this paper highlights the use of application of geospatial techniques for assessing the security risk of vantage points surrounding area of interest where public events are frequently held. The realism of 3D city model using LiDAR (light detection and ranging) and IKONOS satellite data for security hotspot analysis has been the emphasis in this study. Conventionally, the viewshed analysis is one of the practical approach for view impact assessment [4], [13] as well as shooting view's assessment and it is being widely used in military purposes

D. Taniar et al. (Eds.): ICCSA 2010, Part I, LNCS 6016, pp. 331–345, 2010.
© Springer-Verlag Berlin Heidelberg 2010

[17]. Besides, types of firearm also play an important role to determine the possibility of shooting locations because different types of weapons possess specific shooting effective range, ballistic and viewing capabilities. Other external effect such as rainfall is considered to have significant effect towards the shooting effective range limits [7], [8]. Utilization of sniping quality assessment, especially after viewshed and distance analysis is carried out, is believed to be an effective approach to determine the possible area of assault [15]. However, this conventional method of security analysis mentioned above which is based on the manual observation and summation of the information gathered from various sources is less effective and not able to simulate the actual environment condition. On the hand, the fine spatial resolution 3D building model generated from appropriate stereoscopic remote sensing or LiDAR data offer new alternative for deriving terrain information. Utilization of these derived terrain information with spatial modeling, thereby, introduces a new perspective on security hotspot location assessment using geospatial technology applications. More accurate security analysis now can be carried out based on 3-dimensional environment, taking into consideration the X,Y plane coordinates and also the vertical height components of the area of interests. The availability of fine spatial resolution of remote sensing data (acquired both either from airborne and satellite data) could provide information as smallest as sub-meter on the ground and the utility of airborne laser sensing systems to provide height information with accuracy less than 15cm, will eventually lead to the development of more accurate urban city model.

There are 3 ways commonly used to represent geospatial information of the real world which is either in one dimension, two dimensions or three dimensions [9]. The constructions of one and two dimensions to represent the real world are not a big problem at all. However it is quite problematic when it comes to three dimensions because even though, there are a lot of methods been developed, none of it is truly capable to produce a very precise, robust and realistic representation of the real world. In fact the realism of 3D urban city model using geospatial data especially with the recent very fine resolution sensor such as LiDAR, is still considered not matured. There are several approaches that could be used to construct 3D object or features of the real world which are: (i) on-screen digitizing of stereo imagery [3];, (ii) conventional in-situ detailed topographic survey and visualization of surveyed features with the use of commercially available off the shelf software (COTs) such as in [18]; and (iii) generation 3D objects from pre-processed LiDAR data [19], [20]. The first two approaches are very costly in term of requirement of skill operators in either data acquisition and the reconstruction of the objects apart from time consuming in extracting the meticulous urban features. The recent automation of respective systems often used in first two approaches still hinders the operation to operate in fully automatic-mode as interventions of operators are still heavy needed in minimizing ambiguities in model constructed as irregular shape features are plentiful in urban and such objects are cannot perfectly modeled by mathematical geometries. In such a case, the LiDAR footprints or cloud points is the best rapid technique of data capture especially for the vertical variations. However, the clear break lines for features boundaries are still ambigious but can be overcome when overlaid on a fine-resolution image of the corresponding area. Subsequently this study examine the realism of 3D urban city using LiDAR and IKONOS data, which later served as the base of the main aim of this paper to demonstrate a method of utilizing 3D city urban model to assess possible shooting location for security hotspots detection. Fine resolution satellite remote sensing data namely IKONOS and LiDAR acquired using airborne laser system are used to generate the 3D urban city model together with other ancillary data. Multiple criteria analysis is employed to determine the potential shooting locations by ranking the risk. The criteria considered in this study are viewshed, distance, sniping quality, and rainfall effects. Possible shooting locations are then ranked and map in 2D and 3D viewing GIS environment. As such this 3D visualization is very useful in all events emergency mitigation such during riots, civil unrest or even during fire breakouts within high rise buildings in the city. In addition, the emergency exits or evacuation could more effectively plan.

2 Methodology

2.1 Study Area

The selected area for this pilot study is the Dataran Merdeka in Kuala Lumpur, Malaysia (Fig. 1). The focus area for the security analysis is an area within 2 km radius from the centre of the Dataran Merdeka. In fact, the Dataran Merdeka always has frequent usage for various events such as venue for annual Malaysia independent's day and few other national-level celebrations that are involving many high-ranking people. Further, the Dataran Merdeka is surrounded by many high raise buildings which could be a possible place for any assault using long range weapons. In addition, those buildings have been identified to have direct visibility access to the Dataran Merdeka which are considered as the main threat to security aspects. Therefore, the risk of high potential of assaults probability and strategic escape plan are easy. In fact, this place is surrounded by good transportation networks and multi-level roads.

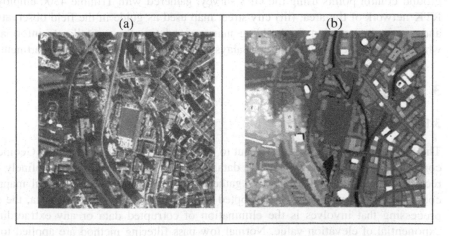

Fig. 1. Study Area: (a) Merdeka Square located in Kuala Lumpur, Malaysia; (b) LiDAR data of the area

2.2 Remote Sensing and Ancillary Data

2.2.1 IKONOS Satellite Data

The 4m spatial resolution IKONOS satellite data in pan-sharpened format are used in the study, chosen due to the high resolution pixel which fits the accuracy of the whole project. The scale for the whole database used in this project is generated at scale of 1:5000; enable the resolution of 4m IKONOS image fits perfectly when combined with other data at the same scale. The image is also used for visualization of the virtual world background.

2.2.2 LiDAR Data

The LiDAR data were obtained by using Leica AL50 LiDAR scanner system. The LiDAR data have accuracy (on hard surfaces) of 30cm at least and point sampling density is sufficient to provide an average post spacing of 1.2 m in the raw DSM. It was provided in raw text format. The LiDAR parameters used for this project are as follows:

- Aircraft speed: 70m//s
- Flying height: 1500 m above ground level
- Scanner field of view (half angle): +16°
- Scan frequency: 14 Hz
- Swath width: 863 m (600 m with a 30% sidelap)
- Pulse repetition rate: 10 kHz
- Sampling density: average 2.4 m

2.2.3 Ancillary Data

The ancillary data of corresponding area used are: (i) the in-situ observation of the texture of the building which have been captured using a non-metric camera,(ii) the ground control points using the GPS survey, gathered with Trimble 4800 employing RTK network of the area; (iii) city street map used as guide in the field observations and source information for building names; and (iv) the rainfall rate information which had been acquired from the Malaysian Meteorological Services Department.

3 Data Processing

3.1 Data Preprocessing

The data preprocessing are carried out to both IKONOS and LiDAR data. Geometric correction is performed to IKONOS data, where the image acquired are refinely corrected using ground control points gathered from GPS survey. The local mapping coordinate system of the city is adopted in this context. For LIDAR data, the preprocessing that involves is the elimination of corrupted data or any extraordinary exponential of elevation value. Normal low pass filtering method are applied to the image for eliminating the corrupted data while extraordinary exponential of elevation value are made by adjusting it manually. First the data are converted to ASCII data, and then the identified exponential elevation values are then altered. Then field verification using GPS will be made to confirm the value where applicable. The geometry of LiDAR data is already in corresponding area of interest as the LIDAR acquisition uses the navigation system tied to reference system based on the local mapping coordinate system. The software used in the data processing are: Trimble Geomatics for reduction of observation of GPS observations; Sketchup 5 for creation of building blocks; Erdas Imagine for digital image analysis and display of end outputs; ArcGIS 9.2 spatial analysis where the multicriteria analysis for security hotspot is performed; and Adobe Photoshop CS for rendering textures of building captured with digital camera shots.

3.2 3D City Urban Model Development and Sniping Hotspot Quality Analysis

The 3D city urban model is developed through the integration of LiDAR, IKONOS data and ancillary data. The geo-rectified IKONOS image were used as a base map for the urban model, while the height information retrieved from the LiDAR is integrated with the base map to build the 3D urban model. The heights of each building were taken from LiDAR while the boundaries of the building were made extracted from IKONOS data. Field work picture were also used as a reference to construct and validate the buildings block created. Fig 2 illustrates the methodology employed in the creation of 3D urban and city block. The crucial steps of the data processing is in the within the generation of 3D terrain reality or surface, and the creation of 3D building blocks within the city. The terrain surface is generated with virtual GIS of the Erdas Imagine from the merged of geometry corrected LiDAR data and IKONOS image, while building blocks is built using Sketch5 software. The texture of buildings is also draped on the building blocks using Sketch5 software at this processing stage. Finally the merging of the surface image generated from fused LiDAR and IKONOS image with the 3D building blocks created fully 3D urban city block.

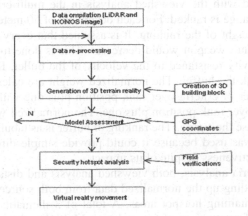

Fig. 2. Flowchart of the methodology

The constructed 3D urban city model were then used as a base for the security hot-spots analysis, where it is performed based on multiple criteria consideration using results obtained from: (i) viewshed analysis; (ii) distance; (iii) types of firearm; (iv) sniping quality assessment ratio; and (v) rainfall rate. The possible sniping location is being analyzed and ranked accordingly from low risk to high risk possible locations. The viewshed and distance analysis are carried out to each building and areas which are based on the VIP places on the centre of the Dataran Merdeka. Before doing the viewshed and distance analyses, the targeted area must be determined (which is the place where most likely the VIPs would be at). The parameters that are taken into account are the offset of target, azimuth and also the vertical angle. Since the target is most likely to be a person, so a minimum 1 meter offset from ground are set to the target point. For the azimuth, the whole 360° angle is considered, whilst the vertical angle is set to full maximum angle 90°. The horizon with 0° is set as the base angle. So the viewshed includes the whole 360° with normal human viewing. Some assumptions were also made to this analysis in order to relate it with logic and real situation. The target point is assumed stationary, so only one target point is needed. Another assumption made is that the target and the assassin are both having direct visibility with each other. Due to this, the angle for viewshed is set to 90° from 0° or horizon. For the viewshed analysis, the output would be in 2D. Therefore, at the end the output it was combined with distance analysis result using multi-criteria analysis. The method used to combine the data is rank sum method. In order to do so, the viewshed layer needed to be rank up. Since there is no significant variation with angle changes, all the viewshed analyses were ranked as 10 (optimum). By doing so, we can emphasize the vantage point.

Distance analysis was made in order to aid and differentiate the analysis of security hotspot with different assault weapon. The output of distance analysis is the potential capability of each selected assault weapon. Each of the firearm effective range is included in distance analysis. Three types of weapon had been identified in this study are: Magnum pistol, M16A2 rifle and Dragunav sniper rifle. These weapons had the effective range of 200m, 460m and 800m respectively. Buffer with regards to the effective range are made in order to establish this analysis. In order to able this analysis output combined with the viewshed analysis in the multi-criteria analysis, each buffer or effective range is ranked. For each decrement of 50 meter from target would also decrease the weight of the ranking. It is assumed that every 50 meter, the effect of each type of assault weapon would decreases. This is done to compensate the effects of air and gravity resistance to the velocity of the bullet. Rank sum method is used in order to rank the buffer. The normalized weight are calculated by diving the difference of number of criteria over rank position plus one with total difference of number of criteria over rank position plus one. The normalized weight is then multiply by 100 to increase the figure. The ranking of buffer is as tabulated in Table 1. The rank sum method was used because it could provide simple direct measurement of each weapon's effectiveness despite of its impact.

In the multi-criteria analysis, both viewshed analysis and distance analysis output are combined by adding up the normalized data from both source; thereby producing a thematic map containing hotspot areas. A total of 3 thematic maps are produced according to type of weapons used for analysis. Multiple criteria analysis is applied taking into account of all the listed factors to highlight all possible security hotspot in the surrounding areas, all generated based on sum rank method [15], given in equation (1). The ranking system is used to portray the level of high risks probability for easy understanding for user.

$$W = \frac{n - r_j + 1}{\sum(n - r_k + 1)} \tag{1}$$

where,

W is the normalized weight for the *jth* criterion;
n are numbers of criteria under consideration; and
r_j, r_k are rank positions of the criterion $k = 1,2,...,n$.

The sniping quality assessment ratio is carried out by modifying the algorithm introduced by Sterren [15] which took into consideration of the blind spot and width of the buildings. The sniping spot quality assessment was made especially to refine the sniper rifle result. With this, each sniping spot can be categorized by its quality. Recent study by Chen [1], show that weight-based multi-criteria analysis offers practical approach in GIS applications.

Table 1. The ranking, weight and normalized weight used in the rank sum method

Distance (meter)	Direct ranking	Weight	Normalized Weight	Normalized weight to 100
50	1	16	0.117647	12
100	2	15	0.110294	11
150	3	14	0.102941	10
200	4	13	0.095588	10
250	5	12	0.088235	9
300	6	11	0.080882	8
350	7	10	0.073529	7
400	8	9	0.066176	7
450	9	8	0.058824	6
500	10	7	0.051471	5
550	11	6	0.044118	4
600	12	5	0.036765	4
650	13	4	0.029412	3
700	14	3	0.022059	2
750	15	2	0.014706	1
800	16	1	0.007353	1
		136	1	100

The quality of each sniping spot are calculated using sniping spot quality; adopting 180° spot-facing while the other 180° as total blind spot. The sniping spot quality's formula is given by dividing the angle of the spot-facing the object with 180°. The categorization of each spot is based on the sniping spot quality. Straight ranking is used for ranking the ratio, as shown in Table 2, where x represent angle at vantage point of the identified risk spot.

Table 2. The categorization of weight according to ratio of degree of spot facing

Ratio (degree/180)	Weight
below 0.25	1
$0.25 < x < 0.5$	2
$0.5 < x < 0.75$	3
$0.75 < x < 1$	4

In order to see the effect of this refinement, the ratio is then multiplied by the score of multi-criteria for each building. This is made to refine the building's hotspot. A building's hotspot should not just be made based on the viewshed and distance analysis only, but it should also include this sniping spot quality because the width of a building itself plays a great role in the hotspot quality. The rainfall effect towards the visibility is relatively proportional, where the effective range of each firearm would be decreased based on three rain types:(i) normal heavy rain (401-700mm); (ii) medium rain (100-400mm); and (iii) light rain or drizzle (less than 100mm). Extreme heavy rainfalls are not considered as all events are cancelled in such a situation. Normal viewing without any interruption of rainfall could give a view up to 800m. However this would decrease with the effect of rainfall. In this study the visibility in rainy condition is taken from the field survey. For normal heavy rain the visibility decrease to 150meter. Medium rain would cause the visibility to decrease to 300m. For drizzle or light rain, the visibility could decrease to 500m only. So each situation of rain is applied to each weapon, minus the effective range of each weapon with the rainfall visibility. In this study it is assumed that the event would go on even if it raining.

4   Results and Discussion

The main purpose of the construction of the building and object in the urban area in 3D is to simulate the situation of hotspot area for security purposes. Even if surveying the vantage point at field, one might not able to get a good analysis for determining the security level hotspot. In order to improve the simulation, the 3 dimensional world or virtual city should be made as real as possible by taking into consideration the orientation and the texture of the building. In order to do so, the building are made according to scale 1:1000 and placed in a geometrically corrected based image. The 3D virtual city model constructed with merged LiDAR and IKONOS image is illustrated in Fig 3. Perfectly textures of buildings were prepared only for all the identified prospective security hotspots for which these hotspots could be verified independently. The texture is captured using camera digital, edited before embedded on to the 3D model. The draped textures are realistic, in fact results when verified at insitu basis are comparable to other related studies on using texture for building façade for building blocks using similar approaches, such in [14, 6, 11].

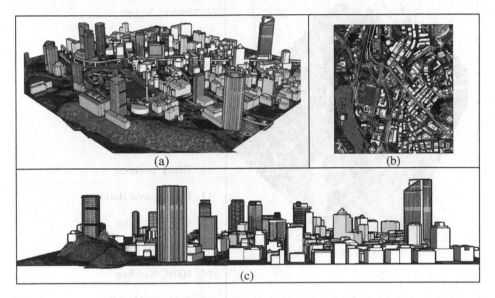

Fig. 3. Constructed virtual 3D city of Kuala Lumpur: (a) isometric view, (b) the top view, and (c) side view

An exploratory analysis of spatial parameters towards building hotspot security under three firearms condition has produced effective results of highlighting possible high risks location of shooting activities. There were 18 possible locations which were identified as high risks for assault positions, taking into consideration of all three types of weapons. Fig.4 shows the results of multiple criteria analysis of the probable security hotspots, vantage points identified as risky spots. Table 3 tabulates the corresponding quantitative scores of the profiling percentage.

Based on the rainfall effect analysis, heavy rain conditions have the potential to reduce the effective shooting range for all the weapons especially the long range sniper rifle. The medium rain, however, only strongly effect the long and medium range weapons, and yield no significant effect towards short range firearms. Based on the information in Table 3, long range sniper weapons are sensitive to all rain condition followed by medium range weapons and short range weapons. In addition, the rainfall condition has resulting to significant effects towards the possible locations of shooting activities for all types of weapons. Table 4 summarizes the rainfall effects towards multiple firearms. Meanwhile, Fig. 5 shows the rate of effects of rainfall to the visibility from the vantage points to the target. Study of Garg and Nayar [12] confirmed with our analysis on vision and rain effects within average high-resolution video data

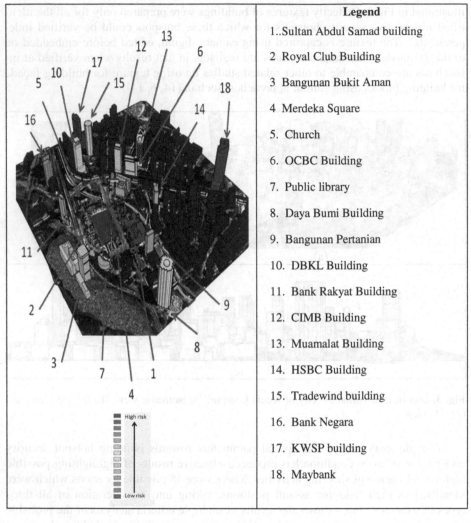

	Legend
	1..Sultan Abdul Samad building
	2 Royal Club Building
	3 Bangunan Bukit Aman
	4 Merdeka Square
	5. Church
	6. OCBC Building
	7. Public library
	8. Daya Bumi Building
	9. Bangunan Pertanian
	10. DBKL Building
	11. Bank Rakyat Building
	12. CIMB Building
	13. Muamalat Building
	14. HSBC Building
	15. Tradewind building
	16. Bank Negara
	17. KWSP building
	18. Maybank

Fig. 4. Multiple criteria analysis results of possible location of potential risk security hotspots visualized in 3D isometric view

captures. Based on the assumption weapon range finders are within these same specifications, it is likely that rainfall effects to visibility are significant and within the range as tabulated in Table 4.

Data processing, particularly the integration of IKONOS and LiDAR data is the most crucial step in producing the 3D urban model. Given the voluminous of the cloud points of the LiDAR data, sampling of these points at regular intervals throughout the area of interest have been the key factor producing 3D city with appropriate break lines for the buildings. We generated 30cm grid of LiDAR points in this study. Conforming LiDAR points to the required geometry of the area is somehow require very high accuracy control points other than very sensitive to its distribution. For the

Table 3. Result of multi-criteria analysis, sniping spot quality assessment and also the percentage of vertical profiling from the identified building to the target. Please refer Fig 4 for locations of buildings.

	Building name	Degree	Ratio	MCA	Total Score	Profiling Percentage
1	Sultan Abdul Samad building	110	0.611	86	52.55	100.00
2	Royal Club Building	63	0.35	79	27.65	86.84
3	Bangunan Bukit Aman	44	0.244	65	15.86	50.20
4	Merdeka Square	30	0.167	79	13.19	100.00
5	Church	17	0.094	72	6.77	29.17
6	OCBC Building	14	0.077	65	5.01	7.69
7	Public library	12	0.067	72	4.82	38.00
8	Daya Bumi Building	12	0.067	58	3.89	68.00
9	Bangunan Pertanian	9	0.05	72	3.60	56.25
10	DBKL Building	10	0.055	58	3.19	70.37
11	Bank Rakyat Building	8	0.044	72	3.17	58.89
12	CIMB Building	7	0.039	65	2.54	13.68
13	Muamalat Building	7	0.039	58	2.26	35.71
14	HSBC Building	4	0.022	72	1.58	29.41
15	Tradewind building	7	0.039	30	1.17	62.96
16	Bank Negara	5	0.027	23	0.62	66.67
17	KWSP building	3	0.017	16	0.27	43.47
18	Maybank	3	0.017	9	0.15	4.65

horizontal accuracy, the root mean square error (RMSE) of 30 checkpoints distributed throughout the generated city block was computed. The RMSE was computed based on common statistical measure as given by equation (2). The RMSE obtained for both x and y coordinates were ± 1.129 and ± 1.288, respectively; and the resultant horizontal accuracy is ± 1.713m.

$$RMSE = \sqrt{\sum_{i=1}^{n} \frac{(x - x_i)^2}{n}} \tag{2}$$

where

x is the coordinate checkpoints from the image sets;
x_i is the coordinates of checkpoints obtained from GPS surveys; and
n is the total number of sample points used in the analysis (30 points in this study)

In the context of vertical accuracy assessment, the method used was based to percentile test and RMSE analysis as suggested by Maune [10] using a set of 30 checkpoints. First the data were subjected to percentile test were employed to eliminate 5 or 10 percentile of errors for any outstanding errors within the histogram of the given specific dataset. Then, RMSE was used to determine the accuracy of 20 checkpoints within the filtered data set against the known locations obtained from the GPS survey. For the vertical accuracy assessment, it is best first to ensure the LiDAR data pass the percentile test, i.e. distribution of checkpoint errors are within 3σ (standard deviations) before being used for further integration with IKONOS to form the 3D urban city model (see Fig 6). Using a total of 30 checkpoints, the standard deviation of the

Table 4. Summary of the rainfall effects to shooting visibilities

Simulated Weapon	Effective Shooting from Optimum Range in metres / % of reduction			
	Max range with no rain	Light rain (< 100mm)	Medium rain (100 – 400mm)	Heavy rain (> 400mm)
Magnum Pistol	200	200 / 0%	184 / 8%	92 / 54%
M16A Rifle	400	400 / 0%	184 / 56%	44 / 89%
Dragunav Rifle	800	312 / 61%	122 / 86%	24 / 97%

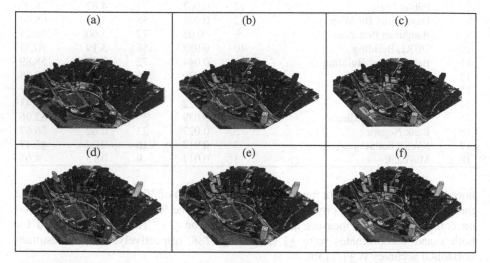

Fig. 5. Rainfall effects to the surrounding possible locations for shooting activities, using: (a) Magnum pistol in heavy rain condition; (b) M16A2 rifle in medium rain condition (c) M16A2 rifle in medium and heavy rain condition; (d) Dragunav rifle in light rain condition; (e) Dragunav rifle in medium rain condition; and (f) Dragunav rifle in heavy rain condition.

checkpoints error is 0.894 and, the as for 3σ the error is 2.608. This indicated that the errors are within the acceptable range, i.e. equivalent to 1.96 x RMSE$_z$. Therefore this confirmed 2.49 meters vertical accuracy at 95 percent confidence level using RMSE procedures with no outliners. Given the LiDAR were integrated with the 4m IKONOS with common resampled grid of 1m, the vertical accuracy achieved is in fact comparable to previous studies generated using airborne aerial photographs [5, 10], and recent studies [16]; [19]; and [6] using LiDAR generated DEM, also reported near similar accuracy range.

In building the virtual city, many problems had arisen and one of the problems is the compatibility between the software with 3 dimensional engines. The market had offered a lot of 3 dimension software but most of it is not as compatible as we can see. For example, we might have software A which is very good in building 3 dimension objects in details but not capable of containing a lot of 3 dimensional objects in it and

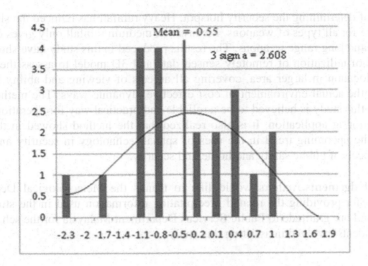

Fig. 6. Histogram of checkpoint errors distribution and mean error

in the other hand we might have software B which doesn't had the capability to build 3 dimensional object as powerful as software A but had a capability to contain a lot of 3 dimensional object at one time. In this situation, one might depend on the application or the motive of the construction of the 3 dimensional objects itself and some tradeoff need to be made. Besides that, not all 3 dimension software can provide full automatic link with the existing projection in order to build a precise simulation. The nearest way to construct the building in the virtual world is by building it based on local mapping coordinate system which are quite similar to the real projection.

Other problem is the compatibility of the 3 dimensional objects built in software with 3 dimension engine with the geographical information system software. It is true that some of the geographical information system had being developed to provide with 3 dimension object but it is not sufficient because some of the software can't support the texture of the real object. The closes it can get is by providing the 3 dimension object with color similar to the texture. It is also observed that some of these geographical information systems, such as Virtual GIS by ERDAS IMAGINE can only support objects that are built with triangulated irregular network (TIN). If not, the 3 dimensional objects will be presented in a wire model; a model which do not have any surface but only line or wire resembling 3 dimensional object built.

5 Conclusion

This paper has demonstrated the use of integrated fine satellite remote sensing with airborne LiDAR data for identifying possible security hotspots in context of snipping from vantage points. The uses of 3D city urban model in the study through the multiple criteria analysis have produced impressive yet effective results. Among all of the buildings, we have identified all possible spots which have high risks of assault probability, and portrayed them in 3D environment which overpowered the conventional method of determining the security hotspot. Heavy rainfall has reduced the shot effective range for all types of weapons. Meanwhile, medium rainfall only gives effects to medium and long range weapons. The results produced in this study have shown huge potential of utilization of remotely sensed data and 3D model to assess the security hotspot location in larger area, covering all aspects of viewing and ability for us to simulate the actual environment in cost effective, dynamic ways. The method introduced in this study is believed to be a reliable and practical way for operational security monitoring application. It is also realized that the method showed in this study will be the upcoming trend in the uses of spatial technology in security analysis in many aspects of public safety and homeland security.

Acknowledgements. Authors would like to thanks the Meteorological Department Malaysia for providing the related precipitation information used in the study. We also extend our gratitude to Public Services Department Malaysia for the scholarships of the students involved in assisting this study.

References

1. Chen, Y., Yu, J., Shahbaz, K., Xevi, E.: A GIS-based sensivity analysis of multi-criteria weights. In: Procs. of 18th World IMACS / MODSIM Congress, Cairns, Australia, July 13-17 (2009), http://mssanz.org.au/modsim09
2. Cucchiara, P., Prati, A., Vezzani, R.: An Intelligent Surveillance System for Dangerous Situation Detection in Home Environments, Dll, University di Mondera e Reggio Emillia, Italy (2004), http://imagelab.ing.unimo.it/pubblicazioni/pubblicazioni/ia2004.pdf
3. Deng, F., Zhang, Z., Zhang, J.: Construct 3D City Model by Multi-Sensor Data. Wuhan University, China (2003)
4. Danese, M., Casas, G.L., Murgante, B.: 3D simulations in environmental impact assessment. In: Gervasi, O., Murgante, B., Laganà, A., Taniar, D., Mun, Y., Gavrilova, M.L. (eds.) ICCSA 2008, Part I. LNCS, vol. 5072, pp. 430–443. Springer, Heidelberg (2008)
5. Frueh, C., Zakhor, A.: Constructing 3D City Models by Merging Aerial and Ground Views. IEEE Computer Graphics and Applications 23(6), 52–61 (2003)
6. Frueh, C., Jain, C., Zakhor, A.: Data Processing Algorithms for Generating Textured 3D Building Facade Meshes from Laser Scans and Camera Images. International Journal of Computer Vision 61(2), 159–184 (2005)
7. Idlahcen, S., Mees, L., Roze, C., Girasole, T., Blaisot, J.B.: Time gate, optical layout, and wavelength effects on ballistic imaging. Journal of the optical society of America A-optics image science and vision 26(9), 1995–2004 (2009)
8. Lilja, D.: Ballistic Effects of Altitude, Temperature and Humidity. Lilja Precision Rifle Barrels Inc., United States of America (2002)
9. Kolbe, T.H., Groger, G.: Towards Unified 3D City Models. Institute of Cartography and Geoinformation, University of Bonn, Germany (2005)
10. Maune, D.F.: Digital Elevation Model Technologies and Applications: The DEM Users Manual. The American Society for Photogrammetry and Remote Sensing, Bethesda, Maryland (2001)
11. Muller, P., Zeng, G., Wonka, P., Van Gool, L.: Image-based procedural modeling of facades. ACM Transactions on Graphics (TOG) 26(3) (July 2007)

12. Garg, K., Nayar, S.K.: Vision and rain. International Journal of Computer Vision 75(1), 3–27 (2007)
13. Ramos, B., Panagopoulos, T.: The Use of GIS in Visual Landscape Management and Visual Impact Assessment of A Quarry in Portugal. In: International Conference on Environmental and Mineral Processing, vol. 1, pp. 73–78. Tzek Republic (2004)
14. Stamos, I., Liu, L., Chen, C., Wolberg, G., Yu, G., Zokai, S.: Integrating Automated Range Registration with Multiview Geometry for the Photorealistic Modeling of Large-Scale Scenes. International Journal of Computer Vision 78(2-3), 237–260 (2008)
15. Sterren, W.V.D.: Terrain Reasoning For 3D Action Games. CGF-AI,Veldhoven, The Netherlands (2001)
16. Sun, W.W., Liu, C., Wu, H.B.: Accuracy evaluation and gross error detection in Digital Elevation Models based on LIDAR data. In: Proceedings of the 8th symposium on spatial accuracy assessment in natural resources and environment sciences, vol. II, pp. 127–133 (2008)
17. Stoltz, V.: DTSS and Visibility Models. Combat Terrain Information System. Presentation Slide (2003), http://www.ctis.com (cited date: July 21, 2007)
18. Takase, Y., Sho, N., Sone, A., Shimiya, A.: Automatic Generation of 3D City Models And Related Applications, CAD Centre Corporation, Japan (2002)
19. Zhou, Q.Y., Neumann, U.: Fast and extensible building modeling from airborne LiDAR data. In: Proceedings of the 16th ACM SIGSPATIAL international conference on Advances in geographic information systems, Irvine, California, November 05-07 (2008)
20. Zhou, G., Song, C., Simmers, J., Cheng, P.: Urban 3D GIS from LiDAR amd digital aerial images. Computers and Geosciences 30, 345–353 (2004)

Towards 3D Tactical Intelligence Assessments for Crime Scene Analysis

Markus Wolff and Hartmut Asche

University of Potsdam, Department of Geography,
Karl-Liebknecht-Strasse 24/25, 14476 Potsdam, Germany
{markus.wolff,gislab}@uni-potsdam.de
http://www.geographie.uni-potsdam.de

Abstract. This paper presents a set of methods and functions to create interactive 3D tactical intelligence assessments by joining analysis of burglary crime scenes and geovisualization issues. For this purpose general spatio-temporal patterns of residential burglary crimes are analysed and subsequently visualised by using three-dimensional geovirtual environments. To allow furthermore for a straightforward portability, an application framework is developed that encapsulates the most important GIS-analysis functions applied. By employing Microsoft's Esri's ArcObjects technology, a standalone GIS-application is programmed that allows even a GIS-untrained user both to conduct initial exploratory data analysis and to prepare the resulting files for 3D-geovisualization. Finally, the application potential of the created 3D tactical intelligence assessments is surveyed by questioning a group of crime mapping and geo-profiling experts.

Keywords: Crime mapping, spatio-temporal analysis, 3D geovisualization, GIS.

1   Introduction

Knowing the spatial distribution of crime scenes is of significant importance for decision makers e.g. engaged in security- or planning agencies. Within the abundant multitude of crime mapping literature diverse methods are described to identify and map spatial hotspots of certain offences. The easiest method to quickly visualise a set of crime scenes is the so-called "pin map" [1]. However, considering the limitations given by the number of offences and the map's scale, those maps are situated only for a first impression of crime scene distributions. To gain deeper insights into crime scene distribution patterns, more sophisticated methods should be applied. Particularly suitable techniques to visualize crime scene densities can be identified within the domain of geostatistics. In this context kernel-density-estimation (KDE) techniques are widely adopted. These techniques transform discrete point distributions of crime scenes to a continuous surface of crime scene densities [2], [3], [4], [5], [6]. A further step of hotspot

D. Taniar et al. (Eds.): ICCSA 2010, Part I, LNCS 6016, pp. 346–360, 2010.

analysis, however, should include statistical tests to verify KDE analysis' reliability. Reference [7], for instance, presents functions for the statistical analysis of crime scene datasets.

While a plethora of studies exist that present geospatial approaches for crime analysis and crime mapping, less studies have been published in the past which deal with the exploration and visualisation of temporal issues in the filed of geospatial crime scene analysis (cf. [8]). Reference [9] gives both an overview of existing studies in the domain of spatio-temporal crime mapping and present further techniques for visualising space and time related issues, as, for instance (map) animations, isosurfaces, comaps and linked plots.

Against this background this contribution presents an approach for crime scene analysis and visualisation by means of coupling spatio-temporal crime scene analysis techniques with 3D geovisualization methods. The approach is characterised by a processing chain that origins in geospatial analysis of residential burglary scene distributions (Section 2.1). Geographic Information Systems (GIS, namely ArcGIS by Esri) are applied for this purpose. Hence identified hotspots are subsequently subject of deeper, primarily temporal, analysis. It is demonstrated how burglary scenes vary over space and time and which buildings are at which time affected by repeat victimisation and which particular modus operandi is being applied (Section 2.2). To allow untrained GIS users as well as GIS experts to explore fundamental spatio-temporal trends in crime scene datasets, a GIS-application is programmed in a parallel step. This application is realised by using Esri's ArcGIS Engine software development framework and is therefore designed as to be a standalone application (.exe).

Subsequent to these analyses, corresponding results have to be communicated to the target audience. Since spatio-temporal analysis can be addressed as multidimensional analysis (with x-, y-features describing the geometry and z-features describing a temporal dimension), results may be represented best possible by using multidimensional visualisation ("Multi-D Vis") techniques. Against this background the paper describes methods for creating interactive four-dimensional map applications. To allow for such sophisticated multidimensional visualisations of spatio-temporal crime scene issues, geovirtual environments (GeoVE, cf. references [10], [11]) can be considered as most suitable. Therefore a last step of the applied processing chain comprises the generation of a three-dimensional GeoVE and the integration of analysis results. This GeoVE is modelled outside the GIS by using specialised 3D visualisation software (namely Autodesk's LandXplorer). As this concept links digital processing and geospatial analysis of crime data with easy-to-comprehend 3D and 4D visualisations respectively, the GIS and VIS (visualisation system) tasks are combined in a specific workflow designed for that purpose. Figure 1 shows a schematic representation of this workflow.

Though hard evidence - that 3D map visualisations generally enable for a faster and more lasting comprehension of geospatial phenomena than a two dimensional map - still has to be showed proof by further studies, one can subsume that interactive visualisations as presented in this paper may facilitate a more intuitive grasp of spatio-temporal information for an untrained map reader. This can be traced back to the fact that the human perception of the real world is basically three-dimensional. Therefore 3D map graphics contributes to reduce the map readers' mental effort since 3D real world features have not to be transformed into 2D map features and vice versa. This leads to an instant grasp of complex geospatial phenomena and thus makes map comprehension more intuitive. Against this background [12] highlights the fact that three-dimensional cartographic visualisations provide "a more intuitive acquisition of space, due to an explicit use of 3D". However, [12] and [13] indicate also disadvantages concerning three-dimensional visualisations as for instance the absence of a single scale in perspective views, occlusion of objects, etc. To evaluate the application potential of developed 3D crime mapping applications, Section 3 contains the interpretation of a survey conducted with crime mapping experts.

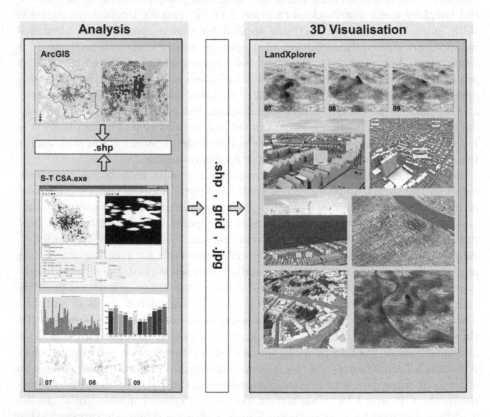

Fig. 1. Workflow as applied in this study. In a first step burglary scene data is preprocessed and spatially analysed within ArcGIS. In a second step the processed files are imported as Esri shapefiles into the programmed application for initial spatio-temporal exploration and temporal KDE analysis. In a third step the resulting files are imported into the VIS-frontend for advanced 3D Visualisation.

2 Spatio-Temporal Crime Scene Analysis and Visualisation

Residential burglary crime scene data analysed in this paper is obtained from the police headquarters of the German city of Cologne (4247 offences). Each individual burglary is represented by a geocoded point having the applied modus operandi (MO) and the time of offence as additional thematic attributes stored in the database. Further datasets used in this study consist of the road network, digital terrain model, 3D city model, aerial photography, digital cadastral map and further vector-based datasets including rivers, administrative boundaries and others. These datasets are used for analysis as well as for creating the three-dimensional geovirtual environment.

2.1 Mapping General Burglary Distribution Patterns

To create first overview maps of crime scene positions the traditional pin-map approach [1] can be used. Figure 2 (left-hand image) shows the application of this method for representing burglary scene positions in the city of Cologne. Though depending the study areas size and the map's scale this kind of visual representation usually does not give much more insights than a rough impression of how crime scenes are distributed in general over the study area. Especially crime scenes affected by repeat victimisation are not visible since that points cover each other. A slightly better suited representation can be achieved by using graduated symbols.

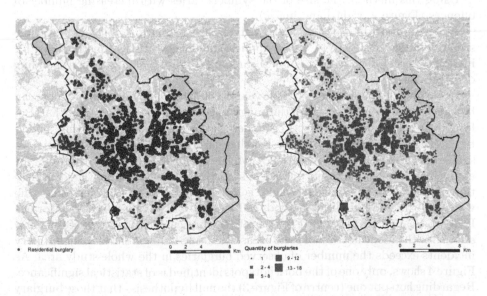

Fig. 2. 2D representation of residential burglaries within the study area for the year 2007 as pin-map (left-hand image) and with graduated symbols (right-hand image)

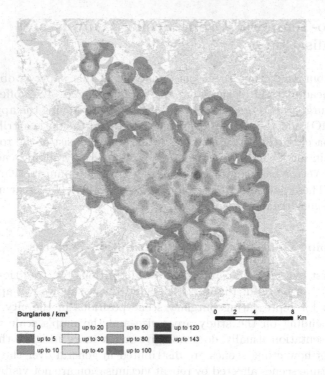

Fig. 3. Two-dimensional kernel-density-estimation map of residential burglaries 2007

Using this method, the size of the symbols varies with increasing number of offences (Figure 2, right-hand image).

A more appropriate method for identifying crime scene distributions and crime scene densities respectively, is the application of geostatistical methods as, for instance, kernel-density-estimation techniques. Figure 3 shows a corresponding density map.

Regarding the period for the whole year of 2007 two main burglary hotspots can be identified, one in the centre of the image and another one in the bottom left. Before identified spots are subject to further spatio-temporal analysis, they should be checked for statistical reliability. For that purpose local indicators of spatial association, the so-called LISA statistics [14], are applied. These indicators allow for analysing geospatial datasets on a local statistical level. Therefore the identification of differences between data values is facilitated on a local scale instead on the wider global scale. From the methods of LISA statistics available (Local Moran's I, Local Geary's C) Getis-Ord (Gi*) statistics are calculated in this study. This allows for the identification of local areas where the number of observed burglary incidents exceeds the number of observed burglaries in the whole study area. As Figure 4 shows, only one of the both hotspots identified is of statistical significance. Regarding hotspot one (centre of Figure 3) the null hypothesis - that those burglary scenes are distributed randomly - can not be rejected with statistical significance (95% confidence level). Otherwise, regarding the distribution of burglary scenes

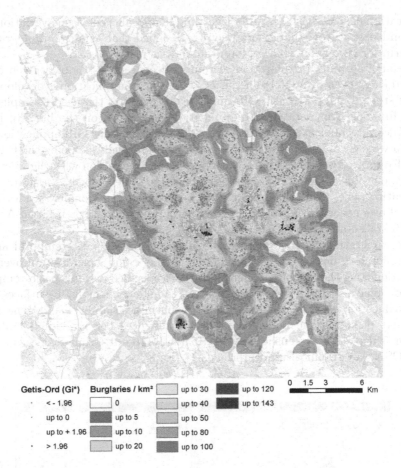

Getis-Ord (Gi*)	Burglaries / km²		
· < - 1.96	0	up to 30	up to 120
· up to 0	up to 5	up to 40	up to 143
up to + 1.96	up to 10	up to 50	
· > 1.96	up to 20	up to 80	
		up to 100	

0   1.5   3   6   Km

Fig. 4. Hotspot surface (year 2007) and corresponding results of LISA statistics. Only the hotspot in the south-west can be certified as statistical significant.

in the south-western hotspot, a statistical significant probability (99% confidence level) verifies that this distribution is not caused by random. Inside this area crime scenes with high numbers of offences are statistical significant surrounded by scenes having high numbers of offences as well.

Since geospatial analysis identified the crime scene cluster in the south-west of Cologne as a statistical significant hotspot area, this region is exemplarily taken for further spatial, but primarily temporal analysis.

2.2 Towards Interactive Spatio-Temporal 3D Tactical Intelligence Assessments

This section describes a set of selected multidimensional geovisualization methods and techniques for representing spatio-temporal characteristics of selected crime scenes. In a first part an application is presented that allows for the initial exploration of some basic features regarding temporal crime scene variations. In a second part a geovirtual environment is designed that acts as an integration-platform for visualizing spatio-temporal analysis results.

To facilitate initial exploration of temporal characteristics of a given crime scene dataset even by an untrained user, a GIS-based application is developed in a first step. To support basic GIS-functionality without the need to implement every function from scratch, the application is designed on the basis of Esri's ArcObjects technology. This approach allows for building GIS-applications by using a wide set of already predefined classes for GIS-analysis. Using the Esri Ar-cGIS Engine software development framework in conjunction with the Microsoft component object model (COM) this application is developed as a stand-alone application (.exe). However, since proprietary ArcGIS functionality is addressed, the end user needs the Esri ArcGIS Engine runtime library or a licensed ArcGIS to be installed at the local machine.

The application focuses on the following options of spatio-temporal analy-sis: Exploratory data analysis through supporting rapid generation of overview charts depicting the number of offences during a specified period, spatio-temporal hotspot analysis through the calculation of time-dependent KDE-surfaces (e.g. one surface for each month to represent monthly variability) and generation of charts depicting the number of burglary offences per individual building. Figure 5 depicts a screenshot of the Spatio-Temporal Crime-Scene-Analyst's (S-T CSA.exe) graphical user interface.

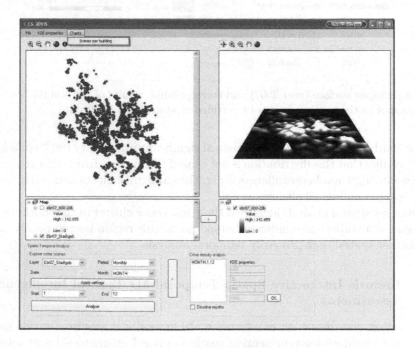

Fig. 5. GUI of the developed application

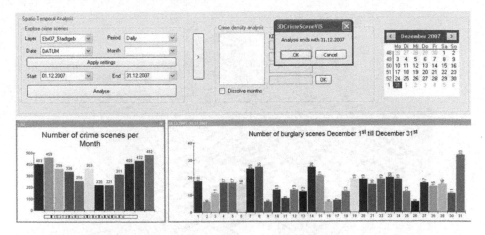

Fig. 6. Charts created by the application. In a first step the period for analysis as well as start- and end-date are specified (upper image). As a result corresponding charts of monthly and daily temporal variations are generated (lower left-hand image and lower right-hand image respectively).

For the purpose of initial temporal data exploration the application provides a temporal-query-module. This function allows for a convenient query of offences' timestamp on monthly or daily basis. Hence the dataset can be explored at different time scales. This results in bar charts showing temporal variations in the frequency distributions of residential burglaries. In this context Figure 6 (lower left-hand image) shows that most burglaries in Cologne are committed during December 2007 (monthly variation). By increasing the temporal analysis scale to the daily level, corresponding daily variations of burglaries are calculated (cf. Figure 6, lower right-hand image). Apparently most residential burglaries in December 2007 are committed on new years' eave. Subsequent to primary temporal data exploration the spatio-temporal spreading of crime scenes is subject to further analysis. To gain insights into the overall dynamics of the underlying burglary crime scenes, spatio-temporal monthly variations of burglary densities can be analysed for instance. For this purpose the application is provided with a KDE-module that facilitates the generation of different hotspot surfaces for a specified time span. The resulting raster files can be used, for instance, as a basis for animated maps that illustrate changing hotspot patterns [15].

Previous analysis (cf. Section 2.1, Figure 4) revealed one statistically relevant hotspot area. This region is exemplarily taken for further spatio-temporal analysis. To visualise the results, another three-dimensional GeoVE is created for this hotspot area (cf. Figure 7).

While hotspot analysis so far revealed distinct regions of different crime scene densities, no evidence is given yet of burglary intensities. In order to initiate crime

Fig. 7. GeoVE of a residential burglary hotspot region with 3D city model and hotspot-map

scene prevention measures e.g., it is an important prerequisite to identify those buildings affected by repeat victimisation. According to [16] repeat victimisation can be defined as "where the same offence occurs a number of times against the same victim (be this a person or an entity like a house)". Concerning the issue of repeat victimisation the following three elements can be considered to be of special interest: location, offence time and applied modus operandi.

A combined analysis of these three elements can be addressed as multi-dimensional since one has to analyse the geospatial dimension (where is the building being burgled located?), the temporal dimension (when and how many times is the building being burgled?) and the thematic dimension (which modus operandi is being applied?). Because of this multidimensional aspect, multidimensional geovirtual environments can be considered as an adequate tool to facilitate intuitive visualisation of repeat victimisation issues.

With the objective of enhancing the existing 3D GeoVE from a predominantly topographic visualisation to an integrative representation of urban three-dimensional tactical intelligence assessment, the geovirtual environment is upgraded with additional spatial and temporal analysis results. To facilitate visual analysis of repeat residential burglary victimisation e.g., respective information is integrated into the GeoVE. First of all, information regarding the building being burgled as well as the modus operandi being applied is subject of analysis. To visualise which building is burgled and which modus operandi is applied, the

Fig. 8. Towards 3D tactical intelligence assessments: 3D GeoVE enhanced with information of repeat residential burglary victimization. The thematic dimension (applied modus operandi) is visualised by dedicated icons. The temporal dimension is visualised on the z-axis by classifying scenes regarding offences weekday.

burglary dataset is linked in a first step to the buildings of the three-dimensional city model. Afterwards it is analysed on what precise weekdays every single building is being burgled. Figure 8 depicts a first approach to visualise multidimensional spatio-temporal issues.

The respective applied modus operandi for burglary offences of 2007 is illustrated by symbols that represent the registered entries "front door", "terrace door", "French window", "window" and "not registered" respectively. To visualise time, the symbols are stacked vertically according to the working day the burglary is committed. Therefore the symbol at the lower end of the pole represents a burglary committed on a Monday, the second lowest symbolises a Tuesday, while the symbol on the top of the pole represents a burglary committed on a Sunday. A gap inside this stack - for instance a missing symbol at the second position - indicates that this building was not burgled on a Tuesday. To alleviate readability and comparability of different stacks, an optional layer (cf. dark blue transparent layer in Figure 8) is used to mark the temporal basement (that is a Monday). It has to be emphasised at this point, that the 3D GeoVE is completely interactive navigable. Therefore an analyst can compare the position of different symbols by individually adjusting viewpoint and perspective.

However, to visualise two or more burglaries that occurred at the same weekday this visualisation is enhanced by adding the respective number of registered offences of that workday to the symbol. Within GIS-processing a function

Fig. 9. Representing repeat burglary victimisation by means of enhancing the GeoVE via combining frequency charts with symbols describing applied modus operandi (right-hand image). The lower left image depicts the integration of further information by using pie-charts.

might assign correct (numbered) symbols to the respective database entries. This enhanced approach is shown by Figure 9 (upper left-hand image): for each building being burgled, charts are produced that indicate the number of offences for that precise building, varying from one residential burglary up to 17 offences in 2007. Combining these representations (right-hand image) allows for visual analysis of both the number and the repeat rate of residential burglaries. Additionally, the lower left image in Figure 9 depicts the integration of further information into the 3D GeoVE. Exemplarily socioeconomic information regarding household age patterns for certain administrative boundaries is integrated.

One shortcoming considering the graphic representations of the last both Figures can be identified in the fact that the pole belonging to the respective MO-symbol is always pointing to the buildings roof - independent from the represented access mode. Unfortunately this restriction is LandXplorer-software intrinsic. However, it would be more reasonable if the pole would optionally point to the 3D building's window or door - depending on the applied modus operandi. A possible solution of this issue could be achieved by using CityGML. With CityGML, both geometry and semantic of a 3D geo-object (for instance a building) can be modelled and described in detail [17]. Therefore, e.g. (French) windows, front- and terrace doors could be modelled for each building separately. Then each of these intelligent buildings would "know" about the position of those elements and whether it serves an access element. Subsequently, it would be possible to use this information to visualise the applied modus operandi in a more appealing manner. For instance, the respective element could be coloured or the pole could point precisely to it.

3   Evaluating Usability and Application Potential Issues

To evaluate the usability of the developed methodology and the interactive intelligence assessments in particular, a survey was conducted during an international crime mapping symposium held at the police headquarters of Cologne in October 2009. Participants of this symposium were predominantly police officers, analysts and decision makers who are using crime mapping techniques during their day-to-day business. Therefore this audience was ranked as to be a well suited target group for surveying usability issues. However, since it was a small group of about just 20 participants, the results are not representative. But still the experts' general opinions and trends concerning usability issues and application potential of the developed 3D crime mapping methods are being reflected. In total 18 participants took part in the standardised questioning via questionnaires.

Although the questionnaire consists of different topics ranging from general map expertise to specific individual crime mapping and 3D skills, within this paper only the users' evaluations regarding 3D crime mapping techniques are analysed and presented. Before handing the questionnaires out to the users, the interactive versions of the 3D tactical intelligence assessments (cf. Figures 7, 8, and 9) were presented in form of a live-demo to the participants.

Summarized, the majority of the participants expressed that the demonstrated 3D visualisation methods are in general meaningful (8 persons) and very meaningful (2 persons) respectively. A third (6 persons) considered them as less meaningful. Regarding the communication of analysis results to third parties and compared to the traditional 2D map, the presented interactive 3D representations are judged as a meaningful completion by the majority (11 out of 18, cf. Figure 10, upper image). However, the potential of presented 3D methods for police day-to-day business was evaluated heterogeneously. Eight persons consider this as "low", five persons expressed a high and another two persons a very high potential (cf. Figure 10, lower image). Summarised, the majority of interviewed experts considers the presented 3D and multidimensional crime mapping techniques as generally meaningful and as a useful completion to the traditional two-dimensional thematic map. Related to their day-to-day business, a narrow majority of experts thinks that such 3D and interactive tactical intelligence assessments are rather of low potential. However, those two experts who state a very high potential for their day-to-day business are also convinced, that presented 3D applications are better suited than a 2D map as well (cf. Table 1). Compared to this two "3D enthusiasts" there is only one "3D pessimist", who sees low potential for day-to-day business and who also expresses that those applications are generally inappropriate (cf. Table 1).

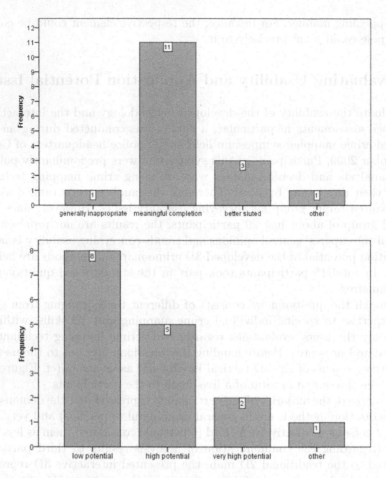

Fig. 10. Frequency charts depicting the response behaviour regarding users' estimations on the communication potential of presented 3D crime mapping application to third parties compared to a traditional 2D map (upper image) and regarding the potential for police day-to-day business (lower image).

Table 1. Response behaviour comparing users' estimations on 3D crime mapping applications' potential for police-related day-to-day business with estimation on 3D crime mapping applications' potential compared to the traditional 2D thematic map

		3D relevance for day-to-day business				
		low potential	high potential	very high potential	other	total
3D relevance as compared to 2D map	generally inappropriate	1	0	0	0	1
	meaningful completion	6	4	0	1	11
	better siuted	0	1	2	0	3
	other	1	0	0	0	1
	total	8	5	2	1	16

4   Conclusion and Outlook

Against the background of geospatial crime scene analysis this paper presented methods and techniques for both spatio-temporal analysis and geovisualization of residential burglaries scenes. For this purpose the presented workflow combines spatio-temporal data exploration and analysis with the visualisation potential of interactive three-dimensional geovirtual environments. It was demonstrated how initial temporal data exploration for both GIS-experts and untrained users is facilitated by a programmed standalone GIS-application. Results of this analysis are passed to a specialised software system for subsequent 3D visualisation. Extending the resulting geovirtual environments by integrating further information leads to the generation of integrative representations of urban three-dimensional tactical intelligence assessments. In a concluding step the application potential of these basically scientific motivated 3D tactical intelligence assessments was surveyed by interpreting the results of questioning crime mapping experts. Although this survey was not representative it could be shown that a majority of experts appreciate these interactive tactical intelligence assessments as (a) meaningful (completion to the 2D map). Within the next steps the survey will be subject to deeper analysis. A possible further step might be to evaluate how potential users judge their interaction-capabilities with the presented system. Combined with the survey this might lead to certain usability guidelines of how to design interactive three-dimensional intelligence assessments.

Acknowledgements. Funding of this study by the German Federal Ministry of Education and Research (BMBF) within the framework of the InnoProfile research group '3D Geoinformation' (www.3dgi.de) is gratefully acknowledged. The author also likes to thank the police headquarters of the city of Cologne for providing extensive burglary crime datasets. Furthermore the author gives a special thank to the municipality of the city of Cologne and to Virtual City Systems, Inc. for providing the 3D city model and other geospatial base data. Finally, the author thanks Autodesk, Inc. for supplying the LandXplorer system.

References

1. Chainey, S., Ratcliffe, J.: GIS and Crime Mapping. John Wiley & Sons Inc., Chichester (2005)
2. McCullagh, M.J.: Detecting Hotspots in Time and Space. In: ISG 2006 (2006)
3. Boba, R.L.: Crime Analysis and Crime Mapping. Sage Publications, Thousand Oaks (2005)
4. Williamson, D., McLafferty, S., McGuire, P., Ross, T., Mollenkopf, J., Goldsmith, V., Quinn, S.: Tools in the spatial analysis of crime. Mapping and analysing crime data. In: Hirschfield, A., Bowers, K. (eds.) vol. 1, p. 187. Taylor & Francis, London (2001)
5. de Smith, M.J., Goodchild, M.F., Longley, P.A.: Geospatial Analysis. Troubador Publishing (2006)

6. Danese, M., Lazzari, M., Murgante, B.: Kernel Density Estimation Methods for a Geostatistical Approach in Seismic Risk Analysis: The Case Study of Potenza Hilltop Town (Southern Italy). In: Proceedings of International Conference on Computational Science and Its Applications (Part I). Section: Workshop on Geographical Analysis, Urban Modeling, Spatial Statistics (GEO-AN-MOD 2008), Perugia, Italy, pp. 415–429. Springer, Heidelberg (2008)
7. Craglia, M., Haining, R., Wiles, P.: A Comparative Evaluation of Approaches to Urban Crime Pattern Analysis. Urban Studies 37(4), 711–729 (2000)
8. Townsley, M.: Visualising space time patterns in crime: the hotspot plot. Crime patterns and analysis 1, 61–74 (2008)
9. Brunsdon, C., Corcoran, J., Higgs, G.: Visualising space and time in crime patterns: A comparison of methods. Computers, Environment and urban Systems 31(1), 52–75 (2007)
10. Fuhrmann, S., MacEachren, A.M.: Navigation in Desktop Geovirtual Environments: Usability Assessment. In: Proceedings of the 20th ICA/ACI International Cartographic Conference, Beijing, China, August 06-10 (2001)
11. MacEachren, A., Edsall, M.R., et al.: Virtual Environments for Geographic Visualization: Potential and Challenges. In: ACM Workshop on New Paradigms for Information Visualization and Manipulation, Kansas City, MO. ACM, New York (1999)
12. Jobst, M., Germanichs, T.: The Employment of 3D in Cartography - An Overview, Multimedia Cartography. In: Cartwright, W., Peterson, M.P., Gartner, G. (eds.) pp. 217–228. Springer, Heidelberg (2007)
13. Meng, L.: How can 3D geovisualization please users' eyes better. Geoinformatics -Magazine for Geo-IT Professionals 5, 34–35 (2002)
14. Anselin, L.: Local indicators of spatial autocorrelation - LISA. Geographical Analysis 27(2), 93–115 (1995)
15. Wolff, M., Asche, H.: Geospatial Crime Scene Investigation - From Hotspot Analysis to Interactive 3D Visualization. In: Proceedings of International Conference on Computational Science and Its Applications (Part I). Section: Workshop on Geographical Analysis, Urban Modeling, Spatial Statistics (GEO-AN-MOD 2009), pp. 285–299. Springer, Heidelberg (2009)
16. Ashby, D., Craglia, M.: Profiling Places: Geodemographics and GIS. In: Newburn, T., Williamson, T., Wright, A. (eds.) Handbook of criminal investigation. Willan Publishing, UK (2007)
17. Kolbe, T.H.: Representing and Exchanging 3D City Models with CityGML. In: Lee, J., Zlatanova, S. (eds.) 3D Geo-Information Sciences, Part I, pp. 15–31. Springer, Heidelberg (2009)

On the Estimation of Fire Severity Using Satellite ASTER Data and Spatial Autocorrelation Statistics

Rosa Coluzzi[1], Nicola Masini[2], Antonio Lanorte[1], and Rosa Lasaponara[1]

[1] CNR-IMAA (Istituto di Metodologie di Analisi Ambientale), C.da S. Loja 85050
Tito Scalo (PZ), Italy
lasaponara@imaa.cnr.it

[2] Archaeological and Monumental heritage institute, National Research Council, C/da
S. Loia Zona industriale, 85050, Tito Scalo (PZ), Italy

Abstract. What are the ecological effects of fires? The evaluation of fire-affected areas and fire severity is of primary importance to answer this question, because fire strongly affects the ecological processes, such as, productivity level, creation of altered patches, modification in vegetation structure and shifts in vegetation cover composition, as well as land surface processes (such as surface energy, water balance, carbon cycle). Traditional methods of recording fire burned areas and fire severity involve expensive and time -consuming field survey. The available remote sensing technologies may allow us to develop standardized burn-severity maps for evaluating fire effects and addressing post fire management activities. This paper is focused on preliminary results we obtained from ongoing research focused on the evaluation of spatial variability of fire effects on vegetation. For the purposes of this study satellite ASTER (Advanced Spaceborne Thermal Emission and Reflection Radiometer) data have been used. Both single (post-fire) and multi-date (pre and post fire) ASTER images were processed for some test areas in Southern Italy. Spatial autocorrelation statistics, such as Moran's I, Geary's C, and Getis-Ord Local Gi index (see Anselin 1995; Getis and Ord 1992), were used to measure and analyze the degree of dependency among spectral features of burned areas.

Keywords: satellite, fire, burned area, Spatial autocorrelation statistics.

1 Introduction

During the last decades, the high number and repeated occurrence of severe wildfires in different regions of the world has strongly heightened the negative effects of fire, which is considered to be one of the most critical factors of disturbance in worldwide ecosystems (1,2). The effects of fires on soil, plants, landscape and ecosystems depend on many factors, among them fire frequency and plant resistance. Fire severity is a qualitative indicator of the effects of fire on ecosystems, whether it affects the forest floor, canopy, etc. Assessing and mapping burn severity is important for monitoring fire effects, for model and evaluate post-fire dynamic and estimating vegetation resilience, which is the ability of vegetation to recover after fire.

In the Mediterranean area, the composition and structure of vegetation are generally strongly shaped by fires, which tend to operate as a selective force, increasing species diversity, or as a filter, favouring the dominance of some species (3).

D. Taniar et al. (Eds.): ICCSA 2010, Part I, LNCS 6016, pp. 361–373, 2010.
© Springer-Verlag Berlin Heidelberg 2010

In the Mediterranean-type communities, post fire vegetation trends have been analysed in a wide range of habitats, although pre- and post-fire investigation has been
generally performed at stand level. Fire-induced dynamical processes are very difficult to study since they affect the complex soil-surface-atmosphere system, due to the
existence of feedback mechanisms involving human activity, ecological patterns and
different subsystems of climate. Therefore, the vegetation patterns constrain fires and
at the same time are constrained by the fire processes that influence them. In operational context, fire severity estimation is critical for short-term mitigation and reha-
bilitation treatments. Traditional methods of recording fire severity involve expensive
and time -consuming field survey.

Remote sensing technologies can provide useful data for fire management from
risk estimation (4,5), fuel mapping (6,7,8), fire detection (9), to post fire monitoring
(10). In particular, satellite data may allow us to develop burn-severity maps (see
11,12,13). The methods generally used to estimate fire severity from satellite are
based on fixed threshold values, which are not suitable for fragmented landscape and
vegetation types, or geographic regions different from those they were devised. A
new approach based on satellite and geo-statistical analysis is herein proposed for
burn severity mapping.

This paper presents our preliminary results obtained from ongoing research based on
the evaluation of spatial variability of fire effects using satellite ASTER (Advanced
Spaceborne Thermal Emission and Reflection Radiometer) data. For the purpose of our
study, satellite –based spectral indices and geospatial statistics were used for some test
areas in southern Italy. In particular, pre-fire and post-fire ASTER derived indices were
processed using spatial autocorrelation statistics, such as Moran's I, Geary's C, and
Getis-Ord Local Gi index (see Anselin 1995; Getis and Ord 1992). Such spatial statistics
enable us to map the areas affected by fire and to estimate the degree of fire severity.

The new approach is independent on sensors used for the evaluation as well as on
vegetation cover types affected by fire. The model could be incorporated directly into
the mapping process from local up to global scale.

2 Data

For the purposes of this study satellite ASTER data have been used. ASTER is a high
resolution imaging instrument flying on Terra, a satellite launched in December 1999,
as part of NASA's Earth Observing System (EOS). It has the highest spatial resolution
(15 meters VNIR) of all five sensors on Terra and collects data in the visible/near
infrared (VNIR), short wave infrared (SWIR), and thermal infrared bands (TIR). Each
subsystem is pointable in the crosstrack direction. The VNIR subsystem of ASTER is
quite unique. One telescope of the VNIR system is nadir looking and two are backward looking, allowing for the construction of three-dimensional digital elevation
models (DEM) due to the stereo capability of the different look angles.

ASTER has a revisit period of 16 days, to any one location on the globe, with a revisit time at the equator of every four days. ASTER collects approximately 8 min of
data per orbit (rather than continuously). Among the 14 ASTER bands in this work
we only considered the three channels in the VNIR region. Two ASTER multispectral images were acquired (14 July 2007 and 30 July 2007). The first one was selected
because closely after the fire event of Maratea (12 July) and it is before the others
three events occurred on 22 and 26 July) 2007, respectively.

3 Method

The method we devised is based on satellite derived spectral indices and geospatial statistics. The new approach is independent on sensors used for the evaluation as well as on vegetation cover types affected by fire. The model could be incorporated directly into the mapping process from local up to global scale.

In this study, both single (post-fire) and multi-date (pre and post fire) ASTER images were processed for some test areas in Southern Italy.

ASTER derived indices were processed using spatial autocorrelation statistics, such as Moran's I, Geary's C, and Getis-Ord Local Gi index (see Anselin 1995; Getis and Ord 1992). Such spatial statistics enable us to map the areas affected by fire and to estimate the degree of fire severity. ASTER-based results were compared with field data provided by the Basilicata regional Forestry Service.

3.1 Spectral Indices

Several vegetation indices were used with ASTER VNIR data in order to map the burnt areas. The SVI (Simple Vegetation Index), TVI (Transformed Difference Vegetation Index), SAVI (Soil Adjusted Vegetation Index) and NDVI (Normalized Difference Vegetation Index) have been applied to the bands 3n and vnir2 of the ASTER images. Moreover, Normalized Difference Burn Ratio has been considered and computed from NIR and SWIR bands. These indices have been compared to each other and with NIR band for burnt area mapping.

Vegetation indices based on ASTER-VNIR are the result of the following formulas:

$$SVI = \frac{NIR}{R} \tag{1}$$

$$NDVI = \frac{NIR - R}{NIR + R} \tag{2}$$

$$SAVI = \frac{NIR - R}{NIR + R + 0,5} \times 1,5 \tag{3}$$

$$TVI = \sqrt{NDVI + 0.5} = \sqrt{\frac{NIR - R}{NIR + R} + 0.5} \tag{4}$$

$$NDBR = (NIR - SWIR)/ (NIR + SWIR) \tag{5}$$

Where R, NIR, SWIR are the Red, Near-Infrared, and SWIR spectral bands, respectively.

ASTER derived indices were processed using spatial autocorrelation statistics.

In this study, both single (post-fire) and multi-date (pre and post fire) ASTER images were processed for some test areas in Southern Italy.

3.2 Spatial Autocorrelation Statistics

Spatial autocorrelation statistics, such as Local Moran's I, Geary's C, and Getis-Ord Local Gi index (see Anselin 1995; Getis and Ord 1992), were used to measure and analyze the degree of dependency among spectral features of burned areas.

Such indices enable us to characterize the spatial autocorrelation within a user-defined distance. For each index, the output is a new image which contains a measure of autocorrelation around the given pixel.

The Moran's I index is defined by formula 6 and 7, respectively, in its global and local definition.

$$I = \frac{N \sum_i \sum_j w_{ij}(x_i - \mu)(x_j - \mu)}{\left(\sum_i \sum_j w_{ij}\right)\sum_i (x_i - \mu)^2} .$$

(6)

where N is the number of observed events, x_i and x_j are the value of considered variable in the location i and j, respectively (with i $\neq$ j), μ is the average of the considered variable, and w_{ij} is the weight.

Classic spatial autocorrelation statistics include a spatial weight matrix that reflects the intensity of the geographic relationship between observations in a neighbourhood.

Such spatial weights matrix indicate elements of computation that are to be included or excluded. In this way it is possible to define ad hoc weights to extract and emphasize specific pattern.

In this study we used local statistics Moran's I, Geary's C, and Getis-Ord Local Gi index (see Anselin 1995; Getis and Ord 1992).

The local Moran's I is given by formula 7

$$I_i = \frac{(x_i - \mu)}{S_x^2} \sum_{j=1}^{N} \left(w_{ij}(x_j - \mu)\right)$$

(7)

where N is the number of observed events, x_i and x_j are the value of considered variable in the location i and j, respectively (with i $\neq$ j), μ is the average of the considered variable, and w_{ij} is the weight.

Moran's I computes the degree of correlation between the values of a variable as a function of spatial lags. This coefficient is structurally comparable to a Pearson's product–moment correlation coefficient and computes the deviation between the values of the variable and its mean.

Moran's I varies from -1 (negative autocorrelation) to 1 (positive autocorrelation).

The Geary's C Index is defined according to formula 8.

$$C = \frac{1}{p} \frac{\sum \sum w_{ij}(x_i - x_j)^2}{\sum (x_j - \mu)^2}$$

(8)

where $p = 2 - \dfrac{\sum \sum w_{ij}}{n-1}$

Geary's c, measures the difference among values of a variable at nearby locations. It behaves somewhat like a distance measure and varies from 0 for perfect positive autocorrelation, to about 2 for a strong negative autocorrelation. In the absence of significant spatial autocorrelation, the expected value is 1.

Spatial autocorrelation statistics such as Moran's I and Geary's C are global in the sense that they estimate the overall degree of spatial autocorrelation for a dataset. The possibility of spatial heterogeneity suggests that the estimated degree of autocorrelation may vary significantly across geographic space.

Local spatial autocorrelation statistics provide estimates disaggregated to the level of the spatial analysis units, allowing assessment of the dependency relationships across space. One of the most widely used local spatial autocorrelation statistics is Getis & Ord (1992). G statistics compare neighborhoods to a global average and identify local regions of strong autocorrelation. Local versions of the I and C statistics are also available.

The Getis and Ord global spatial association measure is defined as follows:

$$G_i^* = \frac{\sum\limits_{j=1}^{n} w_{i,j} x_j - \bar{X} \sum\limits_{j=1}^{n} w_{i,j}}{S \sqrt{\dfrac{\left[n \sum\limits_{j=1}^{n} w_{i,j}^2 - \left(\sum\limits_{j=1}^{n} w_{i,j} \right)^2 \right]}{n-1}}} \tag{9}$$

0where x_j is the attribute value for feature j, $w_{i,j}$ is the spatial weight, n the number of features, X is the average of x_j and

$$S = \sqrt{\frac{\sum\limits_{j=1}^{n} x_j^2}{n} - \left(\bar{X} \right)^2} \tag{10}$$

The Getis-Ord Gi index permits the identification of areas characterized by very high or very low values (hot spots) compared to those of neighboring pixels.

It should be noted that the interpretation of G is different from that of Moran's I. In detail the Getis-Ord Gi enables us to distinguish the clustering of high and low values, but does not capture the presence of negative spatial correlation. the Moran's I is able to detect both positive and negative spatial correlations, but clustering of high or low values are not distinguished:

(i)   Local Moran's I index identifies pixel clustering. It has values that typically range from approximately +1, representing complete positive spatial autocorrelation, to approximately -1, representing complete negative spatial autocorrelation.

(ii) the Local Geary's C index allows us to identify edges and areas characterized by a high variability between a pixel value and its neighboring pixels,

(iii) the Getis-Ord Gi index permits the identification of areas characterized by very high or very low values (hot spots) compared to those of neighboring pixels.

Geostatistical analysis tools are available in several commercial software, such as GIS and image processing. We used ENVI packages for the current study.

The use of all these three indices may improve the map of burnt areas and the classification of fire severity. The efficacy of spatial autocorrelation statistics applied to ASTER images was evaluated from field survey.

4 Results

4.1 The Study Area

The study was carried out in the Basilicata Region (South of Italy) , which in the last years has been characterized by an increasing number of fires, generally occurring during the dry season from July to September.

In particular, we analyze four fire events occurred in the municipality of Maratea (13 ha), Latronico (2 fires, 200 and 261 ha) and Lagonegro (6.5 ha). These areas are characterized by Mediterranean maquis (Maratea), broadleaf forest and transitional woodland-shrub cover (Latronico e Lagonegro).

Fig. 1. Basilicata region and study areas (red circles)

For the purpose of our study, two ASTER multispectral images were acquired (14 July 2007 and 30 July 2007). The first one was acquired closely after the fire event of Maratea (12 July) and   before the others three fire-events (22 and 26 July).

4.2 Results

Figures 2 show the satellite-based analysis performed for some fires occurred in the Maratea and Latronico municipalities.

Figure 2 and 3 show ASTER images (14 July 2007) and spectral indices computed to emphasize burned areas, and results from Local Getis-Ord Gi index, Local Geary's C, Local Moran's I, along with their RGB visualization. Circles indicates the location of fires.

For sack of brevity, we only present the most significant results from spatial correlation analysis, obtained from the NIR channel which, in the current case, enables us to perform the better identification of burned areas.

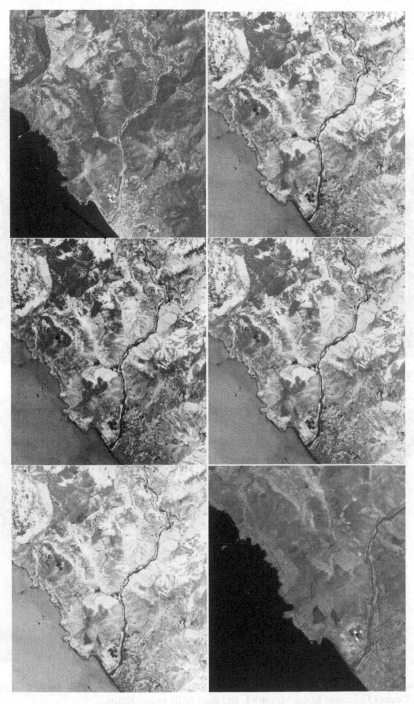

Fig. 2. Maratea fire and ASTER images 14 July 2007. Upper (left) RGB, (right) NDVI. Middle (left) SVI and (right) SAVI. Lower (left) TVI, (right) NIR.

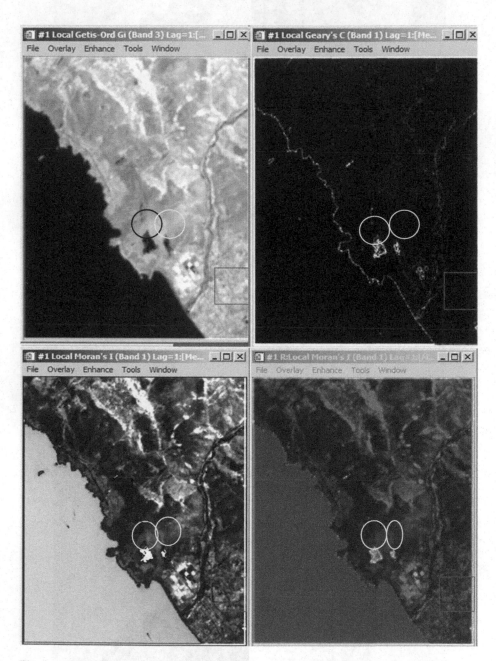

Fig. 3a. ASTER 14 July 2007. Upper (from left to right): Maps from Local Getis-Ord Gi index, Local Geary's C, Lower Local Moran's I, and their RGB visualization.

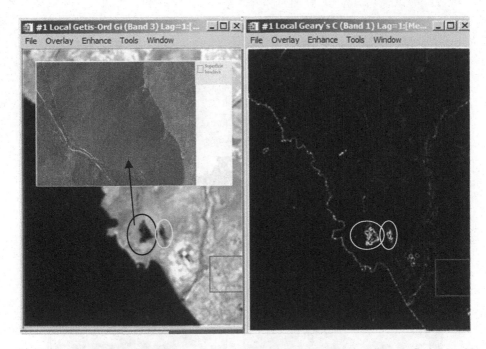

Fig. 3b. ASTER 14 July 2007. zoom of Local Getis-Ord Gi index, Local Geary's C along with map of burned area from field survey made by the Italian Corpo Forestale dello Stato. In the black and yellow circles burned areas.

As expected, we obtain complementary information from the three indices, in particular the most interesting were linked to the edge detection of fire perimeter and the identification of different fire severity, obtained from local Geary's C, Local Moran's I, respectively. Even if the edge identification could be obtained from a number of other algorithms (see for example those provided in Richards,1995), the use of local Geary's index is herein recommended to ensure homogeneity in data processing, weights adopted, and therefore for an easier data interpretation.

The RGB visualization of all the three indices, strongly enhances spatial anomalies and, above all, enable us to well discriminate the scar areas characterized by red and yellow colour (see upper right in figure 3).

Results from Global Positioning System (GPS) campaigns made by the Italian fire Brigate (Corpo Forestale dello Stato) are shown in figure 3. The extension of GPS measurements of burned areas was around 13 ha.

For the two fires occurred in the Latronico municipality we analysed two ASTER multispectral images acquired before (14 July 2007) and after (30 July 2007) the occurrence of fire events (22 and 26 July). Black arrows indicate the location of fires.

AS for the previous case, also for Latronico test cases we only present the most significant results. High satisfactory results were obtained from the comparison of satellite and GPS maps. Fire severity was quite homogeneous for the whole area.

Figure 4 shows maps from Local Getis-Ord Gi index, Local Geary's C, Local Moran's I, along with the map of burned areas from field survey made by fire brigate (Corpo Forestale dello Stato).

Fig. 4a. Latronico Fires Maps from Local Getis-Ord Gi index, Local Geary's C

Fig. 4b. Latronico Fires Maps from Local Moran's I, along with map of burned areas from field survey made by fire brigate (Corpo Forestale dello Stato)

High satisfactory results were obtained from the comparison of satellite and GPS maps. On the basis of method devised (see section 3), it was possible for the considered fires, to classify as high fire severity the brightness pixels and as low severity the darker areas which are indicated in figure 4 by red line.

These preliminary results pointed out that spatial autocorrelation statistics applied to ASTER data allow us to discriminate fire severity and to improve the monitoring of fire effects over time. Such information are effective data source for evaluating erosion/runoff, biomass and carbon issues, and other issues using mapped burn severity.

5   Conclusions and Discussion

The availability of satellite high resolution imagery provide the opportunity to obtain useful information for fire management from the risk evaluation to post fire damage estimation. In particular, satellite data offer the possibility to develop burn-severity maps.

Assessing and mapping burn severity is important for monitoring fire effects, for model and evaluate post-fire dynamic and estimating vegetation resilience, which is the ability of vegetation to recover after fire.

The methods generally used to estimate fire severity from satellite are based on fixed threshold values, which are not suitable for fragmented landscape and do not fit vegetation types, or geographic regions different from those they were devised. A new approach for burn severity mapping from satellite is herein proposed by locally defining severity thresholds through geo-statistical analysis.

In this paper we present our preliminary results obtained from ongoing research based on the evaluation of spatial variability of fire effects using satellite ASTER (Advanced Spaceborne Thermal Emission and Reflection Radiometer) data.

In this study, both single (post-fire) and multi-date (pre and post fire) ASTER images were processed for some test areas in Southern Italy.

ASTER derived indices were processed using spatial autocorrelation statistics, such as Moran's I, Geary's C, and Getis-Ord Local Gi index (see Anselin 1995; Getis and Ord 1992). Such spatial statistics enable us to map the areas affected by fire and to estimate the degree of fire severity. Our results pointed out that spatial autocorrelation statistics applied to ASTER data allow us to discriminate fire severity and to improve the monitoring of fire effects over time. Such information are effective data source for evaluating erosion/runoff, biomass and carbon issues, and other issues using mapped burn severity.

The new approach is independent on sensors used for the evaluation as well as on vegetation cover types affected by fire. The model could be incorporated directly into the mapping process from local up to global scale.

References

1. UNCCD, United Nations Convention to Combat Desertification, report, Paris (1994)
2. FAO, Global forest fire assessment 1990-2000. Forest Resources Assessment Programme, working paper n.55 (2001),
   http://www.fao.org:80/forestry/fo/fra/docs/Wp55_eng.pdf
3. Cochrane, M.A., Alencar, A., Schulze Jr., M.D., Souza, C.M., Nepstad, D.C., Lefebvre, P., Davidson, E.A.: Positive feedback in the fire dynamic of closely canopy tropical forests. Science 284, 1832–1835 (1999)
4. Rauste, Y., Herland, E., Frelander, H., Soine, K., Kuoremaki, T., Ruokari, A.: Satellite-based forest fire detection for fire control in boreal forests. International Journal of Remote Sensing 18, 2641–2656 (1997)
5. Lasaponara, R.: Inter-comparison of AVHRR-based fire danger estimation methods. International Journal of Remote Sensing 26(5), 853–870 (2005)
6. Lasaponara, R., Lanorte, A.: VHR QuickBird data for fuel type characterization in fragmented landscape. Ecological Modelling in press (ECOMOD845R1) 204, 79–84 (2007a)
7. Lasaponara, R., Lanorte, A.: Remotely sensed characterization of forest fuel types by using satellite ASTER data. International Journal of Applied Earth Observations and Geoinformation 9, 225 (2007b)
8. Lasaponara, R., Lanorte, A.: Multispectral fuel type characterization based on remote sensing data and Prometheus model. Forest Ecology and Management 234, S226 (2006)
9. Lasaponara, R., Cuomo, V., Macchiato, M.F., Simoniello, T.: A self-adaptive algorithm based on AVHRR multitemporal data analysis for small active fire detection. International Journal of Remote Sensing 24(8), 1723–1749 (2003)
10. Lasaponara, R.: Estimating Spectral separability of satellite derived parameters for burned areas mapping in the Calabria Region by using SPOT-Vegetation data Ecological Modelling, vol. 196, pp. 265–270 (2006)

11. Gitas, I., Desantis, A.: Remote sensing of burn severity. In: Chuvieco, E. (ed.) Earth Observation of Wildland Fires in Mediterranean Ecosystems, vol. 129. Springer, Heidelberg (2009)

12. Hall, R.J., Freeburn, J.T., de Groot, W.J., Pritchard, J.M., Lynham, T.J., Landry, R.: Remote sensing of burn severity: experience from western Canada boreal fires. International Journal of Wildland Fire 17(4), 476–489 (2008)

13. Richards, G.: A general mathematical framework for modeling twodimensional wildland fire spread. International Journal of Wildland Fire 5(2), 63–72 (1995)

14. Anselin, L.: Local Indicators of Spatial Association LISA. Geographical Analysis 27, 93–115 (1995)

15. Getis, A., Ord, J.K.: The analysis of spatial association by use of distance statistics. Geographical Analysis 24, 189–206 (1992)

Spatial Analysis of the 2008 Influenza Outbreak of Hong Kong

Poh-chin Lai and Kim-hung Kwong

Department of Geography, The University of Hong Kong
Pokfulam Road, Hong Kong SAR
pclai@hkucc.hku.hk

Abstract. The deaths of three children amid a series of recent influenza outbreaks in early March 2008 resulted in the immediate shut down of all kindergartens and primary schools in Hong Kong. While many parents welcome the decision, others queried the judgment given that citizens lack sufficient information to evaluate whether there is an outbreak and must follow actions prescribed by the government. We demonstrated in this paper various techniques to visualize disease distribution and present outbreak data for public consumption. Our analyses made use of affected (case) and non-affected (control) schools with influenza cases in March 2008. A series of maps were created to show disease spread and concentration by means of standard deviational ellipses, grid-based spatial autocorrelation, and kernel density. The generalized data did not permit statistical analysis other than the nearest neighbor distance. We also made suggestions about requirements of additional data and possible directions of disease analysis.

Keywords: GIS, spatial autocorrelation, kernel density mapping, standard deviation ellipse, nearest neighbor distance analysis.

1 Introduction

Following a series of flu outbreaks[1] at schools, a hospital and a nursing home for the elderly since 6 March 2008, the government of the Hong Kong Special Administrative Region (HKSAR) announced on 13 March 2008 to suspend classes of all kindergartens, child care centers, and primary schools for two weeks. The announcement came about after three children were allegedly suspected to die from complications arising from influenza A (H1N1 and H3) [1] [2]. While medical experts reported that the flu strain was not more virulent, the measure to help reduce infections and calm

---

[1] According to the "Guidelines on Prevention of Communicable Diseases in Child Care Centers, Kindergartens, and Schools" by the Center for Health Protection, there is an outbreak from the epidemiological point of view if children or staff members develop similar symptoms one after another and the incidence is higher than usual. More detail is available from http://www.chp.gov.hk/files/pdf/Guild-Booklet-eng.pdf.

D. Taniar et al. (Eds.): ICCSA 2010, Part I, LNCS 6016, pp. 374–388, 2010.
© Springer-Verlag Berlin Heidelberg 2010

public fears has nonetheless received worldwide attention given constant reports on bird flu cases in the region and vivid reminders of the 2003 outbreak of severe acute respiratory syndrome (SARS) [3] [4] [5].

The measure to shut down all schools did lower the disease incidence but received mixed comments from the public [6]. Some argued on hindsight that the move underscored Hong Kong's relative vulnerability to global infectious disease pandemics and perhaps an over-reaction to the influenza threat.

Geographical or spatiotemporal methods may offer insights and suggest solutions to this universal measure of school closures in the territory. Tuckel *et al.* [7] employed the geographic information systems (GIS) technique to revisit the 1918 epidemic pattern of influenza in Hartford. Their study suggested that the use of GIS lends a better understanding of local outbreaks as opposed to viewing the epidemic as a single incident. Venkatachalam and Mikler [8] used a global stochastic field simulation paradigm to model infectious diseases. Other studies [9] [10] also showed that the spatial autocorrelation technique helps to reveal local hot spots of influenza cases and allows geographically focused precautionary measures to take place in due time.

In this paper, we used a number of different methods to investigate outbreak data on affected school locations in March 2008 released by the Hong Kong Center for Health Protection (CHP). We had also some background data for Hong Kong – district boundaries and the extents of populated and non-populated areas. Our analyses included two sets of results for case (affected schools) and control (non-affected schools): (i) maps of standard deviational ellipses, (ii) nearest neighbor distance statistics, (iii) grid-based spatial autocorrelation, and (iv) kernel density maps. We offered our comments on the results and explained choices of the analytical methods and parameters used. We also hope to draw on the complementary roles of various methods which seem to be deficient as the sole measure in decision and policy matters.

2 Methodology

2.1 Data

Three sets of data were compiled: affected schools, non-affected schools, and background (Figure 1). The CHP provided over the Internet daily updates of institutions (including elderly homes, schools, caring centers and hospitals) with flu outbreaks beginning 6 March 2008. The suspected strains of virus for the outbreaks included H1N1 (Brisbane) and H3N2 (Brisbane). The outbreak data for 6-13 March 2008 were assembled to yield a total of 117 cases of affected schools. Data for all schools (kindergarten, primary, and secondary) were compiled from information published on the website of the Hong Kong Education Bureau. The locations of 2045 schools (including the affected) were geocoded to obtain their coordinates for plotting. Background data were obtained from the Survey and Mapping Office of the Lands Department of Hong Kong. They were generalized and reconstituted for this study.

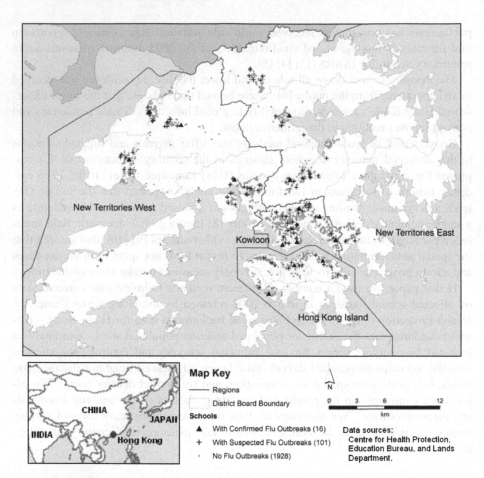

Fig. 1. A spatial distribution of schools with influenza outbreak - Hong Kong 2008

2.2 Analytical Methods

Our analysis involves statistically testing spatial patterns exhibited by case and control data produced by a variety of different methods. We employed ArcGIS, an integrated collection of software for geographical or spatial analyses by ESRI [11], to undertake our investigation. We also utilized GeoDa, which offers various functionalities for spatial analysis and visualization of the analysis results, to conduct spatial autocorrelation analysis [12]. But first, a descriptive analysis of the influenza data was conducted to offer background information for the study.

The method of standard deviational ellipses is an attempt to measure the directional trend of a set of points. A distance of one or two standard deviation will respectively cover approximately 68 or 86 percent of the points under study. The ellipse is based on the mean center of the points and its shape helps project the spread and directionality of the points. The weighted center of the points, adjusted by the size of the schools, is also plotted for comparison. In the weighted case, the center of mass will be pulled towards points representing schools with more student population.

The nearest neighbor distance statistics measures the average distance between points and compares the measurement to the expected measurement of a hypothetical random distribution. The index ranges from 0 to 2.1491 with values less than 1 indicating a clustered pattern, values close to 1 indicating a random pattern, and exceeding 1 indicating a dispersed pattern.

The grid method is a measure of dispersion based primarily on the density of points. Here, we partitioned the study areas into two grid surfaces of cell sizes 1km x 1km and 500m x 500m. Only cells representing populated areas (i.e., excluding country parks and conservation areas) were included in the study. For each cell, the proportion of infection was computed by taking the number of infected schools divided by total schools within a cell. Both grid partitions were within guidelines suggested by researchers, viz. an average of 2 points per cell according to Curtis and McIntosh [13] or 1.6 points per cell by Bailey and Gatrell [14]. Spatial autocorrelation of the grid surfaces were examined using Moran's I and local indicators of spatial autocorrelation (LISA) originally developed by Getis and Ord [15] (see also [16]).

Moran's I values range from -1 to 1 much like the Pearson's correlation coefficient. A value of 1 indicates spatial clustering of like values. A value of -1 signifies spatial dispersion while a zero value typifies spatial randomness. Spatial autocorrelation maps for each grid surface come in pairs – LISA and LISA significance maps. The former categorizes cells into 5 types: High-High (which shows a cell of a high value with adjoining neighboring cells also of high values); Low-Low (which shows a cell of a low value with adjoining neighboring cells also of low values); Low-High (which shows a cell of a low value with adjoining neighboring cells of high values); High-Low (which shows a cell of a high value with adjoining neighboring cells of low values); and not significant (which shows a cell not of the above four types). The latter map shows statistical significance of each cell type.

Kernel density mapping is a partitioning technique where local incidents within a moving 3D kernel of a defined radius or bandwidth are included to compute a density value for each cell in a grid overlaid on the study area [17] [18]. This technique effectively transforms a surface of raw counts into a density or probability surface. The density values are classed and shaded (darker shades to indicate higher values) to highlight hot spots.

3 Results and Discussions

3.1 Background

Our data revealed that the affected schools amounted to about 5.7 percent of the total and more primary schools were affected (Table 1). The Chi-square test was significant and we can be about 99.99 percent confident that the difference between the observed and expected patterns of affected frequencies did not result from mere random variability.

Table 1. Number of affected and non-affected schools by categories of schools

Schools*	Secondary	Primary	Kindergarten	Row Total
Affected (diseased)	16	67	34	117
Not Affected (control)	447	522	959	1928
Column Total	463	589	993	2045

Chi-square = 49.03; df =2; ρ = <0.0001

* School type is based on profile established by the Education Bureau of Hong Kong (http://chsc.edb.hkedcity.net/en/index.php)

Looking at the 2006-2008 statistics released by the CHP [1], the incidence levels in February and March 2008 showed periodicity but the number of occurrences was not as high as those of 2006 and 2007. We must also bear in mind that the strains of viruses were different in these periods. However, the number of outbreaks by institutions did register a noticeable increase.

3.2 Maps of Standard Deviational Ellipses

Figure 2 shows two maps of standard deviation ellipses – one based on locations of controls (non-affected schools) and another on disease incidence (affected schools). The locations of mean and weighted mean centers (the latter adjusted by student population of each school) for the controls were indifferent; however, those of the affected schools were further apart. Because the exact number of infected cases per school was not available, displacement between the mean centers would indicate student population in the direction of the weighted mean center were potentially more susceptible to infection. The skewed nature of the standard deviation ellipse is a general measure of anisotropy or the property of being directionally dependent. By looking at the orientation of the standard deviational ellipses, we can try to predict which areas should prepare for a rise in incidence of influenza.

Point patterns of the infected cases were further analyzed to detect local clustering or hot spots using 1 km as the search radius. The results revealed four hot spots of influenza outbreak. These highlighted locations would be targets for close monitoring of further outbreaks in the neighborhoods.

3.3 Nearest Neighbor Distance Statistics

Figure 3 shows that the nearest neighbor distance for control cases was more compact than infected cases (nearest neighbor observed mean distance of 112 meters compared to 648 meters). The nearest neighbor statistics of 0.24 for control and 0.44 for infected cases indicated point patterns of significant clustering[2]. The results were in

---

[2] The nearest neighbor statistics (observed mean distance / expected mean distance) range from 0 to 2.149. In general: 0 $\rightarrow$ perfect clustering, 1 $\rightarrow$ perfect randomness, 2 $\rightarrow$ perfect even spacing of a grid formation, and 2.149 $\rightarrow$ perfect triangular lattice [19]. Values of 0 to 0.5 indicate high degrees of clustering.

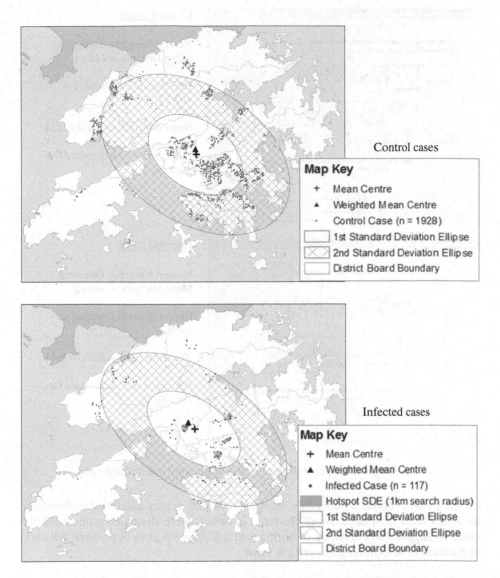

Fig. 2. Standard deviation ellipses by control and infected cases

part due to the sheer difference in number (1928 control versus 117 infected cases) and partly to the locational distribution of schools that were often situated in regions of population clusters.

Comparing Figures 2 and 3, were the number of infected cases to increase in the next few days but the nearest neighbor observed mean distance had remained relatively stable, we would be sure that the newly infected cases would not be too far from existing infected schools in Figure 2. When the observed mean distance of

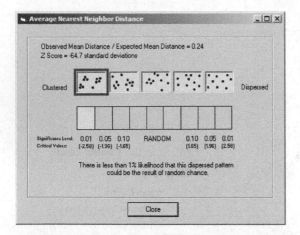

Control cases

Nearest Neighbor Observed
Mean Distance = 112.11

Expected Mean Distance =
463.73

Nearest Neighbor Ratio = 0.24

Z Score = -64.66 Standard Deviations

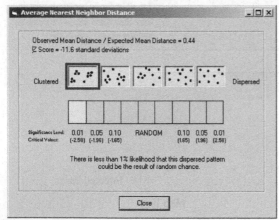

Infected cases

Nearest Neighbor Observed
Mean Distance = 648.92

Expected Mean Distance =
1456.07

Nearest Neighbor Ratio = 0.44

Z Score = -11.52 Standard Deviations

Fig. 3. Nearest neighbor distance analysis by control and infected cases

infected cases becomes noticeably shorter, we would expect additional outbreaks in localities other than the existing clusters. In theory, there should be a threshold distance to suggest the beginning of widespread infection but current research fall short of a means of determining this critical value.

3.4 Grid-Based Spatial Autocorrelation

Point data about schools were aggregated into areal units using grid cells of two different sizes: 1 km x1 km and 500m x500m. The 500m x500m cell contains an average of 120 buildings per cell, thus 'ignoring' the detailed locational information in the observed point distribution (Figure 4). This level of aggregation is a form of data masking [20] to protect against the disclosure of individual identity as revealed by point locations while, at the same time, keeping the number of cell size manageable for desktop computer operations.

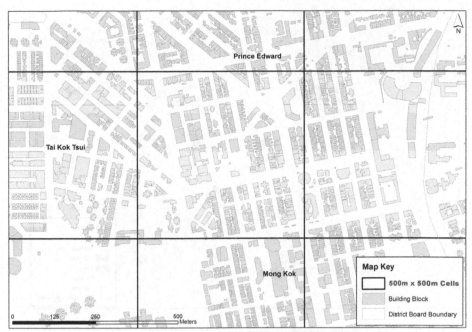

Note: The cell in the center measures 500m x 500m. This cell size covers an average of 180
         buildings for a typical urban area in Hong Kong. Data aggregated at this level should
         be sufficient to safeguard confidentiality of data about individuals.

Fig. 4. Spatial coverage of cells of 500m x 500m

A few patches of 'high-high' occurrences or hot spots were evident from the surface of coarser cells of 1km x 1km (Figure 5). These hot spots were not extensive in
their local coverage and they were buffered by cells of 'low-high' values. The surface
of finer cells manifested similar patterns but the hot spots appeared more disjoint.
These illustrations highlighted the difference of cell sizes on visual impact and analysis. They also brought out the fact that areas of high infection rate were isolated cases
and perhaps not a cause for alarm at this stage. Given that the infection rates were
computed based on institutions and not by residential locations of individuals, the
aggregation might have under-estimated the spatial extent of disease spread.

3.5 Kernel Density Maps

Another method of revealing disease hot spots is by means of kernel density. Figure 6
shows four density surfaces created using different bandwidths (1 km and 500m) and
cell sizes (1km x 1km, 500m x 500m, and 250m x 250m). The choices of bandwidth
and cell size determine the degree of smoothing applied on a point pattern. A larger
bandwidth yields a smoother surface with low intensity levels while a smaller bandwidth a thorny surface with more obvious local variations. Similarly a smaller cell

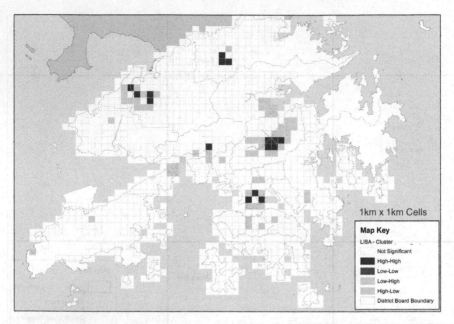

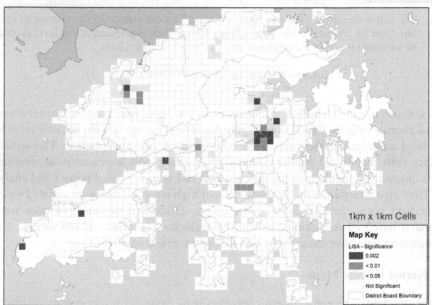

(a) Spatial autocorrelation of quadrat counts of 1km x 1km cells

Fig. 5. Spatial autocorrelation of quadrat counts using two different cell sizes

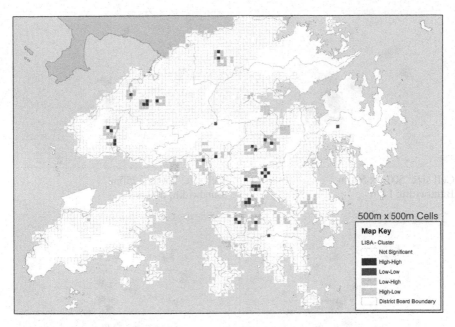

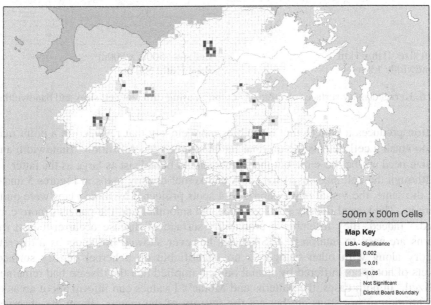

(b) Spatial autocorrelation of quadrat counts of 500m x 500m cells

Fig. 5. (*continued*)

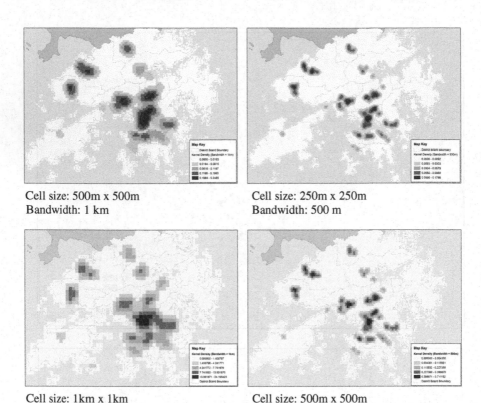

Cell size: 500m x 500m
Bandwidth: 1 km

Cell size: 250m x 250m
Bandwidth: 500 m

Cell size: 1km x 1km
Bandwidth: 1 km

Cell size: 500m x 500m
Bandwidth: 500 m

Fig. 6. Kernel density surfaces of influenza outbreak using different cell sizes and bandwidths

partition produces a pattern that resembles more closely that revealed in a point map but too small a cell defeats the original intent of areal generalization. Bandwidth and cell size need not be the same but the former should be at least as large as the latter.

Although the cell sizes used for LISA and kernel density maps in Figures 5 and 6 were the same, the visual impression of hot spots projected by these maps were quite different. The kernel density surfaces appeared smoother and the patterns more contoured. Indeed, they resemble a probability surface of disease occurrence and the patterns are easy to interpret. LISA maps however showed hot spots as a discrete category along with other categories not identifiable on a kernel density surface. Pockets of hot spots buffered by spatial outliers implied that the disease had remained localized. In both cases, the patterns and Moran's I values can inform about areas of concentration or hot spots are but not the severity of the matter. From the observed pattern, we cannot say for certain that the outbreak needs drastic measures of intervention (such as school closures or designated isolation). Even with daily tracking and reporting of a disease development, the map analysis may detect the occurrence of disease concentration or clustering patterns but still fall short of giving early warning or signal of an outbreak.

4 Observations and Implications

This paper demonstrates that graphic, statistical, and spatial analyses work together to provide clues on clustering tendency and cluster areas. The null hypothesis in point pattern analysis (either a random distribution of points or a homogeneous Poisson distribution) is not appropriate for analyzing cases of a disease which are usually clustered in regions of high population density. The degree of clustering as demonstrated in this paper should be evaluated with respect to the usually non-uniform population distribution.

As one of megacities in the world, Hong Kong's high population concentration and density form a major source of disease burden. Geo-epidemiological models to enable the identification of disease variance in space can help guide interventions for improving the overall conditions of areas with a higher disease burden. A better understanding of spatial distribution of hot and cold spots would help formulate policies to target specific community groups. Here, the spatial process of influenza was examined in terms of variation from Poisson processes. Certain analyses have become more meaningful because of local policies and jurisdiction. For example, movements of primary school students (allocated based on residential locations) are controlled to school districts thereby reducing cross district interaction. Designated isolation of infected primary schools and schools around the hot spots will likely be an effective intervention measure. Other settings such as secondary schools and hospitals with less movement restrains may be modeled in similar fashion but more radical intervention approach may be warranted.

There is no clear cut definition for an outbreak. From the epidemiological point of view, an outbreak occurs if individuals develop similar symptoms one after another and the disease incidence is higher than usual. However, a single case posing major impact to the population at large (such as SARS in 2003) may sometimes warrant intervention treatment for an outbreak. Studies have also indicated that the burden of disease is significantly higher in slums as compared to affluent areas [21] [22] and people of similar socio-economic background and demographic characteristics tend to share similar activity pattern and action space [23] [24] [25]. As such, disease occurrences will likely spread within the community groups. The current intervention practice of a unified policy for an entire city (such as total school closures) may be disruptive to communities not under immediate threat although variable closures may cause confusion and anxiety in practice.

The effectiveness of policies in establishing a functioning health care system depends critically on the capacity of local governments to implement and enforce the policies. Hong Kong's urban health administration, supervision and monitoring are segmented. Time lags between notification of suspected cases and confirmation of statutory notifiable diseases may distort counts. If the different administrations can coordinate their policies, more effective means of communication and intervention strategy can be devised to decrease the likelihood of disease transmission and possibly contain a potential flu pandemic.

Our findings, however, were constrained by the data from the Hong Kong SAR Government. First, we did not have data about the intensity of the infection (e.g. number of individuals reported ill for each institution). Therefore, we were unable to weight severity by institution. Second, our data were at institutional as opposed to individual level. We had no specific data about the infected individuals (e.g. residential location of those infected) and thus unable to delimit their zones of active activity even though residential locations and transport preference have been shown to affect transmission patterns [26]. Third, district boundary is artificial. The presence of such a boundary separating infected and non-infected schools will, in no way, reduce the chance of getting infected. Therefore, district-level aggregation or the modifiable areal unit problem [27] [28] [29] in which health policies are based may be debatable.

The strengths of the study include careful assessment of the aggregation level and comparison of different visualization and presentation techniques. We did demonstrate in this paper that "seeing is believing." Many previous studies on epidemics of respiratory infectious diseases often focused on using deterministic models, charts and tables to analyze the spread of the diseases [30] [31] [32] [33] [34]. They were, however, not able to highlight the spatial characteristics of the diseases. Maps, unlike a printed list of schools, offer a viewable version of the locations or concentrations of a disease which may render a decision, such as school closures, more justifiable. Furthermore, the grid method offers a suitable means of seeing the distribution without disclosing too much detail. For the case of Hong Kong, the opportunity to examine disease by more refined census enumeration units (e.g. tertiary planning units or street blocks) exists to provide fresh insights into the veracity and complexity of the relationship between public health events and neighborhood characteristics. There is further opportunity to apply complex statistical modeling methodology and investigation of cross-level interactions if addresses of the infected subjects were available for geocoding. Such data will allow epidemiologists to see how social mixing patterns might affect disease spread and what measures might protect the public's health.

References

1. CHP: Daily Update of Influenza Situation, http://www.info.gov.hk/healthzone/chp/Flu_dailyupdate_14_3_08_final_en.pdf (Accessed on March 14, 2008)
2. Parry, J.: Hong Kong closes all primary schools in flu outbreak. British Medical Journal 336, 632 (2008)
3. BBC: HK schools close amid flu fears, http://news.bbc.co.uk/2/hi/asia-pacific/7291169.stm (Accessed on March 14, 2008)
4. FOX News: Hong Kong Orders 560,000 Kids to Stay Home for Two Weeks Amid Flu Outbreak, http://www.foxnews.com/story/0,2933,337169,00.html (Accessed on May 5, 2008)
5. TIME: The Hong Kong Flu Scare of 2008, http://www.time.com/time/health/article/0,8599,1722633,00.html (Accessed on May 5, 2008)
6. Cummings, L.M.: Over-securitizing Public Health? The Recent Hong Kong Flu Case, March 17 (2008), http://ponderingir.wordpress.com/2008/03/17/over-securitizing-public-health-the-recent-hong-kong-flu-case/ (Accessed on April 5, 2008)
7. Tuckel, P., Sassler, S., Maisel, R., Leykam, A.: The diffusion of the influenza pandemic of 1918 in Hartford, Connecticut. Social Science History 30(2), 167–196 (2006)

8. Venkatachalam, Mikler: Modeling infectious diseases using global stochastic field simulation (2006), http://ieeexplore.ieee.org/stamp/stamp.jsp?arnumber=1635 909&isnumber=34297 (Accessed on November 15, 2008)
9. Crighton, E.J., Elliott, S.J., Moineddin, R., Kanaroglou, P., Upshur, R.E.G.: An exploratory spatial analysis of pneumonia and influenza hospitalizations in Ontario by age and gender. Epidemiology and Infection 135(2), 253–261 (2007)
10. Greene, S.K., Ionides, E.L., Wilson, M.L.: Patterns of influenza-associated mortality among US elderly by geographic region and virus subtype, 1968–1998. American Journal of Epidemiology 163(4), 316–326 (2006)
11. ESRI: ArcGIS 9.2 Desktop Help (2008), http://webhelp.esri.com/arcgisdesktop/9.2/index.cfm (Accessed on March 3, 2008)
12. Anselin, L., Syabri, I., Kho, Y.: GeoDa: an introduction to spatial data analysis. Geographical Analysis 38(1), 5–22 (2006)
13. Curtis, J.T., McIntosh, R.P.: The interrelations of certain analytic and synthetic phytosociological characters. Ecology 31, 434–455 (1950)
14. Bailey, T.C., Gatrell, A.C.: Interactive Spatial Data Analysis. Longman Group Limited, Essex (1995)
15. Getis, A., Ord, J.K.: The analysis of spatial association by use of distance statistics. Geographical Analysis 24, 189–206 (1992)
16. Anselin, L.: Local indicators of spatial association – LISA. Geographical Analysis 27, 93–115 (1995)
17. Levine, N.: CrimeStat: A Spatial Statistics Program for the Analysis of Crime Incident Locations. Ver. 3.1, Ned Levine & Associates, Houston, TX, and the National Institute of Justice, Washington, DC (2007)
18. Ratcliffe, J.: Spatial Pattern Analysis Machine, http://jratcliffe.net/ware/spam1.htm (Accessed on October 15, 2007)
19. Taylor, P.J.: Quantitative Methods in Geography – An Introduction to Spatial Analysis, pp. 156–162. Houghton Mifflin Company, New Jersey (1977)
20. Rushton, G., Armstrong, M.P., Gittler, J., Greene, B.R., Pavlik, C.E., West, M.M., Zimmerman, D.L.: Geocoding in cancer research: a review. American Journal of Preventive Medicine 30(2), S16–S24 (2006)
21. Reddy, S., Shah, B., Varghese, C., Ramadoss, A.: Responding to the threat of chronic diseases in India. The Lancet 366(9498), 1744–1749 (2003)
22. Agtini, M.D., Soeharno, R., Lesmana, M., Punjabi, N.H., Simanjuntak, C., Wangsasaputra, F., Nurdin, D., Pulungsih, S.P., Rofiq, A., Santoso, H., Pujarwoto, H., Sjahrurachman, A., Sudarmono, P., von Seidlein, L., Deen, J.L., Ali, M., Lee, H., Kim, D.R., Han, O., Park, J.K., Suwandono, A., Ingerani, O.B.A., Campbell, J.R., Beecham, H.J., Corwin, A.L., Clemens, J.D.: The burden of diarrhoea, shigellosis, and cholera in North Jakarta, Indonesia: findings from 24 months surveillance. BMC Infectious Diseases 5, 89 (2005)
23. White, S.E.: Action space, human needs and interurban migration. The Professional Geographer 29(1), 47–52 (1977)
24. Joseph, A.E., Poyner, A.: Interpreting Patterns of Public Service Utilization in Rural Areas. Economic Geography 58(3), 262–273 (1982)
25. Lee, R.E., Cubbin, C., Winkleby, M.: Contribution of neighbourhood socioeconomic status and physical activity resources to physical activity among women. Journal of Epidemiology and Community Health 61, 882–890 (2007)
26. Lai, P.C., So, F.M., Chan, K.W.: Spatial Epidemiological Approaches in Disease Mapping and Analysis: A handbook on operational procedures. CRC Press, Boca Raton (2009)
27. Openshaw, S.: The Modifiable Areal Unit Problem. Geobooks, Norwich (1984)
28. Holt, D., Steel, D.G., Tranmer, M.: Area homogeneity and the modifiable areal unit problem. Geographical Systems 3, 181 (1996)

29. Rushton, G.: Improving the geographical basis of health surveillance using GIS. In: Gatrell, A.G., Loytonen, M. (eds.) GIS and Health, ch. 5. Taylor & Francis, London (1998)
30. Dye, C., Gay, N.: Modeling the SARS epidemic. Science 300, 1884–1885 (2003)
31. Lipsitch, M., Cohen, T., Cooper, B., Robins, J.M., Ma, S., Jams, L., Gopalakrishna, G., Chew, S.K., Tan, C.C., Samore, M.H., Fisman, D., Murray, M.: Transmission dynamics and control of severe acute respiratory syndrome. Science 300, 1966–1970 (2003)
32. Ng, T.W., Turinici, G., Danchin, A.: A double epidemic model for the SARS propagation. BMC Infectious Diseases 3, 19 (2003)
33. Riley, S., Fraser, C., Donnelly, C.A., Ghani, A.C., Abu-Raddad, L.J., Hedley, A.J., Leung, G.M., Ho, L.M., Lam, T.H., Thach, T.Q., Chau, P., Chan, K.P., Lo, S.V., Leung, P.Y., Tsang, T., Ho, W., Lee, K.H., Lau, E.M.C., Ferguson, N.M., Anderson, R.M.: Transmission Dynamics of the Etiological Agents of SARS in Hong Kong: Impact of Public Health Interventions. Science 300, 1961–1966 (2003)
34. Shannon, G.W., Willoughby, J.: Severe acute respiratory syndrome (SARS) in Asia: a medical geographic perspective. Eurasian Geography and Economics 45(5), 359–381 (2004)

Spatial Components in Disease Modelling

Kim-hung Kwong and Poh-chin Lai

Department of Geography, the University of Hong Kong, Pokfulam, Hong Kong
h0110454@hkusua.hku.hk, pclai@hkucc.hku.hk

Abstract. Modelling of infectious diseases could help gain further under-standing of their diffusion processes that provide knowledge on the detection of epidemics and decision making for future infection control measures. Con-ventional disease transmission models are inadequate in considering the diverse nature of a society and its location-specific factors. A new approach incorporating stochastic and spatial factors is necessary to better reflect the situation. However, research on risk factors in disease diffusion is limited in numbers. This paper mapped the different phases of spatial diffusion of SARS in Hong Kong to explore the underlying spatial factors that may have interfered and contributed to the transmission patterns of SARS. Results of the current study provide important bases to inform relevant environmental attributes that could potentially improve the spatial modelling of an infectious disease.

Keywords: Spatial model, GIS, SARS, Risk factors.

1 Introduction

Acute respiratory infections were transmitted through aerosol transmission of respi-ratory secretions from coughing and sneezing. Conditions such as overcrowding and poor personal hygiene tend to facilitate the transmission of respiratory diseases [1]. Education about personal hygiene and simple intervention measures such as washing hands can help to minimize disease incidence [2][3][4]. A model of SARS transmis-sion by Riley *et al.* [5] suggested that the spread of SARS is highly geographical and localized such that a complete ban on travel between local districts could expect to reduce the transmission rate by 76%. Therefore, a closer examination of the SARS occurrences in space and time could provide a better understanding of the spatial diffusion patterns and possible environmental factors contributing to such patterns. Besides, an enhanced understanding of the spatial spread could extend knowledge on the detection of epidemics and help advice infection control and intervention meas-ures. It is also known that conventional disease transmission models are inadequate in considering the diverse nature of a society and its location-specific factors [6][7][8]. This research made an attempt to map different phases of the spatial diffu-sion of SARS in Hong Kong to identify the underlying spatial factors attributing to

D. Taniar et al. (Eds.): ICCSA 2010, Part I, LNCS 6016, pp. 389–400, 2010.
© Springer-Verlag Berlin Heidelberg 2010

its transmission patterns. Results from the study offer useful guidance about the selection of environmental risk factors for inclusion in the spatial modelling of an infectious disease.

2 "Space" as an Element in Disease Modelling

Various efforts have been made to simulate the outbreaks of SARS using mathematical methods [5][9][10][11][12]. Many of the models were based on the deterministic approach, such as SEIR, which incorporates the susceptible population (S), exposed/infected population (E), infectious population (I), and the recovered (immune) / removed (death) population (R) [5][10][12]. SEIR models explain the diffusion of a disease among the four population groups.

SEIR and other related models often require little data, are relatively easy to set up, and can generally simulate infectious disease dynamics among the population [13]. Such models, however, do not consider dynamic elements transpired by population mobility and social mixing; both of which are largely influenced by socio-economic and environmental factors. Small and Tse [14] explained that these conventional models have an underlying assumption that each member of the entire population has an equal chance of being infected. Such an assumption ignores the complex socio-demographic and environmental factors afflicting the transmission course of a disease among various subgroups (e.g., the wealthy, middle class, and the disadvantaged). A typical mathematical model suggests that a disease epidemic would ultimately infect the entire population [10][12]. The reality is that certain communities may be affected less by an epidemic. For example, SARS cases seemed to cluster in several disease "hot spots" in Hong Kong [15]. Jefferson et al. [16] also reported that simple physical interruptions, such as systematic education on personal hygiene and isolation of infected patients, were effective in preventing the spread of respiratory diseases. Hence, Dye and Gay [9] concluded that the next generation of disease models should include spatial processes and stochastic factors to tender a better solution to the problem.

The Geographic Information System (GIS) technology is well suited for analysing epidemiological data and characterising the spatio-temporal patterns of epidemics [15][17]. Epidemiological data often have a spatial context, such as the residential or work addresses of patients and the spatial patterns associated with a disease. Efforts have been made to incorporate the dimension of space into disease simulation. Sattenspiel and Dietz [7], for example, created an epidemic model that accounts for geographic mobility of the population in different regions. Despite the assumptions of a single trip and a static population, their model was regarded superior to the conventional SEIR models because it considered in calculating the transmission risk both epidemic and behavioural processes, as well as environmental factors. Small and Tse [8] modelled the spread of SARS using a small world model to simulate its spatial diffusion using the network structure. However, their model assumed that the environmental factors and population composition within the small world were homogenous. Meng *et al.* [18] tried to employ spatial analysis to investigate and understand factors affecting the spatial transmission process of SARS in Beijing. They identified population density as a significant factor for the spatial diffusion in this case. However, "population density" alone may not reveal overcrowding conditions at the micro-level, especially in places like Hong Kong where a mixed land use is not uncommon and where non populated country parks are adjacent to urbanized areas.

Riley [17] documented four kinds of models (patch, distance, group and network) for the transmission of infectious diseases. He applied these models to simulate various disease outbreaks in the UK and found the group model to be the most suitable for human-to-human transmission of influenza. Watkins *et al.* [19] also tried to model infectious disease outbreaks using a GIS to incorporate traditional SEIR models in their simulations. Their examples also showed that the establishment of a spatial model for contagious diseases (such as SARS) was essential in understanding how the disease spread through time and space. Furthermore, Hsieh *et al.* [20] highlighted the importance of creating distinct and explicit spatial models for the understanding of the specific patterns of transmission of SARS in each region or country.

A new approach seems necessary to address the location-specific as well as environmental and socio-demographic risk factors for communicable diseases. However, only a limited number of studies (such as Lau *et al.* [3]) has identified some risk factors for the SARS transmission in Hong Kong. This study is an attempt to isolate risk (or stochastic) factors to model the transmission dynamics of a disease in space. The study is based on data collected for the 2003 SARS outbreak of Hong Kong.

3 Research Method

Our approach attempts to extract features in space that contribute towards social mixing. We argue that social mixing is a function of transport infrastructures and can also be reflected through certain social-economic indicators.

3.1 Study Area and Data Period

The study area covers the whole territory of Hong Kong and the data include 1,707 confirmed cases of SARS occurring between February and June 2003. We divided the SARS epidemic into four phases and by spatial units of 18 districts to explore its spread across space and time.

1) Early phase, with cases admitted on or before March 10, 2003 (when patients in room 8A of the Prince of Wales Hospital were isolated);
2) Diffusion phase, with cases admitted between March 11 and March 17 inclusive

3) SSE phase, with cases admitted between March 18 (when the Super Spreading Event or SSE at the Amoy Garden was estimated to begin according to Riley *et al.* [5]) and March 30 inclusive;
4) Post-SSE phase, with cases admitted between March 31 (when Amoy Garden residents were segregated) and June 2 (last case admitted and end of the 2003 SARS epidemic of Hong Kong).

3.2 Research Hypotheses

Our research hypotheses are as follows:
1) H_0: There is no relationship between disease spread and transport infrastructure
   H_A: Disease spread follows the pattern of transport infrastructure
2) H_0: There is no relationship between disease incidence and various socio-economic characteristics (refer to section 3.3 for such characteristics)
   H_A: Disease incidence correlates with various socio-economic characteristics

3.3 Data Processing

We obtained the SARS data from the Hong Kong Hospital Authority. A patient record includes an identifier, residential address, hospital admission date, onset date of symptoms, hospital admitted to, as well as health conditions at admission. Personal particulars of individuals were stripped and their residential addresses were replaced with geo-coordinates, with no information about flat numbers and building names, to ensure data privacy.

We employed the 2004 geographical data (B5000 for the whole of Hong Kong) acquired from the Lands Department the Hong Kong Special Administrative Region (HKSAR) government for spatial analysis and spatial modelling of SARS. The Ar-cGIS 9.0 geographic information system software was used as a platform for data input and manipulation. Maps were created to reveal the locations of SARS cases. Aggregation of cases to the 18 districts level was also made to extract potentially risky districts during various phases of the SARS epidemic in 2003.

Demographic and census data of the general population were abstracted from the 2001 Population Census (in street block or small tertiary planning unit levels (STPU)) compiled by the Census and Statistics Department of the HKSAR government [21]. We incorporated such data to investigate possible socio-economic factors that might have affected the spatial distribution of SARS. As the human-to-human transmission of SARS is through close contacts, variations in the socio-economic constructs by different spatial units might influence its spatial distributional patterns [4]. Grids of 150m x 150m were created. SARS data and census data were spatially joined to the grid level for analysis. We examined the relationship between the SARS incidence and the following socio-economic characteristics as stipulated in hypothesis 2 above.

a) percentage of population with tertiary level education
b) percentage of population aged under 15
c) percentage of population aged over 65

d)   non-working population
e)   median household income
f)   median personal income
g)   average number of rooms per household
h)   net residential density

We followed the Irish government's guidelines [22] when defining net residential density because there is no such guideline in Hong Kong. Non populated areas (such as country parks) were excluded in our analysis. The reason for not using population density directly is because many areas in Hong Kong are of the mixed land use type (e.g. inner city areas of Kowloon and northern Hong Kong Island where residential areas are mixed with commercial / retail uses). Moreover, some residential areas are also situated adjacent large plots of non populated country parks (please refer to Figure 3 for such situations in Kowloon and the Hong Kong Island) which are often included in the total area of specific administrative districts or planning units. Population density in these areas will therefore be under-represented and not reflecting truly how crowded a place is.

Statistical methods, including Pearson's correlation co-efficient, were employed to determine the significance of various environmental and demographic factors contributing to the spatio-temporal transmission of SARS.

4   Results and Discussion

4.1 Spatio-Temporal Diffusion of SARS

Figure 1 maps the four phases of the 2003 SARS epidemic outbreak in Hong Kong. It seems that disease cases were concentrated in the Sha Tin district in the first phase or the early stage (Figure 1a) before spreading to the North and South in phase 2 or the diffusion stage (Figure 1b). A concentration of SARS cases remained apparent in both Sha Tin (13.6% of 1515 cases) and Kwun Tong (34.2% of 1515 cases) districts in phases 3 and 4 (Figures 1c and 1d) when SARS became widespread throughout the whole territory of Hong Kong.

An interesting point to note is that the north-south linear spread pattern in the early stages of the epidemic, as illustrated in Figures 1a and 1b, corresponds to the East Rail line which is a heavily used mass transit railway connecting Kowloon and the Northeast New Territories (Figure 2). It appears that transport might have an essential role in facilitating disease spread. A previous study of SARS transmission in China also confirmed that modern public transport has a vital part in spreading contagious diseases like SARS [23]. The study reported that SARS had two major hotspots in Guangdong and provinces near Beijing. Intersections of national highway, in particular, were a high risk factor for the spatial diffusion of SARS. While an appropriate test of significance is not available, the visual evidence derived of the SARS data in our study does suggest that the null hypothesis 1 is not substantiated.

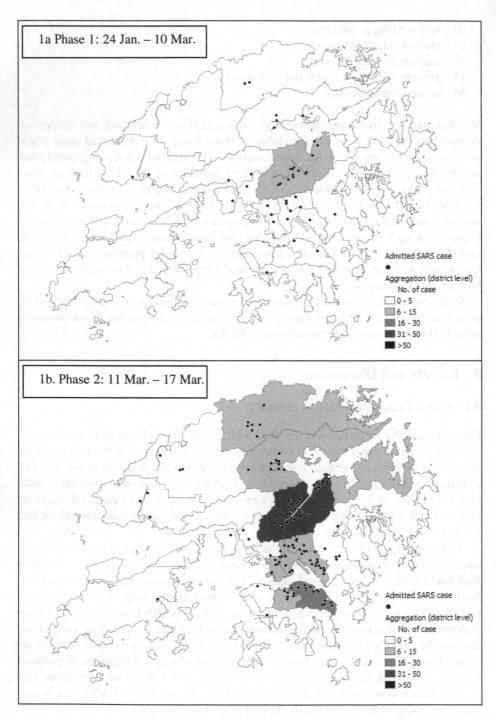

Fig. 1. Diffusion patterns in four phases of the SARS epidemic in 2003

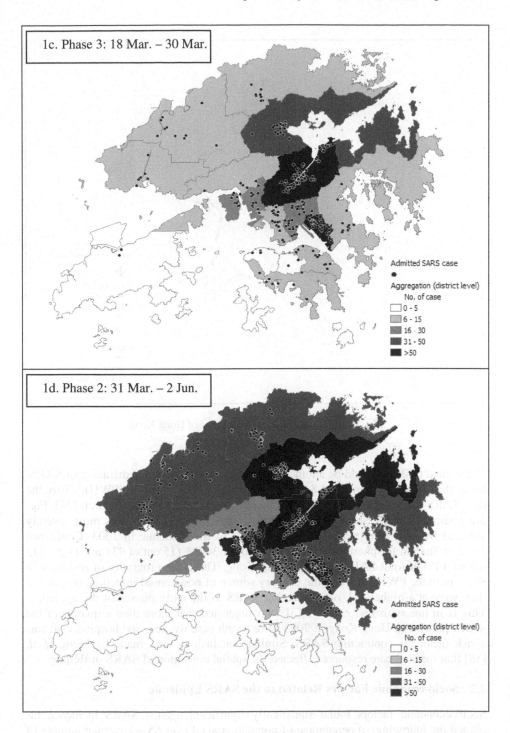

Fig. 1. (*continued*)

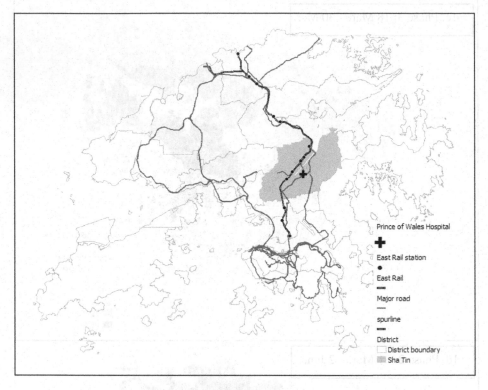

Fig. 2. Major transport infrastructures of Hong Kong

Medical facilities could be another important contributor to the diffusion of SARS. More than 10 workers in room 8A of the Prince of Wales Hospital (PWH), where the first SARS patient was admitted, were infected with SARS in early March [24]. Figure 1 shows that the Sha Tin district, where the PWH is located, was most severely affected by SARS during the first two phases of the epidemic in 2003. Confirmed cases in Sha Tin for phases 1 and 2 accounted for 34.9% (15 out of 43) and 28.2% (42 out of 149) of total SARS cases in Hong Kong. The close proximity of residents in Sha Tin to the PWH, which is the primary source of nosocomial infection, meant that they were at a higher risk of contracting SARS in the early phases of the epidemic. This is in line with Lau *et al.* [2][3] who suggested that more than a quarter of the SARS patients in Hong Kong in 2003 were health care workers and hospital visit was a risk factor for contracting SARS. Similar conclusions were made by Meng *et al.* [18] that medical care resources affected the spatial contagion of SARS in Beijing.

4.2 Socio-economic Factors Related to the SARS Epidemic

Socio-economic factors found statistically significant against SARS incidence included the following: c) percentage of population aged over 65, g) average number of

Table 1. Pearson's Correlation Co-efficiency results between socio-economic factors and occurrence of SARS, SARS cases in a grid (150m x 150m) as the dependent variable

Variables	Co-efficiency	Sig.	N
Grids with SARS cases only			
c) % of the population over 65 years old	.062 (*)	.025	1316
g) Average no. of rooms per household	-.098 (**)	.000	1316
h) Net residential density	.204 (**)	.000	1316
All grids (excluding country parks)			
c) % of the population over 65 years old	-.020 (**)	.001	28303
g) Average no. of rooms per household	-.098 (**)	.000	28303
h) Net residential density	.390 (**)	.000	28303

** Correlation is significant at the 0.01 level (2 tailed).
* Correlation is significant at the 0.05 level (2 tailed).

rooms per household, and h) net residential density (Table 1). All other variables did not exhibit a statistically significant relationship with the occurrence of SARS. Table 1 also shows that net residential density had a significant positive correlation with the occurrence of SARS.

Figure 3 is a map of SARS cases plotted over residential density in the city centres of Hong Kong (Kowloon and the Hong Kong Island). It illustrates that disease cases were concentrated mostly in areas of high residential densities. Areas with lower residential densities in Figure 3 (such as 1 - Kowloon Tong, 2 - Southern District, and 3 - mid-levels) had fewer cases throughout the 2003 epidemic as shown in Figure 1. This observation matches that of a study by Meng *et al.* [18] who demonstrated that population density was an important factor affecting the spatial diffusion of SARS in Beijing. The average number of rooms per household was also found to have a statistically significant negative correlation with SARS because this factor is likely associated with residential density. People must share a room with their family members given fewer rooms per household in places with a high residential density. The percent of elderly population (over 65 years old) was statistically significant at the less stringent 95% instead of 99% confidence level. While the elderly have been found more susceptible to various types of infectious diseases including SARS [25][26][27], their less active social role could have ameliorated the chance of contracting a contagious disease.

The results indicate that the null hypothesis 2 can be rejected for socio-economic characteristics of net residential density, average number of rooms per household, and elderly population. In other words, these three characteristics exhibited statistically significant correlation with the occurrence of SARS in Hong Kong. These social-economic factors could be used to explain the transmission patterns of the 2003 SARS epidemic.

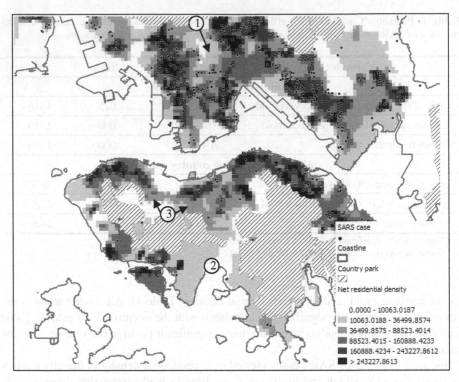

Fig. 3. Residential density and SARS cases (Kowloon and Hong Kong Island)

5 Conclusion

New and re-emerging of infectious diseases post challenges and threats to the health systems of many countries. While medical treatment of patients with contagious diseases has been top priority in curtailing epidemics, surveillance and early warning are equally important [1]. Deterministic and mathematical models of communicable diseases are not adequate as a decision tool because they fall short of providing information about an epidemic form the spatial perspective. Moreover, these models are not able to account for stochastic factors that influence the spatial dispersion of a disease outbreak. Previous studies of the diffusion of SARS in Hong Kong and Beijing have shown evidence of geographical concentrations of SARS cases [15][18]. Further efforts to incorporate stochastic events in modelling the spatio-temporal transmission of an infectious disease such as SARS are therefore necessary.

GIS provides an integrated platform for the examination of spatio-temporal diffusion of a disease. This research studies SARS diffusion in space and various temporal phases of the 2003 epidemic using the GIS technology. We have identified some environmental and demographic factors deemed important in affecting the spatial transmission of SARS. Obtaining results that are in line with similar studies in other places, our study concluded that environmental factors (in this case, transport infrastructure and hospital locations) played a key role in shaping the diffusion pattern of

SARS. Certain socio-economic factors (i.e., average number of rooms per household, percentage of elderly population, and net residential density) were found to correlate positively with the occurrence of SARS in Hong Kong, indicating their potential influence in the disease transmission.

The research findings set the groundwork for the construction of a combination of stochastic and geographical-based models to simulate the transmission patterns of an infectious disease in space and time. Previous studies have documented deficiencies of deterministic models in addressing spatial differences and severity of an epidemic. This research mapped different development phases of the SARS epidemic in Hong Kong and employed the Pearson's correlation to isolate environmental factors and socio-economic factors of significant pertinence to the disease. The results are useful in paving the ways forward to study disease transmission in space and time. Future studies may take heed of our research findings to construct spatial models of disease transmission. The risk factors identified in this study could be incorporated in the modelling process to improve model predictability.

References

1. Connolly, M.A., Gayer, M., Ryan, M.J., Spiegel, P., Salama, P., Heymann, D.L.: Communicable diseases in complex emergencies: impact and challenges. Lancet 364, 1974–1983 (2004)
2. Lau, J.T.F., Lau, M., Kim, J.H., Wong, E., Tsui, H.Y., Tsang, T., Wong, T.W.: Probable secondary infections in households of SARS patients in Hong Kong. Emerg. Infect. Dis. 10, 235–243 (2004a)
3. Lau, J.T.F., Tsui, H., Lau, M., Yang, X.: SARS transmission, risk factors, and prevention in Hong Kong. Emerg. Infect. Dis. 10, 587–592 (2004b)
4. World Health Organization: Severe Acute Respiratory Syndrome (SARS): Status of the Outbreak and Lessons for the Immediate Future, vol. 2007 (2003)
5. Riley, S., Fraser, C., Donnelly, C.A., Ghani, A.C., Abu-Raddad, L.J., Hedley, A.J., Leung, G.M., Ho, L.M., Lam, T.H., Thach, T.Q., Chau, P., Chan, K.P., Lo, S.V., Leung, P.Y., Tsang, T., Ho, W., Lee, K.H., Lau, E.M.C., Ferguson, N.M., Anderson, R.M.: Transmission dynamics of the etiological agents of SARS in Hong Kong: impact of public health interventions. Science 300, 1961–1966 (2003)
6. Dushoff, J., Levin, S.: The effects of population heterogeneity on disease invasion. Mathematical Biosciences 128, 25–40 (1995)
7. Sattenspiel, L., Dietz, K.: A structured epidemic model incorporating geographic mobility among regions. Mathematical Biosciences 128, 71–91 (1995)
8. Small, M., Tse, C.K.: Small world and scale free model of transmission of SARS. International Journal of Bifucation and Chaos 15, 1745–1755 (2005a)
9. Dye, C., Gay, N.: Modeling the SARS epidemic. Science 300, 1884–1885 (2003)
10. Lipsitch, M., Cohen, T., Cooper, B., Robins, J.M., Ma, S., James, L., Gopalakrishna, G., Chew, S.K., Tan, C.C., Samore, M.H., Fisman, D., Murray, M.: Transmission dynamics and control of severe acute respiratory syndrome. Science 300, 1966–1970 (2003)
11. Ng, T.W., Turinici, G., Danchin, A.: A double epidemic model for the SARS propagation. BMC Infectious Diseases 3, 19 (2003)
12. Shannon, G.W., Willoughby, J.: Severe acute respiratory syndrome (SARS) in Asia: a medical geographic perspective. Eurasian Geography and Economics 45, 359–381 (2004)
13. Trottier, H., Philippe, P.: Deterministic modeling of infectious diseases: theory and methods. The Internet Journal of Infectious Diseases 1 (2001)

14. Small, M., Tse, C.K.: Clustering model for transmission of the SARS virus: application to epidemic control and risk assessment. Physica A - Statistical Mechanics and Its Applications 351, 499–511 (2005b)
15. Lai, P.C., Wong, C.M., Hedley, A.J., Lo, S.V., Leung, P.Y., Kong, J., Leung, G.M.: Understanding the spatial clustering of severe acute respiratory syndrome (SARS) in Hong Kong. Environmental Health Perspectives 112, 1550–1556 (2004)
16. Jefferson, T., Foxlee, R., Del Mar, C., Dooley, L., Ferroni, E., Hewak, B., Prabhala, A., Nair, A., Rivetti, A.: Physical interventions to interrupt or reduce the spread of respiratory viruses: systematic review. British Medical Journal 336, 77–80 (2008)
17. Riley, S.: Large-scale spatial-transmission models of infectious disease. Science 316, 1298–1301 (2007)
18. Meng, B., Wang, J., Liu, J., Wu, J., Zhong, E.: Understanding the spatial diffusion process of severe acute respiratory syndrome in Beijing. Public Health 119, 1080–1087 (2005)
19. Watkins, R.E., Eagleson, S., Beckett, S., Garner, G., Veenendaal, B., Wright, G., Plant, A.J.: Using GIS to create synthetic disease outbreak. BMC Medical Informatics and Decision Making 7 (2007)
20. Hsieh, Y., Chen, C., Hsu, S.: SARS outbreak, Taiwan, 2003. Emerg. Infect. Dis. 10, 201–206 (2004)
21. Census and Statistics Department HKSAR: Hong Kong 2001 Population Census - TAB on CD-ROM and MAP on CD-ROM. Census and Statistics Department HKSAR, Hong Kong (2001)
22. Government of Ireland: Residential Density – Guidelines for Planning Authorities, vol. 2008 (1999)
23. Fang, L.Q., de Vlas, S.J., Feng, D., Liang, S., Xu, Y.F., Zhou, J.P., Richardus, J.H., Cao, W.C.: Geographical spread of SARS in mainland China. Trop. Med. Int. Health 14, 14–20 (2009)
24. Hong Kong Economic Times (香港經濟日報): Over 10 staff in Prince of Wales Hospital were infected (威院10多員工 集體染病住院). Hong Kong Economic Times, March 11 (2003) (香港經濟日報). Hong Kong Economic Times, Hong Kong, A18 (2003) (in Chinese)
25. Lau, A.L.D., Chi, I., Cummins, R.A., Lee, T.M.C., Chou, K.L., Chung, L.W.M.: The SARS (Severe Acute Respiratory Syndrome) pandemic in Hong Kong: Effects on the subjective wellbeing of elderly and younger people. Aging Ment. Health 12, 746–760 (2008)
26. Osterhaus, A.: New respiratory viruses of humans. Pediatr. Infect. Dis. J. 27, S71–S74 (2008)
27. Zhou, L.L., Ni, B., Luo, D.Y., Zhao, G.Y., Jia, Z.C., Zhang, L.Y., Lin, Z.H., Wang, L., Zhang, S.L., Xing, L., Li, J.T., Liang, Y.F., Shi, X.F., Zhao, T.T., Zhou, L.Y., Wu, Y.Z., Wang, X.L.: Inhibition of infection caused by severe acute respiratory syndrome-associated coronavirus by equine neutralizing antibody in aged mice. Int. Immunopharmacol. 7, 392–400 (2007)

Ordered Polyline Trees for Efficient Search of Objects Moving on a Graph

Thuy Thi Thu Le and Bradford G. Nickerson

Faculty of Computer Science, University of New Brunswick
P.O. Box 4400, Fredericton, N.B. Canada E3B 5A3
{m6839,bgn}@unb.ca

Abstract. We discuss a spatio-temporal data structure to index objects moving on a graph. It is designed to efficiently answer rectangle R plus time instance and time interval queries about the past positions of moving objects. Such data structures are useful, for example, when searching which vehicles moving on a road network in specific areas at specific times. Unlike other data structures that use R-trees to index bounding boxes of moving object trajectories, our data structure indexes oriented line segments representing positions of moving objects at different times. For n moving object instances (unique entries of moving objects) on a graph with E edges, we show that $O(log_2 E + |L|log_2^2(n/E) + k)$ time is required to answer a rectangle R plus time interval query, for $|L|$ the number of edges intersected by R and k the number of line segments containing moving object instances in range. Space $O(n^2/E + E)$ is required in the worst case to store n moving object instances in E ordered polyline trees. Space $\Omega(n + E)$ is required to store the history of all n moving object instances.

1   Introduction

A significant challenge in spatio-temporal databases is how to index moving objects to improve the response time for query processing. Indexing can be done on either current and future positions of moving objects, or historical positions of moving objects [16]. Our research addresses the latter category. Queries on historical data are likely to be used in applications such as planning, event reconstruction and training. Most previous work for indexing moving objects assumes free movement of the objects in space (e.g., [2], [12], [14], [17], [18]). If movement is restricted to edges of a graph, the index should be able to use less storage than would be required if objects were free to move anywhere in space. We address the problem of indexing moving objects on a graph (possibly disconnected) defined by its edges and vertices. The graph can be non-planar as it is when representing road networks [5].

There is some existing work on indexing objects moving on a graph, including MON-tree [3], PPFI [6], FNR-tree [7], and [13]. The common point of these data structures is to combine several R-trees to index moving objects on a fixed network. A network is indexed by an R-tree [15] [10] while moving objects are

D. Taniar et al. (Eds.): ICCSA 2010, Part I, LNCS 6016, pp. 401–413, 2010.

indexed on a forest of R-trees, whose roots are linked to leaf nodes of the network tree. A moving object is represented as a (space × time) rectangle whose one side is a time interval and whose other side is a position interval of that moving object. The disadvantage of these data structures is that the number of retrieved objects for a query can be much more than the exact result. When a moving object rectangle intersects a (space × time) query rectangle, we still do not know for certain whether this moving object is in range or not. The time complexity of this approach is controlled by the number of (space × time) moving object rectangles intersecting the (space × time) query. Fig. 1 show an example of 14 moving objects, and Fig. 2 shows a query rectangle $R=([23,25],[0.62,0.75])$, respectively. There are 6 moving objects having their begin or end points falling inside the edge. Eight moving objects $o_6, o_8, ..., o_{14}$ move across the entire edge. A diagonal line segment also represents the direction of moving objects at a constant velocity. Diagonal line segments from upper left to lower right represent objects moving from the right to left direction. When rectangles are used to index these moving objects, five rectangles representing five moving objects o_5, o_7, o_9, o_{11} and o_{13} intersect with the shaded query rectangle R as shown in Fig. 3. However, only two moving objects o_5 and o_7, whose rectangle's diagonal line segment intersect with R, are actually in range. Note that the nine other moving objects $o_1, .., o_4, o_6, o_8, o_{10}, o_{12},$ and o_{14} are not shown in Fig. 3 because their rectangles do not intersect with R. In the worst case, all moving object rectangles on an edge intersect the query rectangle R, but none of the moving objects are in range.

We propose a new data structure that allows us to exactly retrieve moving objects for a query. Instead of using R-trees to index bounding boxes of moving objects, our data structure indexes oriented line segments representing positions

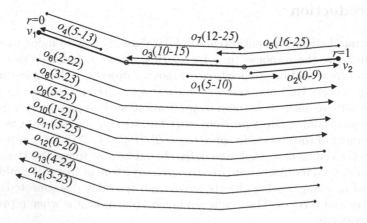

Fig. 1. An example of 14 moving objects on edge connecting two vertices v_1 and v_2. Each directed polyline represents a position interval of a moving object with a direction. The two numbers in parentheses represent time intervals of corresponding moving objects.

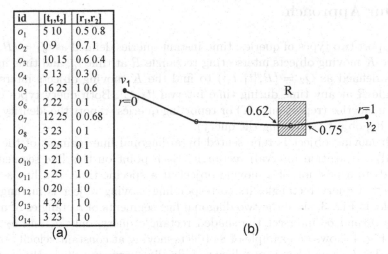

id	[t₁,t₂]	[r₁,r₂]
o_1	5 10	0.5 0.8
o_2	0 9	0.7 1
o_3	10 15	0.6 0.4
o_4	5 13	0.3 0
o_5	16 25	1 0.6
o_6	2 22	0 1
o_7	12 25	0 0.68
o_8	3 23	0 1
o_9	5 25	0 1
o_{10}	1 21	0 1
o_{11}	5 25	1 0
o_{12}	0 20	1 0
o_{13}	4 24	1 0
o_{14}	3 23	1 0

(a)

(b)

Fig. 2. (a) 14 moving objects (from Fig. 1) described by a table. (b) rectangle query R, where R intersects the edge at the position interval $[r_1, r_2] = [0.62, 0.75]$ and the time interval query is $[t_1, t_2] = [23, 25]$.

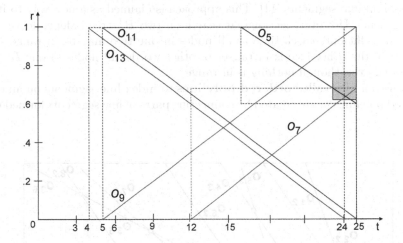

Fig. 3. Five $[t_1^j, t_2^j], [r_1^j, r_2^j]$ rectangles represent five moving objects o_5, o_7, o_9, o_{11}, and o_{13} from Fig. 2(a). The solid line segments illustrate diagonal line segments of rectangles (shown by dashed lines). The shaded rectangle is a query rectangle.

of moving objects at different times. With this new data structure, we can answer a rectangle R plus time interval query in $O(log_2 E + |L| log_2^2(n/E) + k)$ time, where n is the number of moving object instances (unique entries of moving objects) on a graph with E edges, $|L|$ is the number of edges intersected by R and k is the number of line segments containing moving object instances in range. This approach improves our previous research [8] by accounting for both range $[r_1, r_2]$ and $[t_1, t_2]$ interval intersections properly with one data structure.

2   Our Approach

We support two types of queries: time instant queries defined as $Q_1 = (R, t_q)$ to find the K moving objects intersecting rectangle R at time t_q, and time interval queries defined as $Q_2 = (R, [t_1, t_2])$ to find the K moving objects intersecting rectangle R at any time during time interval $[t_1, t_2]$. Both query types can be counting queries (report only K) or reporting queries (report the identity of the K moving objects satisfying the query).

Each moving object is represented by a diagonal line segment of the (time interval) × (position interval) rectangle. Each point on this line segment corresponds to a position of a moving object at a specific time. If a line segment intersects a query rectangle, its corresponding moving object is in range. For example, in Fig. 3, since the two diagonal line segments of rectangles of moving objects o_5 and o_7 intersect the shaded rectangle query, only o_5 and o_7 are in range. Fig. 4 shows an example of 8 objects moving at constant velocity over an entire edge. Our problem is now how to index line segments efficiently to achieve an efficient search on moving objects. Instead of being represented by bounding rectangles and indexed by an R-tree, line segments can be indexed by two B^+-trees, one to store x−coordinates and the second to store y−coordinates of end points of all line segments [11]. This approach is claimed as a new way to index line segments. However, rectangular search on two B^+-tree independently may result in inefficient search time as all nodes in one tree may be in range while nothing in the other tree is in range. In other words, all nodes of one B^+-tree are visited even though nothing is in range.

We use an idea called **ordered polylines** to index line segments on an edge. Ordered polylines p_i are created by connecting parts of line segments formed from

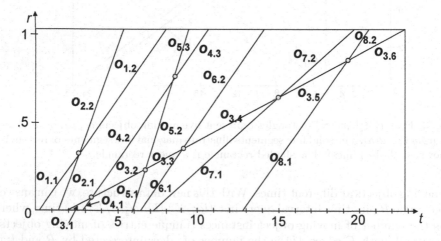

Fig. 4. Line segments represent 8 moving objects traveling at a constant velocity over an edge in direction from $r = 0$ to $r = 1$. $o_{j.1}$, $o_{j.2}$.., belong to the line segment representing moving object o_j.

their intersection (with each other and with the $r = 0$, and $r = 1$ boundaries). For example, the first four ordered polylines in Fig. 4 are $p_1 = \{o_{1.1}, o_{2.2}\}$, $p_2 = \{o_{2.1}, o_{1.2}\}$, $p_3 = \{o_{3.1}, o_{4.2}, o_{5.3}\}$, and $p_4 = \{o_{4.1}, o_{3.2}, o_{5.2}, o_{4.3}\}$. We assume that objects move from $r = 0$ to $r = 1$ in a monotonic fashion. This assumption provides the basic for one data structure. For objects (e.g., o_5, o_{11}, o_{13} in Fig. 3) moving from $r = 1$ to $r = 0$, the ordered polylines would divide the (t, r) space in a monotonic decreasing fashion.

In a real situation when we consider the historical position of vehicles moving on a road network, most of them travel from the start to the end of the edge representing a road. Others may start to move or stop in the middle of the road. We consider all positions of moving objects in our data structures. Ordered polylines also work for objects moving on a road, then stopping for a period of time, then moving again. For objects not moving over the entire edge (e.g., o_9, o_{10}, and o_{11} in Fig. 5), we add one (or two) line segment(s) to their line segments' endpoint(s) so that the connected parts from these original line segments reach the $r = 0$ and $r = 1$ boundaries. The extending line segment starts from one endpoint, whose r-coordinate is not 0 or 1, to a point having r-coordinate=0 or r-coordinate=1, and t-coordinate falling half-way between the end points of the two adjacent line segments. Fig. 5 shows an example of three extended line segments for three objects o_9, o_{10}, and o_{11}.

Ordered polylines are arranged as a balanced search tree based on each p_i dividing the space. Points to the left of p_i are guaranteed to be in the left subtree of the node containing p_i; similarly, points to the right of p_i are in the right subtree of the node containing p_i.

In the worst case, every line segment representing a moving object instance intersects the line segments representing all other moving object instances on

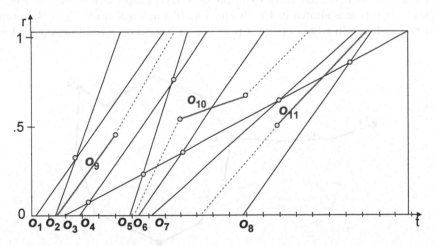

Fig. 5. Line segments represent all situations of moving objects. Objects o_9, o_{10}, and o_{11} are extended, and induce new ordered polylines that account for intersections with ordered polylines spanning the entire edge (i.e. with $r \in [0, 1]$).

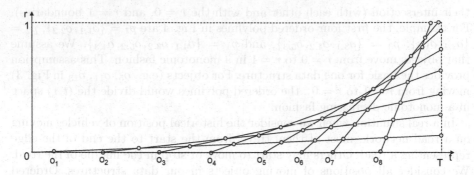

Fig. 6. Example of 8 polylines representing 8 moving object instances $o_1, ..., o_8$ in the worst case, where each object instance intersects 7 others in time

the same edge (see Fig. 6). For g_i moving object instances on edge i, this worst case results in $O(g_i^2)$ line segments, with each ordered polyline requiring $O(g_i)$ line segments. The number of ordered polylines is still precisely g_i. We thus need $O(log(g_i))$ time to find which line segments of a single ordered polyline intersect the Q_2 query. As we show in Section 4, For a single edge e_i containing g_i moving object instances, the time to answer a Q_2 query in the worst case is $O(log(g_i)^2 + k)$, where k is the number of ordered polylines in range.

3   The Primary Data Structure

Our data structure contains a graph strip tree, which spatially indexes edges of a fixed graph with E edges. An example of a fixed graph G is shown in Fig. 7. A graph strip tree is shown in Fig. 8 and Fig. 9. Each leaf node C_i of the graph strip tree indexes an edge e_i (e.g., a polyline, or a road on a road network). Leaf

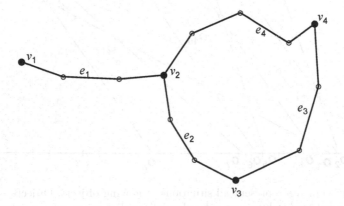

Fig. 7. Example graph G with 4 edges $e_1, ..., e_4$ and 4 vertices $v_1, ..., v_4$

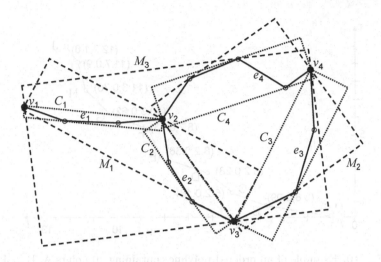

Fig. 8. Edges of graph G (Fig. 7) are represented as strip trees, with $C_1, ..., C_4$ representing the root bounding boxes for each strip tree. The strip trees are merged bottom up in pairs to construct a graph strip tree.

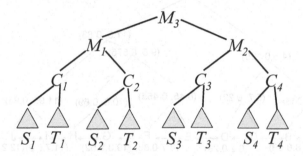

Fig. 9. The graph strip tree corresponding to the graph in Fig. 8. Each leaf C_i points to strip tree S_i representing edge e_i, and ordered polyline tree T_i indexing moving objects on e_i.

nodes C_i point to the strip tree [1] S_i spatially indexing e_i and to an ordered polyline tree T_i indexing line segments representing moving objects on e_i.

In order to index an ordered polyline (Fig. 10), we use a one-dimensional range tree [4] to index its points. Since points (t, r) in an ordered polyline are monotonically increasing in both t and r values, we can choose either t or r as the key of the range tree without changing its structure. In our range tree, a leaf node of the tree contains two values t and r of a point, and an internal node T^j contains two average values $(\bar{t}, \bar{r})$, which are the average of the (t, r) values in the rightmost leaf node in the left subtree of T^j and the leftmost leaf node in the right subtree of T^j. All leaf nodes are threaded. Fig. 11 shows the range tree indexing the ordered polyline in Fig. 10.

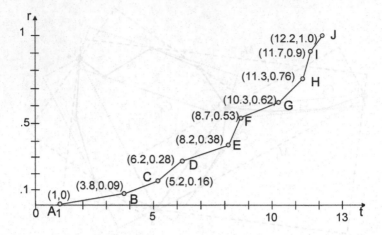

Fig. 10. Example of an ordered polyline containing 10 points A, B,.., J

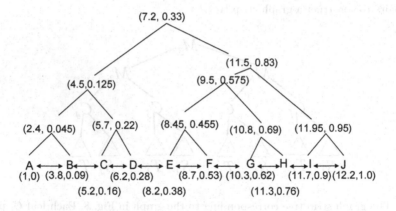

Fig. 11. Range tree indexing the ordered polyline shown in Fig. 10

4   Search Complexity

Searching for moving objects intersecting a query rectangle R and a time interval $[t_1, t_2]$ starts at the root of the strip tree, and returns a list L of edges intersecting R. Searching each of the $|L|$ ordered polyline trees requires $O(log_2^2(\frac{n}{E}) + k)$ time in the worst case, assuming an expected equal number of moving objects on each edge, for n the total number of moving object instances [9].

Theorem 1. *For a single ordered polyline p_i containing w_i points, the time to search for line segments of p_i intersecting a Q_2 query is $O(log(w_i) + a)$, for a the number of line segments intersecting Q_2.*

Proof. A query $Q_2 = (R, [t_1, t_2])$ is transformed to $Q_3 = [t_1, t_2] \times [r_1, r_2]$ queries by finding the positions r_1, r_2 that span the query rectangle R (see Fig. 2(b)). Searching for segments of an ordered polyline intersecting a query $Q_3 = [t_1, t_2] \times [r_1, r_2]$ starts from the root of the range tree, then goes to the left child or the right child based on the $(\bar{t}, \bar{r})$ values. When a leaf node is reached, we follow the threads from the current leaf to check for the intersection between the query and line segments.

At an internal node, the $(\bar{t}, \bar{r})$ values are compared to the $[t_1, t_2]$ and $[r_1, r_2]$ ranges of the query rectangle Q_3. We follow the proper path based on the following four cases:

1. If $\bar{r} \in [r_1, r_2]$ ($\bar{t} \in [t_1, t_2]$), and $\bar{t} \notin [t_1, t_2]$ ($\bar{r} \notin [r_1, r_2]$), we travel down based on the $\bar{t}(\bar{r})$ value. For example, with the query rectangle R_1 in Fig. 12, we travel down to the left child from the root node.
2. If $\bar{r} \notin [r_1, r_2]$ and $\bar{t} \notin [t_1, t_2]$, we identify the following two cases:
   a. if $(r_1 > \bar{r}$ and $t_1 > \bar{t})$ or $(r_2 < \bar{r}$ and $t_2 < \bar{t})$, we follow the right or left child, respectively. For example, with the query rectangle R_2 in Fig. 12, we travel down to the right child from the root node.
   b. if $(\bar{t} > t_2$ and $\bar{r} < r_1)$ or, $(\bar{t} < t_1$ and $\bar{r} > r_2)$, we halt. For example, with the query rectangle R_3 in Fig. 12, we halt because no line segment of the polyline intersects with R_3.
3. If $\bar{r} \in [r_1, r_2]$ and $\bar{t} \in [t_1, t_2]$, we travel down the left side of the current node until reaching a leaf node l. We then check the intersection of the segments threaded from l (e.g., to the right direction) until we reach a line segment that does not intersect Q_3. For example, with the query rectangle R_4 in Fig. 12, we travel down to the leaf node D, then report moving object instances of line segments DE, EF, and FG in range.

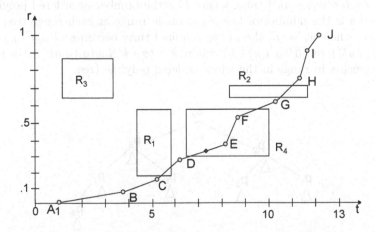

Fig. 12. Examples of four different positions of Q_3: $R_1, .., R_4$, resulting in four different cases of travel down the range tree in Fig. 11. The diamond at location (7.3, 0.33) illustrates the position of the root node of the range tree.

We know that w_i is the number of indexed points on a range tree, and that a range tree is a balanced binary search tree. In the worst case, when the root node meets the fourth case above, the time required is $O(log_2(w_i) + a)$, where w_i is the number of points in the ordered polyline p_i, and a is the number of line segments intersecting Q_3.

In the worst case (illustrated in Fig. 6), $w_i = O(g_i)$, where g_i is the number of object instances on edge e_i, and the above required time becomes $O(log_2(g_i)+a)$. In the best case, assuming objects are all moving at the same velocity, the number of indexed points w_i in the range tree is 2, and a single line segment intersection with Q_3 suffices to answer the query.

Theorem 2. *For a single edge e_i containing g_i moving object instances, the time to answer a Q_2 query in the worst case is $O(log(g_i)^2 + k)$, where k is the number of line segments in range.*

Proof. An ordered polyline tree T_i indexes ordered polylines p_i as a balanced search tree based on each p_i dividing the space into a left and right part. The left part and right part have an equal number of ordered polylines. Each internal node contains a range tree indexing line segments of one ordered polyline, and points to left and right subtrees that recursively subdivide the space by ordered polylines. Each leaf node also contains a range tree for an ordered polyline. Fig. 13 shows the ordered polyline tree indexing the 8 ordered polylines shown in Fig. 4.

Since an ordered polyline tree is a balanced search tree, and indexes g_i ordered polylines p_i, its height is $log_2(g_i)$. From theorem 1, searching a range tree at each node on the ordered polyline tree takes $O(log(g_i) + a)$ time in the worst case. Therefore, searching the ordered polyline tree for moving object instances intersecting Q_2 requires $O((log_2(g_i) + k')(log(w_i) + a))$, or $O(log(g_i)log(w_i) + alog(g_i) + k'log(w_i) + ak')$ time, where k' is the number of ordered polylines in range, and a is the number of line segments in range at each range tree. In the worst case, when $w_i = g_i$, the above required time becomes $O(log^2(g_i) + (a + k')log(g_i)+ak')$, or $O(log^2(g_i)+k)$, where $k = (a+k')log(g_i)+ak'$ is the number of line segments in range in the whole ordered polyline tree.

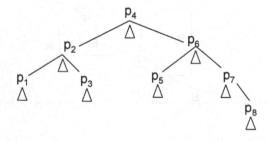

Fig. 13. Ordered polyline tree indexing the 8 ordered polylines shown in Fig. 4. Ordered polyline $p_7 = \{o_{7.1}, o_{3.5}, o_{8.2}\}$.

Many line segments of the same moving object instance can be found in range, so duplicates of moving object instances in the query answer can occur. In the best case, when an ordered polyline is an line segment representing a moving object instance $w_i = 2$, the above required time becomes $O(log(g_i) + k)$, where k is the number of moving object instances in range.

The time to search the graph strip tree is $O(log_2 E + |L|)$, where we assume that searching a single strip tree to see if it intersects R requires $O(1)$ time. This is a reasonable assumption based on actual road network statistics. For example, the number of edges in the entire road network of Canada [19] has $E = 1,869,898$, with an average of 7.32 segments per edge. If we assume a merged strip tree with $E = 2,000,000$, with each strip tree requiring 1,000 bytes (a generous allocation), a main memory size of 2 GB will suffice to hold the merged strip tree.

We assume that there are n object instances moving on E edges of a graph over a time domain $[0, T]$. Assuming the n object instances are uniformly distributed among E edges, the expected number of moving object instances on one edge is $\frac{n}{E}$. Combining these assumptions with Theorem 2 leads to the following theorem:

Theorem 3. *There exists a data structure indexing objects moving on a graph that answers a Q_2 query in expected time $O(log_2 E + |L|log_2^2(\frac{n}{E}) + k)$, for k the number of line segments in range.*

In the best case, when $w_i = 2$ (i.e., each ordered polyline is a line segment), searching an ordered polyline requires $O(1)$ time; thus, the expected time is $\Omega(log_2 E + |L|log_2(\frac{n}{E}) + k)$, for k the number of object instances in range.

Assuming the number of moving object instances n is much greater than the number of edges E on the graph (i.e., $n \gg E$), we expect the search time to be dominated by the time $O(|L|log_2^2(\frac{n}{E}))$ to search L ordered polyline trees.

5   Space Complexity

The space for an ordered polyline tree in the best case (one line segment per ordered polyline) is $O(g_i)$, versus the worst case (see Fig. 6) where the space required is $O((g_i)^2)$. We assume E edges stored in the graph strip tree require $O(1)$ space for each edge. Assuming n moving object instances are uniformly distributed among E edges, the expected number of moving object instances on an edge is $\frac{n}{E}$. Each of the E ordered polyline trees requires $O((\frac{n}{E})^2)$ space, assuming the worst case illustrated in Fig. 6 occurs; thus, the space required for the graph strip tree is $O(\frac{n^2}{E} + E)$. In the best case, each edge stores $\frac{n}{E}$ segments, giving a $\Omega(n + E)$ bound on the required space.

6   Conclusion

We present a new data structure for efficient search of objects (e.g. vehicles) moving on a graph. The underlying graph can be nonplanar, or even disconnected. Our data structure is a combination of strip trees and ordered polyline trees. Strip trees are used for spatial indexing of the graph edges. Each strip tree (at leaf level) represents a polyline (corresponding to a road or road segment in a road network). Ordered polyline trees are used to index the trajectories of moving objects on one of the graph edges.

Unlike previous data structures using rectangles to represent moving objects, we use diagonal line segments. The main advantage of our data structure is that it can answer a rectangle R plus time interval $[t_1, t_2]$ query with polylogarithmic and output sensitive search time. There are some other advantages for our data structure. First, the strip trees (indexing the graph geometry) and the ordered polyline trees (indexing line segments representing moving objects) are independent. One can update the ordered polyline trees without changing the strip tree spatial index for edges, or update a strip tree when an edge geometry changes, without affecting other edge strip trees. Second, since moving objects on a graph edge belong to a strip tree, we can easily answer queries which count moving objects on a single edge. For example, we can count how many vehicles move on a specific road at a specific time or during a specific time interval.

An open problem is how to efficiently index ordered polylines representing moving object instances so as to achieve an I/O efficient worst case optimal search complexity, and how to build an I/O efficient data structure to achieve a polylogarithmic search time on a set of moving object instances.

References

1. Ballard, D.H.: Strip trees: a hierarchical representation for curves. Communications of ACM 24(5), 310–321 (1981)
2. Chon, H.D., Agrawal, D., Abbadi, A.E.: Query processing for moving objects with space-time grid storage model. In: MDM 2002: Proceedings of the Third International Conference on Mobile Data Management, Washington, DC, USA, p. 121. IEEE Computer Society, Los Alamitos (2002)
3. de Almeida, V.T., Güting, R.H.: Indexing the trajectories of moving objects in networks. GeoInformatica 9(1), 33–60 (2005)
4. de Berg, M., van Kreveld, M., Overmars, M., Schwarzkopf, O.: Computational Geometry Algorithms and Applications. Springer, Heidelberg (2000)
5. Eppstein, D., Goodrich, M.T.: Studying (non-planar) road networks through an algorithmic lens. In: ACM GIS 2008, November 5-7, pp. 1–10 (2008)
6. Fang, Y., Cao, J., Peng, Y., Wang, L.: Indexing the past, present and future positions of moving objects on fixed networks. In: CSSE 2008, Washington, DC, USA, pp. 524–527. IEEE Computer Society, Los Alamitos (2008)
7. Frentzos, E.: Indexing objects moving on fixed networks. In: Hadzilacos, T., Manolopoulos, Y., Roddick, J., Theodoridis, Y. (eds.) SSTD 2003. LNCS, vol. 2750, pp. 289–305. Springer, Heidelberg (2003)
8. Le, T.T.T., Nickerson, B.G.: Efficient Search of Moving Objects on a Planar Graph. In: ACM GIS 2008, Irvine, CA, USA, November 5-7, pp. 367–370 (2008)
9. Le, T.T.T., Nickerson, B.G.: Data Structures for I/Os Efficient Search of Moving Objects on a Graph. Technical report, TR09-192, Faculty of Computer Science, UNB, Fredericton, Canada, 14 pages (April 2009)
10. Leutenegger, S., Lopez, M.A.: Chapter 12 - Handbook of Data Structures and Applications (2005)

11. Lin, H.-Y.: Using b+-trees for processing of line segments in large spatial databases. J. Intell. Inf. Syst. 31(1), 35–52 (2008)
12. Ni, J., Ravishankar, C.V.: Indexing spatio-temporal trajectories with efficient polynomial approximations. IEEE Transactions on Knowledge and Data Engineering 19(5), 663–678 (2007)
13. Pfoser, D., Jensen, C.S.: Indexing of network constrained moving objects. In: Proceedings of the 11th ACM GIS, New Orleans, Louisiana, USA, November 07 - 08, pp. 25–32 (2003)
14. Pfoser, D., Jensen, C.S., Theodoridis, Y.: Novel approaches in query processing for moving object trajectories. In: VLDB 2000, Proceedings of 26th International Conference on Very Large Data Bases, Cairo, Egypt, September 10-14, pp. 395–406. Morgan Kaufmann, San Francisco (2000)
15. Rigaux, P., Scholl, M., Voisard, A.: Introduction to Spatial Databases: Applications to GIS. Morgan Kaufmann, San Francisco (2000)
16. Saltenis, S., Jensen, C.S., Leutenegger, S.T., Lopez, M.A.: Indexing the positions of continuously moving objects. In: SIGMOD Conference, Dallas, Texas, United States, May 15 - 18, pp. 331–342 (2000)
17. Song, Z., Roussopoulos, N.: Hashing moving objects. In: Tan, K.-L., Franklin, M.J., Lui, J.C.-S. (eds.) MDM 2001. LNCS, vol. 1987, pp. 161–172. Springer, Heidelberg (2000)
18. Song, Z., Roussopoulos, N.: Seb-tree: An approach to index continuously moving objects. In: Chen, M.-S., Chrysanthis, P.K., Sloman, M., Zaslavsky, A. (eds.) MDM 2003. LNCS, vol. 2574, pp. 340–344. Springer, Heidelberg (2003)
19. Statistics Canada. 2009 road network file, http://www.statcan.gc.ca (last accessed: September 21, 2009)

Compactness in Spatial Decision Support: A Literature Review

Pablo Vanegas[1,3], Dirk Cattrysse[1], and Jos Van Orshoven[2]

[1] Centre for Industrial Management, Katholieke Universiteit Leuven,
Celestijnenlaan 300A, 3001 Heverlee - Leuven, Belgium
Pablo.Vanegas@cib.kuleuven.be, Pablo.Vanegas@ucuenca.edu.ec,
Dirk.Cattrysse@cib.kuleuven.be
[2] Department of Earth and Environmental Sciences, Katholieke Universiteit Leuven,
Celestijnenlaan 200E, 3001 Heverlee - Leuven, Belgium
Jos.VanOrshoven@ees.kuleuven.be
[3] Facultad de Ingeniería, Universidad de Cuenca,
Cdla. Universitaria Av. 12 de Abril s/n, Cuenca, Ecuador

Abstract. The development of Spatial Decision Support Systems (SDSSs) which explicitly consider spatial relations has had a significant growth over recent years. The main intention of this paper is reviewing spatial optimization approaches for identifying *contiguous and compact* areas fulfilling particular criteria. These approaches explicitly consider *topological spatial relations* between geographical entities (cells, lines, points, areas). In this direction, spatial optimization techniques as heuristics, meta-heuristics, and mathematical programming are reviewed. Since the application fields, the nature of the approaches, the data format, and the size of the reviewed works are very diverse, high level comparison is made in order to identify critical issues regarding the identification of contiguous and compact areas in digital geographical information.

1 Introduction

1.1 Justification

The speedy progress of computational facilities has contributed to the development of sophisticated systems like those devoted to Decision Support. A Decision Support System (DSS) implies a computer program that: assists individuals or groups of individuals in their decision process, supports rather than replaces judgments of individuals, and improves effectiveness rather than efficiency [25], i.e. emphasizes effective impact rather than performance. A Spatial Decision Support System (SDSS) is different from a DSS in the fact that it is used to support decision processes where the spatial aspect of a problem plays a decisive role [43]. A SDSS is defined as an interactive, computer-based system designed to support users in achieving effective decision-making by solving semi structured spatial problems [31].

D. Taniar et al. (Eds.): ICCSA 2010, Part I, LNCS 6016, pp. 414–429, 2010.
© Springer-Verlag Berlin Heidelberg 2010

Even considering the fact that last developments of Geographic Information Systems (GIS) irrefutably have contributed to improve geo-spatial information processing, and to develop SDSSs; *historically, most models have dealt with the spatial data aspatially. The important spatial interactions between elements were usually not dealt with; and in Multi-Criteria Decision Analysis spatial influence or requirements have not often been explicit criteria in developing the solution* [23]. Moreover, there are authors [17,8,42] arguing that GIS capabilities are not enough to contribute to the solution of some kind of problems where the analytical and dynamic modelling aspects are crucial. In this sense, coupling GIS with analytical tools and dynamic modelling is proposed in several applications (e.g. [28,7,21,27]) as means to obtain useful methodologies to deal with *spatial analysis* in problems encompassing e.g. contiguity, compactness and clustering.

1.2 Objectives

The main intention of this paper is reviewing approaches to geographically identify *compact* areas fulfilling multiple on-site criteria. Compactness implies *contiguity*, and both of them are based on *adjacency* topological spatial relationships. Identification of compact areas has became a major issue in decision support systems. The problem is complex since the searched sites can be composed either by polygons or points in vector representations, or by a set of cells in raster maps. High quality or optimal compact sites can be relevant from e.g. economical, conservation, or management point of view.

While the second section introduces general definitions of techniques applied in spatial optimization in general; the third section looks over different approaches specifically dealing with contiguity and compactness. Finally, section 4 discusses the reviewed applications and section 5 draws the conclusions.

2 Definitions

Although this document makes use of terminology that could be intuitive, it is important to define some concepts in order to clarify the contributions for identifying compact areas in geo-data sets as part of decision support processes. A site is contiguous if one can walk from an identified location to another without leaving the site [54]. Since the notion of compactness is associated with firmly packed sites, *some of the earliest attempts to develop a compactness index relied on perimeter to area ratios* [30].

Compactness belongs to the Automatic Zoning Problem (AZP), defined by [38] as a hard optimization problem, in which N building blocks are aggregated into M zones such that some function (or functions) on the M zone data is (are) optimized subject to various constraints on the topology of the M zones and/or on the nature of the data they generate. Compactness is an issue that belongs to *optimization spatial analysis* which in turn applies diverse analytic and computational techniques in order to find optimal or near to optimal solutions to problems involving geographical objects (cells, lines, points, areas).

2.1   Spatial Relations

Although some approaches for *spatial analysis* [29] explicitly consider *relations* between spatially distributed entities, other approaches process the descriptive data attached to these entities. Three classes of *Spatial Relations* (SR), namely metric, order and topology have been distinguished based on the type of functions or relation associated with a set of objects [14]. Topology is a mathematical concept that has its origin in the principles of object adjacency and connectedness [44]. Topology describes the relationship between an object and its neighbors [1], relationships which are invariant under geometric transformations such as translation, rotation, and scaling [14]. Moreover, *Topological relations* can be defined through the three components of an object, that is, the interior, boundary and exterior [40]. *Adjacency* is a kind of topological relationship, which is applied in issues of *compactness*, *fragmentation*, and *clustering*. A simple example is shown in figure 1. While in the left hand side the set of nine black cells forms a compact patch, the black cells in the right hand side are fragmented. A region is more compact when the selected cells share more common borders with other selected cells. In this way, while the area is constant, *adjacency* leads to a shorter perimeter.

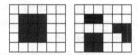

Fig. 1. Compactness vs. fragmentation

2.2   Techniques Applied in Compact Site Location

Heuristic Methods. A heuristic is a problem-specific way of directing problem solving. Since in the worst case exact algorithms need exponential time to find the optimum, approximate methods, often called heuristic methods or simply heuristics, seek to obtain good, that is, near-optimal solutions at relatively low computational cost without being able to guarantee their optimality [12]. When the heuristics are general-propose methods that can guide different problems to find high quality solutions, those are called meta-heuristics, defined [22] as solution methods that orchestrate an interaction between local improvement procedures and higher-level strategies to create a process capable of escaping from local optima and performing a robust search of a solution space. Examples of meta-heuristics are among others: genetic algorithms, tabu search, simulated annealing, multi-agent systems, and guided local search.

Simulated Annealing. The analogy between combinatorial optimization and physical process of crystallization is applied [26] to introduce the concept of annealing in combinatorial optimization. The crystallization process inspired [35] to propose a numerical optimization procedure which starts from an initial solution with energy level $f(0)$. A small perturbation to the initial solution brings the system to a new energy level $f(1)$. If $f(1)$ is smaller than $f(0)$ then the new solution obtained through the perturbation (state change) is accepted. If $f(1)$ is greater than $f(0)$, the new solution is accepted if the probability of acceptance given by the Metropolis criterion [2] $(f(0) - f(1)/S_0)$ is greater than a random number drawn from a uniform [0,1] distribution. Next, the freezing parameter (S_0) is slightly decreased and a new perturbation is performed. This process is repeated until a given number of iterations is reached or until change occurrences are very rare. The decrease of the freezing parameter is usually done only once every L iterations using a constant multiplication factor: $S_{i+1} = r * S_i$, with $0 < r < 1$.

Genetic Algorithms. The original motivation for the GA approach was a biological analogy. In the selective breeding of plants or animals, for example, offspring are sought that have certain desirable characteristics that are determined at the genetic level by the parents' chromosomes combine [41]. GA as they are know today were first described by John Holland in the 1960s and further development by Holland and his students and colleagues at the University of Michigan in 1960s and 1970s [36]. To search a space of solutions (or a space of hypotheses), GA define three elements: *chromosomes/genotype* (Individual solutions to a problem), *population* (set of chromosomes), and *generations* (iterations which allow the population to evolve). Genetic Algorithms provide an approach to learning that is based loosely on simulated evolution [37]. The algorithm starts with a randomly generated population of μ chromosomes. Fitness of each chromosome is calculated, and the next generation is created with *search operators* applied to the chromosomes of the current population to generate λ offspring. Individuals of the λ offspring and μ parents, or only individuals of the λ offspring, are considered to create the population of the new generation. This process is iterated until one or more highly fit chromosomes are found in the population. *Search operators* are classified in two categories: *mutation* operators modify an individual to form another; *crossover* operators generate one or more offspring from combinations of two parents [13].

Tabu Search. Local Search (LS) algorithms start from a candidate solution and moves to a neighbor solution that is better, and stops when all neighbors are inferior to the current solution. Since local search can be trapped in local optima, to improve its effectiveness, various techniques have been introduced over the years. Simulated Annealing (SA), Tabu Search (TS), and Guided Local Search (GLS) all attempt to help [48]. Tabu Search uses tabu lists (memory) to avoid cycling back to previous solutions. In fact, basic TS can be seen as simply the combination of LS with short-term memories [19]. A neighborhood is formally defined [13]: for any solution s of S, a set $N(s) \subset S$ that is a set of the neighboring solutions of s. The neighboring solutions, $N(s)$, are feasible solutions generated with the application of a move (or modification) m to s

$(m \oplus s)$, where a move m belongs to a set M. *TS* makes an "intelligent" choice of a solution from $N(s)$. Random selection or the analysis of subsets of M is proposed by some authors in order to accelerate the evaluation. This method for neighbor selection is associated with a decrease in quality, because the chosen solutions could have lesser quality than those selected in a complete examination of the neighborhood. This limitation encourages avoiding local optima because it generates certain diversity in the visited solutions, in this way the benefit is at global level.

Exact Methods. Exact methods include enumeration and mathematical programming, as well as many specialized algorithms that have been developed for particular optimization problems [52].

Mathematical Programming. Linear and Integer Programming (LP/IP), belonging to the Mathematical Programming methods, can find optimal (or exact) solutions. The simplex algorithm solves Linear Programming (LP) problems. LP is defined [53] as an optimization problem which: 1) attempt to maximize (or minimize) a linear function of the decision variables (objective function); 2) the values of the decision variables must satisfy a set of constraints and each constraint must be a linear equation or a linear inequality; and 3) a sign restriction is associated with each variable, for any variable x_i, the sign restriction specifies that x_i must be either nonnegative ($x_i \geq 0$) or unrestricted in sign (urs). While in pure integer programming all variables are integers, in mixed integer programming only some variables are integers. Spatial optimization is one of the fields where LP/IP has been successfully applied.

Enumerations Methods. Enumeration methods evaluate all candidate solutions (explicit enumeration - brute force), or select a set of efficient solutions (implicit enumeration), and select the one that optimizes specific criteria. Since the computational cost of this sort of search is proportional to the number of candidate solutions, it is typically applied in limited sized problems (small number of candidate solutions).

3   Compact and Contiguous Site Location Approaches

3.1   Heuristic Approaches

To deal with the problem of generating compact and contiguous districts while providing population equality and maintaining jurisdictional boundaries, an Optimization Based Heuristic is developed [34] based on a mathematical model [18], and with capabilities of considering many potential districts. The problem is represented with a graph, where each node is associated with the population of a county (unit), and an edge exists when two geographical units are neighbors. A penalty cost is assigned to every potential district that measures its "non-compactness" from an ideal district; this penalty cost is minimized. The non-comptacness of a district is measured by how far units in the district are from a central unit (u). The central unit is the node which minimizes: $\sum_{j \in V'} S_{uj}$, where V' is the set of nodes in a district. Since it is not possible to enumerate all possible districts (exponential to the number of populations units), the model uses the *column generation* methodology [3] to generate them "as needed". To ensure contiguity the model requires the district to be a subtree of a shortest path tree rooted at u. To enforce the shortest subtree requirement, a constraint is added to control that a node j is selected only if at least one of the nodes that is adjacent to it and closer to u is also selected [34].

To explicitly manage the shape in site allocation problems, the Parameterized Region-Growing (PRG) [6] is proposed as a fusion of two ideas: Simple Region Growing (SRG) and Parameterized Shape Growing (PSG). The SRG algorithm iteratively adds the most suitable neighboring cell; if two or more cells have equal suitability then the one closest to the seed is chosen. The PSG algorithm uses the same incremental process as the SRG but with a shape-suitability score determined by the distance and direction of the cell to the seed. The length of the diagonal of the enclosing rectangle $(diag)$ is used to normalize the score [6]. PRG combines SRG and PSG through a weighted average of the two scores. The simulated problems generated promising regions with a specific shape when an operator chooses the approximate location, shape and orientation of the regions. Nevertheless, an appropriate parameter setting is required.

Another heuristic approach, the Patch Growing Process (PGP) [8] generates feasible patches with reference to a seed cell which must have a high suitability score and must not be located within w cells of the boundary of the study area. This w value is the seed expansion, and defines the number of cells above and below, and left and right away from the seed cell; for example $w = 1$ implies three by three initial seed patch. Once the seed patch is defined, the neighbors to the patch are placed on a list in a random order. Each cell in the list is analyzed in terms of the number of edges e, that it shares with the current patch (from 1 to 4). The composite suitability of the cell i (CS_i) is defined by $CS_i = Suit_i + N.e_i$, where $Suit_i$ is the suitability value of the cell itself, N the weight attached to the number of edges shared with the existing patch. Then the list of neighboring cells is ordered according to the composite suitability. Although the cells with the same composite value appear as a group, they are in random order inside the group. Next, the top X percent of the cells on this list are added to the patch. The X and N parameters are the most important, N *rewards the compactness of the overall shape that would result once the highest X percent of the perimeter cells are joined to the growing patch* [8]. The results are graphically illustrated, and show that the X and N parameters effectively control the compactness of the grown regions. The PGP algorithm [8] is the base of a new Heuristic solution Method for Site Location (HMSL) [45] including Multi-Criteria Decision Analysis, and where the seed patches are automatically generated through a quadtree-based search. The authors compare the results with the objective value obtained with an Integer Programming (IP) formulation, and report that the heuristic results are near to optimal.

3.2   Meta-heuristics

One of the firsts evolutionary approaches [4] for locating optimal sites generates candidate sites through a Parameterized Region Growing (*PRG*) process. This process considers both, spatial and aspatial criteria to compute the suitability score of cells. The approach starts with a single cell and iteratively adds the neighboring cells with the highest score. The numeric string in the proposed genetic algorithm is made up of 10 numbers, one for each *PRG* parameter. While crossover operation exchanges one or more numbers, the other operators do generate new numbers but change only one number in a string [4]. The raster maps used for experimentation are 80x80 grids, and are grouped in two classes: homogeneous and heterogeneous. With fixed shape and trade-off parameters, the *GA* found 24 solutions as good as the ones obtained with an alternative exhaustive search method (15 out of 20 in homogeneous maps and 9 out of 20 in heterogeneous maps). The Genetic Algorithm for Patch Design (*GAPD*) [5] is proposed later to explicitly handle both dynamic and static criteria. It generates parameter strings according to which PRG grows multiple patches over the input maps.

When objectives conflict, it is often impossible to find a single optimum that dominates all other solutions [55]. In this sense, the notions of Pareto Optimal and Pareto Front are introduced according to the concepts presented by [39]. In the approaches proposed with *GA*, Pareto optimum means the current optimum, and consequently the non-dominated solutions only apply to the solutions that have been found in the current population [55]. Due to the recombinations in the different iterations the entire population reaches or approaches the Pareto Front. In the case study of [55], the goal is to find a set of contiguous places that minimize total cost and maximize proximity to certain facilities. An undirected graph is used to represent each feasible solution where each vertex represents a cell in the space, and an edge the connection between two cells (considering 4-connected regions only). The experiments were carried out with a 128x128 grid of cells. The proposed approach was able to generate the Pareto Front for each multi-objective site-search test.

There also exist several approaches for searching optimal location in spatial data represented with vector models. Genetic Algorithms are applied to allocate a contiguous set of land parcels using a graph representation to capture the spatial characteristics of a valid solution [54]. An attribute vector $A = (c(v_1), \cdots , c(v_i), \cdots , c(v_n))$ is the cost for the i_{th} vertex [54]. In this way it is possible to define the objective function as minimizing the sum of costs for all vertices in a solution V'. Initial sites are created with relatively regular shapes; each site starts from a seed vertex and continues to create a contiguous partial site until an entire site is built. The recombination operation is carried out through the local search algorithm based on the concept of a neighborhood of a solution S. While in a first stage this algorithm finds a movable vertex that can be removed from the site but avoiding non-contiguity, in a second stage vertices are found which can be added to the site without resulting in a non-contiguous site. The mutation process selects the vertex in the site with the lowest cost value and uses it as a new seed to create another site. Forty five problems ranging from $100x100$ to $500x500$ total vertices were tested, varying also the number of vertices to be allocated (p). CPU time to solve each problem increases with p, i.e. the time used to solve problems for different values of n remains approximately the same for a fixed value of p.

Evolutionary computation has also been applied in landscape ecology. The optimization procedure presented by [47] comprises in a first stage a simulation analysis of incremental removal of forest patches. Multiple simulations and Principal Component Analysis (PCA) capture the relative influence of two landscape ecology metrics: the Mean Proximity Index (MPI) and the Mean Nearest Neighbor Distance $(MNND)$. Since in previous studies, remnant patch size and relative proximity were key determinants of species abundance, a genetic algorithm is formulated by [47] to maximize the total extension of a network of remnant forest fragments selected on the basis of their relatively proximity and size. A string with length equal to the number of candidate patches and with 0 - 1 (0 = patch not selected, 1 = patch selected) values represent the initial population. The relative performance or "fitness" for each candidate landscape is evaluated by a particular landscape ecology metric or by a linear combination of metrics [47].

Simulated annealing is applied by [2] to allocate NxM pixels with K different types of land use. The distribution is prepared according to a probability P_k $(k = 1, \cdots, K)$ representing the proportion of land that must be allocated with land use k. Additionally, a development cost is assigned to each potential land use. These costs vary with location because they may depend on specific physical attributes of the area [2]. The initial development cost $(f(0))$ is associated with a random distribution of the K land uses over the area. A new development cost $(f(1))$ is obtained through a swap of the land uses of two randomly selected cells. Whether the cost $f(i + 1)$ is smaller than the cost $f(i)$ the cell change is accepted [2]. When $f(i + 1)$ is greater than $f(i)$ the cell change is accepted according to the probability of acceptance given by the Metropolis criterion. Afterwards, the cost function is expanded in order to add spatial compactness criteria by adding a non-linear neighborhood objective to the objective function. The proposed approach was tested on different areas ($10x10$, $50x50$, $250x250$, $300x300$), where the optimization time increases rapidly with grid size, requiring few hours to solve the largest problem.

Greedy search and simulated annealing methods to construct spatially cohesive reserve areas have been compared [33]. While the simulated annealing implementation is similar to a previously proposed approach [2], the greedy search algorithm updates an existing solution by adding one unreserved site. The new solution is called a neighboring solution, and its generation is repeated until no further decrease in the objective function value is possible. An iterative improvement is included in order to fulfill the constraint included in the objective function, which specifies a minimum area required for specific flora or fauna species (conservation value). The initial solution consist of all unreserved sites. Sites are only added to the solution and never removed. On the other hand the simulated annealing approach can reject the new solution. Although both algorithms gave similar solutions, simulated annealing usually gave better results in terms of minimizing the combined cost function (minimizing total reserve area and minimizing total boundary length).

3.3 Mathematical Programming

Spatial optimization has been widely applied in biological sciences. Four linear programming examples have been formulated [24] in order to account for biological dispersal. The constraints relate population in an habitat area in a time period (t) to the populations in other areas in a previous time period $(t-1)$. In addition they take account of the population growth and the immigration dispersion. Although the four linear models require stronger assumptions regarding ecosystem function and behavior, according to the authors the methods are applicable in the context of an adaptive, learning process in order to take advantage of the optimization methodology, and make progress either in learning about the ecological system or in managing it.

The Maximal Covering Location Model ($MCLM$) [9] minimizes the number of facilities to cover each and every demand point on a network. $MCLM$ is modified [11] to determine the optimal deployment of available fire-fighting vehicles. The modified model differs from the classical $MCLM$ in that it considers a different time limit for each class, where time limit represents the only time during which fire suppression can be effective. These time limits were calculated taking into account the type of vegetation, wind direction, and slope. The demand points, and at the same time candidate locations of the network were created from a set of vertices automatically generated by a GIS software. Previous to locate the vertices, a suitability map is constructed combining vegetation and slope type layers. Contiguous blocks belonging to the same suitability class are joined together to form a sub-region; the more valuable a sub-region is, the greater coverage (more demand points) it needs. Finally, the resolution (distance between vertices) is settled according to the suitability of each sub-region, in this way more valuable sub-regions have more vertices. This proposal was applied in a case study, where it was possible to see that the non-uniform distribution of the demand points is promising in facility location models, and that it could be useful also for other applications like deployment of water reservoirs and fuel breaks.

In order to reduce vulnerability of *elements* like species, communities, and endemic plants, a mathematical model is developed [10] for selecting sites for diversity conservation (Biodiversity Management Areas - *BMAs*). Since this approach does not contemplate spatial relations, the solutions are composed of isolated planning units. To avoid fragmentation, [16] formulate a mathematical model including in the objective the minimization of the outside perimeter of selected areas. Outside perimeter only counts those edges of a planning unit that are not shared in common with another selected planning unit in a cluster, and therefore, compact clustering is encouraged [16]. The model requires the definition of a binary variable (Z_{ij}) which is allowed a value of 1 if adjacent planning units i and j are both selected. In addition, the model includes two constraints to assure that shared edges are only subtracted from the objective if both planning units that share the edge are selected. The main conclusion of the authors is that the model can produce dramatic reduction in perimeter of the reserve system at the expense of relatively small increases in area and suitability index.

A mosaic of n cells can be represented (e.g. [49], [42]) as a planar graph with vertices and edges. The directed arcs of a planar graph and of its dual[3] are used to enforce contiguity in both spanning trees of the graph (a spanning tree uses $n - 1$ edges to connect all n vertices of a graph). The interwoven structure, obtained from the complementary nature of primal and dual graphs, prevents cycles in both trees. The formulation of a land acquisition problem is then stated by [50] as the problem of finding an optimal subtree of a spanning tree with a planar graph. Contiguity of the subtree is enforced by requiring the subtree to be a subset of the spanning tree backbone in the primal graph, and by specifying that the difference between the number of vertices and number of edges in the subtree must equal 1. Later, the acquisition of convex areas was faced by [51] with base on the definition of half-plane: a set of cells that can be specified in terms of a boundary line with known slope, direction, and an intercept position. The direction indicates the side of the boundary to which the cells belong. The main constraints enforce the mutually exclusive relation between half-planes and cells: *by selecting a cell, none of cells contained in that half-plane may be selected, and by selecting a half-plane, none of cells contained in that half-plane may be selected* [51]. The experimentation reveal that computing times are sensitive to three other factors: number of half-planes, region size, and whether or not some cells ("seeds") are selected in advance of performing the optimization.

In the mathematical formulation proposed by [45], compactness is achieved by increasing the number of boundaries that a selected cell shares with other cells that are also selected as part of the solution. This formulation implies the reduction of the patch perimeter, while the area is constant. In the same direction [46] present an Integer Programming Formulation (IP) for combining compactness and flow minimization requirements. This work allocates a predefined number of cells satisfying the following criteria: 1) minimize flow reaching the outlet of a watershed, 2) maximize/minimize intrinsic characteristics of the cells, and 3) form a compact patch. Although the core structure of the IP formulation can be applied for different sorts of flow and intrinsic characteristics, it is targeted to a reforestation application. The proposed approach is applied to perform several experiments in two watersheds in South Dakota in the USA for searching a given number of best cells (1) minimizing sediment reaching the watershed outlet,(2) maximizing the on-site environmental criteria, and (3) forming a compact patch.

3.4   Enumeration Methods

To solve land allocation problems, an interactive multi-objective optimization algorithm is develop [20] to operate over a grid of cells. Each cell is designated

---

[3] Given a planar graph G, its dual has a vertex for each plane region in G, and an edge for each edge in G shared by two neighboring regions.

as feasible or infeasible for the proposed land development. In addition, some cells are designated as amenity (desirable to have them in close proximity) and some cells as detractors (opposite to amenity). The algorithm finds a contiguous set of exactly k feasible cells. To solve the problem, four objectives functions are implemented: minimize cost of acquisition and development, minimize amenity distance, maximize detractor distance, and minimize the product of the perimeter and diameter of the set of allocated cells (compactness objective). The algorithm developed by [20] identifies a subset of efficient solutions (partial generation of the efficient set). The algorithm has four steps: 1) Initialization, find an initial efficient solution; 2) Selection, present the most preferred vector of objective function values to the decision maker, and request the selection of one objective function to be improved over its current level; 3) Optimizations, solve the single objective sub-problem; 4) Evaluation, if step 2 determines new efficient solutions, return to step 1 unless the decision maker is satisfied with the current subset of efficient points. The case study uses an area represented by 900 cells. Seven problems were solved specifying one function as objective, and desired levels values for the other three functions. In none of these problems the time response was slow enough to make the interactive use of the program impractical.

4   Discussion

Spatial Optimization based on mathematical programming is an active research area, where several models have been developed taking into account topological relations. Special attention was given to models dealing with *compactness*, and theoretical approaches have been proposed to consider other spatial aspects like perforation [42]. Mathematical formulations targeted to the location of *contiguous and compact* sites are applied in problems with sizes ranging from 100 to 4900 units whereas the required computation times vary from few seconds to hours. Although the number of units is small, some approaches are successfully applied on vector information at a regional level. It implies that mathematical approaches can be applied even to large regions when they are represented by an appropriate number of units. Table 1 shows the heuristics, meta-heuristics, and mathematical programming approaches dealing with compactness. This table makes use of a referential size as an indicator of the total number of objects subject to analysis. Table 1 shows that the referential size of mathematical approaches is kept small with respect to the ones in the heuristics and meta-heuristics. Since mathematical methods are able to generate exact solutions, these methods are very useful for the evaluation of non exact methods and in situations when the computation time is not a relevant issue (e.g. for planning activities). Moreover, mathematical formulations can act as optimality references for evaluating non-exact methods. Since compactness modeled by means of mathematical programming require a high amount of computational resources to achieve optimal solutions, the development of parallel computing and the generation of innovative models will contribute to improve the efficiency

Table 1. Summary of the work with regard to compactness

	Referential size	Size units	Predefined seed	Time	Time units
Heuristics					
Mehrotra and Johnson 1998	46	counties	N	5	minutes
Brookes 2001	300	cells	Y	-	-
Church et al 2003	23000	cells	Y	-	-
Vanegas et al 2008	4900	cells	N	1	second
Metaheuristics					
Brookes 1997	6400	cells	Y	-	-
Brookes 2001	372890	cells	Y	36	hours
Xiao et al 2002	16384	cells	N	-	-
Aerts and Heuvelink 2002	2500	cells	N	few	hours
McDonnell et al 2002	2160	cells	N		
Greedy				1	second
Simulated Anealing				96	seconds
Li and Yeh 2004	22500	cells	Y	4 – 13.6	hours
Venema 2004	162	patches	N	-	-
Stewart et al 2005	1600	cells	N	15-18	minutes
Xiao 2006	250000	cells	N	2268	seconds
Mathematical Programming					
Hof and Bevers 2000	1689	cells	N	-	-
Dimopoulou and Giannolkos 2001	160	cells	N	1.5	minutes
Fischer and Church 2003	776	planning units	N	7 s – 98 h	Seconds - hours
Williams 2003	1024	cells	Y	220	minutes
Shirabe 2004	100	cells	N	0.19 – 87882	wall clock
Vanegas et al 2008	4900	cells	N	540 - 28450	seconds
Enumeration Methods					
Hof and Bevers 2000	900	cells	N	16.8	seconds

of spatial optimization models. Taking into account that these alternatives are not easy to achieve, it is important to come across other approaches able to balance accuracy and efficiency. Several authors suggest the study of approximate methods in order to find feasible and near-to-optimal solutions.

Since Genetic Algorithms follow the concept of solution evolution by stochastically developing generations of solution populations using a given fitness statistic [32], they are a suitable approach to reach equilibrium between performance and optimality when the problems are large or non-linear. Although *LP* approaches can find optimal solutions (compact patches) through a straightforward search in adjacent basic feasible solutions, the improvements in the objective function value can be too slow. In this sense, the stochastic nature of *GA* (achieved through the genetic operators) can improve the performance of the search. Nevertheless, the reviewed *GA* solutions dealing with *compactness* are applied in relatively small sized problems. The biggest reviewed problems use *GA* combined with local search, and require the specification of seed points. GA are population-based metaheuristics, i.e. exploration oriented. They allow a better diversification in the whole search space [15]. Similar performance to GA is obtained with simulated annealing approaches, which were not applied on large sized problems at a regional level either. The very small times required by the greedy and simulated annealing approaches in [33] are also explained by the fact that the design of the reserve areas requires the analysis and improvement of one solution instead of a population of solutions. Single-solution based metaheuristics are exploitation oriented; they have the power to intensify the search in local regions [15].

The idea present in some *GA* approaches, which use a seed or a central unit as the starting point to define efficient compact patches, is also used in pure heuristic approaches. This sort of techniques has been applied on raster and vector data models, and the results obtained in some cases are superior to other approaches, and are at least practical to use in other cases. This paper reviews also heuristics approaches searching for compact areas. Some of these apply region growing and greedy algorithms as central processes in order to locate sites meeting a desired shape and size. In these algorithms the selection of a seed patch is a key issue. Its selection determines the final location of the sites looked for. The condition of being problem-based approaches is the most important advantage of pure heuristics, and in the case of the problems presented here the results are adequate from the performance point of view. Although in the studies we reviewed the solutions are near to the optimal because of the seed point selected by the user, most of them do not include an analysis of how far or near from optimality the solutions are.

One of the main characteristics of the heuristic approaches is that in most of the cases they make use of a starting *seed* area. Particularly remarkable is the referential size of the problem tackled by Church et al. (2003) [8] and the time required by Vanegas et al. (2008) [45]. The last includes an automatic generation of seed patches. Regarding to the meta-heuristics, table 1 shows that most of the approaches do not make use of a *seed* region. But the works of Brookes (2001) [5] and Xiao et al. (2006) [54] are capable to deal with the largest amount of data (372890 and 250000 cells respectively), potentiality based mainly on the predefinition of seed regions in the case of [5] and on the capacity for automatically generate seeds in the case of [54].

The enumeration method applied by Gilbert et al. (1985), the only one which was accessible, shows also good performance results. Although the reference size of the problem is not large, the short computation time makes it a promising method. The good performance is explained by the fact that the algorithm is specially developed to tackle the problem at hand, i.e. this enumeration method is also a problem-specific solution type.

5   Conclusions

Although the objectives of the reviewed studies, particularities of the application fields, and computational equipments are very diverse, relevant conclusions can be drawn regarding the location of contiguous and compact sites. As can be seen, LP/IP formulations are not only adequate for situations when the problem can be represented with an appropriate number of geographical entities, but they also play an important role in the evaluation of approximate solutions.

It seems that automatic generation of seed regions are a crucial issue to increase the size of the analyzed problems. Seeds generation is equivalent to identify local minima solutions, from which at least near to global optimal solutions can be achieved. Therefore the study and evaluation of seed generation techniques seem to be valuable in order to improve the solution space search and in turn the quality of the resulting contiguous and compact patches. The efficiency of population based metaheuristics can be increased through the combination and exploration of the high quality seed solutions. In the same direction, the effectiveness of single solution based metaheuristics can be improved through the exploitation of these seed solutions.

References

1. Abdul-Rahman, A., Pilouk, M.: Spatial Data Modelling for 3D GIS. Springer, Heidelberg (2008)
2. Aerts, J., Heuvelink, G.: Using simulated annealing for resource allocation. Geographical Information Science 16, 571–587 (2002)
3. Barhart, C., Johnson, E.L., Nemhauser, G.L., Savelsbergh, M.W.P., Vance, P.H.: Branch-and-price: column generation for huge integer programs. Operations Research 46, 316–329 (1998)
4. Brookes, C.J.: A genetic algorithm for locating optimal sites on raster suitability maps. Transactions in GIS 2, 201–212 (1997)
5. Brookes, C.J.: A genetic algorithm for designing optimal patch configurations in gis. Geographical Information Science 15, 539–559 (2001)
6. Brookes, C.J.: A parameterized region growing program for site allocation on raster suitability maps. International Journal of Geographical Information Science 11, 375–396 (2001)
7. Bryan, B., Perry, L., Gerner, D., Ostendorf, B., Crossman, N.: An interactive spatial optimisation tool for systematic landscape restoration. In: Complexity and Integrated Resources Management, Biennial conference of the International environmental Modelling and Software Society (2004)
8. Church, R., Gerrard, R., Gilpin, M., Stine, P.: Constructing cell-based habitat patches useful in conservation planning. Annals of the Association of American Geographers 93, 814–827 (2003)
9. Church, R., ReVelle, C.: The maximal covering location model. Regional Science Association 32, 101–118 (1974)
10. Church, R.L., Stoms, D., Davis, F., Okin, B.J.: Planning management activities to protect biodiversity with a gis and an integrated optimization model. In: Proceedings of the Third international conference/workshop on Integrating GIS and environmental modeling (1996)
11. Dimopoulou, M., Giannoikos, I.: Spatial optimization of resources deployment for forest-fire management. International Transactions in Operational Research 8, 523–534 (2001)
12. Dorigo, M., Stutzle, T.: Ant Colony Optimization. The MIT Press, Cambridge (2004)
13. Dréo, J., Petrowski, A., Siarry, P., Taillard, E.: Metaheuristics for Hard Optimization, Methods and Case Studies. Springer, Heidelberg (2006)
14. Egenhofer, M.J.: A final definition of binary topological relationships. In: Litwin, W., Schek, H.-J. (eds.) FODO 1989. LNCS, vol. 367, pp. 457–472. Springer, Heidelberg (1989)
15. El-Ghazali, T.: Metaheuristics, From Design to Implementation. Jonh Wiley and Sons Inc., Chichester (2009)
16. Fischer, D.T., Church, R.L.: Clustering and compactness in reserve site selection: An extension of the biodiversity management area selection model. Forest Science 49, 555–565 (2003)

17. Fischer, M., Nijkamp, P.: Geographic information systems and spatial analysis. The Annals of Regional Science 26, 3–17 (1992)
18. Garfinkel, R.S., Nemhauser, G.L.: Optimal political districting by implicit enumeration techniques. Management Science 16, 495–508 (1970)
19. Gendreau, M.: An Introduction to Tabu Search. In: Handbook of Metaheuristics, pp. 37–54. Kluwer Academic Plublishers, Dordrecht (2003)
20. Gilbert, K.C., Holmes, D.D., Rosenthal, R.E.: A multiobjective discrete optimization model for land allocation. Management Science 31, 1509–1522 (1985)
21. Gilliams, S., Van Orshoven, J., Muys, B., Kros, H., Heil, G.W., Van Deursen, W.: Literature review for afforest. decison support systems and spatial decision support systems (dss and sdss). Technical report, Katholieke Universiteit Leuven, Laboratory for Forest, Nature and Landscape Research (2002)
22. Glover, F., Kochenberger, G.A.: Handbook of Metaheuristics. Kluwer Academic Plublishers, Dordrecht (2003)
23. Hilla, M.J., Braatenb, R., Veitchc, S.M., Leesd, B.G., Sharmad, S.: Multi-criteria decision analysis in spatial decision support: the assess analytic hierarchy process and the role of quantitative methods and spatially explicity analysis. Environmental Modeling and Software 20, 955–976 (2005)
24. Hof, J., Bevers, M.: Direct spatial optimization in natural resource management: Four linear programming examples. Annals of Operations Research 95, 67–91 (2000)
25. Janssen, R.: Multiobjective decision support for environmental problems. Kluwer Academic publishers, Dordrecht (1992)
26. Kirkpatrick, S., Gelatt, C.D., Vecchi, M.P.: Optimisation by simulated annealing. Science 220, 671–680 (1983)
27. Ligmann-Zielinska, A., Church, R., Jankowski, P.: Sustainable urban land use allocation with spatial optimization. In: Geocomputation 2005. University of Michigan, Eastern Michigan University, Ann Arbor (2005)
28. Ligmann-Zielinska, A., Church, R., Jankowski, P.: Development density-based optimization modeling of sustainable land use patterns. In: Proceedings of the 12th International Symposium on Spatial Data Handling (2006)
29. Longley, P.A., Goodchild, M.F., Maguirre, D.J.: Geographic Information Systems and Science, 2nd edn. John Wiley and Sons, Ltd., Chichester (2005)
30. Maceachren, A.M.: Compactness of geographic shape: Comparison and evaluation of measures. Geografiska Annaler 67, 53–67 (1985)
31. Malczewski, J.: GIS and Multicriteria Decision Analysis. John Wiley & Sons, New York (1999)
32. Mardle, S., Pascoe, S.: An overview of genetic algorithms for the solution of optimisation problems. Computers in Higher Education Economics Review 13, 16–20 (1999)
33. McDonnell, M.D., Possingham, H.P., Ball, I.R., Cousins, E.A.: Mathematical methods for spatially cohesive reserve design. Environmental Modeling and Assesment 7, 107–114 (2002)
34. Mehrotra, A., Johnson, E.L.: An optimization based heuristic for political districting. Management Science 44, 1100–1114 (1998)
35. Metropolis, N., Rosenbluth, A., Rosenbluth, M., Teller, A., Teller, E.: Equation of state calculations by fast computing machines. Journal of Chemical Physics 21, 1087–1092 (1953)
36. Mitchell, M., Forest, S.: Genetic algorithms and artificial life. Artificial Life 1, 267–289 (1994)

37. Mitchell, T.: Machine Learning. McGraw-Hill Science/Engineering/Math, New York (1997)
38. Openshaw, S.: Developing GIS-relevant zone-based spatial analysis methods, ch. 4, pp. 55–74. Wiley, Chichester (1996)
39. Pareto, V.: Manual of Political Economy. Augustus M. Kelley, New York (1971)
40. Pullar, Egenhofer, M.: Towards formal definitions of topological relations among spatial objects. In: Third International Symposium on Spatial Data Handling, Sydney, Australia, pp. 225–242 (1988)
41. Reeves, C.: Genetic Algorithms. In: Handbook of Metaheuristics, pp. 55–82. Kluwer Academic Plublishers, Dordrecht (2003)
42. Shirabe, T.: Modeling topological properties of a raster region for spatial optimization. In: Proceedings of the 11th International Symposium on Spatial Data Handling (2004)
43. Uran, O., Jansen, R.: Why are spatial decision support systems not used? some experiences from netherlands. Computers, Environment and Urban Systems 27, 511–526 (2003)
44. Van-Orshoven, J.: Introduction to spatial data modelling and functionality of geospatial technology. Department of Earth and Environmental Sciences. K.U. Leuven (2007)
45. Vanegas, P., Cattrysse, D., Van Orshoven, J.: Comparing exact and heuristic methods for site location based on multiple attributes: An afforestation application. In: Gervasi, O., Murgante, B., Laganà, A., Taniar, D., Mun, Y., Gavrilova, M.L. (eds.) ICCSA 2008, Part I. LNCS, vol. 5072, pp. 389–404. Springer, Heidelberg (2008)
46. Vanegas, P., Cattrysse, D., Van Orshoven, J.: Compactness and flow minimization requirements in reforestation initiatives: an integer programming formulation. In: Gervasi, O., Taniar, D., Murgante, B., Laganà, A., Mun, Y., Gavrilova, M.L. (eds.) Computational Science and Its Applications – ICCSA 2009. LNCS, vol. 5592, pp. 132–147. Springer, Heidelberg (2009)
47. Venema, H.D., Calami, P.H., Fieguth, P.: Forest structure optimization using evolutionary programming and landscape ecology metrics. European Journal of Operational Research 164, 423–439 (2004)
48. Voudouris, C.: Guided Local Search. In: Handbook of Metaheuristics, pp. 185–218. Kluwer Academic Plublishers, Dordrecht (2003)
49. Williams, J.C.: A linear-size zero-one programming model for the minimum spanning tree problem in planar graphs. Networks 39, 53–60 (2001)
50. Williams, J.C.: A zero-one programming model for contiguous land acquisition. Geographical Analysis 34, 330–349 (2002)
51. Williams, J.C.: Convex land acquisition with zero-one programming. Environmental and Planning, Planning and Design 30, 255–270 (2003)
52. Williams, J.C., ReVelle, C.S.: Applying mathematical programming to reserve site selection. Environmental and Modeling Assessment 2, 167–175 (1997)
53. Winston, W.L.: Operations Research, Applications and Algorithms. International Thomson Publishing (1994)
54. Xiao, N.: An evolutionary algorithm for site search problems. Geographical Analysis 38, 227–247 (2006)
55. Xiao, N., Bennett, D.A., Amstrong, M.P.: Using evolutionary algorithms to generate alternatives for multiobjective site-search problems. Environment and Planning 34, 639–656 (2002)

An Architecture and a Metamodel for Processing Analytic and Geographic Multilevel Queries

Diego Martins Vieira Barros and Robson do Nascimento Fidalgo

Federal University of Pernambuco, Informatics Center
Av. Professor Luís Freire s/n, 50740-540 Recife, Brazil
diego.martins1@gmail.com, rdnf@cin.ufpe.br

Abstract. Analytic and geographic decision support queries are characterized by performing spatial analysis on data aggregated at different levels of detail and are typically large and complex to be written from scratch (manually) by a non-specialist user. Considering that decision support tools are in evidence and many databases (DB) have information with some geographic reference, non-specialist users of these DB need analytic and spatial decision support tools to better analyze DB information. In this context, Spatial On-Line Analytical Processing (SOLAP) tools have received a lot of attention. Nevertheless, as there is no *de jure* standard language for OLAP yet, like standard SQL is to Relational Database Management Systems (RDBMS), these tools are dependent on specific OLAP languages, Application Programming Interface (API) and servers. In order to propose an alternative to this problem, this paper presents an Analytic and Geographic Information Service (AGIS). Our proposal is based on open and extensible standards (i.e. it is not based on an OLAP server) to offer a service that provides multilevel analytic functions that aim to enrich the set of functionalities of Geographic Information Systems (GIS). In order to do this, AGIS 1) abstracts the complexity of generating analytic and geographic decision support queries and 2) is independent of hardware and software platform. To satisfy these goals, a three-tiered architecture and a metamodel were defined and implemented. As a proof of concept, a study case to analyze the electrical energy situation in Brazil was implemented using our proposal.

Keywords: Architecture, Decision Support, GIS, Metamodel, Multilevel Aggregation.

1 Introduction

Analytic queries, different from transactional queries (e.g. how many products are in stock?), are characterized by performing analysis on data aggregated at different levels of detail (e.g. what is the sum of sold products by state and city?). In this context, the analytic and geographic processing area is in evidence, especially because many databases (DB) have information with some geographic reference (e.g. streets, cities, zip codes) and therefore need spatial operations (e.g. adjacency, intersection and distance) to better analyze them. In this area, Spatial On-Line Analytical Processing (SOLAP) tools [1,2,3] have received a lot of attention. A SOLAP tool can

D. Taniar et al. (Eds.): ICCSA 2010, Part I, LNCS 6016, pp. 430–444, 2010.

be shortly described as an analytic and geographic tool that aims to integrate the functionalities (i.e. multidimensional and multilevel operations) of On-Line Analytical Processing (OLAP) [4,5] with the functionalities (i.e. spatial operations) of Geographic Information Systems (GIS) [6]. However, as there is no *de jure* standard language for OLAP yet, like ISO/IEC SQL [7] is to Relational Database Management Systems (RDBMS) and ISO/OGC SQL [8] is to Spatial DBMS (SDBMS), these SOLAP tools are dependent on specific OLAP languages and servers. It is important to observe that, according to ISO/OGC [8], its spatial SQL specification extends the conventional ISO/IEC SQL specification to define a standard SQL schema that supports storage, retrieval, query and update of geographic feature collections via the SQL Call Level Interface.

Moreover, as queries for spatial analysis are typically large and complex (i.e. these involve many selections, projections, aggregations and joins) and the effort to write these queries from scratch (manually) is not a trivial task for a non-specialist user, this paper proposes a three-tiered architecture and a metamodel for implementation of a service called Analytic and Geographic Information Service (AGIS). The AGIS three-tiered architecture presents overall definitions of its components and it was designed to provide a high cohesion and a weak coupling between its subsystems. In turn, the AGIS metamodel gives engineers and developers a better understanding of AGIS metadata, which describes the constructors and the restrictions needed to generate queries for analytic and geographic multilevel processing. We highlight that the task of defining AGIS metadata is normally done by engineers and developers (not by the end user), because this task requires familiarity with XML and database administration.

According to He [9], a service is a unit of work done by a service provider to produce results requested by the service requestor. Thus, AGIS aims to provide a service that: 1) abstracts the complexity of writing analytic and geographic multilevel queries by the generation of these queries according to ISO/OGC SQL syntax and 2) is independent of hardware and software platform because its implementation uses consolidated and non-proprietary standards, which also makes its proposal more easily deployable and extensible.

The remain of this paper is organized as follows: section 2 introduces the basic concepts of OLAP and spatial queries; section 3 proposes the AGIS architecture and metamodel; section 4 shows the case study used as a proof of concept; section 5 discuss some related work and finally section 6 presents the conclusions and future work.

2   Basic Concepts

OLAP tools [4,5] perform multilevel aggregation operations like: drill down (i.e. data disaggregation to a level immediately below – e.g. total sales from *Country* level to *State* level), roll up (i.e. data aggregation to a level immediately above – it is the opposite of drill down), drill down across (i.e. data disaggregation to any level below – e.g. total sales from *Country* level to *City* level) and roll up across (i.e. data aggregation to any level above – it is the opposite of drill down across). Note that these operations can be applied in a geographic theme/level (as in the examples above) or in a geographic feature (e.g. total sales in the states of *Brazil* feature).

A typical OLAP aggregate query would be: "What is the total sales by product category, store name and year?". Note that analytic queries aim at computing measures by one or more dimensions of analysis. Then, this query requires the SUM aggregate function on the measure *sales*, using the columns of the tables (i.e. elements of dimensions) in GROUP BY clause. Fig. 1 illustrates a way to write this query.

```
SELECT P.category, S.name, T.year, SUM(SA.price)
  FROM Product P, Shop S, Time T, Sales SA
 WHERE P.product_key = SA.product_key
   AND S.shop_key = SA.shop_key
   AND T.time_key = SA.time_key
 GROUP BY P.category, S.name, T.year
```

Fig. 1. OLAP SQL Query

GIS tools [6] enable analysis of geo-referenced data, making geographic processing possible. For this, these tools apply spatial operations (e.g. topological, directional and metric) on geometries. A typical GIS query would be: "What is the average sales by store for stores located in cities adjacent to Recife city?". Note that, in this query, it is necessary to use *ST_TOUCHES* spatial function. Fig. 2 illustrates a way to write this query.

```
SELECT S.name, AVG(SA.price)
  FROM Shop S, Sales SA, City C1, City C2
 WHERE S.shop_key = SA.shop_key
   AND S.city_key = C1.city_key
   AND C2.name = 'Recife'
   AND ST_TOUCHES(C1.geometry, C2.geometry)
 GROUP BY S.name
```

Fig. 2. GIS SQL Query

As we can see in Figures 1 and 2, the effort to write these queries from scratch (manually) is not a trivial task for a non-specialist user (particularly if it is necessary to write queries for analytic and geographic multilevel processing). Then, next section defines AGIS architecture and metamodel to provide a service that abstracts the complexity of writing these queries.

3 AGIS

This section proposes the AGIS architecture, which was designed so that its components are decoupled with the use of API, facilitating its extensibility and reuse. Moreover, this section also proposes the AGIS metamodel, which defines the metadata that provides support for abstracting the generation of analytic and geographic multilevel queries.

3.1 Architecture

Fig. 3 shows the three-tiered architecture of AGIS, where the AGIS Client tier interacts with the AGIS Server tier via the AGIS-API and the AGIS Server tier interacts with the Data Server tier via standard database API. The remain of this section discusses and presents the components of the AGIS Architecture.

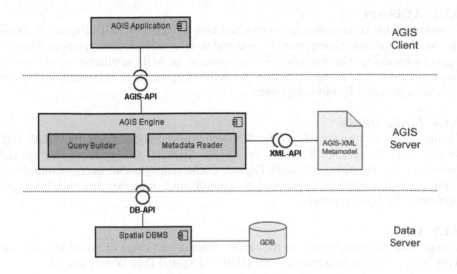

Fig. 3. AGIS Architecture

3.1.1 AGIS Application
Component that corresponds to an application for requesting the service provided by the AGIS Engine. This component can be a GUI (Graphical User Interface) implemented as a Web client, desktop or another application (e.g. a service, a system or a program).

3.1.2 AGIS Engine
Component that is responsible for 1) generating queries for analytic and geographic multilevel processing and 2) sending these queries to the SDBMS that executes them. This component, through its programming interface (AGIS-API component), receives a set of query parameters sent from an AGIS Application and returns the query result to it. The functionalities of this component are possible because it provides the multilevel aggregation operations (i.e. drill down [across] and roll up [across] operations). The AGIS Engine consists of two subcomponents: Metadata Reader and Query Builder, which will be described below.

3.1.3 Metadata Reader
Component to access and provide AGIS metadata. For example, the next level above or below a current level, the index and the name of measures columns in a query and the key fields to define joins between the tables of a Geographic DB (GDB).

3.1.4 Query Builder

Component that generates SQL queries with multilevel aggregations (i.e. with GROUP BY clause) and geographic restrictions (i.e. with spatial operators). This component interacts with Metadata Reader component to request AGIS metadata that gives the descriptions needed to generate analytic and geographic multilevel queries according to ISO/OGC SQL syntax.

3.1.5 AGIS-API

Component that corresponds to the programming interface of AGIS Engine. It allows the AGIS Application component to send and receive requests for operations like data aggregation and spatial restriction. For example, so an AGIS application send requests for drill down or roll up operations to AGIS Engine, it is necessary to use the interfaces provided by this component.

3.1.6 Spatial DBMS

Component that corresponds to the SDBMS, which must support ISO/OGC SQL syntax (e.g. PostgreSQL/PostGIS or Oracle Spatial) and will process queries generated and submitted by AGIS Engine. Cache management, query optimization, transaction management, concurrency control and integrity functionalities are performed by this component.

3.1.7 GDB

Component that corresponds to the tables (schema and data) of AGIS architecture. This component can be a transactional GDB or a Spatial Data Warehouse [10].

3.1.8 AGIS-XML Metamodel

Component that corresponds to the XML repository of metadata (according to AGIS metamodel – see section 3.2), which defines the metadata needed to generate queries for analytic and geographic multilevel processing. In other words, this component defines the metadata that describes how GDB component (i.e. their tables and their columns) must be organized to allow the generation of queries for analytic and geographic multilevel processing.

3.1.9 DB-API and XML-API

Components that correspond to the programming interfaces used to access the SDBMS (e.g. JDBC or ODBC) and the AGIS-XML Metamodel (e.g. DOM or SAX), respectively.

3.2 AGIS Metamodel

This section proposes the AGIS metamodel, which specifies the metadata that describes how AGIS Engine must understand the GDB schema to generate analytic and geographic multilevel queries. In order to provide a specification using a notation independent of technology, Fig. 4 shows AGIS metamodel using UML class diagram notation. The remain of this section presents the AGIS metadata elements and its relationships.

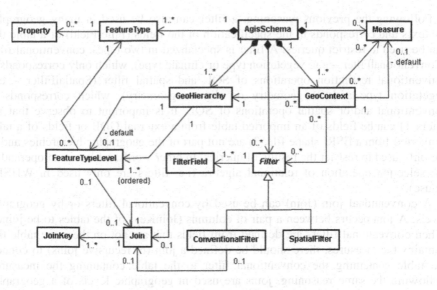

Fig. 4. AGIS Metamodel

The AGIS schema (AgisSchema) element is the root of the proposed metamodel. It is a composition of: 1) a set of feature types (FeatureType) from Open Geospatial Consortium (OGC) [11], where each feature type represents a geographic layer/theme that can be analyzed; 2) a set of geographic hierarchies (GeoHierarchy), where each geographic hierarchy defines the position in which the feature types should be processed in an aggregation operation; 3) a set of measures (Measure), where each measure represents a fact (measurable value that varies over time [4]) to be aggregated/analyzed; 4) a set of filters (Filter), where each filter corresponds to a set of fields (FilterField) from a table of the BDG that can be used as a selection/restriction criterion; and 5) a set of geographic contexts (GeoContext), where each geographic context corresponds to an analysis view.

A geographic hierarchy has a set of ordered geographic levels (FeatureTypeLevel) and it can have a default geographic level. Each geographic level is associated with a feature type (i.e. a geographic layer/theme) and represents the position of the feature type in the hierarchy. Examples of geographic levels can be Region, City, Country and State. As an example of a geographic hierarchy, we can consider H1: Country > State [default] > City. The specification of a default geographic level is optional and aims to facilitate the specification of queries, because it avoids the need of defining the initial geographic level to submit a query to AGIS Engine.

Geographic context is a denomination given to an analysis scope that corresponds to an abstract container, which has a geographic hierarchy and can have a set of measures, a set of filters and a default measure. For example, we can define a geographic context C1 from the geographic hierarchy H1, measures such as Area [default] and Rainfall, and filters like Vegetation Type, Climate Type and their geometries. Similarly to a geographic hierarchy, the definition of a default measure is optional and aims to facilitate the specification of queries, as it avoids the need of defining a measure to submit a query to AGIS Engine.

Following the previous reasoning, a filter can also be used in many geographic contexts and corresponds to the specification of the fields (FilterField) of a table that can be used to restrict queries. A filter is specialized in two types: conventional filter (ConventionalFilter – e.g. vegetation type or climate type), which only corresponds to conventional restriction operations of SQL and spatial filter (SpatialFilter – e.g. vegetation type and its geometry or climate geometry), which corresponds to conventional and/or spatial operations of SQL. It is important to observe that the filters 1) can be fields of an imported table from a external GDB or fields of a table converted from a ESRI shape file, 2) are not part of the geographic hierarchies and 3) are only used to restrict the results of queries. In other words, a filter is an operand of the selection operation of relational algebra (i.e. filters are only used in WHERE clause).

A conventional join (Join) can be used by conventional filters or by geographic levels. A join occurs between a pair of columns (JoinKey) of the tables to be joined. When conventional filters are defined from fields that are not on the same table that contains the measures, there should be defined a join (or recursive joins) to connect the table containing the conventional filter to the table containing the measures. Following the same reasoning, joins are used in geographic levels of a geographic hierarchy in two situations: 1) to make the connection between the table containing the geographic level with the lowest granularity and the table containing the measures and 2) to make the connection between two levels of a geographic hierarchy defined from normalized tables. Note that this second situation often happens in transactional DB, which are highly normalized. However, this situation hardly happens in a Data Warehouse, because its dimensions are usually denormalized.

Finally, feature types can have a set of properties (Property), which corresponds to a set of additional information about a particular theme/layer that can be returned in query results (e.g. political party and name of the Mayor of a City feature type). It is important to observe that 1) a property is an operand of the projection operation of relational algebra (i.e. properties are only used in SELECT clause), 2) properties are not part of geographic hierarchies and 3) there is no restriction to define a GDB column both as a filter and as a property. Fig. 5 shows fragments of a XML Schema that corresponds to the AGIS-XML Metamodel component of Fig. 3.

```
<xs:complexType name="T_MetadataElement">
  <xs:sequence>
    <xs:element ref="Name"/>
  </xs:sequence>
</xs:complexType>
<xs:complexType name="T_FeatureType">
  <xs:complexContent>
    <xs:extension base="T_FeatureTypeAttr">
      <xs:sequence>
        <xs:element ref="Source"/>
        <xs:element ref="ThematicIdentifier"/>
        <xs:element ref="GeoAttribute"/>
        <xs:element ref="Property" minOccurs="0" maxOccurs="unbounded"/>
      </xs:sequence>
    </xs:extension>
  </xs:complexContent>
</xs:complexType>
```

```xml
<xs:complexType name="T_Property">
  <xs:complexContent>
    <xs:extension base="T_MetadataElement">
      <xs:sequence>
        <xs:element ref="Column"/>
      </xs:sequence>
    </xs:extension>
  </xs:complexContent>
</xs:complexType>
<xs:complexType name="T_Filter" abstract="true">
  <xs:complexContent>
    <xs:extension base="T_FilterAttr">
      <xs:sequence>
        <xs:element ref="Source"/>
        <xs:element ref="FilterField" maxOccurs="unbounded"/>
      </xs:sequence>
    </xs:extension>
  </xs:complexContent>
</xs:complexType>
<xs:complexType name="T_SpatialFilter">
  <xs:complexContent>
    <xs:extension base="T_Filter">
      <xs:sequence>
        <xs:element ref="GeoAttribute"/>
      </xs:sequence>
    </xs:extension>
  </xs:complexContent>
</xs:complexType>
<xs:complexType name="T_ConventionalFilter">
  <xs:complexContent>
    <xs:extension base="T_Filter">
      <xs:sequence>
        <xs:element ref="Join" minOccurs="0"/>
      </xs:sequence>
    </xs:extension>
  </xs:complexContent>
</xs:complexType>
<xs:complexType name="T_Join">
  <xs:sequence>
    <xs:element ref="RightTable"/>
    <xs:element ref="JoinKey" maxOccurs="unbounded"/>
    <xs:element ref="Join" minOccurs="0"/>
  </xs:sequence>
</xs:complexType>
<xs:complexType name="T_GeoHierarchy">
  <xs:complexContent>
    <xs:extension base="T_GeoHierarchyAttr">
      <xs:sequence>
        <xs:element ref="DefaultLevel" minOccurs="0"/>
        <xs:element ref="FeatureTypeLevel" maxOccurs="unbounded"/>
      </xs:sequence>
    </xs:extension>
  </xs:complexContent>
</xs:complexType>
```

```
<xs:element name="FeatureType" type="T_FeatureType"/>
<xs:element name="Property" type="T_Property"/>
<xs:element name="SpatialFilter" type="T_SpatialFilter"/>
<xs:element name="ConventionalFilter" type="T_ConventionalFilter"/>
<xs:element name="Join" type="T_Join"/>
<xs:element name="GeoHierarchy" type="T_GeoHierarchy"/>
```

Fig. 5. Fragments of AGIS XML Schema

4 Case Study

As a proof of concept of our proposal, this section presents a case study that implements the AGIS Architecture using Java Enterprise Edition (Java EE). This makes this instance of AGIS architecture portable among operating systems and environments that support Java EE. Furthermore, an instance of AGIS Metamodel is implemented in XML.

In order to show that AGIS provides analytic and geographic multilevel queries abstracting the complexity of defining joins in a normalized schema, a subset of a transactional GDB about the Brazilian Electric Sector was used. Aiming to allow non-specialist users to interact with the AGIS Engine, a simple Java client (AGIS WEB) was implemented and is presented below. The other components were implemented using the following technologies: 1) Query Builder – Standard Java EE API; 2) Metadata Reader and XML-API – W3C DOM API for Java; 3) AGIS XML Metamodel – XML Schema; 4) Spatial DBMS – PostgreSQL/PostGIS and 5) AGIS-API and DB-API – JDBC. In sequence, the next subsections present the logical schema of the used GDB, the instantiation of a XML document validated against the AGIS XML Schema and a query example.

4.1 AGIS WEB

This tool was implemented using open technologies like Java Server Faces (JSF), Google Maps API and Google Chart API. Fig. 6 shows six enumerated areas of AGIS WEB graphical interface. Area 1 shows a set of tabs that allow the parameter definition (i.e. geographic context, aggregation type, measures, filters and properties) to submit a query. Area 2 displays the query result on map. Area 3 is displayed by clicking with the mouse on a geographic feature and shows the query result associated with the geographic feature. Area 4 displays the caption of the range of values given by the measure selected as an indicator to color the map. Area 5 displays the query result in table format. Area 6 displays the query result in chart format. The results shown on map, on table and on chart are updated synchronously.

4.2 Geographic Database

Fig. 7 shows the logical schema of a GDB with information from the Brazilian Agency of Electric Energy. The GDB has information about hydro and thermal power stations, substations, transmission lines, reservoirs, etc., which allow analyzing the situation of generation and transmission of electric energy in Brazil.

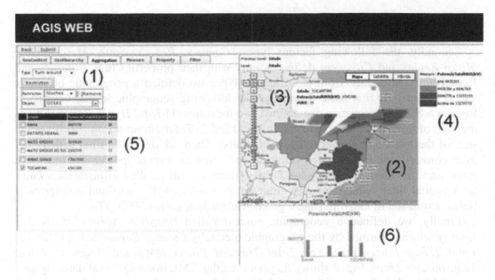

Fig. 6. AGIS WEB Graphical Interface

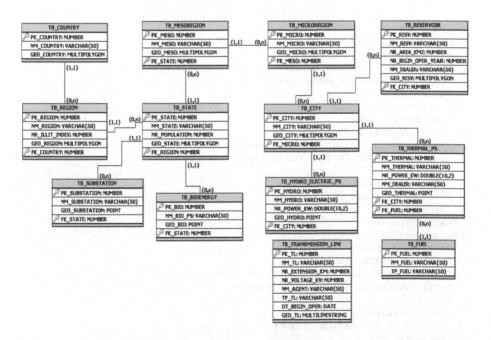

Fig. 7. GDB Logical Schema

4.3 Metadata

In order to allow the AGIS Engine to provide analytic and geographic multilevel queries over the GDB presented above, firstly it is necessary to instantiate the AGIS XML Metamodel, defining geographic contexts, geographic hierarchies, measures, feature types, properties and filters. It is important to observe that all metadata must be defined prior to use any AGIS application.

Secondly, the following feature types: *Country, Region, State, Meso-Region, Micro-Region* and *City* were defined jointly with their properties (e.g. *Illiteracy* and *Population*). After this, from these feature types we defined a geographic hierarchy called *Country Region State* formed by the following geographic levels: Country > Region > State. In sequence, we defined two measures: 1) *Total Hydro Power (kW)* as the sum of hydroelectric power (in kilowatts) and 2) *Total Thermal Power (kW)* as the sum of thermoelectric power (also in kilowatts). Then, we defined a filter called *Fuel* as a conventional filter, which refers to fuel used in thermal power stations, with *name* and *type* fields. Furthermore, we also defined a filter called *Transmission Lines* as a spatial filter, which refers to transmission lines, with *agent* and *voltage (kV)* fields, expressed in kilovolts, and a geometric attribute called *GEO_TL*.

Finally, we defined a geographic context called *Brazilian Agency of Electric Energy* which is formed by the geographic hierarchy *Country Region State*, measures *Total Hydro Power (kW)* and *Total Thermal Power (kW)* and filters *Fuel* and *Transmission Lines*. Fig. 8 shows fragments of the XML document (validated against the AGIS XML Schema) with some of these settings.

```
<FeatureType id="country">
  <Name>Country</Name>
  <Source>TB_COUNTRY</Source>
  <ThematicIdentifier>NM_COUNTRY</ThematicIdentifier>
  <GeoAttribute>GEO_COUNTRY</GeoAttribute>
</FeatureType>
<FeatureType id="region">
  <Name>Region</Name>
  <Source>TB_REGION</Source>
  <ThematicIdentifier>NM_REGION</ThematicIdentifier>
  <GeoAttribute>GEO_REGION</GeoAttribute>
  <Property>
    <Name>Illiteracy</Name>
    <Column>NR_ILLIT_INDEX</Column>
  </Property>
</FeatureType>
<FeatureType id="state">
  <Name>State</Name>
  <Source>TB_STATE</Source>
  <ThematicIdentifier>NM_STATE</ThematicIdentifier>
  <GeoAttribute>GEO_STATE</GeoAttribute>
  <Property>
    <Name>Population</Name>
    <Column>NR_POPULATION</Column>
  </Property>
</FeatureType>
<GeoHierarchy id="countryRegionState" hasAll="true">
  <Name>Country Region State</Name>
  <FeatureTypeLevel featureType="country"/>
  <FeatureTypeLevel featureType="region"/>
  <FeatureTypeLevel featureType="state"/>
</GeoHierarchy>
```

```
<Measure id="totalHydroPower">
  <Name>Total Hydro Power (kW)</Name>
  <Column>NR_POWER_KW</Column>
  <Aggregator>SUM</Aggregator>
  <Table>TB_HYDRO_ELECTRIC_PS</Table>
</Measure>
<ConventionalFilter id="fuelFilter">
  <Name>Fuel</Name>
  <Source>TB_FUEL</Source>
  <FilterField>
    <Name>Name</Name>
    <Column>NM_FUEL</Column>
  </FilterField>
  <FilterField>
    <Name>Type</Name>
    <Column>TP_FUEL</Column>
  </FilterField>
  <Join>
    <RightTable>TB_THERMAL_PS</RightTable>
    <JoinKey>
      <LeftColumn>PK_FUEL</LeftColumn>
      <RightColumn>FK_FUEL</RightColumn>
    </JoinKey>
  </Join>
</ConventionalFilter>
<SpatialFilter id="transmissionLinesFilter">
  <Name>Transmission Lines</Name>
  <Source>TB_TRANSMISSION_LINE</Source>
  <FilterField>
    <Name>Agent</Name>
    <Column>NM_AGENT</Column>
  </FilterField>
  <FilterField>
    <Name>Voltage (kV)</Name>
    <Column>NR_VOLTAGE_KV</Column>
  </FilterField>
  <GeoAttribute>GEO_TL</GeoAttribute>
</SpatialFilter>
<GeoContext>
  <Name>Brazilian Agency of Electric Energy</Name>
  <GeoHierarchyUsage geoHierarchy="countryRegionState"/>
  <MeasureUsage measure="totalHydroPower"/>
  <MeasureUsage measure="totalThermalPower"/>
  <FilterUsage filter="fuelFilter"/>
  <FilterUsage filter="transmissionLinesFilter"/>
</GeoContext>
```

Fig. 8. Fragments of AGIS XML Instance

4.4 Query Example

Once instantiated the metadata, the AGIS WEB client can be used to graphically define query parameters (e.g. geographic context, measures and spatial operations) and, using AGIS-API, to submit them to the AGIS Engine, which queries the AGIS-XML Metamodel to get the metadata needed to generate the request query. After the query is generated, the AGIS Engine sends it to be processed by the SDBMS, gets the result and returns them to AGIS WEB. Considering this context, the next subsection shows an example of an analytic and geographic multilevel query.

4.4.1 Analytic and Geographic Multilevel Query

"Being in geographic context *Brazilian Agency of Electric Energy* and in geographic level *Country* of geographic hierarchy *Country Region State*, what is the total power in kW by region for hydroelectric power stations located in the regions of Brazil?".

The corresponding ISO/OGC SQL query generated by the AGIS Engine is displayed in Fig. 9.

```
SELECT R.NM_REGION, R.GEO_REGION, SUM(HE.NR_POWER_KW)
  FROM TB_COUNTRY C, TB_REGION R, TB_STATE S, TB_MESOREGION ME,
       TB_MICROREGION MI, TB_CITY CI
  LEFT OUTER JOIN TB_HYDRO_ELECTRIC_PS HE ON (CI.PK_CITY = HE.FK_CITY)
 WHERE C.NM_COUNTRY = 'Brazil'
   AND C.PK_COUNTRY = R.FK_COUNTRY
   AND R.PK_REGION = S.FK_REGION
   AND S.PK_STATE = ME.FK_STATE
   AND ME.PK_MESO = MI.FK_MESO
   AND MI.PK_MICRO = CI.FK_MICRO
 GROUP BY R.NM_REGION, R.GEO_REGION
 ORDER BY R.NM_REGION
```

Fig. 9. Generated SQL Query

Fig. 10 shows the result of AGIS query execution. To achieve this result, a drill down operation on *Country* geographic level where the country name is *Brazil* was requested.

Fig. 10. Drill down on *Country* geographic level

5 Related Work

The related literature of analytic and geographic decision support area discusses several works about SOLAP tools/environments. Some relevant proposals of SOLAP work [1,2,12,13,14,15,16] were investigated and we identified that these works make use of proprietary technologies or are implemented using an OLAP server to perform analytic and geographic multilevel processing. As there is no *de jure* standard language for OLAP yet, these works are dependent on specific OLAP languages, Application Program Interface (API) and servers. Specifically the following proposals have the limitation of being based on proprietary technologies, namely: JMap [13,14], GeWOlap [2] and OLAP for ArcGIS [15]. In addition, the following works are dependent on a particular OLAP server, named: GOLAPA [1], GeoMondrian [12], JMap and GeWOlap. These points differentiate these SOLAP proposals from AGIS proposal, which aims to provide a service to perform analytic and geographic multilevel processing without dependence on an OLAP server. Then, the AGIS proposal should not be considered as a SOLAP solution. That is, our proposal is a service that is based on open and extensible standards to provide multilevel analytic functions that aim to enrich the set of functionalities of GIS applications.

6 Conclusion

The main contributions of this article are 1) the definition of a three-tiered architecture (AGIS Architecture), made up of several components that are based on open and extensible standards and 2) the specification of a metamodel (AGIS Metamodel), which defines the metadata that describes how the AGIS Engine must understand the GDB schema to generate analytic and geographic multilevel queries. In this context, the AGIS proposal made possible to perform analytic and geographic multilevel queries, without needing to write manually these queries. Therefore, our work showed feasible for the purpose that it was intended. That is, it provides a service to support geographic decision making that abstracts the complexity of writing theses queries and eliminates the use of proprietary technologies.

Despite having been achieved the goals of this work, some topics for future research are: 1) the implementation of a geographic hierarchy among spatial objects (i.e. using contains spatial relationship), because the current version only supports hierarchies among geographic themes/levels and 2) the use of AGIS with huge databases in order to deeply check its processing performance.

References

1. Fidalgo, R.N.: Uma Infra-estrutura para Integração de Modelos, Esquemas e Serviços Multidimensionais e Geográficos. Doctorate Thesis, Federal University of Pernambuco, Recife, PE (2005)
2. Bimonte, S., Tchounikine, A., Miquel, M.: Spatial OLAP: Open Issues and a Web Based Prototype. In: 10th AGILE International Conference on Geographic Information Science, p. 11 (2007)

3. Rivest, S., Bédard, Y., Proulx, M., Nadeau, M., Hubert, F., Pastor, J.: SOLAP technology: Merging business intelligence with geospatial technology for interactive spatio-temporal exploration and analysis of data. ISPRS Journal of Photogrammetry & Remote Sensing 60(1), 17–33 (2005)

4. Kimball, R., Ross, M.: The Data Warehouse Toolkit: The Complete Guide to Dimensional Modeling. John Wiley & Sons, Inc., New York (2002)

5. Thomsen, E.: OLAP Solutions: Building Multidimensional Information Systems. John Wiley & Sons, Inc., New York (1997)

6. Worboys, M., Duckham, M.: GIS: A Computing Perspective, 2nd edn. CRC Press, Inc., Boca Raton (2004)

7. ISO/IEC 9075. Database Language SQL, International Standard ISO/IEC 9075:1992, American National Standard X3.135-1992, American National Standards Institute, New York, NY (1992)

8. ISO 19125-2. Geographic information – Simple feature access – Part 2: SQL option, International Standard ISO 19125-2:2004, ISO (2004)

9. He, H.: What is Service-Oriented Architecture? O'Reilly Media, September 30 (2003), http://webservices.xml.com/pub/a/ws/2003/09/30/soa.html

10. Fidalgo, R.N., Times, V.C., Silva, J., Souza, F.F.: GeoDWFrame: A Framework for Guiding the Design of Geographical Dimensional Schemas. In: Kambayashi, Y., Mohania, M., Wöß, W. (eds.) DaWaK 2004. LNCS, vol. 3181, pp. 26–37. Springer, Heidelberg (2004)

11. OGC, OpenGIS® (2009)

12. GeoMondrian Project, http://www.geo-mondrian.org

13. Kheops JMap, http://www.kheops-tech.com/en/jmap

14. Kheops JMap Spatial OLAP, http://www.kheops-tech.com/en/jmap/solap.jsp

15. ESRI OLAP for ArcGIS, http://www.esri.com/software/arcgis/extensions/olap

16. Bimonte, S.: On Modelling and Analysis of Geographic Multidimensional Databases. In: Data Warehousing Design and Advanced Engineering Applications: Methods for Complex Construction. Idea Group Publishing, USA (2008)

Transferring Indicators into Different Partitions of Geographic Space

Christine Plumejeaud[1], Julie Prud'homme[2],
Paule-Annick Davoine[1], and Jérôme Gensel[1]

[1] LIG, Laboratoire d'Informatique de Grenoble
681 rue de la Passerelle, Domaine Universitaire BP 72,
38 402 St Martin d'Hères cedex, France
{Christine.Plumejeaud,Jerome.Gensel,
Paule-Annick.Davoine}@imag.fr
[2] UMR 6012 ESPACE CNRS – Université d'Avignon,
74, rue Louis Pasteur, 84029 Avignon cedex 1, France
jul.prudhomme@gmail.com

Abstract. Nowadays, spatial analysis led on complex phenomenon implies the usage of data available on heterogeneous territorial meshes, that is to say misaligned meshes. Then, combine these data requires the transfer of each dataset into a common spatial support that can be exploited. This is known as the Change Of Support Problem (COSP). However, it appears that transfer methods are numerous, and they are often linked with a regression model, and other parameters whose selection and tuning may not be straight forward for a non-expert user. Furthermore, the process is also very dependent from both the nature of the data to be transferred and their quality. This paper first proposes a brief overview of some available transfer methods, giving the premises for the characterization of each method. A use case illustrates a transfer operation, and reveals its main difficulties.

Keywords: Territorial mesh, spatial analysis, statistical datasets, downscaling, aggregation, interpolation.

1 Introduction

Very often, spatial geo-referenced data related to a certain phenomenon of interest (sociological, environmental, or political one) are collected on a support (that is to say a set of geo-referenced locations) which is not the one on which the phenomenon is actually active, observable, or even studied. For instance, temperatures are measured at some punctual locations, whereas this phenomenon is a continuous field, operating on the ground of the Earth, modeled here as a planar surface. Moreover, considering the tremendous increase of the number of data sources of these last past years, researchers in Social Sciences or Geography often have to combine data coming from different kinds of support. For instance, in order to measure the green impact of human's activities, one need to combine data associated with economic basins together with gridded land cover data extracted from some processing on spatial images. In

D. Taniar et al. (Eds.): ICCSA 2010, Part I, LNCS 6016, pp. 445–460, 2010.
© Springer-Verlag Berlin Heidelberg 2010

those cases, the analysis and the interpretation of data require the harmonization of data supports, that is to say to transfer data inside a common support so that heterogeneous data and supports can be compared. These problems are identified in the class of *Change Of Support Problems* (COSP) [1].

A lot of previous works have studied and proposed methods for transferring data between different supports [16], [17], [24]. Usually, those studies focus on the side effects of the proposed transformation. Those side effects are mainly caused by the change of scale and the change of shape of the support. This problem is known as the MAUP (*Modifiable Areal Unit Problem*) [25], [9]. However, to our knowledge, there is no system offering a classification and a characterization of those methods, which could handle a part of the advanced knowledge in spatial analysis or in mathematical fields of expert users. Yet, some attempts into this direction have been made [16], [0], [10].

Our global objective is to show that such classification and characterization of transfer methods can be exhibited, in order to automate their execution by an interactive system dedicated to expert users. This paper aims at exposing our ideas and a methodology allowing the automatic transfer of data between heterogeneous supports.

First, we make a brief survey of spatial analysis methods that can be used to transfer data from one support to another. Then, we identify a list of basic characteristics that should be known and selected by the user (cost calculation, complexity of the algorithm, side-effects and parameters of the method, etc.), together with their meaning. Finally, the estimation of population performed on the districts of the city of Grenoble in France, illustrates the transfer mechanism through the examples of two methods.

2 The Change of Support Problem

Geographical information is associated with a set of locations that can be modeled using objects, characterized by their geometry and some coordinates described into a mathematical space. For this space, a metric is supplied in order to get a measure of the interaction between objects. This set of mathematical objects is known as the *support* of information. Generally, and for sake of simplicity, the mathematical space that is used is a planar Euclidian space, that is to say a Cartesian 2-space, the Euclidian distance function being then used as length-metric. Nevertheless, many interesting methods, based for example on spherical spaces [29], and/or other kind of distances, can express the interaction between locations in a more suitable way when human geography is concerned. For instance, the use of a road distance-time matrix between locations, or of an orthodromic distance, allows a more realistic analysis. But most of the methods that are defined on specific spaces or specific distances require intensive computing, and have not been disseminated yet inside the GIS community [23].

In a planar Euclidian space, one can consider various kinds of support: points, lines, or surface. In our study, we limit our proposal to data linked to surfaces (often called "areal zonings"). In fact, a *tessellation* is applied to the projection of the geographic space onto a plane surface. This tessellation constitutes the support, that is to say a gridded representation of a plane surface into disjoint polygons. These polygons are usually squared (raster), triangular (TIN), or hexagonal ones. A 2D tessellation involves the subdivision of a 2-dimensional plane into polygonal tiles (polyhedral blocks) that completely cover the space. The term *lattice* is sometimes used to describe the complete division of the plane into regular or irregular disjoint polygons. A lattice is said to be regular when one can observe the repetition of some identical shape over the space. For example, a *grid* is a regular polygonal lattice. On the opposite, a *mesh* is a kind of irregular lattice, composed of polygons that have various shapes and size. We use the term of *"discontinuous mesh"* in order to designate an irregular tessellation of space, that does not fully cover the plane. This case occurs, for instance, when defining some employment basins on a given territory: basins limits usually form a lace of this territory.

Some meshes may be nested into other meshes: then the upper level mesh can be built from territorial units of the lower level, using aggregation rules that have to be established. For instance, the Nomenclature of European Territorial Units (NUTS) relies on a hierarchical structure: units of NUTS2 level, corresponding to regions (*régions* in France), are built by aggregation of units of NUTS3 level, corresponding to departments (*départements* in France). If the hierarchy is *strict* (each unit has only one superior unit) and *onto* (any unit of a non-elementary level is composed of at least one unit of the lower level), the transfer of absolute quantitative data from lower levels to upper levels is made straightforwardly by additive operations (addition, maximum, minimum) on data accounted on each unit of the lower level [31]. Finally, two meshes are said to be *misaligned* if one is *not* nested in the other and if their boarders cross each other. This is the case when considering, for instance, administrative units and river catchments on a given territory (a portion of space). In general, they are misaligned because, at some level, a river crosses several administrative units, and its catchments may overlap with several administrative units. In this study, we focus on methods for transferring quantitative data (whether they are absolute or ratio) between two misaligned meshes. Indicator and variable are here considered as synonyms and refer to a property which is considered of interest for any territorial unit of the support.

Based on the vocabulary introduced by [21], the term "change of support" is used when some data is known on a source support, and this data is transferred onto a target support, using some methods whose complexity is variable. This problem is also known as « *spatial rescaling* » [24], or « *downscaling* », since the major difficulty lies in the disaggregation of a variable on a finer scale support that is misaligned with the source support. Transfer techniques are also named « *cross-area aggregation* » [14], or « *areal interpolation* » [11], [12], or « *polygon overlay* ».

The relative scale of meshes is a substantial aspect of the transfer: from one mesh to another, the average area of each unit (or cell) differs, and even inside a given mesh, the degree of variability of these areas is not constant also. When the average area of units of a mesh A is lower than the average area of units of a mesh B, A is said to be finer that B. When most of the units of the mesh A are nested inside units of the mesh B, the situation allows us for aggregating A values into B, with a margin of error, due to the little sub-set of A units that may cross the boarder of B.

Transfer methods from one support to another are thus based on the establishment of an intermediate support, nested inside the target mesh, in the case where this mesh is finer than the source mesh. Then, possible operations are:

- *Disaggregation* which reallocates data on objects of smaller size (either punctual or polygonal), fully included into the units of the source support and into the units of the target support, through the creation of a least common spatial denominator between the source and the target supports.

- *Aggregation* which cumulates data of the source units into the target units, following a geometric inclusion rule. This operation is used after a disaggregation in order to get an estimation of the variable on a misaligned mesh, or when passing from a lower scale to an upper scale in case of hierarchical organization.
- *Interpolation* which builds a density surface using data associated with a punctual or a polygonal support. The support of this density surface is a regular mesh as finer as possible.

Interpolation is generally integrated into a sequence of operations, where data is first reduced to a seedling of points, then interpolated, and finally re-aggregated into the target support. Indeed, the amount of data accounted on a polygon can be considered as concentrated into the center of this polygon, which can be the centroid, or a point inside the corresponding unit that have been selected by the user due to its fitness regarding the study needs: the biggest town, the lowest altitude point, etc. In general, the computed surface aims at giving a continuous representation of discrete or punctual measures. Since this surface is associated with a fine discretization of the space, on which one can sum data of cells, according to their spatial inclusion into the target units, this enlarges considerably the set of available methods for transferring data between misaligned supports.

Figure 1 shows that these three operations that are closely linked to the nature of both source and target supports. All these transformations have also a side effect on the analysis of data, due to the change of size and shape of the support. This is mainly due to the lost of variance on data when grouping units into larger units, which is known as the aggregation or scale effect. Also, alternative formations of units produce different results and inferences: this is called the grouping or zoning effect [25].

We present in the following subsections a synthetic overview of various transfer technique families, and we try to link them with a set of useful criteria for the user.

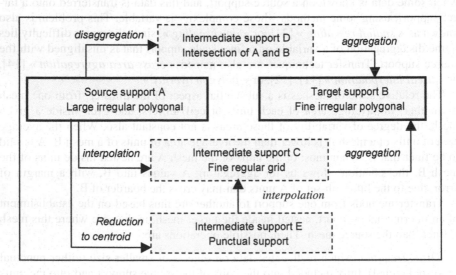

Fig. 1. Support transformations for data transfer

The characterization of the support, for both source and target, can be helpful in the selection of one particular kind of transformation. Yet, the type of variable to be transferred also plays a key role: a relative variable (a ratio) cannot be manipulated in the same way as an absolute quantitative variable (that is to say a count on units), in particular through aggregation operations. The sum of lower units rates is not equal to the upper unit rate. There are few methods adapted to ratio manipulation, and often, one has to operate separately on the both components of a ratio. In the same way, some ancillary data can be used to adjust the transfer, considering that those data may have a spatial correlation with the data to be transferred.

2.1 Aggregation

About aggregation methods, we could have mentioned the regionalization method, the optimization and simulated annealing methods [26], or the clustering methods. However, these techniques aim at building a new mesh according to constraints given by the user (similarity, homogeneity, continuity, etc.) But, since our goal is to transfer a variable towards a target mesh whose borders are defined, we focus on the technique of data-matrix aggregation. Data-matrix is data supported by a grid. In Figure 1, it corresponds to the transformation of the support C into the support B. The idea is to aggregate variables, which are known on a grid support into a target mesh. By superimposing a target mesh on the grid support, one can accumulate the values of the cells considering their spatial inclusion into units of the target mesh, and thus determine the value of the variable in the target support, within a margin of error. This error depends on the weight of the cells of the intermediate mesh and on the process used to reallocate a cell to a unit of the target-mesh. For instance, if the cell mostly belongs to the polygon of the target mesh, the total weight of the cell is assigned to the cell itself, or else it is reallocated proportionally to the surface of the intersection between the cell and the polygon. To reduce as much as possible the error, the intermediate mesh must be as fine as possible. Also, much of the variability in the information is lost since information is re-aggregate in bigger sized and differently shaped units (scale and zoning effect). This kind of method is widely used in the environmental domain – where data on raster support abound – when data must be transferred into socio-economic meshes like the NUTS (Nomenclature of Territorial Units for Statistics) [15], [30].

2.2 Disaggregation

Simple Areal Weighting
This method enables the transfer of variables between two non-nested meshes by means of an intermediate support D, resulting of the intersection between the source and the target supports. It assumes the uniformity of the density of the variable in each unit. The ventilation of the variable is done proportionally to the surface of the intersection between the source mesh and the target mesh. It is easy to implement and does not require a big data sample. The algorithm is available in most of the GIS. However, the strong assumption of the uniformity of the density of the variable prevents the method from taking into account the local variations of data inside units.

Modified Areal Weighting – Regression
This method assumes that a spatial correlation holds between a set of variables [7]: one must identify an ancillary data (called *predictor*) spatially correlated with the variable to be transferred, and whose distribution must be known on both the source and the target supports. Then, the reallocation of the variable on the intermediate support D integrates an assumption about the similarity of the distribution (spatial correlation) between the variable and the ancillary variable (the predictor). In a first step, the spatial correlation model has to be established on the source support. The second step solves a linear regression between the predictor (whose distribution is known on the target support) and the variable to be estimated. An example of this method is provided by [13]. This study highlights that the choice of the regression form between the two variables can be crucial for results accuracy.

Modified Areal Weighting – Control Zones
This is an enhanced version of simple areal weighting, which make use of an ancillary data known on control zones, which constitutes a third support in addition of the source and target support [16]. This third support can be a set of geographic objects (like buildings for example) that forms a finer mesh whose units are almost all in-cluded into both the source and the target support units. Generally, density of the ancillary data on those control zones is said to be constant [19], and through a mathematical expression of the relation existing between the ancillary data and the data to be transferred, it is possible to compute the data on those control zones, and then to re-aggregate into the target support. This method is frequently used because its results are considered to be close to reality. For example, in environmental domain, the trend is to use land use data issued from regular grids composed of pixels of 1ha as control zones [15], [30]. Indeed, numerous variables are directly linked to the land use category: population lives on urban areas, pesticides are spread on agricultural areas, etc.

2.3 Interpolation

The purpose of interpolation is to give the value of a function $F(x,y)$ for any point M whose coordinates are (x,y), using a sub-set of observed values f_i at locations M_i, where i varies from 1 to n. Interpolation builds a continuous surface, based on a fine discretization of space. Depending on the algorithm used, discretization can result in a regular grid, or a triangularization of space. This allows then to aggregate computed values into the target units, by summing values associated to cell grids or triangles, or whatever polygonal shape, that are included into to each target unit. There are many methods [2], and [35] lists the following criteria to distinguish between them:

-   The property of the algorithm: *determinist* or *stochastic*. In the first case, the esti-mation tries to adjust a mathematical function with regard to a set of samples, whereas in the second case, a probabilistic rule models the phenomenon and pro-vides directly an estimation error.
-   The accuracy of the estimation: sometimes these algorithms build a mean density surface, which does not pass through all samples f_i. The ones that compute a value $F(x_i, y_i)$ equal to f_i are said to be *exact*.

- The spatial extent: this makes the difference between *global* or *local* methods. In the first case, a function models the phenomenon on the whole area, whereas in the second case, estimations are computed within the local neighborhood of each sample f_i.

The current presentation is non exhaustive, and we describe here just a sub-set of available methods, in order to illustrate the criteria listed above. Some kinds of methods are just mentioned, with their references. Also, we do not describe some descriptive methods aiming at discovering spatial or spatio-temporal correlation between variables, using either global indices (like Moran), or local indices (like LISA). Indeed, those methods do not make any estimation, even though they are very useful to find spatio-temporal cluster of similar data, and can help also in the determination of ancillary data.

First, we present *parametric regression* methods since many other spatial analysis methods end the steps of their calculus by a linear or a polynomial regression. The produced surface will be described by a unique formula (they are global, deterministic and exact methods). In fact, in those cases, the surface or curve ignores micro-fluctuations, and generalizes the phenomenon. However, the algorithm is simple, and many libraries propose scripts or methods to compute it.

Trend Surface Analysis (Global Polynomial Surface)
Based on a linear combination of polynomial functions, whose degree must be chosen by the user, this interpolation method corresponds to a least square approximation. A linear regression is a special case where the degree is equal to one. Thus, the surface is modeled by:

$Z = F(x,y) = b_0 + b_1 x + b_2 y + b_3 xy + b_4 x^2 + b_5 y^2 + ...$

Parameters of the model (b_0, b_1, b_2, b_3, b_4, b_5, ...) are computed by a least square method, which aims at minimizing the error between the predicted value Z and the samples f_i by minimizing the sum (1):

$$\sum_{i=1}^{n}(Z_i - f_i)^2 . \qquad (1)$$

In Figure 1, this method follows the step A to E (centroid reduction), and then E to C (surface computing). The choice of the degree determines the cost of the computation, both increase with the degree, and the interpretation complexity. Most often, the chosen degree varies from 3 to 5. Like any parametric regression, this method is not well suited in cases where data distribution is sparse and irregular through space [35].

Non-parametric regression methods involve nearly no a priori assumptions about the underlying functional form. At each point M of the support C, such models compute a local distribution function $F_i(x, y)$, based on a weighting of f_i by a coefficient λ_i, assuming that such weights decrease with the distance to the point M (2).

$$F_i(x,y) = \sum_{i=1}^{n} \lambda_i f_i . \qquad (2)$$

This hypothesis is based on the first law of geography stated by Tobler: "Everything is related to everything else, but near things are more related than distant things". The following constraints remain valid for all methods: the sum of weights is equal to one, each weight is always positive or null, and their value depends on the distance between M and the sample f_i. Such models are much more flexible, due to their local nature, and are capable of capturing subtle spatial variations. However, until recently non-parametric models have not been as widely applied as parametric models because of their high computational cost and their great statistical complexity. But thanks to the advances of intensive computing, research is very active in this domain. In this category, one finds:

-       Splines [8], which are based on a polynomial regression by pieces, with a constraint of continuity, derivability and smoothing of the surface.
-       Kernel smoothing methods - (for which many implementations and variations have been published, such as Potential Maps [27]) – which assume that a shape (Gaussian, exponential, disk, etc.) controls the distribution around a neighborhood of each computed point M, decreasing with distance. They require choosing a scope, defining the mean average distance of the influence of each point on its neighborhood.
-       Regression with Topological maps, that are a kind of neural-network based algorithms (Self-Organizing Maps) [3].

We present here a basic one, the Inverse Distance Weighting, and some variants that are very often implemented inside GIS, providing a quick overview of spatial variability, identifying zones with high or low values.

Inverse Distance Weighting (IDW)
The IDW method belongs to the family of spatial filters (or focal functions), being determinist and local. Like kernel smoothing methods, a shape for the phenomenon diffusion is selected by the user, and decreasing with distance. IDW assigns to each λ_i of (2) a value that is proportional to the inverse of the distance d powered by n, d being the distance from the computed M to the sample f_i, as shown in the equation (3)

$$\lambda_i = \frac{k}{d_i^n} . \tag{3}$$

Triangular Irregular Network (TIN) is a particular case of *IDW*, where $n=1$ in (3), and every λ_i is null excepted for the three nearest neighbors: those neighbors are defined by a triangulation of space based on *Thiessen* polygons.

For *IDW* computing, a very fine grid is superimposed onto the source support, (see step A to C on Figure 1), and each cell of C is initially valued with a value proportional to the intersected area of units of the support A. Then, $F_i(x,y)$ is computed in each cell, taking into account the neighborhood through a given scope. This is a very fast computing method, but producing maps with a "Bull's-eye" effect around the point of measure. The Shepard's method [33] and its derivates adapt this method, in order to suppress the "Bull's-eye" effect by using a local least square regression.

Pycnophylactic Interpolation
The pycnophylactic method is another deterministic method, local but exact. Proposed by [34], it aims at producing a smoothed surface from data known on areal zoning, but preserving the total mass of data accounted on source units. It looks like spatial filtering into its first step: a very fine grid is superimposed onto the source support, (see the step A to C of Figure 1), and each cell is initially valued with a value proportional to the intersected area of units of the support A. Then a filter window is moved along the grid to smooth the values, computing the average values of adjacent cells (4 or 8 cells). However, at each iteration, this method constrains the new accounts in order to guaranty the continuity of the surface, as well to preserve the mass accounted on source units. The process ends when a limit for precision is reached (defined by the user). The main drawback of this method is to rub out sudden changes (e.g. local pockets of high population density within a cell) [28], because it works by assuming a uniform variation of the variable density.

In addition, all deterministic methods have two major defaults: first, it is impossible to get an idea on the estimation reliability; secondly, the knowledge about the spatial distribution of measures is not used. *Geostatistical methods* (amongst which Kriging, and all its variants) provide a model of the error, and take benefit of the knowledge about spatial distribution of samples.

Kriging
Kriging is a global and exact stochastic method. Very frequently used and implemented in GIS, it avoids the MAUP. A South-African engineer, M. Krige, has invented this technique, in order to compute the spatial distribution of gold from a set of drilling mining (punctual support). Matheron [22] has formalized the approach with a mathematical theory: it computes the best linear unbiased estimator, based on a stochastic model of the spatial dependence, quantified either by the variogram or by the expectation and the covariance function of the random field. The first step establishes a model of the spatial distribution, based on the variance and a distance function. The second step integrates this spatial similarity model into a simple linear regression model. There are various kriging forms, depending upon statistical characteristics of studied variable: stability through time, heteroscedasticity, etc. [6]. The main drawback of this method is that it requires numerous samples as input. Furthermore, many datasets do not have a clear spatial dependence model.

2.4 Synthesis

Some common characteristics or parameters should be outlined amongst the various transfer methods. First, considering simple aggregation or disaggregation methods, the strategy of reallocation of the variable to the units of the target support is very dependant on the nature of the variable: for a continuous variable, such as forest land use, one should use the areal weighed reallocation. But for a policy related variable, such as number of hospitals, a reallocation based on the major belonging of units sounds more appropriate.

Interpolation methods, and even complex disaggregation methods, often use regression model based on a function which models the diffusion phenomena, that the user has to provide, based on its own assumptions and knowledge. This is the case for kernel smoothing methods, disaggregations by regression, or focal functions. The user has to provide a scope (the mean neighborhood to be accounted for estimation) for those methods. Then, the user has to select a type of distance (simple contiguity, Euclidian, orthodromic, etc.) and be aware of the topology of the space.

The user may like to express some preferences. For example, only geostatistic methods (such as kriging) provide automatically an error estimation. For the others, the user should compare results of various models to each other in order to check whether convergence can be reached, which is a more tedious task. The user may also give the priority to the computing time: global regression methods or focal functions are generally very efficient, whereas kernel smoothing methods are much more time consuming.

3   A Case Study: The City of Grenoble, France

3.1   Context

In the city Grenoble, the partition (exactly the tessellation) that is used for urban development, political action and spatial planning is the district mesh. Composed of 20 districts, this district mesh corresponds to the actual structure of the urban area of Grenoble, since each unit presents of certain degree of homogeneity, in terms of buildings, urban activities, and the socio-demographic profile of population. But this mesh, created during the eighties, is misaligned with the IRIS mesh, which is a prior official mesh used by the INSEE (the French national institute of statistics) to publish statistical accounts of population (see Figure 2).

Knowledge about population of districts is a crucial problem when dealing with planning urban development. Then, we have to cope here with an estimation problem, that requires the selection of the best-fitted method. Here, two question are raised: amongst all methods previously presented, which ones could be applied? Are their results equivalent?

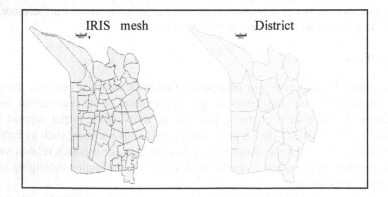

Fig. 2. Different partitions of the city of Grenoble

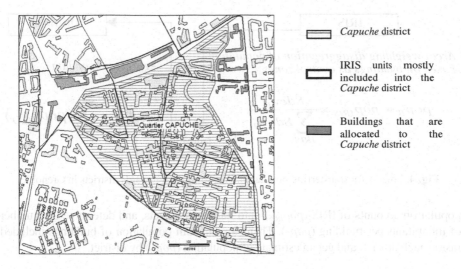

Capuche district

IRIS units mostly included into the Capuche district

Buildings that are allocated to the Capuche district

Fig. 3. Overestimation of population accounts using the simple areal weighting on the *Capuche* district

Clearly, in this case study, data supports are misaligned meshes (IRIS being considered as the source support, and district mesh as the target support). In order to achieve the transfer of data from IRIS to the district mesh, the technical municipality services in charge of the urban management and planning make use of a simple areal weighting method. The reallocation rule assigns accounts of one source unit to the target unit which overlaps it the most. Accounts on districts are obtained by the summation of IRIS units accounts that are, in the majority, spatially included into target units. As an example, the *Capuche* district (a central district on Figure 3) illustrates this algorithm. Composed of many IRIS units, which are not always fully included inside the target unit, the estimation of the population of the *Capuche* district comprises a great number of persons living in buildings belonging to another district. This increases in a tremendous way the estimated account of population on the *Capuche* district.

This example shows the limits of a transfer method based on the simple areal weighting disaggregation. It allocates very frequently some source units to one single target unit, whereas they should be shared between many target units. It seems that it is really important to propose another method, yielding more accurate results on the district mesh. So, we propose an experiment based on the Modified Areal Weighting method using control zones.

3.2 Using Building Footprints as Control Zones

If we assume that weighted estimates can improve the reliability of the statistics, we propose to create a population potential for each residency building. Figure 4 illustrates the process for transferring IRIS population data towards Grenoble districts. Using building elevation and floor height, depending on the age of the buildings, we can estimate the number of floors for each one, and compute the developed area $Sdev_B$ (number of floors multiplied by footprint area). This is used to weight the disaggregation of

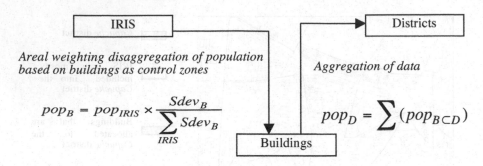

Fig. 4. Process for transferring population data from IRIS towards districts in Grenoble

population accounts of IRIS (pop_{IRIS}) onto buildings objects, and determine the number of inhabitants per building (pop_B). Then, we can sum population of buildings included inside each district, and get an estimate of population (pop_D) by district.

3.3 Analysis of the Results

Figure 5 shows a map of population accounts on the district mesh, obtained either by the simple areal weighting disaggregation, or by the modified areal weighting disaggregation, using buildings as control zones.

It can be noticed that both methods provide very similar results on a sub-set of districts, while, on other districts, a significant difference is measured (up to 3500 inhabitants for the biggest difference). The *Capuche* district, which is a typical case of a district which intersects many IRIS units, is also one of the zones presenting a very significant difference between both methods (almost 3800 inhabitants of difference). In the *Villeneuve_VO* district, a significant difference (1106 inhabitants) can be noticed as well, but in favor of the modified areal weighting disaggregation, based on buildings as control zones. This was very likely to happen since this unit has a high density of buildings.

In order to assess estimates, we have at our disposal data provided by the French National Institute of Socio-Economic Studies (INSEE in French) at district level, and obtained by a census relevant only on one district, *Villeneuve_VO* and especially on *La Bruyère* area.. Indeed, *La Bruyère* is an area which is in *Villeneuve* district but not in IRIS *Villeneuve_VO*. Thus, the difference between them is used as a reference for the comparison of the results. This area includes miscellaneous types of housing (large group, mean group, individual [5]).

The comparison of our results with those data (Table 1) shows that the results based on simple areal weighting disaggregation method are closer to reality (which is 458 inhabitants in *La Bruyère* area). Concretely, these inhabitants are not recorded in the district to where they belong (equipments, policies etc.).

This result can be explained by a deeper study, which shows that footprint of building is in this case not a good ancillary data for computing the developed area in this district, having modern architecture. Indeed, the spatial images processing, that provides the building footprint, takes into account the numerous terraces, balustrades,

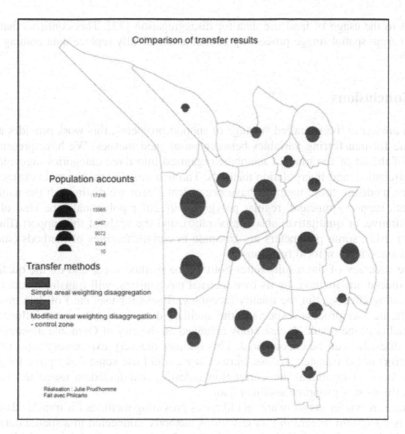

Fig. 5. Comparison of population estimations in Grenoble: simple areal weighting (upper half-disk) versus modified areal weighting disaggregation (lower half-disk)

Table 1. Comparison of population estimations in *La Bruyère* area with disaggregation methods

census data on *La Bruyère* area	Simple areal weighting disaggregation	Modified areal weighting disaggregation
458	602	1107

recess or projections of buildings in this district. This increases artificially the extent of their footprint. This method has an underlying hypothesis of constant population density between buildings, which is wrong. In this example, housing accounts per building may have been a better ancillary data.

As a conclusion, this study case reveals that a transfer based on modified areal weighting with control zones is not always closer to census data than a simple areal weighting method. This result was not expected, but it corroborates other studies linked to the usage of land use data for disaggregation [32]. This confirms that data issued from spatial image processing cannot automatically replace data coming from census.

4   Conclusions

As an answer to the so-called "change of support problem", this work provides a first scheme for transferring variables between misaligned meshes. We have presented a state of the art of the transfer methods, organized into three categories: aggregation, disaggregation, and interpolation methods. Through this review, the main characteristics for modeling these methods have been highlighted: we distinguish the nature of the data support (punctual, regular polygonal, irregular polygonal), the kind of data (quantitative, or qualitative, absolute or ratio), and the scale of the support (finer or larger). Also, some parameters are common to certain families of methods (such as kernel smoothing or focal functions).

The accuracy of the results relies both on the method used, and on the quality of data. Indeed, the method, by its own internal mechanisms, will transform data (scale and zoning effects). But the quality (accuracy, fitness for use, etc.) of data involved into the transfer process (especially the ancillary data) has also a great influence on the quality of the result. A case study achieved on the city of Grenoble illustrates the difficulties that can be encountered. This outlines the very exploratory aspect (trials and error) of the transfer process. Further work could use some descriptive modeling methods (local or global autocorrelation indexes), and metadata usage in order to select the most appropriate ancillary data.

There are numerous software and libraries providing methods for transfer data, but there is no system integrating these various methods, connected to a spatial database, and offering some kind of assisted workflow for data transferring process between supports. This preliminary study will be used to design a task model (an object- oriented model describing a hierarchy of transfer methods, together with their conditions of use). This task model could be at the core of a system controlled by the user. For instance, the user could interact to establish the strategy for the task activation, and give some inputs linked to his/her own knowledge and expertise about data. This system should allow for estimation of missing data, or combination of heterogeneous data, linked with various territorial zonings.

References

1. Arbia, G.: Statistical Effect of Data Transformations: A Proposed General Framework. In: Goodchild, M., Gopal, S. (eds.) The Accuracy of Spatial Data Bases, pp. 249–259. Taylor and Francis, London (1989)
2. Arnaud, M., Emery, X.: Estimation et interpolation spatiale : méthodes déterministes et méthodes géostatiques, Paris, Hermès (2000) (in French)
3. Badran, F., Daigremont, P., Thiria, S.: Régression par carte topologique. In: Thiria, S., et al. (eds.) Statistiques et méthodes neuronales, pp. 207–222 (1997) (in French)
4. Bracken, I., Martin, D.: The generation of spatial population distributions from census centroid data. Environment and Planning A 21, 537–543 (1989)

5. CERTU, Méthodes d'estimations de population, Lyon (2005) (in French)
6. Cressie, N.: Statistics for spatial data. John Wiley and Sons, New-York (1991)
7. Droesbeke, J.-J., Lejeune, M., Saporta, G.: Analyse statistique des données spatiales, Paris, Technip (2006) (in French)
8. Dubrule, O.: Two methods with differents objectives : splines and kriging. Mathematical geology 15, 245–255 (1983)
9. ESPON 3.4.3, The modifiable areas unit problem, Luxembourg, Final report (2006)
10. EUROSTAT European Commission Statistical Office – EUROSTAT, GIS Application Development, Final Report (1999)
11. Fisher, P.F., Langford, M.: Modelling the errors in areal interpolation between zonal systems by Monte Carlo simulation. Environment and Planning A 27, 211–224 (1995)
12. Flowerdew, R., Green, M.: Statistical methods for inference between incompatible zonal systems. In: Goodchild, M., Gopal, S. (eds.) The accuracy of spatial data bases, pp. 239–247. Taylor and Francis, London (1989)
13. Flowerdew, R., Green, M.: Developments in areal interpolation methods and GIS. The Annals of Regional Science 26, 76–95 (1992)
14. Fotheringham, A.S., Brunsdon, C., Charlton, M.: Quantitative Geography, pp. 59–60. Sage, London (2000)
15. Gomez, O., Paramo, F.: The Land and Ecosystem Accounting (LEAC) methodology guidebook, Internal report (2005),
    http://dataservice.eea.europa.eu/download.asp?id=15490
16. Goodchild, M.F., Anselin, L., Diechmann, U.: A general framework for the areal interpolation of socio-economic data. Environment and Planning A, 383–397 (1993)
17. Gotway, C., Young, L.: Combining incompatible spatial data. Journal of the American Statistical Association 97(458), 632–648 (2002)
18. Grasland, C.: A la recherche d'un cadre théorique et méthodologique pour l'étude des maillages territoriaux. Entretiens Jacques Cartier, Les découpages du territoire, Lyon (décembre 2007) (in French)
19. Langford, M., Unwin, D.J.: Generating and mapping population density surface within a GIS. The Cartographic Journal 31, 21–26 (1992)
20. Marceau, D.: The scale issue in social and natural sciences. Canadian Journal of Remote Sens 25(4), 347–356 (1999)
21. Markoff, J., Shapiro, G.: The Linkage of Data Describing Overlapping Geographical Units. Historical Methods Newsletter 7, 34–46 (1973)
22. Matheron, G.: Principles of geostatistics. Economy geology 58, 1246–1266 (1963)
23. Miller, H.J.: Geographic representation in spatial analysis. Journal of Geographical Systems 2(1), 55–60 (2000)
24. Nordhaus, W.D.: Alternative approaches to spatial rescaling. Yale University, New Haven (2002)
25. Openshaw, S., Taylor, P.: A Million or so Correlation Coefficients. In: Wrigley, N. (ed.) Statistical Methods in the Spatial Sciences, pp. 127–144. Pion, London (1979)
26. Openshaw, S.: Building an automated modelling system to explore a universe of spatial interaction models. Geographical Analysis 20, 31–46 (1988)
27. Plumejeaud, C., Vincent, J.-M., Grasland, C., Bimonte, S., Mathian, H., Guelton, S., Boulier, J., Gensel, J.: HyperSmooth, a system for Interactive Spatial Analysis via Potential Maps. In: Bertolotto, M., Ray, C., Li, X. (eds.) W2GIS 2008. LNCS, vol. 5373, pp. 4–16. Springer, Heidelberg (2008)
28. Rase, W.D.: Volume-preserving interpolation of a smooth surface from polygon-related data. Journal of Geographical Systems 3, 199–213 (2001)

29. Raskin, R.G.: Spatial Analysis on a Sphere: A Review. National Center for Geographic Information and Analysis, Technical Report (1994)
30. Reibel, M., Agrawal, A.: Areal Interpolation of Population Counts Using Pre-classified Land Cover Data. Population Research and Policy Review, 619–633 (2007)
31. Rigaux, P., Scholl, M.: Multi-scale partitions: application to spatial and statistical databases. In: Egenhofer, M.J., Herring, J.R. (eds.) SSD 1995. LNCS, vol. 951, pp. 170–183. Springer, Heidelberg (1995)
32. Schmit, C., Rounsevell, M.D.A., La Jeunesse, I.: The limitations of spatial land use data in environmental analysis. Environmental Science & Policy 9(2), 174–188 (2006)
33. Shepard, D.: A two-dimensional interpolation function for irregularly spaced data. In: Proc. 23rd Nat. Conf. ACM, pp. 517–523. Brandon/Systems Press Inc., Princeton (1968)
34. Tobler, W.A.: Smooth pycnopylactic interpolation for geographical regions. Journal of the American Statistical Association 74, 519–530 (1979)
35. Zaninetti, J.M.: Statistique spatiale, méthodes et applications géomatiques, Paris, Hermès (2005) (in French)
36. Zhang, Z., Griffith, D.: Developing user-friendly spatial statistical analysis modules for GIS: an example using ArcView. Computer, Environment and Urban Systems (1993)

A Model Driven Process for Spatial Data Sources and Spatial Data Warehouses Reconcilation

Octavio Glorio, Jose-Norberto Mazón, and Juan Trujillo

University of Alicante, Spain
Department of Software and Computing Systems
Lucentia Research Group
{oglorio,jnmazon,jtrujillo}@dlsi.ua.es
www.lucentia.es

Abstract. Since the data warehouse integrates the information provided by data sources, it is crucial to reconcile these sources with the information requirements of decision makers. It is specially true when novel types of data and metadata are stored in the data sources, e.g. spatial issues. In this way, spatial requirements have to be conformed with the available spatial metadata in order to obtain a data warehouse that, at the same time, satisfies decision maker spatial needs and do not attempt against the available metadata stored in the data sources. Therefore, in this paper, we have based on multidimensional forms and some spatial and geometric considerations to define a set of Query/View/Transformation (QVT) relations to formally define a set of rules that help designers in this tedious and prone-to-fail task. The novelty of our approach is to consider an hybrid viewpoint to develop spatial data warehouses (SDW), i.e., we firstly obtain the conceptual schema of the SDW from user requirements and then we verify its correctness against spatial data sources by using automatic transformations. Finally, the designer could take decisions to overcome the absence or incompactibility of certain spatial data by using our Eclipse CASE tool.

Keywords: Spatial Data Warehouses, Geographic Information, Data Sources Reconcilation.

1 Introduction

Many years of data collection in very different systems and domains have generated significant volumes of heterogeneous information. Information that not only have to be stored, although it is required in analysis processes. Data warehouses (DW) are systems that store and explore huge quantities of information from many data sources. Therefore, these systems are suitable to cover current information requirement scenarios. For this purpose, the data is structured following the multidimensional paradigm. These structures are more intuitive for designers

D. Taniar et al. (Eds.): ICCSA 2010, Part I, LNCS 6016, pp. 461–475, 2010.
© Springer-Verlag Berlin Heidelberg 2010

and faster for exploring tools. The most typical tools for interactively explore the data warehouse are the BI (Bussiness Intelligence) systems which include different analysis techniques such as OLAP (On-Line Analytical Processing) or data mining.

Data warehouses repositories also contain a lot of spatial data that are not used to their full potential and part of their richness is simply left out. For example, traditional data fields such as customer or stores locations are represented by its address in an alphanumeric text. Due to this representation, there are some limitations while analyzing data and interesting insights could be losed. Spatial Data Warehouses address these limitations and integrate spatial data in their multidimensional (MD) structures by extending this model in order to add spatiality at the conceptual level. In this paper, we understand spatial data as which one whose represent geometric characteristics of a real world phenomena. In order to do so, they have an absolute and relative position, an associated geometry and some descriptive attributes.

Since the DW integrates several data sources, the development of conceptual MD models has traditionally been guided by an analysis of these data sources [6,1,7]. Considering these data-driven approaches, MNFs (multidimensional normal forms) have been developed [9] to reason, in a rigorous manner, about the quality (faithfulness, completeness, avoidance of redundancies, summarizability) of a conceptual MD model derived from operational data sources.

Nevertheless, in these data-driven approaches the requirement analysis phase is overlooked, thus resulting in an MD model in which the user needs and expectations may not be satisfied [22]. To overcome this problem, several approaches [22,19,13,2] advocate a requirement-driven DW design process. However, hardly any of these approaches considers the data sources in the early stages of the development. Therefore, the correctness of the MD model with respect to the data sources cannot be assured and the DW repository cannot be properly populated from these data sources.

In order to reconcile these two points of view (data-driven and requirement-driven), a Model Driven Architecture (MDA) [16] framework for the development of DWs has been described in [3]. Within this approach a conceptual MD model of the DW repository is developed from user requirements. This MD model must be then conformed to data sources in order to assure its correctness. Finally, in [12], we focus on presenting a set of Query/View/Transformation (QVT) relations in order to check the correctness of the MD conceptual model against the available data sources.

However, for the best of our knowledge, there is not an approach that considered traditional spatial multidimensional elements (e.g., spatial level or measures) correctness against the available data sources. Therefore, designers have to affort the tedious and prone-to-fail task of satisfy decision makers spatial needs and do not attempt against the available metadata stored in the spatial data sources.

The motivation of our approach is as follows: since the SDW integrates spatial information provided by spatial source databases, it is important to check (in early stages of the development) if the requirement-driven spatial MD conceptual model agrees with the available spatial data sources in order to assure that the SDW repository will be properly populated from spatial data sources.

To illustrate these benefits, consider the following running example. We assume that the conceptual model for the sales domain shown in Fig. 1 has been derived from analysis requirements *without* taking spatial data sources into account. The notation of Fig. 1 is based on a UML profile for geographical MD modeling (GeoMD) presented in [4] (see Section 3.2 for details).

The figure models *Sales* facts which are composed of several measures (*Unit Sales, Store Cost* and *Store Sales*) and described by dimensions *Store, Product, Time,* and *Customer.* In this example we only have expanded *Store* dimension to simplify. There we have different hierarchy levels (*City* and *State*) and one (*Store* level) that is spatial (described by a point geometry). As domain external geographic information, we have the *Airport* layer that describe the points corresponding to airports.

Supose now that we take in account the spatial data available (see Fig. 11) to populate the SDW. There, we required the airports and the stores geographic description but there are some details: (i) airports are not in the data sources, (ii) stores are not described as points, and (iii) there are some spatial data that have not been considered in the conceptual model and could be usefull. Therefore the GeoMD model shown in Fig. 1 should be improved in a number of ways to obtain the "better" model shown in Fig. 2. Indeed, in this paper we show how to apply QVT relations to obtain the model shown in Fig. 2 from the model shown in Fig. 1 by taking spatial source databases into account.

The remainder of this paper is structured as follows: Related work is put into perspective next. Our approach is presented in Section 3 by describing spatial data source model as well as spatial MD model, and defining QVT relations. The application of sample QVT relations is illustrated in Section 4. The paper ends with conclusions and suggestions for future work in Section 5.

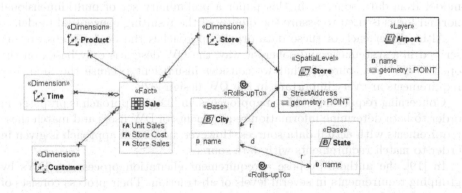

Fig. 1. GeoMD model for sales domain

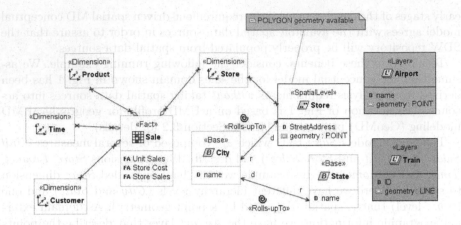

Fig. 2. Improved GeoMD model for sales domain

2   Related Work

In this section, we briefly describe the most relevant approaches for both data-driven and requirement-driven DW development.

Concerning data-driven approaches, in [1], the authors present the Multidimensional Model, a logical model for MD databases. The authors also propose a general design method, aimed at building an MD schema starting from an operational database described by an Entity-Relationship (ER) schema.

In [6], the authors propose the Dimensional-Fact Model (DFM), a particular notation for the DW conceptual design. Moreover, they also propose how to derive a DW schema from the data sources described by ER schemas. Also in [21], the building of a conceptual MD model of the DW repository from the conceptual schemas of the operational data sources is proposed.

In [7], the authors present a method to systematically derive a conceptual MD model from data sources. In this paper a preliminary set of multidimensional normal forms is used to assure the quality of the resulting conceptual model.

Although in each of these data-driven approaches the design steps are described in a systematic and coherent way, the DW design is only based on the operational data sources, what we consider insufficient because the final user requirements are very important in the DW design [22].

Concerning requirement-driven approaches, in [22] an approach is proposed in order to both determine information requirements of DW users and match these requirements with actual data sources. However, no formal approach is given in order to match requirements with data sources.

In [19], the authors propose a requirement elicitation process for DWs by grouping requirements in several levels of abstraction. Their process consists of identifying information that supports decision making via information scenarios. In this process, a Goal-Decision-Information (GDI) diagram is used. Although the derivation of GDI diagrams and information scenarios is described, the relationships between information scenarios and requirements are not properly specified. Moreover, requirements are not conformed to data sources in order to obtain a conceptual MD model.

In [2], the authors present a framework to obtain a conceptual MD model from requirements. This framework uses the data sources to shape hierarchies and user requirements are used to choose facts, dimensions and measures. However, the authors do not present a formal way to conform data sources and the MD conceptual model.

As a survey, we wish to point out that these requirement-driven approaches do not formalize the relation between the data sources and the requirements to verify and enforce the correctness of the resulting DW. Therefore, in [12] we have proposed to use MNFs [9] in a systematic manner, thus formalizing the development of the DW repository by means of (i) obtaining a conceptual MD model from user requirements, and (ii) verifying and enforcing its correctness against the operational data sources. However, for the best of our knowledge, there is not an approach that considered traditional spatial multidimensional elements (e.g., spatial level or measures) correctness against the available data sources. Therefore, designers have to affort the tedious and prone-to-fail task of satisfy decision makers spatial needs and do not attempt against the available metadata stored in the spatial data sources.

3   Checking Correctness of the Conceptual Spatiality

In this section, we present our approach to check the correctness of the spatial elements (spatial levels and measures and geographic layers) in a conceptual GeoMD model with respect to the spatial source databases. To this end, we present a set of QVT relations able to check if the spatial conceptual elements could be populated from the geometric descriptions available in the data sources. But also, if some usefull spatial data of the data sources have not been considered in the conceptual schema.

Our approach consists of three main phases as shown in Fig. 3. The process start with a GeoMD model and a spatial data source model. The data source model is described using CWM and the different elments are marked as spatial dimensional elements (fact, dimension, spatial measure and so on). The GeoMD model have been designed without taking account the data source. Once the initial models have been defined the process start applying a first set of QVT relations (*Required matching*). This set tags GeoMD model elements as *required* if the conceptual element doesn't fit in the spatial data source. For example, in Fig. 2, *Airport* layer is not present in the data sources of Fig CWM ex and is colored red and tagged as *required*. Then, the same set is applied in the other direction (*Supplied matching*) and the GeoMD model elements are tagged as *supplied* if some spatial data has not been taken in consideration at conceptual level. For example, in Fig. 2, the *Train* layer had been added as one possible extra geographic information and is colored blue and tagged as *supplied*. Finally, a relations set (*Geometry warning*) check the geometric description of the

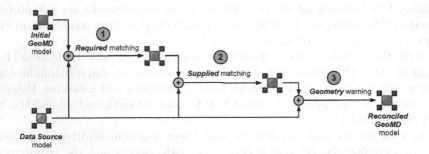

Fig. 3. Our approach for reconcile spatial elements with the data sources

matched elements and add some warning comments to the GeoMD elements if some inconsistencies have been detected. For example, in Fig. 2, the *Store* spatial level is described by a point geometry but in the data source it is described by a polygon. This situation could be easily solved if the designer is warned, for example, calculating the centroid of the polygon and using it as the required point description. Therefore, a warning comment colored in green is added to the GeoMD element. In the following subsections we present the spatial data source model and the GeoMD conceptual model, as well as the set of QVT relations.

3.1 Spatial Data Source Model

We assume that the data source model is the relational representation of the data sources. In particular, we use the CWM (Common Warehouse Metamodel) relational metamodel [15] in order to specify this data source model. The CWM relational metamodel is a standard to represent the structure of data resources in a relational database and allows us to represent tables, columns, primary keys, foreign keys, and so on. Since every CWM metamodel is MOF-compliant [15], it can be used as source or target for QVT relations [17].

On the other hand, this data source model must be marked before the QVT relations can be applied. Marking models is a technique that provides mechanisms to extend elements of the models in order to capture additional information [16,14]. Marks are used in MDA to prepare the models in order to guide the matching between them. A mark represents a concept from one model, which can be applied to an element of other different model. These marks indicate how every element of the source model must be matched. In our approach, the data source model is marked by appending a suffix to the name of each element according to the GeoMD conceptual model. In particular, we assume that the data source tables corresponding to MD model elements Fact, Dimension, and Base are marked with _FACT, _DIM, and _BASE, respectively, while data source columns corresponding to FactAttribute, DimensionAttribute, and Descriptor are marked with _MEASURE, _DA, and _D, respectively. Finally, we assume that a table corresponding to a geographic layer element is marked with

_LAYER. The spatial columns data types are marked as one of those geometric types supported (*POINT*, *LINE*, *POLYGON* and *COLLECTION*).

3.2   Geographic Multidimensional Model, GeoMD

The conceptual modeling of the SDW repository is based in a UML profile that join several ones. Those are one for MD modeling presented in [11], another one for spatial multidimensional levels and measures modeling, and a last one for geographic information modeling presented in [5]. This model also encourage the avaiability of the different spatial elements in the data sources. Therefore, we have also add to the main UML Profile some mark up elements used to describe whether the spatial data is available or not. An overview of our final UML profile is given in Fig. 4 and we have following described in depth the different elements:

Multidimensional elements: The necessary elements in order to represent main MD properties at the conceptual level had been presented for us in [10]. There the MD schemas correspond to UML class diagrams in which the information is clearly organised into facts and dimensions. These facts and dimensions are modeled by *Fact* (represented as ▦) and *Dimension* (⌂) stereotypes, respectively. Facts and dimensions are related by shared aggregation relationships (the Association UML metaclass) in class diagrams. While a fact is composed of measures or fact attributes (*FactAttribute*, **FA**), with respect to dimensions, each aggregation level of a hierarchy is specified by classes stereotyped as *Base* (**B**). Every *Base* class can contain several dimension attributes (*DimensionAttribute*, **DA**) and must also contain a *Descriptor* attribute (*Descriptor*, **D**). An association stereotyped as *Rolls-upTo* (*Rolls-upTo*,◉) between *Base* classes specifies the relationship between two levels of a classification hierarchy. Within it, role *R*

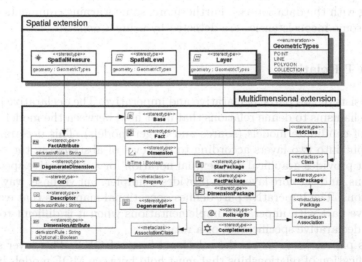

Fig. 4. Extension of the UML with the stereotypes corresponding to the GeoMD model

represents the direction in which the hierarchy rolls up, whereas role D represents the direction in which the hierarchy drills down.

Spatial elements: In [3] we have introduced the required spatial elements related to the multidimensional structure. Those are the spatial level and the spatial measure. The first one is an extension of the *Base* class because it also represents a hierarchy level. In the same way, the spatial measure is an extension of the *FactAttribute* class because it also represents an analysis variable. These spatial level and spatial measure are modeled by *SpatialLevel* ▱ and *SpatialMeasure* (✦) stereotypes. In [5] we have added an element representing external geographic information. We have presented a new element either using the previously presented because the geographic information is related to other spatial elements by coexisting in a same reference system and it has nothing to do inside the multidimensional logical structures Thus, we decide to separate this different kind os spatial data. For example, an spatial level describing a city is logically associated to the dimension and other levels structures. However, an spatial element added only for applying some geometric conditions (e.g., selecting sales made made near an airport) have not to be associated to the MD logical structures. This new element is modeled by *Layer* (▱) stereotype.

Once the different spatial elements had been presented, the geometric description have to be done. For this purpose, every spatial element have a *geometry* attribute. All the allowed geometric primitives have been grouped in a enumeration element named *GeometricTypes*. Those are *POINT, LINE, POLYGON* and *COLLECTION* but more could be easily added. These primitives are included on ISO [8] and OGC [18] spatial standards, in this way we ensure the final implementation in standard platforms. More types could be easy added if they are supported by these standards. All the spatial elements presented also have an attribute (*status*) that allows to be tagged with a status according to reconcile matching with the data sources. Furthermore, some warning comments could be added if some inconsistencies are detected by using *Comment* class.

3.3   QVT Relations

QVT consists of two parts: declarative and imperative. The declarative part provides mechanisms to define relations that must hold between the model elements of a set of candidate models (source and target models). This declarative part can be split into two layers according to the level of abstraction: the relational layer that provides graphical and textual notation for a declarative specification of relations, and the core layer that provides a simpler, but verbose, way of defining relations. The imperative part defines operational mappings that extend the declarative part with imperative implementations when it is difficult to provide a purely declarative specification of a relation.

In this paper, we focus on the relational layer of QVT. This layer supports the specification of relationships that must hold between MOF models by means of a relations language. A relation is defined by the following elements:

- **Two or more domains:** each domain is a set of elements of a source
  or a target model. The kind of relation between domains must be specified:
  checkonly (C), i.e., it is only checked if the relation holds or not; and enforced
  (E), i.e., the target model can be modified to satisfy the relation.
- **When clause:** it specifies the conditions under which the relation needs to
  hold (i.e. precondition).
- **Where clause:** it specifies the condition that must be satisfied by all model
  elements participating in the relation (i.e. postcondition).

In the following, each QVT relation is described: CheckSpatiality_1, CheckSpa-
tiality_2, CheckSpatiality_3, CheckGeometry_1, CheckGeometry_2 and Check-
Geometry_3. The *Required matching* and *Supplied matching* sets are composed
by CheckSpatiality_1, CheckSpatiality_2, CheckSpatiality_3 and the *Geometry
warning* set is composed by CheckGeometry_1, CheckGeometry_2 and Check-
Geometry_3.

Throughout the checks, we assume that the names of corresponding elements
in both models are equal (apart from the previously added marks) according to
a linguistic approach based on name similarity [20]. This issue is captured in the
when clause of each relation.

CheckSpatiality_1. This relation do the bidirectional matching between spatial
levels and spatial data sources. In Fig. 5 it is shown the diagramatic representation of the QVT relation. Since both domains are check-only, it is only checked
whether there exists a valid match that satisfies these relations without modifying any model if the domains do not match. This transformation relation is used
in the *Required matching* and *Supplied matching* sets just deciding the direction
of the matching. If the check fails in the direction UML to CWM, we tag the
failed elements as *required.* If the QVT fail in the other direction, the elements
are tagged as *supplied.*

The elements related to the GeoMD conceptual model are the following: a
SpatialLevel (s), a Descriptor (de) and a GeometricType. These elements must
be matched against a set of elements of the data source model: a table (t) with a

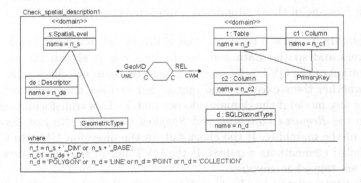

Fig. 5. QVT relation for SpatialLevel matching

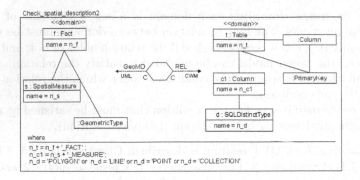

Fig. 6. QVT relation for SpatialMeasure matching

column (c1) which is part of the primary key. This table is marked as a Dimension or Base (n_t) and the column (c1) is marked as a Descriptor (n_c1). There is also a column (c2) which is functionally determined by the SQLDistinctType (d) marked as one of those supported geometric types (n_d).

CheckSpatiality_2. This relation do the bidirectional matching between spatial measures and spatial data sources. In Fig. 6 it is shown the diagramatic representation of the QVT relation. Since both domains are check-only, it is only checked whether there exists a valid match that satisfies these relations without modifying any model if the domains do not match. This transformation relation is used in the *Required matching* and *Supplied matching* sets just deciding the direction of the matching. If the check fails in the direction UML to CWM, we tag the failed elements as *required*. If the QVT fail in the other direction, the elements are tagged as *supplied*.

The elements related to the GeoMD conceptual model are the following: a Fact (f), a SpatialMeasure (s) and a GeometricType. These elements must be matched against a set of elements of the data source model: a table (t) with a column which is part of the primary key. This table is marked as a Fact (n_t). There is also a column (c1) which is functionally determined by the SQLDistinctType (d) marked as one of those supported geometric types (n_d).

CheckSpatiality_3. This relation do the bidirectional matching between geographic layers and spatial data sources. In Fig. 7 it is shown the diagramatic representation of the QVT relation. Since both domains are check-only, it is only checked whether there exists a valid match that satisfies these relations without modifying any model if the domains do not match. This transformation relation is used in the *Required matching* and *Supplied matching* sets just deciding the direction of the matching. If the check fails in the direction UML to CWM, we tag the failed elements as *required*. If the QVT fail in the other direction, the elements are tagged as *supplied*.

The elements related to the GeoMD conceptual model are the following: a Layer (l) and a GeometricType. These elements must be matched against a set

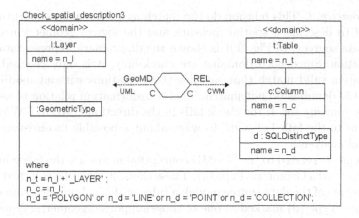

Fig. 7. QVT relation for Layer matching

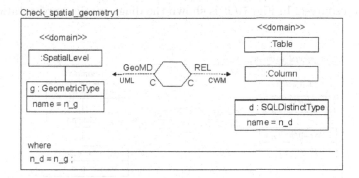

Fig. 8. QVT relation for geometry type matching

of elements of the data source model: a table (t) with a column (c1), this table is marked as a Layer (n_t). The column c1 is functionally determined by the SQLDistinctType (d) marked as one of those supported geometric types (n_d).

CheckGeometry_1. This relation do the matching between the conceptual geometry used to describe a spatial level and the logical geometry used in the spatial data sources. In Fig. 8 it is shown the diagramatic representation of the QVT relation. Since both domains are check-only, it is only checked whether there exists a valid match that satisfies these relations without modifying any model if the domains do not match. This transformation relation is used in the *Geometry warning* set. If the check fails in the direction UML to CWM, we add a comment to the failed element to warn about a possible inconsistency during the spatial analysis.

The elements related to the GeoMD conceptual model are the following: a SpatialLevel and a GeometricType (g). These elements must be matched against a set of elements of the data source model: a table with a column determined by the SQLDistinctType (d) marked as one of those supported geometric types (n_d).

CheckGeometry_2. This relation do the matching between the conceptual geometry used to describe a spatial measure and the logical geometry used in the spatial data sources. In Fig. 9 it is shown the diagramatic representation of the QVT relation. Since both domains are check-only, it is only checked whether there exists a valid match that satisfies these relations without modifying any model if the domains do not match. This transformation relation is used in the *Geometry warning* set. If the check fails in the direction UML to CWM, we add a comment to the failed element to warn about a possible inconsistency during the spatial analysis.

The elements related to the GeoMD conceptual model are the following: a SpatialMeasure and a GeometricType (g). These elements must be matched against a set of elements of the data source model: a table with a column determined by the SQLDistinctType (d) marked as one of those supported geometric types (n_d).

CheckGeometry_3. This relation do the matching between the conceptual geometry used to describe a geographic layer and the logical geometry used in the spatial data sources. In Fig. 10 it is shown the diagramatic representation of the

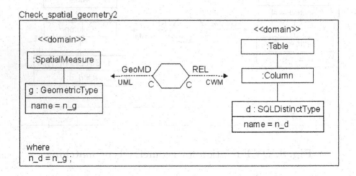

Fig. 9. QVT relation for geometry type matching

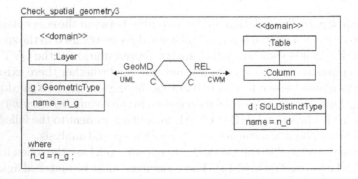

Fig. 10. QVT relation for geometry type matching

QVT relation. Since both domains are check-only, it is only checked whether there exists a valid match that satisfies these relations without modifying any model if the domains do not match. This transformation relation is used in the *Geometry warning* set. If the check fails in the direction UML to CWM, we add a comment to the failed element to warn about a possible inconsistency during the spatial analysis.

The elements related to the GeoMD conceptual model are the following: a Layer and a GeometricType (g). These elements must be matched against a set of elements of the data source model: a table with a column determined by the SQLDistinctType (d) marked as one of those supported geometric types (n_d).

4   Sample Applications of QVT Relations

In this section, we show how our QVT relations are properly applied to assure the correctness of the GeoMD conceptual model of the SDW repository against spatial data sources. We use the sample scenario previously introduced in the Introduction (see Fig. 2). The spatial data source model (already marked) is shown in Fig. 11.

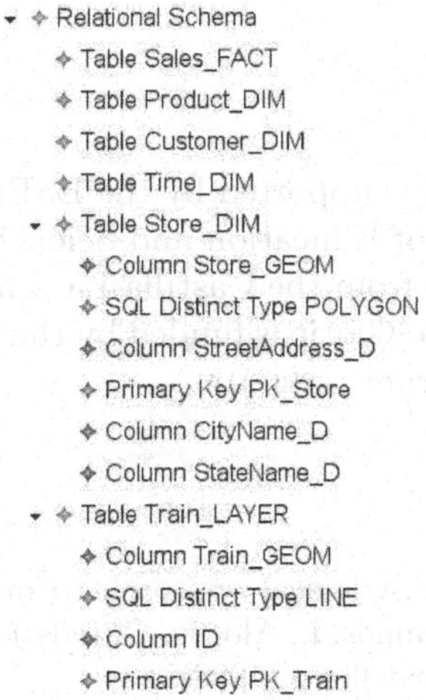

> ▾ ✦ Relational Schema
>   ✦ Table Sales_FACT
>   ✦ Table Product_DIM
>   ✦ Table Customer_DIM
>   ✦ Table Time_DIM
>   ▾ ✦ Table Store_DIM
>   ✦ Column Store_GEOM
>   ✦ SQL Distinct Type POLYGON
>   ✦ Column StreetAddress_D
>   ✦ Primary Key PK_Store
>   ✦ Column CityName_D
>   ✦ Column StateName_D
>   ▾ ✦ Table Train_LAYER
>   ✦ Column Train_GEOM
>   ✦ SQL Distinct Type LINE
>   ✦ Column ID
>   ✦ Primary Key PK_Train

Fig. 11. Spatial data sources model for our example

Due to space restrictions, we only describe a subset of the applied relations. These QVT relations are as follows:

CheckSpatiality_3. This relation checks that the Store_DIM table, the Store_GEOM (of SQLDistinctType type) and StreetAddress_D columns correspond to the Store spatial level and the StreetAddress descriptor.

CheckGeometry_1. This relation checks that the marked SQLDistinctType of column Store_GEOM correspond with the GeometricType of the Store spatial level.

5   Conclusions and Future Work

In this paper, we have presented an approach to assure the correctness of spatial MD elements (spatial level, spatial measure and geographic layer) of the SDW repository according to the spatial data sources that will populate this repository. This approach is outlined as follows: we firstly obtain the MD conceptual schema of the SDW from user requirements and then we verify its correctness against spatial data sources by using a set of QVT relations. Furthermore, QVT relations allow us to integrate this approach into an MDA framework for the development of DWs.

Our immediate future work is to develop automatic mechanism in order to also obtain spatial data source models from geographic information systems workspaces. In such way, more spatial data sources could be verify against conceptual models. Another future topic, is the integration of raw data that could not be stored in traditional repositories platforms but could be usefull combines with the spatial analysis.

Acknowledgments

This work has been partially supported by the ESPIA project (TIN2007-67078) from the Spanish Ministry of Education and Science and by the QUASIMODO project (PAC08-0157-0668) from the Castilla-La Mancha Ministry of Education and Science (Spain). Octavio Glorio is funded by the University of Alicante under the 11th Latin American grant program.

References

1. Cabibbo, L., Torlone, R.: A logical approach to multidimensional databases. In: Schek, H.-J., Saltor, F., Ramos, I., Alonso, G. (eds.) EDBT 1998. LNCS, vol. 1377, pp. 183–197. Springer, Heidelberg (1998)
2. Giorgini, P., Rizzi, S., Garzetti, M.: Goal-oriented requirement analysis for data warehouse design. In: DOLAP, pp. 47–56 (2005)
3. Glorio, O., Trujillo, J.: An MDA Approach for the Development of Spatial Data Warehouses. In: DaWaK, Turin, Italy, pp. 23–32 (2008)
4. Glorio, O., Trujillo, J.: Designing data warehouses for geographic olap querying by using mda. In: ICCSA, vol. (1), pp. 505–519 (2009)
5. Glorio, O., Zubcoff, J., Trujillo, J.: A model driven framework for geographic knowledge discovery. In: Geoinformatics 2009, pp. 1–6 (2009)
6. Golfarelli, M., Maio, D., Rizzi, S.: The Dimensional Fact Model: A conceptual model for data warehouses. Int. J. Cooperative Inf. Syst. 7(2-3), 215–247 (1998)
7. Hüsemann, B., Lechtenbörger, J., Vossen, G.: Conceptual data warehouse modeling. In: DMDW, p. 6 (2000)

8. ISO, International Organization for Standardization, http://www.iso.org
9. Lechtenbörger, J., Vossen, G.: Multidimensional normal forms for data warehouse design. Inf. Syst. 28(5), 415–434 (2003)
10. Luján-Mora, S., Trujillo, J., Song, I.-Y.: A UML profile for multidimensional modeling in data warehouses. Data Knowl. Eng. 59(3), 725–769 (2006)
11. Luján-Mora, S., Trujillo, J., Song, I.-Y.: A UML profile for multidimensional modeling in data warehouses. Data & Knowledge Engineering (2006) (In Press)
12. Mazón, J.-N., Trujillo, J., Lechtenbörger, J.: A set of qvt relations to assure the correctness of data warehouses by using multidimensional normal forms. In: Embley, D.W., Olivé, A., Ram, S. (eds.) ER 2006. LNCS, vol. 4215, pp. 385–398. Springer, Heidelberg (2006)
13. Mazón, J.-N., Trujillo, J., Serrano, M., Piattini, M.: Designing data warehouses: from business requirement analysis to multidimensional modeling. In: REBNITA, pp. 44–53 (2005)
14. Mellor, S., Scott, K., Uhl, A., Weise, D.: MDA distilled: principles of Model-Driven Architecture. Addison-Wesley, Reading (2004)
15. Object Management Group. Common Warehouse Metamodel Specification 1.1. Visited (January 2006), http://www.omg.org/cgi-bin/doc?formal/03-03-02
16. Object Management Group. MDA Guide 1.0.1. Visited (January 2006), http://www.omg.org/cgi-bin/doc?omg/03-06-01
17. Object Management Group. MOF 2.0 Query/View/Transformation. Visited (January 2006), http://www.omg.org/cgi-bin/doc?ptc/2005-11-01
18. OGC, Open Geospatial Consortium, http://www.opengeospatial.org
19. Prakash, N., Singh, Y., Gosain, A.: Informational scenarios for data warehouse requirements elicitation. In: Atzeni, P., Chu, W., Lu, H., Zhou, S., Ling, T.-W. (eds.) ER 2004. LNCS, vol. 3288, pp. 205–216. Springer, Heidelberg (2004)
20. Rahm, E., Bernstein, P.A.: A survey of approaches to automatic schema matching. VLDB J 10(4), 334–350 (2001)
21. Tryfona, N., Busborg, F., Christiansen, J.G.B.: starER: A conceptual model for data warehouse design. In: DOLAP, pp. 3–8 (1999)
22. Winter, R., Strauch, B.: A method for demand-driven information requirements analysis in data warehousing projects. In: HICSS, p. 231 (2003)

ISATEM: An Integration of Socioeconomic and Spatial Models for Mineral Resources Exploitation

Fenintsoa Andriamasinoro, Daniel Cassard, and Bruno Martel-Jantin

BRGM - Mineral Resources Division,
BP 36009 Cedex 2, 45060 Orléans, France
{f.andriamasinoro,d.cassard,b.martel-jantin}@brgm.fr

Abstract. In the spatial-integrated socioeconomic model field, a multi-agent approach is appropriate for supporting applications modelled at a detailed territory scale, but it is less used than other approaches when supporting applications modelled at a larger scale. One possibility would be to have a more generic platform that is capable of supporting both levels. Moreover, at the spatial level, integration of dynamic spatial data and, in our case, spatial shape data should be reinforced so that, at any moment during a simulation, a user should be capable of exporting the temporal evolution of the spatial state as a (new) shape map, exploitable in a GIS tool. This paper aims to contribute to the improvement of these two aspects. We began the study with ADK, an existing agent platform, ending up with a new platform known as ISatEM. Our thematic interest is the field of mineral resources exploitation.

Keywords: Spatial shape data, socioeconomic model, simulation, agent, component, mineral resources exploitation.

1 Introduction

Socio-economic modelling can be described as the representation of the relationship between economic activity and social life [10]. Spatial-integrated socioeconomic models (hereafter SISM) are models that often concern the management of natural resources, in which economic or social activities often apply pressure to a geographical space, measured at the territory scale where the social actors are situated. SISM application domains are various: not just water resources [13], bioenergy [16], fisheries [19], etc., but also mineral resources exploitation [1]. Mineral resources exploitation is a SISM composed of socioeconomic actors performing a set of tasks[1], starting from the production of ores, continuing through their transport to the transformation area and ending with the (second) transport of the final product to the area of consumption, where it is either sold and used. The study scale may be micro (local site scale), medium (regional) or macro (national). Socioeconomic impacts are jobs and incomes. Spatial interests are transport distance (impacting on cost), environmental impact (generally due to production and transport) and also spatial (re)distribution of production centres and resources availability [9].

---

[1] At the application level, some tasks may be abstracted if not necessary for the modelling.

D. Taniar et al. (Eds.): ICCSA 2010, Part I, LNCS 6016, pp. 476–490, 2010.

Designing a SISM involves the selection of the appropriate modelling approach, depending on the application territory scale. A multi-agent system (hereafter MAS) [20] is often used, especially if the application territory is defined at a micro scale [5][11]. At a larger scale, other approaches, such as dynamic systems [13], may be more appropriate even if a MAS is still acceptable. Besides, simulating a SISM results in a constant evolution of the state at both socioeconomic and spatial levels. As such, simulation is a way to constantly acquire new temporal data for these levels. In particular, at a spatial level, it should be possible for the simulation user, at any time during an ongoing simulation, to export this dynamic spatial data as (new) shape map data. Consequently, the user, after importing these successive maps in a Geographic Information System (GIS) tool, will be presented with a superposition of files showing the spatial state of one system at different times.

By focusing, at an application level, on the field of mineral resources exploitation, the objective of the work described in this paper is to present and discuss our contribution to two aspects: (a) the improvement of a multi-agent model, formerly designed to support applications modelled at a micro-territory scale, to a more generic object model, capable of also coping with an application modelled at a larger territory scale; and (b) the improvement of the conceptual integration of dynamic spatial shape[2] data in a SISM, as explained in the previous paragraph. In this paper, shape object refers to these spatial entities having line, circle and polygon forms, and a shape map only refers to ESRI® shape file specification, composed of the three files shp (for entity geometry), dbf (for entity attributes) and shx (for the indexes).

Our approach is to start, as an initial case-study, with an existing multi-agent system known as ADK (for Agent Developer Kit) to finally end up with a new resulting model and simulation platform known as ISatEM (Integrated Systems applied to Exploitation of Mineral resources). Temporal storage of the simulated SISM data is the main issue that must be handled during the work.

Section 2 presents ADK. Section 3 presents our proposal, ISatEM, which is then discussed in Section 0. Section 5 concludes the paper and outlines perspectives.

2 ADK: An Initial Case Study

ADK was developed by Calderoni [5] with the idea of simulating a society of artificial agents. ADK contains three of the main components generally found in Multi-Agent Systems: agents, objects and environment. At a spatial level, ADK uses shape format to model its data. The agent behaviour is based on the triad "perception-deliberation-action". Messages exchanged inside ADK are then called percepts. At each simulation time step, percepts are propagated throughout the environment according to the previous state of the system. For example, a visual percept, which contains the position of an agent or an object, is propagated so that all agents can behave accordingly, regarding what to do and where to go.

Scope of the ADK approach. The ADK approach is appropriate for applications modelled at a very detailed scale, such as robot foraging problems [5], [11]. In the

---

[2] The choice of shape spatial format was made only because it was of interest to us. A discussion about which is better, grid or shape spatial format, is beyond the scope of this paper.

domain of mineral resources exploitation, it is also appropriate for applications such as the exploitation of quartz at the scale of Rantabe in Madagascar [2] or artisanal and small-scale gold mining at the Alga site in Burkina Faso [3] (let Asgma). At a larger application scale (cf. Section 3.1), the ADK approach may still be employed, but it may be cumbersome to use the above triad to model an application at such a level: it does not provide more information to the application and it may overburden the simulation performance.

State of the art regarding spatial representation. Regarding the spatial level, the fact that ADK uses shape format is interesting for our purpose but it has some limitations. To ascertain the details of these limitations, let us focus on the application of ADK to Asgma.

Asgma is a mineral resources exploitation that is composed of a task sequence, from shaft *extraction* to successive *treatments* of *crushing, grinding, sluice washing, winnowing* and *mill grinding*. Each task is performed by a *team* of actors. Transport is carried out by boys with carts. The Asgma model is a SISM, the socioeconomic part of which is modelled in [3].

The spatial representation of Asgma is shown in Fig. 1. In detail, Fig. 1.a shows the content of the unique file, designated asgma.ads that ADK uses to initialise the simulation illustrated in Fig. 1.b. Lines starting by # are comments. Only position, nb_agents, id and dimension properties concern the spatial initialisation.

The formal syntax of each line in asgma.ads is described in Equation 1, in which expressions written in "[ ]" are optional.

$$\text{classId: } (\text{prop}_1 \text{ val}_{11} \text{ [val}_{12}]) \text{ [(prop}_2 \text{ val}_{21} \text{ [val}_{22}])] \tag{1}$$

Fig. 1.b shows agents having a circular shape and task areas having a polygonal shape. We can see that spatial dynamic representation exists, in particular in the transport process: not only can the conveyor agent move but it is also possible to track the spatial evolution of such movement.

However, the spatial information presentation is currently approximate: in asgma.ads, the content is set by the user according to his/her own perception. Regarding the conveyor movement in particular, the conveyor goes in a straightforward manner, from the shafts to the crushing area whereas, in real-field, the conveyor cart actually follows determined paths that should allow the model to evaluate the transport cost. These limitations are due to two reasons: not only did real-field data collection in the upstream phase not consider spatial aspects [12], but even if this was the case, ADK cannot read data from a shape map (these two actions should both exist). As a result, the economic impact of the transport activity in the Asgma network could not be modelled, as noted in [3].

Besides, ADK displays all polygonal shapes, obligatory in the same form (cf. Fig. 1.b). This is because the position parameter only has two values, which actually refer to the barycentre of each task area polygon. All polygon drawings start from this barycentre. All other coordinates that should exist in a polygon are ignored.

Finally, it is not possible for ADK to store the temporal evolution of spatial data during a simulation [3] [5]. When a simulation stops and ADK is closed, all simulated data is lost.

```
#display ----
monitor: (res 10) (per 10) (mdp 30) (out 30000);

#agent environment size ----
field: (dimension 70.0 75.0) (tim 91) (acc 18) (nb_day 9200);

#ore extraction areas (the three shafts on the left) ----
shaft: (position -22.5 20.0) (nb_agents 5) (id shaft1) (type sz) (depth 100);
shaft: (position -25.5 15.0) (nb_agents 5) (id shaft2) (type fm) (depth 75) ;
shaft: (position -26.5 11.0) (nb_agents 5) (id shaft3) (type fm) (depth 87);

#transport headquarters (in the middle) ----
conv:  (position -15.0 22.0) (nb_agents 1) (id conveyor_HQ);

#ore treatment areas (on the right) ----
millg: (position 14.0 8.0)  (nb_agents 2) (id mill_grinding_area);
winn:  (position 16.0 5.0)  (nb_agents 2) (id winnowing_area);
wash:  (position 22.0 12.0) (nb_agents 5) (id washing_area);
grind: (position 15.0 17.5) (nb_agents 22)(id grinding_area);
crush: (position 9.0 20.0)  (nb_agents 6) (id crushing_area);
```
(a)

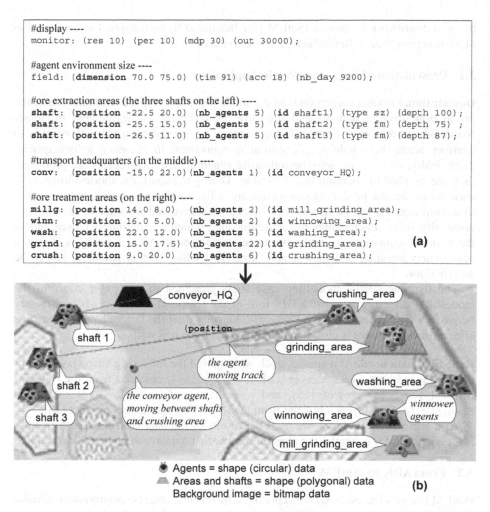

● Agents = shape (circular) data
▲ Areas and shafts = shape (polygonal) data   **(b)**
Background image = bitmap data

Fig. 1. (a) Content of the file asgma.ads, which launches the Asgma simulation illustrated in (b)

3 ISatEM: A Proposal

Due to a real-word demand, in the field of mineral resources management, a new application called FlowMod, defined at a regional scale, has to be modelled. Since the modelling process at this scale requires going beyond a multi-agent approach, an improvement needs to be made to have a framework that is conceptually capable of supporting both FlowMod and Asgma applications and of having a better data storage mechanism regarding the previous ADK limitations. A collection of real-field data should also be made to avoid an approximate spatial representation, as was explained concerning Asgma. Section 3.2 describes how we conceptually translate from ADK to the new framework known as ISatEM (for Integrated System applied to Exploitation of Mineral resources). Beforehand, let us introduce FlowMod.

3.1 Presentation of the Larger-Scale Application

Description. FlowMod corresponds to the modelling and *prospective* simulation of the production (from a quarry) and the flow management of aggregates[3] in Seine-Normandie, a region of France. If we compare Asgma and FlowMod with regards to territory scale, the whole Asgma system is equivalent, in FlowMod, to one quarry. Technically, FlowMod models the following situation: after aggregates are produced, they are supplied to communities[4] by trucks. During transport, the shortest itinerary is chosen because the producing companies are obliged to keep transportation distances to a minimum for the large volumes of materials involved in order to remain economically viable. Each quarry has a lifetime after which it is definitely closed, unless the regional administrative authority agrees to re-open it. After a quarry is closed, a new quarry resource and then a new itinerary leading to that resource, has to be searched for.

The dynamic spatial modelling case study presented in this paper concerns the modelling and exportation to a GIS tool of the temporal evolution of the itinerary between a given community and a quarry, knowing that the latter changes over time after a previous quarry is closed and assumed not to be renewed.

Real-field data used. At a spatial level, we acquired the following shape layers, temporarily noted here layer_name{form}: quarry{point}, obtained from the 'GIS for Mineral resources' project [15], and community_node{point}, road{line}, and road_node{point} layers, obtained from the Route500® numerical product [18].

At a socioeconomic level, we used the results of the data collection performed in [4], containing, for example, the average income that a quarry exploitation can bring.

3.2 From ADK to ISatEM

ISatEM resumes the essential concepts of ADK (agents, objects, environment, simulation and behaviour), with the difference that the concept of agents and objects is generalized to that of components that may be *spatial* or *transversal*. The ADK environment then becomes an ISatEM environment for components.

The concept of spatial components. A spatial component is a dynamic entity composed of *input ports* (which receive events), *fire ports* (which send events), *behaviour* and *properties*. There are two generic properties: a *spatial property* designated Geometry, which may be a *line*, *circle* or *polygon* and a *behavioural property* designated state. The possible values for state are contained in a static property designated possible states. All non-generic properties are either *socioeconomic properties* or *component properties*, i.e. properties referring to other components. Geometry, state

---

[3] Aggregates are unconsolidated materials used as one of the main components of concrete and as foundations for road and railway infrastructures.

[4] In France, a "community" corresponds to an administrative unit at a town scale.

and *socioeconomic* properties are called *temporal properties*, namely properties whose value can evolve over the simulation time.

An output fire port takes the form of FireEvent(), where Event$_y$ is the event to be sent from that port. Symmetrically, an input event port is associated with the function that should be performed on receiving the associated event. It takes the form of On-EventX(). There is *always* at least one input port named OnTimeChanged(), which continuously receives the system timer event at each simulation time step. The current value of state determines the *unit* goal and then the *unit* behaviour (which may include a thinking process if the component represents a cognitive agent) to be adopted during that time step, after which state is re-evaluated by a StateTransition() function, invoked after OnTimeChanged ().

In FlowMod, spatial components are Quarry (circle), RoadNode (point), Road (line), Community (circle), Itinerary (line) and Truck (polygon). It may be noted that only the four first components have a corresponding shape map of real-field data.

Fig. 2 illustrates what a spatial component is. As an example in FlowMod, the Quarry component is shown (in a simplified way, for space reasons).

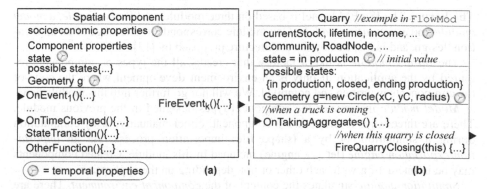

Fig. 2. The generic scheme of a spatial component (a), followed by an example from the FlowMod application: the quarry component (b)

From the behavioural points of view, a quarry is an entity in which behaviour is driven by the goal to produce the necessary aggregates needed by its corresponding community while avoiding having too much stock of non-consumed production. Likewise, a truck conveys the maximum of aggregates in a day to maximize its profits while trying to diminish as much as possible the quantity of CO_2 produced, and a community tries to acquire the appropriate quantity of aggregates corresponding to its population's needs (local building of houses or roads, etc).

Transversal components. A transversal component is a component with the following differences compared to a spatial component: (a) it has a global view to all spatial components, allowing it to perform a computation involving all of the latter elements, and (b) it does not have state and Geometry properties.

In `FlowMod`, transversal components are:

- `ItinerarySearch`, which looks for the itinerary and the quarry that should supply a community requiring aggregates: research criteria are the existence of a non-used quarry and the shortest itinerary between it and the community.
- `TruckManager`, which adds or removes a truck, depending on the quantity produced for a community.
- `CO2Evaluator` (and resp. `FlowEvaluator`), which computes, at each `On-TimeChanged`(), all the CO_2 released by the production and the transport processes (resp. that computes the quantity of aggregates conveyed by trucks).

During a simulation, the `OnTimeChanged`() of all transversal components is always run before that of spatial components.

3.3 A Global View of the ISatEM Architecture

At a generic level, ISatEM is composed of three packages: a *kernel*, a *user interface* and a *document*, as detailed below and illustrated in Fig. 4.

The kernel. The ISatEM kernel is based on three modules: a *library module*, a *model module* and a *simulation module*. One module corresponds to one stage of an application design, and is inspired by the architecture proposed by [17].

The *library module* is like a factory that creates all the types of components required by the application. It only is an environment development where the code of the components is written and compiled. We will not go further into this module here.

Model module instantiates the component types designed in the previous module. There are three ways to instantiate a component: either manually, or by computation during a simulation, or by a (shape file) importation process, via an *importation/exportation engine* (let I/E engine) included in this module. Created components may be in interaction with each other or not, depending on the application.

Simulation module simulates the content of the *component environment*. There are three modes of simulation: the *none mode*, during which nothing is saved during the simulation, the *execution mode* during which, at each time step of the simulation, the value of each temporal property of each component is saved "online" by a *property logger*, and the *replay mode*, which reviews the simulation at the "offline" phase, only by retrieving the corresponding property values of the current simulation time, previously saved. In that mode, it is possible to go back and forth during the simulation, without performing any computation from the beginning again.

The user interface (UI). This contains the interface of the functions described above. Furthermore, it contains (a) a *map displayer*, which shows all shape maps imported by the I/E engine via a *layer manager*, and (b) a *comment editor*, at the user's disposal. Simulation and model modules have the same UI as is presented in Fig. 3.

The ISatEM document. An ISatEM document contains all the data corresponding to an application. When the ISatEM software starts, no application is actually loaded until the ISatEM document containing that application is opened by the user, (exactly like a user opens an MS-Word® document in MS-Word® software). An ISatEM document is a container, in the form of a ZIP file, generated by ISatEM, and containing the following files:

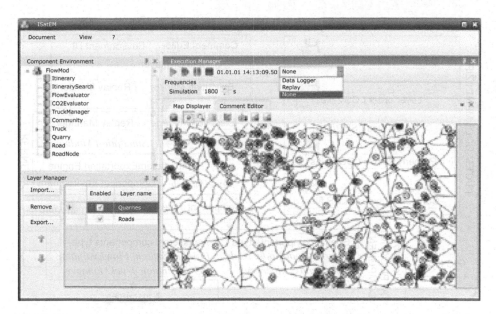

Fig. 3. The user interface of both model and simulation modules. Are displayed: at top left, all `FlowMod` components; at bottom, two shape layers (quarries and roads); at top right, the simulation time as well as the simulation time step and the three simulation modes.

- The files generated/used by the *property logger* during the execution mode. There is one file per component, as formalized later in Equation 2. The files are in CSV (Common-Separated Values) format.
- A list of the current imported shape files.
- The files currently managed by the comment editor. They are in HTML format.
- A file storing the current order in which layers of imported shapefile are successively displayed, from top to bottom, as in a GIS tool. For example, in Fig. 3, the `quarry` layer is above the `road` layer (cf. the layer manager view).
- All classes designed by the library module. They are stored in a simple object (binary) file, to which we allot the extension .LBR (referring to the *library* term).

Organisation of the property logger files. The organisation of the information in the CSV file managed by the property logger is inspired from that of `asgma.ads` with, in addition, the introduction of temporal values. However, one CSV file corresponds not to the whole simulation, as in `Asgma`, but to one component only.

Equation 2 explains the process, where expressions in "[ ]" are optional. As an example: for a quarry (a circle shape) designated q2, having an initial stock of 1000 tonnes, and being capable of producing 0.5 tonnes of aggregates per simulation time unit, we will have the information below inside the file named `quarry.q2.csv` after one simulation time step, and under the execution mode.

```
0, stock, 1000
0, circle, 700, 240, 4
1, stock, 1000.5
1, circle, 700, 240, 4 // the same because the quarry does not move
```

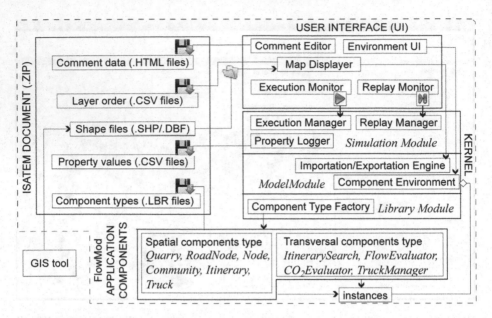

Fig. 4. Illustration of the general architecture of ISatEM (the area inside the dashed line)

// Recall of Equation 1, applied to `asgma.ads`
  classId: (prop$_1$ val$_{11}$ [val$_{12}$]) [(prop$_2$ val$_{21}$ [val$_{22}$])]

// Transformation for the CSV file
  classId
    $\rightarrow$ a CSV file named classId.componentId.
(prop$_1$, val$_{11}$, [val$_{12}$])   (2)
    $\rightarrow$ currentTime, prop$_1$, val$_{11}$, [val$_{12}$]
    $\rightarrow$ and written on a whole line
// Regarding the `Geometry` *property, we have*
  currentTime, "circle", xCentre, yCentre, radius // for circles
  currentTime, "polygon", x$_0$, y$_0$, x$_1$, y$_1$, x$_2$, y$_2$ [, …, x$_n$, y$_n$] // for polygons
  currentTime, "line", x$_a$, y$_a$, x$_b$, y$_b$ [, …, x$_m$, y$_m$] // for lines

3.4 Generation of New Dynamic Shape Data

The only mechanism that drives the dynamic (i.e. the evolution of the system state) of ISatEM is the simulation of the content of the component environment. The full process is presented in Fig. 5 and explained in the next paragraph.

If the user wants to evolve the state of entities contained in a shp/dbf file, he/she has to (a) import the map into ISatEM via the I/E engine and (b) select the area of interest (let aoi) from the maps, via the *map displayer*. This selection transfers the content of each entity in the shp/dbf files to a created instance of the corresponding spatial component as follows: the shp content is transferred to the Geometry property

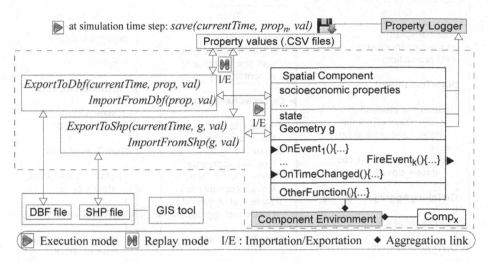

Fig. 5. The mechanism of the importation/exportation engine (the area inside the dashed line)

of that component and the dbf content to the socioeconomic properties. For example, the content of a quarry entity from the shp/dbf layer is transferred to an instance of quarry component, a sample of which has been described in Fig. 2.a. Next, during simulation, values of these spatial components will evolve via their interaction to other spatial components and via the action of transversal components. At any time, the temporal property values of these spatial components can be exported to a new shape file.

As a result, a user can export two types of (new) shape data layers, classified in the way the corresponding upstream components have been created:

- *Existing evolved layers*, viewed as the temporal evolution of the initial imported shape, at the time t where it is exported.
- *New layers*, resulting from the exportation of instances of spatial component types that are not initialised by a previous importation process but by computation during the simulation. It is, in FlowMod, the case for the Itinerary (cf. Fig. 6, simplified for space reasons) and Truck layers.

Fig. 7 illustrates the general shape data generation mechanism, from the importation of layers to the generation and exportation of the new successive Itinerary layers over time. The left part of Fig. 7 is an abstract view of Fig. 6.

Note that the state property is not manipulated by the I/E engine. State is pre-initialised in the component type declaration (e.g. in the quarry component, the initial value of state is in_production, as illustrated in Fig. 2.b), is saved by the property logger during simulation, and is not concerned by the exportation process.

3.5 Results

Let us take a scenario where, each time an aggregate supplying the community of Rouen (Seine-Maritime) has produced over 100 days it is closed and is not renewed.

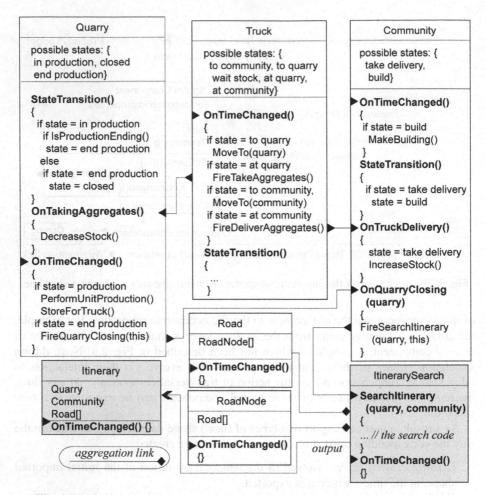

Fig. 6. Block diagram of how an Itinerary component is generated during simulation

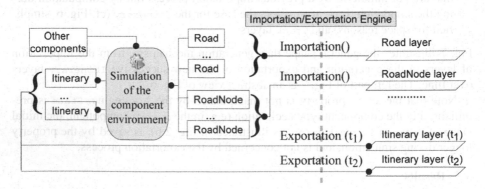

Fig. 7. Mechanism for generation of the Itinerary shape layers over time, starting from the importation/exportation engine, to the simulation of the content of component environment

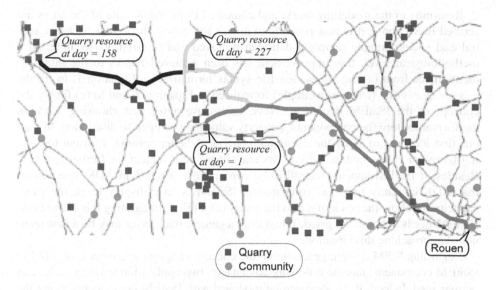

Fig. 8. Result of the exportation of three itinerary layers to three successive resources, obtained during one simulation. The start of the itinerary is the Rouen community.

As explained before, this situation systematically involves the search for a new quarry and itinerary after 100 days. At each newly found itinerary, the `Itinerary` layer is exported and integrated in a GIS tool where, for better visibility, only the itinerary starting from Rouen is kept. In ISatEM, time for exportation is not important as long as exportation is made inside the itinerary lifetime. The simulation time step is 30 minutes. Fig. 8 shows the final result visible in the GIS tool, after three exportations.

4 General Discussion

The result illustrated in Fig. 8 is still being adjusted and validated by the domain experts, regarding the itinerary search rules (the quarries found are not always exactly those expected by them) and the simulation lifetime: at present, we are able to stabilise tests of up to around 15,000 time steps (i.e. 300 days of 30 minutes) with the replay mode. However, this current validation does not affect the capacity of the system to generate new shape data by simulation, whatever the simulation mode.

In a more general manner, Isatem can be viewed as a complement to a GIS tool. It generates new dynamic spatial information by simulation, can display such information by itself (e.g. truck moving) and can store and reproduce the action (via the replay mode). However, Isatem cannot analyze spatial data to the same extent as a GIS. Inversely, a GIS can represent spatial information but in a static way only. One solution is to make them operate in close collaboration since, in the end, they are both data providers and analyzers at their respective levels. As one result, the quality of a map to be produced as a decision aid support, for example, can be the result of its iterative design between both tools.

Returning to the modelling work, and compared to the ADK state of the art as described in Section 2, it is now possible to import and export shape files. Besides, spatial and socioeconomic temporal data can be saved and restored at any time. At a methodological level, this improvement has been achieved thanks to the improvements made from (a) the `asgma.ads` file syntax formalized in Equation 1, to (b) the `quarry.q2.csv` file (taken as example) formalized in Equation 2, and to (c) finally the concept of the ISatEM document. Nevertheless, we agree that choosing .CSV as the format to store the components' property value may be open to discussion. In fact, our first idea was to apply the document concept. A better optimized format for saving temporal values undoubtedly exists and should be a subject for further research. Besides, if ISatEM appears overall to be conceptually better than ADK, one feature that ADK currently only has compared to ISatEM is, at a display level, the ADK capacity to follow the track of a moving entity (cf. Fig. 1). Integrating this feature into ISatEM needs to be investigated. Integrating a generic track layer may be a first manner of approaching this situation.

Regarding SISM design, generalizing the concept of agents and objects of ADK to ISatEM components has the following advantage[5]: two application territory scales can be managed. Indeed, if `FlowMod` can be modelled with ISatEM components, using the ISatEM component to model ADK architecture (recall the presentation in Section 2), then the `Asgma` application is still feasible. The result is shown in Fig. 9 where a `PerceptsPropagator` is transversal and an `ADKAgent` is spatial.

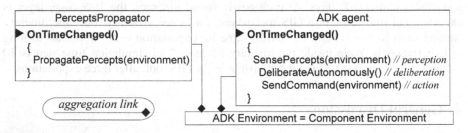

Fig. 9. Design of the ADK architecture using the ISatEM component. The 'perception-deliberation-action' triad as well as the propagator concepts of ADK are still present.

The notion of components may lead the reader to think about the DEVS (Discrete EVent System specification) components [8], widely used in modelling and simulation contexts, integrating space [e.g. 19]. The reason we do not use DEVS is a visualization issue: we want to see the *continuous* movement of our trucks in the system, as has been done with the conveyor in `Asgma` (cf. Fig. 1). We think that DEVS is not the appropriate approach for that purpose, unless the duration of the internal state transition of the DEVS component is statically set to that of the simulation time. But in such case, the actual interest of using DEVS formalism is diminished.

---

[5] Another interest of this change is that it offers the possibility of supporting other SISM applications based on approaches other than a multi-agent approach, such as for example the system dynamics approach as used by [13].

5 Conclusions and Perspectives

Summary. Spatial-integrated socioeconomic models (SISM) are models that can represent the relationship between economic activity, social life and the pressure social actors apply to the geographical space containing them. Although a multi-agent approach is often used to support applications modelled at a detailed territory scale, it may be less appropriate when an application is modelled at a larger scale. Moreover, since SISM is a spatial model, conceptual integration of dynamic spatial data and, in our case, spatial shape data should be reinforced.

By focusing on the domain of mineral resources exploitation, we have proposed, in this paper (a) to improve a multi-agent model to obtain a more generic object model that is capable of also supporting applications modelled at a larger scale, and (b) to integrate the mechanism of dynamic spatial shape data, in which the temporal evolution of the spatial state of an ongoing simulation can be exported at any time, as (new) shape data stored in a map exploitable in a GIS tool. Our approach was to start from an existing multi-agent platform known as ADK, ending up with a new platform known as ISatEM.

Perspectives. Although ISatEM seems to be a better result for us, regarding dynamic spatial modelling, ADK still has the capacity to follow the track of a moving component, a feature that ISatEM does not yet integrate. The integration of such a feature constitutes the first perspective for ISatEM. The other perspective is the integration of what we call *indicator display*. An indicator is one component property, the evolution of which a user wants to visualize via one feature of the shape representing this component in a screen. A shape feature may be a *width* (for a line), a *surface size* (for a polygon and circle), or a *colour* (for all of them). Features may be combined if possible. During a simulation, when an indicator evolves, the corresponding shape feature also evolves. It results in a display of dynamic spatial shape data information, even on non-moving shapes. For example, the colour of a quarry shape may evolve according to its current stock (the indicator). Regarding the mineral resources field, one technique of selecting indicators is presented in [6].

References

1. Andriamasinoro, F., Angel, J.M.: High-Level vs. Low-Level Abstraction Approach for the Model and Simulation Design of Ultra-pure Quartz Exploitation in Northeastern Madagascar. In: Joint Conference on Multi-Agent Modelling for Environmental Management (CABM-HEMA-SMAGET), Bourg St-Maurice, France, March 25-28 (2005)
2. Andriamasinoro, F., Angel, J.M.: Modeling the Ultra-pure Quartz Exploitation in Northeastern Madagascar: Impact of the Activity on the Socio-Economical Situation of the Population. Journal of Socio-Economics 36(2), 311–329 (2007)
3. Andriamasinoro, F., Jaques, E., Pelon, R., Martel-Jantin, B.: Artisanal and Small-scale Gold Mining in Alga (Burkina Faso): Building a Decision-Aid Model for Development and Governance. In: The Summer Computer Simulation Conference (SCSC 2005), Philadelphia, Pennsylvania, USA, July 24-28, pp. 292–297. CD-Rom (2005), ISBN 1-56555-299-7
4. Andriamasinoro, F., Orru, J.F.: Collecte de données socioéconomiques sur les exploitations de granulats dans la boucle d'Anneville-Ambourville (Seine-Maritime). Technical report, BRGM/RP-57465-FR, 105 pages (2009)

5. Calderoni, S.: Ethologie Artificielle et Contrôle Auto-Adaptatif dans les Systèmes d'Agents Réactifs: de la Modélisation à la Simulation. PhD Thesis, University of La Réunion, 175 pages (2002)
6. Chamaret, A., Récoché, G., O'Connor, M.: Proposal for a top-down/bottom-up approach to build up indicators of sustainable development for use in the mining industry in Africa. In: The SDIMI conference 2005, Aachen, May 18-20 (2005)
7. Courdier, R., Guerrin, F., Andriamasinoro, F., Paillat, J.M.: Agent-based simulation of complex systems: application to collective management of animal wastes. Journal of Artificial Societies and Social Simulation 5(3) (June 30, 2002)
8. Dalle, O., Zeigler, B.P., Wainer, G.A.: Extending DEVS to support multiple occurrences in component-based simulation. In: 40th Conference on Winter Simulation, Miami, Florida vol. 933-941 (2008), ISBN:978-1-4244-2708-6
9. Deschamps, Y., Milesi, J.P., Hocquard, C., Bouchot, V., Salpeteur, I., Pelon, R., Ralay, F.: Germanium potential in Africa: a predictive approach methodology. In: 21st CAG21 - Colloquium of African Geology, Maputo - Mozambique, July 03-05 (2006)
10. Haberl, H., Gaube, V., Díaz-Delgado, R., Krauze, K., Neuner, A., Peterseil, J., Plutzar, C., Singh, S.J., Vadineanu, A.: Towards an integrated model of socioeconomic biodiversity drivers, pressures and impacts. A feasibility study based on three European long-term socio-ecological research platforms. Ecological Economics 68(6), 1797–1812 (2009)
11. Hugues, L., Drogoul, A.: Synthesis of Robot's Behaviors from few Examples. In: IEEE/RSJ International Conference on Intelligent Robots and Systems, IROS 2002 (2002)
12. Jaques, E., Zida, B., Billa, M., Greffié, C., Thomassin, J.F.: Artisanal and small-scale gold mines in Burkina Faso: today and tomorrow. In: Hilson, G.M. (ed.) Small-Scale Mining, Rural Subsidence and Poverty in West Africa, ch. 10, pp. 114–134 (2006)
13. Lanini, S., Courtois, N., Giraud, F., Petit, V., Rinaudo, J.D.: Socio-hydrosystem modelling for integrated water-resources management – The Herault catchment case study, southern France. Environmental Modelling and Software 19(11), 1011–1019 (2004)
14. Le Page, C., Bousquet, F., Bakam, I., Bah, A., Baron, C.: CORMAS: A multiagent simulation toolkit to model natural and social dynamics at multiple scales. The ecology of scales, Wageningen, the Netherlands, June 27-30 (2000)
15. Leistel, J.M.: SIG Ressources Minérales Françaises - Architecture et mode d'emploi des applications de saisie. Technical report, BRGM/RP-54545-FR, p. 67 (2005)
16. Madlenera, R., Domacb, J.: Introduction to the special section Modeling socio-economic aspects of bioenergy use: methodologies, case studies, and policy evaluation and guidance. Energy Policy 35(12), e1–e4 (2007)
17. Serment, J., Espinasse, B., Tranvouez, E.: For a generic software architecture facilitating environmental decision support system development: Illustration with the Camargue Ecosystem. In: The Joint Conference on Multi-Agent Modelling for Environmental Management (CABM-HEMA-SMAGET), Bourg St-Maurice, France, March 25-28 (2005)
18. The Route 500® numerical product, http://www.cartosphere.com/en/ign_route500.htm
19. Versmisse, D., Macher, C., Ramat, E., Soulié, J.C., Thebaud, O.: Developing a bioeconomic simulation tool of fisheries dynamics: a case study. In: Proceedings of the International Congress on Modelling and Simulation, International Society for Computer Simulation, Christchurch, New Zealand, December 10-13 (2007)
20. Wooldridge, M.: An Introduction To Multiagent Systems, p. 340. John Wiley & Sons, Chichester (2002)

Scale-Dependency and Sensitivity of Hydrological Estimations to Land Use and Topography for a Coastal Watershed in Mississippi

Vladimir J. Alarcon and Charles G. O'Hara

GeoSystems Research Institute, 2 Research Blvd., Starkville MS 39759, USA
{alarcon,cgohara}@gri.msstate.edu

Abstract. This paper investigates the effect of land use and digital elevation models spatial resolution and scale on the simulation of stream flow in two coastal watersheds located in the Mississippi Gulf Coast (USA). Four elevation datasets were used: USGS DEM, NED, NASA's SRTM and IFSAR (300, 30, 30, and 5 meter resolution, respectively). Three land use datasets were included in this study: USGS GIRAS, NLCD, and NASA MODIS MOD12Q1 (400, 30, and 1000 m resolution, correspondingly). The Hydrological Program Fortran (HSPF) was used for estimating stream flow in the two watersheds. Results showed that swapping datasets in a factorial design experiment produce equivalent statistical fit of measured and simulated stream flow data. The results also showed that HSPF-estimated stream flows are not sensitive to scale and spatial resolution of the datasets included in the study.

Keywords: Watershed hydrology, hydrological simulation, HSPF, MODIS, DEM, land use.

1 Introduction

Hydrologic modeling at the watershed scale involves managing large volumes of meteorological, topographical, land use, and water quality data. The management of these large data volumes usually requires linking Geographical Information Systems (GIS) and hydrological models. GIS programs are used for extracting and summarizing weather and physiographic information from digital datasets, and to set-up initial hydrological model's applications that are further refined in later steps of the hydrological modeling process. With the advent of Internet, the ever-growing availability of computational resources, and the demand of users, private or public-domain databases can be accessed directly (from within the GIS programs) and different datasets can be easily downloaded for geo-processing. In particular, topographical and land-use/land-cover datasets are downloaded for the purposes of watershed delineation, land use characterization, geographical positioning of hydro-chemical point sources, etc.

The spatial variability of the physical characteristics of the terrain influences the flow regime in watersheds. It has been investigated from the theoretical and the numerical point of view [1]. Several other researches have explored the sensitivity of

D. Taniar et al. (Eds.): ICCSA 2010, Part I, LNCS 6016, pp. 491–500, 2010.

hydrological estimations to topographical or land use datasets. Few, however, have assessed the sensitivity of hydrological estimations to combined swapping of topographical and land use datasets. This paper explores the effects of using several different combinations of topographical and land use datasets in hydrological estimations of stream flow. The Hydrological Simulation Program Fortran (HSPF, [2]) is used for modeling the hydrological processes. The Better Assessment Science Integrating Point & Nonpoint Sources (BASINS) GIS system [3] is used to perform most of the geospatial operations although GEOLEM [4], ArcGis and ArcInfo were also used to complement geospatial processing that was not available in BASINS. This research is part of several studies being undertaken in the Northern Gulf of Mexico region [5][6].

2   Methods

2.1   Study Area

Two main river catchments in Saint Louis Bay watershed at the Mississippi Gulf Coast were the focus of this study (Figure 1).

The Jourdan River catchment drains approximately 88220 ha and it is the largest contributor of flow to the St. Louis Bay, with an average stream flow of 24.5 m³/s. The

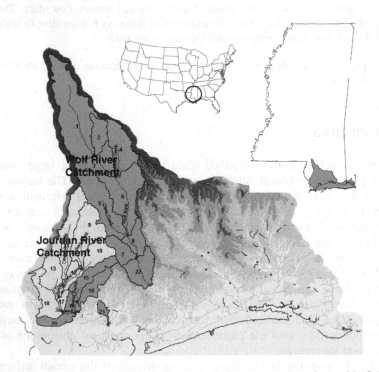

Fig. 1. Wolf River and Jourdan River catchments. Both catchments are located in Saint Louis Bay watershed, Mississippi Gulf Coast, USA.

Wolf River flows into St. Louis Bay from the east (Figure 1). The Wolf River catchment drains slightly more than 98350 ha with an average stream flow of 20.1 m^3/s.

2.1 Topographical Datasets

The topographical digital datasets (also known as Digital Elevation Models, DEM) used in this research were: USGS DEM, NED, and NASA's SRTM and IFSAR. USGS produces five types of elevation data: 7.5-minute, 7.5-minute-Alaska, 15-minute-Alaska, 30-minute, and 1-degree DEMs. In this research, 1-Degree DEMs corresponding to the 3 arc-second (or 1:250,000-scale) USGS topographic map series were used. The National Elevation Data (NED) database provides a seamless mosaic elevation data having as primary initial data source the 7.5-minute elevation data for the conterminous United States [7]. NED has a consistent projection (geographic), resolution (1 arc second, approximately 30 m), and metric elevation units [8]. The NASA Shuttle Radar Topography Mission (SRTM), in collaboration between the National Aeronautics and Space Administration (NASA) and the National Imagery and Mapping Agency (NIMA), collected interferometric radar data, which has been used by the Jet Propulsion Laboratory (JPL) to generate a near-global topography data product for latitudes smaller than 60 degrees. Intermap's Interferometric Synthetic Aperture Radar (IfSAR) Digital Elevation Models [9] are topographical data for 7.5-minute by 7.5-minute units (corresponding to the USGS 1:24,000 scale topographic quadrangle map series) comprising elevations at 5 meter postings. DEMs are intensively used in water resources modeling. Watershed delineation and digital stream (rivers) definition depend heavily on those DEMs. Figure 2 shows all topographical datasets after being geo-processed for the study area. The theoretical link between the digital elevation model and the parameters of the Hydrological Simulation Program Fortran (HSPF) is well described in [10].

2.2 Land Use Datasets

Three land use datasets were included in this study (Figure 2): USGS GIRAS, USGS NLCD, and NASA MODIS MOD12Q1. All the datasets were downloaded from public land use databases in the US that provide several different types of land-use/land- cover digital maps.

The USGS GIRAS is a set of maps of land use and land cover for the conterminous U.S. delineated with a minimum mapping unit of 4 hectares and a maximum of 16 hectares (equivalent to 400 m spatial resolution), generated using the Geographic Information Retrieval and Analysis System (GIRAS) software. Today, they are widely known as the USGS GIRAS land use datasets.

Derived from the early to mid-1990s Landsat Thematic Mapper satellite data, the National Land Cover Data (NLCD) is a 21-class land cover classification scheme applied consistently over the United States. The spatial resolution of the data is 30 meters and mapped in the Albers Conic Equal Area projection, NAD 83.

The NASA MODIS MOD12Q1 Land Cover Product (MODIS/Terra Land Cover, 1000 m spatial resolution) [11] is provided by NASA through several internet portals. The land use map is classified in 21 land use categories, following the International Geosphere-Biosphere Program land cover classification. The map covers most of the

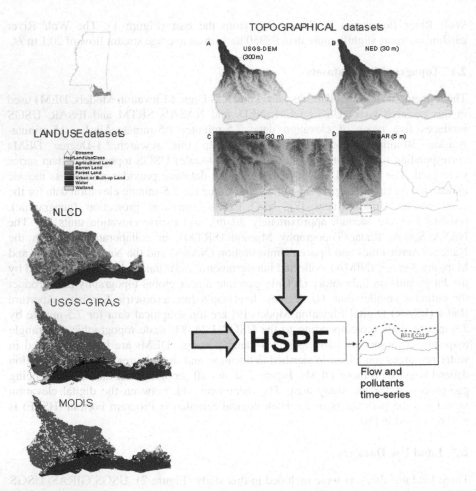

Fig. 2. Datasets used in the study. Topographical: USGS DEM, NED, NASA's SRTM and IFSAR (300, 30, 30, and 5 meter resolution, respectively). Land use: USGS GIRAS, NLCD, and NASA MODIS MOD12Q1 (400, 30, and 1000 m resolution, correspondingly).

globe and is updated every year. All the land use datasets included in this research were geo-processed for achieving the same number of land use categories (agricultural, barren, forest, urban, water, and wetland land use classes), so that the summarization of land use information was consistent for input into HSPF, and subsequent comparison of HSPF output.

2.3 Hydrological Model

Hydrological modeling of the Jourdan and Wolf watersheds is performed using the Hydrological Simulation Program Fortran (HSPF). HSPF is a computer model designed for simulation of non-point source watershed hydrology and water quality. Time-series of meteorological/water-quality data, land use and topographical data are used to estimate stream flow hydrographs and polluto-graphs. The model simulates interception, soil moisture, surface runoff, interflow, base flow, snowpack depth and water content, snowmelt, evapo-transpiration, and ground-water recharge. Simulation results are provided as time-series of runoff, sediment load, and nutrient and pesticide concentrations, along with time-series of water quantity and quality, at any point in a watershed. Additional software (WDMUtil and GenScn) is used for data pre-processing and post-processing, and for statistical and graphical analysis of input and output data.

2.4 Geo-processing and Hydrological Modeling

Figure 3 summarizes the geo-processing steps and hydrological modeling approach.

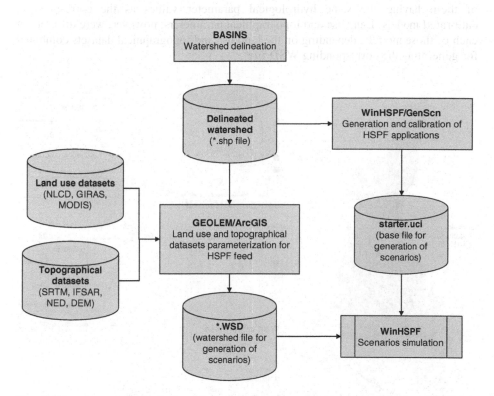

Fig. 3. Flowchart of the geo-processing steps for generating the hydrological model's data input. BASINS, GEOLEM, ArcGIS, and Arc Info were used. These GIS systems extracted land use and topographical information for input into HSPF.

BASINS was used for downloading basic data and delineating the catchments included in this study. The creation of the initial HSPF models was done using the WinHSPF interface included in BASINS. The generated HSPF models (one for Jourdan River catchment and another for Wolf's, Figure 4) were calibrated for stream flow using the NED and NLCD datasets combination, and the USGS stream flow gauge stations at Catahoula (02481570), Lyman (02481500), and Landon (02481510) (shown in Figure 4). The User Control Input (UCI) files resulting from the calibration (one per each catchment) were used to modify the HSPF's starter.uci file (this file is used by the HSPF program to generate a HSPF model). In this research, two starter.uci files were created (for each of the watersheds under study). These files allowed preserving the hydrological parameters (resulting from the hydrological calibration process) constant.

The delineated catchments were used as geographical containers for further geoprocessing. GEOLEM and ArcGIS were used to parameterize land use and topographical information from the datasets described in sections 2.1 and 2.2. The parameterization was summarized in several *.wsd watershed files (12 per catchment) for different combinations of land use and topographical data. These watershed files and the starter.uci files were used for generating 12 HSPF models per catchment, each of them having the same hydrological parameter values as the corresponding calibrated models. Land use and topographical parameters, however, were different in each of those models, depending on the land use and topographical datasets combined for generating the corresponding WSD file.

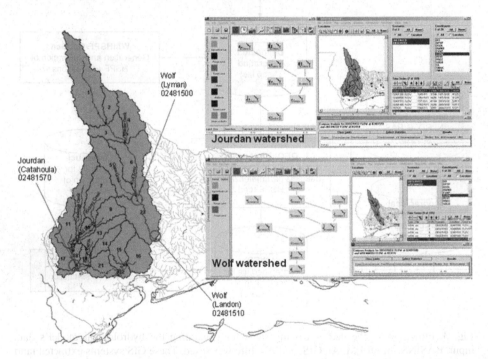

Fig. 4. HSPF models for Jourdan and Wolf watersheds. USGS stream flow gauge stations at Catahoula, Lyman, and Landon were used for hydrological calibration of the models.

3   Results

After calibrating and validating the HSPF applications to Jourdan and Wolf watersheds using the finest resolution datasets (NED and NLCD combined), HSPF was used to simulate stream flow hydrographs for each of the 12 combinations shown in Tables 1 and 2. Those simulated stream flow hydrographs were compared to measured stream flow and the following best-fit coefficients were assessed: coefficient of determination (r^2); Nash-Sutcliff model fit efficiency (NS). The Nash-Sutcliffe coefficient (NS) [12] represents the fraction of the variance in the measured data explained by the model. The NS ranges between minus infinity to one. A NS value of one represents perfect fit. Nash-Sutcliffe coefficient has been used by many researches and is considered one of the best statistical for evaluation of continuous-hydrograph simulation programs [13][14]. The NS is given by the following equation:

$$NS = 1 - \frac{\sum\limits_{j=1}^{n}(O_j - S_j)^2}{\sum\limits_{j=1}^{n}(O_j - \overline{O}_j)^2}.\qquad (1)$$

In Formula (1), O_j is the observed stream flow at time step j; $\overline{O}$ is the average observed stream flow during the evaluation period; and S_j is the simulated stream flow at time step j.

The results summarized in Tables 1 and 2, and depicted in Figure 5, show that scale and spatial resolution of topographical and land use datasets do not affect the quality of statistical fit between simulated and measured stream flow data. In fact, the NS and r^2 values for Jourdan River (0.72 and 0.76, respectively) in the base-case scenario (i.e., using NED topography and NLCD land use) are the lowest statistical fit coefficient values. However, the narrow range of NS and r2 values for all the experiments performed for the Jourdan River watershed ($0.72 \leq NS \leq 0.75$; $0.76 \leq r^2 \leq 0.80$) would not allow pointing the best combination of land use and topographical datasets.

Table 1. Results of statistical fit between simulated and measured stream flow for Jourdan River watershed

Model fit efficiency (Nash-Sutcliff, NS)			
	MODIS (1000 m)	GIRAS (400 m)	NLCD (30 m)
USGS DEM (300m)	0.75	0.74	0.75
NED (30m)	0.73	0.72	0.72
SRTM (30m)	0.73	0.72	0.72
IFSAR (5m)	0.74	0.73	0.73
Coefficient of determination R^2			
	MODIS (1000 m)	GIRAS (400 m)	NLCD (30 m)
USGS DEM (300m)	0.8	0.8	0.79
NED (30m)	0.77	0.78	0.76
SRTM (30m)	0.77	0.77	0.76
IFSAR (5m)	0.78	0.78	0.77

Table 2. Results of statistical fit between simulated and measured stream flow for Wolf River

Model fit efficiency (Nash-Sutcliff, NS)			
	MODIS (1000 m)	GIRAS (400 m)	NLCD (30 m)
USGS DEM (300m)	0.82	0.76	0.81
NED (30m)	0.81	0.81	0.8
SRTM (30m)	0.81	0.81	0.8
IFSAR (5m)	0.82	0.82	0.81

Coefficient of determination R^2			
	MODIS (1000 m)	GIRAS (400 m)	NLCD (30 m)
USGS DEM (300m)	0.83	0.83	0.82
NED (30m)	0.82	0.82	0.82
SRTM (30m)	0.82	0.82	0.82
IFSAR (5m)	0.83	0.83	0.82

Jourdan River watershed

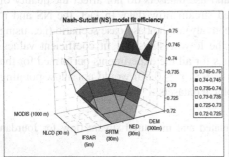 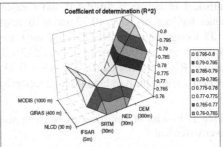

Wolf River watershed

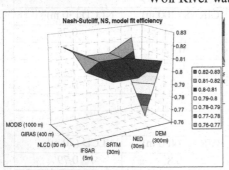 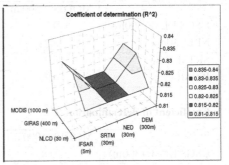

Fig. 5. Graphical comparison of statistical fit results for Jourdan and Wolf watersheds. Nash-Sutcliff (NS) and r^2 coefficients are show in the vertical axis.

In the case of measured and simulated stream flow time-series comparison for Wolf River watershed, the range of values for NS and r^2 is equivalent to that of Jourdan River watershed: $0.76 \leq NS \leq 0.82$; $0.82 \leq r^2 \leq 0.83$.

In particular, the combination of moderate resolution topographical datasets (such as SRTM, 30 m) and coarse resolution land use datasets (such as MODIS, 1000 m) produce good statistical fit between simulated and measured stream flow hydrographs. Model fit coefficients (r^2 and NS) for the MODIS-SRTM combination range between 0.73 and 0.81. Interestingly, the coarsest resolution datasets (MODIS and DEM) do not provide the worst statistical fit between measured and simulated stream flow.

4 Conclusions

The results from this research show that scale and spatial resolution of digital land use and topography datasets do not affect the statistical fit of measured and simulated stream flow time-series, when using the Hydrological Program Fortran (HSPF) as the hydrological model recipient of land use and topographical data. In fact, this research shows that when the input to HSPF comes from the coarsest spatial resolution datasets (MODIS land use and USGS DEM topography), HSPF simulated stream flow show equivalent statistical fit to measured stream flow as when finer spatial resolution datasets are combined. This suggest that stream flow simulation is not sensitive to scale or spatial resolution of land use and/or topographical datasets.

Since HSPF is a lumped-parameter hydrological model, the summarization of physiographic information (before it is input to the model) is a required step. This pre-processing of raw land use and topographical data (re-classification, averaging of data per sub-basin, etc.) may be a factor that explains the insensitivity of simulated stream flow to land use and topographical datasets swapping, when using HSPF. Future studies should explore the effects that this swapping may have when using distributed hydrological models.

All the hydrological models generated in this research were developed using mainly precipitation and evapo-transpiration time-series data, primarily because HSPF only requires those time-series for simulation of stream flow. For future water quality modeling of the Jourdan and Wolf watersheds, other weather time-series data (such as temperature, etc.) will be included.

A thorough study on the relationship of soil moisture and overestimation/ underestimation of stream flow will also be included in future researches.

Acknowledgements. This study has been part of the NASA Rapid Prototyping Capability (RPC) for Earth-Sun System Sciences project, at Mississippi State University. The authors are grateful to the editors and three anonymous reviewers for their constructive comments and valuable ideas on earlier versions of the manuscript.

References

1. Manfreda, S., Rodriguez-Iturbe, I.: On the Spatial and Temporal Sampling of Soil Moisture Fields. Water Resources Research 42(5), W05409.1–W05409.10 (2006)
2. Bicknell, B.R., Imhoff, J.C., Kittle, J.L., Jobes, T.H., Donigian, A.S.: HSPF Version 12 User's Manual. National Exposure Research Laboratory. Office of Research and Development U.S. Environmental Protection Agency (2001)

3. Environmental Protection Agency: BASINS: Better Assessment Science Integrating Point & Nonpoint Sources: A Powerful Tool for Managing Watersheds, http://www.epa.gov/waterscience/BASINS/
4. Viger, R.J.: GEOLEM: Improving the Integration of Geographic Information in Environmental Modeling Through Semantic Interoperability. Master's Thesis, University of Toronto, Canada (2004)
5. Alarcon, V.J., McAnally, W., Diaz-Ramirez, J., Martin, J., Cartwright, J.: A Hydrological Model of the Mobile River Watershed, Southeastern USA. In: Maroulis, G., Simos, T.E. (eds.) Computational Methods in Science and Engineering: Advances in Computational Science, vol. 1148, pp. 641–645. American Institute of Physics (2009)
6. Alarcon, V.J., McAnally, W., Wasson, L., Martin, J., Cartwright, J.: Using NEXRAD Precipitation Data for Enriching Hydrological and Hydrodynamic Models in the Northern Gulf of Mexico. In: Maroulis, G., Simos, T.E. (eds.) Computational Methods in Science and Engineering: Advances in Computational Science, vol. 1148, pp. 646–650. American Institute of Physics (2009)
7. Environmental Protection Agency: USGS 30 Meter Resolution, One-Sixtieth Degree National Elevation Dataset for CONUS, Alaska, Hawaii, Puerto Rico, and the U. S. Virgin Islands, http://www.epa.gov/waterscience/basins/metadata/ned.htm
8. USGS: Earth Resources Observation and Science, http://edc.usgs.gov/products/elevation.html
9. Intermap Technologies Inc.: IFSAR product handbook, http://www.intermap.com/images/handbook/producthandbook.pdf
10. Alarcon, V.J., O'Hara, C.G., McAnally, W., Martin, J., Diaz, J., Duan, Z.: Influence of elevation dataset on watershed delineation of three catchments in Mississippi, http://www.gri.msstate.edu/research/nasa_rpc/papers/AWRA_elevation_2006.pdf
11. NASA: MODIS MOD12 Land Cover and Land Cover Dynamics Products User Guide, http://www-modis.bu.edu/landcover/userguidelc/lc.html
12. Nash, J.E., Sutcliffe, J.V.: River flow forecasting through conceptual models, part I: a discussion of principles. Journal of Hydrology 10, 282–290 (1970)
13. Engelmann, C.J.K., Ward, A.D., Christy, A.D., Bair, E.S.: Application of the BASINS database and NPSM model on a small Ohio watershed. Journal of the American Water Resources Association 38(1), 289–300 (2002)
14. Legates, D.R., McCabe, G.J.: Evaluating the use of "goodness-of-fit" measures in hydrologic and hydroclimatic model validation. Water Resources Research 35(1), 233–241 (1999)

Using MODIS Land-Use/Land-Cover Data and Hydrological Modeling for Estimating Nutrient Concentrations

Vladimir J. Alarcon, William McAnally, Gary Ervin, and Christopher Brooks

GeoSystems Research Institute, Northern Gulf Institute, Mississippi State University,
2 Research Blvd., Starkville MS 39759, USA
{alarcon,mcanally,ervin,brooks}@gri.msstate.edu

Abstract. This paper presents results on nutrient concentrations estimations in the Upper Tombigbee watershed (northern Mississippi-Alabama region, USA). It details the hydrological model development and its use for providing stream flow, runoff, and nutrient concentrations (total phosphorus, TP, and total nitrogen, TN) for subsequent biological studies. Geographical locations of data collection on fish and mussel were used to perform a watershed delineation of the area of study. The delineated catchment was enriched with land use information from USGS GIRAS (1986) and NASA MODIS MOD12Q1 (2001-2004) datasets. An increase of 34% in agricultural lands is shown to have occurred from 1986 to 2003. The Hydrological Program Fortran (HSPF) was used for estimating stream flow and run-off rates for two hydrological models (one per each land use dataset). Export coefficients representative for the regions were used for estimating TN and TP concentrations. It is shown that only maximum concentrations of total nitrogen and total phosphorus have increased from 1986 to 2003. The percent increase ranges from 5 to 16% when comparing a sub-set of sub-basins, and 34% to 37% when taking into account all sub-basins. This seems to be consistent with the increase in agricultural areas in the same time period.

Keywords: Watershed hydrology, hydrological simulation, water quality, HSPF, MODIS, land use.

1 Introduction

The United States has a land area of about 0.9 billion hectares, from which about 20 percent is cropland, 26 percent permanent grassland pasture and range land, and 28 percent forest-use land. Land used for agricultural purposes in 1997 totaled nearly 1.2 billion acres, over (52 percent of total U.S. land area) [1]. Cropland, grassland pasture, and range accounted for most of the land used for agricultural purposes, but land used for agricultural purposes also included forest land used for grazing and land in farmsteads, farm roads, and farm lanes [1]. Land use in the Southeastern United States is predominantly covered by forests and agricultural lands [1].

D. Taniar et al. (Eds.): ICCSA 2010, Part I, LNCS 6016, pp. 501–514, 2010.

It is widely recognized that water quality and flow regime (amounts, timing, and variability in flow) influence the ecological "health" of aquatic biota [2], [3]. In watersheds such as the Upper Tombigbee, where agricultural land use can comprise 50% or more of land cover, sediment and nutrient runoff can seriously degrade the ecological quality of aquatic environments [2].

While it is desirable to count with as much data as possible characterizing the water quality of a watershed or a river, data on nutrient loads to rivers from non-point sources are particularly difficult to find. Moreover, setting up field surveys for collecting nutrient data require extensive use of personnel and resources making it an impractical alternative. A technique that would combine remotely sensed land use data and export coefficients for estimating nutrient loads seems to be particularly attractive given the geographical extent that is covered by land use maps. There are several recent examples of this type of approach for estimating nutrient loads in watersheds located abroad [4][5][6], but there are no recent studies of this type in the USA.

For purposes of connecting hydrological processes to biological system response studies in the Upper Tombigbee watershed (Mississippi-Alabama, USA), a hydrological model of the watershed was developed. This paper details the hydrological model development and its use for providing stream flow, runoff, and nutrient concentrations to establish relationships between stream nutrients, runoff and discharge, and biotic data. Data for fish and mussel collections (provided by the Mississippi Museum of Natural Science) guided the watershed segmentation process. The Hydrological Simulation Program Fortran (HSPF) [7] is used for estimating water quantity, and export coefficients are used for calculating nutrient concentrations.

2   Methods

2.1 Study Area

The Upper Tombigbee watershed is located in Northwestern Alabama and Northeastern Mississippi, USA (Figure 1).

The watershed drains approximately 1390325 ha and it is a main contributor of flow to the Mobile River, with an approximate average stream flow of 169 m^3/s.

2.1 Topographical and Land Use Datasets

The topographical dataset used in this research was the United States Geological Service (USGS) DEM, which corresponds to the 3 arc-second (1:250,000-scale, 300 m spatial resolution) USGS topographic map series. A seamless topographical dataset was produced by "mosaicking" several DEMs that covered the area. ArcInfo (GRID) was used to fill grid cells with no-data values (*con*, *focalmax*, and *focalmean* commands were used.) Figure 2 shows a flowchart of the processing steps and the resulting topographical dataset.

Two land use datasets were used in this study (Figure 3): USGS GIRAS, and NASA MODIS MOD12Q1. The USGS GIRAS is a set of maps of land use and land cover for the conterminous U.S. delineated with a minimum mapping unit of 4 hectares and a maximum of 16 hectares (equivalent to 400 m spatial resolution). The

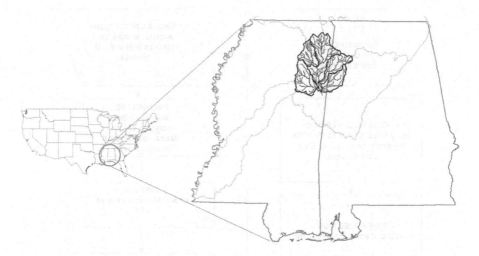

Fig. 1. Upper Tombigbee watershed, located in the northern Mississippi-Alabama region (USA)

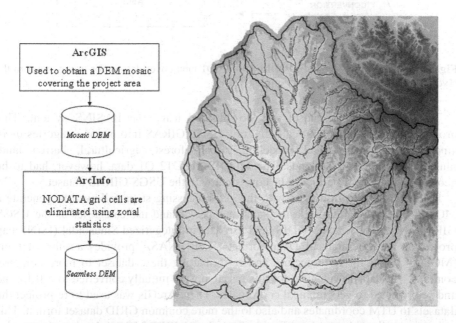

Fig. 2. Geo-processing of the topographical dataset (USGS DEM) used in the study

NASA MODIS MOD12Q1 Land Cover Product (MODIS/Terra Land Cover, 1000 m spatial resolution) [8] is provided by NASA through several internet portals. The land use map is classified in 21 land use categories, following the International Geosphere-Biosphere Program (IGBP) land cover classification. The map covers most of the globe and is updated every year.

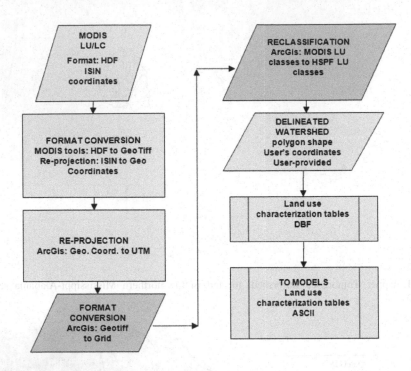

Fig. 3. Geo-processing steps of MODIS MOD12Q1 land cover dataset for use as input to the Hydrological Simulation Program Fortran (HSPF)

The USGS GIRAS dataset was downloaded using the BASINS system. This program reclassifies automatically the raw USGS GIRAS into major categories more amenable for hydrological modeling: urban, forest, agricultural, barren land, rangeland, water, and wetlands. The MODIS MOD12 Q1 data, however, had to be geo-processed for the dataset to be consistent with the USGS GIRAS dataset.

Figure 3 shows a flowchart with the geo-processing steps followed to generate a MODIS land use dataset with the same number of land use categories as the USGS GIRAS. NASA provides MODIS land use data in Integerized Sinusoidal (ISIN) map projection and Hierarchical Data Format (HDF). NASA provides a suite of tools (MODIS Tools) for re-projecting and re-formatting these dataset to more common contexts. The data downloaded for this research were initially converted to .tiff format and re-projected to geographical coordinates. Then, ArcGis was used to re-project the datasets to UTM coordinates and also to the more common GRID dataset format. This new format allowed a re-classification from the 21 IBEP MODIS land use categories to the USGS-GIRAS-HSPF categories.

ArcGIS was also used to extract land use characterization tables per sub-watershed and per land use datasets (either USGS GIRAS or MODIS). These tables were further processed to be in a format (ASCII) and data structure friendly to the hydrological model.

While the higher-resolution land use maps of the National Land Cover Dataset (NLCD) may have been used in this study (e.g., NLCD 1992 or NLCD 2001), these land use maps are outside the time intervals of interest for this study (2002-2004 and 1977-1982). Another option would have been using raw LANDSAT reflectance data and producing land use maps for the time intervals of interest (trying to replicate the process of producing NLCD maps) but this was unachievable since those maps would have required ground-truthing in large geographical regions.

2.5 Biological Data and Watershed Delineation

Geographical locations of field-collected data on fish and mussel (provided by the Mississippi Natural Heritage Program, Mississippi Museum of Natural Sciences) were used to delineate the watershed under study. The data were screened to determine sub-watersheds, within the upper Tombigbee River basin, that contained at least four sampled species per sub-watershed. Only samples collected during 2002-2004 and 1977-1982 were used for these analyses. The 2002-2004 time period coincides with data collection of MODIS MOD12 Q1 land use data. The 1977-1982 time period coincides with the period of data collection for the USGS GIRAS (1986) land use data.

2.3 Hydrological Modeling and Nutrients Estimation

Hydrological modeling of the Upper Tombigbee watershed is performed using the Hydrological Simulation Program Fortran (HSPF). HSPF is a computer model designed for simulation of non-point source watershed hydrology and water quality. Time-series of meteorological/water-quality data, land use and topographical data are used to estimate stream flow hydrographs and polluto-graphs. The model simulates interception, soil moisture, surface runoff, interflow, base flow, snowpack depth and water content, snowmelt, evapo-transpiration, and ground-water recharge. Simulation results are provided as time-series of runoff, sediment load, and nutrient and pesticide concentrations, along with time-series of water quantity and quality, at any point in a watershed. Additional software (WDMUtil and GenScn) is used for data pre-processing and post-processing, and for statistical and graphical analysis of input and output data.

All preprocessed physiographic (land use, topography) and meteorological information was set up to be read by the Better Assessment Science Integrating Point and Nonpoint Sources (BASINS) system [9]. From within BASINS, two initial HSPF hydrological model applications were generated: one using USGS GIRAS land use data, and the other using the MODIS land use datasets. Data from the USGS stream flow gauge station located in Luxapallilla Creek (USGS 2443000) was used to calibrate the models.

Nutrients (total nitrogen, TN, and total phosphorus, TP) concentrations were estimated using export coefficient for the region [10]. Table 1 show export coefficient values used in this research. Although HSPF could have been used for this estimation, the lack of measured nutrient concentrations for the study area did not allow water quality modeling.

Table 1. Export Coefficients used in the study in kg/ha-year (after [9])

Land use category	Average TP	Average TN
Row Crops	4.46	16.09
Non Row Crops	1.08	5.19
Forested	0.236	2.86
Urban	1.91	9.97
Pasture	1.5	8.65
Feedlot/Manure Storage	300.7	3110.7
Mixed Agriculture	1.134	16.53

3 Results

Figure 5 shows the results of the geo-processing of MODIS land use data. For the purposes of comparison the figure includes the USGS GIRAS land use dataset for the region of study. The land use categories to which the MODIS MOD 12Q1 datasets were reclassified are also shown. Although land use MODIS data for years 2001 through 2004 were generated, the figure only shows resulting datasets through 2003.

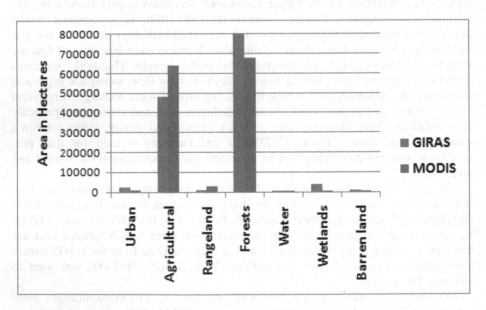

Fig. 4. Comparison of GIRAS (1986) and MODIS (2003) land uses for the Upper Tombigbee watershed area. Notice that in the period 1986 to 2003 agricultural lands and forest lands increased. Since those land use categories are dominant, the coarse spatial resolution of MODIS land use data (1000 m) would not affect the quantification of land use changes as reported in the literature [11].

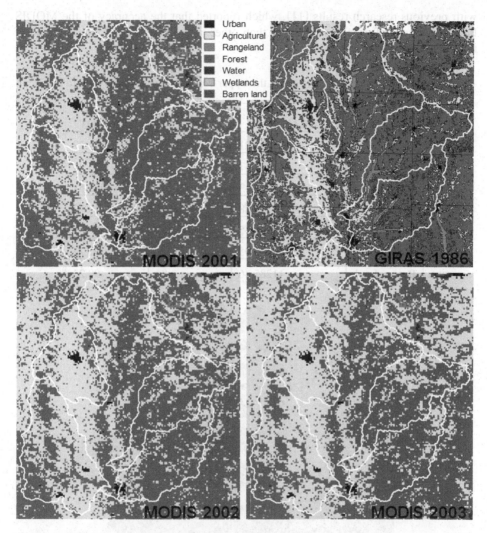

Fig. 5. Geo-processed MODIS MOD 12 Q1 land use datasets for year 2001 through 2003. Notice the increase in agricultural areas from the 1986 (GIRAS, upper left corner) to 2003 (MODIS, lower left corner).

As can be observed in Figure 4, and Table 2, from 1986 to 2003 agricultural lands increased in almost 34%, forest lands decreased in 16% and range-land almost quadruple in size. Interestingly, urban areas decreased in 50%, as well as water bodies. However, due to the coarse spatial resolution of MODIS land use data (1000 m), the land use area values for categories rangeland, water, wetlands and barren should be taken as coarse approximations. Within the context of this research (non-point source hydrological and water quality processes) the percent-change values associated with forest and agricultural lands are the most important. This is consistent with previous research results [11], which reported that the accuracy of the MODIS land cover type of cropland is higher than other categories when cropland is one of the dominant land cover types.

Table 2. Percent change in land use in the Upper Tombigbee watershed (1986 to 2003)

LAND USE	GIRAS 1986	MODIS 2003	% Change 1986-2003
Urban	22792.21	10991	-51.77
Agricultural	479521.47	642173	33.91
Rangeland	8029.43	29108	262.51
Forests	805819.88	678665	-15.77
Water	3034.75	1288	-57.55
Wetlands	40652.95	1717	-95.77
Barren land	11285.46	86	-99.23

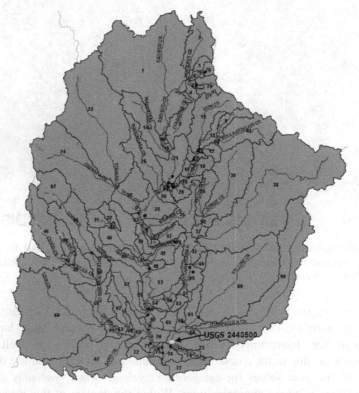

Fig. 6. Watershed delineation results of the Upper Tombigbee River watershed. Each sub-basin contains at least four sampled species per sub-watershed (represented as colored dots.

Considering that the accuracy of the MODIS MOD12 Q1 land cover product is relative to the spatial distribution of features of the land cover patches [11], and that the vast geographical areas associated with agriculture and forests are dominant in the Upper Tombigbee watershed, the estimations of land use coverage from MODIS datasets for this research is considered satisfactory.

Figure 6 shows the final result of the watershed delineation process. Sampling points of mollusk and fish data are represented in various colors. The generation of sub-watersheds was performed trying to capture the distribution of biological data throughout the study area. A total of 97 sub-watersheds were produced.

Once an optimum watershed delineation was achieved, HSPF was launched from within BASINS to initialize the HSPF model application. The initialization was done for each of the land use datasets used in this study (GIRAS and MODIS). Hence, two hydrological models were set-up with two different time periods of simulation: 1980-1990, and 1996-2006. Figure 3 shows the location of the stream flow gauge station used for hydrological calibration (Luxapallilla Creek, USGS 2443500).

The configuration of the HSPF model for the Upper Tombigbee watershed is shown in Figure 7. Results of the hydrological calibration performed for the two hydrological models are also shown in the figure. Correlation coefficient (r^2) values of 0.94 and 0.63 were calculated for the models corresponding to 1995-2007 and 1977-1982 periods of analysis, respectively, showing good agreement of measured and simulated stream flow data.

Stream flow and run-off time-series simulated by the two calibrated hydrological models for the watershed under study were used in conjunction with export coefficients (reported in the literature) to estimate concentrations of total nitrogen (TN) and total phosphorus (TP). These estimations were performed only for selected sub-watersheds. Biological criteria for subsequent studies were followed in the selection of sub-basins.

Figures 8 and 9 show estimated total nitrogen (TN) and total phosphorus (TP) concentrations. Tables 3 and 4 compare nutrient concentration values for sub-basins 43, 51, and 54 (common sub-basin among the GIRAS and MODIS analyses). Average and 3rd-quartile total phosphorus (TP) concentrations were not found to differ greatly when using either land use dataset (GIRAS or MODIS). Only maximum concentrations show to have increased from 6% to 16% (Table 3).

Total nitrogen (TN) concentrations for sub-basins 43, 51 and 54, follow the same trend as those of phosphorus (Table 4). Only maximum TN concentrations were found to have increased when using MODIS land use data (with respect to TN concentrations estimated using GIRAS land use data). Percent increments in TN concentration values are in-between 5% to 15%.

When taking into account all sub-basins, average TP concentrations estimated using the GIRAS dataset range from 0.31 to 1.23 mg/L, while maximum concentrations range from 1.51 to 5.66 mg/L. Concentration values calculated using the MODIS dataset are not noticeably higher. Average values are between 0.07 to 1.2 mg/L, and maximum values from 0.5 to 7.78. While average values did not seem to show an overall increase, maximum TP concentrations seem to have increased in about 37 %. Correspondingly, average TN concentrations range: 1.88 – 4.72 mg/L (when using GIRAS), and 0.9 – 4.48 mg/L (when using MODIS). Maximum TN concentrations are between: 8.96 – 21.58 mg/L (when using GIRAS), and 6.15 – 28.94 mg/L (when using

MODIS). Again, the increase in maximum TN concentrations seems to be of about 34%. This increase in maximum concentrations seems to correlate with the increase in agricultural areas from 1986 to 2003 for the Upper Tombigbee watershed, showed in Table 2.

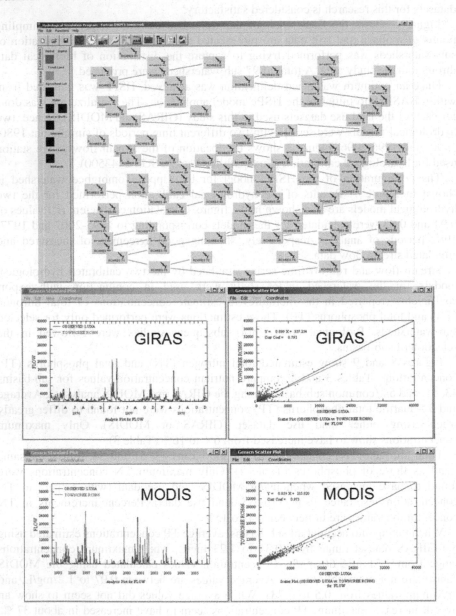

Fig. 7. HSPF model for the Upper Tombigbee watershed and results of the hydrological calibration

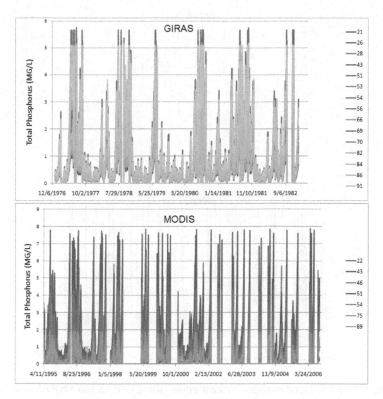

Fig. 8. Estimated total phosphorus concentrations (using GIRAS and MODIS land use)

Table 3. Total phosphorus concentrations in (mg/L)

Sub-basin	Average GIRAS	Maximum GIRAS	3 quartile GIRAS
43	0.43	2.04	0.62
51	1.11	5.26	1.66
54	0.80	3.75	1.12
Sub-basin	Average MODIS	Maximum MODIS	3 quartile MODIS
43	0.33	2.17	0.51
51	0.88	6.09	1.17
54	0.68	4.36	1.06

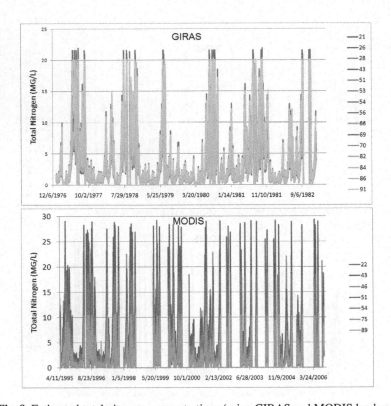

Fig. 9. Estimated total nitrogen concentrations (using GIRAS and MODIS land use)

Table 4. Total nitrogen concentrations in (mg/L)

Sub-basin	Average GIRAS	Maximum GIRAS	3 quartile GIRAS
43	2.30	10.91	3.32
51	4.40	20.94	6.61
54	3.53	16.65	5.00
Sub-basin	Average MODIS	Maximum MODIS	3 quartile MODIS
43	1.76	11.42	2.69
51	3.42	23.70	4.55
54	2.98	19.07	4.62

4 Conclusions

The methodology presented in this research for the introduction of land use data from MODIS MOD 12Q1 into the Hydrological Program Fortran (HSPF) is shown to be successful. MODIS datasets for 2001 through 2004 were geo-processed and the results are shown to be consistent with historical trends in land use for the region of Upper Tombigbee watershed. This research shows that from 1986 to 2003 agricultural lands increased in almost 34%, forest lands decreased in 16%, and range-land almost quadruple in size. Land use change trends for areas of minor extent (urban, wetlands, barren) in the region were not correctly detected due to the coarse spatial resolution of the MODIS datasets (1000 m).

The watershed delineation process, guided by geographical locations of sampling points of mollusk and fish data, allowed the generation of sub-watersheds that captured the distribution of biological data throughout the study area. A total of 97 sub-watersheds were produced that contained at least four sampled species per sub-watershed.

A comparison of nutrient concentration values for sub-basins 43, 51, and 54 (common sub-basin among the GIRAS and MODIS analyses) showed that average and 3rd-quartile total phosphorus (TP) concentrations do not differ greatly when using either land use dataset. Only maximum concentrations showed to have increased from 6% to 16%. Similarly, only maximum total nitrogen (TN) concentrations were found to have increased when using MODIS land use data (with respect to TN concentrations estimated using GIRAS land use data). Percent increments in TN concentration values are in-between 5% to 15%. When taking into account all sub-basins, average and maximum TP and TN concentration values were not noticeably different. However, maximum TP and TN concentrations seem to have increased in about 37 % and 34%, respectively, from 1986 to 2003. This increase in maximum nutrient concentrations seems to correlate with the 34% increase in agricultural areas in the Upper Tombigbee watershed, from 1986 to 2003.

Acknowledgements. This study has been supported by a grant from the Northern Gulf Institute, Mississippi State University. The authors are grateful to the editors and three anonymous reviewers for their constructive comments and valuable ideas on earlier versions of the manuscript.

References

1. Vesterby, W., Krupa, K.S.: Major Uses of Land in the United States. Resource Economics Division, Economic Research Service. U.S. Department of Agriculture. Statistical Bulletin No. 973 (1997)
2. Allen, J.D.: Stream ecology: Structure and function of running waters. Chapman & Hall, Oxford (1995)
3. Karr, J.R., Chu, E.W.: Restoring life in running waters. Island Press, Washington (1999)
4. Liu, R., Yang, Z., Shen, Z., Yu, S.L., Ding, X., Wu, X., Liu, F.: Estimating nonpoint source pollution in the upper Yangtze River using the export coefficient model, remote sensing, and geographical information system. Journal of Hydraulic Engineering 135(9), 698–704 (2009)

5. Liu, R., He, M., Wang, X.: Application of the export coefficient model in estimating nutrient pollution of Dahuofang Reservoir Drainage Basin, Daliao River, China. In: 2nd International Conference on Bioinformatics and Biomedical Engineering, iCBBE, pp. 3645–3648 (2008)

6. Ierodiaconou, D., Laurenson, L., Leblanc, M., Stagnitti, F., Duff, G., Salzman, S.: Multitemporal land use mapping using remotely sensed techniques and the integration of a pollutant load model in a GIS, vol. 289, pp. 343–352. IAHS-AISH Publication (2004)

7. Bicknell, B.R., Imhoff, J.C., Kittle, J.L., Jobes, T.H., Donigian, A.S.: HSPF Version 12 User's Manual. National Exposure Research Laboratory. Office of Research and Development U.S. Environmental Protection Agency (2001)

8. NASA: MODIS MOD12 Land Cover and Land Cover Dynamics Products User Guide, http://www-modis.bu.edu/landcover/userguidelc/lc.html

9. Environmental Protection Agency: BASINS: Better Assessment Science Integrating Point & Nonpoint Sources: A Powerful Tool for Managing Watersheds, http://www.epa.gov/waterscience/BASINS/

10. Lin, J.P.: Review of Published Export Coefficient and Event Mean Concentration (EMC) Data. Wetlands Regulatory Assistance Program ERDC TN-WRAP-04-3 (September 2004)

11. Haobo Lin, H., Wang, J., Jia, X., Bo, Y., Wang, D.: Evaluation of MODIS land cover product of East of China, http://www.igarss08.org/Abstracts/pdfs/2400.pdf

Geometrical DCC-Algorithm for Merging Polygonal Geospatial Data

Silvija Stankute and Hartmut Asche

University of Potsdam, Department of Geography,
Karl-Liebknecht-Strasse 24/25, 14476 Potsdam, Germany
{silvija.stankute,gislab}@uni-potsdam.de
http://www.geographie.uni-potsdam.de

Abstract. Geospatial data integration technology involves fusing equivalent objects from multiple datasets. Due to different acquisition methods of geospatial data, new problem cases arise in data integration systems and thus the complexity of the integration approach increases. There are many data homogenization methods, which determine the assignment of objects via semantic similarity. The algorithms for polygonal geospatial data integration, presented in this paper, are based on geometrical comparison between two datasets. The objective of these algorithms is the assignment of geospatial elements representing the same object in heterogeneous datasets. Depending on semantic information in geospatial data the polygonal shapes have different spatial extent. For this reason two kinds of polygonal geospatial data were analyzed. The methods are discussed and first results are presented.

Keywords: data fusion, data integration, vector data, homogenization, heterogeneous geospatial data, data conflation.

1 Introduction

Data fusion is the process of combining the information from two or more geospatial datasets. The objective of this process is to make an improved dataset, which is more superior to the source dataset in respect of either spatial or attributive properties. Therefore the spatial accuracy and consistency of the output dataset increases. The input datasets used in the fusion or the integration process describe the same area in the real world, but have varieties in density and accuracy of given information. Different geospatial data providers collect data applying diverse methods. Therefore the same object or the same area is represented differently and thus has different geometrical characteristics. That requires an increased complexity of the integration approaches, because many nontrivial problems arises from it, which need special handling in the pre-processing steps (see 3.1).

Finding a suitable geospatial dataset for a particular project or specific application is very difficult, because available datasets are often incomplete and/or inconsistent. A good solution could be the self-acquisition of missing semantic

D. Taniar et al. (Eds.): ICCSA 2010, Part I, LNCS 6016, pp. 515–527, 2010.

information, but it is very time-consuming and costly. A combination of two or more different datasets is desirable resulting in an output dataset, which fulfills the demands of the particular application. Furthermore this combination allows for an incorporation of suitable features contained in the input datasets, which are needed by the new application, only. The problems occurre during the use of data from two or more different providers of geospatial data. In particular these are topological problems, which are inadmissible in geographic information systems (GIS) according to international conventions and standards for GIS-data and GIS-applications (e.g. ISO 19111, ISO 19126). For instance geometrical overlapping of two or more different object types can occur, which is not allowed, but causes nontrivial problems during data processing.

Further, the level of geometrical details is different, also. The density and the type of semantic information corresponding to the same object in geospatial datasets from heterogeneous sources are different. Another good solution can be the combination of two ore more datasets resulting in only one end-dataset containing the desired geographical and semantical information with increased precision and quality, respectively, which is our approach presented in this paper. In this way the geodata fusion opens new GIS application fields.

In this paper an algorithm is presented and implemented showing the approach to data optimization and data integration. This is applicable to polygonal geospatial data, only. The rest of the paper is organized as follows. After investigation of related works made by other scientists, we describe our approach methodology in detail in chapter 3. Thereby in 3.1 we go into details of necessary data formats and polygon types and in 3.2 of polygon centres and important assignment, which is very important in our polygonal data fusion approach. Taking geospatial data of an area under investigation we present first test results of the polygonal fusion process applying our approach in chapter 4. The paper closes with the summary, the concluding remarks and the future outlook.

2   Related Work

Several approaches for data homogenization problems make use of semantic similarity between geospatial data from different sources. Rodríguez and Egenhofer [1] presented an approach to computing semantic similarity that relaxes the requirement of a single ontology and accounts for differences in the levels of explicitness and formalization of the different ontology specifications. A semantic method for geospatial information integration was proposed by Torres et al. [2]. This consists of providing semantic descriptions, which explicitly describe the properties and relations of geographic objects represented by concepts, whereas the behaviour describes the semantics of objects. Ontologies have been used in [3], also, where spatial conceptualizations were integrated with temporal and thematic dimensions at the domain level, and where the context-aware framework was exploited to meet the requirements of a varied and distributed user community with differing objectives.

An algorithm dealing with polygons with non-stable borders was introduced in [4]. Sehgal, Getoor and Viechnicki propose in [5] an approach introducing a method for combination of different features in order to perform accurate resolution.

3   Methodology

The approach presented here is based on a direct comparison of geometrical structures. The objective of data integration is finding corresponding features from two different geospatial datasets. During the fusion of two datasets it is absolutely necessary to find/determine the correct relation between objects contained in these datasets. The geometrical information serve as the relation. Thus, an identical coordinate system as a frame of reference is one of the most important requirements to the input datasets used in the data fusion process.

In order to be applicable in our data fusion approach, each input dataset has to meet some requirements. The geospatial data have to refer to a common coordinate system and must represent the same investigation area. The demand on the user is the knowledge about the kind of semantic information and the geospatial objects which have to be merged from both input datasets. Fig. 1 shows the general workflow for our data fusion algorithm. In the first step all input datasets are checked to meet the set requirements. Beside the problems arising from different data acquisition methods, often input data have different and nonstandard storage format, which makes the read in step nontrivial. Therefore in the pre-processing step the data format of all input datasets have to be unified. So, the pre-processing step includes the conversion to an uniform data format, the transfer to the same coordinate system, the verification and a potential geometrical correction. Next workflow step is the assignment between two particular features and objects of different datasets, respectively. The assignment is performed under consideration of certain criteria set by the user. This part of the workflow is the most difficult part, depending on the level of structural similarity. In the last step, the user can choose the components, which have to be transferred. These can be only geometric components, only semantic components (attributes) or both components together. This workflow shows the general steps of data integration only and is valid for all geospatial data types

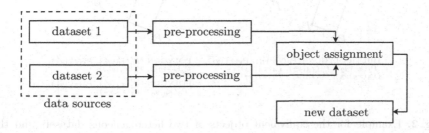

Fig. 1. General workflow for data fusion

(polygon, line and point). The algorithm presented in this paper is applicable to polygonal data, only. The fusion of linear structures has been presented in our previous works [6].

3.1 Data Format and Polygon Types

All input datasets are stored differently. That means the datasets have different data format, so that the same object in the real world can be stored as a single or as a multiple polygon in a dataset. Figure 2 shows two heterogeneous datasets for the same area. On the left hand side the area is represented using multiple polygon data type. The same area in the another dataset is represented with the single polygon data type. In the pre-processing step these datasets have to be converted to a common data format.

The polygonal geospatial datasets consist of several polygons. Each polygon is a closed plane defined by the n-tuple $P := (P_0, P_1, ..., P_n), P_i \in \mathbb{R}^2, 0 \le i \le n$, $n \in \mathbb{N}(0, 1, 2)$, with $n \ge 2$ vertices. A Polygon with respect to geospatial data can be convex or concave, single or multiple, or have an island (see fig. 3) and is always topologically closed. The latter must be stored using the multiple polygon data type, otherwise it would be stored as several different polygons. A planar polygon is convex if every interior angle is less than 180°. All diagonals of a convex polygon lie entirely inside the polygon. A concave polygon has at least one angle greater than 180° and is opposite of a convex polygon [7]. At least one diagonal in a concave polygon lies outside itself.

The polygonal geometry may not be ambiguous, because it can lead to data processing problems, so that always the polygonal geometry must hold for P_i, P_j $\in \mathbb{R}^2, P_i \ne P_j(P_0, P_n)$ in order to be unique. Therefore the input data sets are being checked for the geometry uniqueness during the pre-processing step and potential geometrical ambiguities are reduced to unique single geometries. Thereby no attributive data is lost, because it is transferred to the residual geometry.

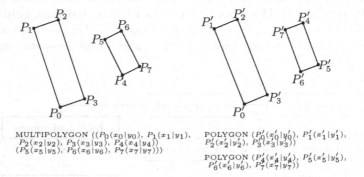

MULTIPOLYGON $((P_0(x_0|y_0), P_1(x_1|y_1), P_2(x_2|y_2), P_3(x_3|y_3), P_4(x_4|y_4)) (P_5(x_5|y_5), P_6(x_6|y_6), P_7(x_7|y_7)))$

POLYGON $(P_0'(x_0'|y_0'), P_1'(x_1'|y_1'), P_2'(x_2'|y_2'), P_3'(x_3'|y_3'))$

POLYGON $(P_4'(x_4'|y_4'), P_5'(x_5'|y_5'), P_6'(x_6'|y_6'), P_7'(x_7'|y_7'))$

Fig. 2. Example for the equivalent objects of two heterogeneous datasets and their description in ASCII format. Left: multipolygonal data type, right: single polygonal data type.

Fig. 3. Types of polygons: a) convex and single, b) concave and multiple parts, c) with island

The pre-processing step is not only the coordinate transformation and the verification of the geometrical inconsistency, but also the feature/data sorting inside the input datasets. For the reason that our algorithm is based on the direct coordinate comparison (DCC) all coordinate information of polygonal geospatial input data are converted and stored in ASCII format as a list (L_1) of data blocks (see fig. 2). The first point in the block is the start point $P_0(x_0|y_0)$ of the polygon. Because of performance reasons, before the coordinate search the unsorted list L_1 is being sorted to a sorted list L_2. The sorting process involves the start points of each polygon, only. For the later accurate polygon assignment we need to create an additional list L_3, where all coordinate pairs are sorted according to the x-value. Thereby all start points and the affinity of corresponding polygons are stored. After the pre-processing step the polygon assignment follows.

3.2   Centres of Polygons and Polygon Assignment

The most important step of the geospatial data fusion process is the determination of the relation between two corresponding structures representing the same object in the real world. Depending on the kind of the polygon the method for finding this relation is different. To find equivalent objects from heterogeneous geospatial datasets the centre of polygons have to be determined first.

The terms centre and centroid are connected with a variety of different meanings and formulas. The most used centres are: mean centre (MC), minimum bounding rectangle centre (MBR) and centroid (C). The centroid is also known as the centre of gravity and is often defined as the nominal centre of gravity for an object or a group of objects. The centre of gravity represents the point about which the polygon would balance, if it would be made of a uniform thin sheet of material with a constant density [7].

For calculating the centroid $C(x|y)$ of an irregular (non-self-intersecting) polygon its area A is needed to be calculated. We consider a polygon made up of line segments between n vertices $(x_i|y_i)$, $i = 0$ to $n-1$, $n \geq 2$, $x, y \in \mathbb{R}^2$, $n \in \mathbb{N}$. The last vertex $(x_n|y_n)$ is assumed to be the same as the first $(x_0|y_0)$, i.e. P_0 and P_n are directly connected, so that the polygon is closed. The polygon area A is given by

$$A = \frac{1}{2} \sum_{i=0}^{n-1} |(x_{i+1}y_i - x_iy_{i+1})|. \tag{1}$$

Its centroid is $C(x|y)$ where

$$C_x = \frac{1}{nA} \sum_{i=0}^{n-1} |(x_i + x_{i+1})(x_i y_{i+1} - x_{i+1} y_i)| \tag{2}$$

and

$$C_y = \frac{1}{nA} \sum_{i=0}^{n-1} |(y_i + y_{i+1})(x_i y_{i+1} - x_{i+1} y_i)|. \tag{3}$$

n is the number of vertices of the polygon and $(x_n|y_n)$ is assumed to be $(x_0|y_0)$ as in (1). The mean centre of polygon is not the same as the centroid of the polygon and MC is given by:

$$MC(x|y) = \left(\sum_{i=0}^{n-1} \frac{x_i}{n}, \sum_{i=0}^{n-1} \frac{y_i}{n} \right), \ MC \in \mathbb{R}^2. \tag{4}$$

The minimum bounding rectangle centre is defined by

$$MBR(x|y) = \left(\frac{x_{max} - x_{min}}{2}, \frac{y_{max} - y_{min}}{2} \right), \ MBR \in \mathbb{R}^2 \tag{5}$$

and formes the bounding geometry by the minimum and maximum $(x|y)$ coordinates. Figure 4 shows an example of MBR centres of simple polygon data.

Which kind of centre is being calculated depends on the polygon under investigation. For convex polygons as centre is calculated the MBR point using (5), otherwise the MC point applying (4) or the C point using (2) and (3), respectively. For the calculation of polygon centres the original input data list L_1 is being used (see 3.1). In the next step the polygons from the source input dataset (SDS) and from the target input dataset (TDS) have to be assigned among each other. The SDS is defined as the dataset from where the geospatial information is taken (e.g. thematic information) and the TDS is defined as the dataset to which the geospatial information taken from the SDS is being transferred,

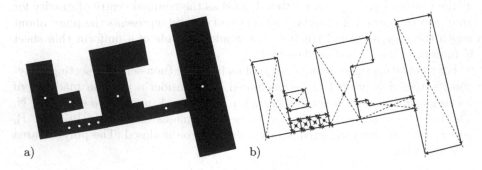

a)   b)

Fig. 4. Definition of the MBR centres of non-self-intersecting polygons

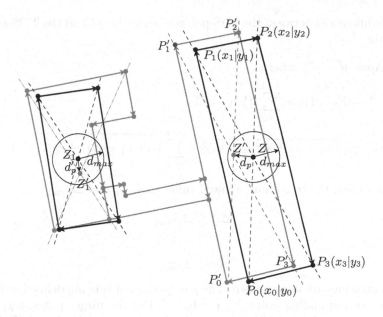

Fig. 5. Assignment of polygons by means of the MBR centres

i.e. the expanded dataset. In the assignment process the distance d_p,where p is
the current polygon under test, between Z^s and Z^t is being calculated as

$$d_p = |Z^t - Z^s| = \sqrt{(y_t - y_s)^2 + (x_t - x_s)^2}, \qquad (6)$$

where Z^s is the first centre of the SDS and Z^t the centre of all other potentially
equivalent polygons from the TDS.

The seek condition is $min(d_p) \leq d_{max}$, where d_{max} is the user-defined radius
of the circle which covers a certain set of Z_c-points, where $c = MC, MBR$ or
C (see fig. 5). Thus the seek circle delimitates the maximum allowed distance
deviation between the source polygon centre Z_{xy}^s and the target polygon centre
Z_{xy}^t. Once Z_{xy}^s and Z_{xy}^t are found, an accurate assignment is being applied in
the next step. Thereby the following polygon properties of found potentially
equivalent polygons are being compared:

- perimeter,
- area,
- polygon extent.

The differences between the calculated area values using (1) of the SDS-polygon
area A^s and the TDS-polygon area A^t

$$\Delta A = |A^t - A^s| \qquad (7)$$

and the differences between the SDS-polygon perimeter p^s and the TDS-polygon perimeter p^t

$$\Delta p = |p^t - p^s|, \text{ where}$$

$$p^{t,s} = |P_n - P_0| + \sum_{i=0}^{n-1} |P_{i-1} - P_i| \tag{8}$$

$$= \sqrt{(x_n - x_0)^2 + (y_n - y_0)^2} + \sum_{i=0}^{n-1} \sqrt{(x_{i+1} - x_i)^2 + (y_{i+1} - y_i)^2}$$

may not exceed the maximum allowed values ΔA_{max} and Δp_{max}:

$$\Delta A \leq \Delta A_{max} \tag{9}$$

and

$$\Delta p \leq \Delta p_{max}. \tag{10}$$

These two values are user-defined. The polygon extent is being defined as follows. First the corresponding point P_i^t, $i = 0...n - 1$ of the target polygon p_t to the start point $P_0^s(x_0|y_0)$ of the source polygon p_s have to be found. It is very improbable, that the start point $P_0^t(x_0|y_0)$ of the target polygon is close to the start point $P_0^s(x_0|y_0)$. During the data acquisition the polygons are differently recorded. So, the polygons representing the same object can have wrong vertex ordering (clockwise or anti-clockwise) and/or start points on different polygon sides, i.e. $P_0^s \neq P_0^t$. That implies a possibly very large distance value d_0 between the start points of compared polygons (see fig. 6). Figure 6 illustrates in a good way, that $P_0^t(x_0|y_0)$ and $P_0^s(x_0|y_0)$ are often not in close neighbourhood to each other, although the corresponding polygons have to be assigned to each other, because they represent the same object. The closest point obviously can be any polygon vertex $P_i^t(x_i|y_i)$. Therefore all distances from $P_0^s(x_0|y_0)$ to each vertex of the target polygon must be calculated in order to find the corresponding start point P_i^t of the target polygon, which is found for the minimum distance d_{min}.

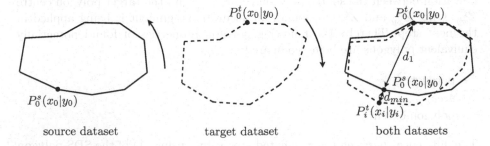

source dataset   target dataset   both datasets

Fig. 6. An example of polygons from source and target datasets representing the same object. The distance d_0 between start points is very large due to different data acquisition methods.

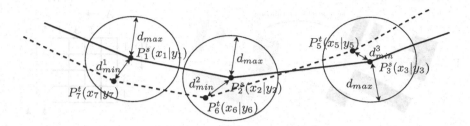

Fig. 7. Verification of the accurate assignment

After determination of the relation between the start points of the source and target polygon, the direction of the rotation has to be checked. The vertices of the polygons are sorted. Therefore the vertex ordering is the same in source and target polygon, if the first point of the source polygon is a close neighbour of the first point of the target polygon, so that both polygons have the clockwise ordering. If the first point of the source is a close neighbour of the last point of the target point, than the vertex ordering is wrong and has to be corrected. After a potential correction of the vertex ordering, only (for performance reasons) the first five distances between corresponding points of the source and target polygons are calculated and their sum is built.

$$d^1_{min} + ... + d^5_{min} \leq d_{max} \text{ where } d_{max} \text{ is user-defined} \tag{11}$$

Using the condition (11) we are defining a polygonal shape similarity coefficient $\bar{d}$, which is small for similar structures and large for diverging structure shapes and is given as

$$\bar{d} = \frac{1}{5} \sum_{i=1}^{5} d^i_{min} \leq \overline{d_{max}} \tag{12}$$

where $\overline{d_{max}}$ is the similarity deviation limit. The polygonal assignment is successful if all conditions (9), (10), (11) and (12) are fulfilled. Fig. 7 shows this process.

After the accurate assignment of all source and target polygons among each other, the topological relation between the source and the target dataset is assured, so that the following transfer of the desired geometrical and semantical information is an easy step. This is simply done by inserting or deleting selected rows in the attribute table (geometrical data transfer) and/or selected columns (semantical data transfer). This step is followed by a post-processing step in which the set output data format and other user options (e.g. data clipping) are applied on the final dataset.

4   Results

After implementing all steps of our approach (pre-processing / input data correction, centre calculation, accurate polygon assignment, data transfer) we made

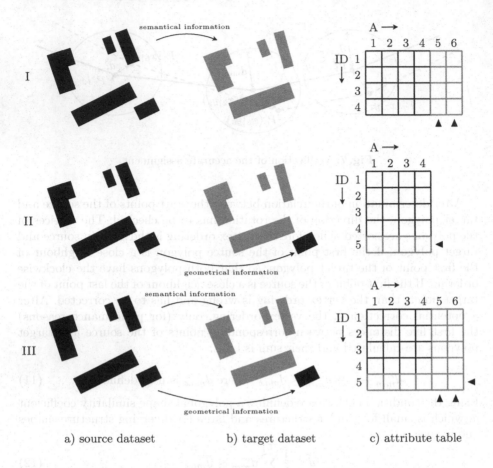

a) source dataset   b) target dataset   c) attribute table

Fig. 8. Options for transferring geometrical or/and semantical information: black polygons - source dataset, grey polygons - target dataset, A - different semantical attributes, ID - number of shapes, black left/up arrow - added semantical or/and geometrical information

first geometrical and/or semantical information transfer runs. Figure 8 shows which user options for information transfer are available. In this example an original input target dataset has four shapes (polygons) with ID number which corresponds to the geometrical information. Each object represented by a shape carries four attributes.

In case *I* the available target dataset is being extended with semantical information *A*1 and *A*2 without changing the geometry. This option completes the target dataset on the semantical level (new columns in the attribute table). If the geometry has no accuracy lacks, this option is to be preferred for data fusion. In case *II* a target dataset is extended with new geometrical information. The semantical information remains unaffected. So, the attribute table obtains new rows representing new shapes. The transfer of semantical and geometrical

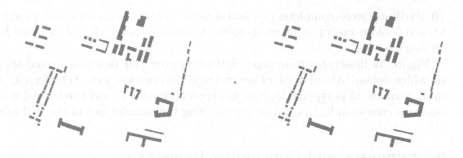

Fig. 9. Input datasets: a) source dataset, b) target dataset

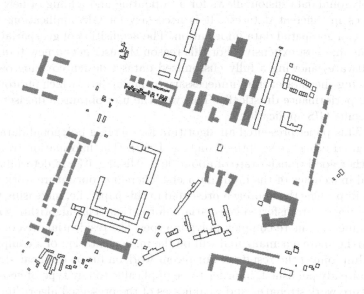

Fig. 10. Transferring of geometrical and semantical information: grey - target dataset, white - new shapes inserted from source dataset

information in case III results in an increased quality of the input dataset. Applying this option the most information are transferred, but the user must accept partially incomplete semantical information, because the new geometry had never existed in the target dataset, so that it can not have the semantical information, which have the original geometry entries in the target dataset. That applies to case II, also.

For testing the algorithm two input datasets were used. The source dataset had 58 shapes and only three attributes, whereas only one had complete values for all 58 geometry entries. Another two attributes were given for one geometry entry. The rest of 57 shapes had not this information. The second input dataset had 306 shapes, which carried semantical information of 12 attributes.

10 attributes were complete, one had 4 values, only and another one 19 values. Figure 9 shows both test input datasets. In order to cover all test cases we have chosen case *III*.

Figure 10 illustrates the target dataset in grey and new transferred shapes in white colour. About 96% of geometrical information were transferred. The main problem of polygonal assignment errors (about 4%) was the large distance between corresponding polygons representing the same object in the real world.

5 Summary and Concluding Remarks

Polygonal data fusion allows for an updating and adding of new geospatial features in different datasets. It is necessary for GIS applications, which require special geospatial data information. The acquisition of geospatial data is mostly time and cost expensive. For this reason the user gets a new tool (data merging software) allowing a fully customized dataset design covering own needs, only, freeing the dataset from unnecessary (generic) data, which improves the processing performance drastically. This way the user obtains a dataset defined for his specific GIS application.

This paper presented an algorithm for merging polygonal data. It was implemented using the scripting language PERL. The information transfer achieves a rather good transfer rate of about 96%. Missing 4% are determined by topological inaccuracy of the input datasets. Therefore, our future work will be focused on improving the approach presented in this paper, i.e. increasing the quality and accuracy of transferred geospatial information. This algorithm will be advanced for merging more complex polygon types, like residential area or landscape use. Furthermore our main goal will be the implementation of a comprehensive algorithm joining the results of our recent work on fusion of linear structures, which is already published, in order to be applicable to any type of geospatial data. In future work strengths and weaknesses of the presented algorithm will be proved by analysing more complex application examples.

References

1. Rodríguez, M.A., Egenhofer, M.J.: Determining Semantic Similarity Among Entity Classes from Different Ontologies. IEEE Transactions on Knowledge and Data Engineering 15(2), 442–456 (2003)
2. Torres, M., Levachkine, S., Quintero, R., Guzmán, G., Moreno, M.: Geospatial Information Integration Based on the Conceptualization of Geographic Domain. In: Proceedings of the 16th ACM SIGSPATIAL International Conference on Advances in Geographic Information Systems (2008)
3. Kemp, Z., Tan, L., Whalley, J.: Interoperability for geospatial analysis: a semantics and ontology-based approach. In: Proceedings of the Eighteenth Conference on Australasian Database, vol. 63, pp. 83–92 (2007)
4. Klajnsek, G.: Merging a set of polygons with non-stable borders. Central European Seminar on Computer Graphics (2000)

5. Sehgal, V., Getoor, L., Viechnicki, P.D.: Entity resolution in geospatial data integration. In: 14th International symposium on advances in Geographic Information system (ACM-GIS 2006), pp. 83–90 (2006)
6. Stankute, S., Asche, H.: An Integrative Approach to Geospatial Data Fusion. In: Gervasi, O., Taniar, D., Murgante, B., Laganà, A., Mun, Y., Gavrilova, M.L. (eds.) Computational Science and Its Applications – ICCSA 2009. LNCS, vol. 5592, pp. 490–504. Springer, Heidelberg (2009)
7. De Smith, M., Goodchild, M.F., Longley von Troubador, P.A.: Geospatial Analysis: A Comprehensive Guide to Principles, techniques and Software Tools. Matador, Market Harborough (2009)

Geospatial Semantics: A Critical Review

Pasquale Di Donato

Sapienza University of Rome, LABSITA
Piazza Borghese 9, 00186 Rome, Italy
pasquale.didonato@uniroma1.it

Abstract. Current approaches to semantics in the geospatial domain are mainly based on ontologies, but ontologies, since continue to build entirely on the symbolic methodology, suffers from the classical problems, e.g. the symbol grounding problem, affecting representational theories. We claim for an enactive approach to semantics, where meaning is considered to be an emergent feature arising context-dependently in action. Since representational theories are unable to deal with context and emergence, a new formalism is required toward a contextual theory of concepts. SCOP is considered a promising formalism in this sense and is briefly described.

Keywords: Semantics, experiential realism, enactive cognition, non-representational formalism, quantum like formalism.

1 Introduction

The current scene of Geographic Information (GI) is characterised by the provision of services, in a distributed information systems environment, that enable to integrate distributed information resources.

Dealing with data integration basically implies addressing two main types of heterogeneity: data heterogeneity and semantic heterogeneity. Data heterogeneity refers to differences in data in terms of data type and data formats, while semantic heterogeneity applies to the meaning of the data [1]. Semantic heterogeneities may be classified in two macro-categories: naming heterogeneities, where different words/expressions are used for the same (semantically alike) concept, and conceptual heterogeneities, where different people and/or disciplines have a different interpretation/conceptualisation of the same "thing" [2].

The Open Geospatial Consortium and the ISO TC 211 provide specifications and standards supporting the deployment of geospatial web services. These specifications and standards address the interoperability issue at syntactic level, but are limited in terms of semantics and do not provide a consistent model for the semantics integration/composition of geospatial services.

Coping with semantic interoperability is a challenging task, since it has more to do with how people perceive and give meaning to "things", rather then with integrating software components through standard interfaces [3].

Semantics deals with aspects of meaning as expressed in a language, either natural or technical such as a computer language, and is complementary to syntax which

D. Taniar et al. (Eds.): ICCSA 2010, Part I, LNCS 6016, pp. 528–544, 2010.

deals with the structure of signs (focusing on the form) used by the language itself. In the area of distributed data sources and services, semantic interoperability refers to the ability of systems to exchange data and functionalities in a meaningful way. Semantic heterogeneity occurs when there is no agreement of the meaning of the same data and/or service functionality.

Data creation happens in a context or in an application domain where concepts and semantics are clear to the data creator, either because they are explicitly formalised either they are naturally applied due to a yearly experience. But with distributed data resources this context is missed and unknown to the end user. This means that, in order to achieve semantic interoperability, semantics should be formally and explicitly expressed [4].

Current approaches to overcome semantic heterogeneities rely on the use of ontologies and reasoning engines for concepts matching among different ontologies. The main drawback is that ontologies, being forms of a priori agreements, are decontextualised and decontextualise experience; instead our assumption is that semantics reconciliation depends on contextual human sense-making. This claims for a new formalism for geospatial semantics.

The rest of this paper is organised as follows: section 2 deals with the semantics issue in the broader context of cognitive sciences; section 3 briefly summarises current approaches to semantics in distributed information systems; section 4 summarises current approaches to semantics in the GI arena; section 5 is about future work and introduces SCOP as a formalism for non-representational modelling of geographic information systems.

2   Semantics

There is a general agreement on considering that semantics deals with relationships between linguistic expressions and their meaning; but when it turns do define such relationships opinions highly diverge in a dispute which is mainly philosophical.

Dealing with formal semantics means opting for one of the two following paradigms, and the choice is mostly philosophical:

- Realistic semantics, which comes in two flavours:
  - o   Extensional: in extensional semantics terms of a language **L** are mapped onto a "world" **W**. The main aim is to determine truth conditions for sentences in **L** against **W**. Extensional semantics is rooted in Tarski's model theory for first order logic, where sentences from a language get their meaning via a correspondence to a model assumed to be a representation of the world: meaning is independent of how people understand it;
  - o   Intentional: in intentional semantics the language **L** is mapped onto a set of possible worlds, and the aim continues to be that of providing truth conditions for sentences in **L**;
- Cognitive semantics: in cognitive semantics the meanings of sentences are "mental", and linguistic expressions are mapped onto cognitive structures. According to Gärdenfors [5]: (i) meaning is a conceptualisation in a cognitive model and is independent of truth; (ii) cognitive models are mainly

perceptual; (iii) semantic elements are based on spatial and topological objects, and are not symbols; (iv) cognitive models are image schematic and not propositional; (v) semantics is primary to syntax; (vi) concepts show prototype effects.

In order to analyse the semantics issue in a broader context we need to shift our focus to developments in the field of cognitive science. A critical review of cognitive science evolution can be found, for example, in [6][7][8][9][10][11].

Cognitive Sciences is an interdisciplinary field of investigation, with ideas coming from several disciplines such as philosophy, psychology, neurosciences, linguistics, computer science, anthropology, biology, and physics. The main aim of cognitive sciences is trying to answer questions such as *"What is reason? How do we make sense of our experience? What is a conceptual system and how is organised? Do all people use the same conceptual system?"* [12, xi].

Two main different approaches try to answer these questions in different ways. The traditional approach claims that reasoning/cognition is essentially a form of information processing oriented to problem solving. It comes in two flavours: cognitivism, which sees the human brain as a deterministic machine manipulating symbols in an algorithmic way; connectionism, which uses a sub-symbolic representation and considers cognition as emergent from a network of atomic components (Artificial Neural Networks).

The new approach is characterised by the so-called embodied-embedded mind hypothesis and its variants and extensions, such as situated cognition, and enactivism. Two terms are borrowed from [12] to indicate the two approaches; objectivism for the traditional approach, and experiential realism for the new approach.

2.1 Objectivism

Objectivism assumes that reason and cognition consist of symbols manipulation, where symbols get meaning through a correspondence to the real world (or possible worlds) objectively defined and independent of any interaction with human beings: incidentally this means that cognition is substantially context-free. Since the approach involves computation, it is also known as computationalism [11][5].

The objectivist approach is rooted in the logical positivism wave of analytical philosophy as formalised at the beginning of the 20th century by the Vienna Circle. The assumption is that scientific reasoning is based on observational data derived from experiments: new knowledge is acquired from data through logically valid inferences. Only hypothesis grounded in first-order logic with model-theoretic interpretations – or some equivalent formalism – have a scientific validity.

Objectivism is also reductionist since it assumes that a system can be totally analysed and defined in terms of its components, in a kind of divide et impera process. The main fallacy of the reductionist hypothesis is to give for granted the reversibility of the process, but the hypothesis is not necessarily constructionist: *"... the more the elementary particle physicists tell us about nature of the fundamental laws, the less relevance they seem to have [...] to the rest of science. [...] The behaviour of large and complex aggregates of elementary particles [...] is not to be understood in terms of a simple extrapolation of the properties of few particles. [...] at each level of complexity entirely new properties appear ..."* [13,393].

We may summarise the fundamental views of objectivism/realism/reductionism as follows [12]:

- the mind can be considered as a computer (a Turing machine) manipulating symbols through algorithmic computation based on first-order predicate calculus with a standard model-theoretic interpretation;
- symbols get their meaning in relation to "things" in the real world, thus they are internal representations of an external objective reality independent of human being;
- thought is context-free and disembodied;
- categorisation is the way we make sense of experience and categories are defined via sharing necessary and sufficient memberships properties;
- category symbols are grounded (get their meaning) in categories existing in the world independent of human being.

Dreyfus [9] has strongly criticised the computationalism hypothesis; his criticism is inspired by the heideggerian criticism to the reductionist position of computationalism. According to Heidegger cognition is the result of our experience in *being-in-the-world*, and is grounded in our disposition to react in a flexible way as required by a specific context [7].

Guided by this idea, Dreyfus [9] claims that the representation of significance and relevance is the main problem of computationalism: assuming that a computer stores facts about the world, how can it manage to know which facts are relevant in any given situation?

A version of the relevance problem is the well known frame problem [14][15], i.e. the problem for a computer, running a representation of the world, in managing world changes: which changes are relevant for the new situation? Which have to be retained, since relevant? How to determine what is relevant and what is not? The frame problem may be considered as a manifestation of symptoms of the symbol grounding problem. Harnad [16] questions the claim of computationalism that semantic interpretation of a formal symbolic system is intrinsic to the system itself; instead, he claims that meaningless symbols, manipulated on the basis of their shape, are grounded in anything but other meaningless symbols. Imagine we have a calculator and type `2+2=4`: it is undoubted that this makes sense, but it makes sense in our head and not in the calculator.

Furthermore, a symbolic system is vulnerable to the Searle's Chinese Room argument [17], discussed in [18] as a criticism to the computationalism position according to which an appropriately programmed computer is a mind and has cognitive states.

Another questioned point is related to the traditional view of categories: on the objectivist view a category is defined as a set of "things" that share certain properties, which are necessary and sufficient conditions for defining the category itself. Implications of this position are: (i) members of a category are all equivalent, there is not a better example; (ii) categories are independent of any peculiarity of people doing the categorisation; (iii) new categories are derived through the composition of existing categories on a set-theoretic base.

According to Rosch [19] most categories do not have clear-cut boundaries and exhibit a prototype effect, i.e. some members are better examples of a category than others ("apple" is a better example of the category "fruit" than "fig"). Rosch refers to a perceived world, rather than a metaphysical one without a knower: an object is put in a category on the basis of a *similarity judgement* to the category prototype as perceived by a knower. This means that human capacities to perceive, to form mental images, to organise "things" play their role in categorisation; categories are culture-dependent conventions shared by a given group of people, and become accepted at global level through a communicative process [11][5].

As a first alternative approach to computationalism, connectionism is based on the assumption that we need to simulate the brain structure and functioning in order to understand cognition. Connectionism claims that cognition is the result of the emergence of global states from a network of simple connected components: the focus is primarily on learning, rather than on problem solving. For connectionism, as for computationalism, cognition remains basically a form of information processing: both approaches lack of embodiment and autonomy [18].

2.2 Experiential Realism

Different studies on anthropology, linguistics, psychology shows result in conflict with the objectivist view of the mind; the evidence suggests a different view of human cognition, whose characteristics are briefly summarized:

- Mind is embodied, meaning that our cognitive system is determined by our body. Our thoughts are shaped by our body, by our perceptual system, by our activity and experience in the world: this process is of a physical and social character [12];
- Thought is imaginative, and employs metaphors, metonymies and image schemas [12];
- Thought has gestalt properties, i.e. the way our brain operates is holistic, parallel, and analogue with self-organising tendencies, thus it is not atomistic [12];
- Cognitive models are mainly image-schematic and not propositional [5];
- Concepts show prototype effects [19][5];
- Meaning is a conceptual structure in a cognitive system [5].

Embodied cognition claims that cognitive processes emerge from real-time, goal-directed interactions between agents and their environment.

Experiential realism and the embodied hypothesis root their basis in the heideggerian philosophy. In *Being and Time* [20] Heidegger claims that the world is experienced as a significant whole and cognition is grounded in our skilful disposition to respond in a flexible and appropriate way to the significance of the contextual situation. The world is made up of possibilities for action that require appropriate responses. Things in the world are not experienced in terms of entities with functional characteristics; rather our experience when pressed into possibilities deals directly responding to a "what-for": thus, a hammer is "for" hammering and our action of hammering discovers the readiness-to-hand of the hammer itself. The readiness-to-hand is not a fixed functionality or characteristic encountered in a specific situation; rather it is experienced as a solicitation that requires a flexible response to the significance of a specific context [9]. This is similar to what Gibson would call "affordances" [21]. Affordance is what matter when we are confronting an environment; we experience entities of the environment that solicit us to act in a skilful way, rather than their physical features, which do not influence our action directly.

The notion of "image schemas" has been jointly introduced by Lakoff and Johnson as a fundamental pillar of experiential realism [22]. Image schemas are recurring and dynamic patterns of out perceptual interactions with the world that give coherence to our experience; they are pre-conceptual structures directly meaningful since they are grounded in our bodily experience, and have an inherent spatial structure constructed from basic topological and geometrical structures, i.e. *"container"*, *"source-path-goal"*, *"link"* [5]. Metaphors and metonymies are considered as cognitive operations that transform image schemas from a source to a target mental space. Fauconnier and Turner call this process "conceptual blending" [23]. Since image schemas are conceptual structures, they pertain to a particular individual: the question is how individual mental spaces become shared conventions [24]. Recent studies demonstrate that conventions emerge out of a communicative process between agents [25][26][27].

As Gärdenfors [24] puts it, semantics, thus meaning, is a "meeting of mind" where a communicative interaction enables to reach a semantic equilibrium.

2.3 Enactivism

Several authors [7][9][28][29][30] argue that paradoxically this meeting of mind is what is actually missing in empirical and theoretical investigation of the embodied hypothesis, where the focus is rather on agent's individual cognitive mechanisms as a form of closed sensorimotor feedback loops.

Enactivism is an attempt to move embodied practices beyond their current focus. The term enactivism was first used by Maturana, Varela, Thomson, and Rosch to name their theories and is closely related to experiential realism; it is not a radically new idea, rather it is a synthesis of different ideas and approaches [31]. Enactivism is characterised by five main ideas:

- Autonomy: cognising organisms are autonomous by virtue of their self-generated identity. A system whose identity is specified by a designer cannot exhibit autonomy since it can only "obey" to rules imposed in the design. Autonomous agency emphasises the role of the cogniser in organising its sensorimotor loops and determining the rules of the "game" being played;
- Sense-making: in our being-in-the-world we try to preserve our self-generated identity through interactions and exchanges with the environment which are significant for us. We actively participate in the creation of meaning via our action, rather than passively receive stimulus from the environment and create internal "images" of it. De Jaegher [30] further extends the notion of sense-making into the realm of social cognition: participatory sense-making emerges in a social situation where the active coupling of an agent is with another agent. Each single agent is engaged in its own individual sense-making, but when different agents need to interact, social meaning emerges as the result of the modification and mutual attunement of agents' individual sense-making. This is what Barsalou [32] calls social-embodiment;

- Emergence: the notions of autonomy and sense-making invoke emergence. Autonomy is not a property of something, but the result of a new identity that emerges out of dynamical processes;
- Embodiment: cognition is embodied action, temporally and spatially embedded. Reasoning, problem solving, and mental images manipulation depend on bodily structures;
- Experience: experience is a skilful aspect of embodied activity. As we progress from beginners to experts our performance improves, but experience also changes.

The following table is a short synopsis of the different approaches to cognition:

Table 1. Synopsys of different approaches to cognition (based on [33])

	Computationalism	Connectionism	Embodiment/ Enactivism
Metaphor for the mind	Mind as computer (Turing machine)	Mind as parallel distributed network	Mind inseparable from experience and world
Metaphor for cognition	Rule-based manipulation of symbols	Emergence of global states in a network of simple components	Ongoing interaction with the world and with other agents
The world	Separate and objective. Re-presentable via symbols	Separate and objective Re-presentable via patterns on network activation	Engaged Presentable through action
Mind/body	Separable	Separable	Inseparable

3 Dealing with Semantics in Information Systems

In the domain of distributed information systems the role of semantics for the automatic/semi-automatic exploitation of distributed resources is particularly emphasised. This process requires semantic interoperability, i.e. the capability of an information system to understand the semantic of a user request against that of an information source and mediate among them.

But how can semantics be specified? Uschold [34] proposes the following classification: (i) implicit semantics; (ii) informally expressed semantics; (iii) formally expressed semantics for human consumption; (iv) formally expressed semantics for machine processing. In [35] the following classification is proposed:

- Implicit semantics: is the semantic implicit in patterns in data and not explicitly represented, i.e. co-occurrence of documents or terms in clusters, hyperlinked documents.
- Formal semantics in the form of ontologies: in order to be machine readable and processable, semantics need to be represented in some sort of formalism;
- Powerful (soft) semantics: implies the use of fuzzy or probabilistic mechanisms to overcome the rigid interpretations of set-based formalisms, and enables to represent degrees of memberships and certainty.

In an environment of distributed, heterogeneous data sources and information systems, semantic interoperability refers to the ability of systems to exchange data and software functionalities in a meaningful way; semantic heterogeneity, i.e. naming and conceptual conflicts arises when there is no agreement on the meaning of the same data and/or software functionality.

Explicit and formal semantic is seen as a solution to the problem, and this has motivated several authors to apply formal ontologies [36]. Current practices, thus, rely on ontologies creation and automated resources annotation, coupled with appropriate computational approaches, such as reasoning and query processing, for concept matching among different ontologies and against user queries.

Notwithstanding ontologies are seen as a solution to semantic heterogeneity, the irony is that a clear understanding of ontology itself is far to be achieved [37], and this understanding varies across disciplines.

As philosophical discipline Ontology (with a capital "o") is the study of the *"being qua being"* [38], i.e. the explanation of the reality via concepts, relations, and rules; the term ontology (with a lowercase "o") in the philosophical sense refers to a specific system of categories accounting for a specific idea of the world; in computer science an ontology refers to *"An engineering artifact, constituted by a specific vocabulary used to describe a certain reality, plus a set of explicit assumptions regarding the intended meaning of the vocabulary words"* [38,4].

Ontologies enable to capture in an explicit and formal way the semantics of information sources. In a distributed environment such as the Web, resources are distributed and there is often the need to integrate different information in order to satisfy a user request. Semantic integration of information relies, currently, on ontologies integration: the process requires the identification of concepts similarity between ontologies and against user requests.

There are different ways of employing ontologies for information integration; Wache [39] identifies three framework architectures:

- Single ontology approach: all information sources are related to one common global (top-level) ontology. The approach assumes that all information sources have nearly the same conceptualisation;
- Multiple ontologies approach: each information source has its own ontology;
- Hybrid approach; hybrid approaches try to overcome the drawbacks of the two previous approaches. Each information source is described via its own ontology, but all source ontologies are built from the same global (top-level) ontology.

Semantic similarity measurements play a crucial role in this process, since they provide mechanisms for comparing concepts from different ontologies, and are, thus, the basis of semantic interoperability (a survey of different approaches to measuring similarity is provided in [40]).

Since different ontologies may commit to different conceptualizations and may be implemented with different formalisms, inconsistency is inevitable. Ontology mismatches may be classified in two broad categories [41]:

- Conceptualisation mismatches: are inconsistencies between conceptualisations of a domain, which may differ in terms of ontological concepts or in the way these concepts are related (i.e. in a subsumption hierarchy);
- Explication mismatches: are related to the way the conceptualisation is specified, and occur when two ontologies have different definitions, but their terms, definiens, and concepts are the same.

The information integration process would be straightforward, at a certain degree, if all ontologies would be similar in terms of vocabulary, intended meaning, background assumptions, and logical formalism, but in a distributed environment this situation is hard, if not impossible, to achieve since different users have different preferences and assumptions tailored to their specific requirements in specific domains.

Notwithstanding the efforts to establish standards for ontology languages and basic top-level ontologies, there are still different approaches and heterogeneity between ontologies is inevitable [42].

Ontology approach to semantics is also receiving more foundational criticisms. Gärdenfors [43] advocates, for example, that this approach is not very semantic; at the best it is ontological. Since it continues to build entirely on the symbolic methodology, it suffers from the symbol grounding problem; the question is how expressions in ontology languages may get any meaning beyond the formal language itself: ontologies are not grounded.

Another difficulty with ontologies is that they are decontextualised and decontextualise experience; instead we claim that semantics reconciliation depends on contextual human sense-making. Ontologies are forms of a priori agreements on a shared conceptualisation of a domain of interest, but meaning is an emergent feature arising context-dependently in action and acquired via participatory sense-making of socially coupled agents, rather than defined as symbolic rules [29][30][44][45].

The static nature of ontologies is problematic as long as we consider the temporal extent of the knowledge. The original community that committed to a certain conceptualisation of a domain may evolve as long as new members enter or old members leave it and the commitment changes: this means that a new consensus may arise and invalidate the original ontology. Therefore, the use of ontologies is insufficient in a dynamic situation, where all interpretations may not be anticipated and on-the-fly integration may be needed [46].

Several authors have proposed emergent semantics [47] as a solution; emergent semantics envisions a community of self-organising, autonomous agents interacting in a dynamic environment and negotiating meaning as required for cooperation and communication: this means that meaning emerges in context, but context itself is an emergent property, a feature of interaction of a community of practice [45]. Emergent semantics is dynamic and self-referential, as a result of a self-organisation process; this requires some autonomous behaviour.

Collaborative tagging is a new paradigm of the web, where users are enabled to manage, share and browse collection of resources and to describe them with semantically meaningful freely chosen keywords (tags). These tags cannot even be considered as vocabularies, since there is no fixed set of tags nor explicit agreement on their use. Nevertheless, this set of unstructured, not explicitly coordinated tags evolves and leads to the emergence of a loose categorisation system (folksonomy) shared and used by a community of practice [48]. Collaborative tagging falls within the scope of semiotic dynamics defined as "*... the process whereby groups of people or artificial agents collectively invent and negotiate shared semiotic dynamics, which they use for communication or information integration*" [25,32]. Semiotic dynamics builds on different AI techniques, borrowing also ideas from the embodied hypothesis: the focus, however, is on social, collective, dynamic sense-making. Computer simulations [26][27] have demonstrated that a population of embodied agents can self-organise a semiotic system.

4 Semantics and Geographic Information

Traditionally GIScience has relied on an objectivistic approach to knowledge creation [49]: this view assumes that GISystems represent the "real world" as it is independently of human cognition and perception of it [50]. The focus, therefore, has been ontological in nature more than epistemological; in determining geo-spatial ontologies, the question of "what exists" has gained much attention versus the question of "how what exists is identified and defined [37].

Starting from early 1990s, however, several researchers have focused their attention on the epistemological aspects of GIS, accounting for human cognition and perception. These authors borrow ideas from the experiential realism and the epistemological model introduced by [12], arguing that cognition structures the perception and representation of reality: their work builds on image schemata, conceptual blending, conceptual spaces, and affordances.

Semantic issues have always been a key concern in GIS, since semantic interoperability plays a crucial role for the sharing and integration of geographic information [3]. The use of ontologies is the most applied means to support semantic interoperability, and ontology has been recognized as a major research theme in GIScience [51]. Two main approaches to ontology in GIS may be individuated:

- Philosophical approach: deals with top-level ontologies for the geographic domain, and takes an objectivistic view, i.e. reality as objectively existent independent of human cognition and perception. Some researchers highlight some issues, e.g. vagueness as well as cultural and subjective discrepancies that are difficult to solve: Mark [52] has shown that people from different places and cultures use different categories for geographic features;
- Knowledge engineering approach: deals with ontologies as application-specific and purpose-driven engineering artifacts.

Frank [53] suggests that an ontology for GIS should be built as a coordinated set of tiers of ontologies, allowing different ontological approaches to be integrated in a unified system constituted of the following tiers: (i) Tier 0 – human-independent reality; (ii) Tier 1 – observation of the physical world; (iii) Tier 2 – objects with properties; (iv) Tier 3 – social reality; (v) Tier 4 – subjective knowledge. Frank's five-tier architecture has a lot of commonalities with the four-universes paradigm [54] applied to geographic information by [55]. Inspired by this last work, and based on a realistic view of the world, Fonseca [56], has introduced a five-universes paradigm: (i) physical universe; (ii) cognitive universe; (iii) logical universe; (iv) representation universe; (v) implementation universe. Representing the reality involves the conceptualisation of elements of the physical world via a collective agreement of a community sharing common perceptions; concepts are defined within a community of experts and are organised in a logical framework (ontologies). The representation universe deals with the symbolic description of elements in the logical universe; the implementation universe deals with computational issues.

From a knowledge engineering point of view, ontologies have been applied for (i) geographic information discovery and retrieval [58]; (ii) geographic information integration [39][1]; (iii) GISystems [59][60].

Application-specific, task-oriented, purpose-driven ontologies are aimed at information systems deployment: these ontologies emerge from requirements and contain knowledge limited to a specific area of application.

The main issue with engineering ontologies is grounding: according to the ontology hierarchy proposed in [36], domain and task ontologies are grounded in top-level ontologies. The question is how these top-level ontologies are grounded themselves: this infinite regress should end at some point to an ontology, but this is objectivism/reductionism and we are not in sympathy with this approach. Ontology-based approach to semantics is not very semantic, at the best it is ontological [43].

Borrowing ideas from embodied cognition and cognitive semantics, some authors propose image schemas as grounding mechanism and conceptual spaces as a new representation paradigm. Kuhn [57], for example, proposes image schemas for grounding Semantic Reference Systems. In analogy with spatial reference systems, semantic reference systems are composed of a semantic reference frame and a semantic datum: as the geometric component of geographic information refers to spatial reference systems, the thematic component refers to semantic reference systems. A semantic reference frame acts like a coordinate system as a framework to which terms can refer to get meaning: this reference frame is a formally defined top-level ontology. As a datum in spatial reference systems anchors the geometry model to the real world, a semantic datum grounds the terms of a semantic reference frame using image schemas as grounding mechanism.

Image schemas have been introduced in the geospatial domain by [61], have received formal specifications in [62] and [63], and have been applied, for example, to way finding in [64].

However, the concept of image schemas remain controversial and ambiguous, and disagreements exist in image schemas research between two broadly contrasting approaches: the first approach, located in the context of cognitive psychology and neurosciences, relies on "strong neural embodiment" and sees image schemas as expression of universal principles; the second approach, located in the context of anthropology and cognitive-cultural linguistics, has a more relativistic view of image schema and emphasizes that cognition is situated in socio-culturally determined context [22]. Cross-linguistic and cross-cultural studies [65] show that image schemas, while operating in many languages, are not universal, instead they are culturally situated [66]. On the other hand, the tendency to make universalistic statements is based on few languages, above all English [67].

Some major drawbacks exist in the ontology approach to semantics in terms of dynamicity and context. Ontologies are a priori agreements on a shared conceptualisation of a domain of interest, a form of pre-given, decontextualised knowledge; this is problematic as long as we consider the temporal extent on the knowledge.

There is an empirical evidence of the fact that human manipulation of concepts is facilitated by considering them in relevant context [32]. Current approaches to context, also in the GI field [68][69] are representational, i.e. they assume that context is stable, delimited information that can be known and encoded in just another information layer or another ontology in an information system.

Meaning, instead, is an emergent feature arising context-dependently in action and acquired via participatory sense-making of socially coupled agents, rather than as symbolic rules: context itself is dynamically emergent and not stable [29][30][45].

This claims for non-representational modelling formalisms.

5 Conclusions and Future Work

This work has dealt with semantics and how it is addressed in distributed information system and in the GI domain. Drawbacks of current practices, mainly based on ontologies, have been highlighted. Ontology-based approach to semantics is problematic in terms of dynamicity and context, since ontologies, being forms of a priori agreements, are decontextualised.

Instead we start from the assumption that meaning and context are dynamically emergent from activity and interaction, determined in the moment and in the doing [45]: there is no pre-given knowledge and no fixed properties that can a priori determine what is relevant. Representational theories, i.e. ontology-based approach to semantics, are unable to deal with these issues, and new non-representational formalisms are required.

The State-Context-Property (SCOP) formalism seems promising in this sense. A detailed description of the formalism can be found in [70][71][72][73]: here a brief description is provided.

SCOP is a non-representational formalism, based on a generalisation of mathematics developed for quantum mechanics, that provides a means for dealing with context, concept combination and similarity judgments, toward a contextual theory of concepts.

At conceptual level SCOP falls within the enactive approach to cognition: the main ideas behind it may be summarised as follows:

- Concepts as participatory (ecological view): concepts and categories are participating parts of the mind-world whole;
- Contextuality: context influences the meaning of concepts and needs to be given a place in the description of concepts;
- Concept combination: concept conjunctions exhibit emergent features that traditional theories (representational), are not able to "predict";
- Similarity: similarity judgments are context-dependent.

The description of a concept in SCOP consists of five elements:

- A set of states the concept may assume;
- A set of relevant contexts;
- A set of relevant properties;

- A function describing the applicability of certain properties in a specific state and context;
- A function describing the probability for one state to collapse into another state under the influence of a specific context.

For any concept we may have a number (infinite) of "possible" states, and each state is characterised by a unique typicality for instances and properties. A concept that is not influenced by a specific context is said to be in an *eigenstate*[1] for that context, otherwise it is said to be a *potential state* (superimposition state). A potential state may collapse to another state under the influence of a specific context: for example consider the concept **Tree** that under the context "**Desert island**" might collapse to state **Palm Tree**.

The properties of a concept are themselves potential: they are not definite except in a specific context. If a concept is in an *eigenstate* for a given context, then the latter just detects what the concept is *in acto* [73], but if the concept is in a superposition state, then the context change this state: properties of the concepts may change under the influence of the context from actual to potential and vice versa. Therefore each state of a concept is an *eigenstate* or a superposition state: if it is an *eigenstate* the properties are actual, otherwise most of the properties are potential: a context has the "power" to change a superposition state in an *eigenstate*.

The various states of a concept can be described as a *Hilbert Space*, while the conjunction of two concepts can be modelled as an *entanglement*[2] through the tensor product of the two *Hilbert Spaces* describing those concepts.

Similarity judgments between two concepts are only possible if their respective properties are compatible, i.e. they refer to the same context (refer to [72] for a detailed description of context-sensitive measure of conceptual distance).

Future work will deal with an in depth analysis of the formalism in order to investigate its applicability to GI domain, possibly toward practical applications.

References

1. Hakimpour, F., Geppert, A.: Resolving Semantic Heterogeneity in Schema Integration: an Ontology Based Approach. In: FOIS 2001, pp. 297–308 (2001)
2. Bishr, Y.: Overcoming the semantic and other barriers in GIS interoperability. International Journal of Geographical Information Science 12(4), 299–314 (1998)
3. Harvey, F., Kuhn, W., Pundt, H., Bishr, Y., Riedmann, C.: Semantic Interoperability: a central issue for sharing geographic information. The Annals of Regional Science 33, 213–232 (1999)
4. Kuhn, W.: Geospatial Semantics: Why, of What, and How? In: Spaccapietra, S., Zimányi, E. (eds.) Journal on Data Semantics III. LNCS, vol. 3534, pp. 1–24. Springer, Heidelberg (2005)
5. Gärdenfors, P.: Conceptual Spaces: The Geometry of Thought. The MIT Press, Cambridge (2000)

---

[1] An eigenstate is a state associated with definite properties.
[2] Entanglement means that two states are linked together and it is not possible to describe one state without mention of its counterpart.

6. Anderson, M.L.: Embodied Cognition: a field guide. Artificial Intelligence 149, 91–130 (2003)
7. Froese, T.: On the Role of AI in the Ongoing Paradigm Shift within the Cognitive Sciences. In: Lungarella, M., Iida, F., Bongard, J.C., Pfeifer, R. (eds.) 50 Years of Aritficial Intelligence. LNCS (LNAI), vol. 4850, pp. 63–75. Springer, Heidelberg (2007)
8. Steels, L.: Fifty Years of AI: From Symbols to Embodiment - and Back. In: Lungarella, M., Iida, F., Bongard, J.C., Pfeifer, R. (eds.) 50 Years of Aritficial Intelligence. LNCS (LNAI), vol. 4850, pp. 18–28. Springer, Heidelberg (2007)
9. Dreyfus, H.L., Why Heideggerian, A.I.: Why Heideggerian AI failed and how fixing it would require making it more Heideggerian. Artificial Intelligence 171(18), 1137–1160 (2007)
10. Gärdenfors, P.: Cognitive Science: from computers to anthills as models of human thought (1999)
11. Licata, I.: La logica aperta della mente. Codice Edizioni (2008)
12. Lakoff, G.: Women, Fire, and Dangerous Things. The University of Chicago Press, Chicago (1987)
13. Anderson, P.W.: More Is Different. Science 177(4047), 393–396 (1972)
14. Dennet, D.C.: Cognitive Wheels: The Frame Problem of Artificial Intelligence. In: Hookaway, C. (ed.) Minds, Machines and Evolution, Cambridge University (reprinted in Pylyshyn 1987)
15. McCarthy, J., Hayes, P.: Some philosophical problems from the standpoint of artificial intelligence. In: Meltzer, B., Michie, D. (eds.) Machine Intelligence, vol. 4
16. Harnad, S.: The Symbol Grounding Problem. Physica D 42, 335–346 (1990)
17. Harnad, S.: Computation Is Just Interpretable Symbol Manipulation: Cognition Isn't. Minds and Machines 4, 379–390 (1994)
18. Searle, J.R.: Minds, Brains, and Programs. Behavioral and Brain Sciences 3(3), 417–457 (1980)
19. Rosch, E.: Principles of categorization. In: Rosch, E., Lloyd, B.B. (eds.) Cognition and categorization. Erlbaum, Hillsdale
20. Heidegger, M.: Essere e Tempo. Longanesi (2005), Italian translation of Sein und Zeit (1927)
21. Gibson, J.J.: The theory of affordances. In: Shaw, R., Bransford, J. (eds.) Perceiving, Acting and Knowing, pp. 127–143. Erlbaum, Hillsdale (1977)
22. Hampe, B.: Image Schemas in cognitive linguistics: Introduction. In: Dirven, R., Langacker, R., Taylor, J. (eds.) From perception to meaning: image schemas in cognitive linguistics. Cognitive Linguistic Research, vol. 29, pp. 1–12 (2005)
23. Fauconnier, G., Turner, M.: Conceptual Projection and Middle Spaces. Report 9401 Department of Cognitive Science, University of San Diego (1994)
24. Gärdenfors, P., Warglien, M.: Cooperation, Conceptual Spaces and the Evolution of Semantics. In: Vogt, P., Sugita, Y., Tuci, E., Nehaniv, C.L. (eds.) EELC 2006. LNCS (LNAI), vol. 4211, pp. 16–30. Springer, Heidelberg (2006)
25. Steels, L.: Semiotic dynamics for embodied agents. IEEE Intelligent Systems 21(3), 32–38 (2006)
26. Loula, A., Gudwin, R., El-Hani, N.C., Queiroz, J.: The emergence of symbol-based communication in a complex system of artificial creatures. In: Proceedings KIMAS 2005: Modeling, Evolution and Engineering, pp. 279–284 (2005)
27. Puglisi, A., Baronchelli, A., Loreto, V.: Cultural route to the emergence of linguistic categories. PNAS 105(23), 7936–7940 (2008)

28. Di Paolo, E.A.: Organismically-inspired robotics: homeostatic adaptation and teleology beyond the closed sensorimotor loop. In: Murase, K., Asakura, T. (eds.) Dynamical Systems Approach to Embodiment and Sociality, pp. 19–42 (2003)
29. Di Paolo, E., Rohde, M., De Jaegher, H.: Horizons for the enactive mind: Values, social interaction and play. In: Stewart, J., Gapenne, O., Di Paolo, E. (eds.) Enaction: Towards a New Paradigm for Cognitive Science. MIT Press, MA
30. De Jaegher, H., Di Paolo, E.: Participatory sense-making: An enactive approach to social cognition. Phenomenology and the Cognitive Sciences 6(4), 485–507 (2007)
31. Maturana, H.R., Varela, F.J.: Autopoiesi e cognizione. La realizzazione del vivente. Marsilio (2001), Italian transalation of Autopoiesis and Cognition (1980)
32. Barsalou, L.W., Niedenthal, P.M., Barbey, A., Ruppert, J.: Social embodiment. In: Ross, B. (ed.) The Psychology of Learning and Motivation, vol. 43, pp. 43–92 (2003)
33. Varela, F.J., Thompson, E., Rosch, E.: The Embodied Mind: cognitive science and human experience. The MIT Press, Cambridge (1991)
34. Uschold, M.: Where Are the Semantics in the Semantic Web? AI Magazine 24(3), 25–36 (2003)
35. Sheth, A.P., Ramakrishnan, C., Thomas, C.: Semantics for the Semantic Web: The implicit, the Formal and the Powerful. International Journal on Semantic Web & Information Systems 1(1), 1–18 (2005)
36. Guarino, N.: Formal Ontology in Information Systems. In: Guarino, N. (ed.) Formal Ontology in Information Systems. Proceedings of FOIS 1998, pp. 3–15 (1998)
37. Agarwal, P.: Ontological considerations in GIScience. International Journal of Geographical Information Science 19, 501–536 (2005)
38. Guarino, N.: Formal Ontology, Conceptual Analysis and Knowledge Representation. International Journal of Human and Computer Studies 43(5/6), 625–640 (1995)
39. Wache, H., Vogele, T., Visser, U., Stuckenschmidt, H., Schuster, G., Neumann, H., Huber, S.: Ontology-based Integration of Information – A survey of existing approaches. In: Proceedings of IJCAI, pp. 108–117 (2001)
40. Goldstone, R.L., Son, J.Y.: Similarity. In: Holyoak, K.J., Morrison, R.G. (eds.) The Cambridge Handbook of Thinking and Reasoning, pp. 13–36. Cambridge University Press, Cambridge (2005)
41. Visser, P.R.S., Jones, D.M., Bench-capon, T.J.M., Shave, M.J.R.: An Analysis of Ontology Mismatches; Heterogeneity versus Interoperability. In: AAAI 1997 Spring Symposium on Ontological Engineering (1997)
42. Krötzsch, M., Hitzler, P., Ehrig, M., Sure, Y.: Category Theory in Ontology Research: Concrete Gain from an Abstract Approach. Technical Report, AIFB, University of Karlsruhe (2005)
43. Gärdenfors, P.: How to make the Semantic Web more semantic. In: Vieu, A.C., Varzi, L. (eds.) Formal Ontology in Information Systems, pp. 19–36. IOS Press, Amsterdam (2004)
44. Flender, C., Kitto, K., Bruza, P.: Beyond Ontology in Information Systems. QUT Technical report, FIT-TR-2008-05 (2008)
45. Dourish, P.: What We Talk About When We Talk About Context. Personal and Ubiquitous Computing 8(1), 19–30 (2004)
46. Ouksel, A.M.: In-context peer-to-peer information filtering on the web. SIGMOD Records 32(3), 65–70 (2003)
47. Aberer, K., Cudré-Mauroux, P., Ouksel, A.M., et al.: Emergent Semantics Principles and Issues. In: Lee, Y., Li, J., Whang, K.-Y., Lee, D. (eds.) DASFAA 2004. LNCS, vol. 2973, pp. 25–38. Springer, Heidelberg (2004)

48. Cattuto, C., Loreto, V., Pietronero, L.: Semiotic dynamics and Collaborative Tagging. PNAS 104(5), 1461–1464 (2007)
49. Schuurman, N.: Formalization matters: critical GIScience and ontology research. The Annals of the Association of American Geographers 96(4), 726–739 (2006)
50. Schuurman, N.: Reconciling Social Constructivism and Realism in GIS. ACME: An International E-Journal for Critical Geographies 1(1), 75–90 (2002)
51. Mark, D.M., Egenhofer, M., Hirtle, S., Smith, B.: UCGIS Emerging Research Theme: Ontological Foundations for Geographic Information Science (2000)
52. Mark, D.M., Turk, A.: Landscape categories in Yindjibarndi: Ontology, environment, and language. In: Kuhn, W., Worboys, M.F., Timpf, S. (eds.) COSIT 2003. LNCS, vol. 2825, pp. 28–45. Springer, Heidelberg (2003)
53. Frank, A.U.: Tiers on ontology and consistency constraints in geographical information systems. International Journal of Geographical Information Science 15(7), 667–678 (2001)
54. Gomes, J., Velho, L.: Abstraction Paradigms for Computer Graphics. The Visual Computer 11(5), 227–239 (1998)
55. Camara, G., Monteiro, A.M.V., Paiva, J.A., Gomes, J., Velho, L.: Towards a unified framework for geographical data models. In: Figueiredo, L. (ed.) Proceedings of GeoInfo 2000 Workshop Brasileiro de Geoinformatica, pp. 37–44 (2000)
56. Fonseca, F.T., Egenhofer, M.J.: Semantic granularity in ontology-driven geographic information systems. Annals of Mathematics and Artificial Intelligence – Special issue on Spatial and Temporal granularity 36(1/2), 121–151 (2002)
57. Kuhn, W.: Semantic Reference System. International Journal of Geographical Information Science 17, 405–409 (2003)
58. Klien, E., Einspanier, U., Lutz, M., Hubner, S.: An architecture for ontology-based discovery and retrieval of georgaphic information. In: Proceedings of AGILE 2004, pp. 179–188 (2004)
59. Fonseca, F.T., Egenhofer, M.J., Agouris, P., Camara, G.: Using ontologies for integrated geographic information systems. Transactions in GIS 6, 231–257 (2002)
60. Camara, G., Monteiro, A.M.V., Paiva, J.A., Souza, R.C.M.: Action-Driven Ontologies of the Geographic Space: Beyond the Field-Object Debate. In: GIScience 2000: The First International Conference on Geographic Information Science (2000)
61. Mark, D.M.: Cognitive Image-Schemata for Geographic Information: relations to user views and GIS interfaces. In: Proceedings of GIS/LIS 1989, vol. 2, pp. 551–560 (1989)
62. Rodriguez, A., Egenhofer, M.J.: Image-Schemata-Based Spatial Inferences: The Container-Surface Algebra. In: Frank, A.U. (ed.) COSIT 1997. LNCS, vol. 1329, pp. 35–52. Springer, Heidelberg (1997)
63. Frank, A.U., Raubal, M.: Formal specification of image schemata – a step towards interoperability in geographic information systems. Spatial Cognition and Computation 1, 67–101 (1999)
64. Raubal, M., Egenhofer, M.: Comparing the complexity of wayfinding tasks in built environments. Environment & Planning B 25(6), 895–913 (1998)
65. Choi, S., McDonough, L., Bowerman, M., Mandler, J.: Early sensitivity to language-specific spatial terms in English and Korean. Cognitive Development 14, 241–268 (1999)
66. Correa-Beningfield, M., Kristiansen, G., Navarro-Fernando, I., Candeloise, C.: Image schemas vs "Complex Promitives" in cross-cultural spatial cognition. In: Dirven, R., Langacker, R., Taylor, J. (eds.) From perception to meaning: image schemas in cognitive linguistics. Cognitive Linguistic Research, vol. 29, pp. 343–366 (2005)
67. Zlatev, J.: Spatial Semantics. In: Cuyckens, H., Geeraerts, D. (eds.) Handbook of Cognitive Linguistics, ch. 2

68. Rodriguez, A., Egenhofer, M.J., Rugg, R.: Assessing Semantic Similarity amont geospatial entity class definitions. In: Včkovski, A., Brassel, K.E., Schek, H.-J. (eds.) INTEROP 1999. LNCS, vol. 1580, pp. 189–202. Springer, Heidelberg (1999)
69. Keßler, C., Raubal, M., Janowicz, K.: The Effect of Context on Semantic Similarity Measurement. In: Meersman, R., Tari, Z., Herrero, P. (eds.) OTM-WS 2007, Part II. LNCS, vol. 4806, pp. 1274–1284. Springer, Heidelberg (2007)
70. Aerts, D., Gabora, L.: A theory of concepts and their combination I; The structure of the sets of contexts and properties. Kybernetes 34(1), 167–191 (2005)
71. Aerts, D., Gabora, L.: A theory of concepts and their combination II; A Hilbert space representation. Kybernetes 34(1), 192–221 (2005)
72. Gabora, L., Aerts, D.: Contextualizing concepts using a mathematical generalization of the quantum formalism. Journal of Experimental and Theoretical Artificial Intelligence 14(4), 327–358
73. Gabora, L., Rosch, E., Aerts, D.: Toward an Ecological Theory of Concepts. Ecological Psychology 20(1), 84–116

Modelling Sea Surface Salinity from MODIS Satellite Data

Maged Marghany, Mazlan Hashim, and Arthur P. Cracknell

Institute of Geospatial Science and Technology (INSTEG)
Universiti Teknologi Malaysia
81310 UTM, Skudai, Johore Bahru, Malaysia
maged@utm.my
magedupm@hotmail.com

Abstract. In this study, we investigate the relative ability of least square algorithm to retrieve sea surface salinity (SSS) from MODIS satellite data. We also examine with comprehensive comparison of the root mean square of bias the difference between second polynomial order algorithm and least square algorithm. Both the least squares algorithm and second polynomial order algorithm are used to retrieve the sea surface salinity (SSS) from multi MODIS bands data. Thus, the basic linear model has been solved by using second polynomial order algorithm and least square estimators. The accuracy of this work has been examined using the root mean square of bias of sea surface salinity retrieved from MODIS satellite data and the in situ measurements that are collected along the east coast of Peninsular Malaysia by using hydrolab instrument. The study shows comprehensive relationship between least square method and in situ SSS measurements with high r^2 of 0.96 and RMS of bias value of ±0.37 psu. The second polynomial order algorithm, however, has lower performance as compared to least square algorithm. Thus, RMS of bias value of ± 7.34 psu has performed with second polynomial order algorithm. In conclusions, the least square algorithm can be used to retrieve SSS from MODIS satellite data.

Keywords: least square algorithm, second polynomial order algorithm, MODIS Satellite Data, Sea surface salinity.

1 Introduction

Remote sensing technology has been recognized as powerful tool for environmental dynamic studies. Ocean surface salinity is considered as major element in marine environment. In fact, the climate change, marine pollution and coastal hazardous are basically controlled by the dramatic changes in sea surface salinity (SSS) [2,5]. From an oceanographic viewpoint, salinity is important because together with temperature, it determines water density and thus is intimately linked to the horizontal circulation of the ocean. It also determines the depth to which water, cooled at the surface in winter, can sink. Through its effect on density, it partially controls the stability of the upper mixed layer of the ocean. This in turn has important physical and ecological consequences. Furthermore, it is one of the prime determinants of the environment in

D. Taniar et al. (Eds.): ICCSA 2010, Part I, LNCS 6016, pp. 545–556, 2010.
© Springer-Verlag Berlin Heidelberg 2010

which fish and other marine life live and modulates air-sea interaction including gas
and heat exchange [8]. The conventional method for ocean salinity measurements
that acquired by buoys and oceanographic or commercial ships, remain sparse and
irregular, with large parts of the global ocean never sampled. In addition, weather
conditions can be play tremendous role in achieving the collection of in situ measurements. In these circumstances, scientists have paid a great attention to utilize
satellite data for SSS retrieval [2-4,6,10]. Therefore, acquiring SSS from satellite
measurements would be greatly useful to oceanographers and climatologists. Radiometric accuracy and sensitivity depend on the position of the pixel in the field of view
[4]. In this context, standard mathematical algorithms are required. Previous empirical research provides conclusive evidence on utilizing mathematical algorithm such as
least square algorithm to acquire comprehensive and accurately pattern of sea surface
salinity (SSS) from different remote sensing sensor i.e. passive and active sensors
[11-14]. In this research, we are going to investigate this question that least square
algorithm on the basis of all- inclusive concept, would be a better measure of sea
surface salinity from MODIS satellite data.

2 Previous Research

Scientists have made use of the active passive microwave sensors for acquiring sea
surface salinity. Particularly, advances in microwave remote sensing enable precise
measurements of the brightness temperature of seawater at L-band (□1.4 GHz) to be
acquired over coastal regions from a light aircraft, whereas the Soil Moisture and
Ocean Salinity (SMOS) and Aquarius satellite missions are provided a similar capability over the deep global oceans [6,10]. Modern airborne L-band microwave radi-
ometers therefore, are sensitive enough to detect brightness temperature variations at
better than 0.5-K precision under operational conditions, at typical spatial resolutions
of 1 km, whereas satellite-borne systems are being designed to provide effective 0.1-
K precision, after data averaging, on spatial scales of about 100–300 km [2]. In fact,
scientists have found that SSS retrieval is function of brightness temperature variations. According to Ellison et al.,[4] the relationship between brightness temperature,
sea surface salinity (SSS), sea surface temperature, incidence angle, and antenna po-
larization for a flat calm sea can be obtained from the so-called "flat sea" empirical
emissivity model relationships. Indeed, The brightness temperature at the surface
brightness temperature is proportional to the sea surface temperature and the emissivity. Further, Sonia et al., [12] estimated SSS on a global scale, with a precision over
the open ocean of 0.2 practical salinity units (psu) in 200 × 200 km boxes on a ten-
day average. They, therefore, reported that the remotely sensed SSS should be appropriate for assimilation into ocean circulation models which is based on global ocean
data assimilation experiment. In the case of SMOS, this precision would achieve by
averaging numerous salinity retrievals, as every region of the global ocean can be
visited by SMOS at least once every three days. Generally, monitoring surface brightness temperatures, however, from L-band satellite radiometric measurements is particularly challenging because of their limited resolution (typically 30–100 km) and
L-band measurements over the coastal ocean are contaminated by the nearby land. In
fact, recent global simulations of L-band land brightness temperatures showed a range
of about 140 K to 300 K, compared to approximately 100 K for the ocean [6].

Researchers have found that dissolved salts, suspended substances have a major impacts on the electromagnetic radiation attenuation outside the visible spectra range [14]. In this context, the electromagnetic wavelength larger than 700 nm is increasingly absorbed whereas the wavelength less than 300 nm is scattered by non-absorbing particles such as zooplankton, suspended sediments and dissolved salts [1]. Recently, Ahn et al., [1] and Palacios et al., [13] have derived SSS using colored dissolved organic matter, (a_{CDOM}) from optical satellite data. Ahn et al., [1] have developed robust and proper regional algorithms from large in-situ measurements of apparent and inherent optical properties (i.e. remote sensing reflectance, R_{rs}, and absorption coefficient of colored dissolved organic matter, a_{CDOM}) to derive salinity using SeaWiFS images. Further, Palacios et al., [13] stated that light absorption by chromophoric dissolved organic matter (a_{CDOM}) is inversely proportional to salinity and linear because of conservative mixing of CDOM - rich terrestrial runoff with surrounding ocean water. In this context, Ahn et al., [1] established the robust algorithm based on the absorption coefficients of CDOM, in-situ measurements of salinity that made at 400 nm, 412 nm, 443 nm and 490 nm. Similarly, Palacios et al.,[13] developed   synthetic salinity algorithm simple linear (salinity versus a_{CDOM}) and multiple linear (salinity and temperature versus a_{CDOM}) algorithms were applied to MODIS 250 m resolution data layers of sea surface temperature and absorption by colored dissolved and detritus matter (a_{CDM}) estimated at 350 nm and 412 nm from the Garver - Siegel - Maritorena model version 1 algorithm. Ahn et al., [1] found that the CDOM absorption at 400 nm was better inversely correlated (r^2=0.86) with salinity than at 412 nm, 443 nm and 490 nm (r^2=0.85–0.66), and this correlation corresponded best with an exponential (r^2=0.98) rather than a linear function of salinity measured in a variety of water types from this and other regions. In this context, Palacios et al., [13] stated that light absorption by chromophoric dissolved organic matter (a_{CDOM}) is inversely proportional to salinity and linear because of conservative mixing of CDOM - rich terrestrial runoff with surrounding ocean water using MODIS satellite data.   The study of Palacios et al., [13] showed high correlation using MODIS during both downwelling (simple, β_1 = 0.95 and r^2 = 0.89; multiple, β_1 = 0.92 and r^2 = 0.89) and upwelling periods (simple, β_1 = 1.26 and r^2 = 0.85; multiple, β_1 = 1.10 and r^2 = 0.87) using the 412 nm data layer. Both studies of Ahn et al., [1] and Palacios et al., [13] have agreed that SSS can be derived using optical satellite data based on absorption coefficient of colored dissolved organic matter, a_{CDOM}.

3 Methodology

3.1 In Situ Measurements

The in situ measurement cruises are conducted in two phases: (i) September 2002 which is along the coastal waters of Kuala Terengganu and (ii) October 2003 which is in Phang coastal waters, Malaysia (Fig. 1). In doing so, more than 100 sampling locations are chosen (Fig. 1). The field cruises are conducted separately, area by area on the east coast of Peninsular Malaysia. In fact, it is major challenge to cover a large scale area over than 700 km^2 in short period using conventional techniques.   The hydrolab equipment is used to acquire vertical water salinity profiles (Fig. 2). Every field cruise has been conducted on 6 days in the east coast of Malaysia. For this study the in situ surface salinity (1 meter below sea surface) data are used. In fact, it is expected to have a higher correlation with MODIS reflectance data than middle and bottom salinity column measurements. These data are used to validate the sea surface salinity distributions that derived from MODIS data. In situ measurements are collected near real time of MODIS satellite data overpass. Twenty four sets of Aqua/MODIS level 1 B images are acquired during the in situ salinity measurements.

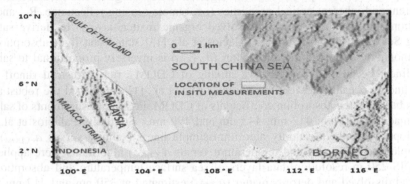

Fig. 1. Sampling Locations

Fig. 2. Hydrolab equipment is used in this study

3.2 Deriving Sea Surface Salinity Algorithm from MODIS Data

The relationship between in situ sea surface salinity (SSS) and radiance in different bands of MODIS can be described by the multiple regression as follows [9,14]

$$SSS = b_0 + b_1 I_1 + b_2 I_2 + b_3 I_3 + \ldots\ldots\ldots + b_7 I_7 + \varepsilon \qquad (1)$$

Equation 1 can be written as

$$SSS_i = b_0 + \sum_{i=1}^{k} b_i I_{ij} + \varepsilon_{ij} \qquad (2)$$

where SSS_i is the measured sea surface salinity, b_0 and b_i are constant coefficient of linear relationship between MODIS radiance data I within multi-channels i and in situ sea surface salinity, $k = 1,2,3,\ldots\ldots\ldots,7$ and ε is residual error of SSS estimated from selected MODIS bands. The unknown parameters in Eq.2, that are b_0 and b_i may be estimated by a general least square iterative algorithm. This procedures requires certain assumptions about the model error component ε. Stated simply, we assume that the errors are uncorrelated and their variance is σ_ε^2.

The least-square estimator of the b_i minimizes the sum of squares of the errors, say

$$S_E = \sum_{j=1}^{k} (SSS_i - b_0 - \sum_{i=1}^{k} b_i I_{ij})^2 = \sum_{j=1}^{k} \varepsilon_j^2 \tag{3}$$

It is necessary that the least squares estimators satisfy the equations given by the k first partial derivatives $\dfrac{\partial S_E}{\partial b_i} = 0$. Therefore, differentiating Eq. 3 with respect to b_i and equating the result to zero we obtain

$$k\hat{b}_1 + (\sum_{j=1}^{k} I_{2j})\hat{b}_2 + (\sum_{j=1}^{k} I_{3j})\hat{b}_3 + \ldots + (\sum_{j=1}^{k} I_{7j})\hat{b}_7 = \sum_{j=1}^{k} SSS_j$$

$$(\sum_{j=1}^{k} I_{2j})\hat{b}_1 + (\sum_{j=1}^{k} I^2{}_{2j})\hat{b}_2 + \ldots + (\sum_{j=1}^{k} I_{2j}I_{7j})\hat{b}_7 = \sum_{j=1}^{k} I_{2j}SSS$$

$$\ldots\ldots\ldots\ldots\ldots\ldots\ldots\ldots\ldots\ldots\ldots\ldots\ldots\ldots$$

$$(\sum_{j=1}^{k} I_{7j})\hat{b}_1 + (\sum_{j=1}^{k} I_{7j}I_{2j})\hat{b}_2 + \ldots + (\sum_{j=1}^{k} I^2{}_{7j})\hat{b}_7 = \sum_{j=1}^{k} I_7 SSS \tag{4}$$

The equations (4) are called the least-squares normal equations. The $\hat{b}_i$ found by solving the normal equations (4) are least-squares estimators of the parameters b_i. The only convenient way to express the solution to the normal equations is in matrix notation. Note that the normal equations (4) are just a $I \times I$ set of simultaneous linear equations in unknowns the parameter $\hat{b}_i$. They may be written in matrix notation as

$$I\hat{b}_i = g \tag{5}$$

where

$$I = \begin{vmatrix} n & \sum I_2 & \sum I_3 & \cdots & \sum I_7 \\ \sum I_2 & \sum I^2_2 & \sum I_2 I_3 & \cdots & \sum I_2 I_7 \\ \sum I_3 & \sum I_3 I_2 & I^2_3 & \cdots & \sum I_3 I_7 \\ \hline \sum I_7 & \sum I_7 I_2 & \sum I_7 I_3 & \cdots & \sum I^2_7 \end{vmatrix}$$

$$
\hat{b}_i = \begin{bmatrix} \hat{b}_1 \\ \hat{b}_2 \\ \vdots \\ \hat{b}_7 \end{bmatrix}
$$

and

$$
g = \begin{bmatrix} \sum SSS \\ \sum I_2 SSS \\ \vdots \\ \sum I_7 SSS \end{bmatrix}
$$

Thus, I is a 7 x 7 estimated matrix of MODIS radiance bands that used to estimate sea surface salinity, and $\hat{b}_i$ and g are both 7 x 1 column vectors. The solution to the least-squares normal equation is

$$
\hat{b}_i = I^{-1} g \tag{6}
$$

where I^{-1} denotes the inverse of the matrix I. Using equation 6 to express into equation 2, then, the sea surface salinity SSS is given as

$$
SSS_i = I_0^{-1} g_0 + \sum_{i=1}^{7} I_i^{-1} g_i I_i + \varepsilon \tag{7}
$$

Then, the empirical formula of SSS (psu) which is based on equations 6 and 7 is

$$
SSS \text{ (psu)} = 27.65 + 0.2\ I_1 - 21.11\ I_2 + 14.23\ I_3 + 62.12\ I_4 + 148.32\ I_5 +
$$
$$
1.22.03\ I_6 + -11.41\ I_7 + \varepsilon \tag{8}
$$

In this study, polynomial regression algorithm is also examined to retrieve SSS from MODIS satellite data. In this context, SSS is estimated using the multiple regression models in Eq. 1 can be also made up of powers several variables

$$
SSS_{Pol} = \beta_0 + \beta_1(SSS) + \beta_2(SSS)^2 + \ldots\ldots + \beta_n(SSS)^n + \varepsilon_{pol} \tag{9}
$$

where SSS is retrieval sea surface salinity from MODIS data using Eq.1, while SSS_{Pol} is sea surface salinity estimated using polynomial regression algorithm and ε_{pol} is residual error of SSS_{Pol} estimated. In addition, β_0 and $\beta_1, \beta_2, \ldots\ldots\ldots, \beta_n$ are unknown parameters that are calculated using polynomial regression algorithm with degree of n. In this study, quadratic model, in two variables SSS and SSS_i is given by

$$SSS_{Pol} = \beta_0 + \beta_1(SSS) + \beta_2(SSS)(SSS_i) +$$
$$\beta_3(SSS)(SSS_i) + \beta_4(SSS)^2 + \beta_5(SSS_i)^2 + \varepsilon_p \qquad (10)$$

In Eq.10 the variable SSS , SSS_i is the interaction between SSS and SSS_i. In Fact, a variable that is the product of two others variables is called an interaction.

3.2 Accuracy Estimation

Following Sonia et al., [12], ε errors that represents the difference between retrieved and in situ SSS are computed within 10 km grid point interval and then averaged over all grid points having the same range of distance to coast, where the bias ε on the retrieved SSS_i is given by:

$$\varepsilon = \frac{\sum_{i=1}^{N} (SSS_{il\,pol} - SSS_{situ})}{N} \qquad (11)$$

where $SSS_{il\,pol}$ is the retrieved sea surface salinity from MODIS satellite data using least square and polynomial regression algorithms, respectively. Further, SSS_{situ} is the reference sea surface salinity on grid point i and N is the number of grid points. Finally, root mean square of bias (RMS) is used to determine the level of algorithm accuracy by comparing with in situ sea surface salinity. Further, linear regression model used to investigate the level of linearity of sea surface salinity estimation from MODIS data. The root mean square of bias equals

$$RMS = [N^{-1} \sum_{i=1}^{N} (SSS_{il\,pol} - SSS_{situ})^2]^{0.5} \qquad (12)$$

The time integrations is performed to determine the possible improvement of RMS. In doing so, simulations and retrievals were performed within a two-month period and for each grid point, the retrieved SSS was averaged over six days during the MODIS satellite passes.

4 Simulation Results

4.1 Results of in Situ Measurements

The salinity water distribution patterns are presented in 2D and 3D plots that have been derived from in situ measurements are illustrated in Figs. 3 and 4. The typical water salinity distributions during the inter-monsoon period of September 2002 of the South China Sea are shown in Figs 3a and 3b, respectively.

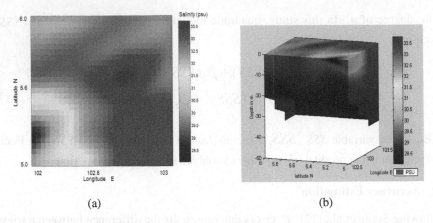

(a)   (b)

Fig. 3. In situ measurements during September 2002 (a) 2D sea surface distribution and (b) 3D salinity pattern variations

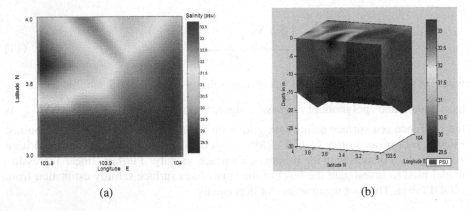

(a)   (b)

Fig. 4. In situ measurements during October 2003 (a) 2D sea surface distribution and (b) 3D salinity pattern variations

In September 2002, both 2D and 3D plots show that the water salinity ranges between 28.5 to 33.6 psu (Figs. 3a and 3b) whereas in October 2003, the water salinity ranges between 29.5 to 33.0 psu (Fig. 4). Both Figs 3a and 4a show the onshore waters salinity are lower than offshore. In this context, Figs 3a and Fig.3b are agreed that the onshore water salinity is ranged between 28.5 to 30 psu during September 2002. In October 2003, however, the onshore water salinity is ranged between 29.5 to 31.0 psu (Fig 4). It is clear that the offshore water salinity is higher than onshore within constant value of 33.5 psu in September 2002 and October 2003, respectively. Further, both September 2002 and October 2003 dominated by tongue of low water salinity penetration of 28.5 and 29.5 psu, respectively along the coastal water. This agrees with the studies of Wrytki, [15]; Zelina et al. [16]; Maged and Mazlan [9].

4.2 Simulation Results from MODIS Data

The sea surface salinity retrieved from MODIS data in September 2002 and October 2003, respectively is shown in Fig. 5. It is observed that the offshore water salinity is higher than onshore. The homogenous offshore water salinity pattern occurred in both September 2002 and October 2003 with maximum salinity value of 33.00 psu and 33.8 psu, respectively. The retrieval SSS patterns from MODIS data confirm the occurrences of tongue of low water salinity penetration along the east coast of Peninsular Malaysia. This may be attributed to the proximity of nearshore waters are close to the rivers such as Kuala Terngganu and Pahang Rivers. The maximum amount of rainfall in the September 2002 and October 2003 are 150 and 300 mm, respectively. This high amount of rainfall is not only dilute the salinity of the surface water but also cause a high amount of fresh water discharges from the rivers are located along the east coast of Malaysian waters into the South China Sea. This confirms the studies of Maged and Mazlan [9]; Maged et al., [8]; Maged and Hussin [7].

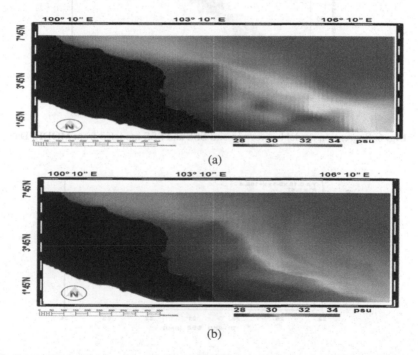

(a)

(b)

Fig. 5. Sea surface salinity estimated from MODIS data (a) September 2002 and (b) October 2003

4.3 Model Validation

Fig. 6 shows the comparison between in situ sea surface salinity measurements and SSS modeled from MODIS data. The blue color exists in Fig.6 is represented sample points of regression. Therefore, regression model shows that SSS modeled by equation 8 is in good agreement with in situ data measurements. The degree of correlation is a function of r^2, probability (p) and root mean square of bias (RMS). The relationship between estimated SSS from MODIS data and in situ data shows positive correlation as r^2 value is 0.96 with p<0.00007 and RMS value of ± 0.37 psu. 2nd polynomial order algorithm, however, shows a poor correlation between in situ SSS and SSS modeled from MODIS as compared to least square methods with RMS value of ± 7.34 psu and r^2 value of 0.67 (Fig. 7).

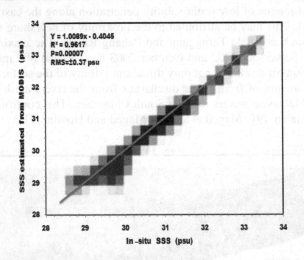

Fig. 6. Regression model between in situ SSS and SSS modeled from MODIS Data

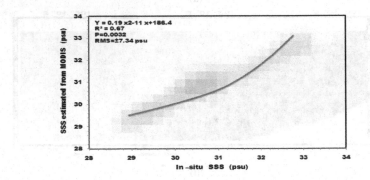

Fig. 7. 2nd polynomial order algorithm between in situ SSS and SSS modeled from MODIS data

5   Summary and Concluding Remarks

The results of the study shows comprehensive using of least square model as compared to 2nd polynomial order algorithm to retrieve sea surface salinity from MODIS satellite data. Further, accurate results of sea surface salinity in recent study can be explained as: using multiple MODIS bands i.e., 1 to 7 bands is a useful extension of linear regression model is the case where SSS is linear function of 7 independent bands. Such a practical is particularly useful when modeling SSS from MODIS data. Further, using least squares method derive a curve that minimizes the discrepancy between estimated SSS from MODIS data and in situ data. This means that using a new approach based on least squares method would be to minimize the sum of the residual errors for the estimating SSS from MODIS data. Further, this study shows the possibilities of direct retrieving of the SSS from visual bands of MODIS satellite data without utilizing such parameter of colored dissolved organic matter, a_{CDOM} [1,13]. However, this study shows differences with Wong et al.,[14] in terms of constant coefficient of linear model and involving the retrieved SSS bias value. In fact, Wong et al., [14] did not take into account the bias value. Under these circumstances, Wong et al., [14] have acquired RMS ±1.63 that is higher than RMS of this study.

In general, the least square algorithm has higher performance as compared to second polynomial order algorithm within RMS of bias value of ± 0.37 psu and r^2 value of 0.96. In conclusions, the least square algorithm can be used as direct method to retrieve SSS from visual bands of MODIS satellite data.

References

[1] Ahn, Y.H., Shanmugam, P., Moon, J.E., Ryu, J.H.: Satellite remote sensing of a low-salinity water plume in the East China Sea. Ann. Geophys. 26, 2019–2035 (2008)

[2] Burrage, D., Wesson, J.: Deriving Sea Surface Salinity and Density Variations From Satellite and Aircraft Microwave Radiometer Measurements: Application to Coastal Plumes Using STARRS. IEEE Transactions on Geosciences and Remote Sensing 46(3), 765–785 (2008)

[3] Ellison, W., Balana, A., Delbos, G., Lamkaouchi, K., Eymard, L., Guillou, C., Prigent, C.: New permittivity measurements of sea water. Radio science 33(3), 639–648 (1998)

[4] Gabarro, C., Vall-llosera, M., Font, J., Camps, A.: Determination of sea surface salinity and wind speed by L-band microwave radiometry from a fixed platform. International Journal of Remote Sensing 25(1), 111–128 (2004)

[5] Hu, C., Chen, Z., Clayton, T., Swarnzenski, P., Brock, J., Muller-Karger, F.: Assessment of estuarine water-quality indicators using MODIS medium-resolution bands: Initial results from Tampa Bay, fL. Remote Sensing of Environment 93, 423–441 (2004)

[6] Klein, L., Swift, C.: An improved model for the dielectric constant of sea water at microwave frequencies. IEEE Transactions. Antennas propagation AP-25(1), 104–111 (1997)

[7] Maged, M., Hussien, M.L.: Upwelling and Downwelling along the Coastal Waters of Kuala Terengganu. Journal of Physical Sciences 15(2), 201–208 (2003)

[8] Maged, M.M., Mohd, N.S., Mohd, L.H., Mohd, I.M.: Seasonal Thermohaline Variation in Coastal Waters off Kuala Terengganu, Malaysia. In: Proceedings of the National Conference on Climate Change, Universiti Pertanian Malaysia, Serdang, August 12-13, pp. 176–175 (1996)

[9] Maged, M., Mazlan, H.: Linear algorithm for salinity distribution modeling from MODIS data. In: CD-ROM Proceeding of IGARSS 2009, Cape Town University, Cape Town, South Africa, July 12-17, pp. 1–4 (2009)

[10] Maes, C., Behringer, D.: Using satellite-derived sea level and temperature profiles for determining the salinity variability: A new approach. Journal Geophysical Research 105(C4), 8537–8547 (2004)

[11] Miller, J.L.: Airborne remote Sensing of Salinity. Backscatter, 24–26 (summer 2000)

[12] Sonia, Z., Boutin, J., Waldteufel, P., Jean-Luc, V., Thierry, P., Pascal, L.: Issues About Retrieving Sea Surface Salinity in Coastal Areas From SMOS Data. IEEE Transactions on Geosciences and Remote Sensing 45(3), 2061–2073 (2007)

[13] Palacios, S.L., Peterson, T.D., Kudela, R.M.: Development of synthetic salinity from remote sensing for the Columbia River plume. J. Geophys. Res. 114, C00B05 (2009)

[14] Wong, M., Kwan, S.H.L., Young, J.K., Nichol, J., Zhangging, L., Emerson, N.: Modelling of Suspendid Solids and Sea Surface Salinity in Hong Kong using Aqua/ MODIS Satellite Images. Korean Journal of Remote Sensing 23(3), 161–169 (2007)

[15] Wyrtki, K.: Physical Oceanography of the South-East Asian Waters. NAGA Report, vol. 2, Univ. Calif Scripps Inst. Ocean., La Joll. (1969)

[16] Zelina, Z.I., Arshad, A., Lee, S.C., Japar, S.B., Law, A.T., Mustapha, N., Maged, M.: East Coast of Peninsular Malaysia. In: Sheppard, C. (ed.) Seas at The Millennium: An Environmental Evaluation. Elsevier Science LTD, London (2000)

Skeleton of a Multi-ribbon Surface

Ivan Mekhedov[1] and Leonid Mestetskiy[2]

[1] Dorodnicyn Computing Centre of Russian Academy of Sciences, Russian Federation
[2] Moscow State University, Russian Federation

Abstract. In this paper, two-dimensional manifolds in three-dimensional Euclidian space are considered in order to single out surfaces whose skeletons fulfill the grass-fire concept. Among such surfaces we distinguish those ones that can be covered by finite number of adjacent patches. We name them multi-ribbon surfaces. We aim to calculate a multi-ribbon surface skeleton by constructing every patch Voronoi diagram in a surface parameter space and merging all Voronoi diagrams. Voronoi diagrams merging technique is proposed. The introduced approach can be applied to the problems of geographic information systems (for example, to street network modeling).

1 Introduction

The concept of medial axis transform is usually concerned with plane shape description. It appears to have been introduced first by Blum in [Blum]. Since then, medial axes together with related concept of skeleton were extensively studied from theoretical and algorithmic points of view. Actually, the difference between medial axes and skeletons is significant only in case of unbordered shapes (such as sphere S^2 in $\mathbb{R}^3$, for example). Such shapes are of not of the main interest in this paper, so further we will use the only concept of skeleton (with the exception of special cases), meaning both skeleton and medial axis.

In practice we consider two and three-dimensional manifolds to undergo skeletonization. This is obvious (but also was proved in [Chaz]) that dimension of an object is higher than the dimension of its skeleton. Following it, the only four cases of dimensional relation between a shape and its skeleton are possible in practical applications.

The first case this is an one-dimensional skeleton related to a planar shape. The strict proof concerned connectivity, finiteness and differentiability properties of such skeleton was first obtained in [C-C-M]. A considerable number of algorithms to compute skeletons of planar shapes has been developed. Early relevant algorithms were presented in [Prep], [Lee]. Most algorithms are based on the property of skeleton being a subset of Voronoi diagram of polygonal domain approximating the source shape.

The second case is related to a two-dimensional skeleton of a solid shape. Algorithms computing skeletons of solid objects are also developed (though the

D. Taniar et al. (Eds.): ICCSA 2010, Part I, LNCS 6016, pp. 557–573, 2010.

amount of research done in the three-dimensional case is smaller). Computation of equidistant surfaces for solid objects was first described in [Hof].

In the third case we have a so-called curved skeleton of a solid shape (see [Cor], for example). Being the set of curves, curved skeleton is not a locus of the centers of maximal balls, as opposed to the canonical concept skeleton. Nevertheless, it is utilized in application as shape descriptor equally with medial axes.

The fourth case is an one-dimensional skeleton of a two-dimensional manifold in three-dimensional Euclidian space. In the paper this case is considered.

One of the first approaches to calculate skeleton of a surface appeared in [Gur]. The geometric object considered by the authors was a trimmed surface patch of non-uniform rational B-spline (NURBS) form bounded by set of disjoint loops, defined in terms of NURBS curves in parametric space of surface patch. The concept of the skeleton of curve surface patch was generalized using the grass-fire analogy and the resulting generalized offset curves on surfaces, defined via minimal paths (geodesics).

To obtain the skeleton of a source surface authors utilized Voronoi diagram calculation for a plain polygonal domain representing surface boundary in the parameter space of surface patch, and used the correspondence function between points of a surface patch and a polygonal figure then.

An $O(n \log N)$ algorithm to calculate the spherical Voronoi diagram of a set of circular arcs on the sphere was presented in [Na].

Despite numerous theoretical investigations into the concept of skeleton of a manifold in $\mathbb{R}^N$ (see [Chaz], for example), still there are no any general computational algorithms for the case of two-dimensional manifold in $\mathbb{R}^3$. We are not going to propose an algorithm of two-dimensional manifold skeleton calculation in the general case. Nevertheless, there exist surfaces that can be covered by finite union of pathes so that the skeleton of every patch can be calculated in a surface parameter space. In this paper, we shall consider two-dimensional manifolds in three-dimensional space in order to single out such surfaces. Also we aim to propose an algorithm of calculation such surfaces skeletons.

Our research was stimulated by the following problem of geoinformatics. Skeleton is a good instrument for describing a street network if streets are presented as a set of polygonal shapes. In [Mekh] such road model was investigated and good results were obtained for city areas where roads intersect at one level (see Fig. 1 (left)). At the same time, shapes that model interchanges (Fig. 1 (middle)) belong to a common class of two-dimensional manifolds in three-dimensional space. Their geographic projection is represented by a finite union of overlapped (in the general case) multiply-connected polygonal domains (see Fig. 1 (right)). Presence of polygon intersections is the certain obstacle in joining of all polygonal domains into entire one and its skeleton calculation.

In the next section, we specify the concept of skeleton of two-dimensional manifold in three-dimensional space and single out the class of surfaces that are analogues of planar shapes from the standpoint of the *grass-fire concept*.

Fig. 1. Left : An example of a skeleton based road model of plain city street network (the dots denote crossroads). Middle: An example of a road surface within a road interchange area. Right: Its plain presentation in a spatial data base (dark parts denote bridges).

2   Specifying the Concept of Skeleton of Two-Dimensional Manifold in Three-Dimensional Space

Let Ω be a piecewise smooth compact connected two-dimensional manifold in three-dimensional euclidian space $\mathbb{R}^3$, and S_Ω be the skeleton of Ω. S_Ω can be canonically defined as a locus of the centers of maximal discs (see [Chaz]). But this definition needs to be specified so that the skeleton corresponds the grass-fire concept. The specified will allows us to operate with the skeleton of a two-dimensional manifold as with the object that can be utilized in applications as a shape descriptor.

Skeleton is defined accurately within the metric, and for its calculation a canonical euclidian distance is not always appropriate. Let us consider a band patch (Fig. 2(a)): the set of points P equidistant from the band boundary in a canonical euclidian metric makes a skeleton edge s having no any correspondence with the band shape. The grass-fire analogy can not be applied, and the skeleton, being formally defined, actually, does not reflect shape peculiarities. So that, the first specification concerning Ω in connection with its skeleton is the requirement on a two-dimensional manifold to be a riemannian manifold with induced inner metric, then every two points on it can be connected by a piecewise smooth curve of finite length. Induced riemannian metric makes S_Ω being the subset of the cut locus of Ω (see [Wolt'78] and [Wolt'93]). The next manifold property to be considered in connection with the concept of skeleton is absence of boundary (closed manifold) or its presence (non-closed manifolds). Let Ω be a sphere S^2 of radius r in $\mathbb{R}^3$, what is S_Ω then? For every point $P \subseteq S_\Omega$ there exists exactly one antipodal point $P_1 \subseteq S_\Omega$ such that distance $d(P, P_1) = \pi r$, and for any other point $P_2 \neq P_1$ distance $d(P, P_2) < \pi r$ (Fig. 2(b)). Then the ball $B(P) \subseteq S_\Omega$ of radius πr is the maximal ball, and, consequently, $S_\Omega = \Omega$. To avoid such cases we require Ω to be a manifold with boundary, and assume its boundary

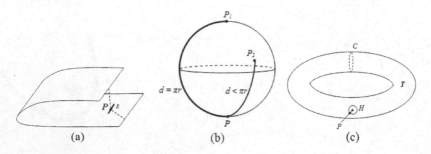

Fig. 2. (a): The set of points P equidistant from a band boundary in euclidian metric forms the skeleton edge s. (b): A radius of a maximal ball on the sphere S^2 is equal to πr. (c): The torus T with a disk cut. Its boundary consists of one loop H. The skeleton S_T is a union of the point P and the loop C, where P is a crossing of T and a line perpendicular to a tangent surface of S_T at the center of H, and C is a "meridian" of T at the maximal distance from the center of H.

is a finite union of disjoint simple compact piecewise smooth closed curves (or, disjoint knots).

Remark 1. Here we distinguish the concepts of skeleton and medial axis. The medial axis is not defined for closed manifolds.

The next requirement to follow the grass-fire concept is orientability of Ω. Imagine a Mobius strip. This is a non-orientable surface, and its skeleton is twice longer than the skeleton of corresponding non-twisted band (lateral cylindric surface). In the second case grass-fire fronts spread along one-side surface (and the skeleton is not a shape descriptor then), while in the first one along two sides simultaneously (skeleton is a shape descriptor).

Thus, we narrow the space of all two-dimensional manifolds in $\mathbb{R}^3$ to the class of piecewise smooth, compact, connected, orientable riemannian manifolds embedded in $\mathbb{R}^3$, with boundary that consists of finite number of disjoint knots. Further we will use the short name for such manifolds, namely *grass-fire surfaces*, since the skeleton of such manifolds is well defined in sense of the corresponding to the grass-fire concept.

Now let us specify the definition of a grass-fire surface skeleton. We pay attention to it because we haven't yet strictly defined the concept of "maximal ball".

Let Ω be a grass-fire surface with an inner riemannian metric M. The distance $\rho(P', P'')$ between two points P' and P'' is defined as the infimum length of all curves connecting P' and P'' in Ω.

The distance $d(P, \partial\Omega)$ between point P and Ω boundary $\partial\Omega$ is imfimum of all distances $\rho(P, Q), Q \in \partial\Omega$.

In metric space (Ω, M) a ball $B_r(x)$ with the center x and the radius $r \geq 0$ is the set $B_r(x) = \{y \in \Omega)|\rho(x, y) \leq r\}$. In this definition, for every point $x \in \Omega$ there exists such $r_0 > 0$ that $B_{r_0}(x)$ covers all Ω. Since that the definition

of a maximal ball needs to be specified. Let us introduce the definition of an
injectivity ball before.

Definition 1. *An injectivity ball $B_r^{in}(x)$ of Ω centered at x is a ball $B_r(x)$ such
that r is the injectivity radius at x.*

Let us remind that the *injectivity radius* at a point $x \in \Omega$ is the largest radius,
r, for which $B_r(x)$ is an embedded ball.

Definition 2. *A maximal ball $B_r^{max}(x)$ of Ω is the injectivity ball $B_r^{in}(x)$ of Ω
such that for any $y \in \Omega$ and any $q \geq 0$ it follows that $B_q^{in}(y) \subseteq B_r^{in}(x)$.*

Such definition of a maximal ball allows us asserting that for any maximal ball
$B_r^{max}(x)$ of Ω a line that connects the center x with the nearest point on $\partial\Omega$ is
a geodesic line (see [Chav], for example).

Given the definition if a maximal ball, we can define the concept of skeleton
of a grass-fire surface.

Definition 3. *The skeleton S_Ω of a grass-fire surface Ω is a locus of the centers
of maximal balls of Ω.*

Now we shall consider the concept of grass-fire surface Voronoi diagram which
is closely related to the concept of the skeleton.

Consider a grass-fire surface Ω. Assume that $\partial\Omega$ consists of finite union of
closed disjoint polygonal chains $L_1, L_2, \ldots, L_N$ (without any requirements to the
surface itself). Every $L_i, 1 \leq i \leq N$, consists of finite union of sites (a site is a
vertex or a segment of a polyline). Denote a union of all sites of all polygonal
chains $L_1, L_2, \ldots, L_N$ as L_S.

Definition 4. *Let us say that an injectivity ball $B_r^{in}(x)$ is incident to the site
$s \in L_S$ if there exists the point $x_1 \in \Omega$ such that $B_r^{in}(x) \bigcap s = \{x_1\}$. That means
that an inner ball and a site have exactly one common point on a surface.*

Definition 5. *Let $s_1, s_2 \in L_S$. If a locus of the centers of maximal balls of Ω
such that every ball, which is incident both to s_1 and s_2, is not empty than we
say this is a bisector $BIS(s_1, s_2)$ of s_1 and s_2.*

Definition 6. *A Voronoi diagram $VD(L_S)$ of the set L_S is a union of all bisectors of Ω: $VD(L_S) = \bigcup_{s_1, s_2 \in L_S} BIS(s_1, s_2)$*

Definition 7. *A Voronoi diagram of a grass-fire surface $VD(\Omega)$ is the Voronoi
diagram of the set of $\partial\Omega$ sites $VD(L_S)$.*

Let us adduce the theorem of the relation between Voronoi diagram and the
skeleton of a grass-fire surface.

Theorem 8. *The skeleton S_Ω of a grass-fire surface Ω is a subset of its Voronoi
diagram $VD(\Omega)$ and consists of and only of non-neighboring sites of $\partial\Omega$ (vertex-
site and segment-site are neighboring sites if they have not null intersection).*

The proof of this theorem is analogous to such for plane figures.

We aim to calculate the Voronoi diagram (and, consequently, the skeleton) of a grass-fire surface. This is a complicated task in the general case since surfaces can have complex shapes. So, we shall consider only those grass-fire surfaces whose skeletons are of application value as shape descriptors (as an example, modeling road networks). In the following sections, we are going to introduce mathematical model of such surfaces and propose an algorithm of their Voronoi diagrams constructing. Let us start with a very simple object – a multi-ribbon in three-dimensional space.

3   Polygonal Multi-ribbon in Three-Dimensional Space and Its Voronoi Diagram Calculation

Road interchanges (Fig. 1 (middle)) can be imagined as attached ribbons in three-dimensional space. This will be our main point in the constructing of the mathematical model of surfaces to undergo skeletonization.

In [Ros] the concept of a polygonal ribbon in three-dimensional space was introduced. A polygonal ribbon was defined to be a sequence of simple planar (but not necessarily coplanar) polygons $P_1, \ldots P_k$ such that each P_i intersects P_{i+1} exactly in a common side, $1 \leq i \leq k - 1$, and the sides which P_i has in common with P_{i-1} and P_{i+1} are distinct. Now let us introduce the definition of a polygonal multi-ribbon.

Definition 9. *A polygonal multi-ribbon* is a union of planar (but not necessarily coplanar) multiply-connected plane polygonal domains $P_1, \ldots P_n$ such that each P_i intersects P_j exactly in a common side, $i \neq j$, and the sides which P_i has in common with P_j and P_k are distinct.

The difference between polygonal ribbon and polygonal multi-ribbon is that the latter one allows ribbon bifurcations, while the first one requires strict sequence of adjacent polygons (Fig. 3), and that multi-ribbon consists of not only simple polygons but also of complex multiply-connected polygonal domains.

Since every polygon in a polygonal multi-ribbon can be developed on plane, the Voronoi diagram of a polygonal multi-ribbon plane development can be computed (as a Voronoi diagram of a multiply-connected polygonal domain), and then mapped onto a multi-ribbon. This technique can be applied only in case of an isometric development. There are two reasons for which a polygonal multi-ribbon can possibly not have an isometric plane multiply-connected polygonal domain:

1. Locally isometric mapping is not homeomorphic, for example, in case of lateral surface of a cylinder and its plane development;
2. Locally isometric mapping is not bijective. An example of the mapping is shown at Fig. 1 (right). "Bridges" parts of projection overlap with "road" parts of projection.

To overcome this obstacle we propose an algorithm that allows constructing Voronoi diagram of union of two adjacent polygons having only their Voronoi diagrams computed (so, we do not need to unite two polygons into one). This allows us to compute Voronoi diagram of every polygon in a polygonal multi-ribbon and merge Voronoi diagrams into one for every pair of adjacent polygons on a plane. The next definition is devoted to the merging concept.

Definition 10. Let P_1 and P_2 be the two multiply-connected polygonal domains with their Voronoi diagram constructed $VD(P_1)$ and $VD(P_2)$. Assume that P_1 and P_2 have the only one common side. The Voronoi diagram of $VD(P_1)$ and $VD(P_2)$ union $VD(P_1 \bigcup P_2)$ is said to be *the merge* of Voronoi diagrams $VD(P_1)$ and $VD(P_2)$ and denoted as $VD(P_1) \bigoplus VD(P_2)$.

Remark 2. The symbol $\bigoplus$ denotes merging process: we do not unite polygons P_1 and P_2 to construct $VD(P_1) \bigcup P_2$, thus, merge is a function of two polygons and two Voronoi diagrams but not a function of a polygon union.

Let us propose the following technique of a polygonal multi-ribbon Voronoi diagram constructing:

1. To compute Voronoi diagram $VD(P_i)$ for every polygon P_i in a polygonal multi-ribbon by means of $VD(P_i')$ constructing where P' is an isometric polygon on a plane;
2. To merge Voronoi diagram $VD(P_i)$ and $VD(P_j)$ for every pair of adjacent multi-ribbon polygons P_i and P_j by means of correspondent Voronoi diagrams $VD(P_i')$ and $VD(P_j')$ merging;
3. Suppose a multi-ribbon polygon P_i has more than one adjacent polygon, for example, P_{i-1} and P_{i+1}, and $VD(P_i)$ and $VD(P_{i-1})$ have already been merged. Then merging of $VD(P_i)$ and $VD(P_{i+1})$ is to be performed via merging of $VD(P_{i+1})$ and $[VD(P_i) \bigoplus VD(P_{i-1})] \bigcap P_i$, i.e. the part of merged Voronoi diagram of P_i and P_{i-1} that lays in P_i.

This technique is demonstrated at Fig. 4.

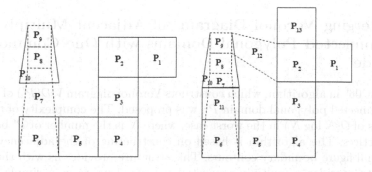

Fig. 3. A polygonal ribbon(left) and a polygonal multi-ribbon(right)

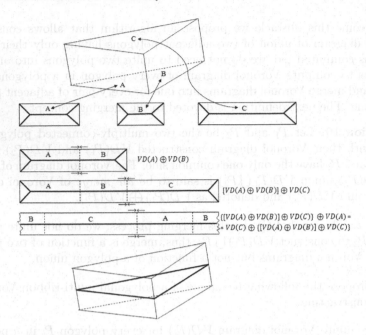

Fig. 4. The technique of a polygonal multi-ribbon Voronoi diagram constructing

Computation of a Voronoi diagram of a multiply-connected polygonal domain is of $O(N \log N)$ complexity in the worst case ([Mest'06]), so we need a merging algorithm of at least the same complexity (not higher). In the next section, such algorithm will be proposed and shown that if P_i' is adjacent to polygons P_{i-1}' and P_{i+1}' then

$$[VD(P_i') \bigoplus VD(P_{i-1}')] \bigoplus VD(P_{i+1}') = [VD(P_i') \bigoplus VD(P_{i+1}')] \bigoplus VD(P_{i-1}')$$
(1)

and thus, the correctness of the point 3 of the proposed technique will be substantiated.

4   Merging Voronoi Diagrams of Adjacent Multiply-Connected Polygonal Domains with One Common Side

In [Mest'06] an algorithm, which constructs Voronoi diagram $VD(P')$ of a multiply -connected polygonal domain P', was proposed. The complexity of the algorithm is of $O(N \log N)$ in the worst case, where N is the number of P' boundary $\partial P'$ vertices. The algorithm is based on constructing of the adjacency tree of polygonal figure boundary contours. This structure provides us with the opportunity to consider a multiply-connected polygonal figure as a simple polygon within the Voronoi diagram constructing process. To construct Voronoi diagram

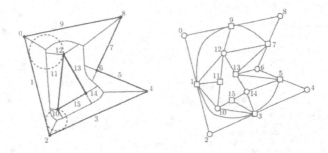

Fig. 5. Left: The Voronoi diagram of a polygonal domain site set. Right: The Delaunay graph of polygonal domain sites (circles denote vertex-sites and squares denote side-sites).

itself there was used the dual structure called Delaunay graph of P' denoted as $DG(P')$. $DG(P')$ is a graph (V, E) where V consists of the sites of P' (sides and vertices), and $E \subseteq V \otimes V$ contains an edge connecting two sites in V if and only if their Voronoi cells have not null intersection. In literature the concept of Delaunay graph related to the set of points [Sier] can be found. The concept of Delaunay graph related to the set of planar convex objects ([Kar'03]) can be found as well. In [Kar'06] the algorithm to transform Delaunay graph to the corresponding Voronoi diagram is described.

The duality of $DG(P')$ and $VD(P')$ is that there exists bijection between these structures elements: every $VD(P')$ vertex with its incident edges and incident faces is assigned to $DG(P')$ face with its incident edges and incident vertices. In [Kar'06] the algorithm to transform Delaunay graph to the corresponding Voronoi diagram is described. In [Mest'06] similar technique is utilized to calculate the skeleton of multiply-connected polygonal domain.

Actually, under the non-degeneracy assumption that no point in the plane is equidistant to more than three sites of P', the Delaunay graph is the Delaunay triangulation of a set of the sites of P' (possibly, with non-straight edges).

At Fig. 5 (left) a polygonal figure is presented. The Voronoi diagram for the set of sites is constructed. The sites are enumerated from 0 up to 15. At Fig. 5 (right) the dual Delaunay graph is shown with the sites enumerated from 0 up to 15.

Let P_1' and P_2' be two adjacent multiply-connected polygonal domains with their Voronoi diagrams constructed. Assume that $DG(P_1')$ and $DG(P_2')$ are also constructed. Let P_1' and P_2' have exactly one common side. That means that three sites of P_1' boundary (two vertices and one side) are confronted with three sites of P_2' boundary (also two vertices and one side). At Fig. 6(a) two adjacent polygons are shown. At Fig. 6(b) you can see their Delaunay graphs with sites enumerated from 1 to 8 and from 9 to 16, respectively, and three pairs of confronted sites: (7,9),(6,10) and (5,11). Voronoi diagrams merging can be reduced to the merging

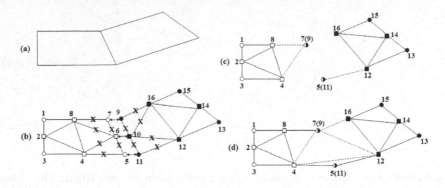

Fig. 6. Left: The Voronoi diagram of the set of the sites of polygonal domain. Right: The adjacency graph of the sites of polygonal domain (circles denote vertex-sites and squares denote side-sites).

of adjacency graphs. Now let us describe the Delaunay graphs merging technique, which involves three steps.

First step : The clearing. Two confronted side-sites are eliminated and all sites incident to the three pairs of confronted sites are eliminated, too. At Fig. 6(b) the sites to be eliminated are denoted by the cross signs.

Second step : The collapsing. Every of two pairs of confronted vertex-sites is collapsed to a single vertex-site. At Fig. 6(c) collapsed vertices are denoted as black-and-white ones.

After these steps are performed we are given 4 connected Delaunay subgraphs. At Fig. 6(c) these subgraphs have the following vertex sets: {1,2,3,4,8}, {7(9)}, {5(11)}, {12,13,14,15,16}.

Third step : The union. Obtained subgraphs are merged into the Delaunay graph. This can be done analogously to the merging of Delaunay graphs of polygonal chains ([Mest'06],[Mest'09]) and similarly to the union of Voronoi diagram of polygonal chains in Lee algorithm ([Lee]).

To perform the union we utilize the technique described in ([Mest'06],[Mest'09]). Given the set of k Delaunay subgraphs, we perform iterative pairwise merging of them. This procedure involves $\lceil \log_2 k \rceil$ steps. At every step the sites in subgraphs are connected so that Delaunay condition is not broken. Thus, in the example at Fig. 6 Delaunay subgraphs $GD(1,2,3,4,8)$ and $GD(7(9))$ are merged, $GD(5(11))$ and $GD(12,13,14,15,16)$ (Fig. 6(c)) are merged as well and two subgraphs: $GD(1,2,3,4,8,7(9))$ and $(12,13,14,15,16,5(11))$ are obtained. Further these subgraphs are merged into the Delaunay graph of $P'_1 \bigcup P'_2$ (Fig. 6(d)).

Total complexity of the technique is $O(N \log N)$ where N is the sum of vertices number of P'_1 and P'_2 boundaries (because the most complex step is the third one).

Those sites of P_1' and P_2' that are not connected with the sites of six confronted, are not changed and are present in the merged Delaunay graph of $P_1' \bigcup P_2'$. Equation (1) is proved then.

5 A Multi-ribbon Surface and Its Voronoi Diagram Calculation

Surfaces which describe road interchanges can be simplistically imagined as a polygonal multi-ribbon. Nevertheless, we assume curvature of considerable surfaces, therefore we shall expand the concept of a polygonal multi-ribbon to the concept of a multi-ribbon surface in three-dimensional space.

Let Ω be a developable grass-fire surface. That means that every point on Ω has a neighborhood isometric to some plain domain (or, equivalent, gaussian curvature in every point equals 0). Assume that Ω is also homeomorphic to some plain figure Φ (a connected compact plain domain bounded by finite number of disjoint Jordan curves). Then Ω can be flattened onto a plane without distortion (i.e. "stretching" or "compressing"). In this case the Voronoi diagram of Ω can be computed in parameter space, and the resulting bisectors can be mapped to three-dimensional space. Now let us state an obvious theorem:

Theorem 11. *Let Ω be a grass-fire surface, Φ is a plain figure, and $\varphi : \Omega \to \Phi$ is an isometry mapping. Then Voronoi diagram $VD(\Omega)$ is an isometric invariant of φ, that is $VD(\Phi) = \varphi(VD(\Omega))$ and $VD(\Omega) = \varphi^{-1}(VD(\Phi))$.*

Since isometry of a surface with riemmanian metric and a plain domain is a homeomorphism then the theorem formulated above can be applied to the compute Voronoi diagram of a surface in parametric space.

Let Ω be a grass-fire surface.

Definition 12. *A polygonal developable patch* of Ω is a compact connected domain $P \in \Omega$ that is isometric to some plain multiply-connected polygonal domain.

Definition 13. Two plane multiply-connected polygonal domains P_1 and P_2 are *adjacent* if their intersection consists of finite number of simple polygonal chains.

Definition 14. Two grass-fire surface polygonal developable patches P_1 and P_2 are *adjacent* if:

1. An intersection of P_1 and P_2 consists of finite number of disjoint knots;
2. There exist adjacent polygonal multiply-connected domains P_1' and P_2' on plane so that P_1 is isometric to P_1' and P_2 is isometric to P_2';
3. $P_1 \bigcup P_2$ is homeomorphic to $P_1' \bigcup P_2'$.

Definition 15. We shall say that a grass-fire surface Ω is a multi-ribbon surface if it can be covered by finite union of adjacent polygonal developable pathes $P_1, P_2, \ldots, P_N$.

An example of a *multi-ribbon surface* is shown at Fig. 1 (middle) (road interchange). An example of a grass-fire surface that is non multi-ribbon one (a torus with removed disk) is presented at Fig. 2(c).

Remark 3. Calculation of a skeleton of a plain domain is based on Voronoi diagram computing. Most algorithms that construct Voronoi diagram deal with polygonal objects. Since that in definition 14 we require plane multiply-connected domains to be polygonal ones.

Thus, a multi-ribbon surface is a curve analogue of a polygonal multi-ribbon in three dimensional space, and the Voronoi diagram merge definition and its constructing technique, described in previous sections, can expanded to such surfaces.

Now let us introduce two more definitions related to Voronoi diagrams merging for the general case.

Definition 16. Let P_1' and P_2' be adjacent multiply-connected polygonal domains in $\mathbb{R}^2$, $P_3' = P_1' \bigcup P_2'$ and $VD(P_1'), VD(P_2'), VD(P_3')$ are their Voronoi diagrams, correspondingly. Then the Voronoi diagram $VD(P_3')$ is said to be *the merge* of Voronoi diagrams $VD(P_1')$ and $VD(P_2')$ and denoted as $VD(P_3') = VD(P_1') \oplus VD(P_2')$.

An analogous definition refers to surface patches:

Definition 17. Let P_1 and P_2 be adjacent patches on a multi-ribbon surface $\mathbb{R}^3$, $P_3 = P_1 \bigcup P_2$ and $VD(P_1), VD(P_2), VD(P_3)$ are their Voronoi diagrams correspondingly. Then the Voronoi diagram $VD(P_3)$ is said to be *the merge* of Voronoi diagrams $VD(P_1)$ and $VD(P_2)$ and denoted as $VD(P_3) = VD(P_1) \oplus VD(P_2)$.

Now let us prove the theorem that will provide us with the opportunity to construct Voronoi diagram of a multi-ribbon surface in its parameter space.

Theorem 18. *Let Ω is a multi-ribbon surface and $P_1, P_2 \in \Omega$ are adjacent polygonal patches. Then a parametrization of $P_1 : P_1' = \varphi(P_1), P_1' \in \mathbb{R}^2$ and a parametrization of $P_2 : P_2' = \psi(P_2), P_2' \in \mathbb{R}^2$ such that $VD(P_1 \bigcup P_2) = \varphi^{-1}\{[VD(P_1') \oplus VD(P_2')] \bigcap P_1'\} \bigcup \psi^{-1}\{[VD(P_1') \oplus VD(P_2')] \bigcap P_2'\}$.*

Proof. P_1 and P_2 are adjacent polygonal patches therefore there exist multiply-connected polygonal domains P_1' and P_2' in parameter space such that P_1' and P_2' are isometric to P_1 and P_2, correspondingly. Let φ and ψ be correspondent isometry mappings. Let

$$\xi(X) : P_1 \bigcup P_2 \to P_1' \bigcup P_2' = \begin{cases} \varphi(X), X \in P_1; \\ \psi(X), X \in P_2. \end{cases} \qquad (2)$$

Since $P_1' \bigcup P_2'$ is homeomorphic to $P_1 \bigcup P_2$ then there exist a path that connects two any points in P_1' and P_2'. For riemannian manifolds with inner metrics $\rho(X_1, X_2) + \rho(X_2, X_3) = \rho(X1, X3)$ if X_2 lays on the curve realizing the shortest distance between X_1 and X_2. Consequently, ξ in (2) is an isometric mapping. That proves the theorem.   □

Note 1. Everywhere the concept of similar mapping instead of the concept of isometric mapping can be used. By similarity we mean isometry accurate within the coefficient.

Thus, a Voronoi diagram of a multi-ribbon surface can be constructed by means of the same technique, which was described in the section 5. The only difference is that adjacent polygons in a parameter space may have more than one common side, and also may have not a side but a part of a side in their intersection. In the next section, we generalize merging process of Voronoi diagrams of adjacent polygonal domains.

6   Merging Voronoi Diagrams in the General Case

Let P'_1 and P'_2 be two adjacent polygons. Assume that $P'_1 \cap P'_2 = [AB] \cap [CD]$ where AB is a side of P'_1 and CD is a side of P'_2. Without loss of generality, the following cases are possible:

1. $A = C, B = D$. This case was considered in the section 4;
2. $A = C, D \in]AB[$ (Fig. 7(a));
3. $C \in]AB[, B \in]CD[$ (Fig. 7(g));
4. $C, D \in]AB[$ (Fig. 7(m)).

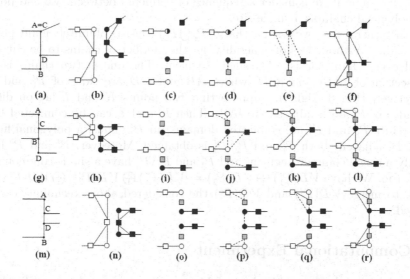

Fig. 7. Merging of Voronoi diagrams of adjacent polygonal figures with their sides [AB] and [CD] intersecting. (a)–(f): The case $A = C, D \in]AB[$. (g)–(l): The case $C \in]AB[, B \in]CD[$. (m)–(r): The case $C, D \in]AB[$.

In the cases 2–4, the technique of $VD(P'_1)$ and $VD(P'_2)$ merging is the same as described in the section 4 except an additional step, which is called the insertion.

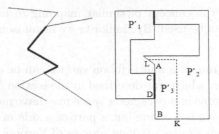

Fig. 8. Merging Voronoi diagrams of adjacent polygons in the general case. Left: two polygonal figures have a common polygonal chain. Right: two polygonal figures have finitely many common polygonal chains.

The insertion step goes just after the collapsing step. At least one and at most two side-sites by positional relationship of points A, B, C and D (such sites are denoted as grey squares at Fig. 7) are inserted. These sites make separate Delaunay subgraphs to be merged with the other subgraphs. The technique for the cases 2–4 involving 4 steps (namely the clearing, the collapsing, the insertion, the union) is illustrated at Fig. 7.

Now suppose two adjacent polygons P_1' and P_2' have a common polygonal chain (Fig. 8 (left)). The technique of $VD(P_1') \oplus VD(P_2')$ constructing in this case is the same if we consider a sequence of segments between two end points of a polygonal chain as a single site.

In the general case, we assume that $\partial(P_1' \bigcup P_2')$ consists of finitely many polygonal chains. Without loss of generality, let the number of chains to be equal to 2 and every chain consist of a single segment. The one of two chains is the intersection of $[AB]$ and $[CD]$ where AB and CD are sides of P_1' and P_2', respectively (Fig. 8 (right)). Suppose that two points K and L lay on different sides of P_2' both adjacent to $[AB]$. Then K and L can be connected by a path (since P_1' and P_2' are connected domains) in P_2'. Thus, a polygonal figure $P_3' \subset P_2'$ adjacent both P_1' and $P_2' \backslash P_3'$ is obtained. Moreover, P_1' and P_3' have exactly a single common segment and P_3' and $P_2' \backslash P_3'$ have a single common segment, too. We have $VD(P_1') \oplus VD(P_2') = [VD(P_1') \oplus VD(P_3')] \oplus VD(P_2' \backslash P_3')$. Thus, to merge $VD(P_1')$ and $VD(P_2')$ the considered above technique can be applied.

7   Computational Experiment

Given the spatial geographic data of Moscow street network, we utilized the proposed algorithm to construct skeleton of a road interchange. At Fig. 1 (middle), real interchange is presented, and at Fig. 1 (right) its projection is shown, and this projection was the source data for us. Though the projection has been already decomposed by an attribute of road and bridge, we still needed the different decomposition since polygons were not adjacent. The decomposition, we have made, is shown at Fig. 9 (left). The obtained skeleton of the projection

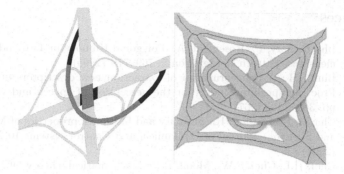

Fig. 9. Left: Road interchange projection decomposed by adjacent multiply-connected polygonal domains (they are of different colors). Right: The computed skeleton (after regularization, i.e. removing noise branches) of a multi-ribbon surface modeling road interchange.

was mapped onto surface (we were given the similarity-keeping projection function). The result is presented at Fig. 9 (right). The computational experiment was conducted using the russian geoinformation system Mappl [mappl].

8   Conclusion

Thus, the following main results were obtained in this paper:

1. The merging technique for Voronoi diagrams of two adjacent multiply-connected polygonal domains was proposed (with $O(N \log n)$ complexity in the worst case);
2. The algorithm of a multi-ribbon surface skeleton constructing was proposed.

This technique can be utilized in algorithms of geographic information systems. One of the main application is construction of a street network model by a set of polygonal road parcels representing roads in various spatial databases.

The following unsolved problems still remain:

1. To find out the criterion of a surface being a multi-ribbon surface (when it can be covered by finite number of special patches?);
2. To develop a technique of decomposition of a multi-ribbon surface into polygonal developable patches.

These problems are of authors interest and will be considered in future works.

Acknowledgements

The research was supported by the Russian Foundation of Basic Researches (grant 08-01-00670).

References

[Ros]   Bhattachary, P., Rosenfeld, A.: Polygonal Ribbons in Two and Three Dimensions. Pattern Recognition 5, 769–779 (1995)

[Blum]   Blum, H.: A transformation of extraction new descriptors of shape. In: Proc. Symposium Models for the perception of speech and visual form, pp. 362–381 (1967)

[Chaz]   Chazal, F., Soufflet, R.: Stability and finiteness properties of Medial Axis and Skeleton. Journal of Dymamical and Control systems 10(2), 149–170 (2004)

[C-C-M]   Choi, H.I., Choi, S.W., Moon, H.P.: Mathematical Theory Of Medial Axis Transform. Pacific Journal of Mathematics 181(1), 57–88 (1997)

[Chav]   Chavel, I.: Riemannian Geometry: A Modern Introduction. Cambridge University Press, Cambridge (1993)

[Cor]   Cornea, N., Silver, D., Min, P.: Curve-skeleton properties, applications and algorithms. IEEE Transactions on Visualization and Computer Graphics 13(3), 530–548 (2007)

[Hof]   Dutta, D., Hoffman, C.M.: A Geometric investigation of the skeleton of CSG objects. In: Ravani, B. (ed.) Proc. 16th ASME Design Automation Conf.: Advances in Design Automation, Computer Aided and Computational Design, Chicago, Ill, vol. 1, pp. 67–75 (1990)

[Gur]   Gursoy, H.N.: Shape Interrogation by Medial Axis Transform for Automated Analysis. PhD thesis, Massachusetts Institite of Technology (1989)

[Kar'06]   Karavelas, M.I.: Voronoi diagrams in Cgal. In: 22nd European Workshop on Computational Geometry, pp. 229–232 (2006)

[Kar'03]   Karavelas, M.I., Yvinec, M.: The Voronoi diagram of Planar Convex Objects. In: Di Battista, G., Zwick, U. (eds.) ESA 2003. LNCS, vol. 2832, pp. 337–348. Springer, Heidelberg (2003)

[Lee]   Lee, D.T.: Medial Axis Transformation of a Planar Shape. IEEE Transactions on pattern Analysis and Machine Intelligence PAMI-4(4), 363–369 (1982)

[Mekh]   Mekhedov, I., Kozlov, A.: Street network model based on skeletal graph. In: Proc. of 19 Int. Conf. Graphicon, pp. 356–359 (2009) (in Russian)

[Mest'09]   Mestetskiy, L.: Continuous morphology of binary images: figures, skeletons and circles. Moscow, FIZMATLIT (2009) (in russian)

[Mest'06]   Mestetskiy, L.: Skeletonization of a multiply connected polygonal domain based on its boundary adjacent tree. Sibirian Journal of Numerical Mathemathics 9(3), 299–314 (2006) (in Russian)

[Mest'08]   Mestetskiy, L., Semyonov, A.: Binary Image Skeleton - Continuous Approach. VISAPP (1), 251–258 (2008)

[Na]   Na, H.-S., Lee, C.-N., Cheong, O.: Voronoi diagrams of the sphere. Computational Geometry 23, 183–194 (2002)

[Prep]   Preparata, F.P.: The Medial Axis of a Simple Polygone. In: Goos, G., Hartmanis, J. (eds.) Lecture Notes in Computer Science: Mathematical Foundations of Computer Science, pp. 443–450 (1977)

[Sier]   Siersma, D.: Voronoi diagrams and Morse Theory of the Distance Function. In: Barndorff-Nielsen, O.E., Jensen, E.B.V. (eds.) Geometry in Present Day Science, pp. 187–208. World Scientific, Singapore (1999)

[Wolt'93]   Wolter, F.-E.: Cut Locus and Medial Axis in Global Shape Interrogation and Representation. In: Design Laboratory Memorandum 92-2. Department of Ocean Engineering, pp. 92–92. MIT Press, Cambridge (1993)

[Wolt'78]   Wolter, F.-E.: Distance function and cut loci on a complete Riemannian manifold. Archiv der Mathematik 32, 92–96 (1978)

[mappl]   http://www.mappl.ru

Multi-criteria Optimization in GIS: Continuous K-Nearest Neighbor Search in Mobile Navigation

Kushan Ahmadian[1], Marina Gavrilova[1], and David Taniar[2]

[1] Department of Computer Science, The University of Calgary, Canada
{kahmadia,mgavrilo}@ucalgary.ca
[2] Clayton School of Information Technology, Monash University, Australia
david.taniar@infotech.monash.edu.au

Abstract. The generalization of existing spatial data for cartographic production can be expressed as optimizing both the amount of information to be presented, and the legibility/usability of the final map, while conserving data accuracy, geographic characteristics, and aesthetical quality. As an application of information system optimization, distributed wireless mobile network serves as the underlying infrastructure to digital ecosystems. It provides important applications to the digital ecosystems, one of which is mobile navigations and continuous mobile information services. Most information and query services in a mobile environment are continuous mobile query processing or continuous k nearest neighbor (CKNN), which finds the locations where interest points or interest objects change while mobile users are moving. In this paper, we propose a neural network based algorithm solution for continuous k nearest neighbor (CKNN) search in such a system which divides the query path into segments and improves the overall query process.

1 Introduction

The current trend on generalization of available spatial data for cartographic queries can be viewed as optimizing both the amount of information to be presented, and the correctness and usefulness of the final map, while conserving data accuracy, geographic characteristics, and aesthetical quality [1,2]. By this work, we aim to target the k nearest neighbor (KNN) search in mobile navigation. In this approach, a set of rules are defined, one for each constraint [3]. Each rule contains a satisfaction function, measuring the degree of violation of the constraint, and one or more actions, which should improve the situation if the constraint is violated. An optimizer kernel has the responsibility of evaluating local and global satisfaction, which is based on artificial neural network, and applying actions to appropriate features to improve the situation. In real generalization scenarios, it is often not possible to avoid some violation of constraints [4], and the goal of the optimizer is to maximize the overall satisfaction.

Most of the tools available in current commercial GIS products process a feature or a feature class at a time, applying a single generalization operation independent of the context, and without considering other constraints that would impact the appropriate representation of the affected features. Even though these tools are effective, applying the initial operation can often expose further problems. Such problems may vary from simplifying a boundary, which may cause a nearby point feature to fall on the

D. Taniar et al. (Eds.): ICCSA 2010, Part I, LNCS 6016, pp. 574–589, 2010.

opposite side of the boundary; to displacing a building away from roads [5,6], which may move it over water.

As a potential application of such an optimization system, distributed wireless mobile networks allow information exchange and information services to be delivered. An application that utilizes such a technology is information services to mobile devices and users through mobile networks [7]. Mobile information services transcend the traditional centralized wired technology into an interactive and wireless environment, which offers cost-effective digital services and value-creating activities for mobile users [8].

One of the most prominent and growing applications of mobile information services is mobile navigation [9], due to the increase of traffic loads and the complexity of road connections. Many mobile users need a kind of applications to help them navigate on crowded roads, guide them the best route and even give answer to their queries. Global Positioning System (GPS) in car navigation systems is a product which can satisfy the mobile users' requirements, such as locating current position, finding the best way from A to B, finding all interest points within a certain range, finding k nearest neighbor (KNN), and so on.

In mobile navigations, continuous monitoring of interest points or interest objects while the mobile user is on the move is an important criterion of mobile navigations. Normally in continuous monitoring, when interest points or interest objects are changed due to the movement of mobile users, the mobile users are notified of these changes. These are known as *split nodes*. Therefore, existing work has been much focused on processing split nodes efficiently.

Different kinds of approaches have well been explored in the last two decades. As a result, numerous conceptual models, multi-dimensional indexes and query processing techniques have been introduced. The most common spatial query is k nearest neighbour search (KNN) [10].

Continuous KNN (abbreviated as CKNN) approaches [9,11] also have attracted some researchers' interest. In order to find split nodes, all existing continuous KNN approaches divide the query path into segments, find KNN results for the two terminate nodes of each segment, and then for each segment find the split nodes. One segment of the path starts from an intersection and ends at another intersection. For every segment, a KNN process is invoked to find split nodes for each segment. If there are too many intersections on the path, there will be many segments, and consequently, the processing performance will degrade. These are the obvious limitations of the current CKNN approaches.

In this paper, we propose an alternative approach for CKNN query processing, which is based on Neural Network. This approach avoids these weakness mentioned above and improves the performance by utilizing Artificial Neural Network according to the better ability of neural network for solving optimization problems. There are varieties of models of chaotic neural networks which have been used for solving optimization problems e.g. Nozawa [12] shows the search ability of chaotic neural network while Chen and Aihara [13] have introduced chaotic simulated annealing (CSA). Their method starts with a large negative self-coupling in the neurons and then gradually decreasing it to stabilize the network. In 1990, Aihara et al. have introduced a chaotic neural network, which exhibits chaotic behaviour using a negative self-coupling and gradually removing it [14]. The model is based on the chaotic behaviour of some biological neurons and has been successfully applied to several optimization problems such as TSP (Travelling Salesman Problem) [15] and BSP (Broadcast Scheduling Problem) [16]. This is method is considered to be a base for all later chaotic neural nets used to solve optimization problems.

The outline of this paper is as follows. In the second section, we have provided a general discussion on GIS Optimization. Section 3 presents the core of our multi criteria optimization. Section 4 is dedicated to methodology utilization for Voronoi-based CKNN and description of the developed algorithm. Finally, future improvements are provided in the concluding section.

2 Background: Constraints and Optimization

The concept of 'constraints' as a way of defining the requirements and goals of generalization has been actively researched for more than a decade [17], and was explored comprehensively. Beard [17] classifies constraints as: Graphical (minimum legible size), Structural (connectivity of roads), Application (importance of information content), or Procedural (transportation generalization comes after hydrography generalization). Constraints were central to the design of the European AGENT project, which prototyped a multi-agent approach to constraint-based generalization [18]. Although powerful, the resultant multi-agent system introduces overheads of complexity and performance, and requires an active object.

The concept of mathematical optimization of a system by convergent evolution has an even longer pedigree, with key points being the Metropolis algorithm [19], and 'simulated annealing' [20]. There have been various academic applications of simulated annealing to generalization, notably for displacement [21].

Statistical optimization (such as simulated annealing) is a useful technique for finding a 'good enough' solution to the class of problems where determining an exact solution would require exploring a combinatorial explosion of possibilities. The classic example is the 'traveling salesman' problem – "Given a number of cities and the costs of traveling from any city to any other city, what is the cheapest round-trip route that visits each city exactly once and then returns to the starting city?" The most direct solution would be to try all the permutations (ordered combinations) and see which one is cheapest (using brute force search), but given that the number of permutations is $n!$ (The factorial of the number of cities, n), this solution rapidly becomes impractical.

One can assume that assessing that geographic generalization (both model generalization and cartographic generalization) is in the same class of combinatorial problem, for which optimization is a good approach. This paper describes an Optimizer component, designed to apply optimization techniques to geographic data in a GIS.

Note however, that unlike previous applications of simulated annealing for generalization, the Optimizer has two significant advantages:

1. When a constraint is violated, the corresponding action is not a random response, as in many Monte-Carlo approaches. Instead, the action routine will apply the logic of generalization (using the spatial knowledge and neighborhood relationships of the GIS object toolkit) and make an intelligent change which is much more likely to result in improvement of overall system satisfaction.

2. Although an action is triggered as a result of a constraint violation by a specific feature, the action routine may well modify other implicated features in order to improve the overall satisfaction. This mechanism helps minimize problems of cyclic behavior, and speeds convergence.

3 Components of Multi-criteria Optimization

The basic concepts and components involved in an optimization solution are as follows:

Area (or Set) of Interest

An area or set of interest is a limited zone containing a limited number of features where we want to solve an optimization problem (a block of buildings delimited by a set of roads in a cartographic generalization for instance). This is the 'context space' for the generalization.

Action

An action is a basic algorithm, designed to improve satisfaction, with the following capabilities: (*i*) Perform its task(s) based on an input feature. It can change several features at a time, and (*ii*) Declare the object classes it deals with and the attributes it needs. Within the Optimizer system, an action is implemented as a geo-processing tool, which is linked via a geo-processing model to a constraint to make a rule.

Constraint

The process is lead by constraints. A constraint: (*i*) provides a measure of satisfaction of a feature based on its environment (meaning that several other features may be involved in satisfaction calculation), and (*ii*) declares the object classes it deals with and the attributes it needs. Within the Optimizer system, a constraint is implemented as a geo-processing tool, which is linked via a geo-processing model to one or more actions to make a rule. Each constraint provides a satisfaction function.

Satisfaction Function (SF)

The degree of satisfaction of a constraint will be a number greater than or equal to zero and smaller than or equal to one. We will call F_i the feature with id equal to i (this *id* defines the class *id* and the object *id*), and $S_c(F_i)$ the satisfaction of constraint c for feature F_i with:

$$0 \leq (S_c(F_i)) \leq 1 \tag{1}$$

By convention $S_c(F_i) = 0$ will represent the case where the constraint is not satisfied at all and $S_c(F_i) = 1$ where the constraint is fully satisfied. Any constraint must implement a Satisfaction Function and will normally provide a User Interface (UI) for the user to define the requirements and tune the satisfaction function using relevant parameter inputs. Here are examples of different curves of satisfaction functions (Figure 1).

Reflex

If implemented simplistically, the system would not respect some 'strict constraints' like "buildings MUST NOT overlap roads". This is because the Optimizer seeks for

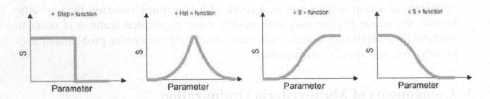

Fig. 1. Satisfaction function curves

the right balance between constraints to reach the best state. Also, we anticipate the need for some data to be strongly linked to others. For instance the category for a building resulting from merging two initial buildings is a function of the initial categories. This function is generally defined by the particular organization's product specifications.

The concept of a reflex is introduced to answer the two above needs. A reflex is a piece of code fired after each data modification. It will be responsible for filtering and modifying the results of the preceding action.

Iteration

Having calculated the initial satisfaction for the set of features, the Optimizer has to choose one feature to become the target for the first iteration. This choice contains a random element, but is biased towards choosing a feature with a low feature satisfaction (tackle the worst problems first). For this feature, the constraint with the worst satisfaction will be chosen, and its actions tried, one by one. If the overall satisfaction improves, then the modifications are kept, else they are discarded.

A target feature for the next iteration is then chosen in a similar manner, and the process repeats. This continues until it reaches stability, or satisfaction gain is sufficiently slow that iteration should stop. Although it is fundamental that the choice of candidate for the next iteration has a random element, we can improve performance by taking advantage of the spatial nature of generalization to bias the selection towards taking nearer candidates first.

Temperature (Simulated Annealing)

In order to avoid being trapped by a local maximum one can use the well known "simulated annealing" technique. This strategy consists in accepting some action with negative ΔS, where ΔS is the difference between the current and previous satisfaction values. The algorithm is the following:

Try actions and calculate best ΔS

if $\Delta S \geq 0$ then accept action modifications, else accept action modification

with probability $\exp\left(\dfrac{\Delta s}{T}\right)$

Decrease temperature T and continue iterations

The concept of temperature comes by analogy with annealing in metallurgy, a technique involving heating and controlled cooling of a material to increase the size of its crystals and reduce their defects. The heat causes the atoms to become unstuck from their initial positions (a local minimum of the internal energy) and wander randomly through states of higher energy; the slow cooling gives them more chances of finding configurations with lower internal energy than the initial one. The decay rate α for temperature is one parameter of the Optimizer. The shape of this decay is exponential: $T^{t+1} = \alpha T^t$. For display convenience we choose to use a temperature starting with value 1 and decreasing toward 0.

Detection of Cyclic Behavior

One classic problem of dynamic systems like the Optimizer is that they can get locked into cycles of repeating states. Solutions to avoid this are however known, including use of taking the Fourier transform of the overall satisfaction and looking for periodicity. We will also learn from the experience of earlier dynamic system approaches to generalization, such as the AGENT prototype.

Using Neural Network for Optimization

In the classical formulation of Hopfield network for optimization problem, Hopfield and Tank [16] proposed a $n \times n$ network to solve a TSP problem, when the input problem size is n cities. The total energy function of their solution is:

$$E = \frac{W_1}{2} \left\{ \sum_{i=1}^{n} \left(\sum_{j=1}^{n} v_{ij} - 1 \right)^2 + \sum_{j=1}^{n} \left(\sum_{i=1}^{n} v_{ij} - 1 \right)^2 \right\} +$$

$$\frac{W_2}{2} \sum_{i=1}^{n} \sum_{k=1}^{n} \sum_{j=1}^{n} (v_{kj+1} + v_{kj-1}) v_{ij} d_{ik}, \tag{2}$$

where, connection weight of v_{ij} indicates that the salesperson visits city i in order j, W_1 is corresponding to the constraints, W_2 is the tour length parameter and d is a two-valued (0 or1) parameter corresponding to connection of neurons. As mentioned previously, this method usually traps into one of many local minima of the energy function since no simulated annealing or noise injection policies have been applied.

4 Voronoi-Based CKNN and the New Applied Algorithm

Continuous k nearest neighbor search is not a novel type of query in a mobile environment, as it has been well studied in the past. Continuous k nearest neighbor (CKNN) [9,11] can be defined as given a moving query point, its pre-defined moving path and a set of candidate interest points, to find the point on the way where k nearest neighbor changes. This is a traditional query in mobile navigation. To get the exact point on the road in short response time is not as easy as we think. The already existing works on CKNN have some limitations as follows.

Firstly, current methods need to divide the pre-defined query path into segments using the intersections on the road. It means that once there is an intersect road in the path, it becomes a new segment, and we need to check whether there is any split nodes on this segment.

Secondly, for every segment we should find KNN for the start and end nodes of the segment. It obviously reduces the efficiency of the performance when the number of intersections on the query path becomes large.

Thirdly, they use PINE (based on Voronoi diagram) to do the KNN for the start and end nodes of each segment. But when doing continuous KNN, DAR/eDAR [11] discards the Voronoi diagram and adopts another method to detect split nodes.

Lastly but not the least, these methods cannot predict where split nodes will appear. In Voronoi-CKNN (VCKNN), it is known even before reaching the point and also it gives the visibility of which interest point is moving out or into the list and at which position the node will become split node.

The VCKNN approach is based on the attributes of Voronoi diagram itself and using *piecewise continuous function* to express the distance change of each border point. At the same time, Dijkstra's algorithm has been used to expand the road network within the Voronoi polygon [10]. In next section we discuss the eDAR algorithm, which is a base for both VCKNN and the proposed algorithm.

4.1 eDAR Algorithm

eDAR algorithm is an enhanced variation of the DAR algorithm [11]. With DAR we maintain two priority queues (PQ_1 and PQ_2) to store the KNNs of each sub-path endpoints (A and B), and two ready-in-queues (RQ_1 and RQ_2). RQ_1 stores all KNNs of B (in PQ_2) but not KNNs of A (in PQ_1) with their shortest path to A, and we do the same for B and RQ_2. Then, if the KNNs in both PQs do not match node names or positions in the PQs, we start from the top of PQ_1 and compute λ (shortest path) for every two consecutive KNNs in PQ_1 and compute λ for the last KNN in PQ_1 and every entry in RQ_1.

λs represent the distances from the start node (i.e., A) to the candidate split points, where this point is on the path between the two interest points (A and B), and at this point the order of the nearest neighbor will change. Finally, we compare all λs and take the minimum λ to be the split point. According to λ we make the changes in the order of PQ_1 queue. If the changes have to be done between the last interest point in priority-queue and ready-in-queue, we pop out the interest point in PQ and bring in the interest point from RQ queue to PQ queue. The computation of λs continues at each step of the algorithm (requiring the use of expensive shortest path algorithm) until PQ_1 matches PQ_2 (i.e., all split points are found).

eDAR, can reduce the number and size of the required queues, and in addition it tries to reduce the number/complexity of distance computations (λs). eDAR maintains two priority queues (PQ_1 and PQ_2) as in DAR. However, it maintains only one ready-in-queue (RQ_1) that stores all KNNs of B (in PQ_2) but not KNNs of A (in PQ_1). For the entries in RQ_1, we store their distances to B (and not to A as in DAR). Note that, by this, we do not need to compute the actual shortest path distances from the KNNs to the entries in RQ_1 as in DAR, we only copy the entries from PQ_2 into RQ_1. Hence it reduces the complexity of the algorithm.

To find the split points on the sub-path we compute λs for all interest points in PQ_1 with all the interest points in PQ_2, regardless of the position of those interest points inside the priorities queues PQ_1 and PQ_2. Note that, in contrary to DAR, eDAR λs are computed only at this step of the algorithm, and the subsequent steps will not require computing any more λs. In addition, we do not need to use the shortest path algorithm to compute such λs.

The next step in eDAR is to reduce/delete some redundant and unnecessary λs, in the sense that they will not produce any real split points. Towards this end, we check if a λ value is negative or greater than the distance of the sub-path (i.e., $d(A, B)$), then it is deleted. This is because they would represent split points that are outside the sub-path; hence they cannot be considered as real split points for the sub-path. In addition, we delete λs which have been computed by the same two interest points, one in PQ_1 and the other in PQ_2, since a split point can only exist between two different interest points.

Finally, we delete duplicate λs since a split point can appear only once between two different interest points. We arrange the remaining λs in ascending order from smallest to biggest in a queue (LQ). All λs are going to represent split points on the sub-path. However, some of them are not real split points (i.e., no change in the order of the interest points would occur). Hence, in the next step we want to identify such λs and remove them from LQ. The remaining λs in LQ would be the real set of split points on the sub-path. If one of the interest points in PQ_1 changes place with one of the interest points in RQ_1, then it will never go back to PQ_1 again. This interest point will not make any further split points on the path. Therefore, once an interest point moves from PQ_1 to RQ_1, we need to remove all the λs computed from that interest point from LQ.

4.2 Comparison (VCKNN vs. DAR vs. IE)

VCKNN [9], DAR [11] and IE [22] are all approaches for CKNN queries. But VCKNN is different from DAR and IE in most of aspects.

Path Division Mechanism

For the same network connection, DAR and IE divide the query path into segments as shown Figure 2, whereas VCKNN processes the path as in Figure 3. Note that in Figure 3, for every intersection in the query path, it becomes a segment. In this example, the query path is divided into 18 segments, as there are as many intersections along the query path.

In contrast, using the same query path, the VCKNN approach has only 5 segments (see Figure 3). The number of segments is determined by the number of Voronoi polygons. Even though there are many intersections in each Voronoi polygon, the VCKNN method will process each Voronoi polygon as a unit, and hence, there is no need to check intersection by intersection.

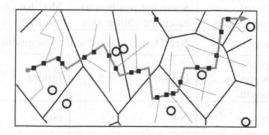

Fig. 2. Segments using DAR and IE

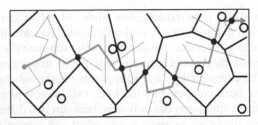

Fig. 3. Segments using VCKNN

KNN Processing

For each segment, DAR and IE use either PINE [11] or VN3 [10] to perform KNN processing for the two terminating nodes (e.g. start and end of the segment). In contrast, VCKNN does not need any algorithm to do KNN on any point on the path. VCKNN finds KNN level by level (from 1^{st}NN, then 2^{nd}NN, then 3^{rd}NN, and so on) for the entire query path. Hence, KNN results can easily be visualized using VCKNN.

Sequence Finding of Split Nodes

DAR and IE use formulas to calculate the distance between two adjacent split nodes. Subsequently, the algorithm finds split nodes one by one. This also means that we do not know the $(k+1)^{th}$ split node until we find k^{th} split node.

In contrast, VCKNN locates split nodes using query point moving distance. For each interval, the algorithm identifies the split nodes directly, which are the nearest distance between the query point and the intersected paths in the Voronoi polygon. Consequently, all split nodes are identified in one go.

Processing Split Nodes

DAR and IE compare the KNN results of the two terminate nodes of each segment to find all split nodes within this segment. On the other hand, VCKNN finds all split nodes top down from 1^{st}NN, and then 2^{nd}NN and so do. The following Table 1 summarizes the differences between DAR, IE and VCKNN.

Table 1. VCKNN vs. DAR vs. IE

	VCKNN	DAR	IE
Query	Continuous k nearest neighbour search		
Basic idea	Monitor border points	Swap the position to calculate split nodes	Monitor candidate POI and use trend to find split nodes
Segment	Ignore	Need to check segment by segment	
Voronoi polygon	Expansion polygon by polygon	Ignore	Ignore
Split node predicable	Yes	No	No
Visible	Yes	No	No
Do KNN	No	Yes	Yes

4.3 VCKNN Algorithm

The benefits offered by the VCKNN processing are supported by the inherent proposition of Network Voronoi Diagram, The VCKNN algorithm [9] is shown in Figure 4.

Algorithm VCKNN (q, k, moving path SE)

Input: k, query point q, moving path SE
Output: Voronoi-CKNN result
1. 1^{st}NN = contain (q) //first NN will be the generator where polygon contains query point.
2.   Initial $CS = \{1^{st}$NN's neighbor generator$\}$.
3. $M = 1$ //M is the level number of NN already found
4.   Result = $\{1^{st}$ NN (moving interval of query point)$\}$//the interval of where query point is valid will be put into the bracket.
5.   If $M>1$ then
6.   For each polygon where SE goes across
7.   Expand q to each border point
8.   Draw a line for each border point & get piecewise func for each border point
9.   Add border to generator distance to the line
10. The lowest line will the 2^{nd}NN. Intersect points will be split nodes. Set $M = 2$
11.   Result = Result +$\{$ 2^{nd}NN(moving interval^1),...,2^{nd}NN(moving interval^n) //moving interval$^{1\sim n}$ is divided by the split nodes.
12.   Do while ($M<K$)
13.   For all intervals which separate by split node
14. $CS = \{CS + M^{th}$ neighbour generator $\}$
15.   For each interest point in CS, draw a line for this interval
16.   The lowest line will be the $(M+1)^{th}$NN.
17.   Result = Result +$\{$ $(M+1)^{th}$(moving interval^1),..., $(M+1)^{th}$(moving interval^n),$\}$
18. $M = M + 1$
19.   Intersect nodes are split nodes
20.   Terminate the algorithm when $M = K$
    End VCKNN

Fig. 4. The VCKNN algorithm

4.4 Neural Network-Based Method

We assume objects move in a piecewise linear manner. In this scenario, an object moves along a straight line with some constant speed till it changes the direction. We use a vector $\vec{x} = (x_1, x_2, ..., x_n)$ to denote the location of a moving object. It is a function of time t and can be written as $\vec{x} = \vec{x}(t_0) + \vec{v}t$ where t_0 is the initial location of the object at some referential instance t_0, and $\vec{v} \in \mathbb{R}^n$ is the velocity vector. In the moving object framework, the KNN problem is defined as: *"Given a set of moving objects and an object at some time instant t, find objects which are the closest to o at time t'*. We choose Euclidean distance here for simplicity and clarity, although any other eligible metric will work under our framework.

Given a set of S moving objects, the KNN of a query object at time t is represented by S_k^o. The k-th neighbor is denoted as $O_k^o(t)$. We use KNN and KNN *set* interchangeably. In order to represent moving objects, we denote the location of an object o at time as loc_o^t. In 2-D space, $loc_o^t = (x_o^t, y_o^t)$, where x_o^t and y_o^t are the coordinate of object o at time t. The term _ is omitted when it is clear from the context. Let $\overrightarrow{v_0}^{(t_1,t_2)}$ denote the velocity vector of object o during time slot (t_1, t_2). The term (t_1, t_2) is omitted when it is clear from the context. The distance between two objects o_1, o_2 at time t is defined as $d_t(o_1, o_2)$. The term t is omitted when there is no confusion.

Based on the VCKNN algorithm the **Neural Network-based** algorithm is proposed as follows:

Step 1: 1st NN

Use the *contain(q)* function to get the Voronoi polygon, which includes the query point. This polygon's generator will be the 1stNN until it moves out from this polygon. We define the energy function of the neural network based on the number of 1stNN within the polygon.

Step 2: Split nodes and recomputed the energy function of neural network.

The intersections between query path and polygon borders are split nodes and the energy function is recomputed.

Step 3: Moving Interval

Moving interval will have segments within the Voronoi polygons and the query path is divided into several *Moving interval*s. For each *Moving interval*, we do the following. From the beginning point of the interval, expand the road network to every border point of this polygon and record the distance. For each border point, monitor the change of the distance. Get the piecewise function for each border point according to query point's moving out distance, and then a set of *candidate interest points (CS)* is initialized that contains all adjacent neighbors of 1st NN.

Step 4: Candidate Interest Points (CS)

Based on the distance of interval the algorithm tries to minimize the energy function in different iterations. The lines would be generated during the evolution of the energy function and based on it; the algorithm will put them into a chart where x is the moving distance of the query point. The energy function of the whole network would be the summation of all query point distances from the set of generators. The energy function is as follows:

$$E = \sum_{j=1}^{k} \sum_{i=1}^{N} Network\_Dist(u, s_i) \tag{3}$$

where, u is the set of generators and s is the query point set.

To get the state change for each neuron and by getting the first derivation of the each node, the state if each neuron at time t is as follows:

$$\frac{du_t}{dt} = \sum_{i=1}^{N} Network\_Dist(u, s_i) \tag{4}$$

If the solution is not feasible for a set of querying points, new node will be add to the network and the network evaluates the feasibility of current solution.

5   Experiments and Validation

We compare the results of neural algorithm with the VCKNN algorithm. We implement the algorithm on a Pentium 4 PC under Windows Vista with Matlab. In our simulations, since each moving object is represented single node in the algorithm, we expect the data structure size of ours is smaller than that of the VCKNN algorithm, although they are of the same asymptotic complexity $O(n)$, where   is the size of the dataset. As a result, neural algorithm's rebuild cost will be lower. However, the Neural-based algorithm leads to significantly more rebuilds. During the time interval of length *evaluation*, there is no rebuild with the algorithm, while there usually are multiple rebuilds with VCKNN algorithm, due to the breaks of the constraints, however, adding new nodes would result in a total rerunning the algorithm. The VCKNN algorithm excels in terms of the overall performance, since the rebuild cost is the dominant factor. Note that in the experiment, we do not consider the initial build.

Also set up a similar experimental environment as follows: our experiments are conducted in a 2-D world with size 1000x1000, where objects are uniformly distributed. The speed of an object is a random variable that satisfies the uniform distribution on (0, 3). We decompose each curve into 4 segments. The segment size is set to be 2 time units. The time between two consecutive updates for an object is uniformly distributed on (0,120) with the average 60. We use 10 seed point nodes and 50000 objects. For the VCKNN algorithm, distance is set to 50. We select the query object randomly, and the query object does not change the object during the experiments. Afterward, we compare the disk accesses of the proposed algorithm with VCKNN algorithm under different values.

From Table 2 and Figure 5, we conclude that the total query response time of neural based method is better than the query response time of VCKNN. On average Neural method is 20 percent faster than VCKNN algorithm. This is because neural algorithm requires computing fewer and requires no expensive shortest path computations. However, as the number of k increases the difference in performance marginally reduces (in terms of percentages).

In general, as the density (number of interest points compared to total number of links in the network) of the data increases, more intersection points are created. Hence, more split points are expected to appear on the path. Despite of the decrement in computation time, the number of KNN queries is more than the VCKNN algorithm. This is due to the incremental nature of the neural algorithm. Each node is added at a time, and if it results in a practical solution then the result is saved. This adding process provides extra overhead to the network.

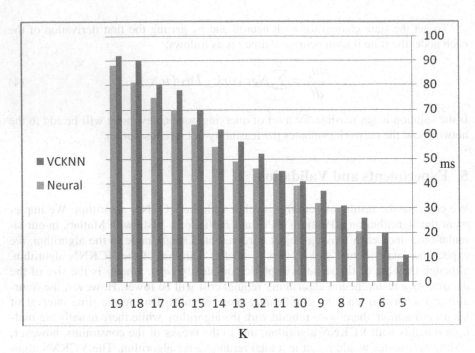

Fig. 5. Computational time for VCKNN and neural algorithms

Table 2. Performance of Neural-based Algorithm to solve Continuous KNN queries

Traveling Path Averaged over 100 queries		K=1	K=3	K=5	K=10	K=20
Entities	Qty (density)	#KNN Queries	#KNN Queries	#KNN Queries	#KNN Queries	#KNN Queries
		Execution Time	Execution Time	Execution Time	Execution Time	Execution Time
Q1	46	24.12	22.96	23.9	22.97	22.5
		13.73	20.11	35.05	70.28	308.12
Q2	173	23.88	22.87	23.22	22.71	23.02
		4.31	8.04	11.47	16.01	40.11
Q3	561	23.15	22.74	22.58	22.31	23.56
		0.74	2.32	4.11	11.08	11.17
Q4	1230	23.06	23.15	22.98	23.31	23.27
		0.32	1.24	1.78	4.64	10.18
Q5	2093	23.71	23.6	23.33	23.2	23.35
		0.14	0.55	0.97	1.94	3.96
Q6	2944	22.34	22.66	22.51	22.69	22.06
		0.12	0.41	0.73	1.31	2.75

Another issue with the neural network is the problem of inaccuracy of split points. While the resulted split points found by the algorithm are very close to the ones found by the VCKNN algorithm, the results are not accurate. This might be a serious issue in applications where the exact points are critical as results of the algorithm. Such an application could be the k nearest airports through a path from a source to a destination.

6 Conclusion and Future Work

In this paper, we have proposed a neural network based approach for continuous k nearest neighbor search according to network distance. The basis of the proposed method is using network expansion within each polygon and drawing line for every border point. Different approaches and applications of GIS have also been discussed and general optimization strategies have been discussed. Implementation and experimental results show that the algorithm is faster comparing to VCKNN (DAR and eDAR) algorithms, however, it suffers from the serious issue of inaccuracy of split nodes which makes the algorithm useless in applications where the exact split nodes is critical. Despite of this, in applications like K-nearest gas satiations or even mobile event points, the algorithm can act very well, especially when the number of query points are high (assume a road with thousands of cars) and the efficiency of algorithm in terms of speed is important.

At the moment, we are trying to utilize the algorithm in another way to enhance find the exact points. By other means finding approximate points, the algorithm would stop and a DAR-like algorithm will find the exact points. This is algorithm is under implementation. One of the main issues in CKNN, particularly using the Voronoi diagram approach, is the storage space. We are planning to manage the storage issue using global indexing which has been shown to be effective in high performance database and mobile database systems [23-27]. Another factor that might help increase performance is by finding patterns of mobile movements [5,6,28]. We also plan to extend the type of queries to other mobile queries suitable for mobile navigations [29-31].

References

[1] Waluyo, A.B., Srinivasan, B., Taniar, D.: Research in mobile database query optimization and processing. Mobile Information Systems 1(4), 225–252 (2005)
[2] Jayaputera, J., Taniar, D.: Data retrieval for location-dependent queries in a multi-cell wireless environment. Mobile Information Systems 1(2), 91–108 (2005)
[3] Mammeri, Z., Morvan, F., Hameurlain, A., Marsit, N.: Location-dependent query processing under soft real-time constraints. Mobile Information Systems 5(3), 205–232 (2009)
[4] Zhao, G., Xuan, K., Taniar, D., Safar, M., Gavrilova, M.L., Srinivasan, B.: Multiple Object Types KNN Search Using Network Voronoi Diagram. In: Gervasi, O., Taniar, D., Murgante, B., Laganà, A., Mun, Y., Gavrilova, M.L. (eds.) Computational Science and Its Applications – ICCSA 2009. LNCS, vol. 5593, pp. 819–834. Springer, Heidelberg (2009)
[5] Taniar, D., Goh, J.: On Mining Movement Pattern from Mobile Users. International Journal of Distributed Sensor Networks 3(1), 69–86 (2007)

[6] Goh, J.Y., Taniar, D.: Mobile Data Mining by Location Dependencies. In: Yang, Z.R., Yin, H., Everson, R.M. (eds.) IDEAL 2004. LNCS, vol. 3177, pp. 225–231. Springer, Heidelberg (2004)

[7] Fülöp, P., Imre, S., Szabó, S., Szálka, T.: Accurate mobility modeling and location prediction based on pattern analysis of handover series in mobile networks. Mobile Information Systems 5(3), 255–289 (2009)

[8] Yamazaki, A., Koyama, A., Arai, J., Barolli, L.: Design and implementation of a ubiquitous health monitoring system. International Journal of Web and Grid Services 5(4), 339–355 (2009)

[9] Zhao, G., Xuan, K., Rahayu, W., Taniar, D., Safar, M., Gavrilova, M., Srinivasan, B.: Voronoi-based Continuous k Nearest Neighbor Search in Mobile Navigation. IEEE Transactions on Industrial Electronics 56 (online since June 2009)

[10] Kolahdouzan, M., Shahabi, C.: Voronoi-Based K Nearest Neighbor Search for Spatial Network Databases. In: Proceedings of VLDB Conference, pp. 840–851. Morgan Kaufmann, Toronto (2004)

[11] Safar, M., Ebrahimi, D.: eDAR Algorithm for Continuous KNN Queries Based on Pine. Int. J. of Information Technology and Web Engineering, IGI Global 1(4), 1–21 (2006)

[12] Nozawa, H.: A neural-network model as a globally coupled map and applications based on chaos. Chaos 2(3), 377–386 (1992)

[13] Chen, L., Aihara, K.: Chaos and asymptotical stability in discrete time neural networks. Phys. D 104, 286–325 (1997)

[14] Aihara, K., Takabe, T., Toyoda, M.: Chaotic neural networks. Phys. Lett. A 144(6-7), 333–340 (1990)

[15] Yamada, T., Aihara, K., Kotani, M.: Chaotic neural networks and the travelling salesman problem. In: Proc. Int. Joint Conf. Neural Networks, pp. 1549–1552 (1993)

[16] Yeo, J., Lee, H., Kim, S.: An efficient broadcast scheduling algorithm for TDMA ad-hoc networks. Comput. Oper. Res (29), 1793–1806 (2002)

[17] Beard, K.: Constraints on Rule Formation. In: Buttenfield, B.P., McMaster, R.B. (eds.) Map Generalization: Making Rules for Knowledge Representation, pp. 121–135. Longman, London (1991)

[18] Lamy, et al.: AGENT Project: Automated Generalization New Technology. In: 5th EC-GIS Workshop, Stresa, Italy (June 1999) http://agent.ign.fr/public/stresa.pdf

[19] Metropolis, N., Rosenbluth, A.W., Rosenbluth, M., Teller, A.H., Teller, E.: Equation of State Calculations by Fast Computing Machines. J. Chem. Phys 21, 1087–1092 (1953)

[20] Kirkpatrick, S., Gelatt, C.D., Vecchi, M.P.: Optimization by Simulated Annealing. Science 220, 671–680 (1983)

[21] Ware, J.M., Jones, C.B.: Conflict Reduction in Map Generalization Using Iterative Improvement. Geoinformatica 2(4), 383–407 (1998)

[22] Papadias, D., Zhang, J., Mamoulis, N., Tao, Y.: Query Processing in Spatial Network Databases. In: Proceedings of the VLDB Conference, pp. 802–813 (2003)

[23] Taniar, D., Rahayu, J.W.: Global parallel index for multi-processors database systems. Information Sciences 165(1-2), 103–127 (2004)

[24] Taniar, D., Rahayu, J.W.: A Taxonomy of Indexing Schemes for Parallel Database Systems. Distributed and Parallel Databases 12(1), 73–106 (2002)

[25] Waluyo, A.B., Srinivasan, B., Taniar, D.: A Taxonomy of Broadcast Indexing Schemes for Multi Channel Data Dissemination in Mobile Database. In: Proceedings of the 18th International Conference on Advanced Information Networking and Applications (AINA 2004), vol. 1, pp. 213–218. IEEE Computer Society, Los Alamitos (2004)

[26] Gómez, L., Kuijpers, B., Moelans, B., Vaisman, A.: A Survey of Spatio-Temporal Data Warehousing. International Journal of Data Warehousing and Mining 5(3), 28–55 (2009)

[27] Taniar, D., Rahayu, J.W.: Parallel database sorting. Information Sciences 146(1-4), 171–219 (2002)

[28] Goh, J., Taniar, D.: Mining frequency pattern from mobile users. In: Negoita, M.G., Howlett, R.J., Jain, L.C. (eds.) KES 2004. LNCS (LNAI), vol. 3215, pp. 795–801. Springer, Heidelberg (2004)

[29] Xuan, K., Zhao, G., Taniar, D., Srinivasan, B., Safar, M., Gavrilova, M.L.: Network Voronoi Diagram Based Range Search. In: Proceedings of the IEEE 23rd International Conference on Advanced Information Networking and Applications (AINA 2009), pp. 741–748 (2009)

[30] Taniar, D., Rahayu, J.W.: Parallel sort-merge object-oriented collection join algorithms. International Journal of Computer Systems Science and Engineering 17(3), 145–158 (2002)

[31] Waluyo, A.B., Srinivasan, B., Taniar, D.: Optimal Broadcast Channel for Data Dissemination in Mobile Database Environment. In: Zhou, X., Xu, M., Jähnichen, S., Cao, J. (eds.) APPT 2003. LNCS, vol. 2834, pp. 665–675. Springer, Heidelberg (2003)

The Application of Disturbance Observer to Propulsion Control of Sub-mini Underwater Robot

Yuyi Zhai[1], Liang Liu[1], Wenjie Lu[1], Yu Li[1], Shiliang Yang[1], and Francesco Villecco[2]

[1] School of Mechatronics andAutomation, Shanghai University
200072, Shanghai., China
yyzhai@mail.shu.edu.cn
[2] Department of Mechanical Engineering, Faculty of Engineering ,
University of Salerno, Via Ponte Don Melillo
84084, Fisciano (SA)-Italy

Abstract. In this paper, the propulsive motility characteristics and the corresponding motion equations of a self-designed sub-mini underwater robot were analyzed. And the disturbance observer was used in propulsive motility control of the underwater robot. According to feedback control principle and dynamic performance index of controlled object, the disturbance observer parameter was designed. Digital simulation of propulsion system indicated that system had a better inhibition effect to the disturbance and the propulsive motility control performance of the underwater robot had also been improved. So all the experimental results showed that the disturbance observer has good robustness, also it is very useful to deal with disturbance rejection, which shows its practical value and good performance in motion control.

Keywords: Disturbance observer, Sub-mini underwater robot, Propulsion control, Simulation platform.

1 Introduction

With the gradual maturity of microelectronics technology, great attention has been paid to sub-mini underwater robots. The propulsion control system of a Sub-mini underwater robot is mainly discussed in this paper.

From the space motion of rigid body and the knowledge of Hydrodynamics, we know that the underwater moving force condition of a sub-mini underwater robot is so complex that it has not been fully understood as yet. On the one hand, underwater motion dynamics of a sub-mini underwater robot has strong nonlinearity. The mathematical model of 6 DOF motion based on the principles of the space motion of rigid body and Hydrodynamics has a high degree of uncertainty. And the robot encounters a number of external disturbances, such as undercurrent, which will directly affect the motion performance of robots. These all determine that the automatic control of a sub-mini underwater robot is very complex and full of challenge. On the other hand, it is hard to obtain accurate mathematical model of a sub-mini underwater robot. The model is so complex that it isn't suitable for the control system design even though the mathematical model obtained is precise enough. So the motion model is necessary

D. Taniar et al. (Eds.): ICCSA 2010, Part I, LNCS 6016, pp. 590–598, 2010.

to be simplified when designing control system, which leads to the error between control system's design model and its mathematical motion model of controlled object, and consequently leads to the uncertainty of this design model. This paper intended to research on the propulsion disturbance control in horizontal plane under the premise of complex spatial motion of a sub-mini underwater robot. The disturbance observer was used in propulsion control of the sub-mini underwater robot to improve the propulsive motility control performance.

2 Propulsive Motility Model of System

Our self-designed sub-mini underwater robot was used as a simulation platform for the study. The propulsive motility of the sub-mini underwater robot adopted two separate motors and the forward, backward, left and right basic movements are carried by changing the angular velocity of two separate motors. In Fig. 1, through establishing the coordinate system, the propelling movement equations of underwater robot can be described [1] .

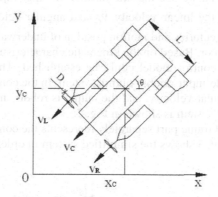

Fig. 1. Propulsive motility model of underwater robot

In Fig.1, v_C is the linear velocity of centroid of underwater robot. v_L , v_R is the linear velocity of left and right motor. D is propeller radius. L is the distance between the two motors. x , y are the two-dimensional plane coordinates of the robot centroid.

Centroid motion equations of underwater robot are as follows:

$$\dot{x}_c = v_c \cos\theta , \quad \dot{y}_c = v_c \sin\theta , \quad \dot{\theta} = \omega$$

$$P = \begin{bmatrix} \dot{x}_c \\ \dot{y}_c \\ \dot{\theta} \end{bmatrix} = \begin{bmatrix} \cos\theta & 0 \\ \sin\theta & 0 \\ 0 & 1 \end{bmatrix} \begin{bmatrix} v_c \\ \omega \end{bmatrix} \tag{1}$$

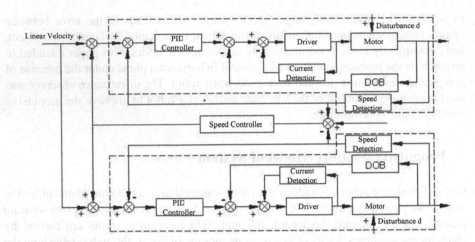

Fig. 2. Structure diagram of propulsion control system of underwater robot

From the equation (1), we see that the desired moving trajectory can be obtained through the control of the linear velocity v_C and angular velocity ω of underwater robot. The different trajectories and motion position of underwater robot are controlled by the left and right motor. Based on the kinematic characteristics of underwater robot and kinematic model, control model could be established. The whole robot motion control became a double-input-double-output system. In the control model, the input is linear velocity and angular velocity, and the output is robots' motor speed. The structure diagram of control system is shown in Fig. 2:

In Fig. 2, the dashed frame part separately represents the control process of left and right motors [2,3,4]. Fig. 3 shows the simplified system in order to analyze its transfer characteristics.

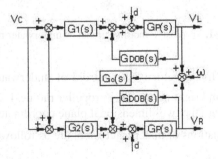

Fig. 3. Block diagram of underwater robot's propulsion control system.

In Fig. 3, $G_1(s)$、$G_2(s)$ are transfer functions of PID controller in propulsion control system; GP(s) is overall transfer function of the motor driver, motors and current detection; GDOB(s) is transfer function of disturbance observer; Gc(s) is transfer function of speed controller.

In control process, the robot encounters a number of external disturbances, such as undercurrent, which affects the robots' motion performance directly. Therefore, these unexpected situations must be well handled by use of disturbance observer, and then the two motors' speed could be controlled precisely.

According to the block diagram of propulsion control system shown in Fig. 3, the response of the two motors' speed in the control system is obtained by the use of Mason formula[5,6], which was equation (2):

$$
\begin{bmatrix} v_L \\ v_R \end{bmatrix} = \begin{bmatrix} \dfrac{G_pG_1(1+G_2G_c)+G_1G_pG_2G_c}{1+G_pG_{DOB}+G_1G_pG_c+G_2G_c+G_2G_pG_cG_{DOB}} & \dfrac{-G_1G_pG_c}{1+G_pG_{DOB}+G_1G_pG_c+G_2G_c+G_2G_pG_cG_{DOB}} \\ \dfrac{G_pG_2(1+G_1G_c)+G_2G_pG_1G_c}{1+G_pG_{DOB}+G_2G_pG_c+G_1G_c+G_1G_pG_cG_{DOB}} & \dfrac{G_2G_pG_c}{1+G_pG_{DOB}+G_1G_pG_c+G_2G_c+G_2G_pG_cG_{DOB}} \end{bmatrix} \begin{bmatrix} v_c \\ \omega \end{bmatrix} \tag{2}
$$

Equation (2) shows that the closed-loop transfer matrix of the propulsion system is a coupling matrix and means the system is a coupling system. Controlling a coupled system is so complex that an output only affected by an input is required in an engineering project. And this controlling style is called decoupling control. So, the system is decoupled in order to simplify the system and shown as equation (3):

$$
\begin{bmatrix} v_L \\ v_R \end{bmatrix} = \begin{bmatrix} \dfrac{G_1G_p}{1+G_pG_{DOB}+G_1G_pG_c} & 0 \\ 0 & \dfrac{G_2G_pG_c}{1+G_{DOB}} \end{bmatrix} \cdot \begin{bmatrix} v_c \\ \omega \end{bmatrix} . \tag{3}
$$

Equation (3) shows that the original propulsion system is equivalent to two single-input single-output systems. Now with taking the underwater robot as the simulation object, the robot control can be transformed into the motor control.

After the simplification, derivation, consult related technical parameters and through experimental test in the control system, the transfer function of controlled object is finally got as equation (4):

$$
G_P(s) = \frac{0.06s + 13.2}{2.07 \times 10^{-5} s^2 + 9.1 \times 10^{-3} s + 18467.8} . \tag{4}
$$

3 Disturbance Observer

Disturbance observer (DOB) can be used to estimate disturbance, and estimation signal will offset input disturbance d_{ex} [7,8,9] .Fig. 4 is the DOB structure diagram:

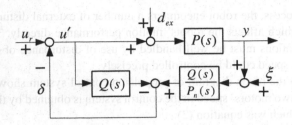

Fig. 4. Usual block diagram of disturbance observer

DOB is accomplished by using the low-pass filter $Q(s)$ and the reciprocal of nominal model $P(s)$. As shown in the Figure, the output of nominal object can be represented in reference to control inputs u_r, external interference signal d_{ex} and noise signal ξ [10,11]:

$$y = [P_n(s)u_r + P_n(s)\{1 - Q(s)\}d_{ex} - Q(s)\xi] \frac{P(s)}{\chi(s)} . \tag{5}$$

In equation (5), $\chi(s) = P_n(s) + [P(s) - P_n(s)]Q(s)$. The signal is lower than the $Q(s)$ cut-off frequency could pass, so that low-frequency interference signal is weakened and the error between controlled object $P(s)$ and nominal model $P_n(s)$ is compensated. The purpose of DOB is to eliminate external interference of controlled object during the motion course [11]. Fig. 5 shows the block diagram of disturbance observer:

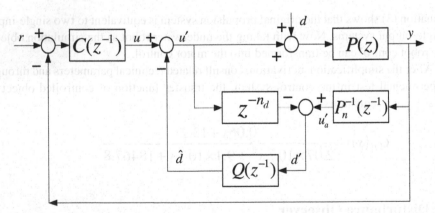

Fig. 5. Block diagram of disturbance observer

In Figure 5, $C(z^{-1})$ is PID controller in the experimental model; $P(z)$ is the controlled object in experimental model; $\hat{d}$ is the estimated value of disturbance;

$P_n^{-1}(z^{-1})$ is the reciprocal of $P_n(z)$, $P_n(z)$ is the nominal model of $P(z)$; n_d is the retardation coefficient of control signal u' and is the compensation signal generated by the controller $C(z^{-1})$ for u; $Q(z^{-1})$ is a low-pass filter with a relative degree n_Q and a cut-off frequency ω_Q. d is an external disturbance. The output y of controlled object passes by $P_n^{-1}(z^{-1})$ to get u'_a and error signal d', then disturbance $\hat{d}$ can be estimated by low-pass filter $Q(z^{-1})$. Through the feedback system, the disturbance is counteracted in order to achieve the desired moving trajectory.

In many motion control systems, the form of nominal model is $\dfrac{K}{(\tau S+1)S}$, and in this case, P_n^{-1} could be approximated by using of impulse response. So there is no limit on the relative degree of Q. But the realization of $Q P_n^{-1}$ required the relative degree of Q should be greater than or equal to P_n.

4 Propulsion System Model Control

According to the inherent correlating parameter of the self-designed underwater robot, open-loop transfer function of controlled object could be calculated as $G_P(s) = \dfrac{0.06s+13.2}{2.07\times10^{-5}s^2+9.1\times10^{-3}s+18467.8}$. Using Z-Transform could get the discrete form of transfer function $P(z) = \dfrac{0.01396z^2}{1.182z^2-2.182z+1}$. In many motion control systems, $P_n(s)$ is a nominal model of controlled object $G_P(s)$ and its general form is $P_n(s) = \dfrac{K}{(\tau S+1)S}$. Checking the technical parameters of motor we could get

$$P_n(s) = \frac{18.8\times10^{-3}}{(9.29\times10^{-3}S+1)S}, \quad \text{then the reciprocal of } P_n(s) \text{ was}$$

$P_n^{-1}(s) = \dfrac{(9.29\times10^{-3}S+1)S}{18.8\times10^{-3}}$. Besides, the key of design lay in the low-pass filter Q. The order of Q must be greater than or equal to the order of nominal model $P_n(s)$, so supposed $Q(s) = \dfrac{1}{(\tau_1 s)^2+2\tau_1 s+1}$ and choose $\tau_1 \approx 10\sim15T_s$ (T_s is sampling period), the discretization of system is made by using of backward difference method based on the experiments.

In the process of simulation, selecting $T_s = 0.001s$, then $\tau_1 = 0.01s$, so

$Q(s) = \dfrac{1}{(0.01s+1)^2}$, and then changing $P_n^{-1}(s)$ and $Q(s)$ on Z-Transform so that

we could get $P_n^{-1}(z^{-1}) = \dfrac{z^2 - 1.898z + 0.898}{1917.6z}$ and $Q(z^{-1}) = \dfrac{9.048z}{(z - 0.9048)^2}$.

These discrete transfer functions were substituted in the digital block diagram of disturbance observer shown in Fig. 5. And based on equivalent transformation and simplification of structure, the two simplified transfer functions, Discrete Transfer Fcn1 and Discrete Transfer Fcn2, were finally obtained in Fig. 6. At last, according to Z plane root locus method and dynamic performance index of controlled object, a suitable PID controller parameters were designed (P=1, i=0.0001, d=2) for ultimate fulfillment of experiment model. Then, with simulation platform of simulink, the digital experiment simulation is carried out to propulsion system. The result is shown in Fig. 6:

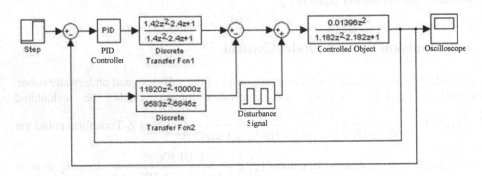

Fig. 6. Digital Simulation Diagram of Propulsion System

In the actual process, a variety of disturbances might be present here such as pulse signal, step signal, random signal. In addition, taking into account the convenience and vivacity of the experimental data analysis, any undercurrent encountered in the motion process was regarded as a pulse signal. Thus, output characteristics were observed through computer simulation technology under a period of 400ms pulse signal given to the system as a disturbance signal in the control process. In the initial phase of the experiment, a unit step signal and a disturbance signal was put into the system and the disturbance signal was high at this time. In the absence of DOB, system was affected by disturbance signal so that the output value became the supposition of two signals. Therefore, the system reached the steady-state value 2 quickly. When t=200ms, systems was affected by the low level part of pulse signal so that its output value became another steady-state value 1. So we can see that, under the disturbance, signal system's output was not normally according to the original signal. The experiment result was showed as Fig. 7:

On the contrary, the system with DOB was affected by the high level of disturbance signals in the initial stage and slightly deviated from the theoretical value and resulted

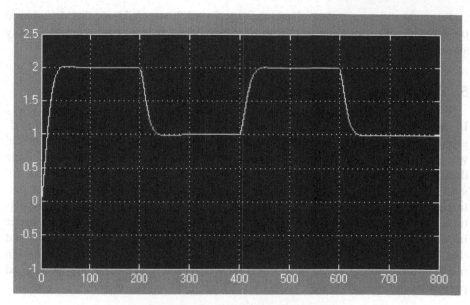

Fig. 7. Experimental results without DOB

in a mutation. Due to the action of disturbance observer, the system spent about 70ms on the resumption of the theoretical value. This explained that the disturbance observer could eliminate the disturbance when disturbed and achieve the precise motion control. The experiment results were showed as Fig. 8:

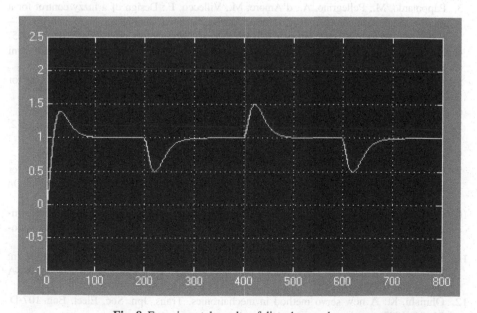

Fig. 8. Experimental results of disturbance observer

From the experimental results in the Fig. 7 and 8, we could see that disturbance observer played a prominent role in the disturbance rejection aspect, which fully showed its practical value in motion control.

5 Conclusion

In this paper, propulsive motility control model was established through the propulsive kinematic model of underwater robot. At the same time, motion control model was analyzed and simplified so that the parameters of the disturbance observer were designed according to controlled object. Make a further simulation to the control system and decide whether to use the experimental results obtained by using disturbance observer controller under the disturbed circumstances. This displayed disturbance observer's significant role in the disturbance rejection aspect and better improvement on the motion performance of underwater robot. The results showed that the design of disturbance observer controller could eliminate control design model's uncertainties in the level of propulsive motility. The controller has a good performance.

References

1. Dai, X.-f., Bian, X.-q.: Simulation on Trajectory Control of A 6-DOF Underwater Vehicle. Journal of System Simulation 13(3), 368–369 (2001)
2. Xing, Z.-W., Zhang, Y., Feng, X.: Position Estimation of Underwater Vehicle Based on Usbl/Doppler. Robot 25(3), 231–234 (2003)
3. Pappalardo, M., Pellegrino, A., d'Amore, M., Villecco, F.: Design of a fuzzy control for a microwave monomode cavity to soot trap filter regeneration. Intelligence in a Small World – nanomaterials for the 21st Century, CRC- Press in Boca Raton, Florida, 1-932078-19-3 (2005)
4. Zhai, Y.-y., Ma, J.-m., Yao, Z.-l., Gong, Z.-b.: Ups and Downs System Design of Sub-Mini Shallow-Water Robot. Optics and Precision Engineering 12(3), 299–302 (2004)
5. Zhai, Y.-Y., Chen, Y., Gong, Z.-B., Tang, H.-B., Ma, J.-M.: Heave Motion Control for Sub-mini Underwater Vehicle. Journal of Applied Sciences 25(2), 189–192 (2007)
6. Sun, D.-b.: Automatic control principle, vol. 1. Chemical Industry Press, Beijing (2002)
7. Gao, J.-y.: The theory the design and realization of computer control system, vol. Version 2. Beijing University of Aeronautics and Astronautics Press, Beijing (2001)
8. Chen, Y.: Blas M.Vinagre & Igor Pldlubny. On Fractional Order Disturbance Observer
9. Kiogtan, K., Henglee, T., Hao, S.: Precision Motion Control with Disturbance Observer for Pulsewidth-Modulated-Driven Permanent-Magnet Linear Motors. IEEE Transactions On Magnetics 39(3) (May 2003)
10. Choi, Y., Yang, K., Chung, W.K., Kim, H.R., Suh II, H.: On the Robustness and Performance of Disturbance Observers for Second-Order Systems. IEEE Transactions On Automatic Control 48(2) (February 2003)
11. Lee, S.-H., Chung, C.C.: Robust Control Using A State Space Disturbance Obserber. In: Proceedings of the 42nd IEEE Conference on Decision and Control Maui, Hawaii, USA (December 2003)
12. Ohnishi, K.: A new servo method in mechatronics. Trans. Jpn. Soc. Elect. Eng. 107-D, 83–86 (1987)

On the Security Enhancement of an Efficient and Secure Event Signature Protocol for P2P MMOGs

Chun-Ta Li[1], Cheng-Chi Lee[2,*], and Lian-Jun Wang[3]

[1] Department of Information Management, Tainan University of Technology
529 Jhong Jheng Road, Yongkang, 710 Tainan, Taiwan, R.O.C.
th0040@mail.tut.edu.tw
[2] Department of Photonics and Communication Engineering, Asia University
500 Lioufeng Road, 413 Taichung, Taiwan, R.O.C.
cclee@asia.edu.tw
[3] Department of Information Management, Yuan-Ze University
135 Yuan-Tung Road, 320 Chung-Li, Taiwan, R.O.C.

Abstract. In 2008, Chan et al. presented an efficient and secure event signature (EASES) protocol for peer-to-peer massively multiplayer online games (P2P MMOGs). EASES could achieve non-repudiation, event commitment, save memory, bandwidth and reduce the complexity of the computations. However, we find that Chan et al. EASES protocol suffers from the passive attack and this attack will make a malicious attacker to impersonate any player to replay the event update messages for cheating. As a result, we introduce a simple countermeasure to prevent impersonate attack while the merits of the original EASES protocol are left unchanged.

Keywords: Cryptanalysis, Hash functions, Massively multiplayer online games, One-time signature, Peer-to-peer networks, Network security.

1   Introduction

An event update is cryptographic protocol by which a player generates an event message and sends it to the server for updating the game states. Traditional massively multiplayer online games (MMOGs) are conventional client-server models that do not scale with the number of simultaneous clients that need to be supported. To resolve conflicts in the simulation and act as a central repository for data, peer-to-peer (P2P) architecture is increasingly being considered as replacement for traditional client-server architecture in MMOGs. P2P MMOGs have many advantages over traditional client-server systems due to their network connectivity and basic network services in a self-organizing manner. Whenever a player wants to play the finger-guessing game, an event message is sent to the server and the server processes all the events and updates the game states

---

* Corresponding author.

D. Taniar et al. (Eds.): ICCSA 2010, Part I, LNCS 6016, pp. 599–609, 2010.
© Springer-Verlag Berlin Heidelberg 2010

to ensure a global ordering for game executions and fair plays. However, P2P MMOGs communicate on the Internet raise the security issues such as cheating, a dishonest player can get valuable virtual items and even be sold for money-making.

Recently, there are more and more efforts mounted to focus on event update protocols for online games in respect to the protection of sensitive communication and the provision of fair play. In 2004, Dickey et al. [3] proposed a low latency and cheat-proof event ordering based on digital signatures and voting mechanism for P2P games. However, Corman et al. later show that Dickey et al.'s protocol is unable to prevent all cheats as claimed, and propose an improvement called secure event agreement protocol [2]. As digital signature requires a large amount of computations. To reduce heavyweight computations in every round of a game session, in 2008, Chan et al. [1] proposed an efficient and secure event signature (EASES) protocol using one-time signature with hash-chain key and claimed that their protocol has low computation and bandwidth costs, and is thus applicable to P2P-based MMOGs. Unfortunately, we find that EASES protocol is vulnerable to an impersonation attack and we will suggest a simple countermeasure to enhance the security of EASES protocol against impersonation attack.

In this paper, we brief review Chan et al. EASES protocol in Section 2 and show the security flaw in Section 3. We proposed a protocol for P2P-based MMOGs in Section 4. Finally, Section 5 is our conclusion.

2   Review of Chan et al. EASES Protocol

Before describing Chan et al. EASES protocol, we define some notations which will be utilized in this paper.

- P_x: the xth player in the game.
- sk_x: player x's private key.
- pk_x: player x's public key.
- $(a||b)$: concatenation of message a and b.
- $H(\cdot)$: a public one-way hashing function.
- $S_{sk_x}(m)$: a message m signed by P_x's private key.
- $D_{pk_x}(m)$: a message m decrypted by P_x's public key.
- K_x^r: one-time signature key of P_x in the rth round.
- U_x^r: an event update of P_x in the rth round.
- δ_x^r: a signature signed by P_x's rth one-time signature key.
- Δ_x: a signature signed by P_x's private key.

EASES protocol is composed of four phases namely, initialization, signing, verification, and re-initialization phase, which are presented in the following subsections.

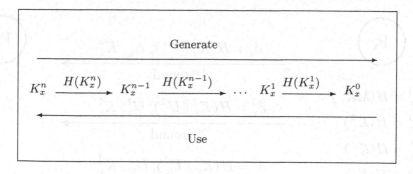

Fig. 1. Construction of hash-chain keys

2.1   Initialization Phase

In the initialization phase, player P_x generates a series of one-time signature keys for a session and performs the following operations:

1. P_x chooses a master key MK_x to compute the nth one-time signature key $K_x^n = h(MK_x)$, where n represents the maximum number of rounds in a session.
2. P_x computes the other rth round one-time signature keys $K_x^{r-1} = H(K_x^r)$, where $r = (n-1), ..., 0$.
3. P_x signs the first one-time signature key by its private key to get the signature $\Delta_x = S_{sk_x}(K_x^0)$. Note that hash-chain keys K_x^r will be used in the reverse order of their production during the subsequent rth rounds, where $r = 0, 1, 2, ..., n-1$.

Figure 1 shows the production of hash-chain keys.

2.2   Signing Phase

If P_x wants to submit event update messages to other online players in a game session with n rounds, he/she performs the following operations:

1. P_x computes the 1st round one-time signature key δ_x^1 by computing $\delta_x^1 = H(K_x^1 \| U_x^1), \Delta_x, K_x^0$, where U_x^1 is P_x's first event update. Then, P_x submits the first round message δ_x^1 to other online players.
2. P_x computes the 2nd round one-time signature key $\delta_x^2 = H(K_x^2 \| U_x^2), U_x^1, K_x^1$ and submits δ_x^2 to other online players.
3. P_x computes the rth round one-time signature key $\delta_x^r = H(K_x^r \| U_x^r), U_x^{r-1}, K_x^{r-1}$ and submits δ_x^r to other online players in the subsequent rth round, where $r = 3, 4, ..., n$.

In Figure 2, we introduce an example to describe the detailed steps of signing phase with transmission action. Suppose there are three rounds in a session and the player P_x sends out the event update messages to the player P_y.

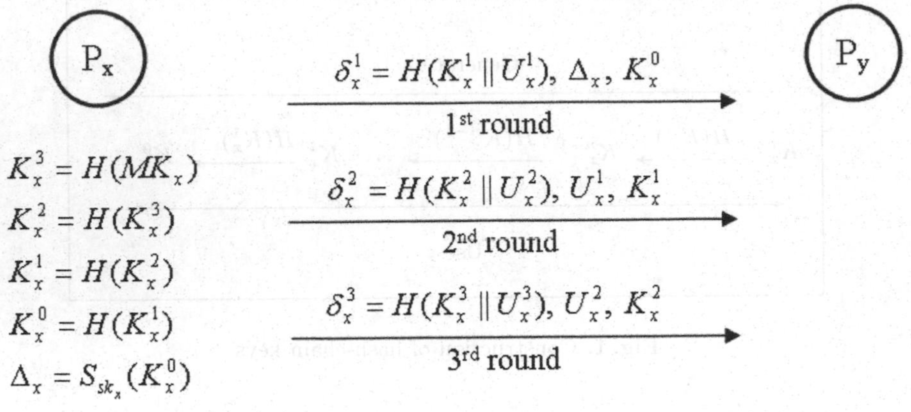

$$K_x^3 = H(MK_x)$$
$$K_x^2 = H(K_x^3)$$
$$K_x^1 = H(K_x^2)$$
$$K_x^0 = H(K_x^1)$$
$$\Delta_x = S_{sk_x}(K_x^0)$$

$\boxed{P_x}$

$$\delta_x^1 = H(K_x^1 \| U_x^1), \Delta_x, K_x^0$$
1st round

$$\delta_x^2 = H(K_x^2 \| U_x^2), U_x^1, K_x^1$$
2nd round

$$\delta_x^3 = H(K_x^3 \| U_x^3), U_x^2, K_x^2$$
3rd round

$\boxed{P_y}$

Fig. 2. Signing phase

2.3   Verification Phase

In the verification phase, online player P_y receives the event update message from the player P_x and performs the following operations:

1. In the first round, P_y first verifies $K_x^0 \overset{?}{=} D_{pk_x}(\Delta_x)$. If it holds, P_y confirms that the key K_x^0 is legitimate; if not, it stops.
2. In the subsequent rth round, P_y verifies $K_x^{r-2} \overset{?}{=} H(K_x^{r-1})$ to check if the signature key K_x^{r-1} is legitimate, where $r = 2, ..., n$.
3. If above holds, P_y verifies $\delta_x^{r-1} \overset{?}{=} H(K_x^{r-1} \| U_x^{r-1})$ to check whether or not the update has been altered. If it passes verification, P_y convinces that no player has tampered with the update from P_x.

2.4   Re-initialization Phase

Whenever P_x wants to extend his/her game session for a few rounds, one basic method is for P_x to start over from the initialization phase to re-generate the new signature keys. However, there is a simple way for P_x to perform the following operations in the nth and $(n + 1)$th round exists.

1. P_x chooses a new master key, MK_x', to generate the new one-time signature keys $NewK_x^0, ..., NewK_x^n$. P_x then hashes the new signature key $NewK_x^0$ with the key $K_x^n = H(MK_x')$ to generate $\delta_x^n = H(K_x^n \| U_x^n \| NewK_x^0)$. P_x sends δ_x^n, U_x^{n-1}, and K_x^{n-1} to other players in the nth round.
2. In the $(n + 1)$th round, P_x computes $\delta_x^{n+1} = H(NewK_x^1 \| U_x^{n+1})$ and sends δ_x^{n+1}, U_x^n, K_x^n, and $NewK_x^0$ to other players.
3. In the $(n + 2)$th round, P_x sends $\delta_x^{n+2} = H(NewK_x^2 \| U_x^{n+2})$, U_x^{n+1}, $NewK_x^1$, and original master key, MK_x, to other players.

Upon receiving new one-time signature keys from P_x, the other player, P_y, should perform the following verifiable operations:

1. In the $(n+1)$th round, P_y verifies $H(K_x^n \| U_x^n \| NewK_x^0) \overset{?}{=} \delta_x^n$ to check if the new signature key $NewK_x^0$ is legitimate.

2. In the $(n+2)$th round, in addition to the regular verifications, P_y must also verify $K_x^n \overset{?}{=} H(MK_x)$. If the above passes verification, P_y confirms the validity of $NewK_x^0$. The series of new one-time signature keys $NewK_x^0, ..., NewK_x^n$ can be used after the $(n+2)$th rounds.

In Figure 3, we introduce an example to describe the detailed steps of re-initialization phase with transmission action.

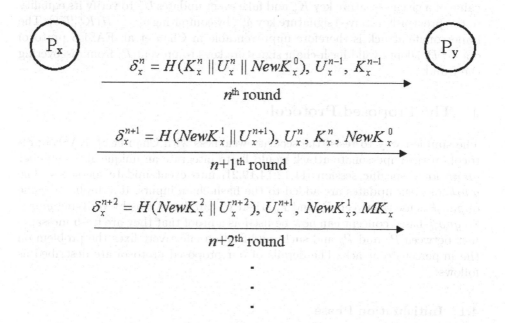

$$\delta_x^n = H(K_x^n \| U_x^n \| NewK_x^0), U_x^{n-1}, K_x^{n-1}$$

n^{th} round

$$\delta_x^{n+1} = H(NewK_x^1 \| U_x^{n+1}), U_x^n, K_x^n, NewK_x^0$$

$n+1^{th}$ round

$$\delta_x^{n+2} = H(NewK_x^2 \| U_x^{n+2}), U_x^{n+1}, NewK_x^1, MK_x$$

$n+2^{th}$ round

.

.

.

Fig. 3. Re-initialization phase

3   Security Analysis of Chan et al. EASES Protocol

In this section, an attacker P_z could impersonate P_x to communication with P_y, and then cheat P_y into believing P_z's fake message. The detailed steps of cryptanalysis of Chan et al. EASES protocol are described as follows.

For passive attacks [4,5,6,7,8,9,10,13,15,16,17,18,19,20], assume an intruder P_z can un-intrusively monitor and collect the communication channels between peer nodes in P2P networks by some way, e.g. eavesdropping the event update messages δ_x^r sent by P_x, where $r = 1, 2, ..., n$. Thus, the one-time signature keys

$K_x^0, K_x^1, ..., K_x^{n-1}, K_x^n$, the signature $\Delta_x = S_{sk_x}(K_x^0)$ and the master key, MK_x, which is transmitted from legal player P_x to other players is collected by P_z during a previous game session. After collecting above communication parameters, P_z can easily impersonate P_x to send forge event updates $U_z^1, U_z^2, ..., U_z^{n-1}, U_z^n$ with valid signature keys $K_x^0, K_x^1, ..., K_x^{n-1}, K_x^n$ to cheat other player P_y in P2P-based MMOGs. Therefore, cheat-prevention thus is not achievable in Chan et al. EASES protocol. Equation (1) shows the fake event message sent by P_z, where $r = 2, ..., n$.

$$\begin{cases} \delta_x^{1'} = H(K_x^1 \| U_z^1), \Delta_x, K_x^0 & \text{in the first round;} \\ \delta_x^{r'} = H(K_x^r \| U_z^r), U_z^{r-1}, K_x^{r-1} & \text{in the } r\text{th round.} \end{cases} \tag{1}$$

Upon receiving event messages from P_z, the other player P_y computes the hash value of a given signature key K_x^r and fake event updates U_z^r to verify its equality to the previously received signature key $\delta_x^{r'}$, by computing $\delta_x^{r'} \overset{?}{=} H(K_x^r \| U_z^r)$. The impersonate attack is therefore unpreventable in Chan et al. EASES protocol due to P_z adopts valid hash-chain signature keys to prevent P_y from discovering the fraud.

4   The Proposed Protocol

The simplest way to resist the security weakness with Chan et al. EASES protocol on the impersonate attack would be to integrate an unique game number $gno\#$ for a specific session [11,12,14,19,21] into event update messages. The $gno\#$ of event updates are added to the hash-chain inputs. If a duplicate value of $gno\#$ is used between P_x and P_y, then P_y can detect this by verifying $gno\#$. So $gno\#$-based concept can now be used as a proof that they are fresh messages just between P_x and P_y and such modification effectively fixes the problem on the impersonate attack. The details of our proposed protocol are described as follows:

4.1   Initialization Phase

The proposed protocol of this phase is extremely similar to Chan et al.'s protocol. The major difference is that the signature, $\Delta_x i$, generated by player P_x is changed as follows: $\Delta_x = S_{sk_x}(K_x^0 \| gno\#)$, where $gno\#$ is an unique game number generated by P_x.

4.2   Signing Phase

If P_x wants to submit event update messages to other online players in a game session with n rounds, he/she performs the following operations:

1. P_x computes the 1st round one-time signature key δ_x^1 by computing $\delta_x^1 = H(K_x^1 \| U_x^1 \| gno\#), \Delta_x, K_x^0, gno\#$. Then, P_x submits the first round message δ_x^1 to other online players.

2. P_x computes the 2nd round one-time signature key $\delta_x^2 = H(K_x^2||U_x^2||gno\#)$, $U_x^1, K_x^1, gno\#$ and submits δ_x^2 to other online players.
3. P_x computes the rth round one-time signature key $\delta_x^r = H(K_x^r||U_x^r||gno\#)$, $U_x^{r-1}, K_x^{r-1}, gno\#$ and submits δ_x^r to other online players in the subsequent rth round, where $r = 3, 4, ..., n$.

In Figure 4, we introduce an example to describe the detailed steps of signing phase with transmission action. Suppose there are three rounds in a session and the player P_x sends out the event update messages to the player P_y.

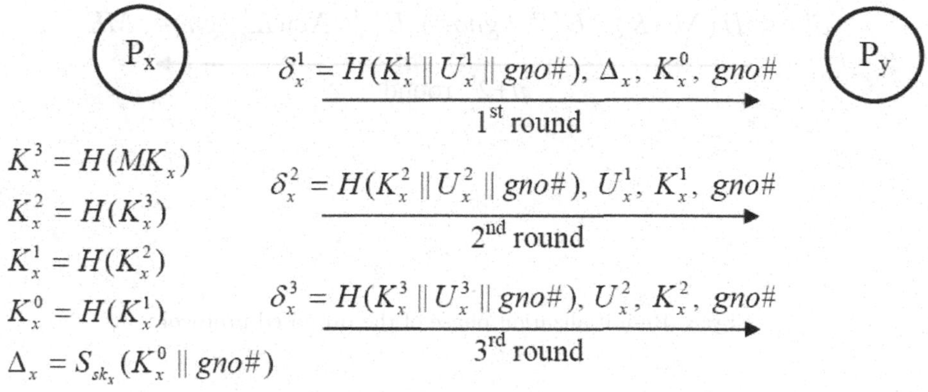

$$K_x^3 = H(MK_x)$$
$$K_x^2 = H(K_x^3)$$
$$K_x^1 = H(K_x^2)$$
$$K_x^0 = H(K_x^1)$$
$$\Delta_x = S_{sk_x}(K_x^0 \parallel gno\#)$$

$$\delta_x^1 = H(K_x^1 \parallel U_x^1 \parallel gno\#), \Delta_x, K_x^0, gno\# \qquad \text{1}^{\text{st}} \text{ round}$$

$$\delta_x^2 = H(K_x^2 \parallel U_x^2 \parallel gno\#), U_x^1, K_x^1, gno\# \qquad \text{2}^{\text{nd}} \text{ round}$$

$$\delta_x^3 = H(K_x^3 \parallel U_x^3 \parallel gno\#), U_x^2, K_x^2, gno\# \qquad \text{3}^{\text{rd}} \text{ round}$$

Fig. 4. Signing phase of the proposed protocol

4.3 Verification Phase

In the verification phase, online player P_y receives the event update message from the player P_x and performs the following operations:

1. In the first round, P_y first verifies $(K_x^0||gno\#) \stackrel{?}{=} D_{pk_x}(\Delta_x)$. If it holds, P_y confirms that the key K_x^0 is legitimate and $gno\#$ is not a duplicate value; if not, it stops.
2. In the subsequent rth round, P_y verifies $K_x^{r-2} \stackrel{?}{=} H(K_x^{r-1})$ to check if the signature key K_x^{r-1} is legitimate, where $r = 2, ..., n$.
3. If above holds, P_y verifies $\delta_x^{r-1} \stackrel{?}{=} H(K_x^{r-1}||U_x^{r-1}||gno\#)$ to check whether or not the update has been altered. If it passes verification, P_y convinces that no player has tampered with the update from P_x.

4.4 Re-initialization Phase

Whenever P_x wants to extend his/her game session for a few rounds, P_x regenerates a new master key and performs the following operations:

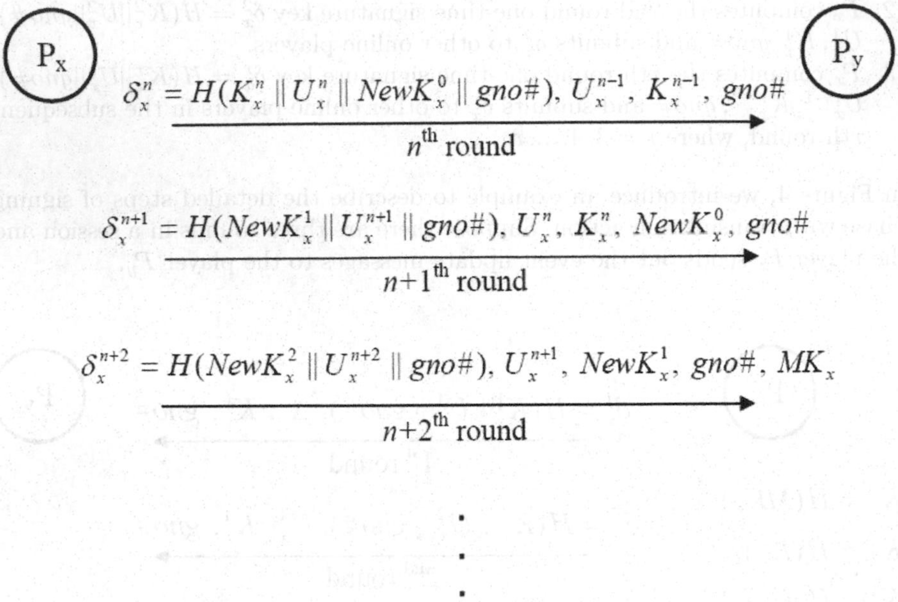

$$\overbrace{P_x}$$ $$\overbrace{P_y}$$

$$\delta_x^n = H(K_x^n \| U_x^n \| NewK_x^0 \| gno\#), U_x^{n-1}, K_x^{n-1}, gno\#$$

$$n^{\text{th}} \text{ round}$$

$$\delta_x^{n+1} = H(NewK_x^1 \| U_x^{n+1} \| gno\#), U_x^n, K_x^n, NewK_x^0, gno\#$$

$$n+1^{\text{th}} \text{ round}$$

$$\delta_x^{n+2} = H(NewK_x^2 \| U_x^{n+2} \| gno\#), U_x^{n+1}, NewK_x^1, gno\#, MK_x$$

$$n+2^{\text{th}} \text{ round}$$

$$\vdots$$

Fig. 5. Re-initialization phase of the proposed protocol

1. In the nth round, P_x chooses a new master key MK_x' and generates the new one-time signature keys $NewK_x^0, ..., NewK_x^n$. P_x then hashes the new signature key $NewK_x^0$ with the key $K_x = H(MK_x')$ to generate $\delta_x^n = H(K_x^n \| U_x^n \| NewK_x^0 \| gno\#)$. P_x sends δ_x^n, U_x^{n-1}, K_x^{n-1} and $gno\#$ to other players in the nth round.
2. In the $(n+1)$th round, P_x computes $\delta_x^{n+1} = H(NewK_x^1 \| U_x^{n+1} \| gno\#)$ and sends δ_x^{n+1}, U_x^n, K_x^n, $NewK_x^0$ and $gno\#$ to other players.
3. In the $(n+2)$th round, P_x sends $\delta_x^{n+2} = H(NewK_x^2 \| U_x^{n+2} \| gno\#)$, U_x^{n+1}, $NewK_x^1$, $gno\#$ and original master key, MK_x, to other players.

Upon receiving new one-time signature keys from P_x, the other player, P_y, should perform the following verifiable operations:

1. In the $(n+1)$th round, P_y verifies $H(K_x^n \| U_x^n \| NewK_x^0 \| gno\#) \overset{?}{=} \delta_x^n$ to check if the new signature key $NewK_x^0$ is legitimate.
2. In the $(n+2)$th round, in addition to the regular verifications, P_y must also verify $K_x^n \overset{?}{=} H(MK_x)$. If the above passes verification, P_y confirms the validity of $NewK_x^0$. The series of new one-time signature keys $NewK_x^0, ..., NewK_x^n$ can be used after the $(n+2)$th rounds.

In Figure 5, we introduce an example to describe the detailed steps of re-initialization phase with transmission action.

4.5   Security Analysis

In this subsection, we shall discuss the enhanced security features. Rests are the same as original Chan et al.'s EASES protocol.

1. The impersonation attack works on Chan et al.'s EASES protocol. However, in our enhanced protocol, it is resisted because the validity of the game sessions can be verified through the unique $gno\#$. If a duplicate value of $gno\#$ is used once again, other players can detect this attack.
2. If an intruder P_z tries to masquerade the valid player P_x, he/she has to prepare a valid message (Δ_x, $gno\#$) with P_x's signature. However, it is impossible for him/her to get the valid Δ_x because he/she does not have P_x's private key sk_x. Only P_x keeps the correct private key for generating a legal signature verifiable by the corresponding public key pk_x.

4.6   Performance Analysis

In this subsection, we show the performance of our improved protocol and compare it with Chan et al.'s EASES protocol in terms of functionality in Table 1. For the total number of hashing operations performed, there are only two hashing operations for each event update in both two protocols. However, in terms of functionality, our improved protocol can resist attacks and threats such as impersonate attacks.

Table 1. Comparisons of ours with Chan et al.'s EASES protocol

Protocol → Functionalities ↓	Chan et al.'s EASES protocol [1]	Our improved protocol
Non-repudiation	Yes	Yes
Event commitment	Yes	Yes
Cheat-prevention	No	Yes

5   Conclusions

In this paper, we have shown that Chan et al. EASES protocol is vulnerable to the impersonate attack and this weakness is due to the fact that the event updates of the communicants are not appropriately encrypted into the exchanged cryptographic messages. To enhance the security of EASES protocol, we have introduced a simple countermeasure to resist our proposed attack. Compared to the previously EASES protocol, the concept of $gno\#$ does not raise any more computation cost. Finally, the proposed protocol not only keeps the original advantages but also improves the security.

Acknowledgements

The authors would like to thank anonymous referees for their valuable suggestions and comments to improve this paper. In addition, this research was partially supported by the National Science Council, Taiwan, R.O.C., under contract no.: NSC 98-2218-E-165-001.

References

1. Chan, M.-C., Hu, S.-Y., Jiang, J.-R.: An efficient and secure event signature (EASES) protocol for peer-to-peer massively multiplayer online games. Computer Networks 52(9), 1838–1845 (2008)
2. Corman, A., Douglas, S., Schachte, P., Teague, V.: A seucre event agreement (SEA) protocol for peer-to-peer games. In: The First International Conference on Availability, Reliability and Security (2006)
3. Dickey, C., Zappala, D., Lo, V., Marr, J.: Low lattency and cheat-proof event ordering for peer-to-peer games. In: Proceedings of the ACM International Workshop on Network and Operating System Support for Digital Audio and Video, pp. 134–139 (2004)
4. Li, C.-T., Hwang, M.-S., Chu, Y.-P.: Further improvement on a novel privacy preserving authentication and access control scheme for pervasive computing environments. Computer Communications 31(18), 4255–4258 (2008)
5. Li, C.-T., Hwang, M.-S., Chu, Y.-P.: A Secure and Efficient Communication Scheme with Authenticated Key Establishment and Privacy Preserving for Vehicular Ad Hoc Networks. Computer Communications 31(12), 2803–2814 (2008)
6. Li, C.-T., Hwang, M.-S., Liu, C.-Y.: An Electronic Voting Protocol with Deniable Authentication for Mobile Ad Hoc Networks. Computer Communications 31(10), 2534–2540 (2008)
7. Li, C.-T., Hwang, M.-S., Chu, Y.-P.: Improving the security of a secure anonymous routing protocol with authenticated key exchange for ad hoc networks. International Journal of Computer Systems Science and Engineering 23(3), 227–234 (2008)
8. Li, C.-T., Hwang, M.-S., Lai, Y.-C.: A Verifiable Electronic Voting Scheme Over the Internet. In: Proceedings of the 6th International Conference on Information Technology: New Generations, pp. 449–454 (2009)
9. Li, C.-T., Hwang, M.-S.: Improving the Security of Non-PKI Methods for Public Key Distribution. In: Proceedings of the 6th International Conference on Information Technology: New Generations, pp. 1695–1696 (2009)
10. Wei, C.-H., Chin, Y.-H., Li, C.-T.: A Secure Billing Protocol for Grid Computing. In: Proceedings of the 6th International Conference on Information Technology: New Generations, pp. 320–325 (2009)
11. Li, C.-T.: An Enhanced Remote User Authentication Scheme Providing Mutual Authentication and Key Agreement with Smart Cards. In: 5th International Conference on Information Assurance and Security, pp. 517–520 (2009)
12. Li, C.-T., Hwang, M.-S.: An Online Biometrics-based Secret Sharing Scheme for Multiparty Cryptosystem Using Smart Cards. International Journal of Innovative Computing, Information and Control (2009) (article in press)
13. Li, C.-T., Chu, Y.-P.: Cryptanalysis of threshold password authentication against guessing attacks in ad hoc networks. International Journal of Network Security 8(2), 166–168 (2009)

14. Li, C.-T.: An Efficient and Secure Communication Scheme for Trusted Computing Environments. Journal of Computers 20(3), 17–24 (2009)
15. Li, C.-T., Hwang, M.-S., Chu, Y.-P.: An Efficient Sensor-To-Sensor Authenticated Path-Key Establishment Scheme for Secure Communications in Wireless Sensor Networks. International Journal of Innovative Computing, Information and Control 5(8), 2107–2124 (2009)
16. Li, C.-T., Wei, C.-H., Chin, Y.-H.: A Secure Event Update Protocol for Peer-To-Peer Massively Multiplayer Online Games Against Masquerade Attacks. International Journal of Innovative Computing, Information and Control 5(12(A)), 4715–4723 (2009)
17. Li, C.-T., Lee, C.-C., Wang, L.-J.: A Two-Factor User Authentication Scheme Providing Mutual Authentication and Key Agreement over Insecure Channels. Journal of Information Assurance and Security 5(1), 201–208 (2010)
18. Li, C.-T., Wei, C.-H., Lee, C.-C., Chin, Y.-H., Wang, L.-J.: A Secure and Undeniable Billing Protocol among Charged Parties for Grid Computing Environments. International Journal of Innovative Computing, Information and Control (2010) (article in press)
19. Li, C.-T., Hwang, M.-S.: An Efficient Biometrics-based Remote User Authentication Scheme Using Smart Cards. Journal of Network and Computer Applications 33(1), 1–5 (2010)
20. Li, C.-T., Hwang, M.-S.: A Batch Verifying and Detecting the Illegal Signatures. International Journal of Innovative Computing, Information and Control (2010) (article in press)
21. Hwang, M.-S., Tzeng, S.-F., Li, C.-T.: A New Nonrepudiable Threshold Proxy Signature Scheme with Valid Delegation Period. In: Gervasi, O., Gavrilova, M.L. (eds.) ICCSA 2007, Part III. LNCS, vol. 4707, pp. 273–284. Springer, Heidelberg (2007)

A Stable Skeletonization for Tabletop Gesture Recognition

Andoni Beristain and Manuel Graña

Computational Intelligence Group, Universidad del Pais Vasco

Abstract. An efficient and stable skeletonization consisting of a Voronoi skeletonization following by a two step pruning is presented. The first pruning step removes Voronoi edges crossing the shape boundary. The second follows a Discrete Curve Evolution approach. Both pruning steps can be done very efficiently because entire Voronoi segments are pruned based on tests on points. The algorithm works in realtime and could be used in a gesture recognition interface for tabletop interfaces.

1 Introduction

Tabletop devices are horizontal displays allowing multimodal interaction. A tabletop allows users to interact face to face, acting as a mediator for communication and sharing data items, promoting a cooperative working environment for the completion of a common task. There are examples of tabletops [6,21] where collective work is carried out on the tabletop itself, even when work teams are geographically distant through network communication using other tabletops and/or computers [26,16,20].

Early tabletop systems are the VIDEODESK [12], DigitalDesk [27], Video-Draw and Video Whiteboard [24,25], TeamWorkStation [11,10], DOLPHIN system [23] and Active Desk [8].

The use of natural interaction methods allows complex operations to be carried out by means of actions which are easy to learn and execute for common people, because they find them alike to other gestures of their everyday life, though the implementation of the recognition procedures may be very complex. Here we focus in hand gesture interaction, proposing thre basic gestures: grabbing, pointing and passing a page, and its visual recognition in real time based on object skeletonization. Hand gesture recognition, which is the target application of our work, is scarcely proposed as a mean of interaction in the latest systems. On the contrary, physical actuators are used by many systems. Moreover, in some systems the tabletop itself can even move the actuator [19,18].

The skeleton of a shape is a thinned version of the original shape, a curve whose points are equidistant to opposite sides of the original shape boundary curve [9,7,22]. Skeletons are composed of branches, connected by different joint points. They represent the essential structure of objects and how components

D. Taniar et al. (Eds.): ICCSA 2010, Part I, LNCS 6016, pp. 610–621, 2010.

are connected to form a whole. Therefore, they are proposed for the recognition, classification and retrieval of shapes. According to Blum [2,3], skeletons are shape descriptors specially suitable for the description of biological or amorphous shapes present in nature for which other description schemes based in ordinary geometry are inadequate. However, the main drawbacks for the use of skeletons in pattern recognition is their instability (small shape changes can produce dramatic skeleton changes), structural complexity and lack of real time implementations. Here we address the problem proposing a two stage pruning process that allows real time implementation, provides stable skeletons which are structurally simple and allow the definition of efficient and fast pattern recognition procedures based on graph matching.

Section 2 gives the description of our algorithm. Section 3 gives the recognition results for tabletop interaction hand gestures. Section 4 gives some summary conclussions.

2   Algorithm Description

The initial skeleton computation is base on the Voronoi Tessellation [5,17]. The subsequent pruning procedure is divided into two stages, the first one removing the Voronoi edges not contained inside the shape, and the second one is an enhanced version of the pruning procedure presented in [1], taking advantage of certain characteristics of Voronoi Skeletons.

An image is a function $I : D \to \mathbb{R}$, and a shape is a connected set of pixel sites $F \subseteq D$ which have been identified through some segmentation procedure, which can include holes in it. This segmentation procedure usually adds some kind of noise to the shape boundary. In the continuous case $D \subset \mathbb{R}^2$ a shape is a closed region of the image domain. In the discrete case, the image plane is tessellated into square pixels $D \subset \mathbb{Z}^2$. In this discrete space the shape F is defined as a connected component:

$$F = \forall p, q \in F \exists G = \{g_1, ..., g_n\} \subset F \, s.t. \, (g_1 = p) \wedge (g_n = q) \wedge (\forall g_i \in G \, \|g_i, g_{i+1}|_A),$$
$$(1)$$

where $|a, b|_A$ represents the adjacency relationship between pixels a and b. We consider the shape boundary curves denoted C, which can be constituted by one or several connected components of one-pixel width curves $C = \{C_1, ..., C_n\}$. In the discrete image domain case $C \subset \mathbb{Z}^2$ each of the boundary curves is represented as a sequence of 8-connected pixels $C_i = \{p_1, ..., p_n\}$, so that p_{j+1} is the next neighbor pixel of p_j ($\forall 1 \leq j < n \, |p_j, p_{j+1}|_A$). This sequence corresponds to visiting the pixels in the boundary curve in clockwise or anticlockwise direction, starting from an arbitrary position. Each of the boundary curves is closed so that $|p_n, p_1|_A$. The boundary condition is mathematically stated as follows:

$$\forall p_k \in C \left(\exists q \in F \wedge \exists r \in \overline{F} \, s.t. \, |p_k, q|_A \wedge |p_k, r|_A \wedge (p_k \in F) \right) \qquad (2)$$

2.1   Skeleton Computation Algorithm

Our algorithm follows the next steps:

1. *Shape boundary subsampling:* The shape boundary curves are subsampled along their arclengths to obtain the set of Voronoi sites $V_{sites} \subset C$ which will be used to compute our Voronoi Tessellation. In our implementation and experiments an uniform subsampling is performed keeping one pixel out of four from the initially 8-connected shape boundary curves.

2. *Voronoi Tessellation computation:* The Voronoi edges $S = \{s_{ij} \mid i, j \in V_{sites}\}$ of the Voronoi Tessellation induced by V_{sites} are computed.

3. *Discrete Curve Evolution computation (DCE):* A Discrete Curve Evolution procedure (see appendix A) is performed on the original shape boundary curves C, with a termination criterion of a minimum number of vertices for each boundary curve C_i. The external boundary curve minimum number of vertices is ϕ_E, while the boundary curves of the shape holes have always a ϕ_I number of vertices. In general $\phi_E \gg \phi_I$. A constant threshold can reduce the complexity of further steps for shape recognition, but also limits the maximal detail resolution of a shape.

4. *Pruning:* The spurious Voronoi edges of the external skeleton branches are removed in a two stage pruning procedure. The set of Voronoi edges is sequentially processed checking the next two conditions in order, preserving only the segments fulfilling both of them. Consequently, the final pruned skeleton is defined as:

$$S_{Vpruned} = S_{VA} - S_{VDCE} \tag{3}$$

   (a) *First Pruning Stage:* We only keep the set of Voronoi segments entirely contained inside the original shape F as the initial Voronoi Skeleton as suggested in [4]. This pruning procedure is formally described as:

$$S_{VA} = \bigcup_{i,j \in V_{sites}} (s_{ij} \subset F) \tag{4}$$

   (b) *Second Pruning Stage:* As a second pruning step, we apply a DCE based pruning procedure [1]. First, the convex hull of the DCE polygon (i.e. only the sequence of convex points in the DCE subsampling $C_{DCE} = \{c_1^*, ..., c_{n'}^*\} \subset C$ are used to compose a polygon) is obtained $H_{DCE} = (E_{DCE}, C_{DCE})$, so that each edge $e_i \in E_{DCE}$ is associated to a subsequence of the original shape boundary curve $e_i = \{c_p, ..., c_{p+q}\} \subset C$, such that $c_p = c_i^*$ and $c_{p+q} = c_{i+1}^*$. For $e_{n'}$ the end points are c_1^* and $c_{n'}^*$. Therefore, there will be some j such that $v_i \in e_j$. The function $Edge\,(polygon, point)$ returns the identity of the H_{DCE} edge for a given Voronoi site. Then, the pruning criterion consists of removing the Voronoi segments s_{ij}, whose generative points (i.e., closest Voronoi sites) v_i and v_j correspond to the same edge in H_{DCE}. Mathematically, our pruning procedure can be defined as,

$$S_{VDCE} = \{s_{i,j} \, | Edge \, (H_{DCE}, v_i) = Edge \, (H_{DCE}, v_j)\}$$

where S_{VDCE} is the Voronoi DCE pruned skeleton.

The requirements of the DCE pruning procedure are met by the Voronoi skeletonization procedure, which are: (1) every skeleton point must be the center of a maximal disk and (2) the generative points in the shape boundary curves must be available.

The first pruning phase, described in the step (4.a) of the algorithm, which involves checking if a Voronoi edge is completely contained inside the shape can be performed efficiently because testing if both endpoints of a Voronoi segment are inside the shape is enough to guarantee that the whole segment is contained inside the shape.

The second pruning phase can also be performed efficiently thanks to the definition of Voronoi segment. According to it, every point in a Voronoi segment shares the same pair of Voronoi sites, say v_i and v_j which are also their generative points, used by the DCE pruning procedure, and therefore it is enough to check the DCE condition once for the whole Voronoi segment.

The algorithmic pseudo code specification of the procedure is shown in 1, where $S_{Vpruned}$ is the shape's Voronoi skeleton obtained by our procedure and composed of Voronoi segments s_{ij}, we denote A_I and A_F the end points of a Voronoi segment s_{ij}. And the functions are defined as:

- $Subsample\,(C)$: Obtains a subsampling of the points in the original shape boundary curves C.
- $VoronoiTesselation\,(V_{sites})$: Computes the Voronoi Tessellation on the V_{sites} point set, which includes obtaining the Voronoi segment set.
- $DCE(C)$: Computes the Discrete Curve Evolution procedure for each of the boundary curves in C.
- $P\,(DCE_{convex})$: Is the polygon formed by the convex vertices of the polygon obtained by the $DCE(C)$ function.
- $EndPoints\,(s_{ij})$: Obtains the end points, i.e. Voronoi vertices, of the Voronoi segment s_{ij}.
- $Shape\,(p)$: Returns true if the point p is contained in the shape, and false otherwise.
- $DCECrit\,(s_{ij})$: Performs the adapted version of the DCE pruning procedure. It checks if the generative points v_i and v_j of the Voronoi segment s_{ij} belong to different edges of $P\,(DCE_{convex})$. If so, the function returns true, and false otherwise.
- $ConvexHull(poly)$: Computes the convex hull of a polygon, returning another polygon.

3   Results

The final Voronoi skeleton obtained by means of our algorithm $S_{Vpruned}$ is a connected set, simple and robust under noise. Being the Voronoi skeleton specially

Algorithm 1. Skeletonization procedure

$V_{sites} := Subsample\,(C)\,;$
$V := VoronoiTesselation\,(V_{sites})\,;$
$P\,(DCE_{convex}) := ConvexHull(DCE(C));$
foreach s_{ij} in V do

- $(\alpha_{ij}, \omega_{ij}) := EndPoints\,(s_{ij})\,;$
- if$((Shape\,(\alpha_{ij}))\;AND\;(Shape\,(\omega_{ij})))$
  - if$(DCECrit\,(s_{ij}))\;S_{Vpruned} := S_{Vpruned} \cup s_{ij};$

noisy with many spurious branches (also called hairs) and also highly affected by noise in the shape boundary curves, this result is remarkable. The external branches of the skeleton do not connect with the boundary curves, because the first pruning stage shortens the skeleton ending branches. But the shortening degree is low and limited as it can be appreciated in figure 1.

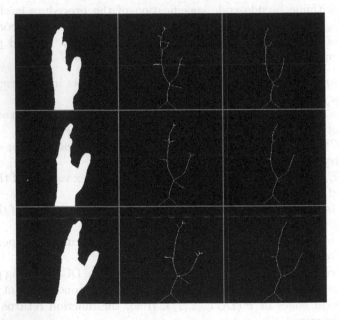

Fig. 1. Left column: Two binary images of the turning page gesture (see section 3.2 below). Middle Column: Skeletons obtained using the implementation of algorithm [1] provided in [1]. Right column: Skeletons obtained using the approach in this paper.

3.1   Real-Time Implementation Results

For the online implementation, a green chroma key was used in our indoor testing environment with conventional office lighting and a Sony EVI D-70 camera.

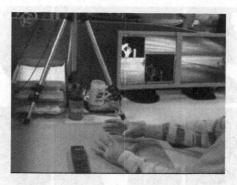

Fig. 2. Realtime prototype. The computer screen shows the online segmentation and skeletonization.

The video resolution used was 320x240 and the prototype implementation steps followed for each image were: (1) Substract the objects on the chroma key using the HSV color space. (2) Threshold the image, obtaining a binary image with the objects on it. (3) Find all the connected components,i.e., shapes, in the image. For each significative (big enough) shape in the image: (a) Obtain the shape boundary point sequence. It is a list of sequences, including the external boundary and the internal boundaries (i.e. holes). (b) Check the size of the holes in the shape to include them or not in the final skeletonization. (c) Compute the skeletonization procedure described in section 2. (d) Show the resulting skeleton on a window.

The realtime prototype is able to compute the proposed skeletonization algorithm at 60 frames per second on a Intel Pentium IV processor (4 GHz.) with 1 GB. memory and Windows XP SP2. Therefore it proves that it is possible to make a realtime implementation of our algorithm. Example images of the prototype is use are shown in figure 2. Our research group web page also hosts a video example showing the realtime performance of our prototype available[1].

3.2 Gesture Recognition Results

We first describe the inhouse hand gesture database used for the validation of the pattern recognition approach, then we comment on the graph matching approach applied, and finally we give some summary gesture recognition results. Our skeletonization approach will be called *Beris*. Comparative results are provided using the algorithm in [1], which will be called *Bai*.

Hand Gesture database for Tabletop Interaction. We have made this image database available[2]. It contains a set of binary images corresponding to

---

[1] http://www.ehu.es/ccwintco/index.php/2009-10-24-video-skeleton
[2] http://www.ehu.es/ccwintco/index.php/GIC-experimental-databases

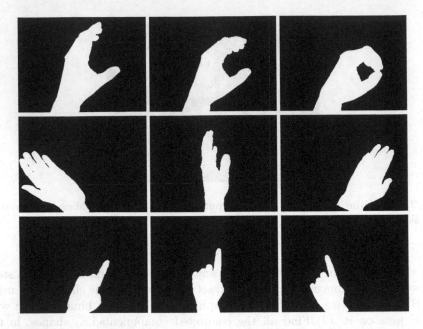

Fig. 3. Hand gestures for natural tabletop interaction, from top to bottom, the sequences correspond to grab

the even frames of the video recordings of three different dynamic hand gestures. The three gestures in the database correspond to basic hand gestures for tabletop interaction: grabbing an object, turning a page and pointing to some object. Examples of the initial, intermediate and final frames of each gesture are shown in fig. 3. This database includes 200 repetitions of the three basic gestures, each repetition represented by a sequence of 15 images, up to a total of 200x3x15=9000 images. All the images are upright oriented, although there are orientation variation in the three dimensions.

Graph matching algorithm. To start with, we consider a conventional mapping of the skeleton into an undirected graph, which can be cyclic or acyclic, depending on the shape having holes or not. Skeleton points are categorized into three categories: *end points* of branches, points with only one skeleton point in their 8-neighborhood, *branch points*, points in a branch with two skeleton points in their 8-neighborhood, and *joint points*, connecting three or more branches, i.e. with more than two points in their 8-neighborhood. A graph G_{skel} will be constructed as follows: the skeleton end points and joint points are the graph nodes, and the skeleton branches correspond to the links of the graph, labeled with the length of the branch. Each node $A = (A_r, A_\theta, A_{dt})$ is characterized by its normalized position in polar coordinates (A_r, A_θ), and its distance transform value A_{dt}. These values are normalized to obtain values in the interval $[0, 1]$.

Algorithm 2. Greedy matching algorithm pseudo code

```
int numMatches=0;
// nodes sort in Nodes(Ti) and Nodes(S)
//such that (n(i).y>n(i+1))OR
//((n(i).y=(n(i+1).y)&&(n(i+1).x<=n(i).x))
foreach n in Nodes(Ti)
          foreach m in Nodes(S)
                  if(notAlreadySelected(m)
                       AND
                  |Neighbors(n)|<=|Neighbors(m)|)
                  {if(ND(n,m)<ND(n,Min))
                                  Min:=m;}
          Match[numMatches]:=(n,Min);
          numMatches:=numMatches+1;
```

The Node Distance (ND) is a mixture of the position distances and the difference on distance transform values. If we have two nodes $A = (A_r, A_\theta, A_{dt})$ and $B = (B_r, B_\theta, B_{dt})$, the distance between them is computed as follows:

$$|A, B|_{ND} = \alpha |A_{dt} - B_{dt}| + (1 - \alpha) \sqrt{A_r^2 + B_r^2 - 2A_r B_r \cos(A_\theta - B_\theta)} \quad (5)$$

so that $|A, B|_{ND} \in [0, 1]$.

Consider that we have a set of template graphs $T = \{T_1, ..., T_n\}$, and a sample graph S. The graph matching problem consists of finding the most similar graph to S in T. For this purpose, we apply a time efficient greedy approach that can be feasible for realtime recognition systems. The pseudo code formulation of our greedy algorithm to match a template graph T_i with a sample graph S is shown in figure 2:

In pseudocode of figure 2, initally nodes in both graphs are sorted by their normalized position, starting from the nodes closest to the image domain boundaries, visiting the graph nodes towards the center of the image domain. The next visited node is matched to the nearest free node in the sense of the Node Distance ND. The Match() structure returned by the algorithm stores the set of node matches between the sample graph and the template graph. Node sorting optimizes the graph visiting process for the hand gesture recognition, which is the intended application. In this context the user arm enters the image from its domain boundaries towards the centere of the image, and the arm's entrance point in the image is used as the origin for the node sorting.

Since the Node Distance $|A, B|_{ND} \in [0, 1]$ with 0 corresponding to the same node, the value $1 - |A, B|_{ND}$ corresponds to the node similarity. Therefore, the Graph Matching is computed in terms of this node similarity. Let us denote number of node matches $M = \#(Match(T_i, S))$ and the distance between the matched nodes. Mathematically, the Graph Similarity (GS) value $GS(T_i, S)$, obtained from the matching $Match(T_i, S) = \{(t_k, s_k); k = 1, ..., M\}$ is defined as,

Table 1. Recognition success of the 3 hand gesture classes

ϕ_E	α	Classifier	Bai	Beris
15	0.25	1NN	72.06	70.74
15	0.25	3NN	80.53	80.21
15	0.25	5NN	83.67	83.81
15	0.50	1NN	78.30	80.73
15	0.50	3NN	87.01	89.17
15	0.50	5NN	89.84	91.96
15	0.75	1NN	82.30	84.78
15	0.75	3NN	90.71	92.27
15	0.75	5NN	**93.25**	**94.57**

Table 2. Total recognition Confusion Matrix for the best case of our algorithm (Beris) with 3 classes: pruning 15, alpha 0.75 and 5NN

	Grab	Point	Turn Page
Grab	**266725**	603	32672
Point	82	**298783**	1135
Turn Page	10607	3731	**285662**

$$GS\left(T_i, S\right) = \frac{2\sum_k \left(1 - |t_k, s_k|_{ND}\right)}{\#T_i + \#S} \tag{6}$$

where $\#T_i$ and $\#S$ are the number of nodes of T_i and S, respectively.

Validation based on k-NN classifiers. The classifiers used are 1-NN, 3-NN and 5-NN, selecting randomly one, three and five gesture samples for each gesture as the class representatives, and classifying the rest of the database into one of the three hand gesture classes. We performed a hundred repetitions of the experiment to estimate the generalization of the classifiers. Total recognition results are shown in table 1, for the 3 hand gesture classes. The confusion matrix for the best results is shown in table 2 for 3 classes.

Several conclusions can be extracted from this tables:

– Our algorithm (*Beris*) outperforms the Bai algorithm recognition in most of cases.
– Higher values of the α parameter in the Node Distance produce better results. This results mean that the geometrical position of nodes is more important for matching than the DT value. In the particular case of this database, all the images in the database are upright oriented.
– As opposed to what intuition suggests, less DCE pruning does not produce better recognition results. This result is related to the maximum complexity of the shapes produces by hands, which is limited. So it seems that higher

DCE pruning parameter values add clutter in the representation, instead of enriching it.
- The confusion between the grab and page turn classes can be explained as follows: We are classifying all the instantaneous poses of a gesture as this gesture. Some of the intermediate poses of these classes are nearly indistiguishable. The classification of these poses can be the surce of confussion.

4 Conclusions

We have presented a skeleton computation algorithm which is a feasible approach for the real time recognition of hand gestures in tabletop interaction systems. We propose a set of three basic hand gestures which could be used for a general tabletop interaction SDK. Our skeletonization approach performs in real time, opening the way for real time gesture interaction. We tested a pattern recognition based on a greedy graph matching algorithm, obtaining good recognition results. Compared with another state of the art skeletonization and pruning algorithm, our approach improved it. Further work will be addressed to the full real time implementation of the pattern recognition approach. We will also perform recognition tests with other datasets and applications. We will explore real time implementations of improved graph representation and graph matching algorithms as a way to augment the approach efficiency and performance.

References

1. Bai, X., Latecki, L.J., Liu, W.Y.: Skeleton pruning by contour partitioning with discrete curve evolution. IEEE Transactions on Pattern Analysis and Machine Intelligence 29(3), 449–462 (2007)
2. Blum, H.: Biological shape and visual science. Theoretical Biology 38, 205–287 (1973)
3. Blum, H.: A transformation for extracting new descriptors of shape. In: Dunn, W.W. (ed.) Models for the Perception of Speech and Visual Form, pp. 362–380. MIT Press, Cambridge (1967)
4. Brandt, J.W.: Convergence and continuity criteria for discrete approximations of the continuous planar skeleton. CVGIP: Image Underst. 59(1), 116–124 (1994)
5. Brandt, J.W., Algazi, V.R.: Continuous skeleton computation by voronoi diagram. CVGIP: Image Underst. 55(3), 329–338 (1992)
6. Chatty, S., Lemort, A., Vales, S.: Multiple input support in a model-based interaction framework, October 2007, pp. 179–186 (2007)
7. Couprie, M., Coeurjolly, D., Zrour, R.: Discrete bisector function and euclidean skeleton in 2d and 3d. Image Vision Comput. 25(10), 1543–1556 (2007)
8. Fitzmaurice, G.W., Ishii, H., Buxton, W.A.S.: Bricks: laying the foundations for graspable user interfaces. In: CHI 1995: Proceedings of the SIGCHI conference on Human factors in computing systems, New York, NY, USA, pp. 442–449. ACM Press/Addison-Wesley Publishing Co. (1995)
9. Hesselink, W.H., Roerdink, J.B.T.M.: Euclidean skeletons of digital image and volume data in linear time by the integer medial axis transform. IEEE Transactions on Pattern Analysis and Machine Intelligence 30(12), 2204–2217 (2008)

10. Ishii, H., Kobayashi, M., Grudin, J.: Integration of interpersonal space and shared workspace: Clearboard design and experiments. ACM Trans. Inf. Syst. 11(4), 349–375 (1993)
11. Ishii, H., Miyake, N.: Toward an open shared workspace: computer and video fusion approach of teamworkstation. Commun. ACM 34(12), 37–50 (1991)
12. Krueger, M.W., Gionfriddo, T., Hinrichsen, K.: Videoplace: An artificial reality. SIGCHI Bull. 16(4), 35–40 (1985)
13. Latecki, L.J., Lakämper, R.: Convexity rule for shape decomposition based on discrete contour evolution. Comput. Vis. Image Underst. 73(3), 441–454 (1999)
14. Latecki, L.J., Lakämper, R.: Shape similarity measure based on correspondence of visual parts. IEEE Trans. Pattern Anal. Mach. Intell. 22(10), 1185–1190 (2000)
15. Latecki, L.J., Lakämper, R.: Application of planar shape comparison to object retrieval in image databases. Pattern Recognition 35, 15–29 (2002)
16. Liu, L., Erdogmus, H., Maurer, F.: An environment for collaborative iteration planning, July 2005, pp. 80–89 (2005)
17. Ogniewicz, R., Ilg, M.: Voronoi skeletons: theory and applications. In: IEEE Computer Society Conference on Computer Vision and Pattern Recognition Proceedings CVPR 1992, June 1992, pp. 63–69 (1992)
18. Pangaro, G., Maynes-aminzade, D., Ishii, H.: The actuated workbench: computer-controlled actuation in tabletop tangible interfaces. In: Interfaces, Proceedings of Symposium on User Interface Software and Technology, pp. 181–190 (2002)
19. Patten, J., Ishii, H.: Mechanical constraints as computational constraints in table-top tangible interfaces. In: CHI 2007: Proceedings of the SIGCHI conference on Human factors in computing systems, pp. 809–818. ACM Press, New York (2007)
20. Pauchet, A., Coldefy, F., Lefebvre, L., Picard, S.L.D., Perron, L., Bouguet, A., Collobert, M., Guerin, J., Corvaisier, D.: Tabletops: Worthwhile experiences of collocated and remote collaboration, October 2007, pp. 27–34 (2007)
21. Scott, S.D., Grant, K.D., Mandryk, R.L.: System guidelines for co-located, collaborative work on a tabletop display. In: European Conference Computer-Supported Cooperative Work, ECSCW 2003 (2003)
22. Siddiqi, K., Bouix, S., Tannenbaum, A., Zucker, S.W.: Hamilton-jacobi skeletons. Int. J. Comput. Vision 48(3), 215–231 (2002)
23. Streitz, N.A., Geisler, J., Haake, J.M., Hol, J.: DOLPHIN: Integrated meeting support across local and remote desktop environments and liveboards. In: Computer Supported Cooperative Work, pp. 345–358 (1994)
24. Tang, J.C., Minnenan, S.L.: Videodraw: A video interface for collaborative drawing. In: Proc. of CHI-1990, Seattle, WA, pp. 313–320 (1990)
25. Tang, J.C., Minneman, S.L.: Videodraw: a video interface for collaborative drawing. ACM Trans. Inf. Syst. 9(2), 170–184 (1991)
26. Tuddenham, P., Robinson, P.: Distributed tabletops: Supporting remote and mixed-presence tabletop collaboration, October 2007, pp. 19–26 (2007)
27. Wellner, P.: Interacting with paper on the digitaldesk. Commun. ACM 36(7), 87–96 (1993)

Appendix

A   Discrete Curve Evolution (DCE)

Discrete Curve Evolution (DCE) [13,14,15] is a shape boundary curve downsampling method that keeps the most meaningful geometrical information for shape recognition. The DCE downsamples iteratively the shape boundary curves' point set, removing the vertex of the current polygonal approximation with less contribution to the global shape at each step of the iteration. The salience of each polygon vertex v_i is given by the relevance value $K(S_i, S_{i+1})$, where S_i and S_{i+1} are the consecutive polygon segments incident to vertex v_i. It is defined as:

$$K(S_i, S_{i+1}) = \frac{\beta(S_i, S_{i+1})l(S_i)l(S_{i+1})}{l(S_i) + l(S_{i+1})}, \tag{7}$$

where $\beta(S_i, S_{i+1})$ is the angle at the common vertex of segments S_i and S_{i+1} and l is the segment length function normalized with respect to the total length of a polygonal approximation to the curve C. The DCE finds the vertex v^* with minimal salience and removes it from the polygonal approximation by the substituting its incident segments by another segment whose endpoints are the other extreme points of these segments.

This algorithm is guaranteed to terminate because the number of initial segments is finite and one segment is removed at each step of the algorithm. It is also proved in [13] that the DCE procedure converges into a convex polygon. Although the original algorithm ends when the convexity of the DCE polygon is achieved, other ending criteria is possible, e.g. defining a constant number of iterations or final segment number. In [15] a more sophisticated criteria is employed based on a threshold value for the difference between the original shape and the DCE approximation.

Author Index